WRIGHTSMAN'S
PSYCHOLOGY
and the LEGAL SYSTEM

EIGHTH EDITION

EDIE GREENE
University of Colorado Colorado Springs

KIRK HEILBRUN
Drexel University

WADSWORTH
CENGAGE Learning·

Australia • Brazil • Japan • Korea • Mexico • Singapore • Spain • United Kingdom • United States

Wrightsman's Psychology and the Legal System, **Eighth Edition**
Edie Greene and Kirk Heilbrun

Publisher: Jon-David Hague

Acquiring Sponsoring Editor: Timothy C Matray

Assistant Editor: Jessica M Alderman

Editorial Assistant: Nicole Richards

Associate Media Editor: Jasmin Tokatlian

Senior Brand Manager: Elisabeth Rhoden

Market Development Manager: Christine Sosa

Art and Design Direction, Production Management, and Composition: PreMediaGlobal

Manufacturing Planner: Karen Hunt

Senior Rights Acquisitions Specialist: Dean Dauphinais

Cover Image: Dragana Gerasimoski/ Shutterstock

For product information and technology assistance, contact us at **Cengage Learning Customer & Sales Support, 1-800-354-9706.**

For permission to use material from this text or product, submit all requests online at **www.cengage.com/permissions** Further permissions questions can be e-mailed to **permissionrequest@cengage.com**

Library of Congress Control Number: 2012951102

Student Edition:

ISBN-13: 978-1-133-95656-3

ISBN-10: 1-133-95656-4

Loose-Leaf Edition:

ISBN-13: 978-1-133-95111-7

ISBN-10: 1-133-95111-2

Wadsworth
20 Davis Drive
Belmont, CA 94002-3098
USA

Cengage Learning is a leading provider of customized learning solutions with office locations around the globe, including Singapore, the United Kingdom, Australia, Mexico, Brazil, and Japan. Locate your local office at **www.cengage.com/global**

Cengage Learning products are represented in Canada by Nelson Education, Ltd.

To learn more about Wadsworth, visit **www.cengage.com/wadsworth**

Purchase any of our products at your local college store or at our preferred online store **www.cengagebrain.com**

Printed in the United States of America
1 2 3 4 5 6 7 16 15 14 13 12

Dedicated to the field of psychology and law—
and to all who have worked to develop it into
the mature discipline it has become.

Brief Contents

Contents

Preface

This is the 8th edition of *Psychology and the Legal System*. Its longevity is a testament to the incisive, rigorous, and accessible presentation of the various aspects of psychology and law by Lawrence Wrightsman and his colleagues over the first five editions. Although Professor Wrightsman is no longer listed as an active author, the 6th, 7th, and 8th editions incorporate his name into the title to honor his many contributions. As in the 7th edition, the sole authors are Edie Greene and Kirk Heilbrun.

We continue to believe that the law is inherently psychological. It is made by people with varying desires and ambitions, interpreted by individuals with different (sometimes contradictory) perspectives, and experienced—either directly or indirectly—by all of us. Both psychology and the law are about motivation and behavior. Indeed, for centuries the legal system has been a powerful influence on people's everyday activities. From the Supreme Court's school desegregation decision of 1954 to its recent decisions concerning the constitutionality of mandatory life without parole sentences for adolescents (all described in this book), the courts have had considerable impact on individual lives.

As we move toward the middle of the second decade of the 21st century, we find it useful to describe the law from the perspective of psychology, a behavioral science that also has a significant applied component. We are not alone. In fact, matters of law and psychology are often cited in the media. Whether they involve training police in specialized responses to individuals with behavioral health problems, criminal trials of the rich and famous, the impact of trauma on human behavior, charges of racism in the criminal justice system, or debates about the utility and morality of capital punishment, headlines and lead stories are often about some aspect of psychology and law. Although this attention appears to cater to an almost insatiable curiosity about crime and other types of legal disputes, it also promotes some ambivalence about the law. Many citizens are suspicious of the police, but police are still the first responders in a crisis. Juries are frequently criticized for their decisions, but most litigants would prefer to have their cases decided by juries rather than judges. Citizens value their constitutionally protected rights, but also demand security in a post-9/11 era. This 8th edition explores these tensions as well as many other captivating and controversial issues that arise at the crossroads of psychology and the law.

The primary audiences for *Psychology and the Legal System* are those students taking a course in psychology and the law, forensic psychology, or the criminal justice system, and others who seek to learn more about the legally relevant science and practice of psychology. This book (and its individual chapters) may also be used as a supplement in psychology courses that emphasize applied psychology, social issues, or policy analysis. In addition, it covers a number of topics relevant to law school courses that introduce law students to social science research findings and applications.

We have attempted to find the right mix of psychology and legal analysis in the text. The book's emphasis remains on psychological science and practice, but we also summarize the legal history of many key topics and present the current status of relevant legal theories and court decisions. Specific recent topics that are covered in some detail in this edition include new forensic assessment measures, verbal and behavioral cues associated with deception, the effectiveness of diversion strategies of mentally ill individuals, cognitive aspects of trial judges' decisions, the effectiveness of problem-solving courts, sentencing of juvenile offenders, and the community-based correctional rehabilitation of adult and juvenile offenders.

We continue to focus on the psychological dimensions of several topics that remain important in contemporary society, just as they were important when previous editions of this text were written. These topics include social influence effects of interrogations (involving children in investigative interviews and adults in interrogation rooms), clinicians' assessments of competence in various domains, reforms to eyewitness identification procedures based on research in perception, memory and social influence, recovery from victimization in light of our understanding of posttraumatic stress disorder, and racial influences on jury decision making. As in previous editions, we have updated each of these topics using the best available scientific evidence that has been published after our most recent edition went to press.

NEW FEATURES AND REVISIONS

We have made the following major changes from the last edition:

- We have made *Psychology and the Legal System* more user-friendly by providing more current examples to illustrate the material in a straightforward and accessible way.

- We have reordered some of the chapters so the information is presented more sequentially, in the order that the issues actually arise in the course of criminal investigations and litigation.

- We have added an entirely new chapter on alternatives to traditional prosecutions, which covers arbitration, mediation, summary jury trials, diversion, specialized police responding, and problem-solving courts.

- In each chapter, case summaries in boxes ("The Case of...") have been updated. These summaries describe cases or trials that illustrate or explain an important legal concept or psychological principle covered in the chapter. Readers will be familiar with many of the recent cases, including those of Jerry Sandusky and Jared Loughner, as well as cases involving the interrogation of terrorist suspects. We also feature the historic cases of Ernest Miranda, Clarence Gideon, John Hinckley, Ted Bundy, and others.

    A few cases are either fictional (such as Dexter Morgan from the popular television series *Dexter*) or composites, but still highly applicable to the chapter material.

- We have added a "critical thought question" at the end of each box. This question is intended to draw upon the material presented in the chapter, allowing readers to apply that material to a specific fact pattern. Although the raw material to answer these questions is available in each chapter, the process of answering each will also require the reader to think in a critical, integrative, and imaginative way.

■ We have updated our focus on the role of psychologists in the legal system and the ethical issues they face. Chapter 1 also introduces the conflicts that pervade a psychological analysis of the law: the rights of individuals versus the common good, equality versus discretion as ideals that can guide the legal system, discovering the truth or resolving conflicts as the goals that the legal system strives to accomplish, and science versus the law as a source of legal decisions. We return to these conflicts several times throughout the book as we apply them to specific issues.

This edition includes a thorough, authoritative revision of every chapter in light of research and professional literature published since the last edition. Highlights include the following:

■ Chapter 1 provides an overview of the field and details the roles that psychologists play in the legal system, including novel aspects of litigation consulting.

■ Chapter 4, on the psychology of police, includes expanded coverage of specialized police responses to individuals in behavioral health crisis.

■ Chapter 5 updates the reforms to lineup procedures in cases involving eyewitness identification based on recent scientific data on eyewitness memory.

■ Chapter 6 covers the psychology of victims of crime and violence. It expands the discussion of posttraumatic stress disorder and the relationship between adverse experience and various outcomes. It also includes a case example of the issues related to political prominence and accusation of sexual assault.

■ Chapter 7, on the evaluation of criminal suspects, includes updated discussion of the detection of deception, including brain-based lie detection.

■ Chapter 9, an entirely new chapter, discusses alternative dispute resolution in the forms of arbitration, summary jury trial, and mediation. It also addresses community-based alternatives to standard prosecution using the Sequential Intercept Model, with a particular focus on specialized police responding (at the earliest stage) and problem-solving courts such as drug court, mental health court, veterans court, and community court.

■ Chapter 11 describes updates on forensic assessment in civil cases, particularly new data on the evaluation of children and parents in the context of child custody litigation.

■ Chapter 12 provides a comparison between decisions made by judges and those made by juries, including some new data on these comparisons.

■ Chapter 13 expands the discussion of juries in the previous chapter to provide more detailed information about the competence of juries—particularly their ability to understand instructions, apply them, and decide complex cases. Juror bias is discussed in light of the recent highly publicized case of Jerry Sandusky and his conviction of multiple counts of sexual abuse of minors.

■ Chapter 14 describes traditional rationales for punishing offenders and also covers restorative approaches that allow victims and offenders to voice their perspectives in order to repair harms and resolve conflicts.

■ The appendices for this book are now available online at www.cengagebrain.com. They include the Ethical Principles of Psychologists and Code of Conduct as well as the Specialty Guidelines for Forensic Psychologists, both of which provide ethical guidance for practice and research in forensic psychology. They also include the Bill of Rights, which describes the amendments to the United States Constitution.

For assistance in preparing this edition, Edie Greene thanks Andrew Evelo and Jessy Quigley, and Kirk Heilbrun thanks Anna Heilbrun. The authors jointly thank their editor, Timothy Matray, for facilitating a smooth and efficient process. They also thank Shiela Mary for photo research, Gunjan Chandola, who coordinated the production, and Kursten Hensl, who wrote the Instructors' Manual. Each was extremely helpful in writing the 8th edition of *Psychology and the Legal System*.

About the Authors

Edie Greene is currently Professor and Chair of Psychology and Director of the Graduate Concentration in Psychology and Law at the University of Colorado (Colorado Springs). She earned her Ph.D. in cognitive psychology and law at the University of Washington in 1983 and served there as postdoctoral research associate between 1983 and 1986. From 1994 to 1995, Greene was a fellow in Law and Psychology at Harvard Law School. She has received several federally funded grants to support her research on legal decision making, eye-witness memory, and psycholegal aspects of aging. Greene received a college-wide award for Outstanding Research and Creative Works in 1999, a university-wide award for Excellence in Research in 2001, and the Chancellor's Award for Distinguished Faculty in 2009. She has been invited to lecture at the National Judicial College and at continuing legal education programs nationwide. She consults with lawyers on various trial-related issues including jury selection, trial strategies, and jury decisions, and has, on numerous occasions, testified as an expert witness on jury behavior and eyewitness memory. In addition to serving as coauthor of the 5th, 6th, and 7th editions of *Psychology and the Legal System*, Greene is the author of a number of articles, columns, and book chapters and co-author of *The Adversary System* (with Frank Strier, 1990) and *Determining Damages: The Psychology of Jury Awards* (with Brian Bornstein, 2003). She has served as President of the American Psychology-Law Society/ APA Division 41 and, in 2008, received the Award for Outstanding Teaching and Mentoring from that Society.

Anna Heilbrun

Kirk Heilbrun is currently Professor, Department of Psychology, Drexel University. He received his doctorate in clinical psychology in 1980 from the University of Texas at Austin, and completed postdoctoral fellowship training from 1981 to 1982 in psychology and criminal justice at Florida State University. His current research focuses on juvenile and adult offenders, legal decision making, and forensic evaluation associated with such decision-making, as well as the diversion of individuals with behavioral health problems from standard prosecution. He is the author of a number of articles on forensic assessment, violence risk assessment and risk communication, and the diversion and treatment of mentally disordered offenders. In addition to serving as co-author for the 6th and 7th editions of *Psychology and the Legal System,* he has published five books (*Principles of Forensic Mental Health Assessment,* 2001; *Forensic Mental Health Assessment: A Casebook,* with Geff Marczyk and Dave DeMatteo, 2002; *Juvenile Delinquency: Prevention, Assessment, and Intervention,* with Naomi Goldstein and Rich Redding, 2005; *Foundations of Forensic Mental Health Assessment,* with Tom Grisso and Alan Goldstein, 2009; and *Evaluations for Risk of Violence in Adults,* in 2009). His practice interests also center around forensic assessment, and he directs a clinic within the department in this area. He is board certified in Clinical Psychology and in Forensic Psychology by the American Board of Professional Psychology, and has previously served as president of both the American Psychology-Law Psychology/APA Division 41, and the American Board of Forensic Psychology. He received the 2004 Distinguished Contributions to Forensic Psychology award and the 2008 Beth Clark Distinguished Service award from the American Academy of Forensic Psychology.

Chapter

1

Psychology and the Law

Choices and Roles

ORIENTING QUESTIONS

1. Why do we have laws, and what is the psychological approach to studying law?
2. What choices are reflected in the psychological approach to the law?
3. How do laws reflect the contrast between due process and crime control in the criminal justice system?
4. What are five roles that psychologists may play in the legal system, and what does each entail?

Consider the following stories, all of which were prominently featured in the news:

- Wearing body armor, a gas mask, and a tactical helmet, and dressed entirely in black, gunman James Holmes opened fire in a movie theater near Denver during the premiere of the Batman movie, *The Dark Knight Rises*. In one of the deadliest shooting rampages in American history, Holmes killed 12 and wounded nearly 60 others. What impelled a quiet, reclusive Ph.D. student, who graduated with honors in neuroscience from the University of California, to kill with such wild abandon? One possibility is that Holmes was distraught over events in his life, prompting his withdrawal from graduate school. Another is that Holmes harbored psychopathic traits that went undetected by those around him.

- A controversial Arizona law requires law enforcement officers to determine the immigration status of any person they detain or arrest if they believe that person is in the country illegally. Psychological research suggests that the law may render residents less likely to report crimes and may subject Hispanic and Hispanic-looking citizens to extra police attention, influencing their perceptions of justice and fairness.

- A drunken driver who killed a 10-year-old boy in suburban Dallas was sentenced to spend 180 days in jail over the next 10 years, including every Christmas Day, New Year's Day, and June 8, the child's birthday. The judge said he wanted to remind the defendant of the family's loss on these important family holidays.

- In late 2011, Representative Marsha Blackburn introduced a bill in Congress dubbed the STRIP act (Stop TSA's Reach In Policy) which would prohibit Transportation Security Administration employees from using the title "officer" and wearing uniforms and badges that resemble those worn by law enforcement personnel. TSA officials claim that uniforms and badges represent "the professionalism of our employees and the seriousness of our work," while consumer advocacy groups claim that TSA workers intimidate passengers by presenting an image of themselves that is untrue. Both assertions involve public perceptions and beliefs—issues that can be examined via psychological research.

These stories illustrate a few of the psycholegal topics that we consider in this book: the motivations of offenders, police–community relations and discrimination, discretion in judges' sentencing decisions, and public perceptions of security and law enforcement officials. They show the real flesh and blood of some of the psychological issues that arise in the law.

THE IMPORTANCE OF LAWS

These examples also illustrate the pervasiveness of the law in our society. But how does the law work? This book will help you understand how the legal system operates by applying psychological concepts, theories, findings, and methods to its study.

Laws as Human Creations

Laws are everywhere. They affect everything from birth to death. Laws regulate our private lives and our public actions. Laws dictate how long we must stay in school, how fast we can drive, when (and, to some extent, whom) we can marry, and whether we are allowed to play our car stereos at full blast or let our boisterous dog romp through the neighbors' yards and gardens. Given that the body of laws has such a widespread impact, we might expect that the law is a part of nature, that it was originally discovered by a set of archaeologists or explorers. Perhaps we think of Moses carrying the Ten Commandments down from the mountain.

But our laws are not chiseled in stone. Rather, laws are human creations that evolve out of the needs for order and consistency. To be responsive to a constantly changing society, our laws must also change. As some become outdated, others take their place. For example, before there were shootings on school grounds, no laws forbade the presence of weapons in schools. But after a series of deadly incidents, laws that banned weapons from school property proliferated. On occasion, the reach of these zero-tolerance policies has been excessive, as Zachary Christie, a Delaware first-grader, learned. Zachary was suspended and ordered to enroll in an alternative program for troubled youths because he took to school a Cub Scout utensil that included a small folding knife. When this sort of overreaching occurs, the public reacts, and the policies are revised again.

Laws Help Resolve Conflict and Protect the Public

Many standards of acceptable behavior—not purposely touching strangers on elevators, for example—seem universally supported. But in some situations, people have differences of opinion about what is considered appropriate and disagreements result. When this occurs, society must have mechanisms to resolve the disagreements. Thus, societies develop laws and regulations to function as conflict resolution mechanisms. Customs and rules of conduct evolve partly to deal with the conflict between one person's impulses and desires and other people's rights. Similarly, laws are developed to manage and resolve those conflicts that cannot be prevented.

Public safety is always an important consideration in a civilized society. In earlier times, before laws were established to deter and punish unacceptable behavior, people "took the law into their own hands," acting as vigilantes to secure the peace and impose punishment on offenders. Now, in the United States and most other nations, all governmental entities—federal, state, county, borough, and municipal, and even some neighborhoods—have enacted laws to protect the public.

The Changing of Laws

The raw material for the construction and the revision of laws is human experience. As our experiences and opportunities change, laws must be developed, interpreted, reinterpreted, and modified to keep up with these rapid changes in our lives. As George Will (1984) put it, "Fitting the law to a technologically dynamic society often is like fitting trousers to a 10-year-old: Adjustments are constantly needed" (p. 6).

The framers of the U.S. Constitution, and even legislators of 30 years ago, could never have anticipated the ways that laws have changed and will continue to change. They probably never contemplated the possibility that advances in neuroscience, for example, would affect how police investigate cases, attorneys represent their clients, and juries and judges make decisions. But brain-imaging technology is now used to detect brain injuries and assess pain in accident sufferers, determine mental state and capacity for rational thought in offenders, and detect lies and deception in suspects under interrogation. Although the correspondence between brain activity and behavior is far from clear at this point, neuroimaging will undoubtedly raise thorny questions for the legal system. New rules, policies, and laws will have to be created to address them.

Similarly, no one could have anticipated the ways that DNA testing would change laws involving criminal investigations. Legislatures have passed statutes that mandate the collection of DNA samples from millions of Americans, including those who have simply been arrested and are awaiting trial. Some of these individuals have objected to having their DNA collected and catalogued. But law enforcement officials claim that widespread testing will help them solve more crimes and exonerate people who were wrongly convicted. (We describe the role of DNA analysis in the exoneration of convicted criminals in Chapter 5.)

Legislators must now consider what, if any, restrictions should be placed on online activities. (Cyberlaw, virtually unheard of 25 years ago, has become an important subfield of the law.) For example, individuals have been convicted of sexually abusing minors after they "sexted" nude and seminude pictures on their cellphones, and drivers have been ticketed for sneaking a peek at their smartphones when stopped at red lights, thereby violating their states' hands-free phone requirements. Should laws regulate these activities? Many people believe that these laws protect the dignity and safety of the public, yet others claim that they interfere with constitutionally protected speech and privacy rights. But most people would agree that vast changes in society have necessitated far-reaching adjustments in the law.

The technological development of the automobile produced several new potential adversarial relationships, including pedestrians versus drivers, and hence new laws. Car accidents—even minor ones—cause conflicts over basic rights. Consider a driver whose car strikes and injures a pedestrian. Does this driver have a legal responsibility to report the incident to the police? Yes. But doesn't this requirement violate the Fifth Amendment to the U.S. Constitution, which safeguards each of us against self-incrimination, against being a witness in conflict with our own best interests?

Shortly after automobiles became popular in the first two decades of the 20th century, a man named Edward Rosenheimer was charged with violating the newly necessary reporting laws. He did not contest the charge that he had caused an accident that injured another person, but he claimed that the law requiring him to report it to the police was unconstitutional because it forced him to incriminate himself. Therefore, he argued, this particular law should be removed from the books, and he should not be jailed on the charge of leaving the scene of an accident. Surprisingly, a New York judge agreed with him and released him from custody.

But authorities in New York were unhappy with a decision that permitted a person who had caused an injury to avoid being apprehended, so they appealed the decision to a higher court, the New York Court of Appeals. This court, recognizing that the Constitution and the recent law clashed with each other, ruled in favor of the state and overturned the previous decision. This appeals court concluded that rights to "constitutional privilege"—that is, to avoid self-incrimination—must give way to the competing principle of the right of injured persons to seek redress for their sufferings (Post, 1963).

These examples illustrate that the law is an evolving human creation, designed to arbitrate between values in opposition to each other. Before the advent of automobiles, hit-and-run accidents seldom occurred. Before the invention of smartphones, texting at stoplights (or worse, while driving) never occurred. However, once cars and smartphones became a part of society,

new laws were enacted to regulate their use, and courts have determined that most of these new laws are constitutional.

THE PSYCHOLOGICAL STUDY OF LAW

Laws and legal systems are studied by several traditional disciplines other than psychology. For example, anthropologists compare laws (and mechanisms for instituting and altering laws) in different societies and relate them to other characteristics of these societies. They may be interested in how frequently women are raped in different types of societies and in the relationship between rape and other factors, such as the extent of separation of the sexes during childhood or the degree to which males dominate females.

Sociologists, in contrast, usually study a specific society and examine its institutions (e.g., the family, the church, or the subculture) to determine their role in developing adherence to the law. The sociologist might study the role that social class plays in criminal behavior. This approach tries to predict and explain social behavior by focusing on groups of people rather than on individuals.

A psychological approach to the law emphasizes its human determinants. The focus in the psychological approach is on the individual as the unit of analysis. Individuals are seen as responsible for their own conduct and as contributing to its causation. Psychology examines the thoughts and actions of individuals—drug abusers, petty thieves, police officers, victims, jurors, expert witnesses, corporate lawyers, judges, defendants, prison guards, and parole officers, for example—involved in the legal system. Psychology assumes that characteristics of these participants affect how the system operates, and it also recognizes that the law, in turn, can affect individuals' characteristics and behavior (Ogloff & Finkelman, 1999). By *characteristics*, we mean these persons' abilities, perspectives, values, and experiences—all the factors that influence their behavior. These characteristics determine whether a defendant and his or her attorney will accept a plea bargain or go to trial. They determine whether a Hispanic juror will be more sympathetic toward a Hispanic defendant than toward a non-Hispanic defendant. They determine whether a juvenile offender will fare better in a residential treatment facility or a correctional institution.

But the behavior of participants in the legal system is not just a result of their personal qualities. The setting in which they operate matters as well. Kurt Lewin, a founder of social psychology, proposed the equation $B = f(p, e)$: behavior is a function of the person and the environment. Qualities of the external environment and pressures from the situation affect an individual's behavior. A prosecuting attorney may recommend a harsher sentence for a convicted felon if the case has been highly publicized, the community is outraged over the crime, and the prosecutor happens to be waging a reelection campaign. A juror holding out for a guilty verdict may yield if all the other jurors passionately proclaim the defendant's innocence. A juvenile offender may desist from criminal behavior if his gang affiliations are severed. The social environment affects legally relevant choices and conduct.

This book concentrates on the behavior of participants in the legal system. As the examples at the beginning of this chapter indicate, we are all active participants in the system, even if we do not work in occupations directly tied to the administration of justice. We all face daily choices that are affected by the law—whether to speed through a school zone because we are late to class, whether to report the person who removes someone else's laptop from a table at the library, whether to vote in favor of or against a proposal to end capital punishment. Hence, this book will also devote some attention to the determinants of our conceptions of justice and the moral dilemmas we all face.

But this book will pay particular attention to the role of psychology in the criminal and civil justice systems and to the central participants in those settings: defendants and witnesses, civil and criminal lawyers, judges and juries, convicts and parole boards. It will also focus on the activities of **forensic psychologists**, professionals who generate and communicate information to answer specific legal questions or to help resolve legal disputes (Heilbrun, Grisso, & Goldstein, 2009; Melton, Petrila, Poythress, & Slobogin, 2007). Most forensic psychologists are trained as clinical psychologists, whose specialty involves the psychological evaluation and treatment of others. Forensic psychologists are often asked to evaluate a person and then prepare a report for a court, and sometimes provide expert testimony in a hearing

or trial. For example, they may evaluate adult criminal defendants or children involved with the juvenile justice system and offer the court information relevant to determining whether the defendant has a mental disorder that prevents him from going to trial, what the defendant's mental state was at the time of the offense, or what treatment might be appropriate for a particular defendant. But psychologists can play many other roles in the legal system, as well. We describe these roles later in the chapter.

BASIC CHOICES IN THE PSYCHOLOGICAL STUDY OF THE LAW

Just as each of us has to make decisions about personal values, society must decide which values it wants its laws to reflect. Choices lead to conflict, and often the resulting dilemmas are difficult to resolve. Should the laws uphold the rights of specific individuals or protect society in general? Should each of us be able to impose our preferences on others, or must we be attentive to other people's needs? You may have pondered this question while stopped at a traffic light next to a car with a deafening subwoofer. One of Madonna's neighbors in a posh New York City apartment building certainly pondered this question. She filed a lawsuit against the pop icon, claiming that her music was so loud that the neighbor had to leave several times a day. Whose rights prevail? A commonly asked question that taps that dilemma is whether it is better for ten murderers to go free than for one innocent person to be sentenced to death. The law struggles with the fact that rights desirable for some individuals may be problematic for others.

This tension between individual rights and the common good is one example of the basic choices that pervade the psychological study of the law. But there are others. In this chapter, we highlight four basic choices inherent in laws and that apply to each of us in the United States, Canada, and many other countries. Each choice creates a dilemma and has psychological implications. No decision about these choices will be completely satisfactory because no decision can simultaneously attain two incompatible goals—such as individual rights and societal rights—both of which we value. These four choices (and the tension inherent in their competing values) are so basic that they surface repeatedly throughout this book.

Consider another choice, that between individual freedom (or discretion) and equality for all. Our society champions both freedom and equality, but it is hard to achieve these aspirations at the same time. Ponder the small-town civic organization that has always had a "males-only" policy at its Friday night dinners and is also a vehicle by which prominent citizens transact their business. The men enjoy the "freedom" to act like "good ole boys" in the company of their own gender. But what if a woman starts a new insurance agency in town? Doesn't she have the right to "equality"—to full and equal participation in the civic organization that is influential in the success of any business in this community? It is hard to see how a resolution of this conflict could fully meet both of these goals (freedom of existing members and equality among all comers). The balance in such cases often shifts from one value to another, emphasizing the attainment of first one and then the other goal.

The First Choice: Rights of Individuals versus the Common Good

Consider the following:

- Smokers have long been restricted to smoky airport lounges and back sections of restaurants, and often huddle together outside of workplace doors. But now smokers are banned from lighting up in some public parks and beaches, and along shorelines and trails. When New York City enacted a ban on smoking in its 1,700 public parks in 2011, Lauren Johnston was ecstatic. She blogged about smokers polluting the air along her running loop. But Bill Saar saw it differently: "It's the most idiotic law they ever made. I've been a smoker for over 20 years. I'm not going to stop," said Saar as he puffed on a cigar while selling figurines in Union Square (Durkin, 2011). Should cities be able to limit smoking in parks shared by all? Whose rights prevail?

- In 2012, six states—Massachusetts, Connecticut, Vermont, New Hampshire, New York and Iowa—as well as the District of Columbia allowed same-sex marriage, and legislatures in Washington State and Maryland passed laws, subject to voter approval, granting same-sex couples the right to marry. Yet laws and

A lesbian couple celebrating their marriage

initiatives passed in several other states barred same-sex couples from marrying. Americans are clearly divided on this issue: According to a 2011 Gallup poll, 53% of Americans favor same-sex marriage, with young people being considerably more supportive than older people. This issue raises complex questions about individual rights to marry whom one wishes versus traditional definitions of the family.

- In a less serious sort of dispute, a growing number of cities have made it a crime to wear "sagging pants," and some cases have actually gone to trial. Three defendants were charged with violating the "decency ordinance" in Riviera Beach, Florida. Their public defenders argued that the law violated principles of freedom of expression. But the town's mayor, Thomas Masters, said that voters "just got tired of having to look at people's behinds or their undergarments ... I think society has the right to draw the line" (Newton, 2009).

Values in Conflict. The preceding vignettes share a common theme. On the one hand, individuals possess rights, and one function of the law is to ensure that these rights are protected. The United States is perhaps the most individualistic society in the world. People can deviate from the norm, or "do their own thing," to a greater degree in the United States than virtually anywhere else. Freedom and personal autonomy are two of our most deeply desired values; "the right to liberty" is a key phrase in the U.S. Constitution.

On the other hand, our society also has expectations. People need to feel secure. They need to believe that potential lawbreakers are discouraged from breaking laws because they know they will be punished. All of us have rights to a peaceful, safe existence. Likewise, society claims a vested interest in restricting those who take risks that may injure themselves or others, because these actions can create burdens on individuals and on society. The tension between individual rights and the collective good is illustrated in the case we describe in Box 1.1.

It is clear that two sets of rights and two goals for the law are often in conflict. The tension between the rights of the individual and the constraints that may be placed on the individual for the collective good is always present. It has factored prominently into various U.S. Supreme Court decisions since the 1960s with respect to the rights of criminal suspects and defendants versus the rights of crime victims and the power of the police.

In the 1960s, the Supreme Court established a number of principles that provided or expanded explicit rights for those suspected of breaking the law. The *Miranda* rule, guaranteeing the right to remain silent (detailed in Chapter 7), was established in 1966. About the same time, the courts required that criminal defendants, in all cases in which incarceration was possible, have the right to an attorney, even if they cannot afford to pay for one. These and other rights were established in an effort to redress a perceived imbalance between a lowly defendant and a powerful government.

But many of these rights were trimmed in subsequent years, when courts frequently ruled in favor of the police. For example, in 1996, the Supreme Court ruled that the police can properly stop a motorist whom they believe has violated traffic laws even if their ulterior motive is to investigate the possibility of illegal drug dealing (*Whren v. United States*, 1996). In 2012, the Court ruled that jail officials can strip search petty offenders even if there is no suspicion they are concealing weapons or contraband (*Florence v. Board of Chosen Freeholders*, 2012).

Two Models of the Criminal Justice System. The conflict between the rights of individuals and the rights of society is related to a distinction between two models of the criminal justice system. This distinction is between the due process model and the crime control model (Packer, 1964). The values underlying each of these models are legitimate, and the goal of our society is to achieve a balance between them. But because different priorities are important to each model, there is constant tension between them.

B o x 1.1 THE CASE OF THE WESTBORO BAPTIST CHURCH: DO INDIVIDUALS HAVE THE RIGHT TO USE OFFENSIVE SPEECH?

In March 2006, Lance Corporal Matthew Snyder, age 20, was killed in Iraq. His funeral was held at a Roman Catholic church in Westminster, Maryland. Protesting outside of the church were seven members of the Westboro Baptist Church, a fringe group based in Topeka, Kansas that attends military funerals across the country to broadcast their belief that God is punishing troops because America tolerates homosexuality. They carry signs that read, "God hates fags" and "Thank God for dead soldiers." Snyder's father sued Westboro, alleging that picketers invaded his privacy and caused emotional distress that compounded his loss. He claimed that he wanted to protect other families from the pain inflicted on his family by members of the Westboro Baptist Church.

But the U.S. Supreme Court ruled against Snyder (*Snyder v. Phelps*, 2011), upholding Westboro's right to freely express itself. In his majority opinion, Chief Justice John Roberts reasoned that the words on Westboro's signs were "matters of public import" and thus were protected by the First Amendment. He wrote that to ensure that public debate is not stifled, even hurtful and offensive speech must be protected. Snyder reacted with sadness, saying there is something very wrong with allowing these protesters to desecrate a Marine's funeral. Westboro vowed to quadruple its efforts at military funerals in the future.

Critical Thought Question
What two values were in conflict in this case?

The **due process model**, favored in the 1960s, places primary value on the protection of citizens, including criminal suspects, from possible abuses by the police and the law enforcement system generally. It assumes the innocence of suspects and requires that they be treated fairly (receive "due process") by the criminal justice system. This model's proponents subscribe to the maxim that "it is better that 10 guilty persons shall go free than that one innocent person should suffer." Thus the due process model emphasizes the rights of individuals, especially those suspected of crimes, over the temptation by society to assume suspects are guilty even before a trial.

In contrast, the **crime control model**, favored in the 1990s, seeks the apprehension and punishment of lawbreakers. It emphasizes the efficient detection of suspects and the effective prosecution of defendants, to help ensure that criminal activity is being contained or reduced. The crime control model is exemplified by a statement by former U.S. Attorney General William P. Barr with respect to career criminals. He noted that the goal is "incapacitation through incarceration" (Barr, 1992)—that is, removing such criminals permanently from circulation.

When the crime control model is dominant in society, laws are passed that in other times would be seen as unacceptable violations of individual rights. The Arizona immigration law described at the beginning of the chapter and similar laws in other states are examples. They raise complicated questions about the rights of individuals to be free from police scrutiny and the obligation of the government to provide safety and security to its citizens.

Despite the drop in crime rates in recent years, vestiges of the crime control model still linger in the United States, more so than in Canada, Europe, or Australia. As we point out in Chapter 14, the United States incarcerates a higher percentage of its citizens than any other country (currently 1 of every 32 Americans are imprisoned or on probation or parole). According to the Center on Juvenile and Criminal Justice, the United States has only 5% of the world's population but nearly 25% of its prisoners.

The global recession may slowly be changing societal options for dealing with crime, however. As federal and state budgets tighten, legislators and law enforcement officials have begun to reevaluate many "tough-on-crime" policies. These strategies boosted spending on prisons but did little to prevent repeat offending by released inmates (Dvoskin, Skeem, Novaco, & Douglas, 2011). Because of reduced resources, officials have become attentive to the need to find cheaper and more effective alternatives for controlling crime and ensuring public safety. Some new programs have already been shown to reduce repeat offending. Crime rates in Texas dropped after it began investing in treatment programs for parolees. The prison population in Mississippi was reduced by 22% after it allowed inmates to earn time off their sentences for participating in educational and reentry programs. Other proven alternatives include providing employment counseling and substance abuse and mental health treatment for inmates, and diverting offenders from the criminal justice system and into community-based treatment programs. We describe many of these alternatives in Chapter 9.

The Second Choice: Equality versus Discretion

Kenneth Peacock was a long-distance trucker who was caught in an ice storm and came home at the wrong time. He walked in the door to find his wife Sandra in bed with another man. Peacock chased the man away and some four hours later, in the heat of an argument, shot his wife in the head with a hunting rifle. Peacock pled guilty to voluntary manslaughter and was sentenced to 18 months in prison. At the sentencing, Baltimore County Circuit Court Judge Robert E. Cahill said he wished he did not have to send Peacock to prison at all but knew that he must to "keep the system honest" (Lewin, 1994). He continued, "I seriously wonder how many men … would have the strength to walk away without inflicting some corporal punishment."

Move the clock ahead one day. A female defendant pleads guilty to voluntary manslaughter in a different Baltimore courtroom. She killed her husband after 11 years of abuse and was given a 3-year sentence, three times longer than that sought by prosecutors (Lewin, 1994). Some people find no inconsistency in the severity of these punishments, believing that each case should be judged on its own merits. However, psychology analyzes these decisions as examples of a choice between the goals of equality and discretion.

What should be the underlying principle guiding the response to persons accused of violating the law? Again, we discover that two equally desirable values— equality and discretion—are often incompatible and hence create conflict. The principle of **equality** means that all people who commit the same crime or misdeed should receive the same consequences. But blind pursuit of equality can lead to unfairness in situations in which the particular characteristics of offender, victim, or offense matter. For example, most people would think differently about punishing someone who killed randomly, ruthlessly, and without remorse, and someone else who killed a loved one suffering from a painful and terminal illness. In this example, discretion is called for. **Discretion** in the legal system involves considering the circumstances of certain offenders and offenses to determine the appropriate consequences for wrongdoing. Psychology provides concepts through which this conflict can be studied and better understood.

The Principle of Equality. Fundamental to our legal system is the assumption advanced by the founders of the American republic that "all men are created equal." In fact, the Equal Protection Clause of the Fourteenth Amendment states that no state shall "deny to any person within its jurisdiction the equal protection of the laws." This statement is frequently interpreted to mean that all people should be treated equally and that no one should receive special treatment by the courts simply because he or she is rich, influential, or otherwise advantaged. We cherish the belief that in the United States, politically powerful or affluent people are brought before the courts and, if guilty, convicted and punished just like anyone else who commits similar offenses. Consider the example of disgraced financier Bernard Madoff. A former chairman of the NASDAQ Stock Exchange, Madoff pled guilty in 2009 to perpetrating the largest investor fraud in history, and exchanged his three homes and a yacht on the French Riviera for a cell in the federal prison system.

Bernard Madoff

But this value of equality before the law is not always implemented. In the last three decades, Americans have witnessed a series of incidents that—at least on the surface—seem to indicate unequal treatment of citizens by the legal system. A common practice among police and state patrols in the United States is *profiling*—viewing certain characteristics as indicators of criminal behavior. African-American and Latino motorists have filed numerous lawsuits over the practice of profiling, alleging that the police, in an effort to seize illegal drugs and weapons or find undocumented immigrants, apply a race-based profile to stop and search them more frequently than White drivers. Said Michigan Congressman John Conyers, Jr., "There are virtually no African-American males—including Congressmen, actors, athletes and office workers—who have not been stopped at one time or another for … driving while black" (Barovick, 1998).

The issue is not limited to driving. It affects people when they shop, eat in restaurants, travel in trains and airplanes, hail a cab, and walk through their neighborhoods. New York City police officers stopped approximately 3 million people between 2004 and 2009, questioning all and frisking and arresting some. But police department statistics show that the stops were not race neutral. Black people accounted for 52% of the stops, and Hispanics for 30%. According to columnist Bob Herbert, "[T]he people getting stopped and frisked are mostly young, and most of them are black or brown and poor … If the police officers were treating white middle-class or wealthy individuals this way, the movers and shakers in this town would be apoplectic" (Herbert, 2010).

Since police agencies have started gathering statistics on the racial makeup of people targeted for traffic stops, border inspections, and other routine searches, and these disparities have come to light, some courts have ruled that a person's appearance may not be the basis for such stops. Psychologists also have a role to play on this issue, gathering data on the psychological consequences to victims of racial profiling, improving police training so that cultural and racial awareness is enhanced, and examining how decision makers form implicit judgments of others on the basis of race.

In keeping with the laudable goal of equality under the law, the U.S. Supreme Court has occasionally applied a **principle of proportionality** to its analysis of cases involving criminal sentencing. This principle means that the punishment should be consistently related to the magnitude of the offense. More

AP Photo/ Louis Lanzano, file

serious wrongdoing should earn more severe penalties. If a relatively minor crime leads to a harsh punishment, then the fundamental values of proportionality and, hence, equality have been violated.

The principle of proportionality has influenced the way that juvenile offenders are sentenced. Recognizing that impulsiveness and psychosocial immaturity render juveniles both less culpable and more likely to be rehabilitated than adult offenders, the U.S. Supreme Court has overturned harsh sentences for juvenile offenders in the quest for equality. Individuals who commit murder before the age of 18 cannot be subjected to the death penalty (*Roper v. Simmons*, 2005) nor automatically sentenced to life without the possibility of parole (*Miller v. Alabama*, 2012). The Court has determined that because juveniles sentenced to life in prison would spend more years and a larger percentage of their lives behind bars, that sentence is disproportionately harsh and not equal to a life sentence received by adults. We describe the case that led to that ruling in Box 1.2.

Although the Supreme Court's decision in the case of *Miller v. Alabama* seems consistent with a due process perspective that emphasizes individual rights, the Court has also upheld the constitutionality of three-strikes laws that reflect the crime control model's goal of keeping lawbreakers off the streets. These laws require that criminals convicted of a third felony, no matter how minor, be sentenced to 25 years to life in prison. The court decided that this punishment is not disproportionate to the severity of a third felony offense (*Ewing v. California*, 2003). So, even the highest court in the land struggles with the meaning of equality and its application to diverse sets of facts.

The Value of Discretion. Although equality often remains an overriding principle, society also believes that in certain circumstances, discretion is appropriate. Discretion refers to judgments about the circumstances of certain offenses that lead to appropriate *variations* in how the system responds to these offenses. It acknowledges that rigid application of the law can lead to injustices.

Many professionals in the legal system have the opportunity to exercise discretion, and most do so regularly. Police officers show discretion when they decide not to arrest someone who has technically broken the law. They show discretion when they calculate the level of fines for speeding. (Incidentally, saying "I'm sorry" actually results in lower fines [Day & Ross, 2011]!) Prosecutors exercise discretion when they decide which of many arrestees to charge

---

B o x 1.2 THE CASE OF EVAN MILLER: LIFE SENTENCES FOR JUVENILE OFFENDERS ARE EXCESSIVE PUNISHMENT

On July 15, 2003, 52-year-old Cole Cannon knocked on the door of his neighbor's trailer in the small town of Speake, Alabama, asking for some food. That trailer belonged to the family of 14-year-old Evan Miller, an active drug user being raised in an extremely abusive family and suffering from mental health problems. After Cannon had eaten, Miller and a friend accompanied him back to his trailer, intending to get him drunk and rob him. The three played drinking games and smoked marijuana, and when Cannon passed out, Miller began hitting him, first with his fists and then with a baseball bat. The friends then set fire to Cannon's trailer, where he died of smoke inhalation.

Miller was charged with murder in the course of arson and was tried as an adult, subject to all the penalties of adult felons. After he was convicted, the judge imposed a mandatory sentence of life without parole. Miller's appeal focused on his immature judgment and lack of moral sense. His attorneys argued that such a severe sentence was a form of cruel and unusual punishment, banned by the Eighth Amendment.

The case was eventually decided by the U.S. Supreme Court. Among the documents that justices considered was a report submitted by a group of psychological scientists, summarizing research relevant to adolescent development. It concluded that (1) adolescents are less mature than adults in ways that make them less culpable, and (2) it is not possible to predict with any reliability whether a particular juvenile offender is likely to reoffend violently (American Psychological Association, 2011). In her majority decision, Justice Elena Kagan acknowledged that youths are different from adults, given their "diminished culpability and heightened capacity for change." She concluded that laws that mandate life sentences, when applied to juvenile offenders, are unconstitutional. Miller's case was referred back to the courts in Alabama for reconsideration of his life sentence.

Critical Thought Question
According to the Supreme Court, why does a sentence of life without parole constitute cruel and unusual punishment when applied to a juvenile offender?

and for what particular crime. Juries exercise discretion in not convicting defendants who killed under circumstances that may have justified their actions (e.g., self-defense, heat of passion). A jury may opt to exercise discretion when it deliberates the fate of community watch volunteer George Zimmerman, charged in the shooting death of an unarmed teenager, Trayvon Martin, in 2012. Zimmerman claimed that he acted in self-defense.

Parole boards also have the opportunity to exercise discretion when they decide whether to commute a death sentence to life imprisonment (a process called granting clemency) or to allow an execution to proceed as planned. The Georgia Board of Pardons and Parole faced that stark choice in 2011 when it had to decide whether death row inmate Troy Davis, who had been convicted for murdering a police officer, should be executed by lethal injection or allowed to

---

B o x 1.3 THE CASE OF TROY DAVIS AND A PAROLE BOARD'S DISCRETION

Former President Jimmy Carter, Pope Benedict XVI, the Indigo Girls, Nobel Laureate Desmond Tutu, former FBI director William Sessions, Amnesty International, and former Georgia Supreme Court justices may not agree on much. But in 2011 they all called for a stop to the pending execution of Georgia death row inmate Troy Davis, whom they claimed was an innocent man. Davis was convicted of murder in the 1989 shooting death of off-duty Savannah police officer Mark MacPhail and sentenced to death. Over the course of 20 years, Davis maintained his innocence, and his claim was bolstered by the possible confession of another person and by the recantation of seven eyewitnesses who said they lied during Davis' trial because they were threatened by an alternate suspect. Some jurors who convicted Davis signed affidavits declaring that they doubted his guilt.

In Georgia, the authority to commute a death sentence into a less severe sentence rests with the Georgia

Board of Pardons and Paroles. (In some states, governors have this discretion.) That board had declined to commute Davis' sentence once before. With an execution date pending and all other options exhausted, Davis' attorneys appealed one last time to the five-member board, which conducted a hearing in which it heard from Davis's attorneys and supporters, and from prosecutors and MacPhail's relatives. Despite doubts about Davis's guilt, his surprising assortment of supporters, and petitions, rallies, and vigils held around the world on his behalf, the board denied Davis's request. He was executed in September, 2011.

Critical Thought Question
Explain why the Georgia Board of Pardons and Paroles may not have been willing to grant clemency to Troy Davis in 2011.

Supporters of Troy Davis

live. This case, described in Box 1.3, raises interesting questions about both discretion and the possibility of error in the criminal justice system.

Discretion may be most obvious in the sentences administered by judges to convicted criminals. In many cases, judges are able to consider the particular circumstances of the defendant and of the crime itself when they determine the sentence. It would seem that this use of discretion is good, yet as we describe in Chapter 14, it can also lead to **sentencing disparity**, the tendency for judges to administer a variety of penalties for the same crime. The contrasting sentences handed out by judges in the Baltimore cases we described earlier provide one example of sentencing disparity.

Sentencing disparity is also apparent in the penalties given to African Americans and members of other minority groups. African Americans are imprisoned at rates five to seven times higher than those of White Americans partly due to disparities in arrests for drug crimes. Police concentrate their attention on drugs that Blacks sell, and the penalties for possessing these drugs are severe (Tonry, 2010). Sentencing disparities can also be seen for Hispanics: one in six Hispanic males and one in 45 Hispanic females can expect to be imprisoned in his or her lifetime, more than double the rates of those who are not Hispanic (Mauer & King, 2007).

A simple explanation for this disparity is **racial bias**, whereby police officers, prosecutors, jurors, and judges use an individual's race as a basis for judgments of his or her behavior. But the situation may actually be more complex. Some studies have shown that once decision makers are made aware of the potential for racial bias, they can largely avoid it, and racial injustices in the criminal justice system have declined in recent years (Spohn, 2000).

A subtler, more insidious form of race-based judgment may be prevalent in the justice system, however. Social psychological research has shown that individuals of the same race may be stereotyped and discriminated against to different degrees, depending how "typical" of their group they appear. African Americans who possess more Afrocentric facial features may be subjected to more prejudicial treatment. An analysis of criminal sentencing in Florida showed that among Black defendants, those with more distinctive Afrocentric features were given longer sentences than those with less distinctive Afrocentric features (Blair, Judd, & Chapleau, 2004). Even more troubling, in death penalty cases involving White victims, the likelihood of a Black defendant being sentenced to death is influenced by whether he has a stereotypically Black appearance (Eberhardt, Davies, Purdie-Vaughns, & Johnson, 2006).

To counteract sentencing disparity, many states implemented what is known as **determinate sentencing:** the offense determines the sentence, and judges and parole commissions have little discretion. But judges were frustrated by the severe limitations imposed on their discretion by determinate sentencing. One federal judge who resigned his appointment in protest said, "It's an unfair system that has been dehumanized. There are rarely two cases that are identical. Judges should always have discretion. That's why we're judges. But now we're being made to be robots."

The pendulum has now swung away from determinate sentencing and toward allowing judges more discretion. Permitting judges more leeway to consider factors such as the defendant's background, motivations for committing the crime, and any psychological disorders may strike a balance between the uniformity that determinate sentencing imposes and the judicial discretion that many judges prefer.

The Third Choice: To Discover the Truth or to Resolve Conflicts

What is the purpose of a court hearing or a trial? Your first reaction may be "To find out the truth, of course!" Determining the truth means learning the facts of a dispute, including events, intentions, actions, and outcomes. All this assumes that "what really happened" between two parties can be determined.

Finding out the truth is a desirable goal, but it may also be lofty and, sometimes, downright impossible. The truth often lies somewhere between competing versions of an event. Because it is difficult for even well-meaning people to ascertain the facts in certain cases, some observers have proposed that the real purpose of a hearing or trial is to provide social stability by resolving conflict. Supreme Court Justice Louis Brandeis once wrote that "it is more important that the applicable rule of law be settled than [that] it be settled right" (*Burnet v. Coronado Oil and Gas Co.*, 1932). This is a shift away from viewing the legal system's purpose as doing justice toward viewing its goal as "creating a sense that justice is being done" (Miller & Boster, 1977, p. 34).

Because truth is elusive, the most important priority of a hearing or a trial may be to provide a setting in which all interested parties have their "day in court." Justice replaces truth as the predominant goal. In fact, attorneys representing the opposing parties in a case do not necessarily seek "the truth." Nor do they represent themselves as "objective." They reflect a different value—the importance of giving their side the best representation possible, within the limits of the law. (The Code of Ethics of the American Bar Association even instructs attorneys to defend their clients "zealously.") Because lawyers believe the purpose of a hearing or trial is to win disputes, they present arguments supporting their client's perspective and back up their arguments with the best available evidence.

One argument in favor of the adversary system, in which a different attorney represents each party, is that it encourages the attorneys to discover and introduce all evidence that might induce the judge or jury to react favorably to their client's case. When both sides believe that they have had the chance to voice their case fully and their witnesses have revealed all the relevant facts, participants are more likely to feel they have been treated fairly by the system, and the system is more likely to be considered an effective one. This is an important part of a theory known as **procedural justice**, a concept presented in Chapter 2.

"Conflict resolution" and "truth," as goals, are not always incompatible. When each participant ensures that his or her concerns and supporting documentation are presented in court, the goal of learning the truth becomes more attainable. But frequently a tension between these goals exists, and in some instances, the satisfactory resolution of a conflict may be socially and morally preferable to the discovery of an objectively established truth. Yet resolving conflict in a hurried or haphazard manner can have a downside, as illustrated by the experience of Richard Jewell.

Jewell was a security guard at the 1996 Summer Olympics in Atlanta. Shortly after a bombing that disrupted the Games, the Federal Bureau of Investigation (FBI) began to question Jewell, who discovered the bomb. Although at first the FBI denied that he was a suspect, they treated him like one, and his name and photograph were widely publicized. The pressure to find the person responsible for this terrifying act—and the desire to give people a sense that no more bombings would occur because the perpetrator had been caught—doubtless influenced the premature focus on Richard Jewell. Despite relentless FBI investigation, no charges were brought against

Eric Rudolph, a North Carolina fugitive, who pled guilty in 2005 to a bombing at the 1996 Olympics in Atlanta

Johnny Crawford/The Image Works

Jewell, and in 2005, Eric Rudolph, a fugitive who lived in the hills of North Carolina for years after the bombing, pleaded guilty to the offense.

Truth versus Conflict Resolution in Plea Bargaining and Settlement Negotiations. The legal system is a massive bureaucracy, and in every bureaucracy there is a temptation to value pragmatic efficiency rather than correct or just outcomes. The heavy reliance on plea bargaining is often criticized because it appears to give priority to conflict resolution over truth seeking. As we describe in Chapter 8, between 90% and 95% of defendants never go to trial; they accept the offer of the prosecutor and plead guilty to a lesser charge. Even some innocent persons plea bargain after being convinced that the evidence against them is overwhelming. Indeed, plea bargaining is an integral part of the criminal justice system. The state benefits by avoiding the expense and trouble of trial and the possibility of an acquittal, and by obtaining the testimony of the accused person against others involved in the crime. The defendant benefits by receiving some kind of reduction in the penalty imposed. In addition to these pragmatic benefits, justice is furthered by a system that rewards a show of remorse (which usually accompanies a guilty plea) and enables the prosecutor and defense counsel, together with the judge, to negotiate a resolution appropriate to the degree of wrongdoing (Kamisar, LaFave, & Israel, 1999). Nonetheless, plea bargaining reveals that the goal of maintaining stability and efficiency in the system is achieved at some cost. That cost is the public's opportunity to determine the complete truth.

The civil justice system uses a procedure similar to plea bargaining to resolve about 90% of the conflicts between a plaintiff and a defendant. **Settlement negotiation** involves a sometimes-lengthy pretrial process of give-and-take, offer-and-demand that ends when a plaintiff agrees to accept what a defendant is willing to offer to end their legal disagreement. It also favors the goal of conflict resolution at the expense of determining what *really* happened.

New Thoughts on Conflict Resolution.   Despite the traditional prominence of adversarial procedures to resolve disputes, many legal problems are actually handled in a nonadversarial manner. Throughout the book we present situations in which people work together in a cooperative way to settle their differences and reach a resolution that is acceptable to all.

Many divorcing couples opt to collaborate rather than contend with each other as they end their marriage. In situations where parents have failed to nurture their children, family court judges temporarily remove children from their homes and provide extensive counseling, education, and other social service interventions to parents, hoping eventually to restore the family unit. In some jurisdictions, people arrested for drug-related crimes are given the opportunity to have their cases resolved in drug courts that focus on treating the underlying problem of addiction, rather than simply punishing the offender. In lawsuits in which plaintiffs are injured due to defendants' negligence and the parties attempt to negotiate a settlement rather than go to trial, these negotiations offer an opportunity for defendants to apologize to plaintiffs. Research shows that apologies may advance settlement negotiations (Robbennolt, 2003), reduce plaintiffs' inclinations to sue (Greene, 2008), and dissipate tension and antagonism in the settlement process (Shuman, 2000).

What these situations have in common is that they do not operate in a zero-sum fashion in which one party wins and another loses. Rather, they attempt to maximize positive outcomes for all concerned, with the objective of keeping the dispute from escalating further and involving more formal adjudication proceedings.

The idea that the law is a social force with consequences for people's well-being, an approach termed therapeutic jurisprudence, is discussed further in Chapter 2. Reform-minded lawyers, jurists, and legal scholars advocate for legal procedures and institutions that facilitate therapeutic ends. They ask how the law can be applied or reformed to enhance individuals' welfare. Therapeutic jurisprudence has been applied in nearly all areas of the law, including criminal law, family law, employment law, probate, health care, workers' compensation, and labor arbitration.

The Fourth Choice: Science versus the Law as a Source of Decisions

When one discipline (in our case, psychology) seeks to understand another (the law), a dilemma is likely to arise because each approaches knowledge in a different way. When asked, "How do you know whether that decision is the right one?" each discipline relies on different methods, even though both share the goal of understanding human experience.

As you read this book you will learn that in many cases the U.S. Supreme Court and other courts have considered data and conclusions presented by psychologists and other social scientists. In several of these, the American Psychological Association (APA) prepared a written document, called an *amicus curiae* ("friend of the court") **brief**, for consideration by an appellate court. Such *amicus curiae* briefs provide the courts with information from psychological science and practice relevant to the issues in a particular case. In many of its decisions (including *Miller v. Alabama*, presented earlier in this chapter), the Supreme Court incorporated input from the *amicus curiae* brief, although in other cases it disregarded the social science data altogether. This inconsistency reflects the fact that the justices sometimes use different procedures and concepts from those of social science in forming their judicial opinions (Grisso & Saks, 1991).

In addition to employing different procedures, each profession may use idiosyncratic or unique concepts to describe the same phenomenon. An attorney

The justices of the U.S. Supreme Court

and a social scientist will see the same event from different perspectives. Neither is necessarily more accurate than the other and their differences are the result of exposure to and training in different points of view. The following subsections illustrate such differences in more detail (see also Ogloff & Finkelman, 1999; Robbennolt & Davidson, 2011).

Law Relies on Precedents; Psychology Relies on Scientific Methods.   In contrast to the law, psychology is generally committed to the idea that there is an objective world of experience that can be understood by adherence to the rules of science—systematic testing of hypotheses by observation and experimental methodology. As a scientist, the psychologist should be committed to a public, impersonal, objective pursuit of truth, using methods that can be repeated by others and interpreting results by predetermined standards. Although this traditional view of psychology's approach to truth is sometimes challenged as naive and simplistic because it ignores the importance of the personal, political, and historical biases that affect scientists as much as nonscientists (Gergen, 1994), it still represents the values and methods in which most psychologists are trained. (It also represents the authors' beliefs that the scientific method and the research skills of psychologists are the most essential and reliable tools available for examining the many important legal questions we address throughout the book.)

By contrast, when they establish new laws, legal experts rely heavily on **precedents**—rulings in previous cases (as well as the Constitution and the statutes) for guidance. **Case law**—the law made by judges ruling in individual cases—is very influential; statutes and constitutional safeguards do not apply to every new situation, so past cases often serve as precedents for deciding current ones. The principle of ***stare decisis*** ("let the decision stand," reflecting the importance of abiding by previous decisions) is also important in this process. Judges typically are reluctant to make decisions that contradict earlier ones, as the history of the Supreme Court's school desegregation cases indicates.

When the U.S. Supreme Court voted unanimously in 1954, in *Brown v. Board of Education*, that public school segregation was contrary to the law, many reports claimed that it "supplanted" or even "overturned" a ruling in the 1896 case of *Plessy v. Ferguson*. But intermediate decisions by the Court permitted this seemingly abrupt change to evolve gradually. A brief history of rulings that led up to the *Brown v. Board of Education* decision illustrates this phenomenon and the way that the law proceeds from case to case.

We begin with the state of Louisiana's dispute with Homer Plessy. During a train trip in Louisiana in the 1890s, Plessy sat down in a railroad car labeled "Whites Only." Plessy's ancestry was mostly Caucasian, but he had one Negro great-grandparent. Therefore, according to the laws of Louisiana at that time, Plessy was considered Black (or *colored*, the term used at that time). Plessy refused to move to a car designated for "colored" passengers, as a recently passed state law required. He took his claim to court, but a New Orleans judge ruled that, contrary to Plessy's argument, the statute that segregated railroad cars by race did not violate the Fourteenth Amendment to the Constitution. In other words, it did not fail to give Plessy "equal protection under the law." Plessy persisted in his appeal, and eventually, in 1896, the U.S. Supreme Court upheld the decision of the judge and the lower courts. Judge Henry Billings Brown, speaking for the majority faction of the Supreme Court, declared that laws that had established separate facilities for the races did not necessarily imply that one race was inferior to the other.

Although this opinion was a far cry from the 1954 *Brown* decision, which highlighted the detrimental effects of segregation on the personality development of Black children, cases decided after *Plessy* and before *Brown* would foreshadow the Court's eventual leanings. One case was brought by George McLaurin, the first Black student admitted to the University of Oklahoma's Graduate School of Education. Although McLaurin was allowed to enroll, he was segregated from all his classmates. His desk was separated from all the others by a rail, to which the sign "Reserved for Colored" was attached. He was given a separate desk at the library and was required to eat by himself in the cafeteria. In the 1950 case of *McLaurin v. Oklahoma State Regents*, the U.S. Supreme Court ruled unanimously that these procedures denied McLaurin the right to equal protection of the law. The Court concluded that such restrictions would "impair and inhibit his ability to study, to engage in discussion and exchange of views with other students." But the Court did not strike down *Plessy v. Ferguson* in this decision.

With a more liberal Court in the 1950s, there was enough momentum to reverse *Plessy v. Ferguson*, however. Chief Justice Earl Warren, who liked to ask, "What is fair?" spearheaded the unanimous decision that finally overturned the idea that separate facilities can be "equal." He wrote that separating Black children "from others of similar age and qualifications solely because of their race generates a feeling of inferiority as to their status in the community that may affect their hearts and minds in a way unlikely to ever be undone" (*Brown v. Board of Education*, 1954).

The school desegregation cases show that lawyers reason from case to case. They locate cases that are similar to the one at hand and then base their arguments on the rulings from these legal precedents. Psychologists, on the other hand, value the scientific method, rely on experimental and evaluation studies, and prefer to gather data that describe large numbers of people. Just as psychologists are cautious of findings based on very small samples, lawyers are hesitant to decide a person's fate on the basis of aggregate data drawn from other people (Ellsworth & Mauro, 1998).

Law Deals with Absolutes; Psychology Deals with Probabilities. Legal questions often require an "either–or" response: A person is either fit or unfit to be a parent; a person was either insane or sane when he or she committed a particular act (Ellsworth & Mauro, 1998). Psychologists are not comfortable reasoning in absolutes. They prefer to think in terms of probabilities (e.g., that a defendant's delusional thinking *could* indicate a psychiatric disorder, that a White eyewitness to a crime is *more likely to* misidentify a Black perpetrator than a White perpetrator). Although the law looks to psychologists for "either–or" answers (e.g., "Is the defendant competent to stand trial?" and "Was the defendant insane at the time of the crime?"), psychologists usually prefer to answer in terms of likelihoods or qualified "maybes." Lawyers may have difficulty with such inconclusive responses because they need a final resolution to a dispute.

Law Supports Contrasting Views of Reality; Psychology Seeks One Refined View of Reality. As indicated earlier, judges and jurors must decide which of two conceptions of the truth is more acceptable in light of conflicting facts. Attorneys assemble all the facts that support their side and argue forcefully that their version of the facts is the correct one. Although this procedure is similar to some scientific activities (a psychologist may do a study that compares predictions from two theories), the psychologist is trained to be objective and open to all perspectives and types of data. The psychologist's ultimate goal is to integrate or assimilate conflicting findings into one refined view of the truth, rather than choosing between alternative views.

Some observers have likened this difference between psychology and law to the difference between scaling a mountain and fighting in a boxing match. As psychologists gain a clearer understanding of a topic (e.g., the causes of elder abuse), they scale a figurative mountain, at the top of which lies true and complete understanding. Although they may never actually reach this pinnacle of knowledge, psychologists highly value the accumulation of data, the development of psychological theory, and the quest for "truth." By contrast, lawyers are less interested in ascertaining the objective truth about a topic and are more concerned with winning against their adversary, resolving a dispute, or, more recently, enhancing the laws' effect on all parties.

Such distinctions only scratch the surface of the differences between law and psychology. In Chapter 2 we consider differing notions of justice in the two fields, and in subsequent chapters we will discuss the implications of these differences. As with the previous choices, selecting one domain over the other does not always yield a satisfactory resolution. The use of both perspectives moves us closer to an adequate understanding than does relying only on one. Both psychologists and lawyers should remain aware of the limits of their own perspective and realize that other viewpoints are essential for a fuller understanding of complex behavioral issues in the law.

But the contrast in knowledge-generating procedures does raise difficult procedural questions. For example, given the differences in approach, how should a psychologist respond to the challenge of studying the law? What roles should the psychologist play in the legal system? What ethical concerns are associated with psychologists' involvement in the legal system?

PSYCHOLOGISTS' ROLES IN THE LAW

Most courses in psychology portray only two roles for psychologists: the scientist, who conducts basic research about the causes and development of behavior, and the applied psychologist (usually a clinical psychologist), who tries to understand and assist individuals or groups in addressing behavioral issues. The possibilities are more elaborate, however, when the psychologist is involved in the legal system. We describe five distinct roles for psychologists in the legal system: basic scientist, applied scientist, policy evaluator, forensic evaluator, and consultant. The work inherent in these roles ranges from isolated academic research in psychology that may be relevant to law, on one end, to active collaboration with people who work in the legal system, on the other end.

As you will see, the five roles vary in several respects. But whatever the role, it carries standards about what is acceptable and unacceptable behavior. Professionals often develop explicit statements of ethical standards of behavior. For psychologists, those principles—known as the Ethical Principles of Psychologists and Code of Conduct—have been published by the American Psychological Association (2012a). They describe a series of broad principles followed by a more specific set of standards. Adherence to the standards is mandatory for psychologists. Among the many topics they cover is when psychologists should terminate treatment and how to do so.

Making the right ethical choice is complicated. Sometimes, the principles specified by these ethics codes conflict with the psychologist's legal responsibilities. The most explicit illustration of this dilemma is the ethical obligation to protect clients' confidentiality when they have threatened to harm others and the legal responsibility to report those threats. This conflict was apparent in the controversial *Tarasoff* decision by the Supreme Court of California, described in Box 1.4.

In the following sections, we describe the various roles that psychologists assume in relation to the legal system and the ethical issues that arise in each context. A footnote on psychologists' relationship to the law: Students often wonder how they can become involved in this field as basic scientists, applied scientists, policy evaluators, forensic evaluators, or consultants. What career paths should one pursue, and what professional opportunities exist at the ends of those trails? How might a developmental psychologist, a cognitive neuropsychologist, or a clinician (for example) interact with the legal system? The website of the American Psychology-Law Society (a division of the APA) has practical and career-related advice for practitioners, educators, researchers, and students (www.ap-ls.org). Those undertaking careers in psychology and law should also familiarize themselves with the ethical requirements pertaining to their professions.

The Psychologist as a Basic Scientist of the Law

A **basic scientist** pursues knowledge for its own sake. Basic scientists study a phenomenon for the satisfaction of understanding it and contributing to

---

B o x 1.4 THE CASE OF TATIANA TARASOFF: THE DUTY TO PROTECT

Few legal decisions have had as much impact on the practice of psychotherapy as the now-famous case of *Tarasoff v. Regents of the University of California*. The decision focuses on the duties required of psychotherapists whose clients threaten violence.

Prosenjit Poddar was a graduate student at the University of California who became infatuated with Tatiana Tarasoff. Poddar was inexperienced in romantic relationships and was confused about Tatiana's on-again–off-again behavior; she was friendly toward him one day but avoided him completely the next night. After Poddar became a client of a psychologist at the university counseling center, he confided that he intended to kill a girl who had rebuffed him. The psychologist told his supervisor of this threat and then called the campus police, requesting that they detain Poddar. They did so but soon released him, believing his promise that he would stay away from Tatiana, who was out of the country at the time. Poddar didn't keep his promise. Two months later, he went to Tatiana's home and stabbed her to death. He was eventually convicted of murder.

Tatiana Tarasoff's parents sued the university, the psychologists, and the campus police for failing to warn them or their daughter about Poddar's threats. The California Supreme Court ruled in the parents' favor by deciding that the university had been negligent. The first *Tarasoff* decision (1974) recognized the duty of a psychotherapist to warn identifiable potential victims of therapy patients when the therapist "knows or should have known" that the patient presented a threat to that victim. The court established a standard that therapists have a duty to use "reasonable care" to protect identifiable potential victims from clients in psychotherapy who threaten violence. A second *Tarasoff* decision in 1976 broadened this duty to include the protection of third parties from patient violence. Courts in several other states have extended this duty to the protection of property and the protection of all foreseeable victims, not just identifiable ones.

The *Tarasoff* case still governs psychologists' conduct in multiple states. Many psychologists feel caught in a no-win situation: They can be held responsible for their clients' violence if they do not warn potential victims, but they can also be held responsible for breaching their clients' confidentiality if they do.

Critical Thought Question
Why is it necessary to specify explicitly what a psychologist must do if he or she hears a client threaten to harm a person or property?

---

scientific advances in the area. They do not necessarily seek to apply their research findings; many have no concern with whether the knowledge they generate will be used to resolve real-world problems. Yet often their results can address important practical issues, including some that arise in the law. For example, though not specifically conducted for use in the courtroom, laboratory research on visual perception can help us understand the accuracy of eyewitness testimony about a crime or accident. Psychologists who test different theories of memory promote a better understanding of whether repression can cause long-term forgetting of traumatic events. Basic research on the relationship between social attitudes and behavior can clarify why people obey or disobey the law. Research in personality psychology can help to show what kind of person will become a follower in a terrorist group and what kind of person will be a leader. Studies of adolescents' brain development may be relevant to their decisions about whether to commit petty crimes. Finally, research can assess whether forensic psychologists' attitudes about the causes of crime affect their professional evaluations of criminal defendants.

The Ethics of the Basic Scientist. Like all scientists, psychologists who do basic research must adhere to standards of conduct in how they undertake and report their studies. In practical terms, this means that they cannot fabricate or forge data, plagiarize, or present a skewed selection of the data to hide observations that do not fit their conclusions. They must treat human subjects in an ethical manner. (All institutions that receive federal research funding have review boards that evaluate the way scientists treat human and animal subjects.) Basic researchers sometimes have a conflict of interest when faced with competing concerns such as honestly reporting their research findings versus making a profit or "getting published." In these situations, they should learn to recognize and be honest about potential conflicts of interest and communicate them to interested parties before undertaking the research.

The Psychologist as an Applied Scientist in the Law

An **applied scientist** is dedicated to applying knowledge to solve real-life problems. Most of the public's awareness of a psychologist's work reflects this role, whether this awareness comes from viewing TV's Dr. Phil or watching a psychologist testify as an expert witness in a dramatized trial. Indeed, an important role for psychologists who are interested in applying the findings of their profession involves serving as an expert witness in a legislative hearing or in a courtroom.

Juries, judges, and legislators cannot be expected to be well versed in every topic from abscesses to zinfandel wine. An **expert witness** is someone who possesses specialized knowledge about a subject, knowledge that the average person does not have. Psychologists may testify as expert witnesses during a trial based on their knowledge, experience, and training regarding psychological issues. The expert's task is to assist jurors and judges by providing an opinion based on this specialized knowledge.

Either side, as part of its presentation of the evidence, may ask the judge to allow expert witnesses to testify. The judge must be convinced that the testimony the expert will present is of a kind that requires specialized knowledge, skill, or experience and that the testimony will help promote better legal decision making. (When psychologists testify concerning a particular individual based on the results of a forensic evaluation, they take on a different role, one we describe later in this chapter.)

The psychological topics that call for scientific expertise are almost limitless. As expert witnesses, psychologists have been called on to testify in many types of cases. For example, expert testimony may be useful in understanding

- Employee discrimination through selection and promotion procedures
- The effects of posting warning signs or safety instructions on potentially dangerous equipment
- The factors that may cause a suspect to make a false confession
- The effects of suggestive questions on children's memory of alleged abuse

The Ethics of the Applied Scientist/Expert Witness. The psychologist as expert witness represents a profession that stands for objectivity and accuracy in its procedures. Even though expert witnesses are usually hired and paid by one side, they are responsible for reporting all their conclusions, regardless of whether these favor the side paying them. Furthermore, it violates the ethical standards of both psychologists and lawyers for expert witnesses to accept payment that is contingent on the outcome of the case.

But achieving objectivity is not easy. When asked to testify as an expert, a psychologist has an ethical responsibility to be candid and explicit with the court about his or her opinions. Yet like other experts, psychologists may be tempted to sympathize with the side that has employed them. Is it possible to increase experts' objectivity? One commentator has proposed using "blinded" experts selected by an intermediary and hired to review the case without knowing which side has requested an opinion (Robertson, 2010). When blinded experts were pitted against traditional experts in a study examining mock jurors' decisions, the former were perceived as more credible and persuasive than the latter (Robertson & Yokum, 2011).

Another ethical dilemma arises whenever the adversary system forces an expert to make absolute "either–or" judgments. Has the pretrial publicity caused potential jurors to be biased against the defendant? In a custody case stemming from a divorce, which parent would be better for the child to live with? Does the evaluation of a defendant indicate that she is mentally ill? In all of these situations, the law requires the psychologist to reach a firm conclusion on the witness stand, regardless of ambiguity in the evidence (Sales & Shuman, 1993). This is an example of the absolute versus probabilistic judgment differences we described earlier in the chapter.

Admissibility of Expert Testimony. In order to maximize the likelihood that expert testimony is based on legitimate scientific knowledge and to exclude "junk science," lawmakers have developed criteria for judges to use when determining whether to allow an "expert" to testify. Each state and the federal government has its own criteria for determining admissibility.

In federal and some state courts, these criteria are informed by a two-prong test developed by the U.S. Supreme Court in a highly influential case, *Daubert v. Merrell Dow Pharmaceuticals, Inc.* (1993). First, the trial judge must determine whether the testimony is relevant and, if relevant, whether it is based on reliable and valid science (Cutler & Kovera, 2011). In essence, judges function as "gatekeepers" who must evaluate potential expert testimony by the standards of science.

Judges have disallowed expert psychological testimony as irrelevant. Consider the case of unlucky Pedro Gil. On a night of wild abandon in the fall of 1993, Gil hoisted a bucket of plaster over the wall of a Manhattan rooftop. It dropped seven stories to the ground and hit and killed a police officer standing on the street below. Gil claimed that he expected the bucket to drop unceremoniously onto an unoccupied street directly below him, rather than to continue forward as it fell and land on the street where the police officer was positioned. To support his naive belief that objects drop straight down, Gil's attorneys attempted to introduce the testimony of a cognitive psychologist, Michael McCloskey, an expert in intuitive physics. He planned to testify that people commonly misunderstand physical laws. The trial judge did not let McCloskey testify, claiming that intuitive physics was irrelevant to the issues under contention. The jury convicted Gil of second-degree manslaughter.

Judges have also disallowed expert testimony as unreliable. Richard Coons, a Texas psychiatrist, testified in death penalty trials that he developed his own methodology to determine whether a defendant poses a risk of future dangerousness. (Prior to sentencing a defendant to death, juries in Texas must agree that there is a probability that he or she poses a continuing threat to society.) Coons considers an offender's criminal history, attitudes toward violence, and conscience, yet he could not show that these factors have been validated by any research or that his predictions are accurate. After an appellate court deemed Coons' testimony unreliable, essentially overruling a trial court judge who had admitted the expert testimony, a defense attorney quipped, "It's overdue."

One clear implication of the *Daubert* decision is that judges must become savvy consumers of science if they are to decide which opinions qualify as "scientific." Since the *Daubert* case, the admissibility of expert evidence has become an important pretrial issue and judges are more likely to scrutinize the reasoning and methodology underlying experts' opinions (Cecil, 2005). This is probably a good thing, because jurors assume that judges carefully evaluate the evidence before admitting it at a trial, and put more weight on expert scientific evidence presented in the context of a trial than the same evidence presented outside of a courtroom context (Schweitzer & Saks, 2009).

The Psychologist as a Policy Evaluator in the Law

In addition to their knowledge of substantive problems, psychologists have methodological skills that they use in assessing or evaluating how well an intervention has worked. Psychologists and other social scientists have been asked so frequently in the last several decades to conduct evaluation studies that a separate subfield called policy evaluation, or evaluation research, has emerged. The **policy evaluator** provides data to answer questions such as, "I have instituted a policy; how do I know whether it was effective?" Or, more laudably, "I want to make a change in our organization's procedures, but before I do, how do I design it so I will be able to determine later whether it worked?"

Psychologists working as policy evaluators might be asked whether changing the laws for teen drivers by restricting the number of passengers they can carry will reduce traffic accidents, whether the chemical castration of released rapists will reduce the rate of sexual violence, or whether changing from automobile patrols to foot patrols will improve relations between police and the community. The methodological skills of a psychologist as policy evaluator are essential in assessing existing programs and policies and designing innovations so that their effects can be tested.

Psychologists have been involved in evaluating policies regarding the use of long-term administrative segregation in prisons. Inmates are typically placed in administrative segregation (involving 23-hour lockdown) for violating prison rules by dealing drugs, fighting, or affiliating with gangs. Despite vocal criticisms that such confinement exacerbates symptoms of mental illness and creates mental illness where none previously existed, there is a dearth of research on the consequences of administrative segregation.

To fill this void, psychologists working as policy evaluators for the Colorado Department of Corrections conducted a study to determine whether (1) inmates in administrative segregation would experience greater psychological deterioration than a comparison group housed within a general population of inmates, and (2) mentally ill inmates would deteriorate at a more rapid rate than non–mentally ill inmates (O'Keefe, Klebe, Stucker, Sturm, & Leggett, 2011). Study participants, all male, were housed in either administrative segregation or the general population as a function of their behavior, although general population inmates were chosen because they were at risk of administrative segregation placement. In this way, the two groups were as comparable as possible. Inmates were evaluated at three-month intervals over a year using standardized self-report tests for constructs such as anxiety, depression, hostility–anger, psychosis, and withdrawal–alienation.

The results were surprising: the segregated groups, as well as the mentally ill comparison group, showed elevated levels on these psychological measures when compared to community samples, but the segregated groups did not deteriorate over time as expected. In fact, the segregated offenders showed the same pattern of change over time as the comparison group, suggesting that change over time on these variables is not related to confinement conditions. These findings may affect future correctional policies regarding both administrative segregation and general inmate populations.

The Ethics of the Policy Evaluator. The psychologist who evaluates the impact of proposed or existing legislation and court or correctional procedures faces ethical responsibilities similar to those of the expert witness. The standard rules of scientific procedure apply, but because of the source of employment and payment, there are pressures to interpret results of evaluation studies in a certain way.

Consider, for example, a large state correctional system that wants to improve its parole process. Correctional officials have identified a problem with releasing those eligible for parole who are heavy drug users. If released into society, they are likely to commit further crimes to maintain their drug habit, and are therefore likely to return to prison. Accordingly, the system seeks to introduce and evaluate an innovative halfway-house program for parolees with a history of narcotics addiction. It hires a policy evaluator to design a study and evaluate the effects of this innovation. The correctional system provides funding to carry out the study, and officials are sincerely committed to its goals. Assume the psychologist concludes that the halfway house does not significantly reduce drug use by parolees. The authorities are disappointed and may even challenge the integrity of the policy evaluator. Yet, as scientists, program evaluators must "call 'em like they see 'em," regardless of the desirability of the outcome.

Even if the program is successful, the policy evaluator faces other ethical dilemmas. To assess such an innovative program, the researcher might have to deny some parolees access to the program and place them in a "status quo" control group. The ethical dilemma becomes more critical when some potentially lifesaving innovation is being evaluated. But often it is only through such research methods that a potentially helpful new program can be convincingly demonstrated to be effective.

The Psychologist as a Forensic Evaluator in Litigation

In addition to evaluating policies and programs, psychologists may be asked to evaluate individuals involved in civil and criminal cases, to report their findings to a judge, and on occasion, to testify about the results in court. Forensic evaluators assess matters such as

- The competence of a defendant to proceed with adjudication of charges (often called "competence to stand trial," although most criminal charges are adjudicated through plea bargaining rather than trial)
- The mental state of a defendant at the time of an alleged offense (often called "sanity at the time of the offense")
- The degree of emotional or brain damage suffered by a victim in an accident
- The effects on a child of alternative custody arrangements after divorce
- The risk of future violent or otherwise criminal behavior
- The prospects for a convicted defendant's rehabilitation in prison or on probation

There are two different ways that mental health professionals become involved in litigation as **forensic evaluators**: they are either court appointed or hired by one of the parties involved in the litigation (defense, prosecution, or plaintiff). Serving in the court-appointed role involves receiving an order from the judge authorizing the mental health professional to evaluate a given individual for a specific purpose. The judge may also specify additional considerations, such as how the results are to be communicated. There is typically an expectation that the resulting forensic evaluation will be considered by the judge without being introduced by either side.

Forensic evaluators for one of the parties involved in the litigation have a different expectation: That particular party may control when (and whether) the forensic assessment findings are actually introduced as evidence in the case. Some referrals for forensic assessment come from attorneys who authorize the evaluations without resorting to any kind of court authority. (This kind of right is usually associated with the defense in a criminal prosecution; the prosecutor cannot request a **forensic mental health**

assessment unless it is approved by the court—and therefore known to the defense.) These tasks will be discussed in much more detail in Chapters 10 and 11 of this book. They are also described in detail elsewhere (Heilbrun et al., 2009; Melton et al., 2007).

The Ethics of the Forensic Evaluator. The ethical considerations associated with the role of forensic evaluator are fairly formal and specifically described in several documents. In addition to the ethical principles disseminated by the APA (APA, 2012a), two other sets of ethical guidelines affect the practice of forensic evaluators. Neither is "enforceable" in the sense that the APA principles are. Nonetheless, both serve as important sources of authority, and may affect the judgments of courts regarding the admissibility and weight of forensic assessment evidence. These two documents are the Specialty Guidelines for Forensic Psychologists (APA, 2012b) and the Guidelines for Child Custody Evaluations in Family Law Proceedings (APA, 2010).

Among the three documents, there is substantial emphasis on providing evaluations that are (1) clear in their purpose; (2) conducted by individuals who are competent by virtue of their education, training, and experience; (3) respectful of appropriate relationships (and that avoid multiple relationships, such as both forensic evaluator and therapist, in the same case); (4) provide the appropriate level of confidentiality consistent with circumstances and the applicable legal privilege; (5) use methods and procedures that are accurate, current, and consistent with science and standards of practice; and (6) communicate appropriately.

Like other expert witnesses, forensic evaluators have an obligation to be objective in their assessments and reporting, yet may be tempted to favor the side that has retained them. This concern is illustrated by a study of how pairs of independent forensic psychologists, retained by opposing attorneys, evaluated a common individual. Despite using a standardized diagnostic test for psychopathy, the psychologists tended to rate the individual in a manner favorable to the side that retained them (Murrie, Boccaccini, Johnson, & Janke, 2008). This sympathy may not even be conscious; instead, the psychologist may simply reach conclusions that are motivated by subtle partisan allegiance to the client. For this reason, adherence to the principles contained in the ethical guidelines is of paramount importance.

The Psychologist as a Consultant in Litigation

The final role for psychologists in the law is that of consultant. The field of **trial consulting** provides one example of this role for psychologists working in the legal arena (see generally Wiener & Bornstein, 2011). Social scientists who began this work in the 1970s used so-called scientific jury selection procedures (further described in Chapter 12) to assist defense lawyers in highly politicized trials resulting from anti-war activities in the United States. Since then, these techniques have been refined and expanded. The national media devoted extensive coverage to the use of trial consultants in the celebrity-status trials of Martha Stewart and O. J. Simpson, and research on community attitudes was influential in the 2001 conviction of a former Ku Klux Klansman for the 1963 bombing of a Birmingham, Alabama church. (We describe this case in more detail in Chapter 13.)

Today the field of trial consulting is a booming business and involves far more than jury selection. Trial consultants also conduct community attitude surveys to document extensive pretrial publicity or to introduce findings as evidence in trials involving discrimination or trademark violation claims (Wiener, 2011; Wingrove, Korpas, & Belli, 2011). They test the effectiveness of demonstrative evidence (Richter & Humke, 2011), provide guidance to attorneys seeking damage awards (Bornstein & Greene, 2011a), and prepare witnesses to testify (Stinson & Cutler, 2011).

There is no expectation of impartiality in any of these roles, as there would be for psychologists acting as basic scientists, applied scientists, policy evaluators, or forensic evaluators. Nor is there an expectation that the consultant must present information in a balanced way. However, the psychologist must still provide the attorney with good information in order to promote more effective performance in litigation. How the attorney decides to use such information is within that attorney's discretion.

Critics have argued that these techniques essentially rig the jury (Kressel & Kressel, 2002) and create a perception that psychologists can manipulate the trial process (Strier, 2011). But at least in the realm of jury selection, it is difficult to determine whether scientific jury selection is more effective than traditional jury selection. Cases that employ scientific jury selection techniques differ in many ways from cases that do not, and "success" is hard to define (Lieberman, 2011). (Does a low damage award or conviction on a less serious charge connote success? Perhaps.) Consultants suggest that they are simply borrowing techniques commonly used in politics and advertising and bringing them into the courtroom. Politicians hire people to help them project a better image, and advertisers try to enhance the ways that retailers connect with consumers. Shouldn't lawyers be able to do the same? Consultants also argue that in an adversarial system, attorneys should be able to use every tool available to them.

The Ethics of the Consultant in Litigation. As we noted earlier, when the psychologist becomes a consultant for one side in the selection of jurors, there may be ethical questions. Just how far should the selection procedures go? Should jurors have to answer consultants' intrusive questions about their private lives? Should consultants be able to sculpt the jury to their clients' advantage? Do these techniques simply constitute the latest tools in the attorney's arsenal of trial tactics? Or do they bias the proceedings and jeopardize the willingness of citizens to participate in the process? These questions deal with fairness, and scientific jury selection may conflict with the way some people interpret the intent of the law.

Returning to the advertising analogy, are psychologists who work for an advertising agency unethical when they use professional knowledge to encourage consumers to buy one brand of dog food rather than another? Many of us would say no; the free-enterprise system permits any such procedures that do not falsify claims. This example is analogous to jury selection because rival attorneys—whether they employ trial consultants or not—always try to select jurors who will sympathize with their version of the facts. Since the adversarial system permits attorneys from each side to eliminate some prospective jurors, it does not seem unethical for psychologists to assist these attorneys, as long as their advocacy is consistent with the law and the administration of justice. The same can be said about consultants retained by attorneys to provide information to enhance the presentation of a case.

When psychologists become trial consultants, they also subscribe to the ethical code of the attorneys, who, after all, are in charge of the trial preparation (Stolle & Studebaker, 2011). The Ethics Code of the American Bar Association (2010) admonishes its members to defend their clients to the best of their abilities, short of lying or encouraging lying. Every litigant—whether a defendant or a plaintiff—regardless of the heinousness of the crime or the nature of the evidence presented, is entitled to the best legal representation possible, including the use of psychological techniques to assess the relative favorability of prospective jurors and to enhance case presentation.

SUMMARY

1. *Why do we have laws, and what is the psychological approach to studying law?*
   Laws are human creations whose major purposes are the resolution of conflict and the protection of society. As society has changed, new conflicts have surfaced, leading to expansion and revision of the legal system. A psychological approach focuses on individuals as agents within a legal system, asking how their internal qualities (personality, values, abilities, and experiences) and their environments, including the law itself, affect their behavior.

2. *What choices are reflected in the psychological approach to the law?*
   Several basic choices must be made between pairs of options in the psychological study of the law.

These options are often irreconcilable because each is attractive, but both usually cannot be attained at the same time. The choices are (1) whether the goal of law is achieving personal freedom or ensuring the common good, (2) whether equality or discretion should be the standard for our legal policies, (3) whether the purpose of a legal inquiry is to discover the truth or to provide a means of conflict resolution, and (4) whether it is better to apply the methods of law or those of science for making decisions.

3. *How do laws reflect the contrast between the due process model and the crime control model of the criminal justice system?*
   The decade of the 1960s represented an era in which due process concerns were paramount and

court decisions tended to favor rights of the individuals, particularly those suspected of crimes, over the power of the police and law enforcement. Since then, the crime control model, which seeks to contain or reduce criminal activity, has been favored by many. But some of the harsh policies and penalties consistent with this perspective, including "three-strikes" laws, have resulted in large increases in prison populations and little reduction in rates of reoffending. The recession is causing legislators and judges to consider community-based alternatives that may control crime more effectively.

4. ***What are five roles that psychologists may play in the legal system, and what does each entail?***
Five possible roles are identified in this chapter: the psychologist as (1) a basic scientist, interested in knowledge related to psychology and law for its own sake; (2) an applied scientist, who seeks to apply basic research knowledge to a particular problem in the legal system (a psychologist serving as an expert witness is an applied scientist in the law); (3) a policy evaluator, who capitalizes on methodological skills to design and conduct research that assesses the effects of policies and program changes in the legal system; (4) a forensic evaluator, who is either appointed by the court or retained at the request of one of the parties in the litigation to perform a psychological evaluation of an individual related to a legal question; and (5) a consultant, who works on behalf of a party or position in litigation. Each role entails its own set of ethical dilemmas.

KEY TERMS

amicus curiae brief
applied scientist
basic scientist
case law
crime control model
determinate sentencing
discretion

due process model
equality
expert witness
forensic evaluator
forensic mental health
  assessment
forensic psychologists

policy evaluator
precedents
principle of
  proportionality
procedural justice
racial bias
sentencing disparity

settlement negotiation
stare decisis
trial consulting

Chapter 2

The Legal System
Issues, Structure, and Players

ORIENTING QUESTIONS

1. What is the difference between the adversarial and inquisitorial models of trials?
2. How do notions of morality and legality differ?
3. How do different models of justice explain people's level of satisfaction with the legal system?
4. What is commonsense justice?
5. How are judges selected and how do their demographic characteristics and attitudes influence their decisions?
6. How does the experience of law school affect its students?
7. What is known about lawyers' professional satisfaction?
8. What factors explain lawyers' overconfidence and how can it be remedied?

To understand how and why psychologists interact with the law, one needs a basic understanding of how the legal system operates. Accordingly, in this chapter, we focus on the legal system itself. We describe the nature of the adversary system and psychological aspects of legality, morality, and justice. We discuss courts and examine the roles played by the major players in the legal system—judges and lawyers. An understanding of the workings of the legal system will help make clear why psychologists are interested in studying and assisting judges, lawyers, and ordinary citizens involved in the law.

THE ADVERSARIAL SYSTEM

In both criminal cases that concern conduct prohibited by law and civil cases that concern disputes between private parties, American legal procedures involve an **adversarial system** of justice. Exhibits, evidence, and witnesses are assembled by representatives of one side or the other to convince the fact finder (i.e., judge or jury) that their side's viewpoint is the truthful one. During a trial, the choice of what evidence to present is within the discretion of those involved in the litigation and their attorneys. Judges rarely call witnesses or introduce evidence on their own.

The adversarial system is derived from English common law. This approach contrasts with the **inquisitorial approach** used in Europe (but not in Great Britain), in which the judge has more control

over the proceedings. Lind (1982) described the procedure in France as follows: "The questioning of witnesses is conducted almost exclusively by the presiding judge. The judge interrogates the disputing parties and witnesses, referring frequently to a dossier that has been prepared by a court official who investigated the case. Although the parties probably have partisan attorneys present at the trial, it is evident that control over the presentation of evidence and arguments is firmly in the hands of the judge" (p. 14). In the inquisitorial system, the two sides do not have separate witnesses; the witnesses testify for the court, and the opposing parties are not allowed to prepare the witnesses before the trial.

The adversarial model has been criticized for promoting a competitive atmosphere that can distort the truth (Lind, 1982). Jurors may have to choose between two versions of the truth, neither of which is completely accurate, because witnesses often shade their testimony to favor the side of the lawyer who interviews them first (Sheppard & Vidmar, 1980).

Research on these contrasting approaches reveals several benefits of the adversarial model, however. A research team led by a social psychologist, John Thibaut, and a law professor, Laurens Walker (Thibaut & Walker, 1975; Walker, La Tour, Lind, & Thibaut, 1974) conducted programmatic research and concluded that the adversarial system led to less-biased decisions that were more likely to be seen as fair by the parties in dispute. One explanation for this more favorable evaluation of the adversarial system is that it is the system with which Americans are most familiar. But people who live in countries with nonadversarial systems (France and West Germany) have also rated the adversary procedure as fairer (Lind, Erickson, Friedland, & Dickenberger, 1978), perhaps because the adversarial system motivates attorneys to identify all the evidence favorable to their side. When law students, serving as research participants, believed that the weight of the information and evidence favored the opposing side, they conducted more thorough investigations of the case. Thus, when the case was eventually presented to the judge, the arguments appeared more balanced than the original distribution of facts would have warranted (Lind, 1975; Lind, Thibaut, & Walker, 1973).

The primary advantage of the adversarial system is that it gives participants plenty of opportunity to present their version of the facts so that they feel they have been treated fairly (Lind & Tyler, 1988). Sheppard and Vidmar (1983) noted that any method of dispute resolution that fosters this belief is more likely to be viewed favorably than alternatives that do not. This finding is consistent with the procedural justice perspective described later in this chapter.

LEGALITY VERSUS MORALITY

Laws are designed to regulate the behavior of individuals—to specify precisely what conduct is illegal. But do these laws always correspond to people's sense of right and wrong?

Consider the case of Lester Zygmanik. Lester was charged with murdering his own brother, George, but only because George had demanded that Lester kill him. A motorcycle accident a few days earlier had left George, age 26, paralyzed from the neck down. He saw a future with nothing but pain, suffering, and invalidism; as he lay in agony, he insisted that his younger brother Lester, age 23, swear he would not let him continue in such a desperate state. (Other family members later verified that this had been George's wish.) So, on the night of June 20, 1973, Lester slipped into his brother's hospital room and shot him in the head with a 20-gauge shotgun. Dropping the gun by the bed, he turned himself in moments later. There was no question about the cause of death; later, on the witness stand during his murder trial, Lester told the jury that he had done it as an act of love for his brother. Because New Jersey had

no laws regarding mercy killing, the prosecution thought a case could be made for charging Lester with first-degree murder.

The state believed it had a good case against Lester. His actions met every one of the elements that the law required for his guilt to be proved. First, there was premeditation, or a plan to kill. Second, there was deliberation (as defined in the New Jersey criminal code—"the weighing of the 'pros' and 'cons' of that plan"). Third, there was willfulness ("the intentional carrying out of that plan"). Lester had even sawed off the shotgun before hiding it under his coat, and he had packed the bullets with candle wax, which compacted the explosion and made it more deadly. Lester forthrightly admitted to his lawyer: "I gave it a lot of thought. You don't know how much thinking I did on it. I had to do something I knew that would definitely put him away" (Mitchell, 1976, p. vii). At his trial, Lester took the stand and described his motivations, explaining that he did what his brother wanted.

If you had been a juror in this trial, how would you have voted? College students usually split just about evenly between verdicts of "guilty of first-degree murder" and "not guilty." Those who vote guilty often hope that the sentence will be a humanitarian one, but they believe it is their duty to consider the evidence and apply the law. Certainly, this was an act of murder, they say, regardless of Lester's good intentions. But those who vote not guilty often feel that it is appropriate, on occasion, to disregard the law when mitigating circumstances are present or when community standards argue for forgiveness.

Both reactions are reasonable, and they illustrate the dilemma between treating similar offenders equally and showing discretion if circumstances warrant. They also demonstrate important differences between judgments based on **black-letter law** and those based on one's conscience or personal sentiments about a given situation. By "black-letter law" (sometimes referred to as the *law on the books*), we mean the law as set down by our founding fathers in the Constitution, as written by legislators, and as interpreted by judges (Finkel, 1995). According to the black-letter law, Lester Zygmanik was guilty. But there is another way to judge his actions—by focusing on his altruistic motives and his desire to help his brother, rather than to harm him.

As Lester Zygmanik's trial began, the prosecutor was confident that he would be found guilty.

The jury, composed of seven men and five women, was tough, conservative, and blue-collar. The judge had even ruled that the term *mercy killing* could not be used in the trial. But after deliberating for fewer than three hours, the jury found Lester Zygmanik not guilty. The jurors focused, apparently, on the relationship between Lester and his brother, and they concluded that Lester had been overcome by grief, love, and selflessness. Their decision implicitly acknowledged that moral considerations such as the commitment to care for others were more important to their decision than the strict guidelines of the law.

Obviously, the Lester Zygmanik trial is not the only one in which a defendant claimed his act was a mercy killing. Helping terminally ill patients to commit suicide (so-called assisted suicide) is usually justified by the "offender" as an act of compassion or mercy, ending the "victim's" pain and suffering. Yet in all but two states—Oregon and Washington—helping someone to commit suicide is a crime. (Even in those states, assisted suicide is legal only if overseen by a physician under narrowly defined circumstances.) Still, many people are loath to call the perpetrators of these acts criminals, and proponents of assisted suicide often hail them as heroes.

Mercy killings and assisted suicides are examples of **euthanasia**, the act of killing an individual for reasons that are considered merciful. They illustrate the often-tragic differences between what an individual feels is the morally right or just thing to do and what the law describes as an illegal act to avoid. Should someone who voluntarily, willfully, and with premeditation assists in killing another human *always* be punished? Or should that person, in some circumstances, be treated with compassion and forgiveness? Many people can imagine exceptional circumstances in which individuals who have technically broken the law should be exonerated. Often, these circumstances involve a lack of intention to harm another person and the desire to help a person who is suffering. The topic of euthanasia highlights the inconsistency between legality and people's perceptions of what is moral, ethical, and just.

Citizens' Sense of Legality and Morality

We might assume at first that what is defined as "legal" and what is judged to be "morally right" would be synonymous. But in the Zygmanik case, what the jury considered to be a moral action and what the system considered the proper legal resolution were inconsistent. Legislators and scholars have argued for centuries about whether the law should be consistent with citizens' sense of morality. In fact, inconsistencies abound. For example, prostitution is universally condemned as immoral, yet it is legal in parts of Nevada and in some European countries. Acts of civil disobedience, whether performed six decades ago in racially segregated buses in Montgomery, Alabama, or more recently to protest U.S. government policies on oil drilling, are applauded by those who consider some laws and policies to be morally indefensible.

Psychologists have now conducted a number of studies that illustrate the differences between citizens' sense of morality and justice, on the one hand, and the legal system's set of formal rules and laws, on the other. At first glance, it may seem nearly impossible to study people's views about the legitimacy of formal laws because there are so many variations in laws and so many different penalties for violating those laws. (Criminal penalties are decided on a state-by-state basis in the United States, so there could be 50 different penalties for the same crime.) Fortunately, though, a large majority of states base their criminal laws on the Model Penal Code drafted by the influential American Law Institute in the 1960s. Thus we can ask whether the principles embodied in the Model Penal Code are compatible with citizens' intuitions about justice and legality. Do people tend to agree with the Model Penal Code or does their sense of right and wrong diverge from this black-letter law? One set of relevant studies has examined the category of attempted crimes and the important role that intention plays in these cases.

Attempted Crimes and the Concept of Intention in Law and Psychology.   Consider the following fundamental question of criminal law: How should attempted (but not completed) crimes be punished? An attempt may be unsuccessful because the perpetrator tries to commit a crime but fails (e.g., he shoots but misses) or because the attempt is interrupted or abandoned (e.g., robbers are about to enter a bank with guns drawn when they see a police officer inside).

The Model Penal Code says that attempts should be punished in the same way as completed crimes. If the offender's conduct strongly corroborates his criminal **intention**—showing that he not merely thought about the crime but actually tried to

B o x 2.1 THE CASE OF RALPH DAMMS AND THE UNLOADED PISTOL

Marjory Damms had initiated divorce proceedings against her husband Ralph, and the two were living apart prior to April 6, 1959. That day, Ralph Damms drove to a location in Milwaukee where his estranged wife usually boarded a bus to go to work. He lured her into his car by falsely claiming that her mother was ill and dying. He then took his wife for a car ride, stopped the car, and brandished a gun. Marjory Damms ran away, but Ralph caught her and raised the pistol to her head. Slowly, deliberately, he pulled the trigger. The gun did not fire. He had forgotten to load it! Two police officers witnessed the event and heard Damms exclaim, after he pulled the trigger of the unloaded gun, "It won't fire. It won't fire." (It was not clear whether the exclamation was made in a tone of assurance, disappointment, surprise, or desperation.) Damms was found guilty of attempted murder, but he appealed his conviction on the ground that it was impossible to kill his wife with an unloaded gun. The appellate court upheld his

conviction, concluding that the mere fact that the gun was unloaded when Damms pulled the trigger did not absolve him of attempted murder if he actually believed the gun was loaded at the time. Intention is the central issue here, and for the charge of attempted murder, it is more important than the consequences of the act. The judge concluded that Damms assumed he had put bullets in the gun. If he had, his wife would have been dead.

Critical Thought Question
Did the jury that convicted Damms and the appellate court that upheld his conviction follow the rule of the Model Penal Code? Do you think jurors should be asked to peer into an offender's mind and guess what he or she was thinking at the time of an attempted but incomplete act? If Damms had known the gun was unloaded, would he still be guilty of attempted murder? How much planning do you think an offender must do in order to be guilty of a crime that he did not complete?

accomplish it—the Model Penal Code decrees that he should be punished to the same degree as the successful offender. Focusing on the central role of intent, the Model Penal Code assigns the same penalty to attempted crimes as completed crimes. Thus, the pickpocket who thrusts his hand into another person's pocket, only to find it empty, is just as guilty (and just as deserving of punishment) as the pickpocket who makes off with a fat wallet. Regardless of the outcome of this act, the pickpocket tried to steal—and so, by definition, a crime was committed. A similar situation arose in the case of *State v. Damms* (1960), described in Box 2.1.

According to the Model Penal Code, an offender who tries but fails is just as culpable as an offender who tries and succeeds. But do ordinary people think about intent and attempted crimes this way? Do they think that *trying* to break into a store is as serious as *actually* breaking into the store?

Psychologist John Darley and his colleagues asked respondents to read short scenarios that described people who had taken one or more steps toward committing either robbery or murder and to assign punishment to those people (Darley, Sanderson, & LaMantia, 1996). They found that people's intuitions differed in predictable ways from the position of the Model Penal Code. In situations where the person depicted in the scenario had taken only preliminary

action (e.g., examining the store he planned to burgle or telling a friend about his plan), few respondents thought he was guilty of any offense, and punishments were generally mild. Yet, according to the Model Penal Code, this person is just as guilty as one who actually completed the burglary. When the scenario described a person who had reached the point of "dangerous proximity" to the crime, punishments increased, but they still were only half as severe as those assigned to the person who actually completed the crime. Apparently people do not accept the view that intent to commit an act is the moral equivalent of actually doing it. Their notions about criminality and the need for punishment were more nuanced, less "black and white" than what the Model Penal Code prescribed.

Psychology's focus on mental states also reflects more differentiations and less clear-cut distinctions than those of black-letter law. Psychology considers a spectrum of behavior, motivated by a variety of influences and ranging from accidents to behavior influenced by stress, peer pressure, or immature judgment, to actions that are deliberate and carefully planned.

Even this continuum may oversimplify variations in intention because it minimizes the importance of environmental and cultural influences that affect people differently. The social context in which behavior occurs can strongly influence a person's intention to behave in certain ways. In some contexts, it can be very hard for an individual to conceive of behavioral options. Therefore, one person's ability to intend a given behavior might be much more limited than that of another person who has more behavioral alternatives.

Psychologists have also studied how people assign causes, including intentions, to the behavior of others. A well-established theory in social psychology, **attribution theory**, allows us to understand how people explain others' intentions. According to the theory, attributions tend to vary along three dimensions: *internality*—whether we explain the cause of an event as due to something internal to a person or to something that exists in the environment; *stability*—whether we see the cause of a behavior as enduring or merely temporary; and *globalness*—whether we see the cause as specific to a limited situation or applicable to all situations. An individual who makes internal, stable, global attributions about an act of misconduct ("He is so evil that he doesn't care what anyone thinks or feels about him") will see an offender as more culpable and more deserving of punishment than a person who offers external, unstable, specific explanations for the same act ("As a result of hanging out with a rough crowd, she was in the wrong place at the wrong time").

When making inferences about what caused another person's behavior—especially behavior that has negative consequences—we tend to attribute the cause to stable factors that are internal to the person. That is, we are inclined to believe that others are disposed to act the way they do. But when our own actions lead to negative outcomes, we are more likely to blame the external environment for the outcome, suggesting an unstable cause for our behavior that will probably change in the future.

Consequences of Citizen–Code Disagreements.
What difference does it make if laws do not comport with people's sense of right and wrong? Can people simply ignore laws they believe to be immoral? Indeed, we can find many examples of situations in which people opt not to obey laws and legal authority. When parents fail to make child support payments or when people violate restraining orders, it is often because they do not accept the legitimacy of a judge's decision. When people use illegal drugs or cheat on their income tax returns, it is often because they do not believe that the laws regulating these behaviors

are just or morally right. During the era of prohibition in the United States, when alcohol consumption was outlawed, honest citizens became "criminals," entire illicit industries were created, and gang membership and gang–related violence increased significantly.

But there may be more significant and more general consequences of discrepancies between citizens' sense of morality and the legal system's sense of legality. For the law to have any authority, it must be consistent with people's shared sense of morality. When that consistency is lacking, citizens may feel alienation from authority and become less likely to comply with laws they perceive as illegitimate (Carlsmith & Darley, 2008). Initial disagreement with one law can lead to contempt for the legal system as a whole, including the police who enforce laws and the judges who punish wrongdoers. If the law criminalizes behaviors that people do not think are immoral, it begins to lose its legitimacy. In the words of Oliver Wendell Holmes, "[The] first requirement of a sound body of law is that it should correspond with the actual feelings and demands of the community" (1881, pp. 41–42).

WHAT IS JUSTICE?

More than 2,000 years ago, at the beginning of the *Republic*, Socrates posed this question and we continue to ponder it today. Definitions of justice have changed throughout history. In the Old Testament and in Homer's *The Iliad*, justice meant something like revenge. By the time of the Golden Age of Athens in the fifth century B.C.E., the concept of justice came to be less about vengeance and more about achievement of the well-being of individuals (Solomon, 1990). The development of Christianity and Islam accentuated a conception of justice within religious traditions of morality. As a result, people began to see matters of social injustice (e.g., the suffering of the poor and the oppressed) as issues of concern, along with offenses against one's person or one's family (Solomon, 1990).

Distributive and Procedural Justice

Our discussion so far has assessed perceptions of legitimacy in the *outcomes* of legal disputes, such as whether the would-be pickpocket who came up empty-handed should be punished as severely as the one who got the loot. This focus on the fairness of the outcome in a legal dispute is the main concern of **distributive justice** models. According to the principles of distributive justice, a person will be more accepting of decisions and more likely to believe that disputes have been resolved appropriately if the outcomes seem just (or if the outcomes—in the same sense as salaries or promotions—seem distributed equitably, hence the term *distributive justice*).

A series of classic studies in psychology and law showed that although distributive justice theories were correct, there was clearly more to the story. This work, conducted by a psychologist and a law professor, suggests that disputants' perceptions of the fairness of the *procedures* are vitally important to the sense that "justice" was done (Thibaut & Walker, 1975). Such an orientation leads us to think of justice not only as punishment for wrongdoing, but also as a process by which people receive what they deserve or are due. **Procedural justice** models suggest that if individuals view the procedures of dispute resolution or decision-making as fair, then they will view the outcome as just, regardless of whether it favors them or not. According to this perspective, an important question in a contested divorce is the means by which each person was wronged. In a dispute with an insurance company over an accident claim, one might ask whether the injured party was treated fairly or unfairly.

Generally, individuals perceive a decision-making process as fair to the extent that they believe they have a voice in how the process unfolds, are treated with dignity and respect during the process, and trust the authorities in charge of the process to be motivated by concerns about fairness (Sydeman, Cascardi, Poythress, & Ritterband, 1997). A full opportunity to state one's viewpoint and to participate actively and personally in the decision makes a strong contribution to an assessment of fairness, probably because it allows people to feel that they retain some control over their affairs (Ebreo, Linn, & Vining, 1996).

Procedural fairness is an important consideration in the resolution of child custody and child support disputes. To the extent that family court judges use fair procedures, they are more successful in creating post-divorce situations in which both fathers and mothers are involved in their children's lives and take responsibility for financial and emotional support (Bryan, 2005). This is true regardless of the outcome.

Thus, fathers, who often lose child custody hearings, are more likely to maintain contact with their children into the future if they believe that the hearing was fair.

These findings also apply in the real-world interactions that occur in police stations and courtrooms. Police officers and judges are not likely to generate warm feelings in the community when they give people less than what those people feel is deserved, or when they limit people's abilities to act as they wish. Do citizens have a better view of police officers and judges (and, by extension, of the entire legal system) if they perceive that they are being treated fairly? Will this make it more likely that they will comply with the law?

To answer these questions, Tom Tyler and Yuen Huo (2002) interviewed individuals in Oakland and Los Angeles who had a recent experience with a police officer or a judge. The researchers asked about the fairness of the outcomes of those encounters with authorities, as well as about the fairness of the procedures that were used to achieve the outcomes. They also measured people's trust in the motives of a particular authority figure by asking participants whether they felt that their views had been considered and whether the authority cared about their concerns.

As one might expect, the favorability of the outcomes shaped participants' responses to this encounter. We feel better about situations and people when we get what we want from those situations and from those individuals. But importantly, the willingness to accept the decision of a police officer or judge was strongly influenced by perceptions of procedural fairness and trustworthiness: When people perceived that police

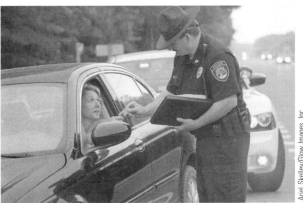

Police officer making a traffic stop

officers and judges were treating them fairly and when they trusted the motives of these officials, they were more likely to accept their decisions and directives.

Procedural fairness also has long-term effects on people's willingness to obey the law. Tom Tyler and his colleagues interviewed people arrested in Australia for drunken driving and tracked their obedience to the law over the next four years (Tyler, Sherman, Strang, Barnes, & Woods, 2007). They found that people who experienced their initial hearings as fair reoffended at approximately 25% of the rate of people who viewed the hearings as less legitimate, even though the hearings typically lasted only a few hours.

The principles and consequences of procedural fairness extend well beyond the confines of a courtroom. How adults, particularly parents, resolve conflicts that inevitably arise in a family influences the behavior of children. One team of researchers asked middle-school students to describe how a recent conflict or disagreement with their parents was resolved: "Did your parents treat you with respect? Were they equally fair to everyone involved?" The students also described mild forms of aggressive behavior—bullying—they had directed at other students. Analyzing these two sets of responses, the researchers determined that higher perceived levels of procedural fairness were associated with lower frequencies of bullying behavior (Brubacher et al., 2009).

Commonsense Justice: Everyday Intuitions about Fairness

Another approach to the study of justice—one closely aligned with the analysis of citizens' agreement with the criminal code—is to learn about the intuitions that average people hold about culpability, fairness, and justice. Psychologist Norman Finkel has examined the relationship between the "law on the books" and what he calls **commonsense justice**—ordinary citizens' basic notions of what is just and fair. Finkel's work has much to say about inconsistencies between the law and public sentiment in the types of cases we have examined in this chapter—assisted suicide and euthanasia—as well as in cases involving self-defense, the insanity defense, the death penalty, and felony murder (Finkel, 1995). Commonsense justice is also reflected in cases in which a jury refuses to convict a defendant who is legally guilty of the crime charged—the phenomenon known as jury nullification.

According to Finkel and others who have studied commonsense justice (e.g., Nadler, 2005), there is evidence that the black-letter law on the books may be at odds with community sentiment. This work is an important contribution to the field of law because it explains *how* people's sentiments depart from legal concepts and procedures. There are three identifiable discrepancies.

1. *The commonsense context is typically wider than the law's.* Ordinary people tend to consider the big picture: Their assessment of the event in question extends backward and forward in time (including, for example, a defendant's conduct prior to the incident and behavior after the crime), whereas the law allows consideration of a more limited set of circumstances. For example, in a date rape case or other case in which the victim and defendant knew each other, jurors would be likely to consider the history of the individuals, both together and apart. Is the incident one in a series of troublesome encounters in a tumultuous relationship? Have these events been alleged by other partners?

Although people contemplate the wider context of the story, the law freezes the frame at the time of a wrongful act and then zooms in on that relatively finite moment. Reasoning that this narrower perspective will result in a cleaner and more precise judgment, the law then asks jurors to determine culpability on the basis of the defendant's actions and intentions within this narrow window. But jurors would often rather learn about the big picture; for many, viewing only the last act does little to reveal the entire drama (Finkel & Groscup, 1997).

2. *Commonsense perspectives on the actions of a defendant and victim are more subjective than the law allows.* In cases that involve two people with a prior history, jurors construct a story about what happened and why. They do this by stepping into the shoes of a defendant and viewing the events through that person's eyes. The stories they construct typically describe the hidden motives of the defendant. But, as Finkel notes, "such a subjective, discretionary enterprise grounds the law not on terra firma but on the unstable and invisible, where all we have are constructions, interpretations and stories constructed by jurors and judges" (Finkel, 1995, p. 327).

The concern is that too much subjectivity will result in lawlessness; that jurors' judgments will be rooted in sentiment rather than in objective evaluations.

But jurors do not yield indiscriminately to their imaginations. In fact, when the individuals in a case are strangers to each other (as is often true), jurors tend to judge the circumstances and the actors' intentions objectively rather than subjectively.

3. *Jurors take a proportional approach to punishment, whereas the law asks them to consider the defendant in isolation.* Imagine a situation in which an armed robber enters a convenience store while his female accomplice watches guard outside the store. Further imagine that things go awry—the robber ends up shooting the cashier, and the cashier dies. The robber has certainly committed a crime, but what about the accomplice?

According to the felony-murder doctrine (which applies in about half the states), the accomplice is as culpable as the triggerman. Yet, as Finkel points out, this egalitarian approach seems to contradict the notion of proportional justice, in which a defendant's actions and intentions are assessed in comparison to others and more culpable defendants are dealt with more severely. Jurors make distinctions among types of crimes and criminals, and they usually want more severe punishment for those they find most blameworthy.

COURTS

We now turn our attention to the reality of resolving legal disputes and the structures our society has enacted to do so. Disputes that reach the legal system are often, though not always, resolved in court. New community-based alternatives to standard prosecutions are increasingly used. **Diversion** to an alternative system may occur upon one's first encounter with a police officer, or when the case is referred to any of several "problem-solving courts" (also called specialty courts). Rather than focusing on punishment for wrong-doing, problem-solving courts deal with the underlying reasons that individuals commit crimes in the first place. Such problem-solving courts include drug court, mental health court, and veterans' court (addressing issues of drug abuse, mental illness, and exposure to trauma, respectively), among others. Chapter 9 describes community-based alternatives, including specialty courts, in detail.

Different kinds of courts have been created to handle specific issues. Because we cover various court cases relevant to psychology throughout this book, an

U.S. Supreme Court building

understanding of the structure of both the traditional and alternative court system will be helpful.

State Courts

Although there are 50 different state court systems in the United States, they all typically include "lower" courts, trial courts, and appellate courts. Lower courts have jurisdiction over specific matters such as probate of wills (proving that a will was properly signed), administration of estates (supervising the payment of the deceased's debts and the distribution of his or her assets), family matters, and cases involving juvenile offenders. Family courts handle cases involving divorce, child custody, and child dependency. Juvenile courts deal with legal questions concerning delinquency. Both family courts and juvenile courts tend to focus on helping people rather than punishing them. In fact, juvenile courts have functioned for many years to protect children from the rough-and-tumble world of adult criminal courts and to resolve cases in a supportive, nonadversarial way.

Trial courts typically decide any case that concerns a violation of state laws. Most criminal cases (e.g., those involving drunken driving, armed robbery, and sexual assault) are tried in state trial courts. For several months in 2011, most of the nation (especially social media) seemed to be riveted by the Florida state court trial of Casey Anthony, who was eventually acquitted of murdering her 2-year-old daughter, Caylee.

State court systems also include one or more courts of appeal, similar to the federal appellate courts, and a state supreme court. Like the United States Supreme Court, state supreme courts review only those cases deemed to be important. Published opinions are found in bound volumes called Reporters, and all opinions are accessible online.

Federal Courts

Federal courts have jurisdiction over cases arising under the Constitution or laws of the United States but typically do not have jurisdiction over cases arising under state law, unless the plaintiff and defendant in a civil case are from different states. Federal courts include trial courts, appellate courts, and the U.S. Supreme Court. When Congress passes a law regarding federal crime (e.g., the statute making identity theft a federal crime), the effect is to increase the caseload of the federal courts.

Federal trial courts are called United States District Courts. There is at least one district in every state; some states (California, for example) have several districts.

The federal appellate courts are called the United States Courts of Appeals. There are 13 federal courts of appeals, divided into geographical "circuits." In population, the largest circuit is the Ninth Circuit, which includes California, and the smallest is the First Circuit, which includes only a few New England states. Appeals are assigned to three-judge panels. The three judges examine the record (documents that the lawyers believe the judges need in order to decide the case), read the briefs (the lawyers' written arguments), and listen to the oral argument (the lawyers' debate about the case) before voting. The panel decides the case by majority vote and one of the judges writes an opinion explaining why the court decided as it did.

The opinions are published in bound volumes called Reporters. Opinions can be accessed online, including through the Westlaw and Lexis computerized legal research services.

The U.S. Supreme Court

Nine justices make up the United States Supreme Court, which has the authority to review all cases decided by the federal appellate courts. But the Supreme Court reexamines only a small percentage of the cases it is asked to consider—cases that the justices view as most significant. The Supreme Court also has the authority to review state court decisions that involve constitutional or federal law issues. Judges and lawyers refer to the latter as *raising a federal question*. A recent case, involving the sale of violent video games to minors, was both legally and psychologically significant and illustrates how a state case raises a federal question. We describe it in Box 2.2.

Justices of the Supreme Court, like other federal judges, are appointed by the president and confirmed by the Senate. Federal judges are granted a lifelong tenure to allow them to be impartial, not influenced by the whims of political or legislative interests. But one of the most important Supreme Court decisions of the past decade tested the independence of the judiciary. We describe the case of Terri Schiavo in Box 2.3.

B o x   2.2   THE CASE OF VIOLENT VIDEO GAMES AND MINORS' FREE SPEECH RIGHTS

Spurred by the efforts of state senator and child psychologist Leland Yee, the California legislature passed a law in 2005 that banned the sale or rental to minors of violent video games that portrayed "killing, maiming, dismembering, or sexually assaulting an image of a human being." Violators could be fined up to $1000. But violent video games such as Grand Theft Auto and Mortal Kombat are big sellers, and video game makers immediately challenged the law in the United States District Court for Northern California, arguing that it restricted free speech rights guaranteed by the First Amendment. The district court judge ruled in their favor, as did the Ninth Circuit Court of Appeals. The U.S. Supreme Court, in a 7–2 ruling, agreed (*Brown v. Entertainment Merchants Association*, 2011), holding that the California law was an unconstitutional infringement on free speech.

Social science played a prominent and controversial role in this case, as both sides enlisted psychologists to comment on the connection between exposure to violent video games and harmful effects on children (Sacks, Bush-man, & Anderson, 2011). Despite strong empirical evidence of increased aggressive behaviors, desensitization to violence, nightmares, and fear of being harmed that result from exposure to media violence (American Academy of Pediatrics, 2009), the Court accepted the video game makers' claim that the relationship is correlational and not causal; in other words, that the studies cannot prove that violent video games actually *cause* minors to act aggressively. They also agreed with the game makers that the law restricted the expression of free speech. But in a forceful dissenting opinion, Justice Stephen Breyer listed dozens of peer-reviewed scholarly articles on this topic, and concluded that the bulk of the evidence supported the claim that violent video games do cause psychological harm to children.

Critical Thought Question
Given that this case involved a California law, why was it tried in federal court, rather than state court? What federal question did it raise?

B o x **2.3** **THE CASE OF TERRI SCHIAVO: A THREAT TO JUDICIAL INDEPENDENCE?**

For a few weeks in March 2005, headlines chronicled the battle over the life and death of Terri Schiavo. In 1990, the 26-year-old suffered a heart attack that caused permanent brain damage, described by her doctors as a "persistent vegetative state." She could breathe on her own and her eyes were open at times, but she could not eat or drink and her responses were random. Michael Schiavo, Terri's husband, claimed she had said she would not want to live "like that," and asked that her feeding tube be withdrawn. But Terri's parents, Bob and Mary Schindler, objected to removal of the feeding tube. The Schindlers and Michael Schiavo fought over Terri for seven years—in state and federal court, the halls of the U.S. Congress, and the court of public opinion. Ultimately, the courts ruled that Michael Schiavo could decide for Terri because she could not decide for herself. The tube was withdrawn on March 14, 2005, and she died two weeks later.

In addition to its public spectacle, the Schiavo case was extraordinary because of the important concerns it raised about the independence of the judiciary from legislative "oversight." In 1998, Michael Schiavo filed a lawsuit to have the tube removed. The Schindlers opposed the request, but a Florida judge ordered the tube removed, and the Florida appellate courts affirmed his decision. The Schindlers didn't give up. They fought this decision in the Florida courts for five years, and when the last appeal was lost and the tube removed for the first time in October 2003, they took their cause to then-Governor Jeb Bush and the Florida legislature. A few days later, the legislature responded with an extraordinary statute ("Terri's Law"), giving the governor the authority to reinsert the feeding tube. Governor Bush signed the law that same day, and the feeding tube was reinserted.

Michael Schiavo then sued the governor in state court, claiming that the legislature and governor had violated the principle of separation of powers as embodied in the Florida Constitution and had encroached on the power and authority of the judiciary. The court agreed, saying it is basic to the American system of government that legislatures pass laws and courts decide cases. By attempting to reverse the decision in the Schiavo case, the legislature had exceeded its authority in violation of the state constitution (*Bush v. Schiavo*, 2004).

After further litigation in both state and federal courts, the tube was removed again in March 2005. But then the U.S. Congress did an extraordinary thing: The Congress passed a law, which President George W. Bush signed, entitled "An Act for the relief of the parents of Theresa Marie Schiavo." The act directed the federal court in Florida to consider the Schindlers' request to have the feeding tube reinserted, notwithstanding the many opinions upholding the decision that the tube be removed. When a judge refused, the Schindlers pressed on, buoyed by throngs of supporters holding vigil outside the hospice where Terri lay. They filed several more appeals and suffered more defeats, including one the day before Terri died. In one of the last opinions in this case, a federal judge scolded Congress for telling a court how to exercise its duties.

Critical Thought Question

How did the Florida legislature and the U.S. Congress attempt to influence the outcome of this case? Why, relevant to judicial independence, are their actions cause for concern?

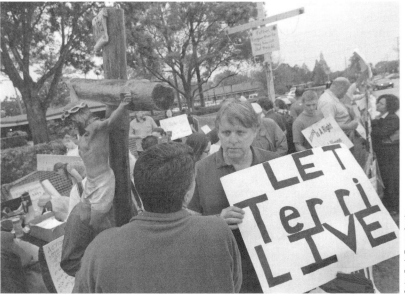

Protesters in the Terri Schiavo case

PLAYERS IN THE LEGAL SYSTEM: JUDGES

Most of us can easily conjure the image of a black-robed judge presiding over a hushed courtroom, approving plea bargains, determining what evidence will be admitted into a trial, and sentencing offenders to lengthy prison terms. To litigants—plaintiffs, defendants, prosecutors, and defense attorneys—indeed, even to the general public, the proclamations of a judge demand deference and, in most instances, respect. His or her words are often the "last words" in a legal dispute. Until recently, we knew relatively little about how judges make decisions, the extent to which their judgments are influenced by personality, attitudes, or past experiences, and how those decisions are constrained by various rules and roles. But psychologists have expressed increasing interest in judicial decision making (Vidmar, 2011). Thus, we are gradually beginning to understand how these robe-cloaked jurists think and how various structural features of the justice system influence their thoughts. One such feature is the means by which judges are selected to serve.

How Are Judges Selected?

We discussed judicial independence—the insulation of judges from the court of public opinion—in the context of the Schiavo case. Though the Schiavo case might suggest otherwise, U.S. federal judges, who are appointed by the president and serve for life, are shielded from the sometimes-fickle inclinations of politicians and the public. They can be removed from office only if impeached for "high crimes and misdemeanors."

The vast majority of state court judges face elections. Typically, the governor makes an initial appointment and the judge is then retained (or not) in a popular election. If retained, the judge serves a number of years, after which he or she again runs for retention. Supporters claim that this system makes judges accountable to the public and that a judge who makes unpopular decisions can be removed from the bench. Of judges surveyed in 10 states, 86% favored retention elections. The judges reported their behavior was improved by knowing that they would have to face the electorate; they were less likely to be arrogant to jurors and litigants and more likely to explain their decisions (Aspin & Hall, 1994).

But like other elections, judicial retention elections may invite pressure from special interest groups. In fact, some judicial races have been hotly contested in recent years, with special interest groups pouring money into advertising, often negative advertising, to elect judges thought to favor their positions. In 2004, Illinois voters experienced what critics called "the race to the bottom": $10 million was spent on a race for the state supreme court, with attack ads featuring the opponent's alleged leniency toward violent offenders in such graphic terms as to almost "make you believe the candidate committed the crime" (Carter, 2005).

There is also concern that judicial elections pose a threat to fairness and impartiality of the courts. The due process clause of the Fourteenth Amendment requires judges to avoid even the appearance of bias. Former president of the American Bar Association, Michael Greco, has said: "When you have interest groups pouring millions and millions of dollars into elections, the impression people get is that judges can be bought and that justice can be bought. The damage that does to the people's confidence in a fair judiciary is incalculable" (Michels, 2006). For this reason, former Supreme Court Justice Sandra Day O'Connor and others have condemned the practice of electing judges.

One judge whose impartiality was seriously questioned is West Virginia Supreme Court Justice Brent Benjamin, who decided a case in favor of a company that contributed $3 million to his election campaign. Many observers thought he should recuse himself (disqualify himself because of his personal involvement with a party in the case). The U.S. Supreme Court tackled the issue in 2009, ruling by a 5–4 majority that Benjamin should have recused himself due to the apparent conflict of interest (*Caperton v. A. T. Massey Coal*, 2009). This case raises some interesting psychological issues, including whether people can overcome their "bias blind spots"—the tendency to see bias in others but not in ourselves (Robbennolt & Taksin, 2010). In fact, judges may have difficulty identifying their biases and making realistic assessments of whether they can set those biases aside.

Standing for election can apparently influence a judge's decisions from the bench. According to one study, judges become more punitive as elections near (Huber & Gordon, 2004). Using sentencing data from more than 22,000 criminal cases in the 1990s, researchers found that judges added more than 2,700 years of additional prison time in aggravated assault, rape, and robbery cases when they were standing for election.

The politicization of judicial races is unfortunate. What is a virtue in a legislative office—keeping a campaign promise—is a vice in a judicial office. Judges who promise in a campaign not to probate offenders either break their promise to the voters by probating an offender who deserves probation, or violate their obligation as judge by denying probation. No judicial candidate should state or imply that he or she would favor one side over the other or decide an issue on anything other than the facts and the law.

There is no easy resolution to the issue of judicial selection. Perhaps the balance between public accountability and judicial independence can be achieved by a system that combines merit appointments with retention elections in which voters are provided with an evaluation of the judge's entire tenure in office by a nonpartisan judicial qualifications commission. Such a system is in place in a handful of states.

Influences on Judicial Judgments

There are at least two schools of thought about whether judges' rulings are influenced solely by the facts of a case and the applicable laws, or whether **extralegal factors** play a role. **Legal formalism** is the perspective that judges apply legal rulings to the facts of a case in a careful, rational, mechanical way, and pay little heed to political or social influences on, or implications of, their judgments. In contrast, **legal realism** holds that judges' decisions are influenced by a variety of psychological, social, and political factors, and that judges indeed are concerned about the real-world ramifications of their decisions.

One caricature of legal realism is that judges are influenced by very personal matters, such as when they last ate. In fact, there is some empirical support of this idea: in their study of successive parole decisions by experienced judges, Danziger, Levav, and Avnaim-Pesso (2011) found that the percentage of favorable rulings dropped from approximately 65% to nearly zero as a morning or afternoon courtroom session wore on, but that the percentage of favorable rulings rose again to about 65% after the judge had taken a food break!

Food matters aside, much evidence suggests that trial judges, as human beings, reflect on their own experiences, assumptions, and biases when reaching decisions from the bench, especially when the decision involves some leeway (e.g., a sentencing range). They may have biases for or against certain groups—homosexual persons, racial minorities, and older adults—that affect the way they process evidence and make decisions. Judges who have been prosecutors may maintain their sympathy with the government's evidence in criminal trials; conversely, judges who were once defense attorneys may be biased in favor of defendants.

One commentator has compared judges to baseball umpires, proposing that although judges' decisions are constrained by procedural rules and precedents, there is still opportunity for personal discretion (Quinn, 1996). This would suggest that the life experiences of judges who are female or members of racial or sexual minorities might predispose them to make decisions that differ from those of their White, male, heterosexual counterparts, particularly in cases related to gender, race and sexual preference (e.g., sexual offenses, harassment, and discrimination).

Although women make up more than half of the U.S. populace, until recently federal judges were almost exclusively male. Racial minorities and avowed homosexuals are also vastly underrepresented on the bench. In fact, not until 2011 was an openly gay man appointed as a federal judge. One reason for the lack of diversity is the life tenure of federal judges, meaning that new judges are appointed only when current judges retire, resign, or die. This imbalance began to change during the presidencies of Jimmy Carter and Bill Clinton and for the first time ever, as of 2010, three women serve as justices of the U.S. Supreme Court.

Although there is a small bit of evidence that judges show **in-group bias** (the tendency to favor one's own group) (e.g., Gazal-Ayal & Sulitzeanu-Kenan, 2010), their decisions generally cannot be predicted from their gender or race alone (e.g., Kulik, Perry, & Pepper, 2003). The powerful forces associated with years of legal education and practice usually trump the influence of personal characteristics. Legal socialization broadens attorneys' knowledge base and increases their respect for precedents and legal compliance. Because judges have typically practiced law for many years before assuming the bench, they understand that personal inclinations cannot dominate their decision making but rather, that they must rule consistently with prior decisions and statutory guidelines (Vidmar, 2011). If they deviate radically from previous decisions, their rulings will be overturned on appeal.

This explains why, in 2011, sponsors of California's same-sex marriage ban lost a request to reverse a decision by former U.S. District Judge Vaughn

Williams. In 2010, Judge Williams ruled that the same-sex marriage ban was unconstitutional, and a few months later, publicly revealed that he is gay. Proponents of the ban argued that because of his sexual orientation, Judge Williams was not an objective arbiter on this issue. But according to James Ware, the Chief Judge of the Northern District of California, Williams was under no obligation to disqualify himself from the case because of his sexual orientation: "It is not reasonable to presume that a judge is incapable of making an impartial decision about the constitutionality of a law, solely because, as a citizen, the judge could be affected by the proceedings" (*Perry v. Schwarzenegger*, 2011, p. 2).

Appellate judges perform different tasks than trial judges and thus may be influenced in different ways by case facts, relevant laws, and extralegal factors. Rather than assessing the credibility of certain witnesses and rendering a verdict, their job is to determine if the law has been correctly applied in previous decisions by trial judges and juries. Although the focus of their work differs from that of trial judges, their decisions can still be analyzed within the perspectives of legal formalism and legal realism. The legal formalism perspective is exemplified by Supreme Court Justice Clarence Thomas's assertion that "There are right and wrong answers to legal questions" (Thomas, 1996). It suggests that judges dispassionately consider the relevant laws, precedents, and constitutional principles, and that judicial bias has no part in decision making. Yet Supreme Court judges tend to vote in predictable ways on cases that reflect basic values such as free speech and civil liberties: Decisions by federal judges appointed by Democratic presidents differ from those of judges appointed by Republican presidents (Tiede, Carp, & Manning, 2010). This suggests that judges' attitudes and predispositions *do* influence their decisions, at least in some kinds of cases. Indeed, most social scientists now reject the legal formalism model and instead favor the legal realism perspective, in which judges view the facts of the case "in light of [their] ideological attitudes and values" (Segal & Spaeth, 1993, p. 32).

How Do Judges Decide?

Cognitive psychologists have proposed various two-process models of human judgment, which are useful for understanding how judges make decisions. Though the details vary, all the models distinguish between **intuitive processes** that occur spontaneously, often without careful thought or effort (as described by Malcolm Gladwell in his best-selling book *Blink*), and **deliberative processes** that involve mental effort, concentration, motivation, and the application of learned rules.

A team of law professors have used a two-process model to explain trial judges' decision making (Guthrie, Rachlinski, & Wistrich, 2007). They claim that although judges try to make decisions by relying on facts, evidence, and legal rules rather than personal biases or emotions, because they are ordinary people (who happen to wear robes), judges tend, like all of us, to have intuitive reactions. And though quick judgments can be overridden by complex, deliberative thoughts, judges must expend the effort to do so.

The researchers asked approximately 300 trial judges to take the Cognitive Reflection Test (Frederick, 2005), a brief test designed to measure intuitive and deliberative processing. Each question has a correct answer that one can recognize on reflection, yet an intuitive—and incorrect—response comes easily to mind. Here is an example:

> A bat and a ball cost $1.10 in total. The bat costs $1.00 more than the ball.
>
> How much does the ball cost?

Many people will immediately say "10 cents." But this intuitive answer is incorrect because if the ball costs 10 cents and the bat costs $1.00 more, the bat will cost $1.10, and together they would cost $1.20, not $1.10. Upon reflection, the correct answer (the ball costs 5 cents and the bat costs $1.05) becomes apparent. Many judges tended to favor the intuitive, rather than the deliberative, response on all questions on the test, though some judges used more deliberate processes. Although judges undoubtedly exercise more care in thinking about issues that arise in their courtrooms than in responding to this short test, they commonly rely on intuitive reactions on the job, as well.

The same team of law professors has shown that judges use intuitive decision processes to respond to suggested damage awards, descriptions of litigants' conduct, and inadmissible evidence (Guthrie, Rachlinski, & Wistrich, 2001; Wistrich, Guthrie, & Rachlinski, 2005). They have even shown that administrative judges, who handle massive numbers of disputes related to environmental safety, labor relations, civil rights violations, and regulatory compliance, and who have vast subject matter expertise, fall victim to the same snap judgments (Guthrie, Rachlinski, & Wistrich, 2009). The authors suggest that judges should verify their intuitive decisions through careful analysis and that the justice system should take steps to make it likely they will do so.

PLAYERS IN THE LEGAL SYSTEM: LAWYERS

Lawyers are plentiful in the United States. Over 70% of the world's lawyers live in the United States, 3 times as many per capita as in Great Britain and more than 25 times as many per capita as in Japan. The American Bar Association (ABA) reported that in 2008, approximately 1 in every 262 Americans was a lawyer, meaning that "every weekday morning 1,143,358 chairs throughout the nation await indentation behind a lawyer's desk" (Kiser, 2010, p. 13).

Lawyers' Work Settings

The legal field permeates the American economy. In 2005, expenditures for legal services were more than twice what the federal government spent on research and development (National Science Board, 2008). The work of lawyers influences everything from "automobile design to pharmaceutical research, from kindergarten field trip waivers to Fortune 500 companies' earnings guidance" (Kiser, 2010, p. 11–12). Given this vast array of legal services, it is not surprising that lawyers work in a wide variety of settings.

Lawyers who work in law firms attend to the needs of the firm's clients. Some of them specialize (e.g., in labor law or intellectual property), and others are generalists, trying to handle most of their clients' legal matters. Some lawyers work for corporations and have only one client—their corporate employer.

Many lawyers work for the government on the federal, state, or local level. Like attorneys for corporations, government lawyers have only one client: the governmental unit for which they work. Prosecutors are government lawyers responsible for prosecuting individuals charged with crimes. Federal prosecutors (called U.S. Attorneys) are appointed by the president, and prosecute people for violating federal laws. The head prosecutors for cities and counties, typically called States' Attorneys or district attorneys, are elected, often

in partisan elections. They prosecute individuals who have allegedly broken city, county, or state laws.

Because many people accused of crime cannot afford to hire a lawyer, most criminal defendants are represented by public defenders who are also government employees. The history of public defenders dates from the 1963 case of *Gideon v. Wainwright*, in which the Supreme Court held that the State of Florida was obligated to pay for a lawyer for Clarence Earl Gideon, a small-town thief who lived on the fringes of society. His story is detailed in Box 2.4.

States responded to the Gideon case by appointing and paying lawyers to represent indigent defendants on a case-by-case basis and by establishing public defender programs, with lawyers hired by the state to represent those who cannot afford to hire them. Public defenders know the law, the system, and the other players in the system (the judge, the prosecutor, the probation officer), and though they have large caseloads, they often obtain excellent results for their clients.

Occasionally one reads of a public defender or appointed attorney who goes far beyond what can reasonably be expected of someone who is overworked and underpaid. Abbe Smith, now a law professor at Georgetown University, has written a book about her experience in representing Patsy Kelly Jarrett over a span of 25 years (Smith, 2008). Smith first met Jarrett in 1980, three years after Jarrett, driver of a getaway car, was convicted of felony murder and was sentenced to life imprisonment in New York. Convinced that Jarrett (whose conviction was based on eyewitness testimony) was innocent, Smith agreed to represent her and became a tireless advocate over the next 25 years, trying to secure Jarrett's freedom. Jarrett's conviction was eventually overturned.

Law Schools and Legal Education

American lawyers of the 18th and 19th centuries typically learned to practice law through the apprentice method: An enterprising young man (the first female lawyer graduated in 1869) would attach himself to an attorney for a period of time, until both he and the lawyer were satisfied that he was ready to be "admitted to the bar." He would then be questioned, often superficially, by a judge or lawyer and pronounced fit to practice (Stevens, 1983).

Powerful forces shaped legal education as we know it today. States began to require those aspiring to be lawyers to pass meaningful examinations. Influenced by the ABA, the states also gradually increased

Box 2.4 THE CASE OF CLARENCE GIDEON, HIS FAMOUS PAUPER'S PLEA, AND THE RIGHT TO AN ATTORNEY

At age 51, Clarence Earl Gideon was tried for breaking into a pool hall and stealing money from a cigarette machine and a jukebox. At his trial, Gideon asked the judge to appoint an attorney to defend him because he had no money to pay for one. The judge, following the laws in Florida, refused.

Gideon did not have a lawyer during his trial. Though no stranger to a courtroom, having been convicted on four previous occasions, he lost this case as well. Eventually, from his prison cell, Gideon filed a pauper's appeal to the U.S. Supreme Court. His contention, laboriously written in pencil and misspelled, was that the U.S. Constitution guaranteed the right of every defendant in a criminal trial to have the services of a lawyer. Gideon's effort was a long shot; well over 1,500 paupers' appeals are filed each term, and the Supreme Court agrees to consider only about 3% of them.

Furthermore, 20 years earlier, in the case of *Betts v. Brady* (1942), the Supreme Court had rejected the very proposition that Gideon was making by holding that poor defendants had a right to free counsel only under "special circumstances" (e.g., if the defendant was very young, illiterate, or mentally ill). Yet, ever since its adoption, the doctrine of *Betts v. Brady* had been criticized as inconsistent and unjust. The folly of requiring a poor person to represent himself is exemplified by Gideon's cross-examination of the most important witness for the prosecution:

Q. Do you know positively I was carrying a pint of wine?

A. Yes.

Q. How do you know that?

A. Because I seen it in your hand. (Lewis, 1964)

When Gideon's case was argued before the Supreme Court in January 1963, he was represented by Abe Fortas, a Washington attorney later appointed to the Supreme Court. Fortas argued that it was impossible for defendants to have a fair trial unless they were represented by a lawyer. He also observed that the "special circumstances" rule was very hard to apply fairly.

In 1963, the Supreme Court ruled unanimously that Gideon had the right to be represented by an attorney, even if he could not afford one. As Justice Hugo Black put it, "[that] the government hires lawyers to prosecute and [that] defendants who have the money hire lawyers to defend are the strongest indications of the widespread belief that lawyers in criminal cases are necessities, not luxuries" (*Gideon v. Wainwright*, 1963, p. 344). Nearly two years after he was sentenced, Clarence Gideon was given a new trial. With the help of a free court-appointed attorney, he was acquitted. The simple handwritten petition of a modest man had forever changed the procedures of criminal trials.

Critical Thought Question

(1) What are some important functions performed by a defense attorney that a defendant such as Clarence Gideon could not provide in his own case? (2) How might this change if Mr. Gideon had been middle class and college educated? (3) What if Mr. Gideon had been a criminal attorney himself? (Why is there an old saying among lawyers that "the attorney who represents himself has a fool for a client")?

AP Photos

Clarence Earl Gideon

the educational requirements for taking these exams, first requiring some college, then some law school, and finally graduation from an accredited law school.

Legal education focuses on fostering analytic skills and deepening one's knowledge of the law, and although it is largely successful in this regard, it may take a toll on students' well-being. Studies show that attending law school tends to undermine students' values, motivation, and mental health (Sheldon & Krieger, 2004; 2007). Prior to law school, students are comparable to students in other professional fields in terms of psychological functioning. But soon after law school commences they report large increases in anxiety, depression, hostility, and paranoia. Some attribute these symptoms to law schools' excessive workload, intimidating teaching practices, competitive grading systems, status-seeking job placement services, and the lack of concern about personal feelings, values, or subjective well-being.

Researchers Kennon Sheldon and Lawrence Krieger (2004, 2007) suggest that psychological dysfunction is related to changes in motivation that occur over the course of one's law school career. They focus on the **self-determination theory of optimal motivation** (Deci & Ryan, 2000), which describes situational and personality factors that cause positive and negative motivation and, eventually, changes in subjective well-being. Sheldon and Krieger (2004) found that the increase in mental health symptoms in the first year of law school was correlated with a decrease in **intrinsic motivation** (engaging in an activity because it is interesting and enjoyable). Over the course of that year, students moved from pursuing their professional goals for reasons of interest and enjoyment (i.e., because of their intrinsic motivation) to pursuing goals that would please and impress others (i.e., for reasons of **extrinsic motivation**). In other words, they felt less self-determined at the end of the year than they had at the beginning. Importantly, students who perceived that faculty supported their autonomy showed fewer declines in psychological well-being in the first year of law school and had higher grades in the third year (Sheldon & Krieger, 2007).

Professional Satisfaction among Lawyers

The practice of law may also be less satisfying than one might hope. Although 80% of lawyers questioned in an American Bar Association–commissioned survey said they were proud to be lawyers and 81% said their work was intellectually stimulating, only about half the respondents voiced satisfaction with their careers, and only 40% would recommend that others pursue law as a career (Ward, 2007). Nonwhite lawyers, whose numbers have been increasing steadily since the mid-1960s, tend to be less satisfied than their White counterparts, although they would still recommend a legal career to others, and tend to regard the law as a promising opportunity for personal and professional growth. Lawyers are generally less satisfied with their jobs than judges or law professors, suggesting that situational forces inherent in the practice of law (e.g., the hierarchical structure of many law firms, the obligation to bill a certain number of hours each week), rather than the discipline itself, may be to blame.

Lawyers who do not possess typical "lawyer traits" may be most discontented by the practice of law. A particular constellation of characteristics distinguishes lawyers from the general adult population: a preference for dominance, competitiveness, the need for achievement, and interpersonal insensitivity (Daicoff, 1999). According to law professor Susan Daicoff, these traits fit well with traditional forms of legal practice that value winning, analytical reasoning, and the elevation of concerns about clients' legal rights (Daicoff, 1999). Certainly not all lawyers possess these traits and not all legal issues require an adversarial, "I win–you lose" mentality. But attorneys who are not highly competitive, achievement-oriented, or motivated by dominance may experience the legal profession as a harsh and inhospitable place to work.

Fortunately, some legal institutions (including specialty courts and juvenile diversion programs) have begun to integrate principles of **therapeutic jurisprudence**, the notion that the law can serve therapeutic purposes, with traditional legal structures and procedures. Therapeutic jurisprudence identifies emotional consequences of legal matters and asks whether the law can be interpreted, applied, or enforced in ways that maximize its therapeutic, or healing, effects. Therapeutic use of the law to enhance people's well-being may promise a less adversarial future for lawyers and the practice of law.

How Do Lawyers Decide?

Although there is little systematic information about how lawyers undertake and perform their work, we are beginning to have a clearer picture of how they make decisions, particularly when the decisions are related to litigation (e.g., whether they should pursue a case on behalf of a client who is eager to sue, or whether to settle a case or go to trial). Underlying these decisions are assumptions about likely outcomes, and recent studies suggest that lawyers are not particularly adept at forecasting case outcomes (e.g., Goodman-Delahunty, Granhag, Hartwig, & Loftus, 2010).

In general, when making predictions or reflecting on past experiences, people tend to be more confident than correct. This **overconfidence bias** applies to people's estimates of the value of their contributions to a group, accuracy of their judgments, and chances of success in a variety of situations. With respect to trial lawyers, it means that they are overly confident of their abilities, including their ability to predict and produce successful case outcomes.

By examining the nature of the decisions that lawyers make and the demands inherent in their professional roles, we can understand why this is true (Greene & Bornstein, 2011). When lawyers decide whether to take on a new client or a new case, they have to make predictions about case outcomes months and years in advance of those outcomes. These are **probabilistic estimates**, in the sense that the correct answer is not yet known. Yet lawyers, like all people, make more optimistic predictions about events in the distant future than in the near future (Gilovich, Kerr & Medvec, 1993) and over time—including hours of strategizing, preparing arguments and locating witnesses—they become increasingly confident that their predicted outcomes are attainable (Trope & Liberman, 2003). What's more, although prediction accuracy can be improved when one learns whether previous predictions were accurate, lawyers rarely get feedback about their decisions. They almost never know what a jury would have awarded the plaintiff had they not agreed to settle the case before trial, or how a particular expert witness might have changed the outcome.

Yet another reason for lawyers' overconfidence is their belief that the outcome of a case is largely under their control. This **illusion of control** means that lawyers may discount the strengths of their adversaries, the whims of the judge, and their own weaknesses, and make predictions of personal success than are higher that may be warranted by reality.

How can lawyers improve their ability to assess the likelihood of future outcomes? A seemingly simple way to gain insight is to discuss the case with peers—other lawyers—who are less invested in the outcome. In a variety of situations that involve probabilistic estimates, both novices and experts have benefitted from the opinion of just one other person, even though they continue to give more weight to their own opinions than to the opinions of others.

The value of seeking feedback from other lawyers was confirmed in a recent study that compared the accuracy of lawyers' individual estimates of damage awards in personal injury cases (e.g., involving car accidents) with estimates made after discussions with others, and with the actual verdict in the case (Jacobson, Dobbs-Marsh, Liberman, & Minson, 2011). When lawyers made individual assessments, only 4% of their predictions were correct, 64% were too low, and 32% were too high. Their predictions were considerably more accurate (i.e., more closely aligned with the actual verdict) when they were able to discuss the case with another lawyer, even though they underweighted that lawyer's estimate relative to their own. The most accurate assessments occurred when two lawyers had to agree on a single, joint estimate. So to the extent that trial lawyers consider and give sufficient weight to a second opinion, they can improve their predictions of future case outcomes.

Are more combined opinions better than fewer? Jacobson and his colleagues addressed that question by statistically creating groups of varying sizes and found that the benefits of additional opinions decreased as the number of the people in the group increased. The "biggest bang for the buck" appears to come from discussing the value of a case with just one other person.

SUMMARY

1. ***What is the difference between the adversarial and inquisitorial models of trials?*** The trial process in the United States and several other countries is

called the adversarial model because all the witnesses, evidence, and exhibits are presented by one side or the other. In contrast, in the inquisitorial model used in much of Europe, the judge does nearly all questioning of witnesses. Although the adversarial model has been criticized for instigating undesirable competition between sides, in empirical studies it has been judged to be fairer and to lead to less-biased decisions.

2. ***How do notions of morality and legality differ?*** What is considered moral is not always what is ruled legal, and vice versa. When determining right and wrong, some people rely on the law almost entirely, but many people have internalized principles of morality that may be inconsistent with the laws.

3. ***How do different models of justice explain people's level of satisfaction with the legal system?*** According to the distributive justice model, people's acceptance of a legal decision is related to whether they think the outcome, or decision, is fair. According to the procedural justice model, fairness in the procedures is a more important determinant of satisfaction. When people think they were treated fairly, they are more accepting of legal outcomes.

4. ***What is commonsense justice?*** Commonsense justice reflects the basic notions of everyday citizens about what is just and fair. In contrast to black-letter law, commonsense justice emphasizes the overall context in which an act occurs, the subjective intent of the person committing the act, and a desire to make the legal consequences of the act proportionate to the perceived culpability of the actor.

5. ***How are judges selected and how do their demographic characteristics and attitudes influence their decisions?*** Federal judges are appointed for life. Most state court judges are appointed and then run on their records in retention elections. Judges' demographic characteristics tend not to influence their decisions, probably because the experiences of law school and years of work as a lawyer are powerful socializing forces. On the other hand, judges' biases and predispositions do tend to influence their judgments.

6. ***How does the experience of law school affect its students?*** Attending law school tends to undermine students' values, motivation, and psychological health because it reduces their intrinsic motivation and sense of self-determination.

7. ***What is known about lawyers' professional satisfaction?*** Although most lawyers think their work is stimulating, fewer would recommend that others pursue a career in the law. Lawyers who do not have typical "lawyer traits" of competitiveness and achievement orientation are less satisfied than those who do.

8. ***What factors explain lawyers' overconfidence and how can it be remedied?*** Lawyers, particularly trial lawyers, are overconfident about their chances of future success because they rarely get useful feedback about their decisions and often assume that they can control case outcomes. Discussing a case with just one other attorney can lead to more accurate predictions about future results.

KEY TERMS

adversarial system
attribution theory
black-letter law
commonsense justice
deliberative processes
distributive justice
diversion
euthanasia
extralegal factors
extrinsic motivation
illusion of control
in-group bias
inquisitorial approach
intention
intrinsic motivation
intuitive processes
legal formalism
legal realism
overconfidence bias
probabilistic estimates
procedural justice
self-determination
theory of optimal motivation
therapeutic jurisprudence

Chapter 3

Psychology of Crime

ORIENTING QUESTIONS

1. Theories of crime can be grouped into four categories. What are they?
2. Among sociological explanations of crime, how does the subcultural explanation differ from the structural explanation?
3. What is emphasized in biological theories of crime?
4. What psychological factors have been advanced to explain crime?
5. How do social-psychological theories view crime?

OFFENDING IN THE UNITED STATES

Crime is a serious problem in our society. How often are crimes committed? What are the important influences to consider in understanding such offending? Questions about the causes of crime are the concern of **criminology**, which is the study of crime and criminal behavior. In this chapter, we summarize the major theories of crime, beginning with a brief review of the historical predecessors of 20th-century criminology. We will give examples of particularly serious and troubling offenses, and discuss why they occur.

Serious Offending

Rates of serious crime have been steadily declining in the United States. This decrease is confirmed by both victimization studies and official police statistics. According to the National Crime Victimization Survey (Bureau of Justice Statistics, 2005b), the rate of violent crime has been dropping since 1999 (Bureau of Justice Statistics, 2010) and decreased substantially (over 8%) between 2008 and 2009.

Despite this downturn in crime rates, many Americans continue to list crime and the fear of crime as one of their most serious concerns. If the rate of crime is declining, why do so many individuals continue to perceive crime as a major threat in their lives? One reason is that the rate of violent crime is still relatively high despite recent decreases: 17 out of every 1,000 residents age 12 or older and living in an urban area were victimized by violent crime in 2009 (Bureau of Justice Statistics, 2010). The average citizen's fear of crime is also heightened by the highly publicized crimes of a few individuals that evoke images of an epidemic of random violence beyond the control of a civilized society. The media, particularly cable networks, provide extensive coverage of heinous crimes, contributing to a heightened state of public fear. Apparently crime coverage "sells." Consider these examples:

- In 2002, John Allen Muhammad and Lee Boyd Malvo terrorized the Washington, D.C. metropolitan area, shooting 13 people at random and killing 10 of them during a three-month crime spree.
- In early 2004, Charles Allen McCoy, Jr., dubbed the Ohio Highway sniper, committed an estimated 24 acts involving firing at cars from an

overpass, killing a woman and terrorizing many more.

Perhaps even more troubling than the overall crime rate or highly publicized crime sprees is the frequency of serious criminal activity among young people. Although the number of serious violent offenses committed by persons ages 12 to 17 declined by 61% from 1993 to 2005, juveniles continue to be responsible for committing about 24% of violent crimes. Specifically, youths under 18 years old commit approximately 12% of sexual assaults, 18% of robberies, and 22% of aggravated assaults.

In 2002, juveniles were involved in approximately 8% of all homicides. Although the number of murders involving juveniles has steadily decreased since 1994, juveniles continued to be involved in high-profile fatal events.

- In February 2009, an eighth-grader named Lawrence King was shot in the head in his Oxnard, California, classroom while classmates looked on, horrified. Police allege that the shooter, 14-year-old Brandon McInerney, and some other boys had previously taunted King because he was gay. At the time of this death, King was living in a shelter for abused and troubled children.
- In 2006, Daytona Beach, Florida, teen Warren Messner and three other boys brutally beat a homeless man to death because they were bored. The boys, who jumped on the man's chest and crushed his ribcage, were sentenced to between 22 and 35 years in prison.
- In April 1999, two students at Columbine High School in Littleton, Colorado, shot 12 of their classmates and a teacher before killing themselves.

School Violence

The public becomes especially fearful about crime when they perceive it is occurring in traditionally safe environments. In the past two decades, crime in the workplace and violence in our schools have caused great national concern. DeKalb, Illinois; Blacksburg, Virginia; Red Lake, Minnesota; and Littleton, Colorado—these four communities share something that sets them apart from thousands of other American towns. In each, one or more

Seung-Hui Cho

AP Photo/Virginia State Police

Statistics about school violence, and the case histories of those boys who have murdered their classmates at school, provide some possible answers. First, according to a national survey of public schools in 1999–2000, 71% of students reported experiencing one or more violent incidents, and 20% reported *serious* violent incidents, which include rape, sexual battery other than rape, physical fighting with a weapon, and robbery with or without a weapon. However, only about 36% of these schools reported one or more of these incidents to the police (National Center for Education Statistics, 2004). These events occurred more often in high schools than in elementary or middle schools, and high schools reported these events to police more often than did elementary or middle schools (National Center for Education Statistics, 2004). One survey conducted in 2001 (National Center for Education Statistics, 2003) revealed that 17% of high school students had carried a weapon (a gun, knife, or club) at least once in the previous month, and about 6% of these students carried the weapon to school. Additionally, in the 2005–2006 school year, 17% of public schools experienced at least one serious violent incident at school. A smaller percentage of primary schools (67%) than middle schools (94%) or high schools (95%) experienced a violent incident in 2005–2006.

School-ground homicides remain very rare, but when they do occur, they attract a great deal of speculation about the motives of the shooters (Cornell, 2006). Based on the small sample of cases, a few common characteristics have been identified in the backgrounds of the boys responsible for school killings (Cloud, 1998; Verlinden, Hersen, & Thomas, 2000). Such boys tend to have

students went to school one day, armed with guns, and proceeded to kill and wound their classmates. The grisly totals from these four shootings: more than 60 dead and dozens wounded.

High-profile shootings occur both in high schools and on college campuses. Seung-Hui Cho was a child of South Korean immigrants who moved to the United States in 1992. In his earlier school days, he was often so uncommunicative that he would not even respond when his teacher took the roll. He enrolled at Virginia Tech. On April 16, 2007, at 7:15 A.M., Cho shot and killed two students in a campus dormitory. Later that morning, he took the two handguns and ammunition he had obtained off campus and went from room to room in Norris Hall, a building on campus. Police responded quickly to an emergency call placed at 9:43 A.M., but by the time they were able to break into the building eight minutes later (Cho had chained several doors shut), Cho and 30 students and faculty members were dead.

The school shooting fatalities had experts, parents, teachers, and youngsters themselves trying to understand what motivates school shootings and what can be done to prevent them. Are school environments to blame? Is the ready availability of guns one explanation? Were the killers mentally ill or emotionally disturbed misfits? Were they driven by violent music and gory video games? Did their parents fail to support and supervise them adequately?

- had more than the usual experience with firearms, showing a persistent fascination with guns

- felt isolated from, rejected by, or even tormented by classmates and had particular difficulty relating comfortably to girls

- been preoccupied with various forms of graphically violent media, including music, Internet sites, and video games

- suffered teasing because of their physical appearance—most of these assailants were either frail or somewhat obese

- had a history of angry brooding, often over their real or perceived status as social outcasts

- developed a detailed plan for their aggression, which was often communicated to others in the days or weeks prior to the event

Whether we will ever be able to explain this kind of crime is not clear. In retrospect, many of these individuals' classmates and teachers report that they now recognize that there were warning signs—although these signs do not necessarily reflect a forthcoming school shooting.

A number of reforms and programs have been attempted: requiring school uniforms, beefing up security measures, passing tougher gun laws, offering violence prevention programs, and restricting access to violent movies, among others. Another practice has involved "profiling" to predict which students are likely to commit violent crimes. However, this practice causes many students to be unjustly targeted, often on the basis of features not related to criminal behavior (e.g., clothing, music preferences). Furthermore, profiling in schools (even if it were very accurate in identifying those who are likely to commit homicides, which it is not) encounters the problem of "low base rates." That is, because school shootings are so rare, profiling would "overpredict," identifying many students who would actually not have committed a shooting.

Instead, some researchers have proposed that increasing communication between students and school administrators may be a more productive approach to resolving the issues surrounding school violence and weapons (Mulvey & Cauffman, 2001). They note, "Students who are committed to school, feel that they belong, and trust the administration are less likely to commit violent acts than those who are uninvolved, alienated, and distrustful … Establishing school environments where students feel connected and trusted will build the critical link between those who often know when trouble is brewing and those who can act to prevent it."

Additional research on secondary school and campus shootings (Cornell, 2003, 2006; Flynn & Heitzmann, 2008; Heilbrun, Dvoskin, & Heilbrun, 2009; Reddy et al., 2001) would suggest several important points:

- The most prevalent problem with aggression in education settings is not shootings. In school contexts, it is bullying; on college campuses it is more likely to be date rape and hazing. Much of this aggression is unreported and hence underestimated by official records.

- Most of those who make implied or direct threats will not go on to commit serious violence. Threatening communications are made for a variety of reasons, including angry disputes, fear, jealousy, and ideology.

- "Zero tolerance" policies are ineffective and have the potential to stigmatize and harm a variety of mistakenly identified individuals.

A different approach, termed **threat assessment**, involves carefully considering the nature of the threat, the risk posed by the individual, and the needed response to reduce the risk of harmful action. Threat assessment has been refined by organizations such as the U.S. Secret Service in their work with threats of targeted violence toward those they protect (such as the U.S. president and vice-president and their families). It can also be modified for use in other settings such as schools and colleges.

Highly publicized acts of violence at school or in the workplace threaten fundamental assumptions about personal security and the safety of our children and have a major effect on how individuals feel about their quality of life. For these reasons, policymakers and social scientists must pay particular attention to workplace and school violence, although neighborhood violence also continues to be a concern.

WHY DOES CRIME HAPPEN?

Behavioral scientists argue that to ease the crime problem, we must first understand its causes. Why does crime happen? What motivates people to commit illegal acts? Bad genes? Inadequate parents? Failed schooling? Twisted impulses? Harsh environments? Delinquent friends? Social disadvantage? Drug addiction? Some combination of these factors? Can crime be predicted from knowing about a person's early life? Or are many people capable of crime under the wrong circumstances—an unfortunate mix of intoxication, anger, and unprotected victims which come together, in the words of novelist Daniel Woodrell (1996), "like car wrecks that you knew would happen … almost nightly, at the same old crossroads of Hormones and Liquor" (p. 27)? Are some crimes, like those of Dexter Morgan (see Box 3.1), so extreme that they defy scientific explanation, or can behavioral scientists make sense of them?

THEORIES OF CRIME AS EXPLANATIONS OF CRIMINAL BEHAVIOR

Theories of crime are as old as crime itself. Aristotle claimed that "poverty is the parent of revolution and crime." But most ancient explanations of crime took a religious tone; crime was either equivalent to or due to sin, a view that was popular throughout the Middle Ages and lives on today in many religious belief systems.

In the 17th century, Sir Francis Bacon argued that "opportunity makes a thief." During the 1700s, philosophers and social critics such as Voltaire and Rousseau emphasized concepts such as free will, hedonism, and flaws in the social contract to explain criminal conduct. These principles ultimately grew into the **classical school of criminology**.

The two leading proponents of classical criminology were the Italian intellectual Cesare Beccaria and the British philosopher Jeremy Bentham, who believed that lawbreaking occurred when people freely chose to behave wrongly when faced with a choice between right and wrong. People chose crime when they believed that the gains from crime outweighed the losses it entailed. Classical theorists were interested in reforming the harsh administration of justice in post-Renaissance Europe, and they believed that punishment of criminals should be commensurate with the crimes committed—that punishment should fit the crime.

Classical theory influenced several principles of justice in Western societies (e.g., the U.S. Constitution's Eighth Amendment ban against "cruel and unusual punishment"). It still exerts an important effect on modern correctional philosophy.

Modern theories of crime developed from the **positivist school of criminology**. Rather than focusing on individuals' free will, positivists emphasized factors that they believed determined criminal behavior. They sought to understand crime through the scientific method and the analysis of empirical data. Some stressed sociological factors, whereas others preferred biological, psychological, or environmental explanations.

An early positivist was Adolphe Quetelet, a Belgian statistician who studied crime data and concluded that crime occurred more often in certain geographic areas and under specific social conditions. Cesare Lombroso (1876) and Raffaele Garofalo (1914), other theorists who relied on scientific data, emphasized the physical characteristics of criminals and proposed a strong biological predisposition to crime. Although the early positivists considered themselves scientists, their methods were crude by current standards and led to conclusions that are not taken seriously today. Positivists believed that punishment should fit the criminal rather than the crime. This position foreshadowed rehabilitation as a correctional priority and the indeterminate sentence as a means for achieving it.

Most modern theories of criminal behavior—including those of biology, genetics, psychology, sociology, economics, anthropology, and religion—are a legacy of the positivist tradition. The validity of these theories varies greatly. Most can account reasonably well for certain types of crime, but none explains all forms of criminality—and some explain very few. Empirical data, rational analyses, moral values, and political ideologies all play a role in shaping preferences for the leading theories in criminology.

For the most part, criminologists have concentrated on those crimes that frighten the average citizen—violent acts (e.g., robbery, rape, assault, and murder) or aggressive behavior against property (e.g., burglary, theft, and arson). But many other kinds of legally prohibited conduct—environmental plunder, price fixing, and business fraud, for example—can cause great damage to individuals and society. (Consider the securities fraud perpetrated by Bernard Madoff, the hedge-fund trader and former chairman of the Nasdaq stock market, who may have plundered up to $50 billion of his clients' money.) However, these crimes are not the typical focus of criminologists, nor are they the kind of offenses considered by the general public when it debates the "crime problem."

Most theories of crime have focused on men. This may be reasonable, given that about three-quarters of all arrests are of men and that almost 85% of violent crimes are committed by men. However, the factors that influence female criminality deserve attention, at least in part because crime by

---

B o x   3.1   THE CASE OF DEXTER MORGAN: A FICTIONAL PSYCHOPATH?

Dexter Morgan is playful, handsome, and has a wonderfully ironic sense of humor. He is the fictional star of novels (*Dearly Devoted Dexter, Darkly Dreaming Dexter, Dexter in the Dark*) and a television series ("*Dexter*"). To his co-workers and fiancée, he is the blood-splatter analyst for the Miami Police Department. Privately, however, he is a selective serial killer who is guided by an internal companion whom he calls "the Dark Passenger." Dexter was trained by his adoptive father, a Miami cop, to present himself as "normal"—and to kill only those who deserve it, according to a strict set of rules designed to avoid detection.

Can a fictional character such as Dexter tell us anything about reality? Are there real-life, nonfictional Dexter Morgans out there? Perhaps not, but reading about and watching Dexter can illustrate genuine phenomena. Engaging in a heinous act such as the killing of neighborhood pets, and needing to be taught to act "as if" one feels certain emotions, are associated with a kind of personality disorder known as **psychopathy**. Dexter's character might meet some of the criteria for this disorder, but does he qualify as a psychopath? Would a real measure of this disorder (the Hare Psychopathy

Michael Hall plays Dexter Morgan

Checklist-Revised, or PCL-R; Hare, 2003) classify the fictional Dexter as a psychopath? Let's consider how some of the PCL-R items might apply.

PCL-R Item	Dexter
Glibness/superficial charm	■ Flirts with women to keep up appearances. ■ Talks his way out of difficult situations easily.
Pathological lying	■ Lies often, but presumably for self-preservation rather than without any understandable motivation.
Conning/manipulative	■ Able to obtain files from clerks with flirting and donuts. ■ Plans his killings carefully, using ruses and cons to capture and subdue his victims.
Lack of remorse or guilt	■ Does not describe feeling these things for his victims. ■ Also does not feel remorse or guilt for anything he does with cow-orkers or his wife or her children, although he feigns these emotions to fit in.

---

females has increased greatly in recent years. The rate of growth in the female inmate population has been substantial in the last two decades; between 1995 and 2008, the number of women in state and federal prisons nationwide increased by 203% (Women in Prison Project, 2009). Despite increases in violent criminal behavior, women are still most often arrested for larceny and theft. Such arrests often involve collaborating with a male partner. One implication of this pattern is that explanations of female crime need to carefully consider the role of coercion, especially as it is exerted in close relationships.

There are four contemporary theories that attempt to explain criminal offending. We group these theories into four categories: sociological, biological, psychological, and social-psychological. There are important distinctions among these four approaches.

Crime may appear to result from an individual's experience with his or her environment. This belief is explained through **sociological theories**, which maintain that crime results from social or cultural forces that are external to any specific individual; exist prior to any criminal act; and emerge from social

PCL-R Item	Dexter
Callous/lack of empathy	■ Shows no empathy for his victims.
Promiscuous sexual behavior	■ No. Dexter describes himself as disinterested in all aspects of sexuality, including both physical and emotional intimacy.
Need for stimulation/proneness to boredom	■ Describes this as a hunger for killing, which he must satisfy periodically. ■ Has a professional position involving the inspection of highly stimulating phenomena (homicide crime scenes). ■ In other respects, however, he is not a great stimulation seeker, nor does he portray himself as easily bored.
Parasitic lifestyle	■ No. He has a steady job and does not rely on others for assistance.
Poor behavioral controls	■ No. He is careful and calculating, the antithesis of an impulsive offender.
Irresponsibility	■ No. He was gainfully employed and does his job well. ■ He is committed to his wife and her family, although not attracted to the intimacy. ■ He uses both his job and his relationships as a cover for his self-designated role as the protector of society from serial killers.
Early behavior problems	■ Showed behavior that could have resulted in arrest (e.g., killing neighborhood pets, taping up and threatening a classmate).
Criminal versatility	■ No. Dexter is a "specialist" whose offending is limited to abducting and killing his victims.

In some respects, the fictional Dexter Morgan (Phillips, 2006) is quite similar to those who have the personality disorder of psychopathy. These similarities are most apparent in his superficial emotions and lack of the capacity for deep emotional attachments. But Dexter does not possess some of the other characteristics and much of the history that are core elements of psychopathy. We might conclude that Dexter Morgan is a charming fictional character who can communicate what it's like to have difficulty feeling deep emotions—but it's not clear whether he would be classified as a psychopath.

Critical Thought Question

Dexter Morgan is obviously very disturbed. Why would he not be classified as a psychopath?

class, political, ecological, or physical structures affecting large groups of people (Nettler, 1974).

Alternatively, criminal behavior may appear to result from an individual's biological characteristics. **Biological theories of crime** stress genetic influences, neuropsychological abnormalities, and biochemical irregularities. But as we shall see, there is little empirical evidence that either sociological or biological theories independently predict criminal behavior. Instead, current theories of crime incorporate a combination of environmental and biological factors to understand the causes of offending behaviors.

Some **psychological theories** emphasize that crime results from personality attributes that are uniquely possessed, or possessed to a special degree, by the potential criminal. For example, some psychological approaches have focused on patterns of thinking—particularly with respect to recognized risk factors such as pro-criminal attitudes or certain kinds of personality disorders.

Social-psychological theories (or social process theories; Nettler, 1974; Reid, 1976) bridge the gap between the environmentalism of sociology and the individualism of psychological or biological theories. Social-psychological theories propose that crime is learned, but they differ from sociological and psychological theories about *what* is learned and *how* it is learned.

Sociological Theories of Crime

Sociological theories may be divided into **structural** and **subcultural explanations**. Structural theories emphasize that dysfunctional social arrangements (e.g., inadequate schooling, economic adversity, or community disorganization) thwart people's efforts toward legitimate attainments and result in their breaking the law. Subcultural theories hold that crime originates when various groups of people endorse cultural values that clash with the dominant, conventional rules of society. In this view, crime is the product of a subculture's deviation from the accepted norms that underlie the criminal law.

Structural Explanations.   A key concept of structural approaches is that certain groups of people suffer fundamental inequalities in opportunities to achieve the goals valued by society. Differential opportunity, proposed by Cloward and Ohlin (1960) in their book *Delinquency and Opportunity*, is one example of a **structural explanation** of crime. This theory can be traced to Émile Durkheim's ideas about the need to maintain moral bonds between individuals in society. Durkheim thought that life without moral or social obligations becomes intolerable and results in **anomie**, a feeling of normlessness that often precedes suicide and crime. One implication of anomie theory was that unlimited aspirations pressure individuals to deviate from social norms.

According to Cloward and Ohlin (1960), people in lower socioeconomic subcultures usually want to succeed through legal means, but society denies them legitimate opportunities to do so. For example, consider a person from Nicaragua who immigrates to the United States because of a sincere desire to make a better life for his family. He faces cultural and language differences, financial hardships, and limited access to the resources that are crucial for upward mobility. It remains more difficult for poor people to obtain an advanced education, despite advances in the practice of need-blind admissions and tuition adjustments based on need that are now offered by some U.S. universities. In addition, crowding in large cities makes class distinctions more apparent.

When legal means of goal achievement are blocked, intense frustration results, and crime is more likely to ensue. Youthful crime, especially in gangs, is one outgrowth of this sequence. The theory of differential opportunity assumes that people who grow up in crowded, impoverished, deteriorating neighborhoods endorse conventional, middle-class goals (e.g., owning a home). Thus, crime is an illicit means to gain an understandable end.

Consistent with this theory of differential opportunity, Gottfredson (1986) and Gordon (1986), a sociologist team, attempted to explain the higher crime rate of lower-class Black youth in terms of their poorer academic performance. Denied legitimate job opportunities because of low aptitude scores or grades, these youth discover that they can make several hundred dollars a week dealing crack cocaine. In fact, with the advent of crack cocaine, arrests of juveniles in New York City, Detroit, Washington, and other cities tripled in the mid- to late 1980s.

The theory of differential opportunity has several limitations (Lilly, Cullen, & Ball, 1989). First, a great deal of research indicates that seriously delinquent youth display many differences from their law-abiding counterparts other than differing educational opportunities, and they tend to show these differences as early as the beginning of elementary school. Second, there is no evidence that lower-class youth find limited success in school to be more frustrating than do middle-class youngsters. On the contrary, the opposite is likely to be true. The assumption that lower-class juveniles typically aspire to membership in the middle class is also unproven. Furthermore, the major terms in the theory, such as *aspiration*, *frustration*, and *opportunity*, are defined too vaguely; the theory does not explicitly explain what determines adaptation to blocked opportunities (Sheley, 1985). Last and most apparent, some crimes are committed by people who have never been denied opportunities; in fact, they may have basked in an abundance of good fortune. Think of Lindsay Lohan's theft charges. Many other examples come readily to mind: the head of a local charity who pockets donations for personal enrichment; the pharmacist who deals drugs under the counter; and the ex-governor of Illinois, Rod Blagojevich, who was removed from office, convicted, and sentenced to prison for attempting to sell the Senate seat vacated by President Obama. Indeed, think of many white-collar offenses, motivated not by lack of opportunity but by the desire to expand substantial opportunities and resources even further.

Subcultural Explanations. The subcultural version of sociological theory maintains that a conflict between norms held by different groups causes criminal behavior. This conflict arises when various groups endorse subcultural norms, pressuring their members to deviate from the norms underlying the criminal law (Nietzel, 1979). Gangs, for example, enforce behavioral norms about how to behave. For many youths, a gang replaces the young person's parents as the main source of norms, even when parents attempt to instill their own values.

This theme of cultural conflict is illustrated by Walter Miller's theory of **focal concerns**. Miller explained the criminal activities of lower-class adolescent gangs as an attempt to achieve the ends valued in their culture through behaviors that appear best suited to obtain those ends. Thus, youth must adhere to the traditions of the lower class. What are these characteristics? Miller (1958) lists six basic values: trouble, toughness, smartness, excitement, fate, and autonomy. For example, lower-class boys pick fights to show their toughness, and they steal to demonstrate their shrewdness and daring (Sheley, 1985). However, the theory of focal concerns does not explain crime by individuals who are not socially disadvantaged, such as the rich hotel owner, the television evangelist, or the Wall Street swindler. In addition, key concepts in the theory are vague.

Like structural theories of crime, subcultural explanations have not demonstrated a strong theoretical or empirical basis. Questions remain: How do cultural standards originate? How are they transmitted from one generation to the next? How do they control the behavior of any one individual? The most troublesome concept is the main one—subculture. Some critics reject the assumption that different socioeconomic groups embrace radically different values.

Biological Theories of Crime

Biological theories of crime search for genetic vulnerabilities, neuropsychological abnormalities, or biochemical irregularities that predispose people to criminal behavior. These dispositions, biological theorists believe, are then translated into specific criminal behavior through environments and social interactions. Research on biological theories commonly focuses on twin and adoption studies to distinguish genetic from environmental factors.

In twin studies, the researcher compares the **concordance rate** (the percentage of pairs of twins sharing the behavior of interest) for **monozygotic twins** (identical twins) and **dizygotic twins** (commonly called fraternal twins). If the monozygotic concordance rate is significantly higher, the investigator concludes that the behavior in question is genetically influenced, because monozygotic twins are genetically identical whereas dizygotic pairs share, on average, only 50% of their genetic material.

In one study of 274 adult twin pairs, participants were asked to complete several questionnaires about past criminal behaviors, such as destroying property, fighting, carrying and using a weapon, and struggling with the police. Results reflected a finding of 50% heritability for such violent behaviors (Rushton, 1996) suggesting that inherited tendencies may play a crucial role in causing crime. However, studies that distinguish between crimes against property and violent crimes against persons have found that although heredity and environment play important roles in both types of crime, the influence of heredity is higher for aggressive types of antisocial behavior (e.g., assaults, robberies, and sexual offenses) than for nonaggressive crimes such as drug taking, shoplifting, and truancy (Eley, 1997).

Adoption studies also support the contention that genetic factors play some role in the development of criminality. Cloninger, Sigvardsson, Bohman, and von Knorring (1982) studied the arrest records of adult males who had been adopted as children. They found that men whose biological parents had a criminal record were four times more likely to be criminal themselves (a prevalence rate of 12.1%) than adoptees who had no criminal background (2.9%) and twice as likely to be criminal as adoptees whose adoptive parents had a criminal history. Other researchers conducted a review of several twin and adoption studies in this area and found similar results (Tehrani & Mednick, 2000).

An interesting possibility regarding a biological contributor to offending was first raised by a 1993 study (Brunner, Nelen, Breakefield, Ropers, & van Oost, 1993). Studying individuals who had committed offenses, the investigators noted five participants who showed both borderline mental retardation and impaired control of impulsive aggression. These individuals each showed a complete absence of activity of a certain enzyme (monoamine oxidase type A, or MAO-A, which affects important neurotransmitters). This absence resulted from a mutation on the X chromosome in the gene coding for MAO-A.

Without replication, this finding—involving a small number of affected individuals—would not have had implications for the broader scientific and legal fields (Appelbaum, 2005). A second study with a large cohort (1,037 individuals followed since birth in Dunedin, New Zealand) has replicated and extended these findings (Caspi et al., 2002). The investigators considered both the levels of MAO-A and the history of maltreatment between the ages of 3 and 11. Using multiple measures of antisocial behavior, they reported that the 12% of their participants who had both low MAO-A and maltreatment accounted for 44% of the total convictions for violent offenses, with 85% of individuals with both low MAO-A and maltreatment later showing some form of antisocial behavior. However, a third study (Stamps, Abeling, van Gennip, van Crachten, & Gurling, 2001) did not support the prospect that this MAO-A gene mutation is a robust explanation for criminal offending—so this hypothesis has not yet been clearly supported by investigators in the field.

Genetic and Biological Influences on Crime: Promising Possibilities. If genetic or biological factors do influence crime, the important question has always been, what influences what? There is a lengthy list of likely candidates (Brennan & Raine, 1997), but five possibilities are emphasized:

1. *Low MAO-A in combination with a history of maltreatment.* Further research is needed, particularly in light of the discussion above, but this initial finding may help to explain how a combination of an adverse experience (child maltreatment) and a biological risk factor (low MAO-A) could affect impulsivity and propensity to antisocial behavior.

2. *Neuropsychological abnormalities.* High rates of abnormal electroencephalogram (EEG) patterns have been reported in prison populations and in violent juvenile delinquents. These EEG irregularities may indicate neurological deficits that result in poor impulse control and impaired judgment. Studies of violent offenders have shown slow-wave EEG patterns indicating underarousal (Milstein, 1988). Although a high percentage of persons in the general population

also have EEG abnormalities, rates of EEG abnormalities are somewhat higher in delinquent youth (Raine, Venables, & Williams, 1989) and impulsive adult offenders (Zukov, Ptacek, & Fischer, 2008).

More promising results have been reported concerning abnormalities in four subcortical regions of the brain—the amygdala, hippocampus, thalamus, and midbrain—specifically in the right hemisphere of the brain, which has been linked to the experience of negative emotions. In one study (Raine, Meloy, & Buchshaum, 1998), brain scans of a group of homicide offenders showed that, compared with normal controls, the offenders experienced excessive activity in the four subcortical structures. Excessive subcortical activity may underlie a more aggressive temperament that could, in turn, predispose an individual to violent behavior.

A review of the neuropsychological literature supports a relationship between deficits in the prefrontal cortex, a region of the brain responsible for planning, monitoring, and controlling behavior, and antisocial behavior (see Raine, 2002). Damage to the prefrontal cortex may predispose individuals to criminal behavior in one of several ways. Patients with impairment in this region of the brain have decreased reasoning abilities that may lead to impulsive decision making in risky situations (Bechara, Damasio, Tranel, & Damasio, 1997). In addition, prefrontal impairment is associated with decreased levels of arousal, and individuals may engage in stimulation-seeking and antisocial behaviors to compensate for these arousal deficits (Raine, Lencz, Bihrle, Lacasse, & Colletti, 2000).

Other lines of research suggest that impaired functioning in the prefrontal cortex contributes to aggressive behavior. Offenders, on average, have about an 8- to 10-point lower IQ (intelligence quotient) than nonoffenders, suggesting that offenders are less able to (1) postpone impulsive actions, (2) use effective problem-solving strategies (Lynam, Moffitt, & Stouthamer-Loeber, 1993), and (3) achieve academic success in schools as a route to socially approved attainments (Binder, 1988).

In one longitudinal study of 411 London boys, a low IQ at ages 8 through 10 was linked to persistent criminality and more convictions for violent crimes up to age 32 (Farrington, 1995). Low IQ is among the most stable of risk factors for conduct disorder and delinquency (Murray & Farrington, 2010). In a recent comparison of intelligence of juvenile offenders within different racial/ethnic groups (Black, Hispanic, and White; Trivedi, 2011), White violent offenders had lower Performance IQ scores than White non-violent offenders. Overall, however, gender, ethnicity, and lower IQ scores also seem to be related in a complex way, indicating the need for further investigation.

3. *Autonomic nervous system differences.* The autonomic nervous system (ANS) carries information between the brain and all organs of the body. Because of these connections, emotions are associated with changes in the ANS. In fact, we can "see" the effects of emotional arousal on such ANS responses as heart rate, skin conductance, respiration, and blood pressure. Some offenders—particularly those whose offending is most chronic—are thought to differ from noncriminals in that they show chronically low levels of autonomic arousal and weaker physiological reactions to stimulation (Mednick & Christiansen, 1977). These differences, which might also involve hormonal irregularities (see the next section), could cause this group of offenders to have (1) difficulty learning how to inhibit behavior likely to lead to punishment and (2) a high need for extra stimulation that they gratify through aggressive thrill seeking. These difficulties are also considered an important predisposing factor by some social-psychological theorists whom we discuss later.

4. *Physiological differences.* A number of physiological factors might lead to increased aggressiveness and delinquency (Berman, 1997). Among the variables receiving continuing attention are (1) abnormally high levels of testosterone, (2) increased secretion of insulin, and (3) lower levels of serotonin (DiLalla & Gottesman, 1991). Research on depleted or impaired action of serotonin has received considerable support as a factor underlying impulsive aggression (Booij et al., 2010).

One study using animal models provides further support for the role of these physiological variables in aggressive behavior. Researchers found that rats with increased production of testosterone and lower levels of serotonin exhibited more aggressive behaviors; these rats displayed an increased number of attacks and inflicted a greater number of wounds on other rats compared to rats with lower testosterone and higher serotonin levels (Toot, Dunphy, Turner, & Ely, 2004). Such findings may be helpful in understanding the biological contributions to human aggression as well. Low levels of serotonin might be linked to aggressiveness and criminal conduct in any of several ways—for example, through greater impulsivity and irritability, impaired ability to regulate negative moods, excessive alcohol consumption, or hypersensitivity to provocative and threatening environmental cues (Berman, Tracy, & Coccaro, 1997).

5. *Personality and temperament differences.* Some dimensions of personality are highly heritable, and thus can be discussed within the scope of genetic influence on behavior. Some heritable dimensions are further related to antisocial behavior. Individuals with personalities marked by undercontrol, unfriendliness, irritability, low empathy, callous unemotionality, and a tendency to become easily frustrated are at greater risk for antisocial conduct (McLoughlin, Rucklidge, Grace, & McLean, 2010). We discuss some of these characteristics more fully in the next section on psychological theories of crime.

Psychological Theories of Crime

Psychological explanations of crime emphasize individual differences in the way people think or feel about their behavior. These differences, which can take the form of subtle variations or more extreme personality disturbances, might make some people more prone to criminal conduct by increasing their anger, weakening their attachments to others, or fueling their desire to take risks and seek thrills.

Criminal Thinking Patterns. In a controversial theory spawned from their frustration with traditional criminological theories, Samuel Yochelson and Stanton E. Samenow (Yochelson & Samenow, 1976; Samenow, 1984) have proposed that criminals engage in a fundamentally different way of thinking than noncriminals. They wrote that the thinking of criminals, though internally logical and consistent, is erroneous and irresponsible. In short, consistent lawbreakers see themselves and the world differently from the rest of us. Yochelson and Samenow described the criminals they studied as very much in control of their own actions, rather than being victims of the environment or being "sick." They were portrayed as master manipulators who assign the blame for their behavior to others. The development of this theory was based on intensive interviews with a small number of offenders, most of whom were incarcerated offenders or men who were hospitalized after having been acquitted of major crimes by reason of insanity. But no control groups of any sort were studied, and the theory itself has not been investigated in a systematic way. We do not know, therefore, how well it applies to most offenders.

However, a much more systematic and scientifically valid approach to investigating the role of offender thinking has been undertaken by Glenn Walters, who for many years served as a psychologist with the Federal Bureau of Prisons. He developed the Psychological Inventory of Criminal Thinking Styles (PICTS), an 80-item self-report inventory that measures cognitive patterns that are supportive of offending. Data from both male and female offenders, as well as meta-analyses, reflect good psychometric properties (internal consistency, test-retest reliability), correlations with previous offending, and modest predictive capacity of future adjustment and release outcome (Walters, 2002). A similar measure (the Measure of Offending Thinking Styles–Revised) was developed as well, also focusing on offender thinking styles, and following a comparable pattern of appropriate scientific development and validation (Mandracchia & Morgan, 2011). This general approach, involving the appraisal of thinking styles and cognitive "errors" among offenders, has added significantly to our current ability to assess offender risk and rehabilitation needs.

Personality-Based Explanations. Most of the influence of personality-based explanations for criminal offending in the last three decades has been provided by the construct of psychopathy, which is discussed in this section. Historically, however, there have been a number of theories of personality that have been offered to help understand offending. These include Eysenck's PEN theory (**psychoticism**, **extroversion**, and **neuroticism**;

Eysenck & Gudjonsson, 1989); Costa and McCrae's five-factor model (Neuroticism, Extraversion, Openness to Experience, Agreeableness, and Conscientiousness; McCrae & Costa, 1990); and Cloninger's seven-factor temperament and character model (Novelty Seeking, Harm Avoidance, Reward Dependence, Persistence, Self-directedness, Cooperativeness, and Self-transcendence; Cloninger, Dragan, & Przybeck, 1993). In some respects, these theories describe overlapping constructs. But which of those are important in understanding antisocial behavior?

A meta-analytic review (Miller & Lynam, 2001) addressed precisely that question. Eight of these dimensions showed some moderate relationship to antisocial behavior. All eight dimensions were measures of either Agreeableness or Conscientiousness, two of the factors in the five-factor model. Those who were low on Agreeableness or low on Conscientiousness were more likely to be involved in antisocial behavior. The other dimensions were less important—so it seems best to conclude that general personality theory has identified two domains (agreeableness and conscientiousness) that are important to understanding criminal offending.

Psychopathy. Many individuals attribute crime to personality defects, typically in the form of theories that focus on the criminal's basic antisocial or psychopathic nature. The concept of *psychopathy* has a long history. As we mentioned previously, this term refers to individuals who engage in frequent, repetitive criminal activity for which they feel little or no remorse. Such persons appear chronically deceitful and manipulative; they seem to have a nearly total lack of conscience that propels them into repeated conflict with society, often from a very early age. They are superficial, arrogant, and do not seem to learn from experience; they lack empathy and loyalty to individuals, groups, or society (Hare & Neumann, 2008). Psychopaths are selfish, callous, and irresponsible; they tend to blame others or to offer plausible rationalizations for their behavior.

The closest diagnostic label to psychopathy is **antisocial personality disorder**. The two disorders are similar in their emphasis on chronic antisocial behavior, but they differ in the role of personal characteristics, which are important in psychopathy but are not among the diagnostic criteria for antisocial personality disorder. About 80% of psychopaths are men, and their acts sometimes are well publicized (see Box 3.2).

Box 3.2 THE CASE OF TED BUNDY: A REAL-LIFE PSYCHOPATH

Born in 1946, Theodore Robert Bundy seemed destined for a charmed life; he was intelligent, attractive, and articulate (Holmes & DeBurger, 1988). A Boy Scout as a youth and then an honor student and psychology major at the University of Washington, he was at one time a work-study student at the Seattle Crisis Clinic. Later he became assistant to the chairman of the Washington State Republican Party. It is probably around this time that he claimed his first victim, a college-age woman who was viciously attacked while sleeping, left alive but brain damaged.

From 1974 through 1978, Bundy stalked, attacked, killed, and then sexually assaulted as many as 36 victims in Washington, Oregon, Utah, Colorado, and Florida. Apparently, some of the women were taken off guard when the good-looking, casual Bundy approached, seeming helpless: walking with crutches, or having an apparent broken arm. He usually choked them to death and then sexually abused and mutilated them before disposing of their bodies in remote areas (Nordheimer, 1989).

Maintaining a charming façade is characteristic of many people with psychopathy; acquaintances often describe them (as they did Bundy) as "fascinating," "charismatic," and "compassionate." Beneath his superficial charm, though, Bundy was deceitful and dangerous. Embarrassed because he was an illegitimate child and his mother was poor, he constantly sought, as a youth, to give the impression of being an upper-class kid. He wore fake mustaches and used makeup to change his appearance. He faked a British accent and stole cars in high school to help maintain his image. He constantly sought out the company of attractive women, not because he was genuinely interested in them but because he wanted people to notice and admire him.

At his trial for the murder of two Chi Omega sorority sisters in their bedrooms at Florida State University, he served as his own attorney. (Bundy had attended two law schools, although he did not graduate from either.) He was convicted; he was also found guilty of the kidnapping, murder, and mutilation of a Lake City, Florida, girl who was 12 years old. Bundy was sentenced to death.

Shortly before he was executed on January 24, 1989, Bundy gave a television interview to evangelist James Dobson in which he blamed his problems on pornography. He said, "Those of us who are ... so much influenced

Serial killer Ted Bundy

by violence in the media, in particular pornographic violence, are not some kind of inherent monsters. We are your husbands, and we grew up in regular families" (quoted by Lamar, 1989, p. 34).

Bundy claimed that he spent his formative years with a grandfather who had an insatiable craving for pornography. He told Dr. Dobson, "People will accuse me of being self-serving but I am just telling you how I feel. Through God's help, I have been able to come to the point where I, much too late, but better late than never, feel the hurt and the pain that I am responsible for" (quoted by Kleinberg, 1989, p. 5A).

The tape of Bundy's last interview, produced by Dobson and titled "Fatal Addiction," has been widely disseminated, especially by those who seek to eliminate all pornography. But Bundy's claim that pornography was the "fuel for his fantasies" should be viewed skeptically. It may merely have been one last manipulative ploy to buy more time. In none of his previous interviews, including extensive conversations in 1986 with Dorothy Lewis, a psychiatrist he had come to trust, did he ever cite "a pornographic preamble to his grotesqueries" (Nobile, 1989, p. 41).

Critical Thought Question
How would Dexter Morgan, a "fictional psychopath," compare with Ted Bundy, who was apparently the real thing?

Psychopathy, as measured by the Hare PCL-R (Hare, 2003), has been well established as a risk factor for offending and for violent offending. Perhaps the best demonstration of this relationship comes from a meta-analysis on this topic (Leistico, Salekin, DeCoster, & Rogers, 2008). The authors integrated 95 nonoverlapping studies ($N = 15,826$ participants) to summarize the relation between the Hare Psychopathy Checklists and antisocial conduct. Their results indicated that higher PCL total scores and the scores on Factor 1 (describing interpersonal characteristics) and Factor 2 (describing chronic antisocial behavior) were moderately associated with increased antisocial conduct. These results depended on the setting from which the participants were drawn. Checklist scores were more strongly associated with offending in the community than with serious misconduct in correctional facilities and secure hospitals.

There are a multitude of theories about what causes psychopathic behavior. One view is that psychopathic persons suffer a cortical immaturity that makes it difficult for them to inhibit behavior. Hare himself has proposed that psychopaths may have a deficiency in the left hemisphere of their brains that impairs **executive function**, the ability to plan and regulate behavior carefully (Moffitt & Lynam, 1994). Considerable research supports a strong relationship between antisocial behavior and impaired executive functioning (Morgan & Lilienfeld, 2000).

Compared to normal controls, psychopaths experience less anxiety subsequent to aversive stimulation and are relatively underaroused in the resting state as well. This low autonomic arousal generates a high need for stimulation. Consequently, the psychopath prefers novel situations and tends to pay less attention to many stimuli, thereby being less influenced by them.

Herbert Quay (1965) advanced the **stimulation-seeking theory**, which claims that the thrill seeking and disruptive behavior of the psychopath serve to increase sensory input and arousal to a more tolerable level. As a result of such thrill seeking, the psychopathic person seems "immune" to many social cues that govern behavior. Eysenck (1964) proposed a theory that emphasizes the slower rate of classical conditioning for persons classified as psychopaths. He argued that the development of a conscience depends on acquisition of classically conditioned fear and avoidance responses, and that psychopathic individuals' conditioning deficiencies may account for their difficulties in normal socialization.

Another popular explanation for psychopathy involves being raised in a dysfunctional family (Loeber & Stouthamer-Loeber, 1986). Arnold Buss (1966) identified two parental patterns that might foster psychopathy. The first is having parents who are cold and distant. The child who imitates these parents develops an unfeeling, detached interpersonal style that conveys a superficial appearance of social involvement but lacks the empathy required for stable, satisfying relationships. The second pattern involves having parents who are inconsistent in their use of rewards and punishments, making it difficult for the child to imitate a stable role model and develop a consistent

self-identity. A child in this situation learns to avoid blame and punishment but fails to learn the finer differences between appropriate and less appropriate behavior. Children with callous-unemotional traits (a central aspect of the adult disorder of psychopathy) were significantly worse compared to those lower on this dimension on stress management, frequency of criminal convictions among parents, and dysfunctional parenting, according to a recent review (McLoughlin, Rucklidge, Grace, & McLean, 2010).

Limitations of Psychopathy in Explaining Offending. The major drawback of psychopathy as an explanation for crime is that it describes only a small percentage of offenders. It might be tempting to classify most offenders as psychopaths and explain their offending with that classification. But most offenders are not psychopathic. One study found that only about 25% of a correctional sample could be classified as psychopathic, and this percentage was even smaller for women than for men (Salekin, Trobst, & Krioukova, 2001). This is generally consistent with other estimates in the literature.

In addition, there is controversy about using the PCL and revised versions of the instrument as diagnostic tools on which legal decisions are based. Although the PCL-R has an excellent inter-rater reliability when carried out in accordance with instructions (indicating that two raters using the PCL-R would tend to reach the same conclusion), a lack of training and possible biases on the part of the clinician may contribute to disparities in scores. Slight differences in scores may account for differences in courts' dispositions of these cases.

However, expert testimony invoking psychopathy may be quite influential. Evidence suggests that expert testimony about an offender's psychopathy or *psychopathic traits* (the preferred term for adolescents showing features of psychopathy) is associated with an increase in severity of the court's disposition (Zinger & Forth, 1998), although other evidence with juveniles suggests that the "antisocial behavior" label has a stronger effect than "psychopathic traits" on the judgments of juvenile probation officers (Murrie, Cornell, & McCoy, 2005). Potential jurors were influenced in their decisions regarding juveniles by descriptions of antisocial behavior, psychopathic traits, and the colloquial use of the term *psychopath* (Boccaccini, Murrie, Clark, & Cornell, 2008).

Furthermore, because the PCL is a self-report measure, the administrator is subject to relying on inaccurate information. As a safeguard against potentially erroneous information, the administrator must have access to collateral information to compare with information obtained from the examinee. Because the number of judicial decisions that rely on the PCL-R appears to be considerable, the ongoing training efforts for this measure are particularly important.

Yet another criticism of the use of these psychopathy assessment instruments in criminal proceedings revolves around their use in cases involving adolescent and female offenders. Although some evidence suggests that these instruments can be successfully used with female offenders (Salekin, Rogers, & Sewell, 1997; Vitale & Newman, 2001) and male adolescent offenders (Corrado, Vincent, Hart, & Cohen, 2004), more research is needed. Nonetheless, it is fair to say that these psychopathy assessment tools offer a valuable way of assessing personal characteristics and history that are related to criminal offending by some offenders. But there are other contributors as well, including social influences, to which we now turn.

Social-Psychological Theories of Crime

Social-psychological explanations view crime as being learned through social interaction. Sometimes called social-process theories in order to draw attention to the processes by which an individual becomes a criminal, social-psychological theories fall into two subcategories: control theories and direct learning theories. **Control theory** assumes that people will behave antisocially unless they learn, through a combination of inner controls and external constraints on behavior, not to offend. **Learning theory** stresses how individuals directly acquire specific criminal behaviors through different forms of learning.

Control Theories. Control theories assume that people will behave antisocially unless they are trained not to by others (Conger, 1980). Young people are bonded to society at several levels. They differ in (1) the degree to which they are affected by the opinions and expectations of others, (2) the payoffs they receive for conventional behavior, and (3) the extent to which they subscribe to the prevailing norms. Some people never form emotional bonds with significant others, so they never internalize necessary controls over antisocial behavior.

Walter Reckless's (1967) **containment theory** is an example of a control theory. Reckless proposed that it is largely external containment (i.e., social pressure and institutionalized rules) that controls crime. If a society is well integrated, has well-defined limits on behavior, encourages family discipline and supervision, and provides reinforcers for positive accomplishments, crime will be contained. But if these external controls weaken, control of crime must depend on internal restraints, mainly an individual's conscience. Thus, a positive self-concept becomes a protective factor against delinquency. Strong inner containment involves the ability to tolerate frustration, be motivated by long-term goals, resist distractions, and find substitute satisfactions (Reckless, 1967).

Containment theory is an "in-between" view, neither rigidly environmental nor entirely psychological. Containment accounts for the law-abiding individual in a high-crime environment. But this theory explains only a part of criminal behavior. It does not apply to crimes within groups that are organized around their commitment to deviant behavior.

The British psychologist Hans Eysenck (1964) proposed a related version of containment theory in which "heredity plays an important, and possibly a vital, part in predisposing a given individual to crime" (p. 55). Socialization practices then translate these innate tendencies into criminal acts. Socialization depends on two kinds of learning. First, **operant learning** explains how behavior is acquired and maintained by its consequences: Responses that are followed by rewards are strengthened, whereas responses followed by aversive events are weakened. Immediate consequences are more influential than delayed consequences. However, according to Eysenck (1964), in the real world the effects of punishment are usually "long delayed and uncertain [whereas] the acquisition of the desired object is immediate; therefore, although the acquisition and the pleasure derived from it may, on the whole, be less than the pain derived from the incarceration which ultimately follows, the time element very much favors the acquisition as compared with the deterrent effects of the incarceration" (p. 101).

Because of punishment's ineffectiveness, the restraint of antisocial behavior ultimately depends on a strong conscience, which develops through **classical conditioning**. Eysenck believed that conscience is conditioned through repeated, close pairings of a child's undesirable behaviors with the prompt punishment of these behaviors. Conscience becomes an inner control that deters wrongdoing through the emotions of anxiety and guilt.

Learning Theories. Learning theory focuses on how criminal behavior is learned. According to Edwin H. Sutherland's (1947) **differential association approach**, criminal behavior requires socialization into a system of values conducive to violating the law; thus, the potential criminal develops definitions of behavior that make deviant conduct seem acceptable. If definitions of criminal acts as being acceptable are strong and frequent, then the person is more likely to commit crimes. It is not necessary to associate with criminals directly to acquire these definitions. Children might learn pro-criminal definitions from watching their father pocket too much change or hearing their mother brag about exceeding the speed limit.

Using the differential association approach, Sutherland and Cressey (1974) proposed various explanations of criminal behavior, including these:

1. Criminal behavior is learned through interaction with other persons in a process of communication.

2. When criminal behavior is learned, the learning includes (a) techniques of committing the crime, which are sometimes very complicated but at other times simple; and (b) the specific direction of motives, drives, rationalizations, and attitudes.

3. A person becomes delinquent because of an excess of definitions favorable to violation of law over definitions unfavorable to violation of law.

Sutherland's theory has been translated into the language of operant learning theory as developed by B. F. Skinner. According to **differential association reinforcement theory** (Akers, Krohn, Lanz-Kaduce, & Radosevich, 1996), criminal behavior is acquired through operant conditioning and modeling. A person behaves criminally when reinforcement for such behavior is more frequent than punishment. Families, peer groups, and schools control most sources of reinforcement and punishment and expose people to many behavioral models (Akers et al., 1996).

Differential association attempts to explain crime in places where it would not, on first blush, be expected (e.g., among lawbreakers who grew up in affluent settings). But it has difficulty explaining impulsive violence, and it does not explain why certain individuals, even in the same family, have the different associations they do. Why are some people more likely than others to form criminal associations?

Social Learning Theory. One answer comes from social learning theory. **Social learning theory** acknowledges the importance of differential reinforcement for developing new behaviors, but it assigns more importance to cognitive factors and to observational or **vicarious learning**. Its chief proponent, Albert Bandura (1986), claimed that "most human behavior is learned by observation through modeling" (p. 47). Learning through modeling is more efficient than learning through differential reinforcement. Complex behaviors such as speech and driving a car require models from which to learn. In all likelihood, so does crime. Observational learning depends on (1) *attention* to the important features of modeled behavior; (2) *retention* of these features in memory to guide later performance; (3) *reproduction* of the observed behaviors; and (4) *reinforcement* of performed behaviors, which determines whether they will be performed again.

The most prominent attempt to apply social learning theory to criminal behavior is Bandura's (1973) book *Aggression: A Social Learning Analysis* (see also Platt & Prout, 1987; Ribes-Inesta & Bandura, 1976). The theory emphasizes modeling of aggression in three social contexts.

1. *Familial influences.* Familial aggression assumes many forms, from child abuse at one extreme to aggressive parental attitudes and language at the other. It is in the arena of discipline, however, where children are exposed most often to vivid examples of coercion and aggression as a preferred style for resolving conflicts and asserting desires.

2. *Subcultural influences.* Some environments and subcultures provide context that supports aggression and an abundance of rewards for their most combative members. "The highest rates of aggressive behavior are found in environments where aggressive models abound and where aggressiveness is regarded as a highly valued attribute" (Bandura, 1976, p. 207).

3. *Symbolic models.* The influence of symbolic models on aggression has been attributed to the mass media, particularly television. A large number of studies have investigated the effects of televised violence on viewers, especially children.

A longitudinal study, conducted over a 15-year period, suggests that there are significant long-term effects from watching violent television in childhood

(Huesmann, Moise-Titus, Podolski, & Eron, 2003). Results from this study revealed a significant relationship between watching violence on television as children and aggressive behavior in adulthood. This pattern held for male and female participants, although the types of aggressive behavior differed. Males engaged in more overt aggression (e.g., domestic violence, physical fights), whereas women engaged in more indirect aggression (e.g., traffic violations). Women who watched violent television as children were also four times more likely than other women to be victims of domestic violence. Furthermore, the study found that early exposure to violence on television significantly predicted aggression in adulthood regardless of the level of aggression the individual displayed in childhood.

Researchers also hypothesized that viewing television violence in childhood can lead to other potentially harmful effects. For instance, children may become desensitized to the effects of violence (e.g., may care less about others' feelings) or experience a heightened fear of victimization. Children younger than 8 years old may be especially vulnerable to the effects of viewing violence because of their cognitive limitations in distinguishing fantasy and cartoon violence from reality. Of more recent interest is the question of whether movies and video games, which often feature much more graphic depictions of violence than those allowed on TV, exert stronger modeling effects on aggression. We describe a relevant case in Box 3.3.

Social learning theory also points to several environmental cues that increase antisocial behavior. These "instigators" signal when it might be rewarding to behave antisocially (rather than risky to do so). One instigator is *models*: observing others and modeling their behavior can influence some, particularly when they have been frustrated or see the aggression as justified. A second (related) instigator is *prior aversive treatment*. People often treat others they way they have been treated. A third is *incentive inducements*, which includes the anticipated rewards of misbehavior. Habitual offenders often overestimate their chances of succeeding in criminal acts and ignore the consequences of failing. A fourth is *instructions*, particularly from one in authority. Milgram's (1963) famous study demonstrating widespread willingness to follow orders to inflict "pain" on another person is a good illustration. Although not a common feature of offending, this kind of influence may play a role in some hate crimes, in which the perpetrator believes he or she is doing the will of a religious or patriotic fanatic. A fifth is *delusions and hallucinations*: individuals occasionally respond aggressively to false beliefs or hallucinated commands that stem from severe mental illness. Finally, there is a strong, positive association between crime and *alcohol or drug use*, especially for violent crime (Parker, 2004; Richardson & Budd, 2003). By depressing a person's responsiveness to other cues that could inhibit impulsive or aggressive behavior, alcohol often leads to an increase in antisocial behavior even though it is not a stimulant. Drug use, by virtue of its cost and deviant status, also acts as a catalyst to or amplifier of criminality, especially property crime.

According to social learning theorists, people also regulate their behavior through self-reinforcement. Individuals who derive pleasure, pride, revenge, or

---

Box 3.3 THE CASE OF "TEENAGE AMUSEMENT," A MURDER, AND A VIDEO GAME

A 2006 report from the National Coalition for the Homeless noted a disturbing trend: there were 122 attacks and 20 murders of homeless people in 2005, several of them by teenage perpetrators. According to the Coalition's executive director, Michael Stoops, "It's disturbing to know that young people would literally kick someone when they're already down on their luck. We recognize that this isn't every teenager, but for some this passes as amusement."

Three teenage perpetrators from Milwaukee—16-year-old Luis Oyola, 17-year-old Andrew Ihrcke, and 15-year-old Nathan Moore—claimed that killing Rex Baum was never part of their plan. But yet, the trio, who had been drinking with Baum at his campsite, suddenly began punching and kicking the 49-year-old man and then hurled anything they could find—rocks, bricks, even a barbeque grill, at the hapless victim. After smearing him with feces, cutting him, and bragging about their actions, they were arrested. One of the teens told police that killing "the bum" reminded him of playing the violent video game "Bumfights," which depicts homeless people pummeling each other to make a few bucks.

Critical Thought Question
What are your hypotheses about the influences on the three adolescents who viciously attacked and killed Rex Baum?

self-worth from an ability to harm or "con" others enjoy an almost sensual pleasure in the way criminal behavior "feels" (Katz, 1988). Conversely, people will discontinue conduct that results in self-criticism and self-contempt.

People can also learn to exempt themselves from their own conscience after behaving antisocially. These tactics of "self-exoneration" assume many forms: minimizing the seriousness of one's acts by pointing to more serious offenses by others, justifying aggression by appealing to higher values, displacing the responsibility for misbehavior onto a higher authority, blaming victims for their misfortune, diffusing responsibility for wrongdoing, dehumanizing victims so that they are stripped of sympathetic qualities, and underestimating the damage inflicted by one's actions.

The major strength of social learning theory is that it explains how specific patterns of criminality are developed by individual offenders. A second strength is that the theory applies to a wide range of crimes. The major limitation of social learning theory is that little empirical evidence indicates that real-life crime is learned according to behavioral principles. Most of the data come from laboratory research where the experimental setting nullifies all the legal and social sanctions that actual offenders must risk incurring. A second problem is that the theory does not explain why some people fall prey to "bad" learning experiences and others resist them. Learning might be a necessary ingredient for criminality, but it is probably not a sufficient one. Individual differences in the way people respond to reinforcement need to be considered. The theory we review next does so.

Multiple-Component Learning Theory. Some theorists have integrated several learning processes into comprehensive, learning-based explanations of criminality (e.g., Feldman, 1977). The most influential and controversial multiple-component learning theory is James Q. Wilson and Richard Herrnstein's (1985) book *Crime and Human Nature.* Wilson and Herrnstein begin by observing that criminal and noncriminal behavior have both gains and losses. Gains from committing crime include revenge, excitement, and peer approval. Gains associated with not committing crime include avoiding punishment and having a clear conscience. Whether a crime is committed depends, in part, on the net ratio of gains and losses for criminal and noncriminal behavior. If the ratio for committing a crime exceeds the ratio for not committing it, the likelihood of the crime being committed increases.

Wilson and Herrnstein argued that several individual differences influence these ratios and determine whether an individual is likely to commit a crime. Like Eysenck, they proposed that individuals differ in the ease with which they learn to associate, through classical conditioning, negative emotions with misbehaviors and positive emotions with proper behaviors. These conditioned responses are the building blocks of a strong conscience that increases the gains associated with noncrime and augments the losses associated with crime.

Another important factor is what Wilson and Herrnstein called *time discounting.* All reinforcers lose strength as they become more removed from a behavior, but people differ in their ability to delay gratification and obtain reinforcement from potential long-term gains. More impulsive persons have greater difficulty deriving benefits from distant reinforcers. Time discounting is important for understanding crime because the gains associated with crime (e.g., revenge, money) accrue immediately, whereas the losses from such behavior (e.g., punishment) occur later, if at all. Thus, for impulsive persons, the ratio of gains to losses shifts in a direction that favors criminal behavior.

Another major component in Wilson and Herrnstein's theory is a set of constitutional factors, including gender, intelligence, variations in physiological arousal, and the aforementioned impulsivity, all of which conspire to make some persons more attracted to wrongdoing and less deterred by the potential aversive consequences of crime.

Of several social factors linked to criminal behavior, Wilson and Herrnstein believe that family influences and early school experiences are the most important. Families that foster (1) *attachment* of children to their parents; (2) *longer time horizons,* where children consider the distant consequences of their behavior; and (3) *strong consciences* about misbehavior will go far in counteracting criminal predispositions.

Research on parenting practices and the quality of the parent–child relationship underscores the relevance of familial interaction to childhood delinquency. Findings from a qualitative study with juvenile offenders and their parents revealed that their familial interactions were characterized by poor communication and high levels of conflict between children and parents. These interactions were associated with children's perceptions of lack of parental concern and warmth (Madden-Derdich, Leonard, & Gunnell, 2002). In addition, an intergenerational study examining the effect of parenting styles on antisocial behavioral patterns across generations suggests that familial interactions have far-reaching implications; parental conflict and highly demanding, unresponsive parents were related to childhood behavioral problems in two successive generations (Smith & Farrington, 2004).

The remedies to these harmful patterns involve warm supportiveness combined with consistent enforcement of clear rules for proper behavior. Unfortunately, individuals whose parents were demanding, unresponsive, and high in conflict are not likely to themselves become parents who are warm, supportive, and consistent in their enforcement of rules. Therefore, many at-risk children face the double whammy of problematic predispositions coupled with inadequate parental control and support.

Biological factors interact with family problems and early school experiences to further increase the risks of poorly controlled behavior. Not only are impulsive, poorly socialized children of lower intelligence more directly at risk for criminality, but their interactions with cold, indifferent schools that do not facilitate educational success can further discourage them from embracing traditional social conformity. Consistent with this part of the theory is a long line of research studies showing that children officially diagnosed with early conduct problems and/or attention deficit/hyperactivity disorder face a heightened likelihood of becoming adult offenders (Slobogin & Fondacoro, 2011).

Because they took hereditary and biological factors seriously, Wilson and Herrnstein have come under heavy fire from critics who portray their theory as purely genetic. It is not. Instead, it is a theory that restores psychological factors (some heritable, some not) and family interaction variables to a place of importance in criminology, which for decades was dominated by sociological concepts.

Social Labeling Theory. The most extreme version of a **social-psychological theory of crime** is the **social labeling** perspective. Its emergence as an explanation reflects frustration about the inability of prior approaches to provide comprehensive explanations and a shift in emphasis from why people commit crimes to why some people are labeled "criminals" (Sheley, 1985).

One illustration of social labeling is the allegation that police use **racial profiling** as a basis for making a disproportionate number of traffic stops of minority motorists, particularly African Americans. This practice has often been justified by police as a tool for catching drug traffickers, but arresting motorists for "driving while black" as a pretext for additional criminal investigations clearly raises the risk of harmful and inappropriate labeling, to say nothing of its discriminatory impact. The outcry over racial profiling has resulted in a call for federal legislation that would prohibit the practice and has led to litigation.

The basic assumption of social labeling theory is that deviance is created by the labels that society assigns to certain acts. Deviance is not simply based on the quality of the act; rather, it stems also from an act's consequences in the form of society's official reactions to it. Social labeling theory makes a distinction between **primary deviance**, or the criminal's actual behavior, and **secondary deviance**, or society's reaction to the offensive conduct (Lemert, 1951, 1972). With regard to primary deviance, offenders often rationalize their behavior as a temporary mistake, or they see it as part of a socially acceptable role (Lilly et al., 1989). Whether or not that self-assessment is accurate, secondary deviance serves to brand them with a more permanent "criminal" stigma.

The main point of the **social labeling theory** is that the stigma of being branded a deviant can create a self-fulfilling prophecy (Merton, 1968). Even those ex-convicts who seek an honest life in a law-abiding society are spurned by prospective employers and by their families and are labeled "ex-cons." Frustrated in their efforts to make good, they may adopt this label and "live up to" its negative connotations by engaging in further lawbreaking (Irwin, 1970). According to this perspective, the criminal justice system produces much of the deviance it is intended to correct.

The social labeling approach raises our awareness about the difficulties offenders face in returning to society. Moreover, it reminds us that some lawbreakers (e.g., those who live in crime-ridden neighborhoods where the police patrol often) are more likely to be caught and "criminalized" than are others. But the social labeling approach does not explain most criminal behavior. Nor is it favored as a serious explanation for criminal offending in the 21st century. Primary deviance (i.e., a law violation in the first place) usually has to occur before secondary deviance takes its toll, and many lawbreakers develop a life of crime before ever being apprehended. Behavioral differences between people exist and persist, despite the names we call them.

INTEGRATION OF
THEORIES OF CRIME

Where do all these theories leave us? Do any of them offer a convincing explanation of crime? Do they suggest how we should intervene to prevent or reduce crime? Although many commentators decry the lack of a convincing theory of crime, knowledge about the causes of serious crime has accumulated and now provides certain well-supported explanations for how repeated, violent criminality develops. Many serious offenders are extraordinarily versatile, with careers that include violent behavior, property offenses, vandalism, and substance abuse.

One implication of this diversity is that individuals travel several causal pathways to different brands of criminality. No single variable causes all crime, just as no one agent causes all fevers or all upset stomachs. However, several causal factors are associated reliably with many types of criminality. Any one of these factors may sometimes be a sufficient explanation for some type of criminal behavior, but more often they act in concert to produce criminality. Our attempt to integrate these various factors (see Figure 3.1) emphasizes four contributors to crime that occur in a developmental sequence.

Our model emphasizes what we believe are the variables best supported by criminological research as causal factors in crime:

1. *Antecedent conditions.* Chances of repeated offending are increased by biological, psychological, and environmental antecedents that make it easier for certain individuals to learn to behave criminally and easier for this learning to occur in specific settings. The leading candidates for biological risk are genetic inheritance, neurochemical abnormalities, brain dysfunction, and autonomic nervous system irregularities.

    Among psychological variables, poor social skills; lower verbal intelligence; personality traits of irritability, impulsiveness, callousness, and low empathy; and deficiencies in inner restraint (or conscience) leave some people well stocked with attitudes, thinking, and motivations that encourage antisocial behavior and that also render them relatively immune to negative consequences for misconduct. These psychological factors may accompany biological risks or may convey their own independent vulnerability to crime.

Finally, certain environments are rife with opportunities and temptations for crime and help translate biological or psychological predispositions toward criminal behavior into ever-stronger antisocial tendencies. Such environments function this way because of social impoverishment and disorganization, fundamental economic inequalities, a tradition of tolerating if not encouraging crime, social dissension and strife, and an abundance of inviting targets and easy victims of crime. Such environments promote offending in those who have a propensity toward crime (Wikstrom, Ceccato, Hardie, & Treiber, 2010).

Within family environments, high levels of mental disorders, criminality, parental absenteeism, and substance abuse also lead to more violence. These links may be forged through any one of several factors: genetic influence, modeling, increased hostility against a constant backdrop of harsh living conditions, disturbed attachments with parents, or lax or overly punitive discipline that does not teach youngsters how to control behavior. Research suggests that early exposure to harsh family living conditions can aggravate some of the biological factors that contribute to aggression, such as a child's physical and emotional reactions to threat (Barnow, Lucht, & Freyberger, 2001; Gallagher, 1996).

2. *Early indicators.* Repetitive antisocial conduct is disconcertingly stable over time. Aggressive children often grow up to be aggressive adults, and the precedents for adult violence and substance abuse are often manifested as aggression in pre-school and elementary school children (Asendorpf, Denissen, & van Aken, 2008; Temcheff et al., 2008). Although there are tests that can identify youth who are at elevated risk for behavioral problems, it remains difficult to predict whether these individuals will commit serious, violent acts later in life (Sprague & Walker, 2000). Relatively few at-risk youth commit serious, violent offenses, but many display major long-term adjustment problems. For instance, youth identified as at risk in childhood may experience drug and alcohol abuse, domestic and child abuse, divorce or multiple relationships, employment problems, mental health problems, dependence on social services, and involvement in less-serious crimes (Obiakor, Merhing, & Schwenn, 1997).

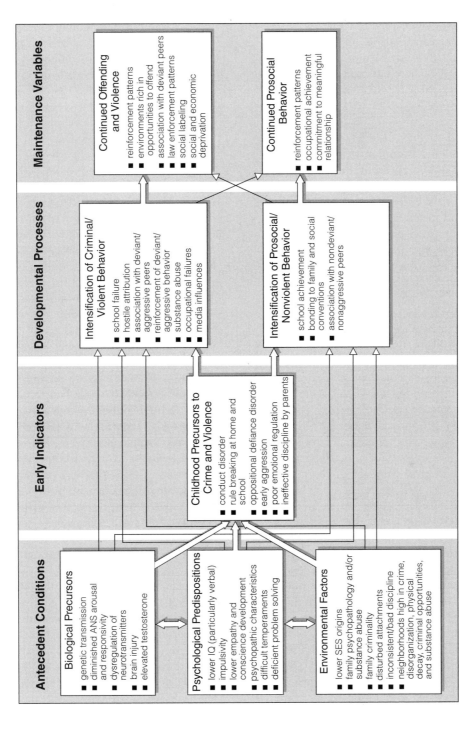

FIGURE 3.1 An integrated model for explaining repeated crime

NOTE: Thick arrows indicate probable paths; thin arrows indicate less likely paths.

Although not all chronic offenders were violent children, many repetitively aggressive adults began to exhibit that pattern early; in fact, most psychologists who study aggression believe that severe antisocial behavior in adulthood is nearly always preceded by antisocial behavior in childhood. These early indicators include officially diagnosed conduct disorder, oppositional defiant disorder, and attention deficit/hyperactivity disorder (Goldstein, Grant, Ruan, Smith, & Saha, 2006; Temcheff et al., 2008). Developmental models have enhanced our understanding of the onset and maintenance of antisocial behavior. For instance, one model suggests two subtypes of adolescent offenders: those who display behavioral problems later in adolescence and desist in early adulthood, and the relatively smaller group who display conduct-disordered behaviors earlier in adolescence that persist into adulthood. Adolescent offenders in the latter group are more likely to develop antisocial personality disorder than those in the former group.

Another model suggests that early emergence of conduct-disordered behavior that is displayed across multiple and diverse settings may predict the development of antisocial personality disorder in adulthood. One study found that early indicators of a diagnosis of antisocial personality disorder included a formal diagnosis of conduct disorder by age 10, participation in frequent and varied conduct-disordered behavior at an early age, and significant drug use in childhood or early adolescence (Myers, Stewart, & Brown, 1998).

Long-term longitudinal studies have demonstrated that aggression in childhood predicts violence in adulthood. Huesmann, Eron, and Yarmel (1987) measured aggression in childhood and tracked the boys and girls for 22 years. They found that aggression began to crystallize around the age of 8 and remained stable into adulthood (Eron, 1990; Huesmann, Eron, Lefkowitz, & Walder, 1984). Aggressive boys turned into men who were more likely to commit serious crimes, abuse their spouses, and drive while intoxicated. Aggressive girls turned into women who were more likely to punish their children harshly. Another 19-year longitudinal study (Asendorpf, Denissen, & van Aken, 2008) followed inhibited and aggressive preschool children into young adulthood. As adults, inhibited boys and girls were delayed in establishing a first stable partnership and finding a first full-time job. However, only the most inhibited children (upper 8%) showed internalizing problems such as self-rated inhibition. Aggressive boys showed more conduct problems, were educational and occupational underachievers, and showed a higher delinquency rate than those rated as nonaggressive as children, even after controlling for gender and socioeconomic status.

3. *Developmental processes.* Whether early indicators of criminal offending harden into patterns of repeated adult crime or soften into prosocial nonviolent conduct depends on several developmental processes. These processes occur in families, schools, peer groups, and the media—and in the thinking of the youth themselves.

Delinquency is often associated with poor school achievement. Grades in school begin to predict delinquency around age 15. As adolescent youth fall further and further behind in school, they have fewer and fewer opportunities or reasons to stay bonded to school and to strive for academic success (Cernkovich & Giordano, 1996). School failure seems to narrow the options for prosocial behavior because it decreases the chances of employability and job success.

Modeling and peer pressure also promote criminality. Crime increases when peers support it, as is sometimes the case in the criminal justice system itself when, by virtue of its official processing of offenders, "beginning" criminals are thrown together with more serious offenders. Furthermore, the more delinquent friends a youth has, the more likely he or she is to behave criminally—at least until age 20 (Monahan, Steinberg, & Cauffman, 2009).

Other research suggests that the association between delinquency and negative peer influences may be even more complex than previously thought. One study found that poor parental monitoring and supervision, as well as increased social stress and poor social skills, affected the relationship between adolescents' delinquent behavior and negative peer affiliation (Kimonis, Frick, & Barry, 2004). On the basis of these findings, the authors concluded that intervening with training in parenting skills and social skills, specifically encouraging more parental involvement and monitoring of their child's behavior, may be especially important in reducing negative peer affiliation and decreasing delinquency.

Modeling influences can also be mediated through the media. One investigator (Murray, 2008) noted that 50 years of research strongly suggested a relationship between TV violence and the increase in aggressive attitudes, values, and behaviors among children. These changes may be mediated by neurological changes in children who view frequent TV violence. It is, of course, difficult to know whether there is a causal relationship between such TV and other media violence and aggressive behavior. What makes this even more difficult is that most of the studies in this area are surveys, rather than controlled experiments. But another set of authors (Glymour, Glymour, & Glymour, 2008) considered these difficulties and concluded, in light of the existing evidence, that there is likely (but not certainly) a causal relationship between exposure to TV violence and subsequent adult aggression. Surprisingly, perhaps, given evidence of this linkage, the U.S. Supreme Court overturned a California law banning the sale of violent video games to children. They opted to protect the free speech rights of video game makers (*Brown v. Entertainment Merchants Association*, 2011).

Another intensifier of aggression is alcohol and substance abuse (Snyder & Sickmund, 2006). Numerous mechanisms could account for the tendency for substance abuse to lead to more crime. Alcohol is a depressant, so it might suppress the ability of certain areas of the brain to inhibit behavior effectively. The more time a youth spends abusing drugs and alcohol, the less time he or she has for prosocial, academic activities. Substance abuse typically results in more associations with deviant peers, thereby increasing the opportunities for antisocial behavior to be reinforced. Repeated substance abuse during adolescence serves as one more "trap" that shuts off many youngsters' options for prosocial behavior. These limits, in turn, increase the reinforcing potential of antisocial conduct.

Unfortunately, these developmental processes tend to compound one another. The impulsive, low-IQ child is more likely to fail at school. School dropouts increasingly associate with antisocial peers. Parents who fail to monitor and

sanction their children when they misbehave tend not to show much concern about what movies their children watch or what video games they play. Finally, early conduct and academic problems are strongly related to later substance abuse. When it comes to crime, at-risk youth stay at risk.

4. *Maintenance factors.* Violent offending can become an entrenched way of life when one or more of the following maintenance factors are in place: The short-run positive payoffs for offending are stronger and more probable than the long-term risks of apprehension and punishment. The person lives in environments that are rich in opportunities for offending and low in the chances of being detected. As a result of the inevitable arrests and incarcerations that repeat offenders experience, their associations with aggressive peers increase, just as contacts with law-abiding citizens decrease. As the long-run consequence of many earlier estrangements from conventional norms and values, delinquents begin to feel growing resentment and contempt for social rules. These maintenance factors do not cause crime so much as solidify it. Once they start to work their influence, the battle is often already lost, because criminal conduct has become a basic part of a person's identity.

An implication of our integrative model is that preventing crime might be a better way of fighting the "crime problem" than rehabilitating criminals. Certainly, with the help of treatment programs that strengthen their social skills, build better cognitive controls, model prosocial behavior, and reinforce law-abiding conduct, some people can "turn around" a life of violent offending (Andrews & Bonta, 2006). But however promising the rates of "success" in correctional rehabilitation might eventually become, it is still likely that some who are arrested and incarcerated will continue to offend throughout their lives.

This should not be surprising. After a protracted history of learning antisocial behavior, rejecting prosocial behavior, and facing closed doors to legitimate opportunity, repeat offenders will not yield easily to attempts to suppress criminal conduct. That is why prevention becomes so important. If most at-risk youth can be reliably identified, we can then intervene in multiple areas—with individuals, families, schools, peer groups, and neighborhoods—to interrupt those processes that eventually ensnare youth into anti-social lifestyles. Brought about by hostile environments and the decisions of youth themselves, these processes include experimenting with alcohol and drugs, dwelling on violent media and subcultures, dropping out of school, failing at legitimate employment, and associating with other law-breakers. They are the pathways to deviance that must be blocked early before they become too well traveled for any change to occur.

SUMMARY

1. ***Theories of crime can be grouped into four categories. What are they?*** The most common theories can be classified into four groups: sociological, biological, psychological, and social-psychological.

2. ***Among sociological explanations of crime, how does the subcultural explanation differ from the structural explanation?*** The structural explanation for crime emphasizes chronic barriers to conventional success that certain people face; these barriers include cultural and language differences, financial hardships, and limited access to those resources crucial to upward mobility. In contrast, the subcultural explanation proposes that certain groups, such as gangs, adhere to norms that conflict with the values of others in society and encourage criminal conduct.

3. ***What is emphasized in biological theories of crime?*** Both genetic and physiological factors are emphasized in biological explanations of criminal behavior. Hereditary factors influence criminal behavior, but the mechanisms through which this influence is exerted are unclear. The most likely candidates involve neurotransmitters, such as serotonin, and certain subcortical and cortical brain structures, particularly the prefrontal cortex, which is responsible for monitoring behavioral inhibition, planning, and decision making. A more specific prospect involves a mutation on the X chromosome in the gene coding for MAO-A, in combination with maltreatment as a child.

4. ***What psychological factors have been advanced to explain crime?*** Psychological theories of criminal behavior emphasize criminal thinking patterns or a personality defect, such as psychopathy.

5. ***How do social-psychological theories view crime?*** Social-psychological theories view criminal behavior as a learned response resulting from classical conditioning, reinforcement, observation or modeling, and social labeling.

KEY TERMS

anomie

antisocial personality disorder

biological theories of crime

classical conditioning

classical school of criminology

concordance rate

containment theory

control theory

criminology

differential association approach

differential association reinforcement theory

dizygotic twins

executive function

extroversion

focal concerns

learning theory

monozygotic twins

neuroticism

operant learning

positivist school of criminology

primary deviance

psychological theories (of crime)

psychopathy

psychoticism

racial profiling

secondary deviance

social labeling theory

social learning theory

social-psychological theory (of crime)

sociological theories (of crime)

stimulation-seeking theory

structural explanations

subcultural explanations

threat assessment

vicarious learning

Chapter 4

Psychology of Police

ORIENTING QUESTIONS

1. What is the role of the police in our society?
2. What procedures are used to select police?
3. How has the training of police officers expanded into new areas?
4. Describe the different activities of the police. Is law enforcement central?
5. What stressors do the police face?
6. What is the relationship between the police and the communities they serve?

In any survey of public concerns, "crime" is usually near the top. This ranking stems from the nature of crime in our country, as well as from the fear that crime typically instills. It is noteworthy that the decreasing crime rate observed over the last 20 years dropped even further in 2009–2010. According to the FBI's annual *Crime in the United States* report (2010), the estimated number of violent crimes reported to authorities in the United States declined in 2010 for the fourth year in a row—and dropped 6.5% relative to 2009. The property crime rate dropped 3.3% compared with 2009, according to the same source. According to the Bureau of Justice Statistics (2010), which calculated violent crime incidence by surveying U.S. households, the violent crime rate in United States (excluding crimes resulting in someone's death) fell 13% in 2010 compared with 2009. The trend toward a lower crime rate is encouraging. Despite such progress, however, the annual economic impact of crime (whether measured in lost cash, damaged property, medical expenses, emotional trauma, or lost income due to injuries) amounts to the billions of dollars.

The road from reporting a crime to convicting and punishing an offender can be long and tortuous, but in most cases the police are the officials in the criminal justice system with whom citizens have the most contact. The police must confront criminal activities face to face, and we expect them to keep our streets safe and our homes secure. They are the "thin blue line" that stands between the law-abiding citizen and public disorder. The visibility of the police is heightened by the uniforms they wear, the weapons they carry, and the special powers they are given. This visibility makes the police convenient targets for the public's frustrations with the criminal justice system. At the same time, many people place enormous trust in the police, and police are the first people whom most citizens call in emergencies. Consequently, there are conflicting attitudes held by many within our society about the police. Some seek protection at all costs; others resist police intrusion and seek to avoid the police; most strike some kind of balance.

Police perform a complex set of tasks in the criminal justice system. To succeed at their jobs, street officers must combine physical prowess, perceptual acuity, interpersonal sensitivity, and intelligent discretion. They need to make quick judgments about all sorts of human behavior, often under very stressful conditions. They should be well versed in the law and should have at least some familiarity with the social sciences. Despite the complexity of these demands, police are usually overworked and underappreciated. These factors, along with the job pressures they face, the criminal offenders they encounter, and the isolated conditions in which they often work, can make officers susceptible to bribery, corruption, and abuses of power.

When we consider the police from a psychological perspective, we encounter various dilemmas. Law enforcement in a democratic society must strike a balance: protecting citizens through crime prevention and investigation while simultaneously respecting constitutional rights. Police officers investigate crime, but they must also make arrests and maintain an image of stability in society. Operating within this balance can be very difficult, particularly when domestic terrorism, cybercrime, and other relatively recent challenges are added to the traditional kinds of criminal offending. But when this balance is not achieved, either effective crime control or civil liberties/criminal rights can suffer.

Another conflict arises when social scientists question the validity of techniques that the police often use, such as lineup identifications and lie detector tests. Last, but of great importance to the police, is the dilemma of equality versus discretion. When should an arrest be made, and when should only a warning be issued? How much force can legitimately be used in an arrest? Should all suspects be treated the same way?

SELECTION OF POLICE OFFICERS

One purpose of this chapter is to examine the police officer from a psychological perspective. How are police officers selected? Do the selection criteria work? Do police officers share certain personality characteristics? How are the police trained, and does training improve their performance on the job? Can the police officer's image in the community be improved?

These questions took on a special urgency in the 1990s as a result of several highly publicized cases in which police officers had brutally beaten suspects in their custody. Many of these cases involved White officers attacking Black citizens, raising the possibility that racial bias was a motive.

Beginning with the prosecution of the Los Angeles police officers who were videotaped beating Rodney King (described in Box 4.2), which was followed by other, similar incidents, concerns have grown over police behavior. For instance, in June 2004, videotapes showed Stanley Miller, a suspect in an auto theft, apparently trying to surrender while Los Angeles officers tackled him and began kicking and repeatedly hitting him in the head (CNN, 2004).

Similar incidents have been reported in several cities throughout the country, including Detroit, New York, Louisville, Pittsburgh, and Miami. Perhaps no case sparked such heated national debate over the relationship between minorities and the police as the assault against Abner Louima, the Haitian immigrant who was beaten and sodomized with a bathroom plunger by

The brutal police assault of Abner Louima by several New York City police officers led to their conviction on federal criminal charges

Stan Honda/AFP/Getty Images

New York City police officer Justin Volpe as a second officer, Charles Schwarz, held Louima down. After Volpe pled guilty, a federal jury convicted Schwarz of conspiracy to sodomize and of violating Louima's civil rights, but it acquitted three other officers who had also been charged in the beating. Although it is tempting to view this case as an isolated incident, similar cases have occurred often enough to raise the possibility that they reflect a broader problem. Are certain police officers prone to these kinds of attacks? If so, can they be identified in advance and screened out of police work?

Psychological evaluation of police personnel began in 1916 when Lewis Terman, the Stanford University psychologist who revised Alfred Binet's intelligence scales to produce the Stanford-Binet intelligence test, tested the intelligence of 30 applicants for police and firefighter jobs in San Jose, California. Terman (1917) found that the average IQ among these applicants was 84 and recommended that no one with an IQ below 80 be accepted for these jobs. A few years later, L. L. Thurstone tested the intelligence of 358 Detroit policemen, using the Army Alpha Intelligence Examination. Like Terman, he reported below-average IQ scores, and he also found that police of higher ranks scored lower than entry-level patrolmen.

Throughout the years, psychologists continued to assess police candidates, although in a way that was often unsystematic and poorly evaluated. As late as 1955, only 14 American cities with populations greater than 100,000 formally tested police candidates; by 1965, 27% of local police agencies reported some psychological evaluation of applicants (Ostrov, 1986). In the 1960s and 1970s, the period when police psychology became an established specialty, several national commissions recommended formal psychological assessment of police personnel in all departments. By the mid-1980s, 11 states required psychological screening of police candidates, and more than 50% of the country's departments psychologically screened beginning police officers (Benner, 1986). By the 1990s, formal assessment of police candidates had become routine, due in part to attempts by municipal governments to prevent or defeat lawsuits claiming that they were liable for dangerous or improper conduct by their police employees. This has continued into the 2000s (Weiss, Hitchcock, Weiss, Rostow, & Davis, 2008).

Psychological evaluation of police applicants can focus on selecting those candidates who appear most psychologically fit or on eliminating individuals who appear least suited for police work. Most selection methods are developed to screen out disturbed candidates, because it is very difficult to agree on the "ideal" police profile. Despite concerns about the validity of psychological evaluations in police selection, a number of experts (Arrigo & Claussen, 2003; Bartol & Bartol, 2006) believe that psychological screening is useful in the selection process and should be included. However, the current standards for screening may not be sufficient. Psychological tests are currently used to assess levels of psychopathology that may interfere with officers' abilities to perform their duties rather than focusing on specific skills or capacities that are directly relevant to police work (see Detrick & Chibnall, 2008; Detrick, Chibnall, & Rosso, 2001).

In general, the courts have upheld the legality of psychological screening of police candidates as long as the evaluation and testing involved do not violate the provisions of various civil rights acts or the Americans with Disabilities Act and are in compliance with federal guidelines.

If it were your task to select police officers from a pool of applicants, what psychological qualities would you look for? Your answers would probably reflect your values, as well as your impression of what police officers do. Among the psychological characteristics usually cited in such a list are the following:

- *Incorruptible:* A police officer should be of high moral character. Reports of officers taking bribes or framing innocent suspects are especially disturbing, because the police officer must treat all citizens fairly within the rules of law.

- *Well adjusted:* A police officer should be able to carry out the stressful duties of the job without becoming seriously and continuously affected by the stress. Officers are always in the public view. They need to be thick-skinned enough to operate without defensiveness, yet they must be sensitive to the needs of others. They also need to cope with the dangers of their jobs, including the constant awareness that injury or death could occur at any time. In 2010, a total of 160 officers were killed in the line of duty, an increase from the 117 killed in 2009.

- *People oriented:* A police officer's major duty is service to others. An officer needs to have a genuine interest in people and compassion for them. At a commencement program of the New York City Police Academy, new officers

were told, "There is one thing we cannot teach you and that is about people. The bottom line is to treat people as people and you'll get by" (quoted by Nix, 1987, p. 15).

- *Free of overly emotional reactions:* Although a degree of caution and suspiciousness may be desirable for the job, the police officer should be free of impulsive, overly aggressive reactions and other responses in which emotions overcome the discipline imposed by training. Restraint is essential because officers are trained to take an active stance in crime detection and are even encouraged by their superiors to be wary of what is happening around them (Barber, Grawitch, & Trares, 2009).

- *Dedicated:* Officers should be committed to their jobs, and not be inclined toward frequent lateness or absenteeism or have personal problems that interfere with this commitment in an ongoing way.

- *Disciplined:* Police officers should be team players, able to function effectively within a chain of command. This includes the ability to give orders to supervisees and accept orders from superior officers.

- *Logical:* Police officers should be able to examine a crime scene and develop hypotheses about what happened and what characteristics might be present in the lawbreaker. This deductive ability is apparent in the actions of Al Seedman, whose work is described in Box 4.1.

Keep these characteristics in mind as we discuss particular approaches to evaluating police candidates. To what extent can each of these characteristics be accurately assessed? There are several reported purposes for evaluating police candidates, including screening out those who are (1) chronically late or absent; (2) disciplinary problems; (3) at risk for inflicting needless harm on citizens; and (4) otherwise reckless or irresponsible (Shusman, Inwald, & Landa, 1984). Psychological evaluation is not likely to identify "ideal" candidates—but it can be used to screen out those with specific problems that would interfere with their effective functioning as police officers.

Psychologists who evaluate police candidates rely on three tools: (1) personal interviews, (2) observations of candidates performing in special situations set up to reflect real-world characteristics of police work,

---

B o x 4.1 THE CASE OF THE UNIDENTIFIED SKELETON

Al Seedman, former chief detective of the New York City Police Department, once explained to an interviewer that he had been helping some detectives from a small Connecticut town investigate a case.

> In the woods just outside town they found the skeleton of a man who'd been dead for three months or so. They figured they'd find out who he was as soon as his family reported him missing, but it's been three months since he was found—which makes six months since he died—and nobody has claimed him. They don't know what to do.... Once I got the answer to one question I was able to give them a method. I asked whether this skeleton showed signs of any dental work, which usually can be identified by a dentist. But according to the local cops, they said no, although the skeleton had crummy teeth. No dental work at all. Now, if he'd been wealthy, he could have afforded to have his teeth fixed. If he'd been poor, welfare would have paid. If he was a union member, their medical plan would have covered it. So this fellow was probably working at a low-paying non-unionized job, but

making enough to keep off public assistance. Also, since he didn't match up to any family's missing-person report, he was probably single, living alone in an apartment or hotel. His landlord had never reported him missing, either, so most likely he was also behind on his rent and the landlord probably figured he had just skipped. But even if he had escaped his landlord, he would never have escaped the tax man. The rest was simple. I told these cops to wait until the year is up. They can go to the IRS and get a printout of all single males making less than $10,000 a year but more than the welfare ceiling who paid withholding tax in the first three quarters but not the fourth. Chances are the name of their skeleton would be on that printout.

(quoted in Seedman & Hellman, 1974, pp. 4–5).

Critical Thought Question
To what extent do you think good police investigative work is a result of training? Experience? Previously acquired skills?

---

and (3) psychological tests. How much emphasis different psychologists place on these tools depends on several factors, including their professional background and training, the resources available for the evaluation, and the focus of the assessment (e.g., different strategies will be used for assessing mental disorders than for predicting what type of person will do best in which kind of position).

A national survey of municipal police departments sought to identify selection and psychological assessment practices for police officers (Cochrane, Tett, & Vandecreek, 2003). Of the 355 police agencies surveyed, a total of 155 (43%) responded. The majority of police departments used selection measures that included a background investigation, medical exam, interview with applicant, drug test, physical fitness exam, and polygraph test. More than 90% required some kind of psychological evaluation of applicants.

The Interview

Personal interviews are the most widely employed tool, despite evidence that interviews are subject to distortion, low reliability, and questionable validity.

The extent to which an interview yields the same information on different occasions or with different interviewers (*reliability*) and the degree to which that information is accurately related to important criteria (*validity*) have not been clearly established for most police selection interviews.

However, there is good evidence that reliability, at least, is increased by the use of **structured interviews**—those in which the wording, order, and content of the interview are standardized (Rogers, 2001). One semi-structured interview for the psychological screening of law enforcement candidates, the Law Enforcement Candidate Interview, uses content from other measures for screening law enforcement personnel and for assessing personality. Modest inter-rater reliability and prediction of performance in the police academy was achieved (Varela, Scogin, & Vipperman, 1999).

Interviews are a necessary part of an evaluation, according to guidelines recommended by police psychologists (Dantzker, 2010). They are also valuable as a rapport-building introduction to the evaluation process. They increase applicants' cooperation at the same time that they reduce apprehension. Interviews are also popular because they are flexible and economical. However, because they are subject to distortions and impression management by candidates, interviews are still more useful for orienting candidates to the evaluation than for predicting subsequent performance.

Situational Tests

Situational tests incorporate tasks that are similar to those that will actually be undertaken by officers on the job. They are designed to predict performance in the training academy and on the job. At one time, this approach was a widely discussed aspect of police selection, involving tasks such as observing patrols, analyzing clues, and discussing cases (see Mills, McDevitt, & Tonkin, 1966). The situational testing approach appears to be less favored than it once was, judging from the dearth of research or even discussion following the Mills et al. (1966) article. Situational *components* of the broader selection process have still been incorporated (Pynes & Bernardin, 1992). But one reason that broader situational testing has become less-frequently employed is its time intensiveness and cost. Accordingly, current situational aspects of screening are more focused, involving tasks such as report writing that are common aspects of police work. (For one part of the National Police Officer Selection Test (POST), see http://www.kacp.cc/misc/post.pdf)

Psychological Tests

Many standardized psychological tests have good reliability and can be objectively scored and administered to large groups of subjects at the same time. Consequently, they are important in police screening. Two types of tests are included in most selection batteries: tests of cognitive or intellectual ability and tests of personality traits, integrity, or emotional stability.

Police officers tend to score in the average to above-average range on intelligence tests (Brewster & Stoloff, 2003), and intelligence tends to correlate fairly strongly with the performance of police recruits in their training programs. However, intelligence scores are only weakly related to actual police performance in the field (Bartol, 1983; Brewster & Stoloff, 2003). These results point to the issue of predicting performance, both in the training academy and on

the job, an important consideration that we discuss in the next section.

The Minnesota Multiphasic Personality Inventory (MMPI; the 1989 revision of this test is called the MMPI-2 and the 2008 revision is the MMPI-2-RF) is the test of personality most often used in police screening; it is followed by the California Psychological Inventory (CPI) and the Sixteen Personality Factor Questionnaire (16PF). Evidence for the validity of these tests in screening out candidates unsuitable for police work is mixed. There is research supporting the validity of the MMPI (Bartol, 1991), the MMPI-2 (Weiss, Davis, Rostow, & Kinsman, 2003), and the CPI (Ho, 2001), although others (e.g., Hogg & Wilson, 1995) have questioned the general value of psychological testing of police recruits.

One personality test developed in 1979 specifically to identify psychologically unsuitable law enforcement candidates is the Inwald Personality Inventory (Detrick & Chibnall, 2002; Inwald, 1992; Inwald, Knatz, & Shusman, 1983). It is a behaviorally-based personality measure designed and validated specifically for use in high-risk occupations, such as law enforcement. Consisting of 26 scales that tap past and present behaviors presumed to have special relevance for law enforcement applicants (Lack of Assertiveness, Trouble with Law and Society, Undue Suspiciousness, and Driving Violations, for example), it can predict poor job performance better than traditional tests of personality and psychopathology such as the MMPI and its revisions (Inwald, 2008). Other measures have also been developed by Inwald, including a predictor of positive work-related characteristics (the Hilson Personnel Profile/Success Quotient) and the Inwald Survey-5 Revised, with additional questions on domestic violence. The development of these measures reflects a trend in the field toward designing and implementing more specialized tests, rather than depending on more general measures of personality and psychopathology.

Another written tool developed for the selection of entry-level police officers is the POST, noted earlier as having a situational component. In addition to incident report writing, the POST measures arithmetic and reading comprehension. It has demonstrated adequate reliability and validity in some research (Henry & Rafilson, 1997; Rafilson & Sison, 1996). It has also been mandated as a statewide screening measure in several states, and adopted by the police chiefs' associations in some jurisdictions.

PSYCHOLOGY OF POLICE **75**

THE VALIDITY OF POLICE SCREENING

Although experts disagree on the usefulness of psychological screening of police, they all agree that good empirical research on this topic is difficult to conduct (Bartol, 1996; Gaines & Falkenberg, 1998; Inwald, 2008). Studying **predictive validity** using actual police performance on the job as the outcome is time-consuming and expensive, so most departments do not do this. Instead, they employ research that examines the relationship between screening results and performance by police recruits in police academies or training schools. This relationship is usually positive, but success or failure in training is of less interest than actual performance as a police officer. One fairly inexpensive form of assessment is to gather peer ratings from trainees as they progress through their training classes together; these ratings have been shown to correlate with job retention of police officers, but not with most other measures of job performance or with supervisor ratings (Gardner, Scogin, Vipperman, & Varela, 1998).

Another problem with studies of validity is that the police candidates who do poorly on screening evaluations are eliminated from the pool of trainees and potential employees. Although this decision is reasonable, it makes it impossible to study whether predictions of poor performance by these individuals were valid.

In addition, applicants for police work, like applicants for most jobs, are likely to try to present an unrealistically positive image of themselves. They may deny or underreport symptoms of mental illness, answer questions to convey a socially desirable impression, and respond as they believe a psychologically healthy individual generally would. If evaluators fail to detect such "fake good" test-taking strategies, they may mistakenly identify some psychologically disturbed candidates as well-adjusted applicants. For these reasons, tests such as the MMPI-2 and the Inwald include various **validity scales** intended to detect test takers who are trying to "fake good" (Baer, Wetter, Nichols, Greene, & Berry, 1995). Research on these scales has shown that they are useful in detecting defensiveness and deception by some candidates for police positions (Detrick & Chibnall, 2008; Weiss et al., 2003).

Finally, selecting adequate criteria to measure effective police performance is notoriously difficult. Supervisor ratings are often inflated or biased by factors that are irrelevant to actual achievements or problems. In some departments, especially smaller ones, the individual police officer will be expected to perform so many diverse functions that it becomes unreasonable to expect specific cognitive abilities or psychological traits to be related in the same way to various aspects of performance. In addition, if we are interested in predicting which officers will act in risky, dangerous, or inappropriate ways, our predictions will be complicated by the fact that such behaviors occur only rarely in any group of people. As a consequence, these assessments, if offering such predictions, will yield many "false positives"—erroneous predictions in which predicted events do not take place.

FITNESS-FOR-DUTY EVALUATIONS

Another type of psychological assessment of police officers is the **fitness–for–duty evaluation**. As a result of stress, a life-threatening incident, a series of problems, injuries, or other indicators that an officer is psychologically impaired, police administrators can order an officer to undergo an evaluation of fitness to continue performing his or her duties.

These evaluations pose difficulties for everyone involved. Administrators must balance the need to protect the public from a potentially impaired officer against the legal right of the officer to privacy and fair employment. Clinicians have to navigate a narrow path between a department's need to know the results of such an evaluation and the officer's expectation that the results will be kept confidential. Finally, the officers themselves face a dilemma: They can be honest and reveal problems that could disqualify them from service, or they can distort their responses to protect their jobs and consequently miss the opportunity for potentially beneficial treatment.

Two different models of fitness-for-duty evaluations have been used. In the first, a department uses the same psychologist to perform the evaluation and to provide whatever treatment is necessary for the officer. In the other, the psychologist who evaluates the officer does not provide any treatment; this avoids an ethical conflict between keeping the therapy confidential (as part of duty to the patient) and disclosing an officer's psychological functioning to supervisors (as part of duty to the department). The second approach is endorsed in the "Guidelines for Fitness for Duty Evaluations" distributed by the Police Psychological Services Section of the International Association for Chiefs of Police (*Psychological Fitness-for-Duty Evaluation Guidelines*, 2004), which was still current in 2011.

TRAINING OF POLICE OFFICERS

Once candidates have been selected, they participate in a course of police training that usually lasts several months. Many major American cities require 24 weeks of training, with 40 hours of training per week. Smaller jurisdictions have training programs averaging 14 to 16 weeks. An increasing number of departments are now requiring that police officers complete at least some college education.

Two types of criticism of police training programs are common. One is that after rigorous selection procedures, few trainees fail the training. In a sample of 93 cadets who began training in 2003, only about 10% either dropped out or failed mandatory academic or physical endurance exercises (Phillips, 2004). Advocates count this rate of success as an indication that the initial selection procedures were valid, but critics complain that graduation is too easy, especially given the burnout rate of on-the-job police officers. The rate of police officers leaving the job during the first 16 months was nearly 25% in one study (Haarr, 2005), a considerably higher rate than the 10% of cadet training dropouts noted in the prior study.

A second criticism is that there is insufficient training in the field, as well as a lack of close supervision of trainees during the time they spend on patrol. The limited time that trainees spend with veteran training officers on patrol may give them a false sense of security and deprive them of opportunities to learn different ways of responding to citizens from various cultural backgrounds or resolving disputes other than through arrests.

However, it is also possible that there are limits to the benefits of extensive supervision by senior officers. It is possible that such contacts teach new officers to be cynical about law enforcement, to "cut corners" in their duties, and, above all, to identify almost exclusively with the norms of police organizations rather than with the values of the larger and more diverse society (Tuohy, Wrennall, McQueen, & Stradling, 1993).

TRAINING IN CRISIS INTERVENTION

The police are often asked to maintain public order and defuse volatile situations involving persons who are mentally ill, intoxicated, angry, or motivated by politically extreme views. Because of the instability of the participants in such disputes, they pose great risks to the police as well as to bystanders. In this section, we examine three types of crisis situations to which police are often called: incidents involving mentally ill citizens, family disturbances, and the taking of hostages. Psychologists have made important contributions to each of these areas by conducting research, designing interventions, and training the police in crisis intervention skills.

Interactions with Mentally Ill Citizens

For the past three decades, several factors have forced mentally ill persons from residential mental health facilities, where they formerly lived, into a variety of noninstitutional settings, including halfway houses, community mental health centers, hospital emergency rooms, detoxification facilities, "flophouses," the streets, and local jails. Deinstitutionalization itself is an admirable goal; spending much of one's life in an institution breeds dependency, despair, and hopelessness. People with mental illness should receive treatment in the least restrictive environment possible, allowing them to function in and contribute to their local communities. However, the evidence on how people with mental illness have fared suggests that deinstitutionalization in the United States has not

Crisis Intervention Team Training for Police

achieved its lofty goals. The problems stem from two fundamental difficulties.

First, even under ideal conditions, severe mental illness is difficult to treat effectively. The impairments associated with disorders such as schizophrenia and serious mood disorders can be profound, and relapses are common. For example, less than a third of non-hospitalized persons with schizophrenia are employed at any given time. Second, sufficient funding for alternative, noninstitutional care has not been provided in the United States. As a result, community-based treatment of severely mentally ill persons seldom takes place under proper circumstances, despite the fact that the economic costs of severe mental disorders rival those of diseases such as cancer and heart disease and could be reduced considerably if proper care were provided.

One consequence of deinstitutionalization is that supervising people with mental illness has become a primary responsibility for the police. In medium-size to large police departments, about 7% of all police contacts involve citizens with mental illness, and it is estimated that the police are responsible for up to one-third of all mental health referrals to hospital emergency rooms. In one survey, 9 out of 10 police officers had responded to a call involving a mentally ill individual in the past month, and 8 out of 10 had responded to two or more such calls in the same time period (Borum, Deane, Steadman, & Morrissey, 1998). Another survey found that 33% of all calls made to a police district in a one-year period were for mental health-related situations (Steadman, Deane, Borum, & Morrissey, 2000). Research on how the police handle mentally ill persons has focused on the discretion that officers use in crisis incidents. Will they arrest the citizen, or will they have the person hospitalized? Will they offer on-the-spot counseling, refer the citizen to a mental health agency, or return the person to a safe place, to relatives, or to friends?

Some research on these questions suggests that the police are reluctant to arrest the mentally ill or to require their emergency hospitalization unless their behavior presents an obvious danger to themselves or others (Lamb, Weinberger, & DeCuir, 2002). These findings are consistent with research on the use of discretion by police in general, which suggests that they tend to avoid an arrest in minor incidents unless the suspect is disrespectful to the officer, the complaining party prefers that an arrest be made, or the officer perceives the benefits of arresting the subject to outweigh the perceived costs.

However, a very large study (Teplin, 1984) clearly indicated that the presence of mental illness increases rather than decreases the probability of arrest. This study assembled a team of psychology graduate students and trained them to observe and code the interactions of police officers with citizens over a 14-month period in two precincts in a large U.S. city. Observers used a symptom checklist and a global rating of mental disorder to assess mental illness in the citizens observed. Teplin studied 884 nontraffic encounters involving a total of 1,798 citizens, of whom 506 were considered suspects for arrest by the police. Arrest was relatively infrequent, occurring in only 12.4% of the encounters; in terms of individuals (some incidents involved several suspects), 29.2% were arrested. The observers classified only 30 (5.9%) of the 506 suspects as mentally ill. The arrest rate for these 30 persons was 46.7%, compared to an arrest rate of 27.9% for suspects who were not rated as having mental disorders. Mentally ill suspects were more likely to be arrested regardless of the type or seriousness of the incident involved.

Teplin (1984, 2000) concluded that the mentally ill were being "criminalized" and that this outcome was the result not only of the provocative nature of their psychological symptoms but also of the inadequacies of the mental health system in treating them, and the lack of training in mental illness for some police officers. As a result, the criminal justice system has become a "default option" for patients whom hospitals refuse to accept for treatment because they are too dangerous to adjust to a hospital setting, are not dangerous enough to be involuntarily committed, or suffer a disorder that the hospital does not treat. Not surprisingly, the rate of severe mental disorders in jail populations, often combined with diagnoses of substance abuse and personality disorder in the same individuals, is alarmingly high. One of the best estimates of the prevalence of individuals with severe mental illness in jails, obtained by administering a structured clinical interview to 822 inmates in Maryland and New York jails, is 14.5% for male inmates and 31% for female inmates (Steadman, Osher, Robbins, Case, & Samuels, 2009).

Another study examined police responses to incidents involving individuals with mental illness in three jurisdictions differing in the level of mental health training that police received. Findings suggested that the jurisdictions with specialized mental health training were especially effective in crisis intervention and made fewer arrests. However, the officers' decisions about how to handle the situation depended on the overall resources available; jurisdictions with mobile crisis units were able to transport mentally ill individuals to treatment locations to ensure that they obtained treatment, while those without crisis units could only refer individuals for treatment (Steadman et al., 2000).

The Memphis Police Department started the Memphis **Crisis Intervention Team** (CIT) program, which has now become known as the "Memphis Model" for crisis intervention (CIT National Advisory Board, 2006). This program was designed to increase officer and consumer safety while attempting to redirect those with mental illness from the judicial system to the mental health system. Along with these broad goals, the program provides law enforcement officers with the tools and skills necessary for dealing with mentally ill persons. Many police departments around the country have started their own CIT programs, some based on this "Memphis Model." A pilot program for police crisis intervention was started in Philadelphia; it made the news because two officers, recently trained in CIT, were able to use their newly acquired skills in communicating with people with mental disorders. Encountering a man who was very depressed and had climbed up on a bridge, these officers talked to him—and convinced him to come down, preventing a possible suicide.

One study (Skeem & Bibeau, 2008) addressed the question of whether CIT intervention decreases the risk of violence. The investigators reviewed police reports ($N = 655$) for CIT events that occurred between March 2003 and May 2005. They were able to classify 45% of these events as reflecting a danger to self, and another 26% as situations in which the individual involved was dangerous to others. The research showed that officers were more likely to use force when the individual was perceived as threatening to others. However, consistent with CIT training, the officers were inclined to use low-lethality force—even when encountering individuals presenting a high risk for violence. Some 74% of these events resulted in hospitalization, while only 4% were concluded by arrest. These results are consistent with the potential for CIT to result in safe and treatment-oriented resolution of high-risk situations involving individuals with mental disorder.

A review of the existing studies on CIT (Compton, Bahara, Watson, & Oliva, 2008) yielded several conclusions. First, this research provided support for the notion that CIT may be an effective way to link individuals with mental illnesses with indicated mental health treatment. Second, the training component of CIT may have a favorable impact on officers' attitudes, beliefs, and knowledge about these interactions; CIT-trained officers report feeling better prepared for their encounters with individuals with mental illnesses. Finally, CIT may have a lower arrest rate and lower associated criminal justice costs than other diversionary approaches.

The importance of evaluating how police interact with individuals with mental illness is underscored by the prevalence of mentally ill offenders in prisons and jails. A study discussed earlier in the chapter (Teplin, 1984) noted the overrepresentation of mentally ill individuals in the justice system. This apparently continues. Using a broader definition of mental health problem than that used by Steadman et al. (2009), the Bureau of Justice Statistics (2006) estimated that 56% of state prisoners, 45% of federal inmates, and 64% of those incarcerated in jails had a mental health problem. Whether one uses the narrow definition (Steadman et al., 2009, of "serious mental illness") or the broader BJS (2006) definition of "mental health problem," the proportion of those incarcerated who have this kind of difficulty is substantial.

The jailing of mentally ill persons does not reflect improper behavior by the police as much as a failure of public policy regarding the treatment and protection of people with chronic mental illness. More and better training of police officers in the recognition and short-term management of mentally ill persons is necessary, but an adequate resolution to this problem requires better organization and funding of special services for those with serious mental illness (Abram & Teplin, 1991; Teplin, 2000).

One possibility is to increase the use of **jail diversion programs** through the use of community-based alternatives for justice-involved individuals with severe mental illness. The first contact between mentally ill individuals in the justice system is most often the police; to the extent that police are trained to use options other than arrest as a result of such encounters, the number of justice-involved mentally ill individuals may decrease (Munetz & Griffin, 2006). A growing body of research, reviewed by Heilbrun et al. (2012), indicates that such diversion, or other community-based services, can be effective in providing needed services to individuals with severe mental illness without a commensurate increase in their risk of reoffending.

Domestic Disturbances

When violence erupts in a family or between a couple, the police are often the first people called to the scene. What will they encounter when they arrive? Are the participants armed? Are they intoxicated or psychologically disturbed? How much violence has already taken place? What is certain is that responding to family disturbances is one of the most dangerous activities that police perform. The level of danger involved when intervening in a domestic dispute is not surprising, considering that strangers (not known to the victim) perpetrated 39% of violent victimizations in 2010—with the remaining 61% of violent offenses perpetrated by family members, neighbors, and others known to the victim (Bureau of Justice Statistics, 2010).

Police spend a great deal of time investigating domestic disturbances, and these are high-risk situations for officers (Ellis, Choi, & Blaus, 1993). A large-scale study investigating the circumstances of 1,550 assaults on police in Baltimore County, Maryland, between 1984 and 1986 (Uchida & Brooks, 1988) indicated that about 25% of these assaults occurred during the investigation of a domestic disturbance. Perpetrators were more likely to use blunt objects than guns or knives. The risk to officers of injury in responding to domestic disturbances include (1) answering the call alone, (2) effort to make an arrest, (3) verbal abuse or physical threat made to officers, (4) intoxication of the disputants, and (5) victim physical injury (Ellis et al. 1993). Some evidence suggests that female officers are at greater risk of assault in such domestic calls (Rabe-Hemp & Schuck, 2007).

Empirical research has contributed to our understanding of domestic violence. We are now better able to recognize the false beliefs about family violence, which are relevant to how such offenses are investigated and prosecuted.

Myth 1: Family Violence Is Perpetrated Only by Men. A recent review of over 200 studies with data on domestic violence by both men and women (Straus, 2011) observed comparable rates for both genders, supporting the "gender symmetry" of violence prevalence in the home. This is an area fraught with debate; some have suggested that this gender symmetry applies to less serious aggression (e.g., slapping, shoving) but not to more severe violence (e.g., choking, punching, use of a weapon). In light of all the research reviewed, however, the author drew two conclusions: (1) domestic violence prevention could be enhanced by addressing programs to girls and women as well as boys and men, and (2) the effectiveness of offender treatment could be enhanced by changing treatment programs to address assaults by both partners when applicable.

Myth 2: Family Violence Is Confined to Mentally Disturbed or Sick People. When we hear or read that a woman has plunged her 2-year-old son into a tub of boiling water or that a man has had sexual intercourse with his 6-year-old daughter, our first reaction might be, "That person is terribly sick!" The portrayal of family violence in the mass media often suggests that "normal people" do not harm family members. In reality, however, family violence is too widespread to be adequately explained by mental illness, although perpetrators of serious domestic violence often experience depression or personality disorder (Andrews, Foster, Capaldi, & Hops, 2000).

Myth 3: Family Violence Is Confined to Poor People. Violence and abuse are more common among families of lower socioeconomic status, but they are by no means limited to such families. There are risk factors associated with poverty (e.g., unemployment, limited education, and sparse social support) that are associated with the risk for family violence (Barnett, Miller-Perrin, & Perrin, 2005; Magdol et al., 1997).

Myth 4: Battered Women Like Being Hit; Otherwise, They Would Leave. This belief combines two myths. First, as noted earlier, family violence is perpetrated by both males and females, although violence by men against women tends to produce more serious injuries. But faced with the fact that many female victims of partner violence do not leave even the most serious of abusers, people seek some type of rational explanation.

A common belief is that women who remain in violent relationships must somehow provoke or even enjoy the violence. This form of "blaming the victim" is not a useful explanation. The concept of

learned helplessness can explain why so many women endure such extreme violence for so long (Walker, 1979). Psychologist Lenore Walker observed that women who suffer continued physical violence at the hands of their partners have a more negative self-concept than women whose relationships are free from violence. She proposed that the repeated beatings leave these women feeling that they won't be able to protect themselves from further assaults and that they are incapable of controlling the events that go on around them (Gelles & Cornell, 1985). Under such circumstances, they give in to the belief that there is nothing they can do to change their circumstances and that any effort at starting a new life not only will be futile but also will lead to even more violence against them.

Myth 5: Alcohol and Drug Abuse Are the Real Causes of Violence in the Home. "He beat up his children because he was drunk" is another popular explanation of domestic violence, and most studies do find a considerable relationship between drinking and violence (Gerber, Ganz, Lichter, Williams, & McCloskey, 2005; Magdol et al., 1997), especially among male perpetrators. Perhaps as many as half of the incidents of domestic violence in the past have involved alcohol or drugs (Gelles & Cornell, 1985); in the case of violence directed toward a spouse, both the offender and the victim may have been drinking heavily before the violence.

This observation appears to be as accurate today as it was nearly 25 years ago. In a longitudinal study considering the relationships among drinking, alcohol-related problems, and recurring incidents of partner violence over a five-year period (Caetano, McGrath, Ramisetty-Mikler, & Field, 2005), investigators found that the rate of domestic violence among men who drink more than four drinks at a time at least once per month was three times higher than that among men who abstain or drink less often and less frequently. This pattern also held for women. But does the substance cause the violence? Some assume that alcohol is a disinhibitor of behavior and that it therefore facilitates the expression of violence. Although there is certainly some truth to this, those who have been drinking may also tend to place more blame on their condition than is justified ("I was drunk and didn't know what I was doing"). Furthermore, those who have trouble controlling their aggressive behavior while drinking can certainly anticipate this and take steps to manage their risk (e.g., drinking in moderation or not at all).

Because of their danger and frequency, family disturbances pose a difficult challenge for the police. Can these encounters be handled in a manner that protects potential victims, reduces repeat offenses, and limits the risk of injury to responding officers?

The first project on crisis intervention with domestic disputes was developed by Morton Bard, a psychologist in New York City. Bard (1969; Bard & Berkowitz, 1967) trained a special group of New York City police officers (nine Black and nine White volunteers) in family disturbance intervention skills for a project located in West Harlem. The month-long training program focused on teaching officers how to intervene in family disputes without making arrests. The training emphasized the psychology of family conflict and sensitivity to cross-racial differences. Role playing was used to acquaint officers with techniques for calming antagonists, lowering tensions, reducing hostilities, and preventing physical violence.

For two years after the training, all family crisis calls in the experimental precinct were answered by the specially trained officers. They performed 1,375 interventions with 962 families. Evaluation of the project concentrated on six desired outcomes: (1) a decrease in family disturbance calls, (2) a drop in repeat calls from the same families, (3) a reduction of homicides in the precinct, (4) a decline in homicides among family members, (5) a reduction of assaults in the precinct, and (6) a decrease in injuries to police officers. But results indicated that the intervention affected only two of these outcomes. Fewer assaults occurred in the precinct, and none of the trained officers was injured (compared with three police officers who were not part of the program but were injured while responding to family disturbances).

Much of the specialized police training during the last decade has been associated with the Crisis Intervention Team approach. (Although work in the 1960s was termed "crisis intervention," the CIT approach of the 2000s is more formal and widespread.) CIT officers are trained to use techniques that facilitate nonviolent resolutions and fewer arrests when individuals have behavioral health problems. Such problems are frequently seen in the course of domestic disturbances.

For a period of time beginning in the 1970s, many police departments shifted policies and advocated the arrest and prosecution of domestic batterers. Is this a better alternative than crisis intervention or counseling?

The first well-controlled evaluation of the effects of arresting domestic batterers was the Minneapolis Domestic Violence Experiment (Sherman & Berk, 1984). In this experiment, police officers' responses to domestic violence were randomly assigned to (1) arresting the suspected batterer, (2) ordering one of the parties to leave the residence, or (3) giving the couple immediate advice on reducing their violence. Judging on the basis of official police records and interviews with victims, subsequent offending was reduced by almost 50% when the suspect was arrested, a significantly better outcome than that achieved by the two non-arrest alternatives. These findings quickly changed public and expert opinion about the value of arresting domestic batterers, and soon many cities had replaced informal counseling with immediate arrest as their response to domestic violence cases.

Since the initial Minneapolis Experiment, at least five other jurisdictions—Charlotte, Colorado Springs, Miami, Omaha, and Milwaukee—have conducted studies designed to test whether arresting batterers is the best deterrent to repeated domestic violence. The results of these projects, collectively known as the Spouse Assault Replication Program, have shown that across all five sites, arresting the violent partner significantly reduced future victimization, independent of other criminal justice sanctions or individual factors (Maxwell, Garner, & Fagan, 2002).

What conclusion should we reach about the value of arrest as a deterrent to future spouse abuse? At this point, the evidence points to the effectiveness of arrest as a deterrent—but such effectiveness is not so powerful as to justify the enthusiastic claims that are sometimes made for arrest programs.

Questions about how best to quell domestic violence illustrate an interesting phenomenon often encountered with social reforms. Social problems and well-intentioned efforts to modify them tend to revolve in cycles rather than moving in a straight line toward progress and increased sophistication. A reform in vogue today, aimed at correcting some social evil, often fosters its own difficulties or inequities and ultimately becomes itself a problem in need of reformation.

Crisis intervention was originally preferred over arrest as a more psychologically sophisticated response by police to family disturbances; however, this intervention fell out of favor and was criticized as an inadequate response to serious domestic violence. Official arrest was then championed as the most effective intervention, but as additional data are gathered about its effectiveness, new questions are raised about whether arrest and prosecution are the best answers for domestic violence.

Hostage Negotiation

Although hostage incidents are at least as old as the description in Genesis of the abduction and rescue of Abraham's nephew Lot, most experts agree that the massacre of 11 Israeli athletes taken hostage and murdered by Palestinian terrorists at the 1972 Munich Olympic Games spurred the creation of new law

Negotiation group, they talk to hostage takers or other criminals or armed suicides

Jochen Tack/Image Broker/Newscom

enforcement techniques for resolving hostage incidents. Developed through extensive collaboration
among military, law enforcement, and behavioral
science experts, these hostage negotiation techniques
are still being refined as more is learned about the
conditions that lead to effective negotiations.

One study of 120 hostage-related incidents found
that the perpetrator used a barricade to separate
himself and his hostage from police in over half of
the incidents (55.8%) (Feldmann, 2001), creating a
complicated situation for negotiation strategies
because police could not be fully aware of the perpetrator's activities and intentions. Soskis and Van Zandt
(1986) have identified four types of hostage incidents
that differ in their psychological dynamics and techniques for resolution (see also Gist & Perry, 1985;
Hatcher, Mohandie, Turner, & Gelles, 1998).

The first type, describing more than half of
hostage incidents, involves *persons suffering a mental
disorder* or experiencing serious personal or family
problems (Feldmann, 2001). In these situations, the
hostage takers often have a history of depression,
schizophrenia, or other serious mental illness, or they
harbor feelings of chronic powerlessness, anger, or
despondency that compel a desperate act. Disturbed
hostage takers pose a high risk of suicide, which they
sometimes accomplish by killing their hostage(s) and
then themselves. In other situations, they try to force
the police to kill them; such victim-precipitated deaths
are termed **suicide by cop**. This underscores the
importance of incorporating mental health consultants'
expertise into the effort to peacefully negotiate and
resolve these hostage situations.

A second common type of hostage situation
involves the *trapped criminal*. Here, a person who is
trapped by the police while committing a crime
takes, as a hostage, anyone who is available and then
uses the hostage to bargain for freedom. Because these
incidents are unplanned and driven by panic, they
tend to be, especially in their early stages, very
dangerous to the victims and the police.

The third type of hostage situation, also involving
criminals, is the *takeover of prisons* by inmates who
capture prison guards or take other inmates as hostages. In these incidents, the passage of time tends
to work against nonviolent resolution because the
hostage takers are violent people, working as an
undisciplined group with volatile leadership.

The fourth type of hostage taking, and the one
that is most widely publicized, is **terrorism**. Terrorists
use violence or the threat of violence "to achieve
a social, political, or religious aim in a way that does
not obey the traditional rules of war" (Soskis & Van
Zandt, 1986, p. 424; see also Lake, 2002). Terrorists
usually make careful plans for the kidnapping of
hostages or the taking of property, and they are typically motivated by extremist political or religious goals.
These goals may require their own deaths as a necessary but "honorable" sacrifice for a higher cause. For
this reason, terrorists are less responsive to negotiation
techniques that appeal to rational themes of self-
preservation. Therefore, new ways of responding to
this type of terrorism must be sought.

One terrorism specialist suggested that a country
has three options in responding. At the lowest level
of response, it may increase its internal security to
prevent further attacks, as anyone who has flown in
an airplane the last few years knows only too well. A
more proactive response may be to attempt to capture
or eliminate the terrorists in a limited operation targeting the leaders of the terrorist organizations. Lastly,
a country may implement a military retaliation with
the aims of eradicating the terrorists and their organizations and deterring future attacks from other groups
(Lake, 2002).

Another approach would involve identifying
those at greater risk for engaging in terroristic activities. A recent review effectively explained why it will
not be possible to develop a specialized risk assessment
measure for terrorists—the conventional strategy of
releasing those "at risk" and observing them to see
who is actually involved in order to validate the measure is not feasible, for obvious reasons (Monahan,
in press). However, the same review considered
the available scientific and cultural evidence and
identified four robust individual risk factors. These
include ideologies, affiliations, grievances, and moral
emotions.

The 2000s have brought additional forms of
terrorism that redefine what it means to be "taken
hostage." For example, **bioterrorism**, in which biological "weapons" such as viruses and bacteria are
released or threatened, could hold far larger populations hostage than conventional guns or bombs. One
study examined public distress following the anthrax-
related incidents that occurred shortly after the
September 11, 2001 attacks. Findings suggested that
even for individuals not actually exposed to the
anthrax, initial media exposure to the anthrax attacks
was a significant predictor of distress. Levels of

distress were especially high when the attacks were first detected (Dougall, Hayward, & Baum, 2005). Effective countermeasures to such threats require new collaborations among law enforcement officials, public health experts, and behavioral scientists.

Successful hostage negotiation requires an understanding of the dynamics of hostage incidents so that these dynamics can be manipulated by the negotiator to contain and ultimately end the incident with a minimum of violence (Vecchi, Van Hasselt, & Romano, 2005). For example, in many hostage situations, a strong sense of psychological togetherness and mutual dependency develops between the hostages and their kidnappers. These feelings emerge from (1) the close, constant contact between the participants, (2) their shared feelings of fear and danger, and (3) the strong feelings of powerlessness induced by prolonged captivity. This relationship, dubbed the **Stockholm syndrome**, involves mutually positive feelings between the hostages and their kidnappers. This term derives from a 1973 event in which hostages held in a Swedish bank developed a close emotional attachment to their captors (Eckholm, 1985). Hostages may come to sympathize with the lawbreakers and even adopt, at least temporarily, their captors' ideological views. The behavior of Patricia Hearst, a newspaper heiress who was kidnapped in 1974 and later helped her captors rob a bank, has been explained through this syndrome. It was also seen in 1985, when 39 passengers from Trans World Airlines (TWA) Flight 847 were detained as hostages for 17 days by hijackers in Beirut. Allyn Conwell, the spokesperson for the hostages in the hijacking, was criticized for his statements expressing "profound sympathy" for his captors' Shiite position, but he explicitly denied that he was influenced by the Stockholm syndrome (Eckholm, 1985).

Hostage negotiators try to take advantage of this dynamic by becoming a part of it themselves. First attempting to become a psychological member of the hostage group who nevertheless maintains important ties to the outside world, negotiators will then try to use their outside contacts to persuade terrorists to bring the crisis to a peaceful end. Successful negotiators make contact with hostage takers in as nonthreatening a manner as possible and then maintain communication with them for as long as necessary. Generally, the negotiator attempts to isolate the hostage takers from any "outside" communication in order to foster their dependency on

the negotiator as the crucial link with other people. Once communication is established, the negotiator tries to reduce the hostage takers' fear and tension so that they will be more willing to agree to a reasonable solution. Negotiators structure the situation in ways that maximize predictability and calm. For example, they may offer help with any medical needs the hostage group has, thereby fostering positive feelings associated with the Stockholm syndrome. Finally, through gradual prompting and reinforcement, the negotiator tries to encourage behaviors that promote negotiation progress (e.g., more conversation, less violence and threats as part of such conversation, and the passage of time without violence).

According to Martin Symonds, a New York psychiatrist and expert on terrorism, the Stockholm syndrome (which is one of several that is known to form among hostages, hostage takers, and negotiators) is more likely to emerge when the hostages are purely "instrumental" victims of no genuine concern to the terrorists except as means to obtain leverage over a third party. In such situations, the captors maintain that they will let their captives go if their demands are met, and the captives begin to (inaccurately) perceive the terrorist as the individual trying to keep the hostages alive. For this reason, it is especially important for the police to determine the motivations of any hostage takers, as well as their specific goals.

Increasingly, police departments have developed special crisis/hostage negotiation teams that usually include a psychologist as a consultant or adviser (Bartol & Bartol, 2006). In this capacity, the psychologist helps select officers for the team, provides on-the-scene advice during hostage incidents, profiles the hostage taker's personality, and assesses the behavior of the hostages themselves.

Do psychologist-consultants make a difference? In the one study evaluating the effects of psychological consultation in hostage incidents, Butler, Leitenberg, and Fuselier (1993) found that using a psychologist resulted in fewer injuries and deaths to hostages and more peaceful surrenders by hostage takers. Empirical evidence regarding the effectiveness of specific negotiation techniques has yet to be gathered (Vecchi et al., 2005), although psychologists have been involved in using "crisis communication" in the course of critical incidents such as hostage situations, kidnappings, suicide threats, and violence in school and workplace (Vecchi, 2009).

THE POLICE OFFICER'S JOB

In the eyes of most citizens, the job of the police officer is to catch criminals and enforce the law, just as the officers on the various *Law and Order* shows do weekly on TV. But the police are responsible for more functions than these. The major duties of the police are divided into three general areas:

- *Enforcing the law*, which includes investigating complaints, arresting suspects, and attempting to prevent crime. Although most citizens perceive law enforcement to be the most important function of the police, it accounts for only about 10% of police activity.

- *Maintaining order*, which includes intervening in family and neighborhood disputes and keeping traffic moving, noise levels down, rowdy persons off the streets, and disturbances to a minimum. It is estimated that 3 out of every 10 requests for police officers involve this type of activity.

- *Providing services*, such as giving assistance in medical and psychological emergencies, finding missing persons, helping stranded motorists, escorting funerals, and rescuing cats from trees.

Much police work is focused on the third category. Should the police spend so much time on community services? The major objections to community services are that they waste police resources and distract the police from the crucial roles of law enforcement and public protection for which they are specially trained. In the 1990s, special initiatives were taken to increase the time police commit to crime-fighting activities. Federal legislation providing funds for cities to hire thousands of new police officers was justified with the promise that additional police would lead to more arrests of criminals. Urban police forces have found that concentrating more police officers in high-crime areas and instructing them to arrest all lawbreakers (even for relatively minor offenses such as loitering and public drunkenness) have resulted in lowered crime rates. This **zero-tolerance** policy demands that police officers concentrate more time on apprehension and arrest activities. Although it was credited with bringing about reductions in crime, the zero-tolerance policy has also been linked to increases in citizen complaints and lawsuits against the police (Greene, 1999). For instance, a 12-year-old boy in Florida was handcuffed after he stomped in a puddle

and splashed his classmates, and a 13-year-old boy in Virginia was suspended and required to attend drug awareness classes after accepting a breath mint from a classmate (Koch, 2000). This policy now appears to have yielded to the provision of more specialized interventions (such as when officers are trained specifically to interact more effectively with citizens with behavioral health problems) and other interventions short of arrest.

There are two advantages to the police continuing to provide an array of social services. First, short of spending massive amounts of money to train and employ a new cadre of community service workers, there is no feasible alternative to using the police in this capacity. Second, by providing these services, the police create a positive identity in the community that carries goodwill, respect, and cooperation over to their crime-fighting tasks.

These "side effects" serve as a buffer that gives the police opportunities to interact with people who are not behaving criminally, thereby reducing the tendency of police to develop cynical, suspicious attitudes toward others. They also may encourage citizens to perceive the police in a less threatening and less hostile manner.

STRESS AND THE POLICE

Not only is the police officer's job composed of multiple duties, but the requirements of these duties may lead to feelings of stress, to personal conflicts, and eventually to psychological problems. Scores of books, technical reports, and journal articles have been written on the causes and treatment of police stress (e.g., Ford, 1998; Harpold & Feemster, 2002; Hille, 2010).

Certainly no one would suggest that a police officer's job is easy. Certain factors make the occupation particularly difficult. One problem that comes with being a police officer is the "life in a fishbowl" phenomenon. Officers are constantly on public view, and they realize that their every act is being evaluated. When they perform their job differently than the public wants, they are likely to hear an outcry of protest. Police are sensitive to public criticism, and this criticism also leads their spouses and children to feel isolated and segregated.

Some have divided the stress of police work into different categories according to the sources of the stress or the type of problem involved. Project Shield, a large-scale study conducted by the National Institute of Justice, asked police officers to respond to a series of questions about the negative effects of stress in several different categories, including psychological, physical, behavioral, and organizational public health (Harpold & Feemster, 2002).

Results from the surveys showed that officers reported an increased vulnerability to alcohol abuse and heightened levels of anxiety within the first five years of employment. In addition, approximately 1% of officers in the study reported having contemplated suicide at some point. Compared to the general population, officers reported more experiences of physical and medical problems over their lifetime, including cancer, heart disease, hypertension, acute migraine headaches, reproductive problems, chronic back problems, foot problems, and insomnia. They also reported increased behavioral problems in their personal lives, such as physical abuse of their spouses and children, as a result of job-related stress. Officers reported the highest levels of organizational, or job-related, stress when faced with making split-second decisions with serious consequences, when hearing media reports of police wrongdoing, when working with administrators who did not support the officers, and when not having enough time for personal or family responsibilities.

According to questionnaire studies of police stress, the following three categories of stress are most commonly encountered by the police:

1. *Physical and psychological threats.* Included here are events related to the unique demands of police work, such as using force, being physically attacked, confronting aggressive people or grisly crime scenes, and engaging in high-speed chases. Danger can emerge from even apparently routine tasks. In 2009, a man wearing a bulletproof vest opened fire on police officers responding to a domestic disturbance call in Pittsburgh. Three officers were killed and two more injured before the shooter could be arrested. Pittsburgh had not had an officer killed in the line of duty in the previous 18 years.

2. *Evaluation systems.* These stressors include the ineffectiveness of the judicial system, court leniency with criminals, negative press accounts of the police, the public's rejection of the police, and put-downs and mistreatment of police officers in the courts. In the United States, many

more police officers die as a result of suicide than of homicide. For instance, in 2010, there were 145 police suicides in the United States, a slight increase over 2009, during which there were 143 (Badge of Life, 2010). By comparison, a total of 56 law enforcement officers were feloniously killed in the line of duty in 2010 (another 72 officers died in accidents while performing their duties, and 53,469 officers were assaulted in the line of duty) (FBI, 2011).

3. *Organizational problems and lack of support.* Examples of these stressors include bureaucratic hassles, inadequate leadership by police administrators, weak support and confused feedback from supervisors, lack of clarity about job responsibilities, and poor job performance by fellow officers. In some studies (Stinchcomb, 2004; Violanti & Aron, 1994), organizational problems proved to be one of the most important sources of stress—more influential even than physical danger, bloody crime scenes, and public scrutiny. A certain degree of stress is inevitable, given the demands on the police. Yet police officers often find it hard to acknowledge that the stressful nature of their job is affecting them. There is a stigma about admitting a need for professional help. Too often, police officers believe that if they acknowledge personal problems or ask for assistance, they will be judged to be unprofessional or inadequate.

These fears are understandable. Officers found to have psychological problems are sometimes belittled by other officers or are relieved of their weapons and badges and assigned to limited-duty tasks. Fear of these consequences induces some officers to hide the fact that they are suffering from job-related stress.

Stressful working conditions also lead to **burnout**, which is "a syndrome of emotional exhaustion, depersonalization, and reduced personal accomplishment that can occur among individuals who work with people in some capacity" (Maslach & Jackson, 1984, p. 134). Emotional exhaustion reflects feelings of being emotionally overextended and "drained" by one's contact with other people. Depersonalization frequently takes the form of a callous or insensitive response to other people, particularly crime victims and others requesting police assistance. Reduced personal accomplishment is manifested in a diminished sense of competence at the end of a day's work with other people (Maslach & Jackson, 1984).

Burnout also affects behavior off the job. In Jackson and Maslach's (1982) study of police officers and their families, emotional exhaustion was found more likely than any other factor to affect behavior at home. Male police officers were described by their wives as coming home upset, angry, tense, and anxious. High rates of substance abuse, domestic battering, and divorce are regarded as occupational hazards of police work. A subsequent study (Hawkins, 2001) replicated Maslach's finding regarding emotional exhaustion, and its relationship to burnout in police. Depersonalization was another factor that was strongly related to burnout among the 452 officers (in four departments) who were surveyed.

Burnout may also result from working many years at the same job. Patrol officers sometimes speak of the "seven-year syndrome." Initially, officers are eager and anxious about their job performance. The tasks are initially interesting and challenging. But after several years, some officers lose interest; the job feels stale. Enthusiasm plummets.

What can be done to reduce stress and burnout in police officers? From their analysis of the research on organizational behavior, Jackson and Schuler (1983) have hypothesized four organizational qualities that increase employee burnout: (1) lack of rewards (especially positive feedback), (2) lack of control over job demands, (3) lack of clear job expectations, and (4) lack of support from supervisors. Although each of these is especially problematic for police officers, certain interventions can reduce the likelihood of burnout. For example, the police officer seldom hears when things go well but often hears of the complaints of enraged citizens. Police officials could create opportunities for citizens to express their appreciation of what police officers are doing daily.

Officers often feel a lack of control in their jobs. They must react to calls; they cannot change the flow of demands. Furthermore, citizens expect them to respond immediately. Although the level of demands cannot be changed, officers can be given greater flexibility in how they respond to these demands. Their daily duties can be restructured so as to increase their sense of choice among activities. The importance of discretion can be emphasized to the officers, because they must exercise such discretion when dealing with suspected offenders. Officers do not always make an arrest, even when they catch a suspect breaking the law.

One strategy for decreasing burnout among police is the use of **team policing**. Team policing involves a partial shift of decision making from a centralized authority to front-line officers and their immediate supervisors, who share the responsibility of setting policing priorities and making management decisions. Teams are often organized around neighborhoods, where they focus their efforts for extended periods of time. Within a neighborhood team, members perform several different functions so that they come to realize how important each team member is to the overall success of the group. In addition, because the team stays in the neighborhood, citizens should come to know the officers more closely and develop a better understanding of them.

In addition to team policing, many police agencies have developed their own stress management programs or referred their officers to other agencies for counseling to reduce burnout. These programs emphasize the prevention of stress through various techniques, including relaxation training, stress inoculation, detection of the early signs of stress, and effective problem solving (see, e.g., the 2004 policy of the Chicago Police Department in the area). As useful as these types of techniques may be, the stigma associated with obtaining mental health treatment may be strong enough to discourage some officers from participating.

But despite attempts to prevent stress and to change organizations in positive ways, some officers will experience stress-related problems that require counseling. Psychological treatment of police officers is complicated because police officers are often reluctant to become involved in therapy or counseling, for several reasons. First, they tend to believe that capable officers should be able to withstand hardships—and failure to do so shows a lack of professionalism or emotional control. Second, police fear that counseling will brand them with the stigma of mental disorder and thus diminish their peer officers' respect for them. Finally, officers are justifiably concerned that the department's need to know their psychological status related to fitness for duty will override their rights of confidentiality and lead to embarrassing disclosures of personal information.

Police departments have developed several alternatives for providing psychological counseling to their officers. Each addresses some of the obstacles that arise in police counseling programs. Peer counseling, involving the delivery of services by police officers, has the potential to overcome the stigma of being involved in treatment with a psychiatrist or psychologist. This approach offers better access to individuals who would otherwise avoid any kind of therapy or counseling; it has contributed to an increase in mental health referrals and a decrease in sick days, poor work performance, and job-related suicide (Levenson & Dwyer, 2003).

A second method is to provide counseling targeted at problems specific to police officers. The most noteworthy example of these focused interventions is with officers who have been involved in the use of deadly force (Blau, 1986). The emotional aftermath of shooting incidents is among the most traumatic experiences the police encounter and can often lead to symptoms of posttraumatic stress disorder. Providing post-incident counseling is a common service of police psychologists; in many departments, counseling for officers involved in shooting incidents is mandatory (Hatch, 2002). The goals of this counseling, which often also relies on peer support, are to reassure officers that their emotional reactions to incidents are normal, to give them a safe place to express these emotions, to help them reduce stress, and to promote a timely return to duty. Many departments also try to make counseling services available to family members of officers who have been involved in traumatic incidents.

There are several ethical considerations involved in psychological counseling for police officers (D'Agostino, 1986), and some of the most difficult concern confidentiality. Police counseling services are usually offered in one of two ways: by an in-house psychologist who is a full-time employee of the police department, or by an outside psychologist who consults with the department on a part-time basis. In-house professionals are more readily available and more knowledgeable about police issues. Outside consultants, because of their independence from the department, may be better able to protect the confidentiality of their clients' disclosures.

POLICE–COMMUNITY RELATIONS

Police officers are justified in feeling that they live in a "fishbowl." Their performance is constantly being reviewed by the courts and evaluated by the public. Several amendments to the U.S. Constitution impose limits on law enforcement officers; such limits are part of the first 10 amendments, known as the Bill of Rights. The Fourth Amendment protects against unreasonable search and seizure of persons or property. The Fifth Amendment provides guarantees for persons

accused of a crime; for example, no such person "shall be compelled in any criminal case to be a witness against himself, nor be deprived of life, liberty, or property, without due process of law." Limits on police activities are frequently reevaluated on the basis of current court interpretations of these amendments. These amendments also have implications for police procedures. Protection against "cruel and unusual punishment" is provided under the Eighth Amendment, and the Fourteenth Amendment guarantees all citizens "due process." These amendments also govern and constrain several police activities.

During the last 35 years, citizens' groups have often been critical of the police. Two types of concerns can be identified. The first deals with the manner in which the police perform certain duties (e.g., arrests and interrogations); the second concerns the prevalence of police brutality.

Historically, the interrogation practices used by the police to elicit confessions from suspects have been a major focus of concern. Police are often criticized for using manipulative tactics to induce confessions from suspects. The most common approach is "to overwhelm the suspect with damaging evidence, to assert a firm belief in his or her guilt, and then to suggest that it would be easier for all concerned if the suspect admitted to his or her role in the crime" (Kassin & Wrightsman, 1985, p. 75). Along with this tactic, police often express concern for the suspect's welfare. Undue physical force is used far less than in the past, but promises of lowered bail, reduced charges, and leniency by the judge, as well as vague threats about harsher treatment, are common. These techniques are sometimes supplemented with exaggerated or trumped-up evidence to scare suspects into confessing (Kassin & Kiechel, 1996). In the post-9/11 environment, the balance between public safety and citizen rights has shifted somewhat. It is challenging—but very important—to see that neither is overwhelmed by the other, and that our efforts to ensure public safety in a free society do not result in behavior that adversely affects the rights of citizens in an important way.

A police technique that has caused widespread concern more recently is racial profiling—the practice of making traffic arrests of a larger percentage of minority than nonminority motorists. Although some law enforcement officials have defended this procedure as a reasonable crime control tool, the public outcry over its potential for abuse has led several states to abandon it. Termed "Driving While Black," the phenomenon of police being more likely to stop African-American drivers is highly problematic, and creates major concerns regarding equal protection under the law for motorists of all races and ethnic groups. There is some evidence that this phenomenon is stronger in local communities than state highway patrols (Warren, Tomaskovic-Devey, Smith, Zingraff, & Mason, 2006).

The second major concern of some community groups is excessive force or brutality by the police (Holmes & Smith, 2008). During the protests of the 1960s that took place in Watts (a section of Los Angeles), in Detroit, and throughout the South, massive demonstrations were held by American citizens, mostly African Americans, against what they believed was racially motivated harassment by the police.

The police officer has come to be viewed in predominantly African-American neighborhoods as a representative of a member of an "out-group," subject to distortions in the same respect that many police officers may view lower socioeconomic status (SES) urban minority citizens in a unitary fashion (Holmes & Smith, 2008). Part of this perception involves the

history of overwhelming authority and power exerted by White males in the United States. Although law enforcement officers are trained to act within legally prescribed boundaries and to do so equally toward all citizens, charges of "police brutality" have continued as concerns in the United States. In 2000, the U.S. Civil Rights Commission, an independent, bipartisan agency established by Congress, reviewed the findings of its 1981 report on police practices and concluded that many of its 1981 findings still applied in alleged police brutality, harassment, and misconduct toward people of color, women, and the poor.

In the past 20 years, the beating or killing of suspects by the police again commanded national attention. For example, the spotlight shone on five New Orleans police officers who, in the aftermath of Hurricane Katrina, were captured on film beating a Black man in the French Quarter and subsequently convicted of criminal charges in this beating. Another particularly vivid case—also involving police brutality filmed by a bystander—involved Rodney King and a 1991 case in Los Angeles (see Box 4.2).

More recent events suggest that the King case was not an isolated incident; minority citizens can point to other cases justifying their concerns that

Box 4.2   THE CASE OF RODNEY KING: VIDEOTAPED POLICE BRUTALITY?

In March 1991, police chased a Black motorist who they alleged was speeding through a Los Angeles suburb in his 1988 Hyundai. As the unarmed man emerged from his car, a police officer felled him with a blast from a 50,000-volt stun gun, and three patrolmen proceeded to beat and kick him while a police helicopter hovered overhead. As a result of this attack, which was witnessed by at least 11 other police onlookers, Rodney King—a 25-year-old man who, it was later learned, was on parole—lay seriously injured with multiple skull fractures, a broken ankle, a cracked cheekbone, and several internal injuries.

The violent arrest of Rodney King

One special feature of this attack was that a nearby citizen captured the entire episode on his video camera; within hours, the tape of this terrifying beating was played across the country on network news programs. Soon thereafter, local, state, and federal agencies launched investigations into the beating and into the entire LAPD. Three of the four officers who were charged with beating King were initially acquitted of all criminal charges, an outcome that shocked millions of Americans. But in a second trial, brought in federal court, two of the officers were found guilty of depriving King of his civil rights and were sentenced to prison.

King was awarded $3.8 million in a civil case and used part of this money to start a record label. He has, since then, been involved with the police on several other occasions, involving several arrests and sentences to prison. King's latest television appearance was on the second season of Celebrity Rehab with Dr. Drew, which premiered in October 2008.

Critical Thought Question
What are the advantages and disadvantages of using physical force in apprehending offenders?

they are often not treated fairly by the police (Weitzer & Tuch, 1999). In 2001, the shooting and killing of Timothy Thomas by Cincinnati police officers sparked riots followed by days of civil unrest (Larson, 2004). In a two-month period prior to the shooting, Thomas, a 19-year-old African-American man, was pulled over a total of 21 times and ticketed for either not wearing a seat belt or driving without a license. Then, in the early morning hours of April 7, 2001, a police officer, who reportedly recognized Thomas from having ticketed him, spotted him outside a local nightclub. When the officer approached Thomas, he ran. The officer called for backup, stating that he was chasing a suspect who had approximately 14 warrants. Thomas ran into a dark alley and the officer followed, firing a single shot that killed Thomas. The officer reported shooting because Thomas was reaching for a gun, but no gun was ever found.

Other cases publicized in the national media include the sodomy and torture of Abner Louima, which we described earlier; the shooting and killing of Amadou Diallo, a West African immigrant, by four plainclothes New York City police officers; and the shooting of Javier Francisco Ovando by two Los Angeles police officers, who then planted a gun on the paralyzed victim to frame him for a crime he did not commit. Even the U.S. Supreme Court has found it necessary to restrict the use of deadly force by police (see Box 4.3).

How can we explain incidents in which officers have used excessive force? One popular explanation is that police excesses stem from the personality problems of a "few bad apples." In this view, brutality reflects extreme aggressiveness and toughness of an authoritarian personality. A contrasting explanation is that brutality is the unfortunate price occasionally paid for situations in which rising numbers of violent, even deadly, criminals demand forceful responses from the police. A third explanation is that police brutality reflects a fundamental sociological pathology—that the deep strains of racism are still apparent in society.

Police brutality is another example of a problem for which psychology seeks explanations in the *interactions* between persons and the situations in which they function, rather than simply in the individual's characteristics or the situational influences. From this perspective, we begin with police officers who typically are strongly committed to maintaining the conventional order and to protecting society. We repeatedly put them into potentially dangerous situations, we arm them well, we urge them to be "tough on crime," and we train and authorize them to use appropriate force. The result of mixing this type of person with these types of situations is not surprising: In some encounters, the police will use excessive force against citizens who are suspected of wrongdoing that threatens public safety. In addition, police justifications for extreme force can be motivated by stereotypes, mistaken information, and the mutual mistrust that can develop between individuals from different cultural and ethnic backgrounds.

B o x 4.3 THE CASE OF EDWARD GARNER AND LIMITS ON THE USE OF DEADLY FORCE

In the 1985 case of *Tennessee v. Garner*, the U.S. Supreme Court struck down a Tennessee law that allowed police to shoot to kill, even when an unarmed suspect fleeing a crime scene posed no apparent threat. In October 1974, Edward Garner, then 15, fled when the police arrived just after he had broken the window of an unoccupied house. He was pursued by Officer Elton Hymon.

As Garner scaled a 6-foot fence at the back of the property, Officer Hymon yelled, "Police—halt!" Garner didn't halt, and Officer Hymon, knowing that he was in no shape to catch the fleeing youth, shot and killed him with a bullet to the back of the head.

Garner's father sued public officials and the city of Memphis, alleging that the police had violated his son's civil rights by the use of excessive force. The city defended itself on the basis of a state statute giving peace officers the right to use deadly force if necessary to stop a fleeing felon. The lower courts agreed with the city, but 11 years later the U.S. Supreme Court struck down the statute in a 6–3 decision (*Tennessee v. Garner*, 1985).

The majority held that shooting a person, even one suspected of a felony, violates that person's Fourth Amendment right to be free from unreasonable searches and seizures. The majority opinion added, however, that deadly force would be justified if the officer had reason to believe that the suspect posed an immediate threat to him or others.

Critical Thought Question
Should facilitating capture of a suspect be justification for using deadly force?

As it turns out, many episodes of police brutality occur following high-speed chases, when (as with Rodney King) police react with violence after pursuing a suspect they consider belligerent or threatening. In a 2000 incident that has been compared to the Rodney King beating, three Philadelphia police officers punched and kicked one man 59 times in 28 seconds while trying to arrest him (Associated Press, 2000). In such tension-charged situations, police are prone to let their emotions dictate their actions. Some police departments are now concentrating on the problem of high-speed pursuits as triggers for police overreaction. They try to teach police to remain focused during these incidents, maintaining the discipline instilled in their training and not responding primarily out of fear or anger.

Since the 1970s, but particularly since the Rodney King episode, a number of attempts have been made to improve police relations with people in the community, especially in neighborhoods with large numbers of ethnic minorities. Over the years, the LAPD has changed from what African Americans referred to as an "occupation force of hardliners" into an organization that actively courts and wins support from its African-American and Latino populations. (This transformation is described in attorney Connie Rice's 2012 book, *Power Concedes Nothing: One Woman's Quest for Social Justice in America.*)

We have already described team policing as one effort to make the police officer's job less stressful and to respond to some community concerns about the way police perform. One important innovation in police work during the last 35 years is **community-based policing**. In this approach, police officers develop a proactive, problem-solving approach with active collaboration from local citizens who support the police in the effort to combat crime, promote safety, and enhance the overall quality of neighborhoods. This type of policing was designed to enhance the working relationship between the police and the public (Zhao, Lovrich, & Thurman, 1999).

In most versions of community policing, there are more foot patrols by officers who stay in the same neighborhoods. As a result, community-based policing seeks to humanize police and citizens in one another's eyes and to broaden the roles that police play in a community. For example, Chicago's version of community policing contains six basic features (Lurigio & Skogan, 1994):

1. *A neighborhood orientation*, in which officers forge friendships with individual residents in a community, identify the "hot spots" for crime, and develop partnerships with community organizations for fighting crime.

2. *Increased geographic responsibility*, which means that officers regularly walk a given neighborhood "beat" and become highly visible, well-known experts about problems in that area.

3. *A structured response to calls for police service*, in which emergency calls are handled by a special-response team, thereby permitting beat officers to stay available for routine calls and maintain a high-profile presence.

4. *A proactive, problem-oriented approach*, whereby more effort is devoted to crime prevention (e.g., closing down drug houses, breaking up groups of loitering youth) than to responding to discrete disturbances or criminal activities.

5. *Brokering more community resources for crime prevention*, as police enlist the help of other city agencies to identify and respond to local community problems.

6. *Analysis of crime problems*, which enables officers to focus their attention on the highest-risk areas by using computer technology to keep accurate track of crime patterns.

Some opponents of the practice have criticized community policing as expensive and as seeking to turn police officers into "social workers with guns" (Worsnop, 1993). Nonetheless, as of 2003, according to the Bureau of Justice Statistics,

- 58% of all departments used full-time community policing officers.

- 60% of departments had problem-solving partnerships or written agreements with community groups, local agencies, or others.

- 43% of departments used full-time school-resource officers.

- 74% of local police departments provided crime prevention education to citizens.

- 37% of residents in 12 cities reported seeing police talking with residents in their neighborhood, and 24% of respondents reporting seeing police facilitating crime watch and prevention activities.

Does community policing work, or is it long on rhetoric but short on success? As with most social

Community policing is a philosophy designed to increase the amount and quality of specific police officers' contact with citizens and to involve police more in crime prevention and community maintenance activities

reform projects, the results have been mixed. Some cities that have introduced community-policing initiatives report large improvements in the public's attitude toward their police departments (Adams, Rohe, & Arcury, 2005; Peak, Bradshaw, & Glensor, 1992) and sizable reductions in rates of serious crimes.

Residents of small to midsize cities were questioned about the effects of community-oriented policing. Findings revealed that awareness of this type of policing, compared to more conventional policing focused on arresting offenders, was associated with greater self-protection efforts (e.g., putting bars on windows), lower fear of crime, and stronger feelings of attachment to the community (Adams et al., 2005). This finding held regardless of the respondents' history of victimization; participants associated community-oriented policing with a lower fear of crime even when they had previously been a victim of crime.

In the early 1990s, the city of Chicago reorganized its police force to incorporate community policing. In a study of the impact of this program, Skogan (2006) considered its impact on crime, neighborhood residents, and the police. The 13-year study revealed distinctive problems for African-American, White, and Latino citizens. Skogan described very substantial improvements in the city's predominately African-American districts, where crime and fear dropped significantly. The city's largely White neighborhoods were already supportive of police, but they also made significant gains in these areas. However, for Latinos, there were differences according to whether the neighborhood contained long-term residents and had been integrated for some time (good outcomes), or comprised predominantly Spanish-speaking people (poorer outcomes on crime, disorder, and neighborhood decay). Although the overall results were promising, it will be important to find a way to assist the city's newest citizens.

Other evaluations indicate that police officers themselves remain skeptical about community policing. In Chicago's program, police officers initially doubted that community-based policing would reduce crime or improve relationships with racial minorities, and believed it would require more work on their part and possibly undercut their authority in the community (Lurigio & Skogan, 1994). In general, police administrators endorse the value of community policing and believe that its advantages (improved physical environment, more positive attitudes toward police, fewer citizen complaints) outweigh its disadvantages (displacement of crime to a non-community-policing area, more opportunities for officer corruption, resistance from rank-and-file officers).

SUMMARY

1. *What is the role of the police in our society?* Policing is necessary in any society concerned with maintaining public order, even though it is important in a democratic society to balance public safety with civil liberties and criminal rights. Police officers daily face the dilemma of equality versus discretion: whether to treat all suspects or lawbreakers equally or to temper justice with mercy.

2. *What procedures are used to select police?* Selection of police officers usually includes the completion of psychological tests and a clinical interview. Another assessment device is the use of situational tests, in which the candidate role-plays responses to real-life challenges that would face a police officer, such as intervening in a dispute between a wife and her husband or writing an incident report. Although responses to these situational

tasks are valuable additions to psychological testing and interviewing, they are also costly and time-consuming.

3. ***How has the training of police officers expanded into new areas?*** Training of police officers usually involves a variety of activities, including criminal law, human relations training, self-defense, and the use of firearms. Most training programs last at least six months. Police officers are now frequently trained in crisis intervention, including handling situations involving individuals with mentally illness, resolving family disputes, and responding to hostage-taking situations.

4. ***Describe the different activities of the police. Is law enforcement central?*** The police officer's job is multifaceted. Law enforcement (including investigation of complaints, arrest and prosecution of suspects, and efforts at crime prevention) accounts for only about 10% of police activity. Maintaining order (intervening in family and neighborhood disputes, keeping traffic moving, responding to disturbances of the peace) accounts

for about 30% of police activity. Providing social services to the community is even more time-consuming.

5. ***What stressors do the police face?*** Three problems are especially significant: the "life in a fish-bowl" phenomenon, job-related stress, and burnout. Job duties and perceptions of police work can be modified to reduce burnout. Special psychological interventions are also available to counteract stress reactions experienced by the police.

6. ***What is the relationship between the police and the communities they serve?*** Some community groups have been critical of police behavior, focusing on unequal and sometimes brutal treatment of the poor and racial minorities. Efforts to improve police–community relations include team policing, crisis intervention training, reorganization of the police department that restructures the traditional chain of command, and community-based policing. These interventions have had some success.

KEY TERMS

bioterrorism

burnout

community-based policing

Crisis Intervention Team

fitness-for-duty evaluation

jail diversion programs

learned helplessness

predictive validity

Stockholm syndrome

structured interviews

suicide by cop

team policing

terrorism

validity scales

zero tolerance

Chapter
5

Eyewitnesses to Crimes and Accidents

ORIENTING QUESTIONS

1. What psychological factors contribute to the risk of mistaken identifications in the legal system?

2. What are the defining features of estimator, system, and postdiction variables in the study of eyewitness memory?

3. How do jurors evaluate the testimony of eyewitnesses, and how can psychological research help jurors understand the potential problems of eyewitness testimony?

4. Can children accurately report on their experiences of victimization? What factors affect the accuracy of their reports? Are they likely to disclose abuse?

5. Can memories for trauma be repressed, and if so, can these memories be recovered accurately?

The police investigate crimes and accumulate evidence so that suspects can be identified and arrested. At the early stages of an investigation, eyewitnesses to those crimes provide important information to police, sometimes the only solid leads. Eyewitnesses also play a vital role in later stages of a prosecution. According to defense attorney David Feige, "It's hard to overstate the power of eyewitness testimony in criminal cases. In thousands of cases every year, testimony of a single eyewitness, uncorroborated by forensic or any other evidence, is used to sustain serious felony charges, including robbery and murder" (Feige, 2006). The National Institute of Justice estimates that approximately 75,000 defendants are implicated by eyewitnesses in the United States every year (Department of Justice, 1999).

But in their attempts to solve crimes—and especially in their reliance on eyewitness observers—police and prosecutors face a number of challenges.

Although many eyewitnesses provide accurate reports, some make mistakes. The recollections of eyewitnesses can lead the police down blind alleys or cause them to arrest the wrong suspect, sometimes resulting in wrongful convictions by judges and juries. A study of actual eyewitness identification attempts showed that one in five eyewitnesses selected an innocent person (Valentine, Pickering, & Darling, 2003).

It is now apparent that eyewitness errors create problems for the justice system (and for the people mistakenly identified!). DNA procedures developed in the 1980s make it possible to take a new look at evidence left at a crime scene. Unfortunately, only a small fraction of crimes—most notably sexual assaults—have DNA-rich evidence, although even when DNA is present, it is often not tested or is destroyed. In 2009, the Supreme Court ruled that states are not required to make DNA evidence available to convicted offenders (*District Attorney's Office for Third Judicial District v. Osborne*, 2009). As a result, many wrongly convicted people have no way to prove their innocence.

When DNA testing is conducted, it sometimes reveals that the person convicted of a crime and incarcerated—sometimes for decades—was not the actual perpetrator. Further analysis of the evidence in these cases often shows that eyewitness errors are to blame. They are a leading cause of wrongful convictions, particularly in sexual assaults and robberies. According to the National Registry on Exonerations, which documented 2000 exonerations between 1989 and 2012, 80% of the exonerations for rapes and robberies involved mistaken eyewitness identifications. According to the Innocence Project, the largest and most prominent organization devoted to proving wrongful convictions, mistaken identifications account for more wrongful convictions than do false confessions, problems with snitches, and defective or fraudulent science combined (Innocence Project, 2008).

Concern about eyewitnesses' accuracy is not restricted to criminal cases or to the identification of persons. The results of civil lawsuits are also often affected by the reports of eyewitnesses (Terrell & Weaver, 2008), and law enforcement officials know that eyewitness descriptions of unusual events cannot always be trusted. Consider the reports from eyewitnesses to the assassination of President Abraham Lincoln, as documented by historian Bruce Catton. All witnesses agreed that John Wilkes Booth pulled the trigger and then leaped from the presidential box where Lincoln was seated and onto the stage. But their descriptions of Booth's actions from that point vary widely:

> … he made a 15-foot leap, ran swiftly off-stage, and vanished … he slid down a flagpole (which did not actually exist), and more or less crept away … [he limped] painfully across the stage moaning incoherently … [he stalked] off calmly, dropping his "*Sic semper tyrannis*" as a good actor might … [he ran] furiously, saying nothing at all … he went off-stage on his hands and knees, making noises … (Catton, 1965, p. 105)

EXAMPLES OF MISTAKEN EYEWITNESS IDENTIFICATION

Cases of wrongful convictions based on faulty eyewitness testimony abound. The ordeal of Calvin C. Johnson, Jr., is a good example. Johnson, a college graduate with a job at Delta Airlines, spent 16 years behind bars for a rape he did not commit. He is not alone. In fact, Johnson was the 61st person in the United States to be exonerated through the use of DNA testing. Tests in Johnson's case proved definitively that he was not the man who raped and sodomized a College Park, Georgia, woman in 1983. Yet the victim picked Johnson out of a photographic lineup and identified him as the rapist at trial. The all-White jury convicted Johnson, who is Black, despite the fact that forensic tests excluded him as the source of a pubic hair recovered from the victim's bed. The jury also apparently chose to disregard the testimony of four alibi witnesses who claimed that Johnson was home asleep at the time. One of the jurors stated that the victim's eyewitness testimony had been the most compelling evidence in the case.

One reason why mistakes are so common is that when eyewitnesses make a tentative identification, police often stop investigating other leads and instead look for further evidence that implicates the chosen suspect. This is an example of **confirmation bias**, whereby people look for, interpret, and create information that verifies an existing belief. In terms of eyewitness identification, the goal of finding the truth is neglected, often unintentionally, in a rush to solve the crime. In Johnson's case, police pushed ahead with the case even after the victim picked someone else at a live lineup (conducted after the photographic lineup). She testified at trial that she had picked the wrong person at the live lineup because looking at Johnson was too much for her: "I just pushed my eyes away and picked someone else," she reported (Boyer, 2000). We chronicle another example of mistaken identification that led to a wrongful conviction and imprisonment, the case of Cornelius Dupree, in Box 5.1.

You might think that people like Calvin Johnson and Cornelius Dupree would have some recourse—that they could get something back for the time they lost in prison. But only 27 states have laws that compensate the wrongly imprisoned, such financial compensation is generally small, and social service assistance is rare. Dupree was lucky: he is eligible for $80,000 per year he spent behind bars as well as job training, tuition credits, and access to medical care. Johnson was not so lucky: he received nothing because Georgia did not have a law providing compensation for people who were wrongly convicted. Unfortunately, many exonerees leave prison with

---

B o x 5.1 THE CASE OF CORNELIUS DUPREE: STICKING WITH THE TRUTH FOR 30 YEARS

Cornelius Dupree, left, prior to testifying at a hearing in which a judge declared him innocent of the crime for which he served 30 years in prison

In Texas, the state that has exonerated more inmates by DNA evidence than any other, Cornelius Dupree waited longer than anyone else—30 years, to be exact—to have his taste of freedom. Dupree was convicted of a 1979 rape and robbery in Dallas in which two men kidnapped a young woman and her male companion in the parking lot of a grocery store, forcing them into the male's car and robbing them as he drove. They eventually released the man and raped the woman in a nearby park. Ten days later, Dupree and a friend were on their way to a party approximately two miles from the grocery when they were stopped and frisked. Their pictures ended up in photo arrays and the female victim identified Dupree as one of the perpetrators. He was convicted and sentenced to 75 years in prison.

Dupree had at least two chances to be paroled and granted his freedom during his years of incarceration, but he had to admit to being a sex offender and attend a treatment program. Successful completion of the program required Dupree to recognize and accept responsibility for the offense, something he simply could not do. "Whatever your truth is, you have to stick with it," stated Dupree shortly after a Dallas judge overturned his conviction in 2011. More than a dozen exonerated former inmates attended Dupree's hearing, welcoming him into their ill-starred club. Fortunately for these men, the Texas legislature passed a generous compensation law in 2009, and the new Dallas district attorney has vowed to cooperate with defense attorneys requesting DNA testing in cases involving other inmates.

Critical Thought Question
What factors may have contributed to Dupree's conviction?

"next to nothing" (Clow, Leach, & Ricciardelli, 2012, p. 330). One commentator has suggested that the new crime is how little some of these lost lives are worth (Higgins, 1999).

HOW MISTAKEN EYEWITNESS IDENTIFICATIONS OCCUR

Mistakes in the process of identification can occur the moment the crime is committed. It may be too dark, events may move too swiftly, or the encounter may be too brief for the victim to perceive the incident accurately. These conditions diminish memory strength. Yet when they are questioned by police, victims are asked to give their impressions of the criminal's height, hair color, voice, and other identifying features. When such descriptions are inaccurate, they hinder the investigation, though *accurate* descriptions can lead

to correct identifications (Meissner, Sporer, & Susa, 2008).

Mistakes can also occur during the investigation of a crime. Police often ask eyewitnesses to examine a series of photos (called a **photographic lineup** or **photospread**) or a physical lineup of suspects and decide whether the perpetrator is present. At this point, eyewitnesses want to help the police solve the crime; they may feel implicit pressure to identify someone, and are likely to assume that the perpetrator is in the lineup. Although accurate identifications are more likely than inaccurate identifications, we know that innocent people are sometimes selected and guilty people are sometimes overlooked.

During trial, jurors may watch an eyewitness confidently identify the defendant as the perpetrator. Not only will they assume that this identification is accurate, but they will also assume that the victim was confident about the initial description or identification of the perpetrator. These assumptions fail to recognize the many problems that can undermine

Sketches based on eyewitnesses' recollections

the accuracy of a criminal identification. We describe several such problems in this chapter.

The study of eyewitness identification grew out of our understanding of the basic principles involved in perception and memory. We are all prone to making errors in perceiving and remembering events that we experience. But eyewitnesses must remember experiences that are typically brief, complicated, and sometimes very frightening. So they are especially prone to error. To illustrate these errors, we consider the steps involved in acquiring and recalling information from the outside world—steps an eyewitness must take to record a memory.

BASIC INFORMATION PROCESSING

We have all had the experience of greeting someone we recognize, only to realize that we were wrong—that the person is actually a stranger. Similar mistakes can be made when crimes are observed. To process information about a crime, we must first perceive a stimulus and then retain it in our minds at least momentarily. But failures and errors can emerge along the way.

Perception

Although our perceptual abilities are impressive (Penrod, Loftus, & Winkler, 1982), we do make errors. We tend to overestimate the height of criminals. We overestimate the duration of brief events and underestimate the duration of prolonged incidents. When watching a short film, we notice more about the actions than about the persons doing the acting.

If a weapon is present when a crime is committed, we may devote more attention to it than to the facial features or other physical aspects of the person who has the weapon. This **weapon focus effect** appears to be caused by **selective attention**: because we have limited attentional capacity and cannot process all of the stimuli available at a given time, we unconsciously select what information to attend to. The threatening aspect of a weapon draws witnesses' attention (Hope & Wright, 2007). This limits the amount of attention they can pay to other aspects of the situation, such as physical features of the perpetrator (Pickel, 2009).

The presence of a weapon can also affect the processing of auditory information. Professor Kerri Pickel and her colleagues showed a film of a man holding either a weapon (e.g., a gun, a switchblade knife) or a neutral object (e.g., a soda pop bottle, a ballpoint pen) and speaking to a woman in such a way that his words were either easy or difficult to understand (Pickel, French, & Betts, 2003). Witnesses had difficulty understanding the man's speech in the latter condition, and the presence of a weapon further impaired their comprehension. A reasonable explanation is that their focus on the weapon and their attempt at language comprehension competed for limited processing time. They had a hard time doing both things at once. In general, when people must divide their attention between two or more stimuli, they are more suggestible (Lane, 2006).

Memory

Cognitive psychologists subdivide the building of a memory into three processes: encoding, storage, and retrieval. We describe the memory of eyewitnesses in each of these three stages.

Encoding. **Encoding** refers to the acquisition of information. Many aspects of a stimulus can affect how it is encoded; stimuli that are only briefly seen or heard cannot be encoded fully, of course. The complexity of a stimulus also affects its encoding. As the complexity of an event increases (consider an earthquake, explosion, or tsunami), some aspects of the event probably will be misremembered, while others will be accurately recalled.

Contrary to what many people believe, a stressful situation does not necessarily enhance the encoding of events. Although mild stress or arousal may indeed

AP photo/Carl Court/PA Wire URN:5529463

heighten alertness and interest in a task, extreme stress usually causes the person to encode the information incompletely or inaccurately (Deffenbacher, Bornstein, Penrod, & McGorty, 2004). Performance on many tasks is best when the level of arousal is sufficient to ensure adequate attention but not so high as to disrupt accuracy.

A study of the accuracy of eyewitness memory in highly stressful military survival school interrogations provides good evidence of the effects of stress on memory (Morgan et al., 2004). Survival school interrogations are one of the greatest training challenges that active duty military personnel experience. (These interrogations are intended to test one's ability to withstand exploitation by the enemy, and to train people to hold up under the physical and mental stresses of capture.) Participants in this study were 500 soldiers, sailors, and pilots who were placed in mock prisoner of war (POW) camps and deprived of food and sleep for approximately 48 hours prior to interrogation. During 40 minutes of intense questioning, half of them were physically threatened and all participants were tricked into giving away information. One day later, they were asked to identify their interrogators from an eight-picture photographic lineup (chance accuracy is therefore 1/8, or 12.5%). The results were startling. Among soldiers who experienced moderate stress without the threat of physical injury, 76% were correct in identifying the target. But only 34% of participants who experienced the high stress of a physically threatening situation were correct.

Characteristics of the witness also affect encoding in a variety of ways. The effects of stress are felt more acutely by those higher in anxiety and neuroticism (Reisberg & Heuer, 2007). We all differ in visual acuity and hearing ability. When we have experience perceiving a stimulus we usually notice its details better than when we perceive something new. This is why experienced judges notice flaws in a gymnast's performance that the rest of us can detect only in a slow-motion replay. Different expectancies about upcoming events also influence how they are encoded; in general, we have a tendency to see what we expect to see.

Storage. The second step in building a memory is the **storage** of stimulus information. How well do we retain what we encode? Many years ago, psychologist Hermann Ebbinghaus showed that memory loss is rapid. This is important for eyewitness accuracy

because it is likely that some time will pass between the commission of a crime and police questioning of eyewitnesses. In one study, eyewitnesses attempted to recall details of a video one, three, or five weeks after viewing it. Eyewitnesses who recalled the video for the first time five weeks after seeing it were significantly less accurate than eyewitnesses who attempted recall after one or three weeks, supporting the notion that memory fades as the **retention interval**, the period of time between viewing an event and being questioned about it, increases (Odinot & Wolters, 2006). Meta-analyses of 53 studies showed that the longer the retention interval, the more memory loss for previously seen faces (Deffenbacher, Bornstein, McGorty, & Penrod, 2008).

A second phenomenon—both surprising and concerning—also occurs during the storage phase. Activities that eyewitnesses carry out or information they learn after they observe an event, termed **post-event information**, can alter their memory of the event. For example, simply talking to other witnesses can introduce new (not always accurate) details into one's memory. A study of actual eyewitnesses at an identification unit in the United Kingdom showed that 88% of cases involved multiple eyewitnesses (Skagerberg & Wright, 2008), suggesting that an exchange of information during the retention interval is a real possibility. We know that most witnesses *do* share information about serious events such as crimes. A survey of Australian undergraduates who witnessed actual assaults or robberies revealed that 86% discussed the event with co-witnesses (Paterson & Kemp, 2006).

The now-classic studies of Elizabeth Loftus (1975, 1979) showed how exposure to post-event information can affect memory. In one study, participants viewed a film of an automobile accident and were asked questions about it. The first question asked either how fast the car was going "when it ran the stop sign" or how fast it was going "when it turned right." Then all subjects were asked whether they had seen a stop sign in the film. In the first group, which had been asked about the speed of the car "when it ran the stop sign," 53% said they had seen a stop sign, whereas only 35% of the second group said they had seen the sign. The effect of the initial question was to "prompt" a memory for the sign. In a second study, Loftus included a misleading follow-up question that mentioned a nonexistent barn. When questioned one week later, 17% of the subjects reported seeing the barn in the original film.

In essence, the new information conveyed as part of a question was added to the memory of the original stimulus. Not surprisingly, post-event information that conforms to one's beliefs is more likely to be integrated into memory (Luna & Migueles, 2008).

Viewing photographs of suspects after witnessing a crime can also impair an eyewitness's ability to recognize the perpetrator's face in a lineup. According to a recent meta-analysis, exposure to photographs reduces both correct identifications (identifying the actual perpetrator when he is present in the lineup) and correct rejections (rejecting the choices in a lineup when the perpetrator is absent), and increases false alarms (identifying someone who is not the perpetrator) (Deffenbacher, Bornstein, & Penrod, 2006). The case of Larry Fuller, described in Box 5.2, provides an example of the effects of post-event exposure to photographs.

Retrieval. The third and final step in establishing memory is the **retrieval** of information. This process is not as straightforward as it might seem. The wording of questions can influence retrieval. For example, consider the question "What was the man with the mustache doing with the young boy?" Assume that the man in question had no mustache. This form of the question may influence memory of the man's appearance. Later, if asked to describe the man, eyewitnesses may incorporate the detail (in this case, the mustache) that was embedded in the original question (Leippe, Eisenstadt, Rauch, & Stambush, 2006). Repeated retrieval procedures—for example, searching

through a series of mug shots before viewing a lineup or seeing a suspect at various pretrial hearings—can increase an eyewitness's susceptibility to suggestion (Chan & LaPaglia, 2011) and inflate a witness's confidence (Odinot, Wolters, & Lavender, 2009).

In recalling information from our memory, we often generate memories that are accurate but are not relevant to the task at hand. Victims sometimes pick from a lineup the person whom they have seen before but who is not the actual criminal. For example, a clerk at a convenience store who is the victim of a late-night robbery may mistakenly identify an innocent shopper who frequents the store. In an actual case, a Los Angeles judge who was kidnapped and attacked while jogging picked a suspect's picture from a photographic lineup. She later stated that she had forgotten that the suspect appeared before her in court for similar offenses four years earlier, and that she had sentenced him to unsupervised probation (Associated Press, 1988). This phenomenon is called **unconscious transference** (not to be confused with the psychoanalytic notion of transference in a therapeutic context). It is one reason that innocent persons are sometimes charged with a crime and eventually convicted.

How Psychologists Study Eyewitness Identification

We have already described studies of various influences on eyewitness memory. We now expand on three

---

Box 5.2 THE CASE OF LARRY FULLER AND THE VICTIM WHO "NEVER WAVERED"

Six o'clock on a foggy April morning in 1981, 45 minutes before sunrise in Dallas. A woman awakens to find a man with a knife atop her. The only light in the room comes from a digital alarm clock. The intruder cuts her and rapes her. Shortly afterwards, hospital personnel collect sperm in a rape kit. Two days later the victim looks at photographs of possible suspects; Larry Fuller's picture is among them. Because she cannot make an identification, the investigating officer recommends that the investigation be suspended. But other detectives persist, showing the victim a second photospread several days later. Importantly, Fuller's picture is the only one in the second photospread that was also in the first. At this point, the victim positively identifies him and he is arrested. Subsequent to a trial during which the prosecution claimed that the victim "never wavered," Fuller is convicted and sentenced to 50 years in prison.

Larry Fuller was 32 years old at the time, raising two young children. He had served two tours of duty in Vietnam where he was shot down several times. After being honorably discharged, he pursued a degree in the arts while working several jobs. From prison he petitioned the Innocence Project to take his case but the Dallas District Attorney's Office opposed requests for DNA testing, as it had done many times before. (That District Attorney has since been replaced.) After a judge ordered testing that excluded Fuller as the perpetrator, he became the 186th person exonerated through DNA analysis.

Critical Thought Question
Why would post-event exposure to Fuller's photograph increase the likelihood that the victim would identify him?

techniques that psychologists use to study eyewitness issues, and describe their advantages and disadvantages. Knowing how the studies are conducted can help you to understand what we can justifiably conclude from them.

Experimental methodology, in which a researcher stages a crime or shows a filmed crime to unsuspecting participant witnesses, is the primary research method. In an experiment, the researcher manipulates some variable (e.g., the presence or absence of an instruction to participant witnesses, prior to viewing a lineup, that the perpetrator "may or may not be in the lineup") and measures its effects (e.g., the likelihood of choosing someone from the lineup). The value of an experiment is that the researcher knows exactly what the witnesses experienced (termed **ground truth**) and can measure, fairly precisely, how the manipulated variable affected what the witnesses remember. In other words, an experiment can establish cause-and-effect relations. But any individual experiment may lack **ecological validity**, meaning that the study may not approximate the real-world conditions under which eyewitnesses observe crimes and police interact with eyewitnesses. Still, if a number of experiments conducted under varying conditions and with different populations tend to reach the same conclusion, we can be fairly certain that the result would apply to the "real world."

A second way to study eyewitness identification is via **archival analysis** that involves after-the-fact examination of actual cases. Archival analyses typically begin with proven wrongful convictions and examine features of the cases that could have led to the mistaken verdicts. A study of the first 200 exonerations based on DNA testing analyzed the evidence that apparently supported the convictions (e.g., eyewitness testimony, forensic evidence) (Garrett, 2008). Archival analyses have confirmed that inaccurate identifications occur when eyewitnesses choose a filler from the lineup (Pezdek, 2012). (Often, fillers are individuals who were incarcerated at the time of the crime.) The value of archival analysis is that it uses real-life situations as the backdrop; the disadvantage is that it can only document what happened in those cases and it cannot explain why.

Field studies combine the rigorous control of an experiment with the real-world setting of archival analyses. Field studies of eyewitness identification examine the procedures used by the police in actual cases. We describe a field study of lineup procedures later in this chapter. A field study may have more ecological validity than an experiment, but it also has a downside. Because

we cannot be certain whether a suspect is guilty or innocent, we cannot distinguish correct identifications of the guilty from incorrect identifications of the innocent.

THE VARIABLES THAT AFFECT EYEWITNESS ACCURACY

Building on the research on basic information processing and using these methodologies, psychologists have identified several other variables that can influence the validity of identifications. Professor Gary Wells, a prolific researcher in the area of eyewitness identification, introduced a useful taxonomy to categorize these variables (Wells, 1978). He coined the term **system variable** to refer to those factors that are under the control of the criminal justice system (e.g., the instructions given to eyewitnesses when they consider a lineup and the composition of that lineup). The term **estimator variable** refers to factors that are beyond the control of the justice system and whose impact on the reliability of the eyewitness can only be estimated (e.g., the lighting conditions at the time of the crime and whether the culprit was wearing a disguise). A third variable—a **postdiction variable**—does not directly affect the reliability of an identification, but is a measurement of some process that correlates with reliability (Wells et al., 2006). The confidence that a witness feels about an identification and the speed with which a witness identifies someone from a lineup are examples of postdiction variables.

Because system variables hold more promise for preventing errors in eyewitness identification (they are, after all, controllable), many psychologists have focused their research efforts on those variables. But research on estimator variables is important because it can help us understand situations in which eyewitnesses experience problems in perception and memory, and studies of postdiction variables allow an after-the-fact assessment of eyewitness accuracy. The next sections review these kinds of variables, all relevant in different ways to our understanding of the psychology of eyewitness identification.

Assessing the Impact of Estimator Variables

We have already described two estimator variables—the witness's stress level at the time of the crime and the presence of a weapon. Other factors also come into play.

Race of the Eyewitness. Eyewitnesses are usually better at recognizing and identifying members of their own race or ethnic group than members of another race or ethnic group. The chances of a mistaken identification have been estimated to be 1.56 times greater when the witness and suspect are of different races than when they are of the same race (Meissner & Brigham, 2001). This phenomenon, termed the **other-race effect**, has been examined extensively in experimental studies involving a variety of racial groups, and archival analysis of DNA exoneration cases shows that it is also a significant problem in actual cases.

Understanding the reasons for the other-race effect has vexed psychologists for some time. Racial attitudes are apparently not related to this phenomenon. (People with prejudicial attitudes are not more likely to experience the other-race effect than are people with unbiased attitudes). Recent explanations of the other-race effect have tended to involve both cognitive and social processes.

Cognitive interpretations hold that there are differences between faces of one race and faces of another race in terms of the variability in features, something called **physiognomic variability**. Faces of one race differ from faces of another race in terms of the *type* of physiognomic variability. For example, White faces show more variability in hair color, and Black faces show more variability in skin tone. For eyewitnesses to correctly identify members of other races, they must focus on the characteristics that distinguish that person from other people of the same race. Thus, Black eyewitnesses would be better off noticing and encoding a White perpetrator's hair color than her or his skin tone, whereas White eyewitnesses could more profitably pay attention to a Black assailant's skin tone. But most of us have more experience with members of our own race, so our natural inclination is to focus on the features that distinguish members of *our own group*. We have less practice distinguishing one member of another race from other people of that race.

These ideas are supported by studies involving sophisticated eye-movement monitoring technology to assess the encoding processes people adopt when viewing own-race and other-race faces. One study showed that we fixate on more, and more distinctive, features when viewing own-race faces than when viewing other-race faces (Goldinger, He, & Papesh, 2009).

Social psychologists have also tried to explain the other-race effect. One reasonable hypothesis is based on social perception and **in-group/out-group differences** (Sporer, 2001). When we encounter the face of a person from another race or ethnic group (the out-group), our first job is to categorize the face as a member of that group (e.g., "That person is Asian"). Attentional resources that are directed toward categorization come at the expense of attention to facial features that would distinguish that person from other members of the out-group. But when we encounter the face of a person from our in-group, the categorization step is eliminated, so we can immediately devote attention to distinguishing that person from other members of the in-group. Because identifying people of other races involves both a cognitive and a social process, both explanations may be right.

Age and Gender of the Eyewitness. Do males make better eyewitnesses than females and do young people make better eyewitnesses than older people? The age and gender of an eyewitness are also estimator variables; we can't control their influence but we can estimate them.

The evidence for gender effects is not overwhelming but tends to indicate an own-gender bias, at least for women. Women are better at recognizing female faces than male faces, whereas men recognize female and male faces equally well (Lewin & Herlitz, 2002).

There is stronger evidence that the age of the eyewitness matters: Older eyewitnesses and young children make more errors than younger and middle-aged adults (Wilcock, Bull, & Vrij, 2007). In addition, the errors of older adults and young children are fairly predictable. They are more likely to choose someone from a lineup from which the culprit is absent and, hence, make more mistaken identifications than young and middle-aged adults (Memon, Bartlett, Rose, & Gray, 2003). But when the lineup contains the culprit, young children and elderly people perform as well as adults. We describe the issues associated with children as witnesses later in the chapter.

Controlling the Impact of System Variables

System variables are those factors in an identification over which the justice system has some control.

In general, system variables tend to come into play after the crime, usually during the investigation. They are associated with how a witness is questioned and how a lineup is constructed and shown to the eyewitness. We have already described two system variables: the influence of post-event information and the effects of questions posed to eyewitnesses. Other system variables are also important. Research on these variables can suggest changes to procedures that investigators use with eyewitnesses.

To explain why system variables and procedures are so important, it may be helpful to draw an analogy to the steps used by researchers doing an experiment (Wells & Luus, 1990). Like scientists, crime investigators begin with a hypothesis (that the suspect actually committed the crime); test the hypothesis (by placing the suspect in a lineup); observe and record the eyewitness's decision; and draw conclusions from the results (e.g., that the suspect was the assailant).

There are certain principles that are essential to good experimental design (e.g., that observers should be unbiased), and violation of those principles affects the usefulness of the experiment's findings. In similar fashion, violating the principles of good criminal investigation affects the results of the investigation. For example, if the suspect appears to be different from the other people in the lineup in some obvious way, or if the person conducting the lineup conveys his or her suspicions to the eyewitness, then the results of that identification procedure can be erroneous. Applying the analogy of an experiment to criminal investigations enables us to evaluate critically the steps involved in these investigations.

REFORMING IDENTIFICATION PROCEDURES

One important aspect of a system variable is that because it is controllable, it can be modified. Because the police want to catch the real culprits and avoid mistakes, they have begun, in recent years, to incorporate procedures recommended by psychologists and others for interviewing eyewitnesses and constructing and presenting lineups. For example, in 1999 the U.S. Department of Justice (DOJ) recommended procedures for collecting eyewitness evidence that were based on psychological research studies. Several state courts have imposed requirements for eyewitness

evidence or restrictions on its use on the basis of social science findings.

The pace of reform will probably speed up in light of a landmark decision by the New Jersey Supreme Court in 2011 (*State v. Henderson*, 2011), issuing in a new set of rules for cases involving eyewitness identifications. Informed by a yearlong study of the scientific research on eyewitness identification by a retired judge, the decision lists more than a dozen factors—many described in this chapter—that judges should consider in evaluating the reliability of an eyewitness's identification. They include the presence of a weapon, other-race identification, length of the retention interval, and behavior of the police, among others. When a defendant presents evidence that a witness's identification may be unreliable, the judge must hold a hearing to consider the issues and must give detailed instructions to the jury about the pitfalls of eyewitness evidence. Because New Jersey was already at the forefront of reforms in identification cases, the decision is expected to have a nationwide impact (Weiser, 2011).

In the sections that follow, we describe some of the scientific findings on system variables that informed the New Jersey Supreme Court's decision. We also describe some of the reforms they suggest. You will notice that the proposed reforms (e.g., warning an eyewitness that the suspect may or may not be in the lineup) come with a trade-off: although they reduce the likelihood of mistaken identifications, they also reduce the likelihood of correct identifications. Whether people are primarily concerned about due process rights of criminal defendants or about crime control and the conviction of guilty offenders, as well as other complicated policy issues, will determine how they value this trade-off (Clark, 2012).

Interviewing Eyewitnesses

The police often want more information from eyewitnesses than those witnesses can provide (Kebbell & Milne, 1998). So they have asked psychologists to devise ways to enhance information gathering. The **cognitive interview**, an interviewing protocol based on various concepts of memory retrieval and social communication, was the result (Fisher & Geiselman, 1992). Before describing the cognitive interview, we describe a standard police interview so you can understand why a new method was needed.

A "standard" police interview relies on a predetermined set of questions with little opportunity for follow-up, an expectation that the witness will be willing and able to answer all of the questions, repeated interruptions, and time constraints. By contrast, in a cognitive interview, the interviewer first engages the witness in order to develop rapport, then asks the witness to provide a narrative account of the event, and finally, probes for details with specific questions. The interviewer allows the witness to direct the subject matter and flow of the questioning, interrupts infrequently, and listens actively to the witness's responses.

Perhaps the most distinctive element of a cognitive interview (and the reason for its name) is its reliance on a set of cues developed from research on memory retrieval. Cognitive psychologists have observed that reinstating the context in which a witness encoded an event increases accessibility of information stored in memory. With this objective in mind, the interviewer may cue a witness to mentally reconstruct the physical and emotional experiences that existed at the time of the crime. The interviewer may direct the witness to form an image of the situation, recollect sights, sounds, smells, and physical conditions (e.g., heat, cold, darkness), and recall any emotional reactions experienced at the time. When the witness has mentally reconstructed the event, the interviewer asks for a detailed narrative and then uses follow-up questions to probe for specific information. Witnesses are sometimes asked to recall events in different temporal orders (e.g., describing the event from the end to the beginning), from different perspectives, or from the point of view of different people.

A meta-analysis of 65 experiments gauged the effectiveness of the cognitive interview. It showed that compared to the traditional interview method, the cognitive interview can generate substantial increases in correct recall, though it can also produce a small increase in incorrect details (Memon, Meissner, & Fraser, 2010). The cognitive interview is especially effective for older adults, who rely more on external cues to retrieve information from memory. Personnel from organizations including the Federal Bureau of Investigation (FBI), Department of Homeland Security, National Transportation Safety Board, and some state and local police departments have been trained on cognitive interviewing procedures. However, other agencies have been slow to adopt them,

perhaps because the cognitive interview is a more demanding interview protocol.

Lineup Instructions

There is ample evidence that when conducting a lineup, an investigator should instruct the witness that the offender may or may not be present (Malpass & Devine, 1981). Without this admonition, eyewitnesses may assume that their task is to pick someone, so they choose the person who looks most like the perpetrator. Evaluating studies on the "might or might not be present" admonition, Professor Nancy Steblay determined that this instruction reduced the rate of mistaken identifications (i.e., saying that the offender was present in the lineup when he was not) by 42% (Steblay, 1997). The rate of accurate identifications is also slightly reduced by the instruction, but that decline is much smaller than the decline in mistaken identifications (Clark, 2005).

The vast majority of police officers report that they give eyewitnesses the option of not making a selection from the lineup (Wogalter, Malpass & McQuiston, 2004). Unfortunately, some detectives also give a pre-admonition suggestion to the eyewitness that the perpetrator is in the lineup ("Surely, you can pick the perpetrator"). When they do so, the beneficial effects of the subsequent admonition ("The suspect might or might not be present") is negated and the likelihood of a false identification increases (Quinlivan et al., 2012).

Lineup Presentation Method

In a traditional lineup, all lineup members are shown to the witness at once. This procedure is termed **simultaneous presentation**. An alternative procedure, used with increasing frequency, is to show lineup members sequentially, one at a time, in a procedure called **sequential presentation**. The witness makes a decision about each lineup member before seeing the next one.

The manner in which a lineup is presented can affect the accuracy of identification. In a field study that compared simultaneous and sequential lineup procedures used by police in four sites across the country, psychologists found that the rates of identifying the suspect did not differ between the two techniques. Importantly though, simultaneous procedures yielded more mistaken identifications of fillers

(18.1%) than did sequential procedures (12.2%) (Wells, Steblay, & Dysart, 2011).

These results are consistent with a recent meta-analysis that compared simultaneous and sequential presentations in studies involving more than 13,000 participant-witnesses (Steblay, Dysart, & Wells, 2011). The chance of mistaken identifications was reduced by 22% when presentations were sequential rather than simultaneous. However, that good news comes with a trade-off: correct identifications were also reduced (by 8%) when lineups were shown sequentially. In general, sequential lineups result in fewer identification attempts, so both mistaken and accurate identifications are reduced (Meissner, Tredoux, Parker, & MacLin, 2005).

Psychologists now suspect that the effects of sequential lineup presentation may depend on how the lineup is constructed and presented (McQuiston-Surrett, Malpass, & Tredoux, 2006). Sequential

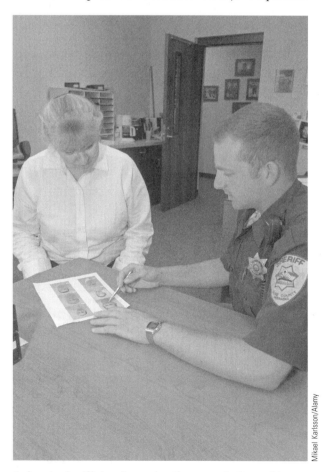

A deputy sheriff showing a simultaneous photographic lineup to an eyewitness

Mikael Karlsson/Alamy

presentation may be advantageous in situations in which the composition of the lineup is unfair—for example, when an innocent suspect matches the description of the perpetrator better than do any of the fillers. In a simultaneous presentation of this lineup, the innocent suspect will stand out and may be misidentified. This is less likely to occur when the same lineup is shown sequentially (Carlson, Gronlund, & Clark, 2008).

Why are there more mistaken identifications in a simultaneous lineup? In the simultaneous presentation of individuals in a lineup, eyewitnesses tend to identify the person who, in their opinion, looks most like the culprit *relative to* other members of the group. In other words, they make a **relative judgment**. As long as the perpetrator is in the lineup, the relative-judgment process works well. But what happens when the actual culprit is not shown? The relative-judgment process may still yield a positive identification, because someone in the group will always look *most* like the culprit (Wells et al., 1998).

Contrast this situation with a lineup in which the members are presented sequentially, one at a time. Here, the eyewitness compares each member in turn to his or her memory of the perpetrator and, on that basis, decides whether any person in the lineup is the individual who committed the crime. In other words, they make an **absolute judgment**. The value of sequential presentation is that it decreases the likelihood that an eyewitness will make a relative judgment in choosing someone from the lineup.

Professor Gary Wells cleverly demonstrated the use of relative-judgment processes in his "removal without replacement" study (Wells, 1993). In this procedure, all eyewitnesses watched a staged crime. Some were shown a photographic lineup that included the actual culprit and five fillers. Another group saw the same photographic lineup with one exception: The culprit's photo was removed and was not replaced with another photo. If identifications of the culprit by the culprit-present group are based solely on their recognition of him, then the percentage of people in that group who identified him *plus* the percentage who said "not there" should be exactly the same as the percentage in the culprit-absent group who said "not there." Wells tested this idea by showing 200 eyewitnesses to a staged crime either a culprit-present lineup or a lineup in which the culprit was absent but was not replaced by anyone else (see Table 5.1). When the culprit was present in

T A B L E 5.1   **Rates of choosing lineup members when a culprit (#3) is present versus removed without replacement**

	Lineup Member						No Choice
	1	**2**	**3**	**4**	**5**	**6**	
Culprit present	3%	13%	54%	3%	3%	3%	21%
Culprit removed (without replacement)	6%	38%	—	12%	7%	5%	32%

SOURCE: "What do we know from witness identification?" from G. Wells. (1993). *American Psychologist, 48,* 553–571.

the lineup, 54% of eyewitnesses selected him, and 21% said "not there." Did 75% of eyewitnesses in the "target-absent" lineup say "not there"? Unfortunately, no. The "not there" response was given by only 32% of people in that group; the others all mistakenly identified someone else from the lineup. Why? Through a process of relative judgment, eyewitnesses apparently select whoever looks most like the perpetrator. The weaker one's memory, the more likely one is to use a relative judgment in this situation (Clark & Davey, 2005).

The Influence of Feedback

Recall our analogy between a criminal investigation and a scientific experiment. One of the cardinal rules of a good experiment is that the person conducting the experiment should not influence the results, a problem referred to as **experimenter bias**. To avoid such bias, experimenters should know little about the study's hypotheses and less about the experimental condition in which any participant is placed. Nearly all clinical drug trials adhere to these rules—neither the patient taking the pills nor the doctor assessing the patient's health know whether the pills are actually a new drug or a placebo. These so-called **double-blind testing procedures**, commonplace in medicine and other scientific fields, have gone largely unheeded in criminal investigations, although some jurisdictions have recently begun to adopt them (Moore, 2007).

The lineup is typically conducted by the detective who selected the fillers and knows which person is the suspect (Wogalter et al., 2004). Does the detective's knowledge of the suspect affect the eyewitness in any way? The answer, based on several recent studies, is yes. A lineup administrator's knowledge of the suspect's identity can increase the likelihood that an eyewitness will choose someone from the lineup (Phillips, McAuliff, Kovera, & Cutler, 1999). This is more likely to occur when the administrator has failed to provide instructions that the suspect may or may not be in the lineup, in which case the eyewitness may presume that the suspect is present and looks to the administrator for cues (Greathouse & Kovera, 2009). Furthermore, eyewitnesses who have frequent contact with the administrator—either because they are in close physical contact or because they have extensive interactions—are likely to make decisions consistent with the administrator's expectations (Haw & Fisher, 2004). An obvious solution to this situation is to have the lineup administered by someone who does not know which person in the lineup is the suspect.

Eyewitnesses sometimes express increased certainty in their identifications as a result of events that happen after they choose someone from the lineup. For example, if eyewitnesses receive confirming feedback from the lineup administrator ("Good, you identified the suspect"), this increases their certainty in their initial identifications, compared to eyewitnesses who received no such feedback (Neuschatz et al., 2007). This inflation of confidence occurs both in experiments and in studies of actual eyewitnesses to real events (Douglass, Brewer, & Semmler, 2009). Remarkably, confirming feedback also bolsters eyewitnesses' retrospective reports of their certainty at the time of the identification, even when the confirming feedback is given a week after the identification (Quinlivan et al., 2009).

Even *without* confirming feedback, eyewitnesses infer from the facts of an ongoing investigation and eventual prosecution that they must have picked the suspect from the lineup. Hence, their confidence increases. This enhanced confidence is troubling because of the repeated finding that the confidence expressed by eyewitnesses during their trial testimony is one of the most compelling reasons why jurors believe such identifications are accurate (Brewer & Burke, 2002). We would expect that the rape victim described in Box 5.2 was more confident of her identification of Larry Fuller at his trial than she was when viewing his photograph.

Witness confidence is a postdiction variable that correlates weakly with witness accuracy. Studies have shown that witness confidence is not a very good predictor of a witness's accuracy unless it is measured immediately after an identification. Some psychologists estimate that eyewitnesses who are absolutely certain of the identifications may be accurate only about 80% of the time (Lampinen, Neuschatz, & Cling, 2012). Another problem with eyewitnesses' confidence is its apparent malleability: After making an identification from a lineup, witnesses who were told that another witness identified the same person became more confident of their identifications (Charman, Carlucci, Vallano, & Gregory, 2010). Furthermore, when witnesses were questioned about a simulated crime scene, their rated confidence depended on whether they might be contradicted by another witness. Confidence increased when there was no chance of contradiction and decreased when there was (Shaw, Appio, Zerr, & Pontoski, 2007).

One result of feedback from the lineup administrator—whether it conveys to the witness that he or she picked the suspect or tells the witness that another person picked the same suspect—is a sense of false confidence. Can the development of false confidence be prevented? Asking witnesses to provide a statement of their degree of certainty *before* giving them any feedback can be an effective way to eliminate the problem of false confidence (Jones, Williams, & Brewer, 2008). This recommendation is among the reforms being incorporated in identification cases.

THE EYEWITNESS IN THE COURTROOM

Despite limitations on the reliability of eyewitness identifications, jurors put a great deal of weight on testimony from an eyewitness. In a study showing this influence, Loftus (1974) gave subjects a description of an armed robbery that resulted in two deaths. Of mock jurors who heard a version of the case that contained only circumstantial evidence against the defendant, 18% convicted him. But when an

eyewitness's identification of the defendant was presented as well, 72% of the mock jurors convicted him. It is hard to overstate the power of confident eyewitnesses to convince a jury of the correctness of their testimony.

Why do jurors have difficulty inferring the accuracy of an eyewitness's memory? In particular, why do they overestimate accuracy? Psychologists have proposed several explanations (see, e.g., Semmler, Brewer, & Douglass, 2012).

- Jurors cannot verify an eyewitness's version of an event against some objective record of what occurred. Instead, they may rely on a positive stereotype about memory credibility. Their baseline expectation is that eyewitnesses are accurate and do not have false memories or make inaccurate identifications.

- Jurors assume that eyewitnesses' testimony is a reflection of their memory quality, and not the way they were questioned or interacted with the lineup administrator. This is an example of the fundamental attribution error: the tendency to assume that the causes of behavior are internal to a person rather than the result of external factors such as the system variables we reviewed in the previous section.

- Finally, as mentioned, jurors over-rely on an eyewitness's confidence when gauging accuracy. They tend to trust both overt statements of confidence such as "I'm sure that's the guy" and subtler indications of confidence such as voice pitch, intonation, and speed.

SAFEGUARDS AGAINST MISTAKEN IDENTIFICATION

Scientists have focused more attention on assessing the effects of various identification procedures than on testing trial processes that could reduce the rates of wrongful convictions (Semmler et al., 2012). But some studies examine ways to counter jurors' over-reliance on eyewitness identification.

One possibility is to inform jurors about whether investigators followed DOJ guidelines for conducting lineups. This would allow jurors to gauge whether the procedures and outcome warrant their trust. A mock jury study tested this idea (Lampinen, Judges,

Odegard, & Hamilton, 2005). Some jurors were informed that detectives violated DOJ guidelines and others were not so informed. Those who learned about guideline violations thought the prosecution's case was weaker and were less likely to convict the defendant, suggesting that failure to adhere to DOJ guidelines could discredit the prosecution.

Until the guidelines are consistently applied or the reforms begun in state courts (including New Jersey) are adopted more broadly, other mechanisms should be available to educate jurors and judges about the problems inherent in eyewitness reports. We discuss three ways this can be done. One proposal limits the testimony of eyewitnesses in particular ways. Another remedy allows psychologists who are knowledgeable about the relevant research on perception and memory to testify as expert witnesses on eyewitness reliability. Finally, judges could instruct juries about the potential weaknesses of eyewitness identifications and suggest how to interpret this testimony.

Limiting Eyewitness Testimony

Suppose that an eyewitness to a convenience store robbery made a tentative identification of a suspect from a lineup, and after being shown a second lineup in which the suspect was the only person repeated, made a more confident identification. A judge could rule that the eyewitness can testify about the initial, tentative identification, but not about the second identification. A prosecutor faced with the exclusion of powerful testimony is likely to pressure the police to use less suggestive procedures in the future (Wells & Quinlivan, 2009).

Expert Testimony

Psychologists occasionally testify about research on eyewitness identification, typically on behalf of the defendant. Their testimony focuses on factors that influence eyewitness accuracy. Such testimony might indicate that (1) extreme stress tends to inhibit encoding, (2) feedback from a lineup administrator can increase an eyewitness's confidence, and (3) differences in the way lineups are constructed and presented to witnesses affect eyewitness accuracy. Note that the expert witness does not tell the jury what to believe about a particular eyewitness or whether the eyewitness is accurate. Rather, the expert's task is to provide the jury with a scientifically based

frame of reference within which to evaluate the eyewitness's evidence.

Studies show that in the kinds of cases where experts typically testify—those that involve questionable viewing conditions or suggestive police procedures—expert testimony tends to sensitize jurors to problems in witnessing and identification procedures rather than to make them generally skeptical of all witnesses (e.g., Devenport, Stinson, Cutler, & Kravitz, 2002). A report of one actual crime lends anecdotal support to the conclusion that the testimony of an expert witness has some impact. Loftus (1984) described the trial of two Arizona brothers charged with the torture of three Mexicans. Two juries were in the courtroom at the same time, one deciding the verdict for Patrick Hanigan, the other deciding the fate of his brother, Thomas. Most of the evidence was from eyewitnesses, and it was virtually identical for the two defendants. However, expert testimony about the inaccuracy of eyewitnesses was introduced in Thomas's trial only. (The jury hearing Patrick Hanigan's case waited in the jury room while this evidence was presented.) Patrick Hanigan was convicted by one jury; his brother was acquitted by the other. This is as close to a "natural experiment" as the legal system has offered for assessing the influence of a psychologist in the courtroom. Unfortunately, even when allowed, expert testimony is an expensive safeguard that is available in only a small fraction of the cases that come to trial each year (Wells et al., 1998). Are there other, more readily available remedies?

Jury Instructions

Another option for alerting jurors to the limitations of eyewitnesses is through a jury instruction delivered by the judge at the end of a trial. The defense typically requests that such an instruction be given, and the judge decides whether to grant the request.

What effects do cautionary instructions have on jurors' beliefs about eyewitness accuracy? Researchers who have tested the impact of a frequently used instruction on eyewitness reliability, the so-called *Telfaire* instruction (*United States v. Telfaire*, 1972), found that it reduced mock jurors' sensitivity to eyewitness evidence, probably because it gives little indication how jurors should evaluate the evidence. However, an instruction that incorporated information likely to be delivered by an expert preserved jurors' sensitivity to the factors that influence eyewitness reliability (Ramirez, Zemba, & Geiselman, 1996).

These findings provide some hints about the type of jury instruction that *could* reduce the likelihood of mistaken convictions in eyewitness cases. Those instructions, as yet untested, are likely to be issue specific, tailored to the facts present in a particular case, and based on scientific research findings. Rather than providing only general directives about eyewitness evidence (e.g., "consider the conditions under which the identification was made"), judges would instruct jurors about relevant scientific findings and inform them how to incorporate this information into their decision making. This approach was advocated by the New Jersey Supreme Court in the *Henderson* case: "We direct that enhanced instructions be given to guide juries about the various factors that may affect the reliability of an identification in a particular case" (p. 123). The Court endorsed directives on lineup instructions, stress, other-race identifications, information received by an eyewitness prior to or after an identification, and weapon focus, among other topics.

CHILDREN AS WITNESSES

Sometimes a child is the only witness to a crime—or its only victim. A number of questions arise in cases where children are witnesses. Can they remember the precise details of these incidents? Can suggestive interviewing techniques distort their reports? Do repeated interviews increase errors? Is it appropriate for children to testify in a courtroom? Society's desire to prosecute and punish offenders may require that children testify about their victimization, but defendants should not be convicted on the basis of inaccurate testimony. In this section we focus on the accuracy of children as witnesses, and on concerns about children testifying in court.

Children as Eyewitnesses to Crimes

Like adults, children are sometimes asked to identify strangers or to describe what they witnessed regarding crimes. In kidnappings and assaults, the child may be the only witness to a crime committed by a stranger. To test children's eyewitness capabilities, researchers create situations that closely match real-life events.

In these studies, children typically interact with an unknown adult (the "target") for some period of time in a school classroom or a doctor's office. They are later questioned about what they experienced and what the target person looked like, and they may attempt to make an identification from a lineup.

Two general findings emerge from these studies. First, children over the age of 6 can make reasonably reliable identifications from lineups, provided that the perpetrator is actually in the lineup and the child had extended contact with the perpetrator (Gross & Hayne, 1996). Second, children are generally less accurate than adults when making an identification from a lineup in which the suspect is absent. In these situations, children tend to select someone from the lineup, thereby making a "false-positive" error (Keast, Brewer, & Wells, 2007). Such mistakes are troubling to the police because they thwart the ongoing investigation.

Psychologists have attempted to devise identification procedures for children that maintain identification accuracy when the suspect is in the lineup but reduce false-positive choices when the suspect is absent. Giving children the option to say "Not sure" combined with instructions informing them of the importance of making a correct decision decreased guessing and the incidence of false identifications (Brewer, Keast, & Sauer, 2010).

Children as Victims of Maltreatment

The most likely reason for a child to become involved with the legal system is that he or she has been maltreated. Here the issue is not who committed the crime. Rather, it is what happened to the child. Psychologists have been particularly interested in the effects—socio-emotional, neurobiological, mental health, *and* cognitive—of maltreatment. In this chapter we focus on the cognitive effects, particularly the implications for memory, of child abuse, including child sexual abuse (CSA).

Most CSA cases rest solely on the words of the victim because these cases typically lack any physical evidence. (The most frequent forms of sexual abuse perpetrated on children are fondling, exhibitionism, and oral copulation.) Yet anyone who has spent time with young children knows that their descriptions of situations can sometimes be fanciful mixes of fact and fantasy. There are concerns about whether preschoolers and even older children can be trusted to provide accurate details and to disclose experiences of abuse. There are also concerns about the accuracy of memory on the part of adolescents and adults who previously experienced maltreatment. Developmental psychologists have investigated these issues over the past few decades. We focus on studies that assess the effects of interviewing techniques on children's memory of events they experienced and that examine patterns of disclosure of maltreatment and the accuracy of memory for abuse.

Investigative Interviews

One feature of CSA cases is crucial to the accuracy of child witnesses: the nature of the investigative interview. Some interviewers now use a structured questioning protocol that first builds rapport between interviewer and child, and then encourages children to provide details in their own words ("Tell me everything that happened from the beginning to the end as best you can remember"). The protocol discourages the use of **suggestive questions** (questions that assume information not disclosed by the child or suggest the expected answer, such as "He touched you, didn't he?").

Investigative interviewers trained in this protocol questioned preschool-aged children who were suspected victims of child abuse. Five-year-olds were able to provide forensically important information in response to **open-ended questions**, and even 3-year-olds were able to share information when invited to elaborate on an earlier response (Hershkowitz, Lamb, Orbach, Katz, & Horowitz, 2012). These findings suggest that central details (the "gist") of victimization experiences can be remembered well when they are elicited by non-suggestive questioning.

After a child has recounted an experience in his or her own words and in response to open-ended questions, investigators may ask specific questions about the event. For example, if a child said that she was touched, a follow-up question might be "Where were you touched?" Although children tend to provide more detail in response to specific questions than to open-ended questions, the use of specific questions comes at a cost: Children are less accurate in answering specific questions. This difficulty is not restricted to very young children. After seeing a stranger in their classroom handing out candy the previous week, two groups of children (4- to 5-year-olds, and 7- to 8-year-olds) were asked specific, misleading questions (e.g., "He took your clothes off, didn't he?"). Older

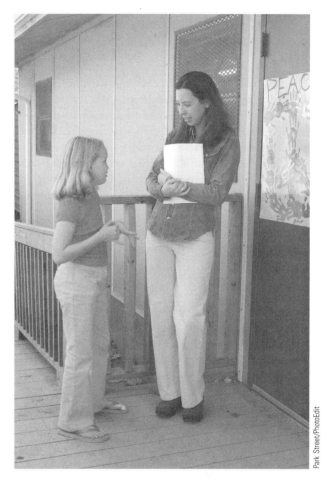

Investigative interviewer questioning a child

children were just as likely as younger children to assent to these suggestions (Finnila, Mahlberga, Santtilaa, Sandnabbaa, & Niemib, 2003). Of course, most interviewers would never intentionally mislead a child, but they may have misinformation or suspicions that could color the nature of the questions they pose.

Children are less accurate in answering specific questions than more general queries because specific questions demand precise memories of events that the child may never have encoded or may have forgotten (Dickinson, Poole, & Laimon, 2005). Additionally, the child may answer a question that she or he does not fully understand in order to appear to be cooperative (Waterman, Blades, & Spencer, 2001). Finally, the more specific the question, the more likely it is that the interviewer will accidentally include information that the child has not stated. Specific questions can easily become suggestive.

A sizeable number of children experience multiple incidents of sexual abuse, and although the central features of the experiences may be constant, peripheral details may change. But before prosecutors can file multiple charges, they must provide evidence that reflects the critical details of each separate incident. In other words, the child has to "particularize" his or her report by providing precise details about each specific allegation (Dickinson et al., 2005). Can a child do this? Studies that examine children's recall of repeated events typically expose them to a series of similar incidents with certain constant features and some details that vary across episodes. Although source monitoring (identifying the source of a memory) improves with age (Quas & Schaaf, 2002), children often recall information from one event as having occurred in another (Brubacher, Glisic, Roberts, & Powell, 2011). In fact, exposure to recurring events is a double-edged sword: Repeated events enhance memory for aspects of the incident that are held constant but impair the ability to recall details that vary with each recurrence (Dickinson et al., 2005).

If they experience multiple incidents of maltreatment, children may be subjected to repeated interviews. One line of research has shown negative effects of repeated interviews on children's memory and suggestibility. In these studies, experimenters describe to children true and false events (e.g., that the child's hand was caught in a mousetrap), imply that the children experienced all of them, and tell the children that their parents or friends said the events had occurred. Approximately one-third to one-half of preschool-aged children provided additional details of the false events (e.g., Bruck, Ceci, & Hembrooke, 2002). A separate line of research has documented beneficial effects of repeated interviews, however. These studies found that children exposed to repeated interviews were not prone to errors. In fact, their memory improved with repeated interviews (e.g., Peterson, Parsons, & Dean, 2004).

What accounts for these conflicting findings? One hint comes from a study that varied the number of interviews and the nature of the questions asked (Quas et al., 2007). In this study, children played alone in a laboratory setting and were questioned either once or three times about what happened while they played. The questions were either biased (implying that the child played with a man) or unbiased. Children interviewed only once by the biased interviewer were most likely to claim they played with a man, and children interviewed on multiple occasions (regardless of the type of question asked) were less likely to do so. This suggests that biased interview questions can lead to false reports in a single interview (Goodman & Quas, 2008).

A robust finding in cognitive psychology, termed the **reminiscence effect**, can explain why multiple interviews might be useful. When people attempt to remember pictures or events they viewed previously, they often report (reminisce) new information on each recall attempt, suggesting that recollection is often incomplete on the first telling and that it is quite normal to produce unrecalled information in later interviews. Reminiscence effects are facilitated by the use of open-ended questions that allow the interviewee to provide information in his or her own words.

Repeated interviewing is necessary when an alleged victim is too distressed to provide useful information initially, when victims fail to disclose abuse that is subsequently documented by medical examinations or suspects' confessions, or when other new evidence comes to light (La Rooy, Katz, Malloy, & Lamb, 2010). A reminiscence effect occurred when a victim of CSA, described in Box 5.3, was interviewed on multiple occasions.

Disclosure of Child Maltreatment

Children are sometimes reluctant to disclose abusive experiences and may even deny them when asked. How likely are children to disclose sexual abuse? Professor Kamala London and her colleagues identified adults with documented histories of CSA and learned that only 33% had disclosed the abuse during their childhood (London, Bruck, Ceci, & Shuman, 2005). This suggests that the majority of children fail to disclose their abuse when they are young and, therefore, that reported cases of CSA are the tip of a large iceberg (Ceci, Kulkofsky, Klemfuss, Sweeney, & Bruck, 2007). But this study also showed that when asked directly about being abused, the vast majority of participants neither denied it nor recanted their stories.

Some studies have focused on what individuals remember about being maltreated. In fact, children can remember significant details of abuse experiences and, if asked directly, can describe them quite accurately. One team of developmental psychologists contacted approximately 200 adolescents and young adults who, during the 1980s, had been involved in a

---

B o x 5.3 THE CASE OF THE 14-YEAR-OLD SEXUAL ASSAULT VICTIM INTERVIEWED TWICE

A 14-year-old girl, whose identity cannot be disclosed for privacy reasons, reported to her mother that the mother's former partner had sexually assaulted her. Independent, external evidence supported her allegation. When prompted by the investigative interviewer, who said, "My job is to talk to people about things that might have happened to them. It's important that you explain to me why you are here today," the victim recounted three different episodes of abuse, disclosing many details in response to open-ended questions. After that interview, the victim told her mother that she had forgotten to mention another abusive experience, so on the next day she was interviewed again, also in an open-ended question format.

Here is an excerpt of what she reported during the initial interview (in regular type) and what she reported for the first time during the second interview (in bold type):

It started when I was about eleven, going on twelve. **He was downstairs with my mum and then he came up to tuck us in like he usually does.** He was in my room. My sister fell asleep and then he took me into a different room. It started from there. He started feeling me. He touched my fanny (vagina) with his hands. He got his finger and rubbed it round my fanny. It was under my clothes. **He had clothes on**...

My mum had gone out. I was upstairs in my room. I think he told me to "get on the bed," so I did and then he started touching me again, and he tried to put his willy inside me, but he couldn't. He touched me with his hands and his willy. He put his hands on my fanny and in my fanny. He put his fingers inside me...

It was downstairs. I was doing my homework or something. He made me watch a video. He sat with me and we watched the video. It had people on it showing sex and things like that. **They had their clothes off. The willy was going in the fanny**...

One day he brought a video camera home. It was upstairs in the bedroom that was my mum's. He switched the video camera on. He told me to take my clothes off so I did. He said to "get on the bed," so I did. He had no clothes on either. He told me to pull his willy up and down. He tried to put his willy inside me again. It hurt. He was on top of me (adapted from La Rooy et al., 2010).

Notice that during the second interview, the girl provided information relevant to an entirely different episode of abuse and that she was able to give additional details about the incidents she had described previously.

Critical Thought Question
What features of these interviews were crucial in allowing the victim to recall what had happened to her?

---

study of the effects of criminal prosecutions on victims of CSA (Alexander et al., 2005). Participants had been 3 to 17 years old at the time of the original data collection. All of them had been sexually abused. Upon renewing contact years later, psychologists provided a list of traumatic events (including CSA) and asked respondents to indicate which events happened to them and, among those events, which was the most traumatic. Respondents who designated CSA as their most traumatic experience were remarkably accurate in reporting details of their experiences. These data suggest that memory for emotional, even traumatic, victimization experiences can be retained quite well even decades after the events occurred.

Still, a subgroup of abuse victims either forgets the abuse or remembers it poorly. Why do some maltreated people have full access to memories of those experiences and others have none? Processes that people use to regulate their emotions—in particular,

their coping strategies—may be implicated (Goodman, Quas, & Ogle, 2010). People who cope with maltreatment by trying to suppress, inhibit, or ignore their thoughts about it may weaken or even eliminate memories of those experiences over time. As a result, they have memory deficits for these traumatic events.

The Child Witness in the Courtroom

Though most child maltreatment cases end in admissions of guilt or plea bargains, tens of thousands of children, often preschoolers, must testify in abuse trials each year. In one study, although only 18% of all CSA cases involved children 5 years old or younger, 41% of the cases that went to trial involved children of this age (Gray, 1993). Two questions arise: What is the effect on the child of having to discuss these issues in court, and how do jurors weigh the testimony of a child witness?

Talking about victimization in a public setting may increase the trauma for many children. Children are especially fearful of confronting the offender (Hall & Sales, 2008). Professor Gail Goodman and her colleagues examined the short- and long-term outcomes for children who testified in CSA cases, initially interviewing a group of 218 CSA victims when their cases were referred for prosecution (Goodman et al., 1992) and reinterviewing many of them 12 years later (Quas et al., 2005). The experience of testifying was quite traumatic for some children. They had nightmares, vomited on the day of their appearance in court, and were relieved that the defendant had not tried to kill them (Goodman et al., 1992). Twelve years later, when compared to a group of individuals with no CSA history, CSA victims who had been involved in criminal cases showed some long-term negative consequences. Most affected psychologically were those who were young when the case started, testified repeatedly, and opted not to testify when the perpetrator received a light sentence.

How do jurors perceive child witnesses? Do they tend to doubt the truthfulness of children's testimony, reasoning that children often make things up and leave things out? Or do they tend to "believe the children," as a popular bumper sticker would like us to do? In mock jury studies, child eyewitnesses are generally viewed as less credible than adult eyewitnesses (e.g., Pozzulo & Dempsey, 2009). But something quite different happens in CSA cases. Here, younger victims are viewed as *more* credible than adolescents or adults, probably because jurors suspect that younger children lack the sexual knowledge to fabricate an allegation (Bottoms, Golding, Stevenson, Wiley, & Yozwiak, 2007). Jurors can recognize the effects of suggestive questioning; mock jurors who read a transcript of a highly suggestive forensic interview tended to discount the child's testimony (Castelli, Goodman, & Ghetti, 2005).

Procedural Modifications When Children Are Witnesses

Judges allow various courtroom modifications to protect children from the potential stress of testifying. One innovation is the placement of a screen in front of the defendant so the child witness cannot see him or her while testifying. This arrangement was used in the trial of John Avery Coy, who was convicted

of sexually assaulting two 13-year-old girls. Coy appealed his conviction on the grounds that the screen deprived him of the opportunity to confront the girls face-to-face, a reference to the **confrontation clause** of the Sixth Amendment that guarantees defendants the right to confront their accusers. The right to confrontation is based on the assumption that the witness will find it more difficult to lie in the presence of the defendant. In a 1988 decision, the Supreme Court agreed with Coy, saying that his right to confront his accusers face-to-face was not outweighed "by the necessity of protecting the victims of sexual abuse" (*Coy v. Iowa*, 1988).

But just two years later, in the case of *Maryland v. Craig* (1990), the Court upheld a law permitting a child to give testimony in a different part of the courthouse and have the testimony transmitted to the courtroom via close-circuit TV (CCTV). The law applied to cases where the child was likely to suffer significant emotional distress by being in the presence of the defendant. *Craig* thus modified the rule of the *Coy* case.

Proponents of CCTV claim that in addition to reducing the trauma experienced by a child, this technology will also provide more complete and accurate reports. Opponents claim that the use of CCTV violates the defendant's right to face-to-face confrontation of witnesses. Several studies have assessed the veracity of children who testify in and out of courtrooms and whether observers perceive differences in their credibility. A common finding is that children give more detailed statements when allowed to testify on CCTV (Goodman et al., 1998). Children also feel less nervous when allowed to testify outside of the courtroom (Landstrom & Granhag, 2010). On this basis, one might argue for its use in every case in which a child feels anxious about testifying. But things aren't quite so simple. Children who testify via CCTV are viewed less positively than children who testify in open court (Landstrom & Granhag, 2010). It appears that jurors want to see children in person in order to assess the truthfulness of their reports. Clearly, the impact of CCTV on jurors' decisions in CSA cases is complex. Perhaps it should be reserved for cases in which the prospect of testifying is so terrifying to children that they would otherwise become inept witnesses—or would not testify at all.

Judges make other accommodations when children must testify. In cases involving CSA, physical abuse, or adult domestic violence, a support person—typically a parent, guardian, or victim assistant—is almost always present with the child to decrease stress and ideally to increase accuracy and completeness (McAuliff, Nicholson, Amarilio, & Ravenshenas, 2012). A growing and controversial trend is to allow children to nuzzle with trained therapy dogs during testimony (Galberson, 2011).

Finally, we should note that although testifying has the potential to inflict further trauma on the child, it can be a therapeutic experience for some children. It can engender a sense of control over events, and if the defendant is convicted, provide some satisfaction to the child. One 15-year-old girl said, "If I, as a young person, were a victim of a sexual abuse or rape case, I would *want* to testify before a full court. I might be scared at first or a little embarrassed, but I'd want to be present to make my assailant look like a complete fool. I'd want to see him convicted—with my own eyes. It would make me stronger" (quoted in Gunter, 1985, p. 12A).

REPRESSED AND RECOVERED MEMORIES

Retrieving memories over short time periods, as eyewitnesses must do, is a complex task. Yet it pales in comparison with retrieving memories that have been stored over lengthy intervals. Two basic processes need to be distinguished in understanding long-lost memories. The first is natural forgetting, which tends to occur when people simply do not think about events that happened years earlier. Just as you might have trouble remembering the name of your fourth-grade teacher, witnesses to crimes, accidents, and business transactions are likely to forget the details of these events, if not the entire event, after the passage of months or years. Such forgetting or misremembering is even more likely when the event is confused with prior or subsequent experiences that bear some resemblance to it. No one disputes the reality of natural forgetting.

Significantly more controversial is a second type of lost "memory"—the memories that are presumed to have been repressed over long time periods. This process involves events that are thought to be so traumatizing that individuals bury them deeply in their unconscious mind through a process of emotionally motivated forgetting called **repression**. For example,

soldiers exposed to the brutal horrors of combat and individuals who experienced a natural disaster such as an earthquake are sometimes unable to remember the traumas they obviously suffered. In such cases, repression is thought to serve a protective function by sparing the individual from having to remember and relive horrifying scenes. These repressed memories sometimes stay unconscious, and hence forgotten, unless and until they are spontaneously recalled or retriggered by exposure to some aspect of the original experience. (The smell of gasoline might remind a soldier of the battlefield, or the sight of an unusual cloud formation might remind an earthquake victim of the sky's appearance on the day of the disaster.) But the notion of repression is highly controversial; some suggest that repression has never been proven to exist and that the inability to remember traumatic effects can be explained by ordinary forgetting.

A related unconscious process is **dissociation**, in which victims of abuse or other traumas are thought to escape the full impact of an experience by psychologically detaching themselves from it. This process is believed to be particularly strong in children, who, because they are still forming integrated personalities, find it easier to escape from the pain of abuse by fantasizing about made-up individuals and imagining that the abuse is happening to those others. Many clinical psychologists believe that such early episodes of dissociation, involving unique ideas, feelings, and behavior, form the beginning of the altered personalities that are found in dissociative identity disorder (formerly called multiple personality disorder).

Repressed Memories and Memory Recovery Therapy

Most of the reports of repressed and recovered memories involve claims of CSA. The theory is that individuals (1) suffered sexual or physical abuse as children, often at the hands of parents or other trusted adults; (2) repressed or dissociated any memory of these horrors for many years as a form of unconscious protection; and (3) recovered their long-lost memories of the abuse when it was psychologically safe to do so.

A widely cited study suggests that it may be possible for people to forget horrible events that happened to them in childhood. Linda Williams (1994) interviewed 129 women who had experienced well-documented cases of CSA. She asked detailed questions about the abuse experiences, which had occurred an average of 17 years earlier. More than one-third of the women did not report the abuse they had experienced in childhood. Of course, this does not prove that the forgetting was due to repression. It is possible that when the abuse occurred, the women were too young to be fully aware of it; in addition, some of the women might have been unwilling to report sexual abuse to an interviewer, who was a relative stranger, even if they did remember it. Yet reports of recovered memories accompanied by corroboration continue to surface (e.g., Colangelo, 2009), supporting therapists' claims about the veracity of these memories.

Sometimes, repressed memories are recovered only after a person participates in "memory-focused" psychotherapy that applies techniques such as hypnosis, age regression, guided visualization, diary writing, or therapist instructions to help clients remember past abuse (Lindsay & Read, 1995). Such "de-repression" techniques have been advocated by popular books on incest (e.g., *The Courage to Heal* by Ellen Bass and Laura Davis, now in its 20th anniversary fourth edition). Some therapists suspect clients of harboring repressed memories of abuse and ask the clients highly suggestive questions, such as "You show many of the signs of childhood sexual abuse; can you tell me some of the things you think might have happened to you when you were a very young child?" Interestingly, people who are likely to seek psychotherapy are also likely to believe that they experienced childhood trauma and abuse they cannot remember (Rubin & Boals, 2010). This finding suggests that some psychotherapy clients may be only too eager to have their suspicions confirmed.

But many researchers and therapists question the validity of memories that resurface years after the alleged incidents and then only after the individual has been in therapy (Gerry, Garry, & Loftus, 2005). (These professionals are not denying the reality of CSA, of course. Not only does it occur, but it is a very serious problem both in the United States and throughout the world. It appears that children who were abused are at increased risk to suffer mental health disorders in adulthood.) The real question is whether allegations of child abuse that first surface only after searching for them in therapy are trustworthy. In a clever study designed to compare memories of abuse recovered in therapy to memories recovered outside of therapy and memories never forgotten,

Professor Elke Geraerts and her colleagues sought independent corroboration of the abuse from other people who were abused by the same perpetrator, individuals who learned of the abuse soon after it occurred, or from perpetrators themselves. They were able to corroborate 45% of the abuse memories that had never been forgotten, 37% of the memories that were recalled out of therapy, but 0% of the memories that were recalled in therapy (Geraerts et al., 2007).

Those who question the validity of repressed memories also point out that most people who suffer severe trauma do not forget the event; in fact, many of them suffer intrusive recollections of it for years afterward. Skepticism is further fueled by the fact that some alleged victims claim to have recalled traumas that happened when they were less than 1 year old. Yet nearly all research on childhood memory and amnesia shows this is not possible, for reasons related to neurological development.

So what should we make of the recollection of past abuse events that a person claims to have repressed for years? Do they stem from actual traumatic events, or are they false memories? If they are false, from where did they originate? Even psychologists are conflicted on these questions. In fact, the Working Group on Investigation of Memories of Childhood Abuse, appointed by the American Psychological Association, was so deeply divided that the group was forced to issue two reports. One report, written by clinical psychologists (Alpert, Brown, & Courtois, 1998), supports the *repression interpretation*: intolerable emotional and physical arousal can lead a child victim to use dissociative coping strategies that may interfere with or impair encoding, storage, and retrieval of memories. A second report, authored by experimental research psychologists (Ornstein, Ceci, & Loftus, 1998), supports the *false memory interpretation*: suggestive and misleading information can degrade memory, memory for traumatic experiences can be highly malleable, and it is relatively easy to create false memories for events that never occurred. According to this perspective, the "repression interpretation does not withstand empirical scrutiny" (McNally & Geraerts, 2009, p. 127.)

Can we be sure that alleged abuses took place? Is it possible that some memories, especially those that appear to have been repressed for years and then recovered—sometimes through aggressive "memory work" therapy—are imagined or made up? Juries

---

B o x 5.4 THE CASE OF FATHER PAUL SHANLEY AND HIS ACCUSER'S RECOVERED MEMORIES

On February 11, 2002, Paul Busa received a phone call from his girlfriend, telling him of a newspaper article that described accusations of CSA against Father Paul Shanley, a controversial and charismatic Roman Catholic priest. With this prompting, Busa began to recall his own abuse at the hands of Father Shanley two decades earlier, memories that he said he had not recalled for years. The accuser then began to speak openly about his abuse and agreed to testify in the criminal case against the former priest. Father Shanley, 74 at the time of the trial, was accused of pulling Busa out of Sunday school classes and raping him in the bathroom, pews, rectory, and confessional booth of the church in Newton, Massachusetts.

At the trial, the alleged victim, a barrel-chested firefighter, gave emotional—even teary—testimony about the multiple incidents of abuse in the church. Busa testified that he was so traumatized by the memories that surfaced years later that he was unable to continue to function at his job, was hospitalized, and was discharged from the Air Force. Despite some inconsistencies in his recollections and testimony from a defense expert witness who explained how false memories can be created in susceptible minds, the jury was apparently convinced by Busa's seemingly heartfelt testimony. They convicted Father Shanley on two counts of rape and two counts of indecent assault on a child. He was sentenced to 12 to 15 years in prison. Yet the controversy still raged. Shanley challenged his conviction but the Massachusetts Supreme Judicial Court affirmed the conviction in 2010.

Charles Krupa/Pool/Reuters/CORBIS

Father Paul Shanley being taken into custody shortly after his conviction on charges of raping an altar boy years before

Critical Thought Question
In his appeal, Shanley argued that the recovered memory evidence should not have been admitted into evidence during his trial because it lacked general acceptance in the relevant scientific community. He enlisted about 100 prominent psychologists and psychiatrists to back him up. They co-authored an *amicus brief,* sometimes referred to as a friend-of-the-court brief, in which they explained current scientific thinking about so-called repressed and recovered memories. Using the information presented in this chapter, summarize their arguments.

---

deciding the fate of some Roman Catholic priests accused of child sexual abuse in the 1990s and 2000s had to grapple with these questions (though most cases of clergy sexual abuse do not involve repressed memories). We describe one such case in Box 5.4.

Creating False Memories

During the 2008 presidential campaign, contender Hillary Clinton described the harrowing experience of landing in war-torn Bosnia under sniper fire in 1996, and running on an airport tarmac with her head down to get to a waiting vehicle. But photographs and video of her arrival showed a very different reality: Clinton greeting smiling Bosnian officials and being kissed by an 8-year-old girl. To what should we attribute Clinton's "memory"? Was this an intentional fabrication to bolster her image as someone who has

undertaken dangerous missions? Or was it a genuinely false memory? In recent years, many psychologists have used laboratory research and real-life cases to document how false memories can be created. There is now general agreement that given the right set of circumstances, people can create memories of incidents that never occurred.

One way that psychologists have been able to implant false memories is by enlisting the help of family members, who suggest to adult research participants that they can recall a fabricated event. In a now-classic study, Loftus and Pickrell (1995), with help from participants' relatives, constructed a false story that the participant had been lost during a shopping trip at the age of 5, was found crying by an elderly person, and was eventually reunited with family members. After reading this story, participants wrote what they remembered about the event. Nearly 30% of participants either partially or fully remembered the made-up event, and 25% claimed in subsequent interviews that they remembered the fictitious situation. Falsely suggesting to research participants that they became sick, years before, after eating a particular food actually influenced their behavior. The suggestion deterred them from eating that food when it was offered (Geraerts et al., 2008).

Psychologists have used other experimental procedures to examine the malleable nature of **autobiographical memory** (memory for one's past experiences). These include asking participants to imagine events that never occurred (Mazzoni & Memon, 2003) and doctoring family photographs by inserting childhood portraits to portray events such as hot-air balloon rides that never took place (Wade, Garry, Read, & Lindsay, 2002). Merely imagining or viewing a photo associated with a fabricated event can dramatically increase the rate of false memories. In one study, researchers provided false suggestions to adults about various school-related pranks (e.g., putting Slime on a teacher's desk in Grade 1 or 2). Some participants viewed group class photos from that time and others did not. The rate of false memory reports was substantially higher among participants who viewed the photographs (Lindsay, Hagen, Read, Wade, & Garry, 2004). This is concerning because some memory-focused therapists recommend that adults who think they have been abused should view family photo albums to cue long-forgotten memories of abuse.

Simply imagining an event from one's past can also affect the belief that it actually occurred, even when the event is completely implausible—for example, proposing marriage to a Pepsi machine (Seamon, Philbin, & Harrison, 2006) or shaking hands with Bugs Bunny at a Disney theme park (Braun, Ellis, & Loftus, 2002). (The Bugs Bunny character was created by Warner Brothers, not Disney.)

How can we account for this "imagination inflation" effect? One possibility is **source confusion**. The act of imagining may make the event seem more familiar, but that familiarity is mistakenly related to childhood memories rather than to the act of imagination itself. The creation of false memories is most likely to occur when people who are having trouble remembering are explicitly encouraged to imagine events and discouraged from thinking about whether their constructions are real. But keep in mind that although false childhood memories can be implanted in some people, the memories that result from suggestions are not always false. Unfortunately, without corroboration, it is very hard to know which distant memories are true and which were implanted via suggestion.

False Memories in Court

Evidence that false memories are a significant problem for the law comes in several forms. First, accusations that arise from recovered "memories" sometimes result in litigation. Because the accused are often related to the victims, other family members may be forced to take sides, causing strain and animosity within a family. On some occasions, though, prosecutors have decided not to pursue cases based solely on repressed memory. Said Patrick Lynch, the Rhode Island Attorney General who dismissed such a case in 2007, "the high burden for admissibility, at trial, of testimony based on repressed memory" would create "a legal impediment that the state is unlikely to overcome" (Zezima & Carey, 2009).

The second problem for the legal system is that some accusers have retracted their claims of repressed memories for abuse. One of the most highly publicized retractions involved another case of alleged priest abuse, this time against Cardinal Joseph Bernardin, who was once the senior-ranking Roman Catholic official in the United States. Ironically, Bernardin was well known for his work helping children who had been sexually abused by priests. His accuser ultimately dropped the lawsuit after admitting that his charges were based on false memories.

Finally, parents have sued therapists who used aggressive memory recovery techniques to help the adult children of these parents recover supposedly repressed memories of CSA. The claims in these malpractice lawsuits usually take the following form: (1) The abuse never occurred, (2) therapists created and implanted false memories of abuse through their uncritical use of memory retrieval techniques, and (3) clients ultimately came to believe the false memories and accused their parents of the abuse. These cases have sometimes resulted in large financial settlements to those who were falsely accused, including Gary Ramona (see Box 5.5).

B o x 5.5 THE CASE OF GARY RAMONA, HIS DAUGHTER'S FALSE MEMORIES, AND THE THERAPISTS WHO SUGGESTED THEM

The first parent who successfully sued a therapist for implanting a false memory of abuse was Gary Ramona, a winery executive from Napa County, California. Ramona accused a family counselor and a psychiatrist of planting false memories in his 19-year-old daughter, Holly, when she was their patient. Ramona claimed that the therapists told Holly that her bulimia and depression were caused by having been repeatedly raped by her father when she was a child. According to Ramona, the psychiatrist gave Holly sodium amytal ("truth serum") to confirm the validity of her "recovered memory."

At their trial, the therapists claimed that Holly suffered flashbacks of what seemed to be real sexual abuse. She also became increasingly depressed and bulimic after reporting these frightening images. But the scientific experts who testified on Ramona's behalf criticized the therapists for using risky and dangerous techniques including suggestive questioning and sodium amytal. The jury decided that Holly's therapists had indeed acted improperly and awarded Gary Ramona damages in the amount of $500,000. In the words of his attorney, "If [therapists] use nonsensical theories about so-called repressed memories to destroy people's lives, they will be held accountable."

Critical Thought Question
What factors may have contributed to Holly Ramona's false memory?

SUMMARY

1. *What psychological factors contribute to the risk of mistaken identifications in the legal system?* Evidence produced by eyewitnesses often makes the difference between an unsolved crime and a conviction. In the early stages of a crime investigation, eyewitness accounts can provide important clues and permit suspects to be identified. But witnesses often make mistakes, and mistaken identifications have led to the conviction of numerous innocent people. Errors can occur at the moment the crime is committed or at any of the three phases of the memory process: encoding, storage, and retrieval. Furthermore, subsequent questioning and new experiences can alter what is remembered from the past.

2. *What are the defining features of estimator, system, and postdiction variables in the study of eyewitness memory?* In describing the factors that affect the reliability of eyewitness memory, psychologists distinguish (1) estimator variables whose impact on an identification can only be estimated and not controlled, (2) system variables that are under the control of the justice system, and (3) postdiction variables that correlate with the accuracy of an identification. Much recent research has focused on a particular set of system variables related to the way lineups are conducted.

3. *How do jurors evaluate the testimony of eyewitnesses, and how can psychological research help jurors understand the potential problems of eyewitness testimony?* Jurors are heavily influenced by the testimony of eyewitnesses, and they tend to overestimate the accuracy of such witnesses, relying to a great extent on the confidence of the eyewitness. To alert jurors to these problems, two types of remediation have been described (in addition to limiting eye-witness evidence when it was gleaned through suggestive procedures). Some trial judges permit psychologists to testify as expert witnesses about the problems inherent in eyewitness memory. Laboratory evaluations of mock juries find that such testimony generally sensitizes jurors to factors that affect an eyewitness's reliability. The other intervention is for the judge to give the jurors a "cautionary instruction," sensitizing them to aspects of the testimony of eyewitnesses that they should consider.

4. *Can children accurately report on their experiences of victimization? What factors affect the accuracy of their reports? Are they likely to disclose abuse?* When children are questioned in a non-suggestive manner and are asked open-ended questions, the resulting report will be more accurate than when suggestive interrogation procedures are

used. Children are also less accurate in answering specific question than more general questions, and sometimes recall information from one event as having occurred in another. Multiple interviews can facilitate memory recall. Most children are able to remember details of their maltreatment and describe them accurately, though victims who suppressed their thoughts about it may have memory deficits.

5. ***Can memories of trauma be repressed, and if so, can these memories be recovered accurately?*** Sometimes, memories of trauma are repressed and later recalled. But the accuracy of repressed

and then recovered memories is suspect when the recollections occur in the context of therapies that use suggestive memory retrieval techniques. Recent research shows that people can "remember" events that never happened, sometimes simply by imagining them. Litigation involving the recovery of repressed memories involves lawsuits brought by victims claiming that therapists led them to believe that they were abused in the past, as well as lawsuits brought by the accused claiming that therapists promoting such false recollections are guilty of malpractice.

KEY TERMS

absolute judgment
archival analysis
autobiographical memory
cognitive interview
confirmation bias
confrontation clause
dissociation
double-blind testing procedures
ecological validity

encoding
estimator variable
experimental methodology
experimenter bias
field studies
ground truth
in-group/out-group differences
open-ended questions
other-race effect

photographic lineup
photospread
physiognomic variability
postdiction variable
post-event information
relative judgment
reminiscence effect
repression
retention interval
retrieval

selective attention
sequential presentation
simultaneous presentation
source confusion
storage
suggestive questions
system variable
unconscious transference
weapon focus effect

Chapter
6

Psychology of Victims of Crime and Violence

ORIENTING QUESTIONS

1. What is the frequency of crime victimization?
2. What types of research have psychologists conducted on victimization?
3. What factors predict the development of PTSD after being a crime victim?
4. What are the components of the battered woman syndrome?
5. How can rape be prevented?
6. What are two types of sexual harassment recognized by the courts?

PERCEPTION OF THOSE WHO EXPERIENCE CRIME AND/OR VIOLENCE

One element of almost every crime is the presence of at least one victim. Even so-called victimless crimes—crimes such as prostitution, ticket scalping, and gambling—have victims, even if they do not immediately recognize it or would not describe themselves that way. The social burdens and psychological costs of these offenses—the squandering of a person's income as a consequence of the inevitable losses from habitual gambling or the physical abuse and underworld crimes that surround prostitution—are often delayed. Ultimately, however, society and individuals are victimized by these crimes.

Society has different reactions toward victims. While most individuals feel sympathy toward them, we also tend to question why they became victims, and sometimes we even blame them for their plight. One reason for this inclination is the need to believe in a "just world." The thought of becoming victims ourselves is so threatening that we feel compelled to find an explanation for why other people are victimized (Lerner, 1980). These justifications often take the form of singling out victims as the primary cause of their own plight.

Such judgments are predicted by the perspective known as attribution theory, which originated with the work of Fritz Heider (1958). Heider stated that people operate as "naive psychologists"; they reach conclusions about what caused a given behavior by considering both personal and environmental factors. Generally, when considering someone else's actions, we use **dispositional attributions** that focus on the person's ability level, personality, or even temporary states (such as fatigue or luck) as explanations for the conduct in question. To explain a person's misfortune as the consequence of his or her physical disabilities, lack of effort, or loose morals reflects a kind of defensive attribution that puts the onus for bad outcomes on the person rather than on the environment. Such reactions help shape our responses to victims. The norms of our society demand that we help others if they deserve our help, but if people are responsible for their own suffering, we feel less obligated to help them (Mulford, Lee, & Sapp, 1996).

The phrase *blaming the victim* was first popularized in a widely read book by William Ryan (1970), in which the author observed that people on welfare were often seen as lazy or shiftless and hence responsible for their fate. An extreme example of blaming the victim was offered by trial attorney Robert Baker, who represented O. J. Simpson in his civil trial for the wrongful deaths of Nicole Brown and Ronald Goldman. His opening statement for the defense included a scorching attack on Nicole Brown, whom he portrayed as a heavy-drinking party girl whose dangerous lifestyle often included companions who were prostitutes and drug dealers. Sometimes by implication and sometimes by direct comment, he communicated that she had many boyfriends and had had at least one abortion. As a trial observer noted, "it was as close to calling her a slut [as one could come] without using the word" (quoted by Reibstein & Foote, 1996, p. 64). Baker demeaned the victim for a reason, of course; he wanted to imply that a sordid lifestyle had led to her becoming involved with someone other than O. J. Simpson and that this supposed individual had killed her (Toobin, 1996). Simpson himself has echoed this claim, stating that he was angry at Nicole because, he felt, her careless lifestyle contributed to her being murdered.

A more recent example of "blaming the victim" may be seen in the wake of the worldwide economic recession of 2008 and the sluggish recovery of the U.S. economy with respect to reemploying many of those who had lost jobs in the recession. Losing a job is a traumatic life event that many would prefer to think could not happen to them. One way to perpetuate this belief is to conclude that those who lost jobs somehow "deserved" it, because they were less capable, industrious, or motivated. This actually combines two beliefs discussed in this book—belief in a just world and a tendency to blame the victim—that may be held to protect individuals from the frightening realization that they are also at risk of losing a job.

TYPES OF VICTIMS

There is no shortage of victims in our society. Estimates of the numbers of children who are sexually abused, of adults who are battered by their partners, and of women and men who are assaulted, robbed, or raped run into the millions each year.

The primary source of information on crime victims in the United States is the Bureau of Justice Statistics' National Crime Victimization Survey, which can be found at www.ojp.usdoj.gov/bjs/. Each year, data are collected from a national sample of 50,000 households on the frequency and consequences of criminal victimization in the form of rape and other sexual assaults, robbery, theft, assault, household burglary, and car theft. From these figures, one can calculate the rate of victimization nationwide. For example, it is estimated that in 2008 (the most recent year for which these statistics are available), approximately 21 million criminal victimizations occurred; 16 million involved property crimes, and 5 million were crimes of violence. Additional statistics on the frequency, consequences, and prevention of criminal victimization can be found at the National Center for Victims of Crime website (www.ncvc.org).

For other offenses, it is difficult to assess the frequency of victimization, but what we do know is that they happen all too often. Included here, for example, are acts of racial or religious discrimination in which the recipient is denied rights that are accorded to others. Homophobic attitudes, teasing, and bullying are frequently reported (Harris Interactive and GLSEN, 2005), and verbal and physical victimization based on sexual orientation has been related to posttraumatic stress symptoms (Dragowski, Halkitis, Grossman, & D'Augelli, 2011). We describe the story of one victim in Box 6.1.

Box 6.1   THE CASE OF MATTHEW SHEPARD: VICTIM OF A HATE CRIME

On a chilly October evening in 1998, two bicyclists riding on Snowy Mountain View Road outside of Laramie, Wyoming saw what they thought was a scarecrow tied to a rough-hewn deer fence. Only after coming closer did the horror set in. This was no scarecrow. This was—or had been—a man. His head had been beaten, his face was cut and covered with blood and tears, and his limbs had been scorched with burn marks. Police believe that Matthew Shepard, a slightly built gay freshman at the University of Wyoming, was lured into a pickup truck by two tall, muscular men who pretended that they, too, were gay. All pretenses vanished as the pair began pounding Shepard on the head with a .357 Magnum revolver, then tied him to the post, beat him relentlessly, and left him to die. He was found 18 hours later, barely alive, and died within days of the beating.

As Shepard's case riveted the nation, state and federal legislators became increasingly concerned about the proliferation of **hate crimes**—criminal acts intended to harm or intimidate people because of their race, ethnicity, sexual orientation, religion, or other minority group status. To date, the federal government and 45 states have enacted laws that allow stiffer sentencing for defendants who choose their victims based on perceptions of at least one of the following: the victim's race, religion, ethnicity, or sexual orientation. Sexual orientation is

Matthew Shepard

specifically identified by 31 states. Wyoming is one of the few states that do not identify any of these factors as exacerbating at sentencing (Anti-Defamation League, 2012).

Critical Thought Question
Why should an offense be considered worse because it is directed toward a member of a minority group?

The Harris survey (Harris Interactive and GLSEN, 2005) involved a nationally representative sample of 3450 students ages 13 through 18, and a nationally representative sample of secondary school teachers. There were several major findings relevant to Lesbian/Gay/Bisexual/Transgender (LGBT) students. Verbal or physical harassment was reported to be a common problem, with 65% of students indicating that they had been harassed during the last year because of appearance, sexual orientation, race/ethnicity, disability, or religion. A total of 39% reported such harassment due to their appearance, and 33% said they were harassed because of their actual or perceived sexual orientation. LGBT students were three times as likely to report feeling unsafe at school (22% versus 7% of non-LGBT students), and 1.5 times as likely to have been harassed (90% versus 62%). More teachers (53%) than students (36%) reported that they considered bullying or harassment to be a "serious problem" at their school.

Technological advancements and cultural changes have brought new forms of victimization to the fore. Identity theft, in which information about an individual's personal and financial life is stolen by computer hackers and then used fraudulently, has become a major fear of people in the 21st century. Cyberstalking is a recently emerged technique favored by some sexual predators as a way to target victims. Cyberbullying can occur through blogs, Facebook, and other social networking sites. The first-ever cyberbullying trial involved a Missouri woman, Lori Drew, who perpetrated a "mean-spirited Internet hoax" (Risling, 2008). Drew created a fictitious 16-year-old boy on MySpace and sent flirtatious messages to her 13-year-old neighbor, Megan Meier, who had apparently been mean to Drew's daughter. But after the "boy" dumped Meier, saying, "The world would be a better place without you," Meier hanged herself in her bedroom closet. Drew was convicted on three misdemeanor charges.

In addition to cyberbullying, psychologists have identified four other subtypes of bullying: physical, verbal, social exclusion, and spreading rumors (Wang, Iannotti, Luk, & Nansel, 2010). Males were more likely to be victims of all types of bullying.

This chapter concentrates on four types of victims and the effects of victimization on them: people who experience adversity and trauma in childhood, targets of sexual harassment, battered spouses, and victims of violent crime—particularly rape, the violent crime

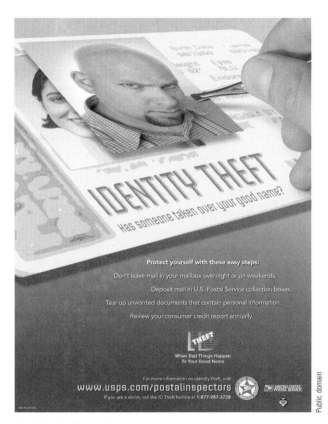

Identity theft warning

that has been studied most often. For each of these, the field of psychology has generated theory and research relevant to the laws and court decisions instituted to protect such victims. The responses of the legal system reflect conflicting views in our society about the nature of victims, especially victims of sex-related offenses. For example, how extreme does a situation need to be before we conclude that sexual harassment exists, and how distressed does the response of the victim need to be? In the case of a battered woman who kills her batterer, will a jury accept a claim of self-defense? Also, why do as many as two-thirds of rape victims never report the attack to the police?

ADVERSITY AND TRAUMA IN CHILDHOOD

There are two kinds of experience that are important to consider in the course of human development. The first involves experiences that are emotionally painful and overwhelming for the individual's capacity to cope effectively. Examples include the abuse of children of various kinds (e.g., sexual abuse, physical abuse, severe neglect). The second refers to the kind of chronic adversity that results from influences such as poverty, racism, and other such longstanding, less acute but more pervasive aspects of the lives of some children. Although adversity may be accompanied by the development of coping strategies, it has a cumulative impact that can affect an individual's development and adult functioning in various problematic ways.

The relationship between traumatic childhood experiences and physical and emotional health outcomes in adult life is at the core of the landmark Adverse Childhood Experiences (ACE) Study. The ACE Study involved the cooperation of over 17,000 middle-aged (average age was 57), middle-class Americans who agreed to help researchers study the following nine categories of childhood abuse and household dysfunction: recurrent physical abuse; recurrent emotional abuse; contact sexual abuse; an alcohol and/or drug abuser in the household; an incarcerated household member; a household member who is chronically depressed, mentally ill, institutionalized, or suicidal; a mother who is treated violently; one or no parents; and emotional or physical neglect. Each participant received an ACE score in the range of 0–9 reflecting the number of the above experiences he or she could claim (Felitti et al., 1998).

The study claims two major findings, the first being that adverse childhood experiences are much more common than anticipated or recognized, even in the middle-class population that participated in the study, all of whom received health care via a large health maintenance organization (HMO). It is reasonable to presume that the prevalence of ACEs is significantly higher among young African-American and Latino males—many of whom live with chronic stress and do not have a regular source of health care.

The study's second major finding is that adverse childhood experiences have a strong relationship to health outcomes later in life. As the ACE score increases, so does the risk of an array of social and health problems such as social, emotional and cognitive impairment; adoption of health-risk behaviors; disease, disability and social problems; and early death. ACEs are strong correlated with adolescent health, teen pregnancy, smoking, substance abuse, sexual behavior, the risk of revictimization, performance

in the workforce, and the stability of relationships, among other health determinants. The higher the ACE score, the greater the risk of heart disease, lung disease, liver disease, suicide, HIV and STDs, and other risks for the leading causes of death (Felitti et al., 1998).

Consequences of Early Victimization

One might wonder whether early victimization experiences increase the likelihood of adolescent and adult criminality. Cathy Spatz Widom (1989, 1992) used court records to identify a group of 908 children in a Midwestern American city who had suffered abuse (i.e., sexual abuse or physical assault leading to injury) or severe neglect (i.e., inadequate food, clothing, shelter, or medical care) between 1967 and 1971. This "abuse/neglect" group was matched to a group of 667 children who had not been exposed to abuse or neglect but who were similar in gender, age, ethnicity, and family socioeconomic status. Matching the abused and nonabused groups on these variables was important, because it enabled Widom to assume that any differences between the groups in terms of violent behavior in adolescence or adulthood were not due to differences in demographic characteristics.

Widom's analysis of police and court records showed that, as earlier research had suggested, abused or neglected children were significantly more likely than the comparison group to have been arrested for violent crimes as juveniles or as adults. In addition, the abused or neglected individuals were, on average, a year younger than comparison subjects at the time of their first arrest and had committed twice as many total offenses over the 15- to 20-year period studied. These differences were seen in boys and girls and in European Americans and African Americans; however, the relationship between abuse and violence was particularly strong among African Americans.

Data on this sample were collected again 22 to 26 years after the abuse or neglect (Maxfield & Widom, 1996). The researchers found that by age 32, almost half of the abused/neglected group (49%) had been arrested for a nontraffic offense. This percentage was considerably greater than for the matched control sample (38%). Furthermore, victims of abuse and neglect were more likely than members of the control group to have been arrested for violent crimes, even after controlling for age, race, and gender.

Widom and her colleagues next examined the impact of sexual abuse, physical abuse, and neglect in childhood on adult mental health outcomes (Horwitz, Widom, McLaughlin, & White, 2001). Findings suggested that both men and women with histories of childhood abuse and neglect displayed increased levels of mood disorders and antisocial personality characteristics when compared with matched controls. The abused and neglected women also reported more alcohol problems than both the men and the matched groups. Although this line of research has suggested a strong association between childhood experiences of abuse and neglect and elevated levels of mental health problems in adulthood, these differences dissipated after controlling for other stressful life events.

Widom and colleagues (Widom, Schuck, & White, 2006) next conducted a follow-up study with these data focusing on potential pathways between childhood victimization and violent criminal behavior, focusing on early aggressive behavior and problematic drinking. They found different pathways for men and women. For men, child maltreatment is related to later aggression toward others as well as later problematic alcohol use. In women, early victimization was directly related to later alcohol problems, which in turn were related to later violence toward others.

Finally, Kaplow and Widom (2007) used these data to identify documented cases of children who were physically and sexually abused and neglected prior to age 12 (N=496), and followed them into adulthood. Earlier onset of maltreatment predicted more symptoms of anxiety and depression in adulthood, even when controlling for gender, race, current age, and other abuse reports. Later onset of maltreatment was associated with more behavioral problems in adulthood.

As disturbing as these results are, they may actually *underestimate* the risks created by childhood abuse. Only offenses that resulted in arrest or trial were included in the studies linking early victimization to later criminality. Undetected or unreported crimes may have been committed by members of the abused/neglected group. These findings highlight the importance of considering early child abuse and neglect as part of a broader constellation of life stressors rather than isolating them as independent predictors of adult outcomes.

VIOLENCE, CRIME, AND POSTTRAUMATIC STRESS DISORDER

The dilemmas confronted throughout this book, especially the quest to preserve both the rights of suspects and the rights of victims, come into sharp focus when we consider the victims of crime, particularly victims of violent crimes such as rape. Until recently, society had not paid much attention to crime victims. Their trial testimony was necessary to obtain convictions, but most of the legal rights formally protected in the adversarial system are extended to defendants, not victims. As a result, the needs and rights of crime victims have often been ignored.

This imbalance began to change in the late 1970s and early 1980s as victim advocacy groups, mental health professionals, police, and court officials all began to acknowledge the need to better recognize and serve crime victims. Several developments reflect the growing stature and influence of the victims' rights movement:

- The emergence of the interdisciplinary field of **victimology**, which concentrates on studying the process and consequences of victimization experiences and how victims (or *survivors*, which is the term preferred by many) recover

- The increasing availability of services to crime victims, including compensation and restitution programs, victim assistance programs in the courts, self-help programs, and formal mental health services

- The expanded opportunity for victims to participate in the trials of their victimizers through mechanisms such as victim impact statements

- The heightened focus on victims brought about by new journals (one example is *Victimology*; another is *Violence and Victims*); organizations such as the National Organization for Victim Assistance; and commissions such as the President's Commission on Victims of Crime (1982) and the American Psychological Association's Task Force on the Victims of Crime and Violence

For their part, psychologists have conducted research on and delivered clinical services to a diverse array of crime victims. Three areas have received special attention: the consequences of physical/sexual abuse on child victims; the role of violent victimization as a cause of psychological disorders, particularly post-traumatic stress disorder; and the psychology of rape. We review the latter two topics in this chapter.

Posttraumatic Stress Disorder

Individuals who suffer a severe trauma and, weeks or months later, continue to experience intense, fear-related reactions when reminded of the trauma, may be experiencing **posttraumatic stress disorder** (PTSD). By definition, such trauma must involve a threat of serious injury or death. We have seen vivid and disturbing examples of PTSD in soldiers returning from the wars in Iraq and Afghanistan. As well, most instances of violent crime qualify as trauma severe enough to trigger PTSD in at least some victims.

The symptoms of PTSD fall into three broad classes (these symptoms must last longer than one month to qualify as PTSD):

1. Frequent re-experiencing of the event through intrusive thoughts, flashbacks, and repeated nightmares and dreams

2. Persistent avoidance of stimuli associated with the trauma and a general numbing or deadening of emotions (feeling detached or estranged from others)

3. Increased physiological arousal resulting in exaggerated startle responses or difficulty sleeping

The case of Joe (Box 6.2) reveals how these diagnostic criteria apply to a real-life case. Sexually abused by parents and older boys, Joe suffered a series of extremely traumatic events and other adverse events throughout his childhood and adolescence. He experienced symptoms including difficulty sleeping, avoidance of people and human relationships, hypervigilance, and nightmares. The correct diagnosis and appropriate treatment resulted in some improvement, but Joe's life was still very difficult.

How common is PTSD? The National Comorbidity Survey Replication (NCS-R) involved interviews of a nationally representative sample of 9,282 Americans who were at least 18 years old. Using criteria from the American Psychiatric Association's DSM-IV-TR (2000), PTSD was assessed among 5,692 participants. The NCS-R estimated the lifetime prevalence of PTSD among adult Americans to be 6.8% (Kessler et al., 2005), with 3.6% prevalence for men and 9.7% for women.

Do military veterans experience PTSD more commonly than individuals in the general population? Using the figures described in the previous paragraph for comparison, the answer is yes. The National Center

---

B o x 6.2 THE CASE OF JOE: ADVERSE EXPERIENCE, MULTIPLE TRAUMAS, AND POSTTRAUMATIC STRESS DISORDER

Joe's life of adverse experience and trauma began in his childhood. He reported that both of his parents sexually abused him. He added that his father once "split my skull … because I was in his way." Joe was a ward of the state and sent to an orphanage as a young child. When he was moved to a wing housing older boys, "I was raped the first night. The rapes continued all throughout my stay at the home."

Today Joe is in his 50s. But the effects of his childhood are still with him. He suffers from posttraumatic stress disorder, which includes intense anxiety, nightmares, constant fear for one's safety, and always being on guard.

Joe attempted suicide for the first time when he was 12, and his adolescence included three more attempts. He ended up leaving the orphanage and hitchhiking around, but says that he still lived in fear, could never relax, and tended to sabotage himself. He tried working so much that he became "sort of a workaholic"; he tried relationships (including a marriage) that didn't work

out, and always assumed that other people didn't want to be around him. He was on workplace disability, seeing therapist after therapist (most frequent diagnosis: chronic depression), when eventually he came in contact with a psychiatrist who spent enough time with Joe and asked the right questions to diagnose Joe with PTSD. He improved a good deal, although he still experiences chronic insomnia. He works with male survivors of abuse through online technology and an in-person support group.

Many think of PTSD as a disorder associated with war. Joe's case demonstrates that it can be associated with adverse experience and trauma at other stages of life as well (Kopfinger, 2007).

Critical Thought Question
Does everyone exposed to life-threatening trauma develop PTSD? If not, why not?

Source: Courtesy of Sunday News, Lancaster, PA.

for PTSD (Department of Veterans Affairs, 2012) provides information about the rates of PTSD experienced by various population subgroups. Among military veterans, the lifetime prevalence rates for Vietnam veterans at the time of the National Vietnam Veterans Readjustment Study (1986–1988) were 30.9% for men and 26.9% for women, and the rates of PTSD experienced at the time of the study were 15.2% for men and 8.2% for women (Kulka et al., 1990). The time-of-study (1995–1997) PTSD prevalence rate for Gulf War veterans was estimated at 12.1% (Kang, Natelson, Mahan, Lee, & Murphy, 2003), and the time-of-study (2008) PTSD prevalence for veterans of Operation Enduring Freedom/Operation Iraqi Freedom at 13.8% (Tanielian & Jaycox, 2008).

Heidi Resnick and her colleagues (Resnick, Kilpatrick, Dansky, Saunders, & Best, 1993) conducted a diagnostic survey of 4,008 females and found that 12% of the sample had symptoms of PTSD at some time in their lives and that 4.6% were currently suffering PTSD symptoms. These percentages suggest that in the United States alone, 11,800,000 women have had PTSD at some time in their lives and that 4,400,000 suffer from it at any given time (Resnick et al., 1993). This is particularly important because PTSD has been shown to be related to suicidal ideation and suicidal attempts (Cougle, Resnick, & Kilpatrick, 2009).

The nature of one's trauma is an important consideration. Military service is a risk factor for PTSD, as may be seen by the elevated "current prevalence" rates cited earlier. Resnick and colleagues (Resnick et al., 1993) found that 26% of women whose trauma was related to crime developed PTSD, whereas only 9% of women who had sustained a noncriminal trauma developed PTSD symptoms. The extent of physical injury during trauma also predicts whether PTSD symptoms will develop. Women who were physically injured by a trauma are more likely to develop PTSD symptoms than those who were not. Victims' perceptions of trauma are also important in determining the likelihood of PTSD. The victim's belief that his or her life is in danger and that he or she has no control over the trauma increases risk for PTSD (Foa & Kozak, 1986; Green, Grace, Lindy, Gleser, & Leonard, 1990; Kushner et al., 1992). One study suggests that cognitive processing during the trauma (such as persistent dissociation) and beliefs after the trauma (such as negative interpretations of trauma memories) predict PTSD symptoms to a

greater degree than objective and subjective measures of the severity of the trauma (Halligan, Michael, Clark, & Ehlers, 2003).

Although traumas are unfortunate facts of life, there is reason to believe that PTSD—in some trauma victims, at least—can be prevented. For one thing, although many persons who experience severe trauma may develop **acute stress disorder** (trauma-related symptoms that last less than one month), most do not go on to develop PTSD. One reason may be that those experiencing trauma, but not PTSD, tend to receive high levels of social support from family, friends, or counselors immediately following the event (Grills-Taquechel, Littleton, & Axsom, 2011). Thus, providing immediate social support for trauma victims may prevent their experiences from progressing into posttraumatic stress disorder.

Two other characteristics distinguish people who develop PTSD from those who do not. Individuals who suffer PTSD often perceive the world as a dangerous place from which they must retreat, and they come to view themselves as helpless to deal with stressors. If these two misconceptions could be eliminated, full-blown cases of PTSD might be prevented in many victims. Edna Foa (well known for her use of exposure therapy—which involves gradually "exposing" individuals to milder forms of the trauma and thereby reducing the associated anxiety—in treating PTSD) has developed a four-session prevention course designed to attack these two misconceptions in women who have been raped or assaulted. Foa includes the following elements in her PTSD prevention course:

1. Education about the common psychological reactions to assault in order to help victims realize that their responses are normal

2. Training in skills such as relaxation so that the women are better prepared to cope with stress

3. Emotionally reliving the trauma through imagery-based exposure methods to allow victims to defuse their lingering fears of the trauma

4. Cognitive restructuring to help the women replace negative beliefs about their competence and adequacy with more realistic appraisals

Foa and her colleagues evaluated these procedures on 10 women who had recently been raped or assaulted and who completed the four-week course. Victims' PTSD symptoms were compared with those of 10 other women who had also been assaulted or raped but who did not take part in the course. At the times of two follow-up assessments (2 months and 5.5 months, respectively, after the assaults) victims who had completed the prevention course had fewer PTSD symptoms than control subjects who had not received treatment. Two months after their trauma, 70% of the untreated women, but only 10% of the treated women, met the criteria for PTSD (Foa, Hearst-Ikeda, & Perry, 1995). These results suggest that a brief program that facilitates emotionally re-experiencing trauma *and* correcting beliefs about personal inadequacy can reduce the incidence of PTSD.

Regardless of whether they result in PTSD, the frequency and consequences of traumatic and other adverse events may be greater than many have thought. As discussed earlier, the Adverse Childhood Experience (ACE) Study (Felitti et al., 1998) found a graded relationship between the number of categories of childhood exposure and each of the adult health risk behaviors and diseases that were studied (including alcoholism, drug abuse, depression, suicide attempts, smoking, poor health, multiple sexual partners and sexually transmitted disease, and severe obesity). Such adverse experiences have particularly been linked to increased risk of PTSD (Breslau et al., 1998; Breslau, Chilcoat, Kessler, & Davis, 1999; Perkonigg, Kessler, Storz, & Wittchen, 2000; Roberts, Gillman, Breslau, Breslau, & Koenen, 2011) as well as anxiety disorders along with lower intellectual functioning (Breslau, Lucia, & Alvarado, 2006).

The question of how such traumatic events affect the risk of antisocial behavior toward others, in the form of juvenile delinquency and criminal offending, is a complex one. In addition to the Widom research described earlier, there is evidence of a relationship between trauma and posttraumatic symptoms in younger cohorts. When adolescents are studied, the evidence suggests that this relationship is similar to the adverse outcomes experienced by adults (Breslau et al., 2006; Cuffe et al., 1998; Giaconia et al., 1995), although adolescents may be particularly vulnerable because the context in which the trauma occurs (often the family) is where the individual continues to live in many instances.

High-risk youths have often been abused or neglected (Swahn et al., 2006). Consistent with this finding, Abram and colleagues (2004, 2007) have conducted large-scale studies of incarcerated youth

and described a substantially elevated risk for traumatic history and psychiatric comorbidity (multiple diagnoses) among such youth. This suggests that early victimization experiences may be related to multiple psychiatric diagnoses and criminal conduct among adolescents.

BATTERED SPOUSES

Prevalence Rates

The extent of physical abuse directed toward spouses and romantic partners in American society is difficult to estimate, but many observe that it is extensive. It has been estimated that some form of physical aggression occurs in one-fourth to one-third of all couples (Straus & Gelles, 1988). More recent estimates suggest that 33% of men and 25% of women have been involved in a physically aggressive altercation, with the most severe episodes occurring in or near a bar for the men and in the home for the women (Leonard, Quigley, & Collins, 2002). One-year prevalence estimates for violence against women in the United States have been described as 0.3% to 4% for severe violence and 8% to 17% for total violence. The prevalence of lifetime domestic violence ranges from 1.9% in Washington State to 70% in Hispanic women in the Southeastern U.S. (Alhabib, Nur, & Jones, 2010).

Although relationship aggression by women against men is as frequent as male-to-female aggression (Magdol et al., 1997), male aggression toward women is significantly more likely to result in serious injuries (Tanha, Beck, Figueredo, & Raghavan, 2010; Tjaden & Thoennes, 2000). About 30% of all the women murdered in the United States each year are killed by their male partners (Kellerman & Mercy, 1992). For this reason, most of the research on relationship aggression has concentrated on male aggression against female partners (Rosenbaum & Gearan, 1999); we echo that emphasis in this chapter.

Despite these disturbing statistics and the continuing research on relationship aggression, myths about battered women still abound. The mass media often pay little attention to this kind of violence (except in highly publicized cases, such as those of Rihanna and Whitney Houston). As a result of mistaken beliefs about battering, some professionals, such as physicians and police, fail to ask appropriate questions when a woman reports an attack by her intimate partner; arrest and prosecution of perpetrators of part-ner violence remain unpredictable; and protective restraining orders against batterers are often not con-sistently enforced.

Myths and Exaggerated Beliefs

Experts emphasize that many oversimplified beliefs, exaggerations, and myths about battered women exist. Follingstad (1994) identified the following misconceptions:

1. Battered women are masochists.

2. They provoke the assaults inflicted on them.

3. They get the treatment they deserve.

4. They are free to leave their violent relationships any time they want to.

5. Violence among intimate partners is not common.

6. Men who are nonviolent in their dealings with outsiders behave the same way in their dealings with their intimates.

7. Middle-class and upper-class men don't batter, and middle-class and upper-class women don't get beaten.

8. Battering is a lower-class, ethnic-minority phenomenon, and such women don't mind because this is a part of their culture.

9. "Good" battered women are passive and never try to defend themselves. (p. 15)

This research examining U.S. perceptions of domestic violence is more than two decades old, so it may not reflect current attitudes in this area. A more recent survey regarding attitudes and beliefs shows that most respondents think of domestic vio-lence as stemming from individual problems, relation-ships, and families, but not from the nature of our society. Not many think that women cause their own abuse, but about 25% believe that some women want to be abused, and most believe that women can end abusive relationships (Worden & Carlson, 2005).

Research conducted in some other countries has yielded somewhat consistent results. For instance, a national study conducted in Singapore found that the overwhelming majority of the 510 participants disapproved of battery, and only about 6% agreed that under some circumstances it is acceptable for a husband to use physical force against his partner (Choi & Edleson, 1996). Another study conducted

with Israeli husbands found that the majority of participants (58%) agreed that "there is no excuse for a man to beat his wife" (p. 199). However, investiga-tors also found that nearly one-third believed that wife beating is justified on certain occasions (e.g., unfaithful sexual behavior, disrespect of relatives) (Haj-Yahia, 2003). The attitudes of this latter group are consis-tent with the belief that women provoke domestic assaults and are treated in the way they deserve.

The misconceptions listed earlier obscure several truths about the plight of battered women: Battered women face many real obstacles that make it difficult for them to leave their abusers, and when they do attempt to leave abusive relationships—as many women do—they often suffer further threats, recrimi-nations, and attacks.

The Causes of Battering

What are the main risk factors for battering? Researchers who have studied the causes of battering have focused on the characteristics of the battering victim, the nature of violent intimate relationships, and the psychological makeup of batterers.

We focus our coverage on batterers. One review points to several risk factors in the lives of batterers as important (Rosenbaum & Gearan, 1999). Although batterers come from all socioeconomic and ethnic backgrounds, they are more likely than nonbatterers to be unemployed, less well educated, members of minority groups, and of lower socioeconomic status. Batterers tend to have been raised in families in which they either suffered physical abuse as children or observed an abusive relationship between their par-ents. Adolescents who later become batterers have experienced a higher rate of conduct problems and are more likely to have engaged in early substance abuse; early experiences with coercive or aggressive behavior may set the stage for similar strategies in adult relationships (Magdol, Moffitt, Caspi, & Silva, 1998). In addition, batterers usually have poor self-concepts, are not very good problem solvers, and often have limited verbal skills. They are prone to extreme jealousy and fear of being abandoned by their partners. As a result, they monitor their partners' activities closely and exert excessive control over their partners' whereabouts and activities. They overreact to signs of rejection and alternate between rage and desperation.

Although research suggests that batterers have many characteristics in common, not all batterers share a common profile. For instance, one comprehensive study revealed three distinct types of batterers: generally violent, psychopathological, and family-only (Waltz, Babcock, Jacobson, & Gottman, 2000). These groups were distinguished by the degree of violence within the relationship and the degree of general violence reported, as well as by personality characteristics. For instance, generally violent batterers displayed the highest levels of aggressive-sadistic behavior, psychopathological batterers exhibited more passive-aggressive/dependent characteristics, and family-only batterers displayed violent behaviors but generally did not hold violence-supportive beliefs and attitudes.

Findings from this study further indicated that differences in life experiences accounted for some of the variations in each of the group's behavior. For instance, when the generally violent batterers and the family-only batterers were compared, both groups were found to have experienced physical abuse as children, but significant differences existed in the frequency and severity of interparental violence witnessed; the generally violent batterers had witnessed more frequent and severe parental violence. These findings suggest that understanding the risk factors associated with batterers may be quite complex.

The Cycle of Violence

Batterers are sometimes described as displaying a **cycle of violence** involving a Jekyll-and-Hyde pattern of emotional and behavioral instability that makes their victims all the more fearful of the battering they believe is inevitable. A man may be loving and attentive to a woman's needs early in their relationship as he cultivates her affection and relies on her to satisfy his dependency needs; however, when disappointments or disagreements occur in the relationship, as they invariably do, a *tension-building phase* begins, characterized by increased criticism of the partner and perhaps even minor physical assaults.

This phase leads to a second stage in the cycle, an *acute battering incident*. By the time this more serious form of aggression occurs, the woman has become too dependent on the man to break off the relationship easily. He has succeeded in controlling her behavior and curtailing her contact with friends who might have possibly helped extract her from her plight. The woman also tends to believe that if only she can find the right way to mollify the man's anger

and reassure him of her faithfulness and obedience, he will change his behavior.

Following a battering incident, a third stage (called the *contrite phase*) occurs, in which the batterer apologizes for his attack, promises never to do it again, and persuades the woman that he is a changed man. Often this is an empty pledge. Indeed, sometimes the humiliation that the man feels over having apologized so profusely to his partner simply fuels more intense anger and violence, and the cycle repeats itself.

How pervasive is the cycle of violence? Even though Walker (1979) portrays it as a significant dynamic faced by battered women, she identified it in only about two-thirds of the 400 women she studied. What the *cycle of violence* may actually be describing is an underlying personality disorder that typifies a certain category of batterer.

According to Donald Dutton (1995, 2000), a psychologist at the University of British Columbia and one of the experts who testified for the prosecution in O. J. Simpson's murder trial, as many as 40% of batterers have the features of **borderline personality disorder**, a severe disturbance that is characterized by unstable moods and behavior. People with borderline personality disorder are drawn into intense relationships in which they are particularly unable to tolerate certain emotions. They are demandingly dependent, which causes them to feel easily slighted, which then leads to jealousy, rage, aggression, and subsequently guilt. These emotional cycles repeat themselves, providing the underlying motivation for the cycle of violence. In addition to emotional instability, batterers are also prone to believing the worst about others; for example, they are quick to attribute hostile intentions to their partners (Eckhardt, Barbour, & Davison, 1998). Dutton traces the origin of this personality disorder to insecure attachments that batterers experienced with their parents, which later cause them to feel intense anger toward partners whenever things go awry in a relationship.

Responses to Victims of Battering

The prevalence of many myths about battered women reflects the negative feelings toward crime victims described earlier in this chapter. A deep uneasiness, even hostility, exists toward some victims of battering (Plumm & Terrance, 2009; Russell & Melio, 2006; Walker, 2009). They may be seen as pathological "doormats" or delusional alarmists "crying wolf" over minor disagreements. When victims retaliate against their abusers—when battered women kill their batterers—they may receive a greater punishment than men who commit acts with similar outcomes. The question of whether women receive harsher sentences than men for domestic homicide is difficult to answer because the circumstances may be quite different. Jenkins and Davidson (1990) analyzed the court records of 10 battered women charged with the murder of their abusive partners in Louisiana between 1975 and 1988; all pleaded guilty or were convicted at trial. Their sentences ranged from five years' probation to life in prison, with half receiving the latter sentence.

Ewing (1987) surveyed 100 women who had killed their batterers. All were charged with murder, manslaughter, or some form of criminal homicide. Most (85) went to trial, and the majority of those who went to trial (65) were convicted. However, the great majority of those convicted (48) received prison sentences of 10 years or less.

Battered Woman Syndrome as a Defense. Only a very small minority of battered women kills their attackers, but these victims receive a great deal of public scrutiny, usually in connection with their trial for murder. When they go to trial, most battered women use either insanity or self-defense as a defense; in either instance, **battered woman syndrome** is likely to be part of the defense. Battered woman syndrome is defined as a collection of symptoms and reactions by a woman to a pattern of continued physical and psychological abuse inflicted on her by her mate. Lenore Walker (1984, 2009), the psychologist who is recognized for naming this syndrome, emphasizes the following elements:

1. As a result of chronic exposure to repeated incidents of battering, the woman develops a sense of learned helplessness, in which she comes to believe that there is nothing she can do to escape from the batterer or improve her life; finally, she gives up trying to make a change.

2. As a result of her social isolation and often her economic dependence on the batterer, the woman falls more and more under his domination. She believes that she has diminished alternatives for solving her problem.

3. As she restricts her outside activities and has less contact with friends or relatives, the woman grows increasingly fearful of the threats and attacks of the batterer. Most of the women Walker interviewed stated that they believed that their batterer would eventually kill them.

4. Trapped in this existence, the woman experiences several emotional and psychological reactions. Her self-esteem is diminished, she feels guilty and ashamed about what she sees as her multiple failures and shortcomings, and she also feels increasing rage and resentment toward her partner, whose control over her seems to grow over time.

5. After years of victimization, the woman grows hypervigilant; she notices subtle things—reactions by the batterer that others wouldn't recognize as a signal of upcoming violence (e.g., her partner's words come faster, he assumes a specific posture, or his eyes get darker). This heightened sensitivity to danger cues often motivates the woman to kill her assailant and accounts for her belief that she acted in self-defense.

Evaluating Battered Woman Syndrome. How have claims of battered woman syndrome fared in court? Does it advance the cause of victims who feel they are forced to retaliate after years of abuse? A battered woman's claim of self-defense often faces both legal hurdles and the skepticism of jurors (Russell & Melio, 2006; Schuller, McKimmie, & Janz, 2004). These obstacles might account for the fact that the majority of battered women charged with murdering their abusive partner are convicted.

Historically, a claim of **self-defense** has applied to homicides in which, at the time of the killing, the individual reasonably believed that he or she was in imminent danger of death or great bodily harm from an attacker. The defense was usually invoked in cases in which a specific attack or fight put defendants in fear for their lives; however, the typical case in which a battered woman relies on a theory of self-defense to clear her of charges of murdering her partner is much different. The violence does not involve a specific episode; rather, it is ongoing. The woman's response may seem disproportionate to what a "reasonable" person believes was necessary; often she kills her abuser while he is unarmed or sleeping.

To help jurors understand how battered woman syndrome leads to a woman's perception that she is acting in self-defense, defendants often try to introduce expert testimony about the characteristics and consequences of the syndrome. Some mock jury research has explored the effect of expert testimony in a criminal homicide case in which the defendant was a battered woman (Schuller et al., 2004). Participants were more inclined to accept the woman's claim of self-defense when they heard from an expert testifying for the defense. In addition, compared to the no-expert control condition, those exposed to expert testimony on battered woman syndrome believed that the defendant's options were far more limited.

It is important to remember that no single set of reactions or characteristics can describe all victims of battering. Although battered women share the experience of being victimized by a violent partner, their reaction to this aggression and how they cope with it takes many different forms. This variation has implications for developing the most effective types of intervention for these women. Rather than assuming that they need traditional services such as psychotherapy or couples counseling, it would be more effective to provide battered women with special advocates who would support these survivors and help them find the resources they need to improve their lives. Just such an intervention has proved very effective in helping bring about changes that allowed battered women to become violence-free (Sullivan & Bybee, 1999). After providing battered women with a personal advocate who helped each one gain access to the resources she needed to reduce her risk of partner abuse, Sullivan and Bybee found that the women who received advocacy services were twice as likely, during the two-year outcome period, to be free of any battering than were women without such a service.

THE PSYCHOLOGY OF RAPE

Historically, rape victims have often been misunderstood, harassed, and neglected. For example, if a rape victim did not resist her attacker, people might incorrectly assume that she wanted to be raped. In contrast, people never raise the question of whether victims wanted to be robbed, or struck by a hit-and-run driver, or have their identity stolen. Furthermore, society struggles over how to deal with convicted rapists. Is rape a sexual crime or an act of violence? Is it the act of a disordered mind or a result of extraordinary circumstances?

Among serious crimes, rape is one of the most appropriate for psychological analysis (Allison & Wrightsman, 1993). Myths abound about the nature of rapists and their relationship to their victims. Rape is a crime in which the interaction between the criminal and his victim is crucial to addressing responsibility and blame (Stormo, Lang, & Stritzke, 1997). Since the 1970s, there has been a good deal of psychological research directed toward understanding sexual assaults (Beech, Fisher, & Thornton, 2003; Ellis, 1991; Hall & Hirschman, 1991; Jones, Wynn, Kroeze, Dunnuck, & Rossman, 2004; Marshall, Fernandez, & Cortoni, 1999). For these reasons, we devote special attention to the crime of rape and its victims. We focus on female rape victims, although the fact that men are also raped should not be overlooked.

Misleading Stereotypes about Rape

Various misleading stereotypes about rape, rapists, and rape victims may incorporate the inaccurate perceptions that victims cannot be raped against their will—or that reports of rape are often exaggerated or even faked. These mistaken perceptions contribute to creating a climate hostile to rape victims, often portraying them as willing participants in or even instigators of sexual encounters. In fact, these attitudes often function as self-serving rationalizations and excuses for blaming the victim.

Rape means different things to different people, and these differing attitudes and perceptions affect behaviors toward both offenders and their victims. Some respondents feel more empathy toward rape victims than others do; some feel empathy toward defendants charged with the crime of rape (Deitz, Russell, & Hammes, 1989; Weir & Wrightsman, 1990). Empathy varies according to an individual's experience as a victim (or a perpetrator); women with victimization experience showed greatest empathy with female victims, while men with perpetration histories showed more empathy for a male perpetrator in one study (Osman, 2011). Thus, the measurement of attitudes about rape can clarify what different people believe about this crime, its victims, and its perpetrators.

What Accounts for Misleading Stereotypes about Rape? Individuals who are unsympathetic to victims and tolerant of rapists also tend to endorse some of the misleading stereotypes about rape described earlier. Such persons have developed a broad ideology that encourages the acceptance of myths about rape (Burt, 1980). This ideology embraces the following beliefs:

1. *Sexual conservatism.* This attitude emphasizes restrictions on the appropriateness of sexual partners, sexual acts, and circumstances under which sexual activity should occur. Burt (1980) observes, "Since many instances of rape violate one or more aspects of this conservative position, a sexually conservative individual might feel so strongly threatened by, and rejecting of, the specific circumstances of rape that he or she would overlook the coercion and force involved, and condemn the victim for participating" (p. 218).

2. *Adversarial sexual beliefs.* This component refers to the belief that sexual relationships are fundamentally exploitive—that participants in them are manipulative, unfaithful, and not to be trusted. To a person holding this ideology, "rape might seem the extreme on a continuum of exploitation, but not an unexpected or horrifying occurrence, or one justifying sympathy or support" (Burt, 1980, p. 218).

3. *Acceptance of interpersonal violence.* Another part of the ideology is the belief that force and coercion are legitimate behaviors in sexual relationships. This ideology approves of men dominating women and overpowering passive partners with violence and control.

4. *Sex-role stereotyping.* The last component of Burt's ideology casts each gender into the traditional mold of behaviors associated with that gender.

Burt constructed a set of attitude statements and administered them to a sample of 598 Minnesota adults to determine whether each of these components contributed to acceptance of myths about rape. When subjects' responses on the ideology clusters were compared to their answers on a scale measuring beliefs in myths about rape, Burt found that three of the four clusters had an impact (sexual conservatism did not). The strongest predictor of believing the myths was the acceptance of interpersonal violence. The subjects, both men and women, who felt that force and coercion were acceptable in sexual relationships were those who agreed with items such as "Women who get raped while hitchhiking get what they deserve" and

"Any healthy woman can successfully resist a rapist if she really wants to."

A review of more than 70 studies that employed a variety of measures of attitudes about rape supports Burt's conclusions (Anderson, Cooper, & Okamura, 1997). Those subjects who are more tolerant of rape are more likely to have traditional beliefs about gender roles, more adversarial sexual beliefs, greater needs for power and dominance, and heightened expressions of aggressiveness and anger. This appears to be true for both men and women, although participants in one study did differ by gender on rape myth acceptance (women were lower), attribution of fault to society (women were higher), and feelings of anger and fear in response to rape (women were higher) (Earnshaw, Pitpitan, & Chaudoir, 2011).

Facts about Rape

As we have seen, mistaken beliefs about rape are related to general attitudes toward law and crime. Still, what are the facts about rape? The United States has one of the highest rates of forcible rape among the world's industrialized countries, although there has been some decrease in the last decade. The FBI estimates that there were 84,767 forcible rapes reported to U.S. law enforcement in 2010. This figure is 5% lower than the 2009 estimate, 10.3% lower than the figure for 2006, and 6.7% lower than that for 2001 (FBI, 2011).

A major study of rape, published in 2000, provided valuable data on the frequency of rape and on women's reactions to this crime. The National Women's Study was organized and funded by several governmental agencies and crime victim organizations. A nationwide, stratified sample of 8,000 adult women and 8,005 adult men were interviewed over the telephone about their experiences as victims of sexual aggression. Since children and adolescents were excluded from the sample, the figures underestimate the total number of rapes, but they do give us an idea of the magnitude of the problem with adults. Among the study's findings are the following:

1. In the sample surveyed, 17.6% of all women said they had been the victim of rape or attempted rape sometime in their lifetime, and 21.6% of these women reported that they were younger than 12 years old at the time of their first rape.

2. Among rape victims, 31.5% reported being physically injured during their most recent rape.

According to the National Violence Against Women Survey, almost 18 million women (and almost 3 million men) in the United States have been raped. In a single year, more than 300,000 women and almost 93,000 men are estimated to have been raped. Women who reported being raped as minors were twice as likely to report being raped as adults (Tjaden & Thoennes, 2006).

Women of all ages, social classes, and ethnic groups are vulnerable to rape. According to the 2010 National Criminal Victimization Survey, the high-risk age groups are children and adolescents for most offenses (sexual as well as nonsexual), as well as women ages 18–24 for rape (National Archive of Criminal Justice Data, 2010). According to the National Violence against Women Study, however, only 19% of the women and 13% of the men who were raped after age 18 said their rape was reported to the police (Tjaden & Thoennes, 2006). Several factors account for the low report rates (Feldman-Summers & Ashworth, 1981): Victims may be convinced that reporting won't help, that they would suffer further embarrassment as a result of reporting, and/or that law enforcement officers would not believe them. Many victims are afraid that the attacker will retaliate if charges are made, and these fears are sometimes justified. According to FBI figures, only about half of reported rapes result in an arrest, and if a male suspect is charged and the female victim is a witness at a trial, the defense attorney may ridicule her testimony and impugn her character.

Motivations and Characteristics
of Rapists

Not all rapists have the same motives. Rape involves diverse combinations of aggressive and sexual motivation and deviant lifestyles for different offenders (Barbaree & Marshall, 1991). Experts have developed typologies of rapists, some proposing as many as nine types (Prentky & Knight, 1991), others as few as two or three (Groth, 1979) (see Robertiello & Terry, 2007, for a review of typologies described over the last 30 years). Most typologies have emphasized four factors that distinguish different types of rapists: (1) the amount and type of aggression the rapist used; (2) when the level of aggression was high, whether it heightened sexual arousal in a sadistic manner; (3) whether the offender showed evidence of psychopathy or antisocial personality disorder; and

(4) whether the offender relied on deviant sexual fantasies to produce sexual arousal. Theories of sexual aggression combine several causal factors into an integrated scheme that accounts for the different types of rapists (Sorenson & White, 1992).

From a somewhat different perspective, Ellis (1989) identified three theories of rape: the *feminist theory*, emphasizing rape as a pseudosexual act of male domination and exploitation of women (Donat & D'Emilio, 1992; White & Sorenson, 1992); the *social-learning approach*, suggesting that sexual aggression is learned through observation and imitation; and the *evolutionary theory*, holding that natural selection favors men who use forced sexual behavior (Buss & Malamuth, 1996).

These different approaches illustrate that rape cannot be easily explained by any one theory, and yet every one of these classification systems fails to capture the full spectrum of behaviors and motivations

Dominique Strauss-Kahn

B o x   6.3   THE CASE OF DOMINIQUE STRAUSS-KAHN: PROMINENCE AND THE ACCUSATION OF SEXUAL ASSAULT

Dominique Strauss-Kahn was in New York City in his role as chief of the International Monetary Fund in May 2011 when he was accused of sexual assault by a hotel housekeeper at the Sofitel Hotel, where he was staying. According to the housekeeper, Strauss-Kahn forced her to perform oral sex and submit to anal sex after emerging naked from his suite's bathroom. Strauss-Kahn was arrested and charged with two counts of criminal sexual act in the first degree, one count of attempted rape, sexual abuse in the first degree, unlawful imprisonment, sexual abuse in the third degree and forcible touching. Prosecutors subsequently became concerned about the history of the housekeeper (she had once reported being sexually assaulted in her native Guinea, but later recanted) and her behavior following the alleged assault. Strauss-Kahn himself had a history that seemed important. The married father of four was nicknamed "The

Great Seducer" and had spoken publicly about his infidelity and affinity for younger women. He was also alleged by French journalist Tristane Banon to have sexually assaulted her during an interview nine years before the New York allegations.

Because prosecutors decided that the testimony that would be provided by the alleged victim in this case would be too weak to withstand cross-examination, they eventually dropped all charges against Mr. Strauss-Kahn.

Critical Thought Question
What are the advantages and disadvantages of admitting into a trial evidence concerning the history of previous allegations of sexual assault by the alleged perpetrator? Of admitting previous allegations of sexual assault made by the alleged victim?

---

that typify rapists. Some of these systems are also limited by the fact that they are based on studies of convicted rapists who have been sentenced to prison. The majority of rapists are never imprisoned for their offenses; fewer than 10% of rapes result in convictions or prison sentences (Frazier & Haney, 1996).

The example provided above describes allegations against Dominique Strauss-Kahn in 2011. We may never know how accurate these allegations were, as prosecutors ultimately dropped the charges. For the sake of discussion, however, assume that the allegations described in Box 6.3 are accurate. How might the typologies discussed in this section apply to Mr. Strauss-Kahn?

Acquaintance Rape and "Date Rape"

The 2000 National Women's Study reported that only 14.6% of rapes were committed by a stranger to the victim; 16.4% were committed by a nonrelative acquaintance; 6.4% by a relative; and 64% by an intimate partner. As of 2008, the estimate for sexual assault committed by a "known" individual is about 70% (Bureau of Justice Statistics, 2011).

The closer the relationship between the female victim and the offender, in general, the greater the likelihood that the police were not told about the assault. When the offender was a current or former husband or boyfriend, about three-fourths of all victimizations were not reported to police. When it was a

friend or acquaintance, most sexual crimes (61% of completed rapes, 71% of attempted rapes, and 82% of sexual assaults) went unreported. But when the offender was a stranger, a different pattern emerged. A total of 54% of completed rapes, 44% of attempted rapes, and 34% of sexual assaults were not reported to the police—meaning that the majority of all forms of sexual assault *were* reported (Bureau of Justice Statistics, 2002).

In general, date rapes differ from sexual assaults by a stranger in several ways. They tend to occur on weekends, between 10:00 P.M. and 1:00 A.M., and they usually take place at the assailant's home or apartment. Date rapes tend to involve situations in which both the attacker and the victim have been using alcohol or drugs but they are less likely to involve the use of weapons; instead, the date rapist employs verbal threats and physical prowess to overpower his victim.

Consequences of Being Raped

Rape victims suffer physical injuries, emotional pain and humiliation, and sometimes-severe psychological aftereffects. Recovery from the trauma of rape can be very slow, and victims often describe a sense that they will never be the same again. Providing psychological assistance to rape victims is of utmost importance.

The plight of rape victims has received increased attention through a number of highly publicized cases in which women have come forward to report their experiences. As these cases have unfolded in the

Kobe Bryant enters the courthouse

public eye, sexual aggression has become a topic of increased discussion among men and women. Highly publicized reports such as the rape charge against Los Angeles professional basketball player Kobe Bryant have helped to focus this nation's attention on matters of sexual conduct and on the plight of the victims of sexual aggression.

One part of this discussion has been a debate about whether the names of victims of sexual assault should be made public. The tradition in this country has been to protect the identity of rape victims by not using their names in media coverage. Still, in the case of Kobe Bryant, both television and online reporting broke with this tradition and published the name of Bryant's accuser, Katelyn Faber. Defenders of this decision argue that not naming rape victims perpetuates the stigma of having been raped, making it more difficult in the long run for victims to come forward and confront their attackers. Critics of the practice claim that publishing the victim's name invades her privacy and perhaps ruins her future because she would forever be branded as a rape victim. According to the National Women's Study, most rape victims prefer not to have their names published; over three-quarters of the respondents said they would be less likely to report a rape if they knew their names would be made public.

How Do Women React to Being Raped?   Burgess and Holmstrom (1974, 1979) offered an early description of symptoms experienced by many rape victims. This pattern—**rape trauma syndrome**—comprises three kinds of reactions: emotional responses, disturbances

in functioning, and changes in lifestyle. The primary emotional response is fear, including fear of being left alone and fear of situations similar to the one in which the rape occurred (Calhoun, Atkeson, & Resick, 1982). Even the most general of associations with the rape or rapist may trigger an emotional response.

Judith Rowland (1985), a deputy district attorney, describes a reaction of a White rape victim, Terri Richardson, as the trial of her alleged attacker began. Her attacker was a Black man.

> [T]he San Diego Municipal Court had one black judge among its numbers. As it happened … his chambers were next door. As Terri and I stood … while the bailiff scurried out to reassemble the jury, this lone black judge was also preparing to take the bench. I was aware of him standing in his doorway, wearing his ankle-length black robes. It was only when his bailiff held the courtroom door open for him and he was striding toward it that Terri saw him. In less than the time it took him to get through the door, Terri had bolted from the corridor, through the courtroom, and into the main hallway. By the time I got to the outside corridor, I found only a group of startled jurors. I located Terri in a nearby ladies' room, locked in a stall, crying. With a bit more comforting, she was able to regain her composure and get through both my direct and the defense's cross-examination with only minor bouts of tears, particularly while describing the attack itself (pp. 166–167).

Guilt and shame are also frequent emotional responses. Victims may blame themselves: "Why was I at a bus stop in a strange part of town?" "Did I check that the back door was locked that night?" They may worry that they didn't resist the attacker vigorously enough. The victim often feels a loss of autonomy and of control over her body. She may no longer trust others, a loss that may never be fully repaired throughout her lifetime. One victim describes the feeling this way: "I never feel safe. I couldn't stand the apartment where I lived, but I'm so afraid to be alone anywhere. I never was like that before. I carry things with me, like kitchen knives and sticks, when I go out" (quoted in Rowland, 1985, p. 146).

The second type of reaction, a disturbance in functioning, also frequently appears among rape victims. Specific disturbances include changes in sleep patterns (insomnia, nightmares, and early awakening); social withdrawal; changes in appetite; and problems in sexual functioning. Women (N=175) who were sexually abused in adulthood were more sexually dissatisfied and nonsensual than women with no history of sexual abuse. Additionally, women with a history of sexual abuse as a child or as an adult were less satisfied with their most recent sexual relationship than women with no history of abuse. These women also tended to have a higher number of unsafe sexual partners (Bartoi & Kinder, 1998). Wolf (2009) studied adult women in Texas (N=64) who were six months post-assault, and found that following a sexual assault, women commonly find themselves struggling with posttraumatic stress symptoms and experience difficulty in coping with normal daily activities. Those with strongly supportive relationships had less severe posttraumatic stress symptoms and were able to function better in daily activities. Unfortunately, however, many women did not receive this kind of support.

Changes occur not only in emotions and general functioning but also in lifestyle. Some victims report obsessively checking doors to make sure they are double-locked; one of the victims whose attacker was prosecuted by Rowland (1985) took 45-minute showers two or three times daily, trying to remove the rapist's odor from her body. Other women make major changes in lifestyle, breaking up with their boyfriends, changing jobs, and moving to new residences. The overall socioeconomic impact of rape can be profound; victims of sexual assault are at greater risk of subsequently losing income, becoming unemployed, and going through a divorce (Byrne, Resnick, Kilpatrick, Best, & Saunders, 1999).

Women who have been sexually assaulted in the past or who were sexually abused as children are two to three times more likely to suffer a subsequent sexual attack than women without prior sexual victimizations (Nishith, Mechanic, & Resick, 2000; Wasco, 2004). Although the reasons for the heightened risk are not clear, one possibility is that some women who have been victimized before are slower to recognize when they are at risk and therefore are more likely to remain in situations where they are vulnerable (Wilson, Calhoun, & Bernat, 1999). Women with more than one sexual victimization across their childhood and adult years are more likely to report unplanned and aborted pregnancies (Wyatt, Guthrie, & Notgrass, 1992).

The impact of rape trauma tends to change over time as well. Ellison and Buckhout (1981) have described the typical rape victim's response as a crisis reaction that unfolds in a series of discrete phases.

The *acute phase* begins with the attack and lasts a few hours or a day. During this acute phase, the primary needs of the victim are to understand what is happening, regain control over her life, predict what will happen next, and air her feelings to someone who will listen without passing judgment (Ellison & Buckhout, 1981). At this point, police officers investigating the crime can either help or hinder the victim, as can medical personnel. For example, a pelvic examination and the collection of any semen samples are necessary at this point because it is unlikely that the suspect can be prosecuted in the absence of such evidence. But the examination may cause a resurgence of the initial feelings of disruption, helplessness, hostility, and violation—a reaction known as **secondary victimization**. In fact, negative experiences with legal and medical authorities have been shown to increase rape victims' symptoms of posttraumatic stress disorder (Campbell et al., 1999).

Within a few hours or days of the attack, many victims slip into a period of false recovery. Denial occurs: "I'm OK; everything is the same as before." Then a secondary crisis occurs—a sort of flashback—in which some of the symptoms of the acute crisis phase, particularly phobias and disturbances in eating and sleeping, return (Ellison & Buckhout, 1981, p. 59). This phase may last for hours or days before another "quiet period" emerges in which the victim feels a range of negative emotions such as loneliness, anger, and guilt.

Because of increased public awareness of the needs of rape victims, rape crisis centers have been established in many cities. These centers provide crisis counseling to victims. Most follow up with at least one further interview (usually by phone), and a third of their clients have from two to six follow-up interviews. The crisis center also checks for pregnancy and sexually transmitted disease.

Long-term counseling for rape victims is more difficult to provide because of the lack of staff at some rape crisis centers and, in some cases, because of a feeling that counseling is no longer needed. A longitudinal study of 20 rape victims (Kilpatrick, Resick, & Veronen, 1981) measured the personality and mood of these victims and of a matched control group at three time intervals: one month, six months, and one year after the rape. Even at a one-year follow-up, many victims continued to suffer emotionally from the sexual assault. Among the major problems were fear and anxiety, often severe enough to constitute a diagnosis of posttraumatic stress disorder. Whether individuals acknowledge a previous sexual assault also makes a difference; unacknowledged victims were nearly twice as likely to report having experienced an attempted rape during the six-month follow-up period (in part because they also reported more risk factors, such as hazardous alcohol use and continuing in their relationship with the assailant) (Littleton, Axsom, & Grills-Taquechel, 2009).

The long-term consequences of rape are also concerning. One study involved interviewing 35 rape victims between 2 and 46 years after their rape and compared their responses to 110 matched, nonabused participants to determine the long-term psychological effects of rape (Santiago, McCall-Perez, Gorcey, & Beigel, 1985). Findings showed that fear and anxiety were significantly higher in the rape victim population, compared to the nonabused sample, regardless of the length of time since their rape. Findings also indicated that the rape victims were significantly more depressed than those who had not been raped and that fear, anxiety, and depression were highest in women who had been raped more than once.

Providing social support is one of the most helpful interventions. The therapeutic power of social support may derive in part from the fact that women, in particular, tend to react to stress by seeking opportunities for attachment and caregiving—or what psychologist Shelley Taylor has termed the *tend-and-befriend* response (Taylor et al., 2000). (Men, on the other hand, are more likely to respond to stress with the well-known "fight-or-flight" strategy.) Therefore, it might be especially useful to female crime victims to have ample opportunities for social support so that their preference to be with others in times of need can be fully addressed.

Rape Trauma Syndrome in Court. Psychologists, along with psychiatrists and other physicians, often testify as expert witnesses in rape trials, especially about the nature and consequences of rape trauma syndrome (Fischer, 1989; Frazier & Borgida, 1985, 1988; Melton et al., 2007). This syndrome is usually thought of as an example of posttraumatic stress disorder, similar to that experienced by veterans of combat, survivors of natural disasters, and victims of other violent crimes. The expert can be of special use to the

prosecution in those trials in which the defendant admits that sexual intercourse took place but claims that the woman was a willing participant; evidence of rape trauma syndrome can be consistent with the complainant's version of the facts (Frazier & Borgida, 1985). In addition, jurors are often not familiar with the reactions that rape victims frequently experience (Borgida & Brekke, 1985), so psychological experts can educate the jury. Courts around the country are divided, however, on the admissibility of such testimony, and the resulting controversy has generated considerable debate.

The main argument against admitting expert testimony on rape trauma syndrome is as follows: The psychological responses of rape victims are not unique to rape and are not uniform, so it is impossible to say with certainty that a woman exhibiting any given set of responses has been raped. Therefore, a psychologist should not be allowed to testify that a woman is suffering from rape trauma syndrome because to do so is tantamount to telling the jury that she has been raped, which should remain a matter for the jury to decide. Many courts also reject expert testimony on rape trauma syndrome on the ground that the reliability of the syndrome has not been established.

Preventing Rape

As we learn more about the frequency and consequences of rape, a primary goal of concerned citizens, law enforcement officials, and social scientists has been to develop effective interventions for preventing rape. Two basic strategies have been emphasized: (1) training potential victims how best to protect

The importance of consent

themselves against rape, and (2) designing effective treatment for rapists so that they do not repeat their crimes.

Training Potential Victims to Reduce the Risk of Rape. If a woman finds herself in a situation in which a man begins to sexually assault her, what should she do? Should she scream? Should she fight back? Should she try to reason with him? Or should she submit to the attack, especially if the assailant has a weapon? There is no uniformly correct response, just as there is no one type of rapist. However, on the issue of passive compliance, a Justice Department survey of over a million attacks (quoted in Meddis & Kelley, 1985) found that women who did not resist a rape attack were twice as likely to suffer a completed rape as women who tried to protect themselves. But though fighting back was more likely to result in rape avoidance, it was also associated with increased physical injury when a weapon was present. Screaming and fleeing when confronted with a weapon was associated with less severe sexual abuse than were pleading, crying, or reasoning.

As we have already seen, national surveys suggest that between one-fifth and one-quarter of college women have suffered a sexual assault and that the majority of victims were acquainted with their assailants before the assault. Research has also uncovered several risk factors associated with sexual assault, including using alcohol and drugs on a date, particularly in an isolated location. Several colleges and universities have incorporated this information about risk factors into rape prevention programs aimed at changing attitudes about sexuality, challenging rape myths and sex-role stereotypes, and improving women's coping responses in potentially dangerous situations.

In the typical rape prevention program, participants discuss several facts and myths about rape, learn how to avoid situations involving heavy use of alcohol, practice resisting pressure for unwanted sexual activity, and role-play other strategies for protecting themselves. The programs try to help women change behaviors and to dispel the notion that victims cause sexual assault. They also strive to minimize the blaming of women that can occur following sexual victimization. One study (Orchowski, Gidycz, & Raffle, 2008) investigated the impact of a sexual assault risk reduction program with a self-defense component for 300 college women. Using a placebo-control group,

the study indicated that this program was effective in increasing levels of self-protective behaviors, self-efficacy in resisting against potential attackers, and use of assertive sexual communication over a four-month period, as well as reducing the incidence of rape among participants over the two-month follow-up. Another study of 500 college women who received a comparable sexual assault risk-reduction program also found an increase in self-protective behavior displayed by program participants during the six months following completion. In this study, however, there were no significant differences between participants and controls in rates of sexual victimization, assertive communication, or feelings of self-efficacy (Gidycz, Rich, Orchowski, King, & Miller, 2006).

Designing Effective Treatments for Rapists. Society is rightfully concerned about the likelihood of sex offenders repeating their crimes. In some states, men convicted of sex crimes are required to complete a sex-offender treatment program before being considered for parole. In such programs, the offender must acknowledge responsibility for his actions and participate in special treatment programs (Glamser, 1997).

The treatment of rapists can involve psychological, physical, and medical procedures; in many treatment programs, different interventions are often combined. On the international scene, neurosurgery and surgical castration have been used, but their effectiveness is unclear. Because of the ethical controversies that surround these procedures, few experts advocate their use in the United States (Marshall, Jones, Ward, Johnston, & Barbaree, 1991).

In the United States it is not uncommon for anti-androgen drugs to be prescribed to sex offenders in order to reduce their sex drive, a procedure sometimes referred to as **chemical castration**. The most common treatment involves giving offenders a synthetic female hormone, MPA, which has the trade name of Depo-Provera. MPA decreases the level of testosterone in the body, thereby decreasing sexual arousal in most men; however, the drug has also been associated with a number of negative side effects, including weight gain, hair loss, feminization of the body, and gall bladder problems.

Anti-androgen treatments have problems other than negative side effects. The rate of men dropping out of such treatment prematurely is very high, and failure to complete treatment is one of the strongest predictors of recidivism for sex offenders (Larochelle,

Diguer, Laverdiere, & Greenman, 2011). In addition, the treatment does not always reduce sexual arousal and sexual offenses. In some men, arousal is not dependent on their level of testosterone, so the drugs have little effect on their sexual behavior. This point is related to the fact that rape is often an act of violence, not of inappropriate sexual arousal; consequently, drugs aimed at reducing sexual desire may be pointing at the wrong target. Even if the drugs inhibit sexual appetites, they may not control violent outbursts. Hence, they would not meaningfully control these offenders.

Another major approach to treating aggressive sexual offenders involves combining several behavior therapy techniques into an integrated treatment package designed to increase offenders' self-control, improve their social skills, modify their sexual preferences, and teach them how to prevent relapses of their offenses. These programs are usually situated in prisons, but they have also been implemented in the community.

These integrated programs employ a wide range of treatment techniques. Sex education and training in social skills are common ingredients because of the widespread belief that sex offenders are often socially incompetent. Biofeedback and aversive conditioning are often used to decrease inappropriate sexual arousal and replace it with arousal to nonaggressive sexual cues. Existing programs appear to be able to produce short-term decreases in recidivism, but long-term improvements have been difficult to achieve. As a result, relapse prevention techniques (which have proved useful in the treatment of drug addictions and cigarette smoking) have been added to some programs. Programs with a cognitive-behavioral orientation have shown effectiveness in reducing subsequent sexual offending against children (Beggs & Grace, 2011).

SEXUAL HARASSMENT

Even though *sexual harassment* has been a significant problem in educational and work environments for many years, the term itself was coined in 1974. At that time, a group of women at Cornell University, after becoming aware that several of their female colleagues had been forced to quit because of unwanted advances from their supervisors, began to speak out against such harassment (Brownmiller & Alexander, 1992). Also in the early 1970s, the United States

Equal Employment Opportunity Commission (EEOC) emerged as a major tool for redressing sexual harassment by employers.

Prevalence Rates

Several cases involving sensational charges of sexual harassment have received widespread attention and focused awareness on the problem of sexual harassment. A well-known case involved the four-year legal battle in which Paula Jones, a former Arkansas state employee, charged that then-governor Bill Clinton pressured her to perform oral sex in a Little Rock hotel room. Although he admitted no wrongdoing and refused to apologize to Jones, President Clinton eventually paid her $850,000 to drop the lawsuit. The consequences of the case went well beyond this, however, in that Clinton's apparently deceitful testimony in the Paula Jones case was a primary impetus for his eventual impeachment.

Talk show host Bill O'Reilly was accused of subjecting the former producer of his television show, Andrea Mackris, to "unwanted sexual conduct" and "a hostile work environment" by detailing his sexual fantasies during multiple phone calls (Spilbor, 2004). About two weeks after the suit was filed and without acknowledging culpability, O'Reilly agreed to pay Mackris approximately $2 million to settle the case (Kurtz, 2004).

How frequent is sexual harassment? A nationwide survey of female psychologists revealed that over half of them had experienced sexual harassment from a psychotherapy client at some point in their careers (deMayo, 1997). A study examining sexual harassment in academic medicine indicated that about half of female faculty experienced some form of sexual harassment, compared to very few male faculty, and these experiences were prevalent across different institutions in the sample and across all regions of the United States (Carr et al., 2000). In addition, a large meta-analysis (Ilies, Hauserman, Schwochau, & Stibal, 2003) used 86,000 respondents from 55 samples to estimate that 58% of women report having experienced potentially harassing behavior, and 24% report having experienced sexual harassment at work.

Sexual harassment is typically assumed to involve a male perpetrator and a female victim, but men also experience sexual harassment. One survey of 480 nursing students and faculty found that although more women than men experienced mild or

Andrea Mackris, who accused Bill O'Reilly of sexual harassment

Talk show host Bill O'Reilly

moderate forms of sexual harassment (e.g., teasing, attempts to initiate romantic relationships), men were more likely to experience severe types of sexual harassment (e.g., intimate touch, forcing the respondent to touch someone else in an intimate way) (Bronner, Peretz, & Ehrenfeld, 2003).

Although popular depictions of sexual harassment of males, such as Michael Crichton's novel *Disclosure* and the movie based on it, feature an aggressive female boss demanding sex from a male subordinate, men more often report that other men sexually harass them. A survey of over 2,000 male workers found that 37% had experienced sexual harassment in the workplace, with 53% of these experiences perpetrated by other men (Stockdale, Visio, & Batra, 1999). Although lewd sexual comments, negative comments about men, and unwanted sexual attention were the most common types of harassment, the form of

harassment that these men found most upsetting involved statements or actions that belittled them for acting too "feminine" or that pressured them to adopt stereotypical "masculine" behavior.

Defining Sexual Harassment

U.S. federal law defines harassment as follows:

> Unwelcome sexual advances, requests for sexual favors, and other verbal or physical conduct of a sexual nature constitute sexual harassment when (1) submission to such conduct is made either explicitly or implicitly a term or condition of an individual's employment, (2) submission to or rejection of such conduct by an individual is used as the basis for employment decisions affecting such individual, or (3) such conduct has the purpose or effect of unreasonably interfering

with an individual's work performance or creating an intimidating, hostile, or offensive working environment (16 Code of Federal Regulations Section 1604.11).

Some of the studies described in this section use the term *sexual harassment* to mean unwanted sexual attention. But sexual harassment also has a specific meaning under the law, as we see in the previous paragraph. Title VII of the Civil Rights Act of 1964 prohibits discrimination in the workplace because of a person's gender. It therefore provides the legal basis for banning sexual harassment, although there is continued confusion about the nature of sexual harassment. "Can I tell my assistant that she looks especially nice today?" "What kinds of jokes are okay at the office party?" Questions like this reflect the uncertainty that men in particular seem to have about the possibility that a comment will be viewed by a woman as sexually harassing if it attempts to reflect a compliment or to be humorous (Terpstra & Baker, 1987).

There are differences between men and women in defining sexual harassment. In some respects these differences are substantial; in other areas, they are minor (Gutek, 1995). For instance, according to a meta-analysis on this topic (Rotundo, Nguyen, & Sackett, 2001), the female–male difference was larger for behaviors that involve hostile work environment harassment, derogatory attitudes toward women, dating pressure, or physical sexual contact (areas in which there were gender differences about what constitutes harassment) than sexual propositions or sexual coercion (topics upon which both men and women seem to agree as they relate to sexual harassment).

One problem with the federal definition of sexual harassment is that it leaves key terms such as *unwelcome* and *unreasonably interfering* open to varying interpretations. When men and women differ in their evaluations of potentially harassing interactions, women are more likely than men to classify a specific act as harassment (Rotundo, Nguyen, & Sackett, 2001). Who, then, determines when an act is harassing—the alleged victim, the alleged perpetrator, or an outside, "neutral" observer?

One contribution of psychological research is to provide information about just what behaviors people consider sexually harassment (Frazier, Cochran, & Olson, 1995). When psychologists study the way individuals define sexual harassment, they usually do

this by presenting participants with a set of facts and asking them whether they believe those facts indicate that sexual harassment occurred. In some studies, the subjects read a summary of the facts; in others they watch or listen to a taped description of the events. For example, Wiener and his colleagues conducted a complex experiment that simultaneously assessed the impact of observers' gender and sexist attitudes on perceptions of allegedly harassing behavior in two workplace situations (Wiener, Hurt, Russell, Mannen, & Gasper, 1997). They classified participants as being either high or low in *hostile sexism* and *benevolent sexism*. Hostile sexism involves antipathy toward women, reflecting a belief that males are superior to women and should be dominant over them. Benevolent sexism is an attitude of protection toward women; it reflects a belief that as the "weaker sex," women need to be shielded from the world's harshness.

In addition to finding that females were more likely than males to find that sexual harassment had occurred in these two situations, Wiener and colleagues (1997) examined the impact of participants' attitudes on their perceptions of sexual harassment. They predicted that those high in hostile sexism would be less inclined to conclude that sexual harassment had occurred. The results supported their prediction. Participants high in hostile sexism were less likely than those who scored low on this dimension to find that the defendant's behavior constituted sexual harassment.

The harasser's status relative to the victim is more influential than gender on perceptions of sexual harassment. In his meta-analysis of 111 empirical studies examining how sexual harassment is evaluated, Blumenthal (1998) found that both men and women were more likely to perceive behavior directed by someone of higher status at someone of equal or lesser rank in the workplace as harassment than if such behavior occurred between peers. This is a reassuring result, given that the law also tends to assign greater liability to a defendant in cases where harassment by a supervisor or manager, as opposed to a peer or coworker, is alleged (Goodman-Delahunty, 1998).

Sexually harassing behaviors can range from lewd and negative comments directed at a person, to more overt overtures for sexual contact such as flirting and uninvited touching, and, finally, to offers of bribes or threats of retaliation in exchange for sexual contact (Fitzgerald, Gelfand, & Drasgow, 1995). As you would expect, reactions to these behaviors vary widely. Fewer than 10% of respondents consider staring, flirting, or nonsexual touching to be harassment, but almost 100% believe that pressure for sexual favors or sexual bribery constitutes harassment (Frazier et al., 1995).

The courts, following federal guidelines, have recognized two types of sexual harassment. The *quid pro quo* type involves sexual demands that are made in exchange for employment benefits; it is essentially sexual coercion. **Quid pro quo** harassment is seen in an implicit or explicit bargain in which the harasser promises a reward or threatens punishment, depending on the victim's response (Hotelling, 1991). When a teacher says to a student, "Sleep with me or you fail this course," it qualifies as *quid pro quo* sexual harassment (McCandless & Sullivan, 1991).

The second, more common type of harassment, usually referred to as **hostile workplace harassment**, involves demeaning comments, acts of touching or attempted intimacy, or the display of provocative photographs or artwork. Under Title VII, it is illegal for employers to create or tolerate "an intimidating, hostile, or offensive working environment." In Paula Jones's lawsuit against former President Clinton, the plaintiff claimed that Clinton's behavior constituted hostile workplace harassment. How is this defined? How disabling must the environment be for the victim? The courts have answered these questions in several relevant cases.

In the 1986 case of *Meritor Savings Bank v. Vinson*, the U.S. Supreme Court recognized for the first time that sexual harassment creating a hostile work environment violates Title VII. Although evidence of repeated offensive behavior or behavior of a severe nature is usually required for the plaintiff to prevail, the effects of such harassment need not "seriously affect [an employee's] psychological well being" or lead the plaintiff to "suffer injury" to constitute *hostile workplace* harassment (*Harris v. Forklift Systems, Inc.*, 1993; see Box 6.4).

B o x 6.4 THE CASE OF TERESA HARRIS: SEXUAL HARASSMENT ON THE JOB

Teresa Harris was the rentals manager at Forklift Systems in Nashville. Her boss (the company president) made a number of suggestive and demeaning comments to her. At first she tried to ignore him, and then she confronted him. He promised to stop, but a month later, in public, he asked whether she had slept with a client to get his account. This was the last straw; after working there two years, Harris quit. She sought relief from the EEOC and the courts, claiming that the boss's behavior had created a hostile workplace. She asked for back wages as part of the litigation.

When she did not receive satisfaction from the lower courts, she brought her appeal to the U.S. Supreme Court, which agreed to hear the case because different circuit courts had been inconsistent in their decisions in such cases. Some courts had adopted a subjective approach, focusing on the impact of the alleged harassment on the plaintiff. Others, taking a more objective approach, had asked whether a reasonable person would have found the environment abusive. Also unclear was the question of degree of impact. Was it sufficient that the environment interfered with the complainant's work performance, or was it necessary for "psychological injury" to have occurred? Even though there is ample evidence that sexual harassment can produce psychological damage (Fitzgerald, Buchanan, Collinsworth, Magley, & Ramos, 1999), should plaintiffs be forced to prove that they were psychologically harmed in order to persuade a jury that the sexual harassment has occurred?

The unanimous decision of the Court, announced by Justice Sandra Day O'Connor, was in favor of Harris and held that it was not necessary for plaintiffs to prove that they had suffered psychological injuries. The Supreme Court decision listed several criteria by which to decide whether an action constitutes sexual harassment, including the frequency and severity of the behavior, whether the behavior was physically threatening or humiliating, and whether it would unreasonably interfere with an employee's work performance.

Prior to this decision there was controversy about whether to assess potentially harassing behavior from the perspective of a "reasonable man," "reasonable person," or "reasonable victim" (Gutek & O'Connor, 1995; Wiener & Gutek, 1999). Justice O'Connor's opinion suggested that if conduct was not sufficiently severe and pervasive as to create an "objectively hostile" work environment as defined by a *reasonable person*, then it was not sexual harassment. The Court's decision reflected an intermediate position; harassment was no longer defined by the responses of a man, but neither could the victim define what is hostile.

Critical Thought Question

If you had been Justice O'Connor trying to determine whether a workplace environment was "objectively hostile," would you have selected the perspective of "a reasonable man," "a reasonable victim," or "a reasonable person"?

Applying Psychological Knowledge to Detecting Harassment

Psychological approaches contribute to our understanding of sexual harassment in two other ways. First, some psychologists have attempted to predict when sexual harassment will occur. Other psychologists have tried to determine the likelihood of a favorable outcome in litigation when a person who alleges sexual harassment files a complaint. We consider these issues next.

When and in what environments is sexual harassment more likely to occur? Pryor, Giedd, and Williams (1995) proposed that certain individuals are inclined toward behavior that would be sexual harassment and that the norms in specific organizations function to encourage the expression of harassment. For example, a factory that permits its workers to display *Playboy* centerfolds or nude calendars in their work areas may encourage harassment on the part of a worker who, in another environment, would not exhibit such behavior. Similarly, a company that provides sexually oriented entertainment at office parties or has work-related parties that exclude one gender is expressing a norm that gives tacit approval to at least some forms of harassment.

Men also differ in their likelihood to harass. Pryor (1987) asked men to imagine themselves in a series of scenarios in which they had power over an attractive woman. In one scenario, for example, the man is a college professor meeting with a female student who is seeking to raise her grade in the class. The subjects were asked to rate how likely they were to engage in an act of *quid pro quo* sexual harassment in each scenario, given that they could do so without being punished. Men who scored relatively high on the Likelihood to Sexually Harass (LSH) scale were more accepting of myths about rape, indulged in more coercive sexual fantasies, and endorsed more stereotypical beliefs about male sex roles (Pryor et al., 1995). They had strong needs to dominate women and to seek sex for the sake of their own gratification. In a series of laboratory experiments, Pryor and his colleagues found that men high in likelihood to sexually harass engaged in harassment in social situations in which harassing behavior was convenient, and under conditions in which local norms encouraged such behavior.

Another study yielded findings consistent with these results using a similar assessment protocol (Begany & Milburn, 2002). This study also indicated that authoritarian personality characteristics (such as a belief in obeying authority above all else) predicted men's self-reported likelihood of engaging in sexual harassment; men who reported higher levels of authoritarian characteristics are more likely to engage in sexual harassment. Other personality characteristics have also been associated with higher scores on the LSH scale, including a less feminine personality, more traditional beliefs about women's roles, more negative attitudes toward women, and less concern with social desirability (Driscoll, Kelly, & Henderson, 1998). Men who are higher in hostility, particularly toward women, are more likely to engage in workplace sexual harassment under conditions of perceived unfairness on the job (Krings & Facchin, 2009).

To determine trends in workplace harassment claims upheld by the Equal Employment Opportunity Commission, a study of such claims from 1992 to 2006 was conducted (Cunningham & Benavides-Espinoza, 2008). Results show a sharp increase during the 1990s, followed by a decline in the 2000s. This observed trend followed the political climate, with more progressive social policies in the 1990s and a more conservative agenda in the 2000s. Particular claims were most likely to succeed when the alleged harassing behaviors were serious, the complainant had supporting witnesses, and the complainant had notified management prior to filing formal charges (Terpstra & Baker, 1988). These findings were consistent with a subsequent analysis of 133 court decisions between 1974 and 1989 (Terpstra & Baker, 1992). In addition to the three criteria distinguishing successful claims found in their prior (1988) study, they also noted that supporting documentation and management's failure to act following notification were important.

OFFENDERS' EXPERIENCE AS VICTIMS OF CRIME AND VIOLENCE

When offenders are at the same time victims, or claim to be victims, society's reaction becomes even more complex, and decisions made by the legal system become even more controversial. Consider the cases of Lorena Bobbitt, Lyle and Erik Menendez, the late Michael Jackson, and Susan Polk. What do these trials have in common? In each case, the defendant or defendants, charged with serious crimes, claimed the role of victim and argued that they were retaliating against an unwanted act or trying to prevent a feared attack. Lorena Bobbitt was outraged over an act earlier that evening that she considered to be spousal rape by her husband John, so while he was sleeping, she cut off his penis. At their trials, the Menendez brothers described episodes of physical and sexual abuse from their father, with their mother as a passive accomplice; fearing the worst, they said, they decided to kill their parents first. Michael Jackson was charged with sexually molesting a young boy and holding his family captive at his "Neverland" ranch. Jackson claimed that the boy and his family had fabricated these accounts in an attempt to obtain money from him. Susan Polk, charged with murder in the death of her 70-year-old wealthy husband, Frank (Felix) Polk, a prominent Berkeley psychologist, claimed that she had long been controlled, abused and battered by her husband, and acted in self-defense when he flew into a rage and attacked her.

How did the juries react to these defenses? Lorena Bobbitt was found not guilty by reason of insanity. Jurors' reactions in the Menendez brothers' trials were more complicated. In the first trials, the jurors could not agree, producing a hung jury. The jurors agreed that each brother was guilty of a crime,

but they could not agree on whether each should be convicted of murder or manslaughter (Thornton, 1995). With each jury deadlocked over the appropriate charge for conviction, the result was a mistrial. At the second trial, both brothers were found guilty of murder and sentenced to life in prison. Michael Jackson was acquitted on all charges after arguing that family members of his alleged victim were essentially con artists trying to take advantage of his celebrity. Susan Polk was convicted of second-degree murder, despite testimony that she suffered from posttraumatic stress disorder as a battered woman.

In cases like those of Bobbitt, Polk, and the Menendez brothers, in which a defendant claims to be a victim, critics are concerned that jurors will be tempted to accept what has been called the **abuse excuse**—"the legal tactic by which criminal defendants claim a history of abuse as an excuse for violent retaliation" (Dershowitz, 1994, p. 3). Although Dershowitz concluded that an increasing number of defense lawyers are using the abuse excuse and that juries increasingly are accepting it, evidence in support of the latter claim is sparse at best. In fact, such defenses seem to be met with increasing skepticism and with a willingness to blame the offender.

SUMMARY

1. *What is the frequency of crime victimization?* According to the National Crime Victimization Survey, there were 16 million property crimes and 5 million violent crimes in the United States in 2008. But these figures underestimate the true extent of victimization that befalls an unknown number of individuals in homes, schools, and the workplace.

2. *What types of research have psychologists conducted on victimization?* Four areas of victimization have received special attention from psychologists: adverse childhood experience; violent victimization and posttraumatic stress disorder, including the psychology of rape; domestic violence (particularly spousal battering); and sexual harassment.

3. *What factors predict the development of PTSD after being a crime victim?* The extent of injury suffered in the crime and the belief that the victim has no control over his or her life heighten the risk of developing PTSD. Cognitive-behavioral

treatments that help restore a sense of control and that help victims re-experience the trauma so that its emotional power is drained are the most effective interventions for preventing and reducing PTSD after a criminal victimization.

4. *What are the components of battered woman syndrome?* Battered woman syndrome consists of a collection of responses, many of which are displayed by individuals who are repeatedly physically abused by their intimate partners. These include learned helplessness, lowered self-esteem, impaired functioning, fear or terror, loss of the assumption of invulnerability, and anger or rage.

5. *How can rape be prevented?* Prevention of rape has taken two routes. One is determination of what responses by potential victims are most effective in warding off a sexual assault. The other is the use of effective treatments for convicted rapists. Anti-androgen drugs, which

reduce sex drive, and a combination of various behavior therapy techniques have shown some effectiveness as treatment for convicted rapists.

6. ***What are two types of sexual harassment recognized by the courts?*** The first type of harassment, *quid pro quo* harassment, consists of sexual demands made in conjunction with offers of benefits in exchange for compliance or threats of punishment if the respondent does not comply. The second type is harassment that creates a hostile work environment; it often involves demeaning comments, acts of touching or attempted intimacy, or the display of provocative photographs or artwork.

KEY TERMS

abuse excuse

acute stress disorder

battered woman syndrome

borderline personality disorder

chemical castration

cycle of violence

dispositional attributions

hate crimes

hostile workplace harassment

posttraumatic stress disorder

quid pro quo harassment

rape trauma syndrome

secondary victimization

self-defense

victimology

Chapter

7

Evaluating Criminal Suspects

ORIENTING QUESTIONS

1. What are some psychological investigative techniques used by the police?

2. What is criminal profiling?

3. What cues do people use to detect deception, and how accurate are these judgments?

4. Is the polygraph a valid instrument for lie detection? What are some problems associated with it?

5. What brain-based techniques are used to detect deception, and how well do they work?

6. How valid is confession evidence? What kinds of interrogation procedures can lead to false confessions?

7. What are some of the reforms proposed to prevent false confessions?

In this chapter, we discuss three additional activities that psychology can provide to assist law enforcement: profiling criminal suspects, assessing the truthfulness of suspects, and evaluating the validity of their confessions. The common thread that ties these topics together is the assumption that psychological theory and techniques can be used to improve police officers' evaluations of criminal suspects.

These contributions occur in a logical sequence. Psychological profiling is usually performed at the beginning of a criminal investigation when the police need help focusing on certain types of people who might be the most likely suspects.

Once suspects have been identified, law enforcement officials use other procedures to determine whether they should be charged. While questioning suspects, police rely on various visual and verbal cues to determine whether they are giving truthful responses. But as you will see, people are not especially adept at detecting deception by relying on these kinds of cues.

Suspects are sometimes given so-called lie detection (or polygraph) tests to provide more information about their guilt or innocence and, sometimes, to encourage them to confess. However, assumptions about the effectiveness of polygraph procedures conflict with some psychological findings about their accuracy. Though results of a lie detection test are sometimes admitted into evidence, many psychologists question the objectivity of the procedure as it is usually administered and, hence, the validity of its results.

Increasingly, law enforcement agents and industry personnel are using brain-based technologies, including neuroimaging and brain wave measurements, to detect deception. Although promising, these techniques have not yet been subjected to the kind of rigorous, real-world testing that is required before they become commonplace investigatory tools.

The police interrogate suspects and encourage them to confess because confessions make it more likely that suspects will be successfully prosecuted and eventually convicted. But in the quest for conviction, confessions can be coerced. Courts have tried to clarify when a confession is truly voluntary, but psychological findings often conflict with the courts' evaluations of confessions.

Thus, a consistent theme throughout this chapter is the conflict between the legal system and psychological science regarding ways of gaining knowledge and evaluating truth. A related conflict involves the competing interests of determining the truth and resolving disputes.

PROFILING OF CRIMINAL SUSPECTS

Do criminals commit their crimes or choose their victims in distinctive ways that leave clues to their psychological makeup, much as fingerprints point to their physical identity or ballistics tests reveal the kind of gun they used? There is some evidence that psychological characteristics are linked to behavioral patterns and that these links can be detected by a psychological analysis of crime scenes. Behavioral scientists and police use **criminal profiling** to narrow criminal investigations to suspects who possess certain behavioral and personality features that were revealed by the way the crime was committed. (Another way to think about profiling is that it involves the attempt to "reverse engineer" a final product—the crime scene—in the attempt to gain leads about the individual[s] who created that final product.)

Profiling, which has also been called "criminal investigative analysis," does not identify a specific suspect. Instead, profilers offer a general psychological description of the most likely type of suspect, including personality and behavioral characteristics suggested by a thorough analysis of the crimes committed, so that the police can concentrate their investigation of difficult cases in the most profitable directions.

(Profiles also help investigators search for persons who fit descriptions known to characterize hijackers, drug couriers, and undocumented aliens; Monahan & Walker, 2005.) The results of a careful profile may provide specific information about suspects, including psychopathology, characteristics of their family history, educational and legal history, and habits and social interests (Woodworth & Porter, 2000). Although profiling can be used in diverse contexts, it is considered most helpful in crimes in which the offender has demonstrated some form of repetitive behavior with unusual aspects, such as sadistic torture, ritualistic or bizarre behavior, evisceration, or staging or acting out a fantasy (Woodworth & Porter, 2000).

A successful profiler should possess several key attributes, including both an understanding of human psychology and investigative experience (Hazelwood, Ressler, Depue, & Douglas, 1995). There is some controversy regarding who should be considered a successful profiler. Because of the importance of investigative experience in criminal profiling, some have suggested that mental health professionals may not be fully qualified to engage in profiling (Hazelwood & Michaud, 2001). Others maintain that clinical (forensic) psychologists possess a level of expertise that contributes to the effectiveness of criminal profiling (Copson, Badcock, Boon, & Britton, 1997; Gudjonsson & Copson, 1997). One survey (Torres, Boccacini, & Miller, 2006) found that only 10% of the psychologists and psychiatrists surveyed reported any profiling experience, and 25% considered themselves knowledgeable about profiling. Although fewer than 25% believed that criminal profiling was scientifically reliable or valid, most felt it had some usefulness in criminal investigation. Certainly any professional who attempts to conduct profiling should be knowledgeable and experienced with offenders and the process of criminal investigation, which typically means that an individual must have experience as a criminal investigator.

Many famous fictional detectives have been portrayed as excellent profilers because they could interpret the meaning of a small detail or find a common theme among seemingly unrelated features of a crime. Lew Archer, the hero in Ross MacDonald's popular series of detective novels, frequently began his search for a missing person (usually a wayward wife or a troubled daughter) by looking at the person's bedroom, examining her reading material, and rummaging through her closet to discover where her

lifestyle might have misdirected her. Lincoln Rhyme, the "criminalist" in Jeffrey Deaver's novels, focuses on learning everything humanly possible from painstaking scrutiny of the crime scene, and using that information to support (or disconfirm) possibilities about potential perpetrators. Profiling has even infiltrated popular culture through TV programs such as *Law and Order* and its offspring (*Criminal Intent* and *Special Victims Unit*), as well as *Criminal Minds*.

One of the earliest cases of criminal profiling involved the 1957 arrest of George Metesky, otherwise known as the Mad Bomber of New York City. Over an eight-year period, police had tried to solve a series of more than 30 bombings in the New York area. They finally consulted Dr. James Brussel, a Greenwich Village psychiatrist, who, after examining pictures of the bomb scenes and analyzing letters that the bomber had sent, advised the police to look for a heavyset, middle-aged, Eastern European, Catholic man who was single and lived with a sibling or aunt in Connecticut. Brussel also concluded that the man was very neat and that, when found, he would be wearing a buttoned double-breasted suit. When the police finally arrested Metesky, this composite turned out to be uncannily accurate—even down to the right type of suit.

Not all early profiles were so useful, however. For example, the committee of experts charged with the task of profiling the Boston Strangler predicted that the killer was not one man but two, each of whom lived alone and worked as a schoolteacher. They also suggested that one of the men would be homosexual. When Albert DeSalvo ultimately confessed to these killings, police discovered that he was a heterosexual construction worker who lived with his wife and two sons (Porter, 1983).

The major source of research and development on criminal profiling has been the FBI's Behavioral Science Unit (the BSU), which has been working on criminal profiles since the 1970s. The BSU is currently one of the instructional components of the FBI's Training and Development Division, located at the FBI Academy in Quantico, Virginia. It provides training, conducts research, and offers consultation in the behavioral and social sciences. The BSU also coordinates with other FBI units, such as the National Center for the Analysis of Violent Crime (NCAVC), which provides operational assistance to FBI field offices and law enforcement agencies (http://www.fbi.gov/hq/td/academy/bsu/bsu.htm). The NCAVC

Public domain

FBI Academy in Quantico, Virginia

now has separate units that focus on crimes against adults, crimes against children, apprehension of violent criminals, and counterterrorism and threat assessment. Its mission combines investigative and operational support, research, and training (without charge), which it provides to federal, state, local, and foreign law enforcement agencies—particularly in the context of investigation of unusual or repetitive violent crimes. The NCAVC also provides support through expertise and consultation in nonviolent matters such as national security, corruption, and white-collar crime investigations.

Following September 11, 2001, the FBI placed a higher priority on counterterrorism (FBI Academy, 2002). Profiling terrorist suspects in the United States has proved challenging, and no reliable profile has been developed. There are a number of reasons for this, described succinctly in a recent review on the topic (Monahan, 2012). The author observes that individual risk factors for criminal behavior (e.g., age, gender, marital status, social class, past crime, major mental illness, and personality) do not serve as risk factors for terrorism. Indeed, while there are some advantages to considering "terrorism" broadly, Monahan describes the strategy of being more specific about types of terrorism, such as suicidal, home-grown, inside, jihadist/Salafist, and so on, as also potentially useful. Finally, he offers four categories of "promising" risk factors in this area: ideology, affiliation, trauma/loss, and disgust. Even focusing

on these more promising strategies, however, would not allow the prospective validation of a risk assessment tool for terrorism. (Imagine "validating" such a tool by administering it to a large number of individuals and releasing some of them to observe how many carried out terrorist activity.) In addition, applying such risk factors in a population in which terrorists are rare, such as the United States, would risk violating Americans' civil liberties and producing an overwhelmingly large number of "false positives" (those who are predicted to present a threat but who actually do not).

Historically, much of the BSU's focus was on violent offenders, especially those who commit bizarre or repeated crimes (Jeffers, 1991). Special attention was given to rapists (Ressler, Burgess, & Douglas, 1988), arsonists (Rider, 1980), sexual homicides (Hazelwood & Douglas, 1980), and mass and serial murderers (Porter, 1983). Interest in these topics continues, particularly in the area of serial and mass murder (Fox & Levin, 2005; Hickey, 2009; Morton & Hilts, 2008; Mullen, 2004). There is also continued interest in the topic of crime scene analysis and offender profiling (Ainsworth, 2001; Owen, 2004; Petherick, 2005). The focus of such work is on describing those who have committed a specific type of offense in order to learn how they select and approach their victims, how they react to their crimes, what demographic or family characteristics they share, and what personality features might predominate among them. For example, as part of its study of mass and serial killers, the FBI conducted detailed interviews with some of the United States' most notorious homicide offenders—among them Charles Manson, Richard Speck, and David Berkowitz—to determine the similarities among them.

Classifying Homicide Offenders: Mass and Serial Murderers

On the basis of this research, behavioral scientists have been able to classify mass murderers and add to the portrait of contemporary homicide offenders. Historically, most homicides have been committed by killers who were well acquainted with their victims, had a personal but rational motive, killed once, and were then arrested. In the past few decades, however, increased attention has been paid to patterns of homicide involving killers who attack multiple victims, sometimes with irrational or bizarre motives, and who are less likely to be apprehended than in former days because their victims are strangers. The criminal trail of these murderers may center on one locale and period of time or cross through different locations and stretch over a longer period of time. This does not mean, of course, that the patterns of homicide offending have necessarily changed. It is quite likely that changes in mass communication technology have changed the *awareness* of homicide offending with multiple victims. (See the "Mass Murder Website" at http://www.fortunecity.com/roswell/hammer/73/index.html for a description of multiple homicide offenders between 1829 and 1996.) Indeed, mass murderers have been a favorite subject of lurid "true crime" books such as *The Only Living Witness* (about Ted Bundy), *The Co-Ed Killer* (Edmund Kemper), *Killer Clown* (John Gacy), and *Bind, Torture, Kill* (Dennis Rader), as well as of more scholarly comparative studies of multiple homicides (Fox & Levin, 1998; Meloy et al., 2004; Morton & Hilts, 2008).

Although experts differ on the precise number of victims to use in defining "multiple homicide," Fox and Levin's (1998) criterion of "the slaying of four or more victims, simultaneously or sequentially, by one or a few individuals" is probably the most widely accepted opinion. It is difficult to estimate how many double homicides are committed each year, but the consensus is that they are increasing, and this increase does not reflect merely greater media attention or police apprehension rates.

Mass murders remain relatively rare, however, which makes it virtually impossible to formulate predictive statistical models that are accurate. The particular problem with trying to predict such rare events is the "false positive" error rate: even approaches that have a good overall accuracy rate will identify a relatively large number of false positives (those who are predicted to be violent, but actually are not). As an alternative to prediction, current research has focused on identifying characteristics of these homicide offenders and examining patterns among individuals. One study comparing 30 adult with 34 adolescent mass murderers found striking similarities between the two groups (Meloy et al., 2004). Three-quarters of the entire sample were Caucasian (75%); the majority of both the adolescents (70%) and the adults (94%) were described as "loners"; almost half of the adolescent sample (48%) and almost two-thirds of the adult sample (63%) demonstrated a preoccupation with

weapons and violence; and about 43% of both groups had a violent history.

Two types of multiple homicides have been identified: mass murders and serial murders. These types share some similarities but are marked by several differences (Meloy & Felthous, 2004). The **mass murderer** kills four or more victims in one location during a period of time that lasts anywhere from a few minutes to several hours. It is estimated that about two mass murders were committed every month in the United States in the 1990s, resulting in the deaths of 100 victims annually (Fox & Levin, 1998). Although most mass murderers are not severely mentally ill, they do tend to harbor strong feelings of resentment and are often motivated by revenge against their victims.

Contrary to popular myth, the majority of mass murderers do not attack strangers at random; in almost 80% of studied mass murders, the assailant was related to or well acquainted with the victims, and in many cases, the attack was a carefully planned assault rather than an impulsive rampage. For every Seung-Hui Cho, who killed 32 people and wounded 25 others in a mass shooting at Virginia Tech in 2007, there are many more people like Bruce Pardo, who, dressed as Santa Claus, opened fire at a Christmas party at the home of his former in-laws and killed nine people before killing himself. Most mass murders are solved by law enforcement; the typical assailant is killed at the location of the crime, commits suicide, or surrenders to police. **Spree killers** are a special form of mass murderers: attackers who kill victims at two or more different locations with no "cooling-off" interval between the murders. The killing constitutes a single event, but it can either last only a short time or go on for a day or more.

Serial murderers kill four or more victims, each on a separate occasion. Unlike mass murderers, **serial killers** usually select a certain type of victim who fulfills a role in the killer's fantasies. There are cooling-off periods between serial murders, which are usually better planned than mass or spree killings. Some serial killers (such as Angel Maturino Resendiz, called the Railway Killer because the murders he was charged with took place by railroad tracks) travel frequently and murder in several locations. Dr. Michael Swango, trained as a physician, is suspected by the FBI of killing up to 60 individuals, typically by poisoning them, between 1981 and 1997. He moved around a great deal, and is suspected of killings in

Dennis Rader, the "BTK Killer"

Illinois, New York, Ohio, and South Dakota—as well as Zimbabwe. Others (such as Gary Ridgway, the so-called Green River Killer, who confessed to killing 48 women, mostly prostitutes, and dumping their bodies along the Green River in Washington) are geographically stable and kill within the same area. The Unabomber, who apparently remained in one place but chose victims who lived in different parts of the country to receive his carefully constructed mail bombs, reflected an unusual combination of serial killer characteristics.

Because they are clever in the way they plan their murders, are capable of presenting themselves as normal members of the community, kill for idiosyncratic reasons, and frequently wait months between killings, serial murderers are difficult to apprehend. It took 30 years for Wichita police to figure out that Dennis Rader, a Boy Scout leader and president of Christ Lutheran Church, was a brutal serial killer who used the moniker "BTK"—an acronym for "bind, torture, kill." He confessed to 10 counts of first-degree murder in 2005.

Social scientists have gained some knowledge about these criminals, who may number as many as 100 in the United States. One study compiled a list of characteristics from 157 serial offenders and found that most were White males in their early 30s (Kraemer, Lord, & Heilbrun, 2004). More than half of the offenders were employed at the time of the offense, and approximately one-third were married. The average offender had an 11th-grade education. Victims of these offenders were most often White

females in their early to mid-30s who were strangers to their killers. More than half of the murders were sexually motivated. These characteristics differ from those of single-homicide offenders, who often know their victims and kill for emotional reasons such as anger or sexual jealousy (Kraemer et al., 2004).

Serial killers tend to select vulnerable victims of some specific type who gratify their need to control people. Consistent with the motive of wanting to dominate people, they prefer to kill with "hands-on" methods such as strangulation and stabbing, rather than with guns, which are the preferred weapons of mass murderers. They are often preoccupied with sexualized or sadistic fantasies involving capture and control of their victims. Many serial killers use pornography and violent sexual fantasies intensively as "rehearsals" for and "replays" of their crimes, and they often keep souvenirs (sometimes in the form of body parts from victims) to commemorate their savage attacks. Despite the apparent "craziness" of their behavior, serial killers are not typically psychotic individuals. Most of them, however, have personality disorders and lack the ability to experience empathy and remorse. In fact, serial killers often revel in the publicity that their crimes receive.

Fox and Levin (2005) have provided examples of different motivations for serial and mass murder (including power, revenge, loyalty, profit, and terror), along with brief vignettes illustrating these motivations (see Table 7.1).

Similar examples of possible motivations for homicide, as well as additional information (e.g., signature aspects of violent crime, staging and undoing at crime scenes, and recommendations for interrogation) are contained in the *Crime Classification Manual* (Douglas, Burgess, Burgess, & Ressler, 2006). As you might suspect, the classification with respect to offender motivation can be complex. For example, was the Virginia Tech shooter Seung-Hui Cho motivated by power? What about revenge? Some evidence suggests that both may have influenced him. This example vividly illustrates the point that many influences and motivations may come together in the rare and tragic context of multiple homicide.

Steps Involved in Criminal Profiling

Douglas, Ressler, Burgess, and Hartman (1986) divided the FBI's profiling strategy into five stages, with a final, sixth stage being the arrest of the correct

TABLE 7.1   **Generic examples of motivations for multiple murder**

Motivations for Multiple Murder	Type of Multiple Murder	
	Serial Murder	**Mass Murder**
Power	Inspired by sadistic fantasies, a man tortures and kills a series of strangers to satisfy his need for control and dominance.	A pseudo-commando, dressed in battle fatigues and armed with a semiautomatic weapon, turns a shopping mall into a "war zone."
Revenge	Grossly mistreated as a child, a man avenges his past by slaying women who remind him of his mother.	After being fired from his job, a gunman returns to the work site and opens fire on his former boss and coworker.
Loyalty	A team of killers turns murder into a ritual for proving their dedication and commitment to one another.	A depressed husband/father kills his family and himself to spare them from a miserable existence and bring them a better life in the hereafter.
Profit	A woman poisons to death a series of husbands to collect on their life insurance policies.	A band of armed robbers executes the employees of a store to eliminate all witnesses to their crime.
Terror	A profoundly paranoid man commits a series of bombings to warn the world of impending doom.	A group of antigovernment extremists blows up a train to send a political message.

SOURCE: From Fox & Levin, 2005, p. 20.

suspect. The six phases, as they evolve in a murder investigation, are as follows:

1. *Profiling inputs.* The first stage involves collecting all information available about the crime, including physical evidence, photographs of the crime scene, autopsy reports and pictures, complete background information on the victim, and police reports. The profiler does not want to be told about possible suspects at this stage, because such data might prejudice or prematurely direct the profile.

2. *Decision process models.* In this stage the profiler organizes the input into meaningful questions and patterns along several dimensions of criminal activity. What type of homicide has been committed? What is the primary impetus for the crime—sexual, financial, personal, or emotional disturbance? What level of risk did the victim experience, and what level of risk did the murderer take in killing the victim? What was the sequence of acts before and after the killing, and how long did these acts take to commit? Where was the crime committed? Was the body moved, or was it found where the murder was committed?

3. *Crime assessment.* On the basis of the findings in the previous phase, the profiler attempts to reconstruct the behavior of the offender and the victim. Was the murder *organized* (suggesting an intelligent killer who carefully selects victims

against whom to act out a well-rehearsed fantasy) or *disorganized* (indicating an impulsive, less socially competent, possibly even psychotic killer)? Was the crime staged to mislead the police? Can details such as cause of death, location of wounds, and position of the body reveal anything about the killer's motivation? Criminal profilers are often guided by the following hypotheses:

- Brutal facial injuries point to killers who knew their victims.
- Murders committed with whatever weapon happens to be available are more impulsive than murders committed with a gun and may reveal a killer who lives fairly near the victim.
- Murders committed early in the morning seldom involve alcohol or drugs.

4. *Criminal profile.* In this stage, profilers formulate an initial description of the most likely suspects. This profile includes the perpetrator's race, sex, age, marital status, living arrangements, and employment history; psychological characteristics, beliefs, and values; probable reactions to the police; and past criminal record, including the possibility of similar offenses in the past. This stage also contains a feedback loop whereby profilers check their predictions against stage-2 information to make sure that the profile fits the original data.

5. *Investigation.* A written report is given to investigators, who concentrate on suspects matching the profile. If new evidence is discovered in this investigation, a second feedback process is initiated, and the profile can be revised.

6. *Apprehension.* The intended result of these procedures, arrest of a suspect, allows profilers to evaluate the validity of their predictions. The key element in this validation is a thorough interview of the suspect to assess the influences of background and psychological variables.

The Validity of Criminal Profiles

Is there any evidence that psychological profiling is valid? Are profilers more accurate than other groups in their descriptions of suspects, or is this activity little more than a reading of forensic tea leaves? Do profilers use a different process in evaluating information than other investigators?

In a review of criminal profiling, Homant and Kennedy (1998) concluded that different kinds of crime scenes can be classified with reasonable reliability and that differences in these crimes do correlate with certain offender characteristics, such as murderers' prior relationships and interactions with victims (Salfati & Canter, 1999); organized versus disorganized approaches; and serial versus single offenders (e.g., Kraemer et al., 2004). At the same time, this research suggests several reasons for caution: (1) Inaccurate profiles are quite common, (2) many of the studies have been conducted in house by FBI profilers studying a fairly small number of offenders, and (3) the concepts and approaches actually used by profilers have often not been objectively and systematically defined. A majority of the psychologists and psychiatrists responding to one survey (Torres et al., 2006) did not view criminal profiling as scientifically reliable or valid (but nonetheless endorsed it as a potentially useful tool in criminal investigation).

One study (Pinizzotto & Finkel, 1990) investigated the effectiveness of criminal profiling as practiced by real-life experts. In this investigation, four different groups of participants evaluated two criminal cases—a homicide and a sex offense—that had already been solved but were completely unknown to the subjects. The first group consisted of four experienced criminal profilers who had a total of 42 years of profiling experience and six police detectives who had

recently been trained by the FBI to be profilers. The second group consisted of six police detectives with 57 years of total experience in criminal investigations but with no profiling experience or training. The third group was composed of six clinical psychologists who had no profiling or criminal investigation experience. The final group consisted of six undergraduates drawn from psychology classes.

All participants were given, for each case, an array of materials that profilers typically use, including crime scene photographs, crime scene descriptions by uniformed officers, autopsy and toxicology reports (in the murder case), and descriptions of the victims. Three tests of profiling quality were used: All subjects prepared a profile of a suspect in each case, answered 15 questions about the identity (e.g., gender, age, employment) of the suspects, and were asked to rank order a written "lineup" of five suspects, from most to least likely to have committed each of the crimes.

The results indicated that, compared with the other three groups, the profiler group wrote longer profiles that contained more specific predictions about suspects, included more accurate predictions, and were rated as more helpful by other police detectives. Profilers were more accurate than the other groups in answering specific questions about the sex offense suspect, though the groups did not differ in their accuracy about the homicide suspect. Similar results were found with the "lineup" identification: Profilers were the most accurate for the sex offense, whereas there were no differences for the homicide case.

This study suggests that profilers can produce more useful and valid criminal profiles, even when compared to experienced crime investigators. This advantage may be limited, however, to certain kinds of cases or to the types of information made available to investigators.

Another study (Canter, Alison, Alison, & Wentink, 2004) tested the "organized/disorganized" dichotomy by using specialized statistics to analyze aspects of serial killing derived from murders committed by 100 U.S. serial killers. There was no distinct subset of offense characteristics associated with organized versus disorganized killings. Researchers did find a subset of organized features (e.g., evidence of planning, bringing a weapon, use of a vehicle) that were characteristic of most serial killings, but disorganized features such as impulsivity, failure to use precautions that would limit evidence left at the scene,

5,5,5. 30

and related behaviors were far more unusual. The investigators suggested that these results cast doubt on whether killings can be reliably and validly classified using this dichotomy.

Based on the absence of empirical scientific data supporting the process of profiling, some (e.g., Note, 2008; Risinger & Loop, 2002) have argued that profiling lacks the requisite scientific support to allow experts to testify to the findings in the course of litigation. Given the limited extent to which the profiling process has been studied, there does not appear to be an adequate scientific foundation for expert testimony. Whether courts admit profiling evidence will probably continue to depend on the particular judge.

How do psychologists themselves view criminal profiling? In a survey of 152 police psychologists, 70% questioned the validity of crime scene profiling (Bartol, 1996). Nonetheless, despite such reservations, profiling continues to be used in law enforcement and is now practiced, in some form or other, in several countries (Woodworth & Porter, 2000).

DETECTING DECEPTION

In the short-lived television crime drama *Lie to Me*, actor Brendan Hines assisted law enforcement by investigating criminals and trying to ascertain their truthfulness. The twist was that he felt a moral imperative to tell the truth himself, to "shoot out the truth" without censoring himself. Unfortunately, such "radical honesty" is far more likely to appear on television than in reality.

People tell lies fairly often—on average, between once and twice a day, according to self-report studies (Hartwig, 2011). They do so for a variety of psychological reasons: so that others will perceive them favorably, to avoid tension and conflict in social situations, and to minimize hurt feelings (Vrij, Granhag, & Porter, 2010). People also lie to conceal their wrongdoings, and successfully detecting these liars can have profound societal benefits. Consider the work of a customs official who intercepts a cache of weapons, a detective who doubts the veracity of a suspected child molester, or an airport security officer who suspects that a passenger about to board a plane harbors ill intent. Consider the fact that each of the 19 terrorists who launched the September 11 attacks lied to

authorities on at least three occasions, and that none of their lies was ever detected (Honts & Kircher, 2011).

Throughout history, many societies have assumed that criminals can be detected by the physical manifestations of their denials. Ever since King Solomon tried to discover which of two women who claimed to be the mother of an infant was lying by watching their emotions when he threatened to cut the baby in half and divide it between them, people have believed that the body will reveal when the mind is lying. People judge others' truthfulness by observing their behavior, often without conscious awareness of doing so. In late-night conversations, parents gauge the veracity of their teenagers' stories about where they had been and with whom. During job interviews, employers make quick judgments of the candor and honesty of prospective employees.

Police officers and other law enforcement officials know that deception is common, and their ability to detect lying has profound implications for the people who pass through the criminal justice system. Being deemed "truthful" can absolve guilty people of suspicion, allowing them to remain on the streets to commit more crimes. Being deemed "deceptive" can launch someone—perhaps an innocent person—into a criminal prosecution and toward eventual conviction and imprisonment. How well law enforcement officials can assess deception is vitally important to the fair and effective operation of the justice system. Fortunately, psychologists have provided tools to help them. In this section, we describe what psychologists have learned about people's ability to detect deception unaided, using only their eyes and ears and relying only on verbal and behavioral cues. This technique—simple observation—is actually the most common form of lie detection (Vrij et al., 2010).

It is difficult to be certain when people are fibbing and when they are telling the truth (at least as they believe it). It is also difficult to assess how people distinguish honesty from dishonesty in others. For this reason, psychological scientists have developed research protocols that mimic real-world lying and truth telling.

In these studies, researchers instruct some participants to lie and others to tell the truth about a particular experience or intention—a film they saw or intend to see, the contents of their pockets, or whether they were involved in or are planning to steal some money. Recent studies have involved more forensically relevant situations such as asking participants to lie about stealing a wallet or to tell the truth about buying a particular product (Hartwig, Granhag, Stromwall, & Kronkvist, 2006). These stories—lies and truths alike—are videotaped and shown to observers who then judge the truthfulness of those statements. Scientists measure the ability to detect deception—that is, to realize that a truthful person is telling the truth and that a liar is lying—as the percentage of correct judgments. In a simple two-alternative forced choice, the chance level of an accurate decision is 50%.

How accurately can people detect deception? In a meta-analysis that evaluated the decisions of nearly 25,000 observers in hundreds of studies, Bond and DePaulo (2006) determined that people are correct only 54% of the time, hardly better than chance. The analysis revealed several other interesting clues to how people judge deception. For example, it uncovered a **truth bias**, meaning that people were biased toward judging statements as being truthful. People tend to take most assertions at face value, assuming that they are true unless their authenticity is called into question for some reason. (Think about asking someone what time it is.) As a result, subjects in the meta-analysis correctly classified 61% of truthful statements as nondeceptive but only 47% of lies as deceptive. Observers are better at detecting truths and lies about what others intend to do in the future than about what they did in the past (Vrij, Leal, Mann, & Granhag, 2011).

Many of the people making judgments in deception studies were college students who had no expertise or specialized training (and perhaps little desire) to do this task well. Might people who have more experience judging deception be better at it? When playwright Tennessee Williams wrote that "mendacity is the system we live in," he may have been referring to people whose occupations expose them to multiple lies on a daily basis: police officers, judges, customs officials, border patrol officers, and the like. Indeed, a classic study supports the idea that it helps to have experience with people who both lie and tell the truth. Ekman and O'Sullivan (1991) found that U.S. Secret Service agents (who frequently interview individuals who may present a threat to the president or vice-president and their families, and must make decisions about the accuracy of those individuals' accounts) were the only

participants—among groups that also included the Central Intelligence Agency (CIA), FBI, National Security Agency (NSA), Drug Enforcement Agency (DEA), California police and judges, psychiatrists, college students, and working adults—who could detect deception at greater than chance levels.

Do this study and others support the idea that being exposed to frequent deceit makes one a better lie catcher? To some extent, yes, although trained observers are only *slightly* better than untrained observers at distinguishing between truths and lies (Vrij et al., 2010). Averaging across various studies, trained observers detected 58% of the truths and lies correctly, whereas untrained observers were correct 53% of the time. But misclassifying deceptive and truthful statements more than 40% of the time means that precious time and resources are being wasted by law enforcement officials relying on mistaken beliefs about cues to deceit.

Distinguishing Liars and Truth-Tellers

How would you expect liars to act? What would you expect them to say? People can fairly easily conjure up an image of liars. Perhaps your image is of people who are shifty, avert their gaze, fidget, and look tense. Are these beliefs correct or are they based on stereotypes and misconceptions?

One reason that people are poor deception detectors is that they tend to focus on the wrong cues when judging another person's truthfulness. Instead of focusing on **diagnostic cues**—cues that can accurately distinguish a truth-teller from an imposter—people tend to fall back on stereotypes and biases about what deceptive behavior looks like.

Studies of beliefs about deception have shown that people (laypeople and experts alike) tend to have mistaken beliefs about nonverbal cues to deception. For example, many people assume that avoiding eye contact is a sign of lying. Yet research on objective, diagnostic cues to deception shows that this trait is not a predictor of deceptive behavior (Sporer & Schwandt, 2007), even in circumstances where liars have a lot to lose—like spouses, money, or reputations. People also mistakenly believe that fidgety movements mean a person is being deceitful. Although a prominent guide to interrogations, Zulawski and Wicklander's *Practical Aspects of Interview and Interrogation* (2001), asserts that a liar's movements tend to be "jerky and abrupt," the data show otherwise.

In fact, psychologists have found very few reliable nonverbal cues to deception. Moreover, nonverbal behavior is influenced by cultural norms. Whereas it is expected for Caucasians look into the eyes of their conversational partners, Japanese consider direct eye contact to be rude, and African Americans avert their gaze more often than European Americans (Johnson, 2006). Furthermore, because people who are asked to tell the truth can be as nervous as liars, using nonverbal cues to detect deception is problematic. As Aldert Vrij, a psychologist at the University of Portsmouth, reminds us, there is nothing as obvious as Pinocchio's growing nose to alert us to a lie.

Psychologists have had more success determining which *verbal* cues are associated with deceptive behavior. For example, because it is difficult to quickly fabricate details that do not exist in memory, a large amount of reported detail should be indicative of truthful reports. Indeed, scientists have learned that truthful statements tend to be longer than lies. And though people are suspicious of memory lapses in the real world, truth-tellers are more likely than liars to say they can't recall certain details. Liars also tend to speak in a higher-pitched voice and make more speech errors (e.g., slips of the tongue, repeated words, and incomplete sentences) than truth-tellers (Sporer & Schwandt, 2006).

Though stereotypic beliefs may hinder our ability to distinguish fabricators from honest responders, **cognitive load interviews** can enhance our ability to make those distinctions. Cognitive load interviews are designed to mentally tax a person so that it becomes difficult to simultaneously answer a question and maintain a lie. Lying is cognitively taxing. Liars must first formulate their fabrications and then remember what they said earlier and to whom. They need to avoid providing any new information to interviewers. Because they know they are being deceitful, they may have to pay more careful attention to their own demeanor and to reactions from the interviewer to see if they are getting away with their lies. Finally, they have to suppress the truth. All of these activities require mental effort which, when compounded by the need to answer interviewers' questions, can confound and confuse deceitful subjects.

Among the techniques that effectively increase cognitive load is asking subjects to recall a series of events in reverse chronological order, and requiring them to perform a secondary task during the interview, such as determining whether a figure that

reappears on a computer screen is similar to a target figure shown earlier. By making a subject think harder in an interview, investigators have been able to more accurately distinguish liars from truthful interviewees (Vrij et al., 2008).

One final approach to detecting deception exploits the fact the liars prepare themselves for anticipated questions by rehearsing—indeed, *over-rehearsing*—their responses. But rehearsal only works when liars correctly anticipate the questions they will be asked. Although they may anticipate certain predictable questions (e.g., "What did you do in the restaurant?"), they typically do not anticipate spatial questions (e.g., "In relation to the front door and where you sat in the restaurant, where were the closest diners?"), temporal questions (e.g., "Who finished their food first, you or your friend?"), or requests to draw the scene. In one study, when observers viewed responses to anticipated questions, they could not distinguish truth-tellers from liars above chance level. But when they viewed responses to unanticipated questions, they correctly classified 80% of the truth-tellers and liars (Vrij et al., 2009). These findings suggest that asking unanticipated questions can be a surprisingly effective way to betray a liar.

Methods of Detecting Deception

Using the Polygraph to Detect Deception. Over the years, people suspected of wrongdoing have faced various tests of their veracity. The ancient Hindus forced suspects to chew rice and spit it out on a leaf from a sacred tree. If the rice was dry, the suspect was deemed guilty. Arabian Bedouins required conflicting witnesses to lick a hot iron; the one whose tongue was burned was thought to be lying (Kleinmuntz & Szucko, 1984). These procedures reflect activity of the sympathetic nervous system (under emotional stress, salivation usually decreases) and thus are crude

A polygraph examination

measures of emotion. But emotion and lying are not the same, and this distinction is at the root of concerns about using the polygraph to detect deception.

For many years, the standard way to assess truthfulness was to measure signs of physiological arousal in combination with a specific questioning strategy. The **polygraph** (sometimes referred to as the *lie detector*) is a computer-based machine that measures blood pressure, electrodermal activity, and respiratory changes during questioning. Unfortunately, the physiological manifestations of various negative emotions (e.g., fear, guilt, anger) are all very similar, suggesting that assessments of a person's credibility based on physiological responses alone may be problematic. Simply being suspected of committing a crime, even if one is innocent, may generate a great deal of surplus emotion that should not be taken as a sign of guilt.

Although scientific research has contributed to the advancement of polygraph techniques over the past half-century, concerns about their validity linger. Nonetheless, the polygraph enjoys fairly widespread application within the criminal justice system, including situations in which an offense has been committed and the issue is whether the suspect was involved, as well as situations in which sex offenders are questioned about whether they committed offenses as yet unknown to authorities (e.g., Have you had unsupervised contact with children over the past three months?) (Meijer & Verschuere, 2010).

Polygraph Techniques. The **Control Question Test** (CQT, sometimes referred to as the *Comparison Question Test*) has become the most popular approach to polygraphic examinations (Meijer & Verschuere, 2010). This exam begins with an interview in which the examiner gathers biographical information from the subject and attempts to impress on the subject that he or she must be honest at all times during the test. The examiner tries to convince the subject that the polygraph is an infallible instrument; this strategy is meant to threaten guilty subjects at the same time that it reassures the innocent.

When the test begins, the polygrapher asks a series of questions and is especially interested in subjects' responses to two kinds of questions. *Relevant questions* inquire about the crime under investigation (e.g., "Did you steal the law school's TV set?"). *Comparison questions* are not directly concerned with the crime under investigation but are calculated to induce an emotional reaction because they cover common misdeeds that nearly all of us have committed (e.g., "Prior to the age of 21, did you ever do anything that was dishonest or illegal?"). Most polygraphers consider a denial to be a "known lie." But subjects *will* deny, thereby providing a characteristic physiological response to a lie.

The expectation is that guilty subjects should be more aroused by the relevant questions (to which they must respond with a lie in order to maintain their innocence), whereas innocent subjects should be more aroused by the comparison questions (because they will worry that admitting to a past misdeed might make them look more like a criminal at the present time). Therefore, this procedure works best when innocent subjects lie or show greater emotional turmoil in response to the comparison questions, and guilty subjects lie and become more emotionally aroused in response to the relevant questions.

An alternative to the CQT is the **Concealed Knowledge Test** (CKT). Both the procedure and the purposes of this method are fundamentally different from the control question approach. The goal is to detect the presence of concealed knowledge in the suspect's mind, not to detect lying. The procedure relies on the accumulation of facts that are known only by the police, the criminal, and any surviving victims. For example, the polygrapher may ask, "In what room was the victim's body found? What strange garment was the victim wearing? What was the victim clutching in his hand?"

The polygrapher creates a series of multiple-choice questions and presents them to the suspect. Each alternative would appear equally plausible to an innocent person. But the true criminal will, in theory, be revealed by heightened physiological reactions that accompany recognition of concealed information. Obviously, this technique can be used only when the details of the crime have been kept from the public. Even then, it is conceivable that the suspect is not the perpetrator but, rather, was told about the crime by the true criminal and therefore possesses concealed knowledge. It is possible that some guilty subjects are so distraught or pay so little attention to the details of their crimes that they actually lack the required information on which this method relies. Some critics of the CKT suggest that it can be conducted properly in only a small percentage of real-life cases.

Regardless of the test used, the final step in a polygraph exam is interpretation of the physiological measurements. Most polygraph examiners are trained to score responses by using a combination of rule-based subjective judgments and objective measures of physiological responses. They may also rely on observations of the subject's behavior throughout the test (Kleiner, 2002).

The Polygraph's Accuracy. Examiners are accurate when they expose liars and believe truthful suspects. They err when they believe that a liar is truthful (a *false negative*) or that a truthful subject is lying (a *false positive*). The level of examiners' accuracy has been a central question in ongoing debates about the validity of the polygraph. Advocates of polygraph procedures, including polygraph examiners themselves, claim very high rates of accuracy. Reid and Inbau (1966) asserted that their success rate was 99%. Relying on laboratory studies in which some participants are instructed to commit a minor crime, others are not, and then all are tested with a CQT, some researchers have found that accuracy rates can be as high as 90% (Offe & Offe, 2007).

A claim of high accuracy—for example, 96% accuracy—can be misleading, however. Imagine that a major theft has occurred in a factory with 50 employees. One is the thief; 49 are honest. The examiner gives a polygraph test to each of the employees, and each denies being the thief. The polygrapher misclassifies one of the innocent people as the thief (false positive). He also fails to detect lying by the true thief (false negative). Thus he has erred in two cases, but he has been correct in classifying the 48 others as truthful. His accuracy rate is 48 of 50, or 96%. But he has still erred on the crucial determination; despite the 96% overall "accuracy rate," his answer to the central question (who stole?) is wrong. A panel of scientists who reviewed studies on the accuracy of the CQT concluded that it could discriminate lying from truth telling at rates above chance, but far below perfection (National Research Council, 2003).

The polygraph has several other shortcomings. First, as we have mentioned, the test cannot distinguish among emotions such as fear, anger, nervousness, and excitement. This means that an innocent person, aware that the question "Did you kill your wife?" is relevant to the investigation, may respond with heightened arousal that stems from nervousness rather than deception. Nonetheless, that heightened response could lead to a false-positive error.

A second concern is that the questioning methods used by polygraphers are not standardized (Ben-Shakhar, 2002). More generally, few professional standards regulate professional polygraphers. Some states have no regulations or licensing requirements whatsoever. This means that the quality of polygraphy can vary widely from one jurisdiction to another.

Another concern is the fact that deceptive subjects can be trained to "beat" the test by taking **countermeasures** to avoid detection. Effective use of countermeasures should increase the rate at which examiners believe that a guilty subject is telling the truth (a false negative). Among the countermeasures suggested online (http://www.wikihow.com/Cheat-a-Poly-graph-Test) are these:

- Develop a breathing strategy by altering the rate of breathing during relevant questions and comparison questions.

- Do complex calculations in your head.

- Prior to the test rub antiperspirant on your fingers and palms.

- Insert a small tack in your shoe and press on it during the comparison questions.

To determine whether using these countermeasures allow subjects to "beat" the test, researchers trained participants to bite their tongue or press their toes to the floor (physical countermeasures) or to count backwards by 7 (a mental countermeasure) during CQT administration (Honts, Raskin, & Kircher, 1994). The mental and physical countermeasures were both effective, enabling approximately 50% of subjects to defeat the test. Moreover, the polygraph examiners were not particularly suspicious; they detected only 12% of the physical countermeasures and none of the mental countermeasures.

The Cheat-a-Polygraph website now warns that astute examiners are wise to these tactics. For example, rather than settling for simple yes–no answers, examiners now ask questions that require detailed responses, demand that subjects remove their shoes, and even require them to sit on pressure-sensitive pads. These counter-countermeasures may effectively eliminate subjects' opportunity to beat the test.

What can one conclude about the validity of the polygraph? Reviewing studies on the accuracy of polygraph examinations—studies undertaken primarily by polygraph examiners conducting tests in the field—a committee of the National Research Council

Box 7.1   THE CASE OF THE MISSING COLLEGE STUDENT AND HER FRIENDS' POLYGRAPH TESTS

Lauren Spierer

AP Photo/Bloomington Herald-Times, Jeremy Hogan

The last time Indiana University sophomore Lauren Spierer was seen alive was in the early morning hours of June 3, 2011, as she walked home alone, barefoot and intoxicated, from a friend's apartment in Bloomington, Indiana. The friend—a 21-year-old student named Jay Rosenbaum, whom the police called a "person of interest" in the case—passed a polygraph exam when questioned about his version of these events. Rosenbaum's attorney forwarded the polygraph results to the police. Another "person of interest," Spierer's boyfriend Jesse Wolff, also apparently passed a polygraph exam. In a message posted on his Facebook page, Wolff insisted that if he had failed the polygraph, everyone in the world would know. Although Bloomington police have not commented on either of these polygraph results, they have not arrested anyone in connection with Spierer's disappearance.

Critical Thought Questions

What role might the polygraph have played in this case? In your opinion, should a test ordered by a defense attorney be given less weight than one ordered by a prosecutor and conducted by a polygrapher employed by the state?

---

expressed concern over the quality of the research and the exaggerated claims of accuracy by some polygraph proponents.

But even the most vocal critics of the polygraph acknowledge that the technique has overall accuracy rates of 65% or better. The question is whether this figure is high enough to justify permitting polygraph data as evidence at a trial or to use it as the primary evidence against a suspect. We think not. Polygraph tests are most valuable at the investigatory stages of a criminal prosecution and as a way to encourage confessions from suspects against whom other incriminating evidence has been gathered. An FBI report found that of 2,641 deceptive criminal polygraph reports, half resulted in the acquisition of information valuable to the investigations in other ways (Warner, 2005). This may be the best use for the polygraph.

How the Polygraph Is Used in Criminal Cases.
There are two ways in which polygraph results can be used in a criminal case. In approximately one-third of the states, a suspect takes a polygraph test with the understanding that the prosecutor will drop charges if the suspect passes the test but may use the results in court if the suspect does not pass. The other way that polygraph evidence is used is when a suspect passes a polygraph exam and tries to have that evidence con-

sidered in an ongoing investigation. Not infrequently, suspects take polygraph exams at the urging of their attorneys, who want to make sure they are telling the truth. Defenders often provide positive test results to the police. We provide an example in Box 7.1.

In states that permit polygraph evidence to be used in trials, judges conduct pretrial hearings to determine whether polygraph results are admissible. Sometimes they allow polygraph evidence. But the United States Supreme Court has declared that a judge's refusal to admit polygraph results did not violate a defendant's rights (*United States v. Scheffer*, 1998). Though binding only on military courts (because the case involved a military rule of evidence), the Supreme Court's decision in *Scheffer* reinforces the general reluctance of judges to admit polygraph results and opinions.

Brain-Based Lie Detection

Rather than relying on measures of physiological arousal as the polygraph does, recent developments in deception detection monitor changes in the brain's activity in response to stimuli. Two of the prominent brain-based methods of lie detection are neuroimaging and brain wave analysis.

Neuroimaging in Deception Detection. Neuroimaging techniques such as **functional magnetic resonance imaging** (fMRI) use scanners fitted with powerful electromagnets to measure blood flow and oxygen utilization in selected parts of the brain. Increases in oxygen consumption and blood flow in a particular part of the brain indicate that that region of the brain is involved when a subject undertakes a certain task. The primary function of fMRI is to diagnose neurological disorders. But because it is highly sensitive to cognitive processes involved in memory (Binder, Desai, Graves, & Conant, 2009) and motivation (Hare, O'Doherty, Camerer, Schultz & Rangel, 2008), it holds promise as a way to monitor deception.

Early studies using fMRI to detect deception typically asked simple questions about one's past experiences or knowledge (e.g., "Who was your best friend in primary school?" "Does a bicycle have six wheels?"). Participants pressed buttons to answer "yes" or "no." Some were told to conceal information by lying in response to specific questions, whereas others were told to respond truthfully. Scientists then compared brain activity in response to truthful answers and lies.

At this point, you may wonder whether lying about the name of a best friend is comparable, in any way, to lying about criminal activity. In doing so, you are asking whether these studies have **external validity**. Many neuroscientists—particularly those who are skeptical that neuroimaging can identify deception—have wondered the same thing.

But scientists have begun to use more realistic methods to simulate the processes of truth telling and lying. For example, one team of researchers asked some research participants to fire a starter pistol with blank bullets in the testing room of a neuroimaging center. Another group of participants did not fire the gun. Prior to fMRI questioning, half of each group was instructed to tell the truth and the other half was instructed to lie when asked, "Did you shoot that gun?" (Mohamed et al., 2006). Results showed that different patterns of brain activation are associated with truth telling and lying. Several brain regions in the frontal, parietal, and anterior cingulate cortex responded more strongly during lies. These brain areas are associated with planning and other high-level executive functions, suggesting that telling lies requires more cognitive effort than telling the truth. Other studies have examined the feasibility of using fMRI to distinguish lies from truths within a single subject. The accuracy of this method ranges from 76% to 90%.

Although fMRI holds some promise as a method of detecting deception, a number of issues have not yet been resolved. It is not clear whether fMRI technology can handle situations in which a subject's response cannot be neatly categorized as the truth or a lie. This occurs when a response is partly true and partly false, when people imagine that a fabricated

fMRI equipment in action

B o x 7.2 THE CASE OF CONTESTED POISONING: MUNCHAUSEN'S SYNDROME BY PROXY OR NOT? CAN fMRI TELL THE DIFFERENCE?

Munchausen syndrome by proxy is a mental health disorder in which parents, guardians, or other caregivers deliberately inflict pain and injury on vulnerable children in order to attract attention to themselves. Perpetrators are overwhelmingly female, and often are mothers of the victims. The disease is difficult to diagnose because many of the child's symptoms could result from organic causes or undiagnosed illnesses. The question posed in a recent case in England was whether a child's poisoning had been carried out by the victim's mother. She was convicted of the charge and served four years in prison.

In a groundbreaking experiment, Professor Sean Spence, a pioneer of fMRI technology to detect deception, examined the woman's brain activity as she alternately repeated her protestations of innocence and her accusers' account of the poisoning (Spence, Kaylor-Hughes, Brook, Lankappa, & Wilkinson, 2008). The tests, repeated four times, showed that her prefrontal and anterior cingulate cortices were activated when she endorsed statements she believed to be false, namely her accusers' versions of the event. In short, the data suggested that she lied when she agreed with her accusers' statements. According to Professor Spence, "[A]t the present moment, this research doesn't prove that this woman is innocent. Instead, what it clearly demonstrates is that her brain responds as if she were innocent … If proved to be accurate, and these findings replicated, this technology could be used alongside other factors to address questions of guilt versus innocence."

Critical Thought Question

A question arises whenever new technology is introduced into legal proceedings: At what point is the technology sophisticated enough to merit its use in investigations and trials? In your opinion, should the answer be different depending on whether the new technology is used for investigative purposes (e.g., to assess suspects' truthfulness), or offered as evidence during a trial (e.g., to show that a witness had lied)?

---

memory is true, and when they consider the possibility of lying but ultimately decide to tell the truth (Appelbaum, 2007). Also, questions remain about the use of fMRI for detecting deception in people with medical or psychiatric disorders, youth, the elderly, and those who take medications or use countermeasures. Despite these lingering concerns, fMRI techniques are being marketed commercially and occasionally used in court. Joel Huizenga, who founded a company called No Lie MRI, asserts confidently, "Once you jump behind the skull, there's no hiding." Not all neuroscientists agree, but fMRI test results were used in the case we describe in Box 7.2.

Brain Wave Analysis in Deception Detection. Imagine that a suspect denies that he or she was at the scene of a crime. Further imagine that he or she is confronted with pictures or verbal descriptions of the scene. New technology that measures brain-wave patterns that occur in response to familiar and unfamiliar images may eventually help investigators determine whether people are being deceptive when they claim, "I wasn't there." This technique, termed **brain fingerprinting**, was the "brainchild" of Lawrence Farwell. It uses an electroencephalogram (EEG) to record electrical activity on the surface of the scalp, reflecting spontaneous activity from the underlying cerebral cortex.

The premise of brain fingerprinting is that the brain houses information about experienced events and emits electrical signals in response to stimuli. A unique brain-wave pattern—the P300 wave—is elicited by a stimulus that is meaningful to the subject. It derives its name from its positive polarity and its occurrence approximately 300–900 milliseconds after the onset of a stimulus. Brain fingerprinting evaluates neural activity to assess how a suspect responds to crime scene details known only to the perpetrator. For example, after showing a suspect a series of common images while measuring P300 waves, investigators might show critical images of the crime scene and compare activation patterns. A guilty person, but not an innocent subject, would react differently to the critical details because they are meaningful. (You can probably see that this protocol borrows heavily from the Concealed Knowledge Test used with the polygraph.)

Researchers estimate the accuracy of brain fingerprinting by asking some participants to lie and others to tell the truth about a witnessed mock crime or autobiographical event when answering questions. They measure detection rates based on the resulting patterns of brain waves. Estimates range from 85% to 95% accuracy in distinguishing liars from truth-tellers under optimized laboratory conditions (Rosenfeld, Soskins, Bosh, & Ryan, 2004), although accuracy drops considerably when the technique is tested in a more realistic mock crime scenario (Mertens & Allen, 2008). The technique's originator, Lawrence Farwell, has patented, developed, and promoted a commercial version of the tool that he claims is 100% accurate (Farwell, 2011) despite limited empirical support (Rosenfeld, 2005).

Brain-Based Lie Detection in Court. Like the polygraph, brain-based technologies could be used in at least two different ways in legal contexts. Defendants and witnesses could try to introduce the results of these tests to bolster their credibility. In the only U.S. case in which brain-based evidence has been admitted in court to address a witness's truthfulness, defendant Terry Harrington's murder conviction was reversed after Lawrence Farwell used brain finger-printing to conclude that the record of the crime stored in Harrington's brain did not match the crime scene, but did match the alibi. When confronted with this information, a key prosecution witness recanted his testimony and admitted that he accused Harrington to avoid being prosecuted (*Harrington v. Iowa*, 2003).

Many people would agree that defendants and witnesses should be able to offer neuroscience evidence to support their version of the facts, so long as that evidence is based on valid and reliable scientific testing procedures. But when one ponders the second use of this type of evidence—demanding that defendants and witnesses be screened for deception—some people will balk. This more controversial use of brain scans and brain-wave analysis could be used as part of the discovery process, for example, during interrogations.

A host of legal issues arise when brain-based techniques are conducted against the wishes of the subject being scanned. What happens if a person refuses to undergo an fMRI or brain wave test? Can his or her credibility be questioned? Some have argued that these practices constitute a "search" of the brain that should be governed by the Fourth Amendment's prohibition against unreasonable search and seizure (Boire, 2005; Farah, 2005). A related question is whether brain-based tests conducted without the consent of the subject violate the protection against self-incrimination guaranteed by the Fifth Amendment. Alternatively, perhaps brain fingerprinting is just another form of physical evidence, similar to DNA or fingerprint evidence.

Although probing a person's brain to detect a lie may seem highly intrusive, the government's interests in crime control and public protection may offset these concerns. How far the law can extend into the realm of exposing (and protecting) private thoughts is unclear. Many commentators urge judges to resist the temptation to admit this evidence until more conclusive data are available (Aronson, 2010) and a team of legal scholars has proposed legislation that would prohibit the use of brain-based lie detection techniques until regulatory systems can be put in place to evaluate and monitor their safety and effectiveness (Greely & Illes, 2007). Perhaps the only certainty is that the controversy over brain-based lie detection systems will continue for some time.

EVALUATING CONFESSIONS

When investigators have a hunch that a person is acting deceptively—due to a "failed" polygraph, neuroscientific test results, or simply through observation and interview—they may target that person for more formal interrogation, with the hope of extracting a confession. Throughout history, confessions have been accorded enormous importance. Many religions maintain that confession is the first step toward redemption and have evolved special rituals to encourage it. Interrogations and confessions also play a role in military and intelligence matters. People detained as terrorist threats in military jails in Afghanistan, Iraq, Guantanamo Bay, and elsewhere have been interrogated by harsh methods, including both physical and psychological torture, which are unacceptable in U.S. criminal courts (McCoy, 2006). But tactics used in military and intelligence-gathering interrogations have been applied in criminal interrogations as well (Evans et al., 2010).

Confessions play a prominent role in the criminal justice system; many consider them to be the most powerful weapon at the state's disposal (Kassin & Gudjonsson, 2004). When the police capture suspects, one of their first acts is to encourage them to confess. A confession will, of course, permit a district attorney or grand jury to bring charges. Even if the suspect later denies the confession and pleads not guilty, the confession can be introduced into evidence at the trial.

Although disputed "confessions" by defendants occur surprisingly often and observers have documented many false confessions (e.g., Drizin & Leo,

2004), the number of false confessions is actually a matter of contention. Prosecutors observe that defendants can easily recant confessions by alleging that police coerced them, but defense attorneys say that false confessions happen more often than prosecutors acknowledge.

Historical Background and Current Legal Standing

Until the mid-twentieth century, many "confessions" came only after intense questioning by the police—questioning that involved promises, threats, harassment, and even brutality. Until 1966, the traditional test for admissibility of a confession in court was voluntariness. A voluntary confession is given without overt inducements, threats, promises, or physical harm. The trustworthiness of a confession was believed to be lost when it was obtained through one or more of those means (*Hopt v. Utah*, 1884).

But assessing the voluntariness of confessions proved difficult for many reasons. The task was highly subjective, and it resulted in countless "swearing contests" between police and suspects about what went on behind the closed door of interrogation rooms. Therefore, in *Miranda v. Arizona* (1966), the Supreme Court held that a confession resulting from in-custody interrogation was admissible in court only if, in addition to being voluntary, it had been obtained after the police had ensured the suspect's protection from self-incrimination by giving the so-called *Miranda* warnings (see Box 7.3). One year later, the Supreme Court extended those rights to juveniles (*In re Gault*, 1967). The *Miranda* warnings are intended to protect suspects from conditions that might give rise to unfounded confessions.

The *Miranda* case did not solve all problems associated with the validity of confessions. Although the warnings add a new element to interrogations, intense and secretive interrogations continue to this day, with the interrogator intent upon persuading the suspect to confess. Furthermore, many suspects waive their *Miranda* rights, and after a suspect voluntarily enters the interrogation room, investigators can use any number of tactics to obtain a confession.

Some suspects waive their rights because they simply do not understand them. Psychologists have documented the problematic vocabulary and terminology of some *Miranda* warnings (the language is not standardized and large variations exist across jurisdictions) (Rogers et al., 2011), and widely held misconceptions about the warnings (Rogers et al., 2010). Other suspects, including those who are young or mentally disabled, waive their rights because they are especially vulnerable to the tactics of a skillful interrogator. In fact, one study that involved review of recorded interrogations showed that 90% of juvenile suspects waived their *Miranda* rights (Cleary et al., 2011). The Supreme Court has stated that judges should take into account a minor's age when determining whether he understood that he was in custody and deserved to be read his *Miranda* rights (*J.D.B. v. North Carolina*, 2011).

Whittling Away at *Miranda*

Miranda v. Arizona (1966) was one of the most controversial decisions of the past century. The Chief Justice at the time, Earl Warren, was castigated in congressional committees and on the floor of Congress (Warren, 1977), and "Impeach Earl Warren" billboards were widely seen. Although the decision has survived for nearly 50 years, it remains controversial to this day. It survived a major challenge in 2000 when the Supreme Court reaffirmed that *Miranda* was a constitutional ruling and that the warnings are part of the national culture (*Dickerson v. United States*, 2000). The *Dickerson* case is a good example of *stare decisis*—the court's preference for maintaining stability in the law through "abiding by settled principle" whenever possible. Given *Miranda's* long-standing acceptance in the United States, the Court opted against changing the law of confessions.

The U.S. Supreme Court has weakened the *Miranda* requirements through a series of other decisions, however. Here are some of the changes:

1. *Confessions that violate* Miranda *may still be used at a trial.* Suppose a person confesses when arrested, and the confession is taken in violation of the *Miranda* warnings. If the defendant testifies to his or her innocence at trial, the prosecutor may use the confession to show that the defendant should not be believed (*Harris v. New York*, 1971).

2. Miranda *does not apply unless the suspect is in the custody of the police.* The Supreme Court has interpreted *custody* in various ways. For example, the Court held that roadside questioning of

---

B o x 7.3 **THE CASE OF ERNESTO MIRANDA AND THE RIGHT TO REMAIN SILENT: CHANGING FOREVER THE FACE OF POLICE WORK**

Ernesto Miranda

One of the best-known U.S. Supreme Court cases decided during the last century, *Miranda v. Arizona* (1966) dealt with the problem of coerced confessions. Late on a Saturday in May of 1963, an 18-year-old woman left her job in downtown Phoenix. As she was walking home, a man grabbed her and dragged her to his car, tied her hands and laid her down in the back seat, then drove to the desert and raped her. As he waited for her to get dressed, he demanded money. She gave him the four $1 bills in her purse.

A week after the rape, the victim's brother-in-law spotted a car like the one she had described. He remembered enough of the license plate for the police to trace the car to Ernesto Miranda. When police located the car, they saw a rope strung along the front seat, just as the victim had described. They put together a lineup, selecting three Mexican Americans to stand with Miranda. But he was the only person with eyeglasses and tattoos—features the victim remembered about her assailant. Still, she couldn't identify anyone.

Frustrated, the police then took Miranda to an interrogation room for what they thought was routine questioning. But the exchanges that occurred in that tiny chamber changed forever the way police interact with citizens. Miranda asked about the lineup: "How did I do?" "You flunked," a police officer replied, and began to question Miranda. No attorneys, witnesses, or tape recorders were present. The police later reported that Miranda voluntarily confessed. Miranda described the interrogation differently:

Once they get you in a little room and they start badgering you one way or the other, "You better tell us ... or we're going to throw the book at you.... And I haven't had any sleep since the day before. I'm tired. I just got off my work, and they have me and they are interrogating me. They mention first one crime, then another one; they are certain I am the person.... Knowing what a penitentiary is like, a person has to be frightened, scared. And not knowing if he'll be able to get back up and go home. (Quoted in Baker, 1983, p. 13)

Whichever story one believes, Ernesto Miranda emerged from the questioning a confessed rapist. In June of 1963, he was convicted of rape and kidnapping, and was sentenced to 20 to 30 years for each charge. He appealed his conviction to the U.S. Supreme Court, and the Court—by a 5–4 vote—concluded that his right against self-incrimination had been violated. Henceforth, they stated, the police must warn suspects of certain rights before starting a custodial interrogation. If these procedures are not followed, any damaging admissions made by suspects cannot be used by the prosecution in a trial.

Ironically, on the night of January 31, 1976, Miranda was playing poker in a flophouse section of Phoenix. A drunken fight broke out and Miranda was stabbed. He was dead on arrival at the hospital. Miranda's killer fled, but his accomplice was caught. Before taking him to police headquarters, a police officer read to him from a card:

You have the right to remain silent. Anything you say can be used against you in a court of law. You have the right to the presence of an attorney to assist you prior to questioning and to be with you during questioning, if you so desire. If you cannot afford an attorney, you have the right to have an attorney appointed for you prior to questioning. Do you understand these rights? Will you voluntarily answer my questions?

Critical Thought Questions
What problems are the *Miranda* warnings intended to solve? What aspects of Miranda's case might have led Supreme Court justices to decide that his confession was not given freely?

---

a motorist stopped for drunk driving is not "custody," even though the motorist is not free to go (*Berkemer v. McCarty*, 1984). Warnings are not required in this circumstance. "Stop-and-frisk" questioning is also usually viewed as noncustodial

because such questioning merely accompanies temporary detentions in public places.

3. Miranda *does not apply unless the defendant is being interrogated*. A volunteered confession is always admissible. Suppose the police arrest a robbery

suspect and decide, for whatever reason, not to question him. On the way to the station, the accused person volunteers that he wouldn't have been caught if he'd kept his mask on. This confession is admissible because it was not in response to police questioning (*Rhode Island v. Innis*, 1980).

The Validity of Confession Evidence

In a perfect world, guilty people would always confess, and innocent people would never do so. Unfortunately, this is far from reality. Scientists know that two kinds of erroneous outcomes are possible: **false denials** (when guilty suspects proclaim their innocence and deny involvement in actual crimes) and **false confessions** (when innocent suspects confess to alleged crimes). False denials occur when crime perpetrators lie by saying "I didn't do it," and false confessions occur when innocent suspects say "I did it" and provide factually untrue descriptions of how and why the crime occurred.

Although false denials occur more often than false confessions, the latter have captured the attention of psychological scientists, lawyers, judges, and the public. Indeed, we focus a great deal of attention on the reasons for false confessions later in this chapter. But it is important to bear in mind that false denials are also critical errors for the criminal justice system and the public. Because they are more frequent than false confessions and can result in the release of guilty and potentially dangerous offenders back into the community, their costs should not be underestimated. As we discuss some of the reasons why false confessions occur, keep in mind that these influences promote confessions by the guilty—important in the investigation and conviction of criminal offending—as well as making false confessions more likely.

Relatively few studies have looked at how guilty suspects tend to lie to authorities, although one recent study involved questioning prison inmates about the strategies they used to tell lies during interrogations (Stromwall & Willen, 2011). It documented both verbal and nonverbal techniques of deception, including providing statements that are close to the truth (but not the *whole* truth), and not giving away any information. These strategies reveal a sophisticated understanding of how to manage impressions and information during an interrogation.

One might ask devoted to uncover little to understanding answers to that ques philosophical agreeme guilty persons to go fi to be convicted," and i many psychology and i ways that the criminal ju cent people (Cutler, 201 ...u, 2011). But it is worth remembering that if society wants the police to refrain from using tactics that yield false confessions, there will be a corresponding reduction in the number of true confessions that lead to the convictions of guilty suspects. Consider, for a moment, the possibility that among those fewer convictions are people who are guilty of multiple counts of sexually abusing children over a period of many years. False denials, like false confessions, come at a cost to society.

Why Do Innocent Suspects Falsely Confess? Why would a truly innocent person falsely confess to a crime that he or she did not commit? How often does this really happen? What are the circumstances that would lead someone to confess falsely? Although it is difficult to gauge the frequency of false confessions, because no agency or organization keeps track of the results of interrogations, scientists do know that they are a global problem (Gudjonsson, 2010). Between 1966 and 2007, there were approximately 250 documented false confessions in the United States (Leo, 2008). Garrett (2008) noted that false confessions were involved in 15–20% of cases in which DNA evidence led to exonerations. These numbers almost certainly understate the problem, because false confessions often are not revealed, and thus go unacknowledged by police and prosecutors and unreported by the media (Kassin et al., 2010). Interrogation-induced false confessions tend to occur in more serious cases like homicides and other high-stakes felonies when the police are under pressure to solve the crime, and thus use more psychologically coercive tactics to wear the suspect down (Gross et al., 2005). Lacking a victim or an eyewitness to describe the crime, the police may need a confession to secure a conviction.

Scientists are now beginning to understand the circumstances that give rise to false confessions. But before we describe them, we ask how one can know

a confession is false. Do we simply
[...]spect or defendant at his or her word
[...] or she alleges that an admission of guilt
[...] wrong? Alternatively, do we need some kind of
evidence that proves, unequivocally, that the defendant could not have committed the crime to which he or she confessed?

Proving That a Confession Is False. There are four ways in which one can be certain that a disputed confession is false (Drizin & Leo, 2004). First, a suspect could confess to a crime that never happened. For example, three mentally retarded defendants (including Victoria Banks) were convicted by an Alabama jury of killing Ms. Banks's newborn child. Only after the three had served time in prison was it determined that Ms. Banks was incapable of giving birth to a child because she had had a tubal ligation operation that prevented her from getting pregnant.

Confessions can be proved to be false in situations where it was physically impossible for a suspect to commit the crime, as, for example, when jail records show that the defendant was incarcerated at the time the crime was committed. Three men suspected of committing crimes in Chicago were actually in jail when those crimes were committed (Drizin & Leo, 2004).

A third way in which a disputed confession can be proved false is that the actual perpetrator is identified and his guilt is objectively established. This happened in the case of Christopher Ochoa, a high school honor student, who confessed to robbing, raping, and murdering a woman in an Austin, Texas, Pizza Hut in 1988. Ochoa, who served 12 years in prison, claims that he confessed in order to avoid the possibility of a death sentence. He was released and exonerated only after the real perpetrator confessed to killing the woman and led authorities to the weapon and the bag in which he had placed the money (Drizin & Leo, 2004).

Finally, a confession is false when there is scientific evidence—most commonly DNA—that definitively establishes the defendant's innocence. For example, three teenagers (Michael Crowe, Joshua Treadway, and Aaron Houser) all falsely confessed to the 1998 murder of Michael's 12-year-old sister Stephanie in Escondido, California. Charges against the boys were dropped only after DNA testing proved that blood found on the sweatshirt of a mentally ill drifter who had been in the neighborhood on the night of the murder was Stephanie's (Drizin & Colgan, 2004).

Few cases involving disputed confessions come with independent evidence that the suspect is innocent, however (Leo, 2008). Rarely will the actual perpetrator come forward to claim responsibility and remove the blame from an innocent confessor, and in most cases there is no DNA evidence to compare to the confessor's DNA. As a result, few confessors can prove definitively that their confessions were false. Even when DNA evidence exonerates a false confessor, prosecutors sometimes refuse to concede innocence (Kassin, 2005). Bruce Godschalk was exonerated after 15 years in prison when DNA testing proved that he was not a rapist. Still, the prosecutor refused to release him after the results were known, claiming that the test was inaccurate and that the tape-recorded confession taken by police detectives should be trusted.

Why would a person confess to a crime he or she did not commit? One reason is to protect someone else (Gudjonsson, 2010). Another reason is to escape the pressures of a harsh interrogation. New studies document the role that psychological coercion can have in inducing suspects to confess, especially when those suspects are particularly vulnerable (e.g., children, adolescents, and those with mental limitations; [Redlich, Hoover, Summers, & Steadman, 2010]). In fact, these studies point to the compounding effects of an interrogator's coercive tactics and a suspect's vulnerable state at the time of questioning.

Inside the Interrogation Room:
Common Interrogation Techniques

Based on his own observations of more than 100 police interrogations and his review of recorded interrogations in several hundred other cases, Professor Richard Leo noted a fundamental contradiction concerning the nature of interrogations: "On the one hand, police need incriminating statements and admissions to solve many crimes, especially serious ones; on the other hand, there is almost never a good reason for suspects to provide them. Police are under tremendous organizational and social pressure to obtain admissions and confessions. But it is rarely in a suspect's rational self-interest to say something that will likely lead to his prosecution and conviction" (Leo, 2008, pp. 5–6).

Because physical intimidation and "third-degree" tactics are virtually nonexistent today, interrogators now use psychologically oriented coercion to overcome the anticipated resistance of suspects and to yield legally admissible confessions (Kassin et al., 2010). Leo (2008) documented a vast array of subtle and manipulative ploys that police use to induce confessions. Most of these techniques are detailed in interrogation training manuals; the most popular are *Criminal Interrogation and Confessions*, currently in its fourth edition (Inbau, Reid, Buckley, & Jayne, 2004), and *Practical Aspects of Interview and Interrogation* (Zulawski & Wicklander, 2001). To fully understand why someone would falsely confess, one must be aware of the techniques of social influence recommended by these manuals and put into practice in interrogation rooms.

One can divide an interrogation into the pre-interrogation "softening up" stage and the interrogation itself. Throughout the encounter, police use well-crafted, deliberate strategies to secure incriminating evidence from suspects.

Pre-Interrogation—"Softening Up" the Suspect. Would you prefer to be "interviewed" or "interrogated?" (Probably the former.) When the police arrange to question a suspect, they may "invite" him or her to the station house because they "just want to ask a few questions" to "clear up a little matter." They may explicitly tell the suspect that they do not consider him or her a suspect. This all sounds innocuous enough. But the police have actually misrepresented the nature and purpose of the "discussion" to disarm the suspect and reduce his or her resistance (Leo, 2008).

When a suspect arrives at the police station for questioning, he or she is typically shuffled off to a small, soundproof room with armless, straight-backed chairs, thereby removing sensory stimulation and distractions. By physically and socially isolating the suspect, the police begin to subtly exert pressure on him or her to talk. The interrogator may then try to soften up the suspect by using flattery, ingratiation, and rapport building—asking benign questions and engaging in pleasant small talk. According to one detective, "I don't care whether it is rape, robbery or homicide … the first thing you need to do is build rapport with that person … I think from that point on you can get anybody to talk about anything." (Leo, 2008, p. 123) All the while, the detective is concealing the fact that he has already determined that the suspect is guilty of a crime and

is intent on extracting incriminating evidence from him or her.

Although the police are required by law to give the *Miranda* warnings prior to questioning, there are various ways they can circumvent these warnings (Wrightsman, 2010). Their intent is to get the suspect to waive his or her rights and begin to talk, thereby increasing the police's chances of hearing incriminating information. Recall that the warnings are required only when the suspect is being interrogated while in custody. By telling suspects that they are not under arrest and are free to go, there is no need to warn them that statements they make may be used against them. Sometimes the police will minimize the importance of the *Miranda* warnings by describing them as a mere bureaucratic necessity or formality. Richard Leo observed a detective who stated, "Don't let this ruffle your feathers or anything like that, it's just a formality that we have to go through, okay. As I said this is a *Miranda* warning and what it says is …" On other occasions, police can persuade the suspect to talk in order to tell "his (or her) side of the story." Almost all suspects waive their *Miranda* rights and talk to interrogators (Leo, 2008). Psychologists have wondered why they do so, especially when they are innocent. We describe relevant research findings later in this chapter.

The Interrogation Itself. During the heart of the questioning, interrogators use a set of carefully orchestrated procedures with the goal to eventually overwhelm even the most reluctant suspect and get him or her to provide incriminating statements. These procedures can be reduced to a few basic strategies. One strategy is the use of **negative incentives** to break down a suspect's defenses, lower his or her resistance, and instill feelings of fear, despair, and powerlessness. Negative incentives are tactics (like accusations, attacks on the suspect's denials, and evidence fabrications) that convey to the suspect that there is no choice but to confess. The police also use **positive inducements** to motivate the suspect to see that an admission is in his or her best interest. All interrogators try, implicitly or explicitly, to send the message that the suspect will receive some benefit in exchange for an admission of wrongdoing (Leo, 2008).

After the suspect has either implicitly or explicitly agreed to talk, the interrogation becomes accusatorial, with the interrogator confronting the suspect with

A handcuffed felony suspect questioned by a Santa Ana, CA, police detective in a specialized interrogation room

Spencer Grant/Photo Researchers, Inc.

a statement indicating absolute belief in his or her guilt. Accusations are one of the most basic tactics in interrogations; police use them routinely and repeatedly. One subtle effect of an accusation is shifting the burden of proof from the state to the suspect. In what may be one of the most "ingenious psychological aspects of American interrogation" (Leo, 2008, p. 135) the suspect must now work to convince the police of his or her innocence.

During questioning, interrogators also frequently challenge denials that suspects make, often by simply cutting them off or expressing disbelief in their

version of events (Kassin et al., 2010), and introduce information, either intentionally or unintentionally, about details of the crime (Garrett, 2010). The effect of these ploys is to undermine suspects' confidence in their memories, which may cause inconsistencies in later retellings of the truth, and false confessions consistent with interrogators' version of the facts.

The most powerful tool in the interrogator's arsenal is the opportunity, often exercised, to present **fabricated evidence**. Even if interrogators have no evidence of suspects' wrongdoing, they can make them believe that they do. They can point to "signs" of nonverbal behavior that indicate guilt, tell suspects that other people including eyewitnesses and accomplices have implicated them, and make up stories about the existence of fraudulent fingerprint evidence or surveillance videos that capture their images. On occasion, a suspect may take a polygraph examination, presented as an opportunity to prove innocence, when all along investigators plan to confront the suspect with evidence of a failed test and urge him or her to confess. The police sometimes use fabricated evidence in order to get a guilty suspect to confess. But such evidence has been at the root of many cases of known false confessions (Garrett, 2010). We describe one case in Box 7.4.

Box 7.4 THE CASE OF FRANK STERLING, FABRICATED EVIDENCE, AND A FALSE CONFESSION

Viola Manville was a spunky, outspoken grandmother who was taking her daily walk along an abandoned railroad bed in suburban Rochester, NY when, in 1988, she was shot twice in the head with a BB gun and beaten to death with a railroad tie. Frank Sterling, a 25-year-old school bus monitor, became an early suspect because his brother was in prison for an attempted sexual assault on the victim three years earlier and police saw a possible motive: they suspected that Frank may have been harboring a grudge against Manville. But he had an ironclad alibi: He'd been on the school bus all morning and he could recite details of the cartoons he had been watching in the afternoon. Since there was no physical evidence linking Sterling to the crime, he was not arrested and the murder went unsolved.

But the police continued to talk to Sterling from time to time. By 1991 he had taken a job as a truck driver, and just after he returned from a 36-hour job, police asked him to come to the station and submit to a polygraph. During the subsequent interrogation, he was told, falsely, that his brother had bragged to fellow inmates

that Frank had killed Manville. Detectives showed him nine pictures of the crime scene to help him "remember" and shared crucial details with him. Finally, after more than nine hours of cajoling, consoling, and suggestive questioning, Sterling complied with their wishes and told detectives that he committed the crime. Although his confession had numerous inconsistencies and was immediately recanted, he was convicted of murder and sentenced to 25 years in prison.

Sterling languished in prison until 2006, when DNA analyses of skin cells left on the victim's clothing excluded him and implicated another early suspect, Mark Christie, in the case. (In the intervening years, Christie had killed a 4-year-old girl.) Christie eventually gave a detailed confession to Manville's murder and in 2010, after spending nearly 18 years in prison, Sterling was officially exonerated.

Critical Thought Question
What police tactics may have led to Sterling's false confession? How do you suspect those tactics influenced Sterling?

Finally, police use positive inducements to persuade suspects that they will benefit from complying with authorities and confessing. This can take the form of providing scenarios to explain or justify the suspect's actions (e.g., suggesting that he or she was probably acting in self-defense or in the "heat of the moment"), or of promising some sort of a deal for confessing. Sometimes detectives simply imply that suspects can go home if they accept interrogators' demands. In another famous case involving false confessions—the Central Park jogger case, in which five young men confessed to brutally raping and beating a female jogger—each suspect confessed in a way that minimized his own involvement, and each thought that after confessing he could go home (Kassin, 2005). A survey of more than 600 police investigators showed that they commonly practice many of these ploys, including physically isolating suspects, establishing rapport, finding contradictions in their accounts, confronting them with evidence of their guilt, and appealing to their self-interest (Kassin et al., 2007).

An Empirical Look at Interrogation Tactics. Psychological scientists have examined some of these interrogation tactics and found surprising results. In this section, we describe studies that explain why innocent people waive their *Miranda* rights; how interrogators' presumption of guilt affects the nature of the questioning, which, in turn, affects the suspect's responses; and how false evidence ploys elicit confessions.

To test the possibility that innocent people are likely to waive their rights and submit to questioning, Kassin and Norwick (2004) conducted a study in which participants were instructed either to steal $100 from a drawer (guilty condition) or to open the drawer but not take any money (innocent condition). When questioned by a "detective" who sought a waiver of their *Miranda* rights, innocent participants were considerably more likely to grant the waiver than those who were guilty, by a margin of 81% to 36%. When asked to explain the reasons for their decisions, 72% of innocent people explained that they waived their rights precisely because they were innocent. A typical comment: "I did not have anything to hide." Innocents may waive their rights and answer questions because they assume, naively, that their innocence will set them free. But ironically, "innocence may put innocents at risk" (Kassin, 2005, p. 224).

Recall that many interrogations begin with the detective issuing a statement of belief in the suspect's guilt. This presumption of guilt can apparently influence the way a detective conducts the questioning, causing the suspect to become defensive or confused, and increasing the chances of a false confession. This phenomenon—referred to as a self-fulfilling prophecy or **behavioral confirmation** (Meissner & Kassin, 2004)—has been demonstrated in a wide range of settings (McNatt, 2000; Rosenthal & Jacobson, 1968). After people form a particular belief (e.g., in the guilt of a suspect), they unwittingly seek out information that verifies that belief, overlook conflicting data, and behave in a manner that conforms to the belief. In turn, the target person (here, the suspect) behaves in ways that support the initial belief.

Psychologists have examined the effects of an implicit assumption of guilt on the behavior of interrogators and suspects, and on judgments of the interrogation by neutral observers. The first section of a multipart study (Hill, Memon, & McGeorge, 2008) asked whether interviewers' assumption of guilt affected the kinds of questions they ask suspects. Prior to formulating their questions, some participant-interviewers were led to believe suspects were guilty of cheating on a test; others believed they were innocent. As expected, expectations of guilt resulted in more guilt-presumptive questions, indicating that confirmation bias led interviewers to seek information confirming their expectations.

In a follow-up study, independent observers listened to audiotaped interviews of "suspects" who had been questioned with either guilt-presumptive or neutral questions, and rated their behavior. Importantly, observers did not hear the questions asked, only the suspects' responses, and none of the responses contained a confession. Still, observers rated the suspects questioned in a guilt-presumptive manner as more nervous and defensive and less plausible than suspects questioned in a neutral manner, and judged the former to be guiltier than the latter.

The presumption of guilt apparently ushers in a process of behavioral confirmation by which the expectations of interrogators affect their questioning style, suspects' behavior, and, ultimately, judgments of the guilt of the suspect. These findings may actually *underestimate* the risks of behavioral confirmation in actual interrogations, where questioning can go on for hours rather than minutes and interrogators have years of experience in questioning suspects, as well as confidence in their ability to get a confession (Meissner & Kassin, 2004).

Finally, we consider the role of **evidence ploys** in eliciting confessions. As we mentioned, it is legal for interrogators to lie to suspects about the existence of evidence linking them to the crime. Researchers have now investigated how these ruses lead people to believe they committed acts they did not actually commit. In one study (Nash & Wade, 2009) participants were falsely accused of cheating on a computerized gambling task. Some were shown a doctored video that portrayed them doing so, and others were only told that their cheating was documented on video. Participants who saw the fake video were more likely to provide confabulated details and confess without resistance. Feeding false information to suspects can apparently cause them to doubt their memories and rely instead on external sources to infer what happened.

So far, we have considered the effects of interrogation on adults accused of committing crimes. But a substantial number of juveniles are also interrogated by police. The training manual (Inbau et al., 2004) suggests that the principles of adult interrogation "are just as applicable to the young ones" (p. 298), and analyses of juvenile interrogations showed that police used many of the same strategies with them, including the possibility that the suspect can go home if he or she tells the police what they want to hear (Reppucci, Meyer, & Kostelnik, 2010). But many juveniles have difficulty understanding the rights accorded to them by the *Miranda* warnings (McLachlan, Roesch, & Douglas, 2011). Some juveniles may be unaware that they are signing a confession because many "confessions" are written by interrogating officers, based on the suspects' verbal account and other evidence. Thus, like adults, juveniles sometimes confess falsely (as did the defendants in the Central Park jogger case). How often does this happen? Of the 125 proven false confession cases compiled by Drizin and Leo (2004), fully 33% involved juveniles.

False Confessions

Innocent people tend to waive their *Miranda* rights, police presume guilt, and interrogators use carefully scripted techniques to elicit confessions. Consequently, detectives draw out confessions from innocent people as well as from the guilty. Yet not all false confessions are alike; they occur for different reasons and can be explained by different situational and dispositional factors. Kassin and Wrightsman (1985) devised a taxonomy of false confessions. Although it has been refined over the years (Kassin & Gudjonsson, 2004), it still serves as a good framework for understanding why false confessions happen.

Some innocent people confess to criminal acts with little prodding. When Charles Lindbergh's baby was kidnapped in 1932, more than 200 people came forward and claimed responsibility. After the murder of child beauty-pageant contestant JonBenét Ramsey had gone unresolved for several years, prosecutors were eager to consider the confession of Mark Karr. But Karr's DNA did not match the sample found on the victim and he was never charged. These **voluntary false confessions** arise because people seek notoriety, desire to cleanse themselves of guilt feelings from previous wrongdoings, want to protect the real criminal, have difficulty distinguishing fact from fiction (McCann, 1998), or, as in one reported case, want to impress a girlfriend (Radelet, Bedau, & Putnam, 1992).

Sometimes suspects confess in order to escape or avoid ongoing aversive interrogations or to gain some sort of promised reward. Legal history is full of examples dating as far back as the Salem witch trials of 1692 during which approximately 50 women confessed to being witches, some after being "tyed … neck and heels till the blood was ready to come out of their noses" (Karlsen, 1989, p. 101, cited by Kassin & Gudjonsson, 2004). The false confessions in the Central Park jogger case were of this sort; each of the defendants said he confessed because he wanted to go home. These confessions are termed **compliant false confessions** because the suspect is induced to comply with the interrogator's demands to make an incriminating statement. They occur when a suspect knows that he is innocent but publicly acquiesces to the demand for a confession because the short-term benefit of confessing—such as being left alone or allowed to leave—outweighs the long-term costs—such as being charged with or convicted of a crime (Madon et al., 2011).

Some suspects confess because they actually come to believe that they have committed the crime. These so-called **internalized false confessions** can be directly related to the highly suggestive and manipulative techniques that interrogators sometimes use during questioning. An internalized false confession can result when, after hours of being questioned, badgered, and told stories about what "must have happened," the suspect begins to develop a profound distrust of his own memory. Being vulnerable, he is then easily influenced by external suggestions and comes to believe that he "must have done it."

We previously described the case of 14-year-old Michael Crowe, who falsely confessed to killing his sister. Despite his initial vehement denials, Michael apparently came to believe, over the course of three grueling interrogations, that he had actually stabbed her: "I'm not sure how I did it. All I know is I did it" (Drizin & Colgan, 2004, p. 141). During the interrogations, detectives told Michael at least four lies: that his hair was found on his sister's body, that her blood was in his bedroom, that all of the doors to the house had been locked, and that he failed a lie detector test. With no memory of the killing but persuaded by these details, Michael was apparently convinced that he had dissociative identity disorder and that the killing was accomplished by the "bad Michael" while the "good Michael" blocked out the crime (Drizin & Colgan, 2004).

Inside the Courtroom: How Confession Evidence Is Evaluated

The first source of error involving confession evidence stems from what happens in the interrogation room. A second source of error occurs when prosecutors, defense attorneys, judges, and especially juries fail to understand why the suspect might have confessed and uncritically accept a false confession as valid. The false confession then sets in motion a chain of events with adverse consequences for the suspect because attorneys, juries, and judges make decisions—about plea-bargaining, convicting, and sentencing—assuming that what the suspect said was true.

Many prosecutors assume that only guilty suspects confess. So when they secure a confession, they tend to treat the suspect harshly, charging him or her with the highest number and types of offenses possible, requesting higher bail, and being reluctant to accept a plea bargain to a reduced charge (Drizin & Leo, 2004). The confession becomes, in essence, the crux of the prosecution's case. Even defense attorneys assume that people who confess are guilty, and urge them to accept plea bargains rather than risk their chances in a trial with confession evidence (Nardulli, Eisenstein, & Fleming, 1988).

Judges are also likely to treat confessors harshly. In cases of disputed confessions, they almost always decide that confessions are voluntary and thus admissible as evidence in a trial (Givelber, 2001). In some cases, a defendant who has confessed will nevertheless enter a plea of not guilty and go to trial. If the jury convicts this defendant, judges are likely to sentence him harshly because they tend to punish offenders who claim innocence, waste resources in a trial, and fail to show remorse or apologize (Leo, 2007).

Confessions are an especially potent form of evidence to jurors, even more influential than eyewitness and character testimony (Kassin & Neumann, 1997), although public perceptions may be shifting a bit. A group of jury-eligible adults recently estimated that approximately one-fifth of confessions are false (Costanzo, Shaked-Schroer, & Vinson, 2010). But jurors are highly likely to convict defendants who have confessed, even when the confession is false. Archival analyses of actual cases in which false confessors pled not guilty and proceeded to trial show that jury conviction rates ranged from 73% (Leo & Ofshe, 1998) to 81% (Drizin & Leo, 2004).

Jurors accept confession evidence because they assume that interrogators are adept at identifying liars (Costanzo et al., 2010) and that suspects would not act against their own self-interests and confess to something they had not done (Kassin et al., 2010). Jurors fail to take the circumstances of an interrogation into account and to discount a confession elicited by high-pressure tactics of interrogators, even when the confession comes through an informant who is motivated to lie (Neuschatz et al., 2008).

When explaining the causes of others' behavior, people often commit the **fundamental attribution error**: They do not give sufficient weight to the external situation as a determinant of behavior; instead, they believe the behavior is caused by stable, internal factors unique to the actor (Jones, 1990). In essence, jurors take a confession at face value, fail to adjust or correct for situational forces on behavior, and assume that if suspects confess, they must be guilty (Wrightsman & Kassin, 1993).

Psychologists sometimes participate in cases of disputed confessions, functioning as consultants to defense attorneys or testifying as expert witnesses in pretrial admissibility hearings and during trials. The objective is to educate jurors and judges about the nature of police interrogations and the dispositional and situational factors that lead to false confessions.

But might there be a more efficient way to prevent wrongful convictions based on false confessions? Wouldn't it be better to assess, early in the investigation of a case, whether a suspect's confession resulted from a coercive interrogation? Several commentators advocate reforming the system with this objective in mind.

Reforming the System to Prevent False Confessions

Recording all police interrogations can provide a complete, objective, and reviewable record of how the suspect was questioned. It can improve the quality of interrogations by deterring manipulative tactics by investigators and frivolous claims of coercion by defendants. It also preserves an objective record of the entire session and avoids "he said/she said" disputes (Kassin et al., 2010). A handful of states require videotaping and a growing number of jurisdictions voluntarily record interrogations.

How the interrogation is recorded is important. Daniel Lassiter and his colleagues have shown that when the camera is focused on the suspect (as is usually done to allow observers to see what the suspect said and did), observers are more likely to judge the confession as voluntary, compared with the same confession recorded from a different camera perspective (e.g., focused equally on the suspect and the interrogator or solely on the interrogator) (Lassiter, Ware, Ratcliff, & Irvin, 2009). This is an example of **illusory causation**—the tendency to attribute causation to one stimulus because it is more conspicuous than others. When the recording shows both the suspect and the interrogator, observers are more attuned to situational pressures exerted by the interrogator. Lassiter (2010) concludes that filming can be an effective tool for recording interrogations, but must be used judiciously.

A more radical reform would reconceptualize the fundamental nature of police interrogations. At present, American interrogation practices are confrontational and accusatorial, and police claim that these techniques are necessary to get reluctant suspects to confess. By contrast, police interviews in the United Kingdom are not coercive or overtly confrontational, and interviewers are not allowed to lie to suspects or present false evidence. The goal is to obtain useful information about a crime, rather than to extract a confession (Gudjonsson & Pearse, 2011). Data are just emerging on the technique's effectiveness. One laboratory study suggests that the nonconfrontational, U.K.-type interviews produce fewer false confessions and more true confessions than accusatory interrogations (Meissner, Russano, & Narchat, 2010) and a meta-analysis that included five observational field studies reached the same conclusion (Meissner & Redlich, 2011). One scholar, a prominent observer of the Supreme Court, advocates that judges take a stand against deception in police interrogations (Wrightsman, 2010).

SUMMARY

1. ***What are some psychological investigative techniques used by the police?*** The police use a variety of techniques to increase the likelihood that suspects will be prosecuted and convicted. Among these are criminal profiling; unaided judgments of deception; the so-called lie detector (technically, the polygraph technique); brain-based techniques for gauging deception; and procedures to induce confessions.

2. ***What is criminal profiling?*** Criminal profiling is an attempt to use what is known about how a crime was committed to infer what type of person might have committed it. Evidence about profiling suggests that it may have some utility as a means of narrowing police investigations to the most likely suspects.

3. ***What cues do people use to detect deception, and how accurate are these judgments?*** People tend to focus on the wrong cues when determining whether another person is telling the truth. Bodily signs like fidgeting and gaze aversion are not generally associated with lying. Verbal cues, including length of utterance and the presence of memory lapses and speech errors, are better indicators. In general, people are not very accurate in discriminating between liars and truth-tellers.

4. *Is the polygraph a valid instrument for lie detection? What are some problems associated with it?* No measure of physiological reactions can precisely distinguish between guilt and other negative emotions, such as fear, anger, or embarrassment. Although polygraph examiners claim high rates of accuracy in distinguishing between subjects who are lying and those who are not, there are several problems with such claims: the misleading nature of "accuracy rates," lack of consistency between the conclusions of different examiners, and suspects' use of countermeasures to "beat the test."

5. *What brain-based techniques are used to detect deception, and how well do they work?* Two techniques, neuroimaging using fMRI and brain fingerprinting using electroencephalograms, record brain activity while people are either lying or telling the truth. Studies show that different patterns of brain activation are associated with truth-telling and lying. Advocates of these procedures promote their effectiveness in detecting deception, but a number of complicating issues have not been resolved.

6. *How valid is confession evidence? What kinds of interrogation procedures can lead to false confessions?* Two kinds of errors arise in the context of confessions: guilty suspects falsely proclaiming their innocence, and innocent suspects falsely confessing. Among the interrogation techniques that can lead to false confessions are prolonged social isolation, confronting a suspect and expressing a belief in his or her guilt, exaggerating or fabricating evidence against the suspect, and offering psychological and moral justification for the offense.

7. *What are some of the reforms proposed to prevent false confessions?* Critics of police interrogations suggest that these interrogations should be recorded in order to improve the quality of questioning, deter police misconduct, and preserve a record that can be evaluated at a later time. A more radical approach would replace the accusatorial style of interrogations with nonconfrontational interviews such as are now being conducted in the United Kingdom.

KEY TERMS

behavioral confirmation

brain fingerprinting

cognitive load interviews

compliant false confessions

Concealed Knowledge Test

Control Question Test

countermeasures

criminal profiling

diagnostic cues

evidence ploys

external validity

fabricated evidence

false confession

false denial

functional magnetic resonance imaging

fundamental attribution error

illusory causation

internalized false confessions

mass murderer

negative incentives

polygraph

positive inducements

serial killers

spree killers

truth bias

voluntary false confessions

Chapter
8

Traditional Prosecutions: Arrest, Bail, Plea Negotiation/ Settlement, and Trial

ORIENTING QUESTIONS

1. What are the major legal proceedings between arrest and trial in the criminal justice system?
2. What is bail, and what factors influence the amount of bail set?
3. Why do defendants and prosecutors agree to plea bargain?
4. What are settlement negotiations, and why are most civil lawsuits resolved through settlement rather than trial?
5. What is the purpose of a trial?
6. What are the steps involved in a trial?
7. How has the introduction of emerging technologies changed the way that trials are conducted?

Between the time that the police make an arrest and a case is eventually resolved at sentencing, traditional prosecutions involve several steps with psychological implications. One feature of traditional prosecutions with obvious psychological overtones is a trial. The grand finale in our adversary system of justice—the trial—is a public battle waged by two combatants (prosecution versus defense in a criminal trial, plaintiff versus defendant in a civil trial), each fighting for a favorable outcome. Trials can be fiercely contested; prosecutors desire convictions, criminal defendants seek their freedom through acquittals, civil plaintiffs want compensation for wrongs they have suffered, and civil defendants hope to be absolved of wrongdoing and not required to pay damages. Psychological issues abound.

Although the trial may be the most visible and dramatic ritual in our system, many other factors play larger—often decisive—roles in determining case outcomes. For example, in the weeks and months following arrest, many criminal cases are simply dismissed for lack of evidence or other difficulties that prosecutors perceive in the case. Of some 49,000 defendants charged with a felony from 1990 to 2002 in the 75 most populous counties in the United States, 24% had their cases dismissed prior to trial (Cohen & Reaves, 2006).

For the vast majority of people charged with crimes and not fortunate enough to have the charges dropped, **plea bargains**, not trials, resolve their cases. Plea bargaining, described in more detail later in the chapter, is a process in which a defendant agrees to plead guilty in exchange for some concession from the prosecutor. Such concessions typically involve a reduction in the type of charge, the number of charges, or the recommended sentence. By pleading guilty, defendants give up their right to a trial, allowing attorneys and judges to move on to other cases. The vast majority of civil cases are also resolved without a formal trial in a process termed *settlement negotiation*, described in more detail in this chapter.

If most cases are settled without a trial, why is our society (including psychologists who work in the legal arena) so fascinated by trials and trial procedures? Without a doubt, there are theatrical aspects to many trials, especially those featured in news media, films, and novels. Trials grab our attention because they vividly portray the raw emotions of sad, distraught, and angry people. Interest in trials is also related to their very public nature; most trials are conducted in open court for all to see. Some are televised or even available for online viewing.

In contrast, negotiations about plea bargains and settlements are largely hidden from public view. Prosecutors offer concessions to defense attorneys over the phone or in courthouse hallways. Defense attorneys convey these offers to their clients in offices or jail cells. Settlement negotiations in civil cases are also conducted in private. In fact, the eventual settlements in civil cases are often never made public.

You may notice that we expend many more pages of this book on psychological issues before and during trials than we do on plea bargains or settlement negotiations. This choice reflects the available data. Like the general public, psychologists are intrigued by the interpersonal dramas and behavioral complexities involved in trials. Thus, psychologists have conducted a great deal of research on trials and have much to say about them. But keep in mind that most cases are disposed of in a different and less public way—through plea bargains and settlement discussions that are core concepts of this chapter.

In addition to plea bargains and settlements, this chapter examines other pretrial proceedings in criminal cases including pretrial motions and bail setting, and outlines the steps involved in a trial. All of these procedures raise important psychological questions that have been addressed through experimentation, observation, or empirical analysis. We preface those issues by describing the customary sequence of pretrial activities in the criminal justice system.

STEPS BETWEEN ARREST AND TRIAL

If the police believe that a suspect committed a crime, they will probably arrest the suspect. However, being arrested for a crime and being charged with a crime are two different events, and a person may be arrested without being charged. For example, the police may arrest drunks to detain them and sober them up, but formal charges might never be filed. Charging implies a formal decision to continue with the prosecution, and that decision is made by the prosecuting attorney rather than the police.

The Initial Appearance

The **initial appearance** is a crucial step in the criminal process. The Fourth Amendment to the United States Constitution requires that any person arrested be brought before a judge within 48 hours of arrest. This is one of the most important protections of the Bill of Rights. In many countries the police arrest people (or "detain" them, a euphemism for arrest) and hold them without charge for extended periods—or indefinitely. In the United States, however, anyone who is arrested must be taken without delay before a judge, an important protection against abuse of power by the police. The primary purpose of the initial appearance is for the judge to review the evidence summarized by the prosecutor and determine whether there is reason to believe that the suspect committed the crimes charged. In addition, the judge will inform defendants of the charges against

them, inform them of their constitutional rights, review the issue of bail, and appoint attorneys for those that cannot afford to hire their own.

The Preliminary Hearing

The next step is the **preliminary hearing**. One of its purposes is to filter out cases in which the prosecution has insufficient evidence. At a preliminary hearing, the prosecution must offer some evidence on every element of the crime charged and the judge must decide whether the evidence is sufficient to pursue the case further. No jury is present and defendants rarely testify or offer any evidence of their own. The judge will sometimes send the case to a grand jury (described next) or reduce the charges, either because he or she believes the evidence does not support the level of crime charged by the prosecutor or because of a plea bargain between the prosecutor and the defense attorney.

The Grand Jury

Consisting of citizens drawn from the community, the **grand jury** meets in private with the prosecutor to investigate criminal activity and return **indictments** (complaints prepared and signed by the prosecutor describing the crime charged). The grand jury may call witnesses on its own initiative if it is dissatisfied with the witnesses presented by the prosecutor. In some states the defendant has a right to testify. In about one-third of the states, a criminal defendant cannot be prosecuted unless a grand jury has found grounds to do so. The remaining states permit the prosecutor to proceed either by grand jury indictment or by a preliminary hearing. In the 2012 case of Trayvon Martin, an unarmed Florida teen who was fatally shot by George Zimmerman, a neighborhood watch volunteer, the prosecutor decided to forego a grand jury investigation and to determine on her own whether to charge Zimmerman. Because local authorities initially opted *not* to press charges, sparking protests nationwide, all eyes focused on the prosecutor's decision. Zimmerman was charged with second-degree murder.

If the grand jury decides there is sufficient evidence to justify the defendant being tried, it issues an indictment. For example, former Penn State football coach Jerry Sandusky was indicted on multiple counts of deviant sexual intercourse, endangering the welfare of a child, indecent assault, and other

Courtroom trial in session

charges, all resulting from his alleged rape of young boys between 1994 and 2009.

Arraignment

A grand jury gives its indictments to a judge, who brings those indicted to court for arraignment. At the **arraignment**, the judge makes sure that the defendant has an attorney and appoints one if necessary. The indictment is then read to the defendant, and the defendant is asked to plead guilty or not guilty. It is customary for defendants to plead not guilty at this time, even those who ultimately plead guilty. The reasons for a not-guilty plea at this stage involve providing opportunities for both plea bargaining and discovery (described next), so that the defendant's attorney can review some of the evidence against the defendant.

Discovery and Pretrial Motions

Defendants and their attorneys want to be aware of the evidence the prosecution will use to prove its case. In civil trials, each side is entitled to **discovery**—that is, each side has a right to depose (or question) the witnesses on the opposing side, and to review and copy documents that the other side might use at trial. In criminal cases, just how much the prosecution must reveal to the defense varies widely. Some states require prosecutors to turn over to the defense all reports,

statements by witnesses, and physical evidence. Most states require only that the prosecutor share certain evidence (e.g., laboratory reports) and evidence that is **exculpatory** (i.e., that tends to show the defendant is not guilty or suggests that prosecution witnesses are not credible). In part because prosecutors failed to share exculpatory evidence, a Colorado man spent eight and a half years in prison for a crime he didn't commit. We describe his case in Box 8.1.

Discovery is a two-way street. In general, states require the defense to turn over the same types of materials that the prosecution must turn over. If the prosecution is required to reveal laboratory reports, the defense will likewise be required to share such reports. In many states, the defense is required to notify the prosecution if it intends to rely on certain defenses, notably insanity and alibi defenses. The reason for requiring such pretrial notice is to give the state an opportunity to investigate the claim and avoid being surprised at trial.

During the discovery phase of the case, both sides file pretrial motions seeking favorable rulings on the admissibility of evidence. Motions commonly filed by the defense are the following:

1. *Motion for separate trials.* When two or more defendants are jointly indicted, one of them can be counted on to request a separate trial, claiming that to be tried together would be prejudicial. Such a motion was granted in the case of Timothy McVeigh and Terry Nichols, who were

In late January, 2008, Tim Masters became perhaps the first person in Colorado to walk up to a counter at the Department of Motor Vehicles and, without first taking a number and waiting in line, get a drivers' license. The crowds of people waiting their turns were happy to give Masters a break; after all, he had been released from prison just a few days before when his murder conviction and life sentence were wiped out by DNA evidence that pointed to another suspect. The DNA testing was the final chapter in a long saga of misplaced hunches, shoddy procedures, and prosecutors' failure to disclose crucial evidence.

In 1987, Masters—then only 15 years old—lived with his father in a trailer outside of Fort Collins, Colorado. A woman's body was found in a field about 100 feet from his home; she had been stabbed and sexually mutilated. Detectives interrogated Masters, who admitted to walking past the body on his way to catch a school bus and failing to report it. They also searched his home, confiscating violent pictures he had drawn in his school notebooks. Over the next several years, prosecutors built a circumstantial case against Masters based on "psychological analysis"

of his drawings, the fact that the murder coincided with the anniversary of his mother's death, and their suspicions. Masters was convicted of murder and sentenced to life imprisonment in 1999.

But several years later, a new team of investigators and attorneys began to glean clues that prosecutors knew more than they revealed in 1987. They learned that police had an alternate suspect back then, something not revealed to the defense. They learned that counter to the judge's orders, prosecutors had taken evidence from the case for their own examination. They alleged that prosecutors deliberately "stonewalled, delayed, and obstructed" in order to preserve the conviction. Eventually, DNA tests excluded Masters as a suspect. His conviction was set aside, he was released from prison, and he finally got the chance to drive.

Critical Thought Questions
What had the prosecutor in this case failed to do, and why was that mistake costly to Masters, and eventually, to the police department, prosecutor's office, and the community?

convicted in separate trials of bombing the federal building in Oklahoma City, killing 168 people. McVeigh was convicted of murder and sentenced to death, but Nichols was convicted of a lesser charge (conspiracy) and sentenced to life imprisonment.

2. *Motion to sever counts.* Suppose the indictment charges the defendant with robbing a convenience store on April 13 and burglarizing a house on April 15. The defendant may request separate trials on these offenses. A defendant may argue that it is prejudicial for the same jury to hear evidence about separate crimes because the jury will be tempted to combine the evidence introduced on the separate crimes to find the defendant guilty of each crime. There is good reason for defendants to be concerned about how a jury will react to multiple charges. Psychological research studies that simulate jury decision making have shown that jurors are more likely to convict a defendant on any charge (e.g., robbery) when it is combined with another (e.g., burglary) than when it is tried alone (e.g., Greene & Loftus, 1985). A review of nearly 20,000 federal criminal trials over a five-year period reached a similar conclusion (Leipold & Abbasi, 2006).

3. *Motion for change of venue.* The defendant may request a **change of venue** (moving the proceedings to a different location) on the ground that community opinion, usually the product of prejudicial pretrial publicity, makes it impossible to seat a fair-minded jury. Psychologists are sometimes involved in analyzing the extent and impact of the publicity on prospective jurors.

4. *Motion to suppress a confession or other statement by the defendant.* The Fifth Amendment protects against self-incrimination, and the Sixth Amendment forbids the use of a statement taken in violation of the right to counsel. One or both of these constitutional provisions may become relevant any time the prosecution offers a confession or other statement by a defendant as evidence of guilt. Typically, defense counsel files a motion alleging that the confession was obtained in violation of the defendant's constitutional rights, the prosecutor files a written response, and the court holds a hearing at which the defendant and police give their versions of the circumstances under which the confession was obtained. The judge decides the issue on the basis of what was said and the credibility of the witnesses. Questions of who

is telling the truth are usually resolved in favor of the police. Criminal defendants who believe that their confessions were coerced or made involuntarily have good reason to try to suppress them, because juries tend to accept a defendant's confession without careful evaluation of the circumstances that led to the confession.

5. *Motions* in limine. Perhaps the most common pretrial motions are those that seek advance rulings on evidentiary issues that will arise at trial. A **motion *in limine*** is simply a request for a pretrial ruling. Suppose, for example, that the defendant was previously convicted of burglary. The judge must decide whether to allow the prosecution to introduce that conviction into evidence in order to discredit the defendant if he chooses to testify. The defendant obviously wants a pretrial ruling on this issue in order to plan the questioning of the jurors and to decide whether to testify. Similarly, the prosecutor may want a pretrial ruling on the admissibility of a certain piece of evidence in order to plan the opening statement.

THE DECISION TO SET BAIL

Judges must decide whether to keep criminal defendants in custody during the lengthy process between arrest and trial or whether to release them into the community with a promise to reappear for subsequent hearings. Judges have many options. In some cases (capital cases and cases in which the defendant poses a serious risk of fleeing or committing other crimes), they can deny bail altogether. Short of denying bail, judges can require that money (or a bail bondsman's pledge) be deposited with the court or that a third person agrees to be responsible for the defendant's future appearances and to forfeit money if the defendant does not appear. When bail is higher than defendants can afford, they have no choice but to remain in jail. Studies of defendants who promised to reappear showed that most defendants did so (Feeley, 1983). Whether bail bonds actually reduce the risk of nonappearance is not clear. Box 8.2 describes techniques that bail bond agents use to ensure that defendants who post bail will show up for court.

In addition to ensuring the defendant's return to court, bail has a secondary purpose: protecting public safety. In fact, bail evolved in the American legal system as an attempt to resolve the basic conflict between an individual's right to liberty on the one hand, and societal rights to be protected from criminal behavior on the other. The Eighth Amendment to the U.S. Constitution says that excessive bail shall not be required, but the Supreme Court has ruled that this provision does not guarantee a right to bail; it simply requires that bail, if any, should not be excessive (*United States v. Salerno*, 1987). Although various laws govern the bail decision, they are typically vague and ill defined, allowing judges considerable leeway in the factors they consider and the way they make the decision about bail.

B o x 8.2 THE CASE OF "LITTLE RANDY" WITHERS AND THE CYBERSEARCH FOR DEFENDANTS ON THE RUN

Bail bond agents like Duane Lee "Dog" Chapman (star of the reality television program *Dog the Bounty Hunter*) are renowned for their diligence in tracking down defendants who have skipped bail and failed to return to court as required. Bonding agents stand to lose the value of the bond posted if the defendant cannot be located, so their financial incentive for locating and returning the defendant to custody is considerable. Although bonding agents have been criticized in the past for strong-arm search-and-return tactics, they increasingly are turning to modern technology to catch defendants on the run. One of those fugitive defendants was "Little Randy" Withers, who was charged with possession of a firearm by a felon and whose picture was included on the website entitled "The World's Most Wanted—Bail Jumpers" (www.mostwanted.org). The 21st century's counterpart to the old "Wanted Dead or Alive" posters of the western frontier, this website describes Withers as a Black male, born on April 28, 1975, 5 feet 7 inches tall, 175 pounds, black hair and brown eyes, residing in Charlotte, North Carolina. Warning that these defendants have "Nowhere to Run! Nowhere to Hide!" the subscribing companies typically offer $1,000 and $2,000 cash rewards for information that leads to the apprehension of the most wanted bail fugitives. They also caution would-be bounty hunters that most of the suspects are armed and should be considered dangerous.

Critical Thought Questions
What are the implications for most defendants, fugitive defendants like "Little Randy" Withers, and the general public when suspects are released on bail prior to trial?

WANTED
BY THE FBI

Hobbs Act Robbery; Using, Carrying, and Discharging a Firearm During and in Relation
to a Crime of Violence - Criminal Homicide; Theft by Unlawful Taking; Robbery

KENNETH JOHN KONIAS, JR.

Konias' Vehicle   Konias' Vehicle

Aliases:
Kenneth Konias, Kenneth J. Konias

DESCRIPTION

Date(s) of Birth Used:	December 8, 1989	**Hair:**	Brown (Very Short / Balding)
Height:	6'0"	**Eyes:**	Brown
Weight:	165 pounds	**Sex:**	Male
NCIC:	W584551583	**Race:**	White
Build:	Thin		
Remarks:	Konias is believed to be in possession of several weapons. He may be driving a tan, 2006 Ford Explorer with license plate GZW-4572. (Shown Above)		

CAUTION

Kenneth John Konias, Jr., an armored car driver, is wanted for his alleged involvement in the murder of his co-worker
and the theft of approximately $2.3 million, all of which occurred during his scheduled shift on February 28, 2012, in
Pittsburgh, Pennsylvania. Konias allegedly shot and killed his co-worker, a fellow armored vehicle employee, before
absconding with the money from the armored car. A local arrest warrant was issued for Konias on February 29, 2012,
in the Commonwealth of Pennsylvania's Pittsburgh Municipal Court on charges of criminal homicide, theft by unlawful
taking, and robbery. On March 2, 2012, a federal arrest warrant was issued for Kenneth John Konias, Jr. in the United
States District Court, Western District of Pennsylvania, Pittsburgh, Pennsylvania, after he was charged with Hobbs Act
robbery and using, carrying, and discharging a firearm during and in relation to a crime of violence.

SHOULD BE CONSIDERED ARMED AND DANGEROUS

If you have any information concerning this case, please contact the FBI's Toll-Free Hotline at 1-800-CALL-FBI; your
local FBI office ; or the nearest American Embassy or Consulate .

HANDOUT/Reuters /Landov

Cybersearch for a wanted suspect

What Considerations Affect the Decision to Set Bail?

Psychologists and other social scientists have examined how judges make bail-setting decisions (e.g.,
Allan, Allan, Giles, Drake, & Froyland, 2005). In particular, they have evaluated the factors that judges
consider and the cognitive processes by which judges
weigh and combine these factors.

Bail decisions are influenced by both legal and
extralegal factors. **Legal factors** are related to the
offense or the offender's legal history; research has
shown that bail is likely to be denied or set very high
when the offense was serious and when the offender
has prior convictions. But because the laws relevant to
bail decisions are ill defined and there is little public
scrutiny of this step in the criminal process, there is
potential for offenders' race and gender—**extralegal
factors**—to affect judges' decisions (Demuth, 2003).
In fact, race and gender had significant impacts on
judges' pretrial release decisions in drug cases in a
mid-sized Pennsylvania county between 2000 and
2003. Black defendants were less likely than other
defendants to be released, and female defendants
were assigned lower bail amounts than males
(Freiburger, Marcum, & Pierce, 2010). These results
are consistent with the **focal concerns perspective**,
which proposes that judges perceive Black offenders
as more dangerous and blameworthy than Whites,
and female offenders as less dangerous and blameworthy than males. These perceptions affect judges'
bail decisions.

Psychologists have assessed the cognitive processes that judges use in determining whether bail should be allowed. In some studies, judges respond to simulated cases presented as vignettes. In other studies, researchers observe judges dealing with real cases in the courtroom (Dhami, 2003; Dhami & Ayton, 2001). In both settings, judges tend to use a mental shortcut called the **matching heuristic**: They search through a subset of available case information and then make a decision on the basis of only a small number of factors (for example, offense severity and prior record), often ignoring other seemingly relevant information. This is not especially surprising; judges' large caseloads force them to make fast decisions, and people often use shortcut reasoning strategies when forced to think quickly.

The opinions of police and prosecutors can also sway judges' decisions about bail. Dhami (2003) analyzed bail-setting decisions in two London courts and found that the prosecutor's request and the position of the police strongly influenced the judge's choices. Judges were less swayed by an offender's risk of committing further crimes while out of jail (Dhami, 2005), raising questions about whether judges are sufficiently concerned about society's right to be protected against the harm caused by defendants on bail. Finally, although judges were highly confident that they had made the appropriate decisions (the overconfidence bias), there was significant disagreement among judges who responded to the same simulated fact patterns, raising troubling questions of fairness and equality.

Does Pretrial Release Affect Trial Outcome?

What if the defendant cannot provide bail and remains in jail until the time of trial? Does this pretrial detention affect the trial's outcome? Clearly, yes. Defendants who are detained in jail are more likely to plead guilty or be convicted and to receive longer sentences than those who can afford bail, even when the seriousness of their offenses and the evidence against them are the same (Kellough & Wortley, 2002). Some data suggest that prosecutors use pretrial detention as a "resource" to encourage (or coerce) guilty pleas. Pretrial detention is likely to cost defendants their jobs, making it harder for them to pay attorneys—so the threat of it may make them more likely to plead guilty. Among defendants who actually go to trial, an accused person who is free on bail

finds it easier to gather witnesses and prepare a defense. A jailed defendant cannot go to his or her attorney's office for meetings, has less time with his or her attorney to prepare for trial, and has less access to records and witnesses. Detention also corrodes family and community ties.

Can High-Risk Defendants Be Identified?

Around 1970, a push began for legislation that would increase the use of **preventive detention**—the detention of accused persons who pose a risk of flight or dangerousness. Civil libertarians oppose preventive detention because it conflicts with the fundamental assumption that a defendant is innocent until proven guilty. But most citizens approve, valuing society's need to be protected from possible future harm over the rights of individual suspects to be free until proven guilty. Although the preventive detention of suspected terrorists is controversial, many people believe that the risk of a large-scale attack similar to 9/11 outweighs suspects' individual rights. The U.S. Supreme Court has taken the view that preventive detention is not a punishment, but rather a regulatory action (like a quarantine) for the public's protection.

Preventive detention assumes that valid assessments of risk and accurate predictions of future dangerous conduct can be made, an assumption that is not always correct (Heilbrun, 2009). Thus, judges have difficulty knowing which defendants are high risk and which can be trusted. In Shepherd, Texas, Patrick Dale Walker tried to kill his girlfriend by putting a gun to her head and pulling the trigger. The loaded gun failed to fire. Walker's original bail was set at $1 million, but after he had been in jail for four days, the presiding judge lowered his bail to $25,000. This permitted Walker to be released; four months later, he fired three bullets at close range and killed the same woman. Afterward, the judge did not think he was wrong in lowering the bail, even though, since 1993, Texas has had a law that permits judges to consider the safety of the victim and of the community in determining the amount of bail. In fact, Patrick Walker had no previous record, was valedictorian of his class, and was a college graduate. Would a psychologist have done any better in predicting Walker's behavior?

Mental health professionals now have the capacity to assess violence risk in some situations, particularly when using specialized tools (see, e.g., Monahan et al., 2005; Otto & Douglas, 2010). There remains a debate about how precise such estimates can be, with some authors identifying the limits of specialized tools and strategies (e.g., Hart, Michie, & Cooke, 2007; Kroner, Mills, & Reddon, 2005).

PLEA BARGAINING
IN CRIMINAL CASES

Most criminal cases—by some accounts, 90–95%—end prior to trial when the defendant pleads guilty to some charge, usually in exchange for a concession by the prosecutor. The extensive use of plea bargaining in the criminal justice system illustrates the dilemma between truth and conflict resolution as goals of our legal system.

Plea bargaining has been practiced in the United States since the middle of the 19th century, and lately it has threatened to put the trial system out of business. Of the estimated 1,132,000 people who were sentenced on felony convictions in 2006, 94% pleaded guilty (Rosenmerkel, Durose, & Farole, 2009). Interestingly, murder defendants were less likely to plead guilty than defendants charged with other violent felonies. Guilty pleas were offered by 89% of robbery suspects but by only 61% of murder suspects. The harsh sentences imposed on most convicted murderers—often life in prison without parole—make it worthwhile for murder defendants to go to trial and hope for sympathetic judges or juries.

Both mundane and serious cases are resolved by plea bargains. In a routine case that would never have been publicized if the defendant had not been a judge, Roger Hurley, a judge from Darke County, Ohio, pled guilty in a domestic violence case. He was accused of grabbing his estranged wife by the neck during an argument and threatening her with a bread knife. According to Hurley, he accepted a plea bargain in order to get on with his life and end the hurt and friction that this incident caused his family. In a more notorious case, James Earl Ray, the assassin of Martin Luther King, Jr., died in prison while serving a life sentence as a result of a plea bargain. The plea deal was not well received: many thought Ray had not acted alone, and the plea agreement meant that the facts would never be aired in a public forum. After Ray's death in 1998, the King family released a

statement expressing regret that Ray had never had his day in court and the American people would never learn the truth about King's death.

The defendant's part of the bargain requires an admission of guilt. This admission relieves the prosecutor of any obligation to prove that the defendant committed the crimes charged. The prosecutor's part of the bargain may involve an agreement to reduce the number of charges or allow the defendant to plead guilty to a charge less serious than the evidence supports. For example, manslaughter is a lesser charge than murder, and many murder prosecutions are resolved by a plea of guilty to manslaughter.

In a common procedure known as **charge bargaining**, the prosecutor drops some charges in exchange for a guilty plea. But charge bargaining may lead prosecutors initially to charge the defendant with more crimes or with a more serious crime than could be proven at trial, as a strategy for enticing defendants to plead guilty. Laboratory research using role-playing procedures (Gregory, Mowen, & Linder, 1978) indicates that "overcharging" is effective; research participants were more likely to accept a plea bargain when more charges were filed against them. The defendants who engage in this type of bargaining may win only hollow victories. Cases in which prosecutors offer to drop charges are likely to be ones for which judges would have imposed concurrent sentences for the multiple convictions anyway.

Plea bargaining may also take the form of **sentence bargaining**, in which prosecutors recommend reduced sentences in return for guilty pleas. Sentencing is the judge's decision, and although judges vary in their willingness to follow prosecutors' recommendations, many simply rubber-stamp prosecutorial sentencing recommendations. In general, defendants can expect that judges will follow the sentences that have been recommended by a prosecutor, and prosecutors can earn the trust of judges by recommending sentences that are reasonable and fair.

Why do defendants plead guilty? There are two primary reasons: because the likelihood of conviction is high, and because, if convicted, they would face lengthy sentences (Bibas, 2004). Some court observers suspect that tougher sentencing laws of the past few decades have allowed prosecutors to gain even greater leverage over criminal defendants, threatening them with mandatory or harsh sentences. So no matter how convinced defendants are of their innocence, they take a risk by turning down plea bargains and facing

---

B o x   8.3   THE CASE OF SHANE GUTHRIE AND THE POWER OF THE PROSECUTION IN PLEA BARGAINING

Shane Guthrie, age 24, was arrested in Gainesville in 2010 and charged with aggravated battery on a pregnant woman and false imprisonment. The charges stemmed from Guthrie allegedly beating his girlfriend and threatening her with a knife. The prosecutor initially offered Guthrie a plea deal of two years in prison and probation. Believing in his innocence, Guthrie rejected that offer, as well as a subsequent offer of 5 years in prison, despite apparently being warned that higher charges would be filed if he refused to accept the offer. But Guthrie's attorney maintained that there was no evidence the girlfriend was pregnant, that she started the fight by hitting Guthrie in the forehead with a pipe and changed her story several times, and that she had been arrested in 2009 for attacking Guthrie and telling police that he struck her.

The prosecutor's response to Guthrie's unwillingness to plead guilty? A year later, he filed more serious charges, including first-degree felony kidnapping, which would have meant life imprisonment if Guthrie, who had already spent time in prison, was convicted. "So what he could have resolved for a two-year term could keep him locked up for 50 years or more" (Oppel, 2011). This case illustrates the power that a prosecutor, who determines what charges to file, has over a defendant's destiny.

Critical Thought Questions
How do the prosecutor's actions in this case differ from the more typical ways that prosecutors handle plea bargains?

---

the possibility of additional charges or mandatory sentences (Oppel, 2011). We describe one such case in Box 8.3.

Defendants have the final say in any decision or plea. Before accepting a guilty plea, judges ask defendants if they made the decision freely and of their own accord. Defense attorneys can have an impact in this decision. Their recommendations interact with the defendant's wishes in complex ways to yield a decision. Defense attorneys gauge whether to recommend a plea offer based on the strength of the evidence against the defendant and the severity of the punishment (Brank & Scott, 2012). When the evidence points toward conviction and the defendant is facing a lengthy prison sentence, defense attorneys will recommend strongly that defendants accept plea offers.

At least in some circumstances, defense attorneys also take their clients' preferences into account. Kramer, Wolbransky, and Heilbrun (2007) had attorneys read vignettes that varied the strength of the evidence against a hypothetical defendant, the potential sentence if convicted, and the defendant's wishes. When the probability of conviction was high and the likely prison sentence was long, attorneys strongly recommended the plea offer, regardless of the defendant's desires. But when the probability of conviction was low and the prison sentence was short, attorneys were willing to consider the defendant's wish to proceed to trial.

Unfortunately, zealous representation by defense attorneys in plea negotiations may not apply to all defendants equally. When she asked defense attorneys from across the country to respond to scenarios that varied the race of the defendant, Edkins (2011) found that the plea deals attorneys felt they could secure for Caucasian clients contained shorter sentences that those they felt they could obtain for African American clients, even though they were slightly more likely to think that the Caucasian clients were guilty. Apparently defense attorneys' own biases may come into play when they advocate for their clients.

Defendants plea bargain in order to obtain less severe punishment than they would receive if they went to trial and were convicted. But why do prosecutors plea bargain? What advantages do they seek, given that they hold the more powerful position in this bargaining situation? Prosecutors are motivated to plea bargain for one or more of the following reasons: (1) to dispose of cases in which the evidence against the defendant is weak or the defense attorney is a formidable foe; (2) to ensure a "win" when their office keeps a record of the "wins" (convictions) and "losses" (acquittals) of each prosecuting attorney in the office; (3) to obtain the testimony of one defendant against a more culpable or infamous codefendant; and most importantly, (4) to expedite the flow of cases for an overworked staff and a clogged court docket.

Plea bargaining serves the need of the defense attorney to appear to gain something for his or her client and the need of the prosecutor to appear fair and reasonable. Both prosecutors and defense attorneys believe they are making the "punishment fit the crime" by individualizing the law to fit the circumstances of the case, and both are comfortable with a system in which most cases are resolved without a clear winner or clear loser. Experienced prosecutors and defense attorneys teach plea bargaining to the rookies in their offices, and lawyers from both sides engage in a ritual of give and take, with changing facts and personalities but with the same posturing and rationalizations. In fact, the procedures are so well known that in some cases no formal bargaining even takes place; everyone involved—prosecutor, defense attorney, defendant, and judge—knows the prevailing "rate" for a given crime, and if the defendant pleads guilty to that crime, the rate is the price that will be paid.

Psychological Influences on the Plea-Bargaining Process

Although there are few empirical studies of plea bargaining, we can generalize from other bargaining situations to understand the role of psychological factors in the process (McAllister, 2008). One factor concerns **framing effects**. Psychologists who study decision making have learned that the way decision alternatives are presented (or framed)—as either *gains* or *losses*—can have a significant impact on a person's choice. Individuals are more willing to take chances when the decision alternatives are presented in terms of gains rather than losses. Imagine that two defendants have been charged with the same crime, each has a 50% chance of being convicted at trial, and, if convicted, each is likely to be sentenced to 20 years in prison. The prosecutor has offered both defendants a deal that would result in only 10 years imprisonment in exchange for a guilty plea. Now imagine that Defendant A's options are framed as a *gain* and Defendant B's options are framed as a *loss*. Defendant A is told that if he went to trial, there would be a 50% chance that he would be acquitted and *gain 10 years* outside of prison compared to the plea-bargain offer. Defendant B is told that if he went to trial, there would be a 50% chance that he would be convicted and *lose an additional 10 years* of life in prison compared to the plea-bargain offer. Although the two situations are identical except for the decision frame, Defendant A is more likely to take his chance at trial and Defendant B is more likely to take the plea bargain to avoid a loss.

Other psychological factors affect and sometimes distort offenders' and attorneys' decisions concerning plea bargains. In general, people tend to be too optimistic about their chances of securing favorable outcomes and are therefore overconfident. The **overconfidence bias** suggests that because defendants and their attorneys believe (incorrectly) that they have a chance to win at trial, they might reject reasonable offers from prosecutors.

Overconfidence skews beliefs about the likelihood of acquittal. Denial mechanisms affect thoughts about one's guilt and the chances for successful plea-bargain arrangements. Offenders often have difficulty acknowledging guilt to their attorneys; some cannot even admit it to themselves (Bibas, 2004). Thinking about one's immoral or illegal actions is painful and depressing, and denial mechanisms allow people to avoid dealing with those thoughts. But denial results in minimizing the harm caused to others and an unwillingness to accept responsibility for wrongdoing. Defendants in denial are unlikely to take a plea bargain even when it is advantageous for them to do so.

Attorneys also tend to be overconfident of their ability to predict case outcomes (Goodman-Delahunty, Granhag, Hartwig, & Loftus, 2010), rendering them less than stellar tellers of the future. Their overconfidence stems from a variety of factors, including the absence of feedback on the accuracy of most predictions (90–95% of cases are never tried!); the belief in their professional prowess; and the related illusion that with hard work and perseverance, they can control the outcome of events (Greene & Bornstein, 2011).

Evaluations of Plea Bargaining

The U.S. Supreme Court has called plea bargaining "an essential component of the administration of justice" (*Santobello v. New York*, 1971), and has stated that defendants have a constitutional right to effective representation in plea negotiations, including competent advice and information about prosecutors' offers (*Lafler v. Cooper*, 2012). Still, plea bargaining remains a controversial procedure. It has been defended as a necessary and useful part of the criminal justice system (American Bar Association, 1993), and condemned as a practice that should be abolished from our courts (Lynch, 2003). Advocates justify the procedure by pointing out that guilty pleas lessen the backlog of cases that would otherwise engulf the courts; facilitate the prosecution of other offenders; and reduce the involvement of criminal justice participants, including (in addition to judges and attorneys) police officers who don't have to spend hours in court testifying, and victims who are spared the trauma of a trial.

Critics urge the abolition of plea bargaining. They claim that (1) improper sentences—sometimes too harsh but more often too lenient—are likely; (2) plea bargaining encourages defendants to surrender their constitutional rights; (3) prosecutors exert too much power in negotiating guilty pleas; and (4) innocent defendants might feel coerced to plead guilty because they fear the more severe consequences of being convicted by a jury.

Data on these contentions are limited, but the available evidence suggests that plea bargaining works as advertised. Defendants who are convicted at trial do indeed suffer more severe sanctions than those who accept plea bargains. In 2006, 89% of felons convicted during a trial were sentenced to jail or prison, compared with only 76% of those who committed the same crime and accepted plea bargains. In addition, judges imposed longer sentences on offenders who went to trial (an average sentence of 8 years and 4 months) than on those who pled guilty (an average sentence of 3 years and 11 months) (Rosenmerkel et al., 2009).

There may be some "dark sides" to plea bargaining, however. It is troubling that adolescent defendants may lack the comprehension skills necessary to intelligently weigh the trade-offs inherent in plea bargaining and to consider the long-term consequences of their decisions (Redlich, 2010). In fact, adolescents may be more likely than adults to accept guilty pleas (Grisso et al., 2003), and among adolescents aged 11–13, the decision to accept a plea bargain is unrelated to the strength of the evidence against them (Viljoen, Klaver, & Roesch, 2005).

Plea bargaining may also work against the long-range goal of achieving justice. It may prevent the families of victims from seeing the defendants "get justice" or hearing them acknowledge full responsibility for their offenses. In 2000, a Missouri man, Terrance Wainwright, was sentenced to life without parole plus 90 years for killing his wife and her 15-year-old daughter. The case seemed closed. But during the appeals process five years later, a prosecutor offered Wainwright a deal to plead guilty to a lesser charge and a reduced sentence, infuriating family members of the victims. According to the father of

the 15-year-old girl, the prosecutor proposed the deal without ever consulting him. To address this concern, victims' rights legislation increasingly ensures that the victim or his or her family has a say in plea bargaining, and some states now involve victims in the plea-bargaining process.

Finally, it is troubling that cases are not always resolved in line with the gravity of the offense. When these "errors" are in the direction of sentencing leniency, they often are attributed to a perceived overload in the prosecutor's office or the courts. A defendant should not be able to plead to a greatly reduced charge simply because the criminal justice system lacks the resources to handle the case. However, the answer to problems of unwarranted leniency is not the abolition of plea bargaining; rather, adequate funding must be provided for the court system, as well as for the correctional system, so that when severe penalties are necessary, severe penalties can be given. In the long run, if plea bargaining serves primarily as a method for managing the underfunded budgets of our courts and correctional systems, it will cease to be a bargain in the larger sense and will become, instead, too great a price for our society to pay.

SETTLEMENTS IN CIVIL CASES

Just as most criminal cases are resolved through plea-bargaining procedures prior to trial, the vast majority of civil disputes are also resolved (or settled) without a trial, typically in private negotiations between attorneys representing the disputing parties. This process is known as **settlement negotiation**. (Attorneys also negotiate with insurers, regulators, and sometimes even with their own clients in an attempt to settle a dispute.) Most divorces, landlord–tenant disputes, claims of employment discrimination, and accident cases are resolved without a trial.

Large class-action lawsuits that may involve hundreds or thousands of plaintiffs are also typically resolved in settlement negotiations. In 2012, attorneys representing the oil giant BP and more than 100,000 Gulf Coast residents and businesses affected by the 2010 Deepwater Horizon oil spill reached a settlement that eliminated the threat of a trial. One commentator suggested that as lawsuits go, "this was going to be the Super Bowl wrapped up in the

World Series—only with much, much more money at stake" (Walsh, 2012).

Lawyers spend considerable time negotiating settlements because they would almost always prefer the certainty of a negotiated compromise to the uncertainty of a jury trial. Because their caseload (or docket) is so large, judges would always prefer that the participants in a civil dispute resolve their differences themselves, without using the considerable resources necessary for a trial.

Disputing parties obviously have different objectives in settlement negotiations. Hence, the attorneys representing these parties will have very different roles to play in the negotiation. In a personal injury case, a common type of civil dispute, plaintiffs' lawyers will try to extract every dollar that a defendant will pay, whereas defendants' lawyers will try to avoid paying all but the minimal cost necessary to settle the case. In the Deepwater Horizon case, plaintiffs' attorneys were motivated to avoid years of uncertain litigation and the possibility of obtaining less money for their clients than they would receive in the settlement, and attorneys representing BP opted to settle in order to avoid having the company's mistakes paraded in open court, particularly in light of ongoing litigation with federal, state, and local governments.

Some lawyers have become highly skilled at negotiating settlements. Consider, for example, the case of Valerie Lakey, who, at age 5, was disemboweled by the suction power of a pool drain pump produced by Sta-Rite Industries. Valerie sat on an open pool drain after other children removed the protective cover that a swim club had failed to install prop-

Informal negotiations on the courthouse steps

erly. Despite 12 prior suits with similar claims, Sta-Rite continued to make and sell drain covers lacking installation warnings. Former North Carolina senator and presidential hopeful John Edwards served as the attorney for plaintiffs Valerie Lakey and her family. After lengthy negotiations that continued "backstage" throughout the trial, Sta-Rite eventually settled and the Lakey family received $25 million, the largest personal injury award in North Carolina history.

What makes some lawyers so skilled at negotiating and winning such large damages? Do they have a knack for deciding whether a case is worth pursuing and an ability to assess accurately what it might be worth? Do they have a particular interpersonal style that facilitates compromise? Or do they have especially shiny crystal balls? In recent years, psychologists, economists, and game theorists (scientists who study behavior in strategic situations) have conducted studies of actual and simulated settlement negotiations (though they have yet to study the crystal-ball hypothesis!) to determine what factors predict settlement amounts.

Factors That Determine Settlement Amounts

The legal merits of the case matter most, of course. In an automobile accident case in which there is strong evidence of the defendant's reckless driving and in which there are obvious and severe injuries, a plaintiff will recover more money than will a plaintiff whose case is weak on liability or damages.

Deepwater Horizon explosion in the Gulf of Mexico

But other factors matter as well. Negotiation theory suggests that outcomes are also influenced by the negotiators' **reservation price**, or bottom line (Korobkin & Doherty, 2009). The defendant's reservation price is the *maximum* amount of money that he or she would be willing to pay to reach an agreement, whereas the plaintiff's reservation price is the *minimum* amount of money that he or she would accept to settle the claim. Say that a plaintiff was injured when a piece of machinery malfunctioned, injuring him or her and resulting in medical and other costs of approximately $100,000. The defendant manufacturer may set a reservation price of $75,000, authorizing the defense attorney to negotiate a settlement that does not exceed that amount, while the plaintiff may set a reservation price of $25,000, meaning that he or she will accept nothing less. Though the parties are not initially aware of one another's reservation prices, they have a $50,000 "bargaining zone" in which to negotiate a compromise. If they fail to reach a compromise, negotiators walk away from the bargaining table and the case goes to trial. Various psychological factors influence reservation points, including perceptions of the likely outcome if the case goes to trial and negotiators' goals and views on the merits of the case.

In considering the merits of their case, plaintiffs, defendants, and attorneys alike are influenced by psychological biases, often referred to as **heuristics** (Greene & Ellis, 2007; Kahneman, 2011). One such heuristic, the **self-serving bias**, occurs when people interpret information or make decisions in ways that are consistent with their own interests, rather than in an objective fashion. When evaluating their cases, involved parties often have difficulty seeing the merits of the other side, believing that the evidence favors their position and that the fairest resolution is one that rewards them. For example, laypeople who were asked to play the role of either the plaintiff or defendant in a personal injury case involving an automobile–motorcycle collision and to assess the value of the case exhibited the self-serving bias. Although all participants had the same information, those who evaluated the case from the perspective of the plaintiff believed a fair settlement in the case was, on average, nearly $18,000 more than the amount suggested by the "defense" (Loewenstein, Issacharoff, Camerer, & Babcock, 1993). Self-serving biases can also lead to impasse because people who are unable to take the perspective of their negotiation opponents are less likely to successfully reach a deal than those who are able to take their opponents' perspective (Galinsky, Maddux, Gilin, & White, 2008).

Another heuristic, termed the **anchoring and adjustment bias**, occurs when negotiators are strongly influenced ("anchored") by an initial starting value and when, in subsequent discussion, they do not sufficiently adjust their judgments away from this starting point. This bias is quite pervasive, and even wildly extreme anchors can influence judgments. People provided higher estimates of the average temperature in San Francisco when first asked whether it was higher or lower than 558 degrees, a number that may have induced people to consider the (unlikely) possibility that San Francisco temperatures are high (cited by Guthrie, Rachlinski, & Wistrich, 2001). In the context of settlement negotiations, the first offer can serve to anchor the final negotiated compromise; the higher the offer, the higher the ultimate settlement (Korobkin & Doherty, 2009).

Many legal disputes involve intense emotions that can also influence the likelihood of resolution. Imagine, for example, the despair and anguish that Rachel Barton Pine must have experienced after being dragged 200 feet underneath a Chicago commuter train in 1995. The then–21-year-old classical violin prodigy had her left leg severed above the knee, lost part of her right foot, and badly injured her right knee as terrified passengers tried to alert the engineer to halt the train. Barton sued the train company for $30 million. After several years of negotiations and 25 operations, she received nearly that amount and gave a sizeable portion to charity.

Emotions on the part of plaintiffs, defendants, and their attorneys all play a role in negotiation. The emotion most closely associated with disputes may be anger; parties involved in settlement discussions often feel resentment, antagonism, and sometimes outright fury. Presumably those expressions would harm the chances for concessions and compromise, and psychological data suggest that they do. Higher levels of anger on the part of negotiators are related to angry responses from the other party (Friedman et al., 2004), less regard for one's adversary (Allred, Mallozzi, Matsui, & Raia, 1997), and a greater frequency of impasse (Moore, Kurtzberg, Thompson, & Morris, 1999). Angry disputants have difficulty resolving their competing claims.

If anger tends to inhibit dispute resolution, do more positive emotions tend to enhance it? The answer is yes; positive emotions such as happiness

Attorney questioning witness during a trial

foster cooperation and concession making (Kopelman, Rosette, & Thompson, 2006), stimulate creative problem solving (deVries et al., 2012), increase the likelihood that parties will disclose personal information (Forgas, 2011), and positively influence negotiators' expectations (Carnevale, 2008). Experiencing positive emotions improves one's chances for successful settlement negotiations.

WHAT IS THE PURPOSE OF A TRIAL?

Sometimes settlement negotiations fail and plea bargains prove to be elusive. In those situations, disputants have no choice but to have their case resolved in a trial, a topic to which we devote the remainder of this chapter. Every trial, civil or criminal, presents two contrasting versions of the truth. Both sides try to present the "facts" in question in such a way as to convince the judge or the jury that their claims are true. The judge or jury must render judgments on the probable truth or falsity of each side's statements and evidence.

The jury system evolved from an ancient ritual during which a defendant stood before a priest, surrounded by friends who swore that the defendant had not committed the crime. But the victim also brought friends who swore to just the opposite (Kadri, 2005). Because this arrangement was not especially satisfactory to anyone, the English monarchy began to have defendants appear in front of a panel of citizens whose

task was to swear to the innocence or guilt of the defendant.

If one is asked about the purpose of a modern trial, the first response might be "to determine the truth, of course." But is this really the prime function of a trial? In fact, trials also serve other purposes: They provide a sense of stability and a way to resolve conflicts so that the disputants can receive satisfaction. Many years ago, Miller and Boster (1977) identified three images of the trial that reflect these contrasting conceptions and that still hold true today.

The Trial as a Search for the Truth

Many people see a trial as a rule-governed event involving the parties' collective search for the truth (Miller & Boster, 1977). This view assumes that what really happened can be clearly ascertained—that witnesses are capable of knowing, remembering, and describing events completely and accurately. Although this image of the trial recognizes that the opposing attorneys present only those facts that buttress their positions, it assumes that the truth will emerge from the confrontation of conflicting facts. It also assumes that judges or jurors, in weighing these facts, can "lay aside their prejudices and preconceived views regarding the case and replace such biases with a dispassionate analysis of the arguments and evidence" (Miller & Boster, 1977, p. 25).

But this image of the trial as a rational, rule-governed event has been challenged on several grounds. Eyewitnesses are not always thorough and accurate reporters, as the legal system would like to believe. Interrogations can sometimes result in false confessions, and jurors are not particularly good at distinguishing false confessions from true confessions. Jurors may have difficulty setting aside their own experiences and prejudices. Although this image of the trial remains as an inspiring ideal, other images need to be considered as well.

The Trial as a Test of Credibility

A second conception—that the trial is a test of credibility—acknowledges that facts and evidence are always incomplete and biased. Hence the decision makers, whether judge or jury, must not only weigh the information and evidence but also evaluate the truthfulness of the opposing sources of evidence (Miller & Boster, 1977). They must focus on the way evidence is presented, the qualifications of witnesses, and the inconsistencies between witnesses. Competence and trustworthiness of witnesses take on added importance in this image.

The image of the trial as a test of credibility also has problems. Both judges and jurors can make unwarranted inferences about witnesses and attorneys on the basis of race, gender, mannerisms, or style of speech. Judges' and jurors' judgments of credibility may be based more on stereotypes, folklore, or "commonsense intuition" than on the facts.

The Trial as a Conflict-Resolving Ritual

The first two images share the belief that the primary function of a trial is to produce the most nearly valid judgment about the guilt of a criminal defendant or the responsibility of a civil defendant. The third image shifts the function of the trial from determining the truth to providing a mechanism to resolve controversies. Miller and Boster (1977) express it this way: "At the risk of oversimplification we suggest that it removes primary attention from the concept of doing justice and transfers it to the psychological realm of *creating a sense that justice is being done*" (p. 34). Truth remains a goal, but participants in the trial process also need both the opportunity to have their "day in court" and the reassurance that, whatever the outcome, "justice was done." In other words, they need closure that only a trial can provide.

A trial conducted in Oklahoma in 2004 exemplified this desire for closure. Several years before,

Oklahoma City bombing suspect Terry Nichols was convicted on federal charges and sentenced to life in prison, rather than to death (his codefendant, Timothy McVeigh, was executed in 2001). An Oklahoma prosecutor, responding to some victims' families who were eager to see Nichols also put to death, charged him in state court with 161 counts of first-degree murder (for the 160 people and 1 fetus who were killed in the blast) and requested the death penalty. But Nichols was again spared execution when this second jury, despite convicting him, deadlocked over his sentence. By law, Nichols was sentenced (again) to life in prison—161 consecutive life sentences, to be exact—and those families hoping for closure were disappointed (again).

The stabilizing function of a trial is worthless, of course, if the public doubts that justice was done in the process. That sense of closure is sometimes missing after a trial; the widespread dissatisfaction in some segments of our society with the outcome of O. J. Simpson's murder trial (Brigham & Wasserman, 1999) ensured continued media interest and public fascination with his actions and statements. The belief that "he got away with murder" even led to proposals to reform and restrict the jury system. Other segments of society were equally dissatisfied with the verdict in Simpson's civil trial, in which he was found liable for the deaths of his ex-wife and her friend Ronald Goldman. Perhaps together, the verdicts in the two trials converged on a reasonable outcome—Simpson probably was the killer, but this couldn't be proven beyond a reasonable doubt, the level of certainty required for a criminal conviction.

These three contrasting images remind us that truth in the legal system is elusive, and that truth seekers are subject to human error, even though the system seems to assume that they approach infallibility. The failure to achieve perfection in our decision making will become evident as we review the steps in the trial process.

STEPS IN THE TRIAL PROCESS

In the next section, we sketch out the usual steps in a trial in brief detail. Though some of these procedures are conducted out of the public eye, they all involve—either implicitly or explicitly—issues of interest to psychologists.

Preliminary Actions

Discovery is the pretrial process by which each side tries to gain vital information about the case that will be presented by the other side. This information includes statements by witnesses, police records, documents, material possessions, experts' opinions, and anything else relevant to the case.

The U.S. Constitution provides criminal defendants with the right to have the charges against them judged by a jury of their peers, though a defendant can decide instead to have the case decided by a judge. If the trial is before a jury, the selection of jurors involves a two-step process. The first step is to draw a panel of prospective jurors, called a *venire*, from a large list (usually based on lists of registered voters and licensed drivers). Once the venire for a particular trial has been selected—this may be anywhere from 30 to 200 people, depending on the customary practices of that jurisdiction and the nature of the trial—a process known as *voir dire* is employed to question and select the eventual jurors. Prospective jurors who reveal biases and are unable to be open-minded about the case are dismissed from service, so the task of jury selection is really one of elimination. Prospective jurors who appear free of these limitations are thus "selected." Voir dire can have important effects on the outcome of the trial.

The Trial

All trials—whether related to criminal law or to civil law—include similar procedural steps. At the beginning of the trial itself, lawyers for each side are permitted to make **opening statements**. These are not part of the evidence, but they serve as overviews of the evidence to be presented. The prosecution or plaintiff usually goes first, because this side is the one that brought charges and bears the burden of proof. Attorneys for the defendant, in either a criminal or civil trial, can choose to present their opening statement immediately after the other side's opening statement or to wait until it is their turn to present evidence.

Some psychologists have wondered whether the timing of the opening statement matters. In other words, would it be preferable for the defense attorney (and more beneficial to the defendant) if the defense's opening statement immediately followed the prosecutor's opening statement or would it be better for the defense attorney to wait until all of the prosecution witnesses have testified? Their study, using a mock jury simulation, varied the timing of the defense opening statement in an auto theft case (Wells, Wrightsman, & Miene, 1985). The results were striking: When the defense opening statement was given earlier rather than later, verdicts were more favorable to the defense, and the perceived effectiveness of the defense attorney was enhanced. Defense attorneys who take their first opportunity to make an opening statement can apparently counter the story told by the prosecutor, or at least urge jurors to consider an alternative interpretation of the evidence.

After opening statements, the prosecution or plaintiff calls its witnesses. Each witness testifies under oath, with the threat of a charge of **perjury** if the witness fails to be truthful. That witness is then cross-examined by the opposing attorney, after which the original attorney has a chance for **redirect questioning**. Redirect questioning is likely if the original attorney feels the opposition has "impeached" his or her witness; **impeachment** in this context refers to a cross-examination that has effectively called into question the credibility (or reliability) of the witness.

The purpose of redirect examination is to "rehabilitate" the witness, or to salvage his or her original testimony. The defense, however, has one more chance to question the witness, a process called **recross** (short for "re-cross-examination"). After the prosecution or plaintiff's attorneys have presented all their witnesses, it is the defense's turn. The same procedure of direct examination, cross-examination, redirect, and recross is used. After both sides have presented their witnesses, one or both may decide to introduce additional evidence and witnesses and so ask the judge for permission to present **rebuttal evidence**, which attempts to counteract or disprove evidence given by an earlier witness.

Once all the evidence has been presented, each side is permitted to make a **closing argument**, also called a summation. Although jurisdictions vary, typically the prosecution or plaintiff gets the first summation, followed by the defense, after which the prosecution or plaintiff responds and has the final word.

The final step in the jury trial is for the judge to give instructions to the jury. (In some states, instructions precede the closing arguments.) The judge informs the jury of the relevant law. For example, a definition of the crime is given, as well as a statement of what elements must be present for it to have occurred—that is, whether the defendant had the motive and the opportunity to commit the crime. The judge also instructs jurors about the standard they should use to weigh the evidence.

With criminal charges, the jurors must be convinced beyond a reasonable doubt that the defendant is guilty before they vote to convict. Although the concept of "reasonable doubt" is difficult to interpret, generally it means that jurors should be strongly convinced (but not necessarily convinced beyond *all* doubt). Each of us interprets such an instruction differently, and this instruction is often a source of confusion and frustration among jurors.

In a civil trial, in which one party brings a claim against another, a different standard is used. A **preponderance of evidence** is all that is necessary for a finding in favor of one side. Usually, judges and attorneys translate this to mean "Even if you find the evidence favoring one side to be only slightly more convincing than the other side's, rule in favor of that side." Preponderance is sometimes interpreted as meaning at least 51% of the evidence, though it is difficult (and potentially misleading) to quantify a concept that is expressed verbally.

The jury is sometimes given instructions on how to deliberate, but these are usually sparse. Jurors are excused to the deliberation room, and no one—not even the bailiff or the judge—can be present during or eavesdrop on their deliberations. When the jury has reached its verdict, its foreperson informs the bailiff, who informs the judge, who in turn reconvenes the attorneys and defendants (and plaintiffs in a civil trial) for announcement of the verdict.

Now that we have detailed the steps involved in trials, we consider the advantages accorded by these procedures to the prosecution and the defense in criminal trials. You will notice that opposing sides have roughly offsetting advantages. For example, the prosecution gets the first and last chance to address the judge or jury, but it also has the burden of proving its case. The defense, on the other hand, is not given the opportunity to speak first or to speak last. But it has the advantage of not needing to prove anything to the judge or jury. If the prosecution is unable to meet its obligation to convince the judge or jury of the defendant's guilt, then the defendant prevails. What other advantages does each side have in a criminal case?

The prosecution, in its efforts to convict wrongdoers and seek justice, has several advantages, including these:

1. It has the full resources of the government at its disposal to carry out a prosecution. Detectives can locate witnesses and subpoena them. The prosecutor can request testimony from chemists, fingerprint examiners, medical examiners, psychiatrists, photographers, or other appropriate experts.

2. In the trial itself, the prosecution presents its evidence before the defense, getting "first crack" at the jury. At the end of the trial, when both sides are permitted closing arguments, the prosecution again gets to go first and also gets the chance to offer a final rebuttal to the defense attorney's closing argument. Therefore, the prosecution has the advantages of both *primacy* and *recency* in its attempts at jury persuasion, and research shows that information presented first (primacy) and last (recency) has more persuasive influence than information presented in the middle of a discussion.

Trial procedures also provide defendants with certain benefits, including the following:

1. The defense is entitled to "discovery"; the prosecution must turn over all exculpatory evidence (evidence that would tend to absolve the defendant), but the defense does not have to turn over all incriminating evidence.

2. If a trial is before a jury, the defense may have more opportunities than the prosecution to remove potential jurors without giving a reason.

3. Defendants do not have to take the stand as witnesses on their own behalf. In fact, they do not have to put on any defense at all; the burden is on the prosecution to prove beyond a reasonable doubt that the defendant is guilty of the crime.

4. Defendants who are found not guilty can never be tried again for that specific crime. For example, retired National Basketball Association star Jayson Williams was acquitted on the charge of aggravated manslaughter in the death of a chauffeur at his mansion. (In a confusing verdict, the jury convicted Williams of trying to cover up the man's death by describing it as a suicide,

hindering apprehension, and fabricating evidence.) But even if clear evidence of Williams' guilt on the manslaughter charge comes to light at some time in the future, he can never be retried for that offense.

Sentencing

If the defendant in a criminal trial is deemed guilty, a punishment must be decided. In the vast majority of jurisdictions, the trial judge decides punishment. In the past, judges have had wide discretion to impose sentences by taking into account all they knew about the defendant and his actions, regardless of whether those actions constituted a crime or were proven to a jury. But in a landmark 2004 decision, the U.S. Supreme Court ruled that judges may not increase defendants' sentences on the basis of what they perceive as aggravating factors (circumstances that seem to make the "crime" worse). In *Blakely v. Washington* (2004), the Court reserved those determinations for juries.

The ruling came from a case in which the defendant, Ralph Blakely, pled guilty to kidnapping his estranged wife, a crime that carried a penalty of 53 months. But the judge, after deciding that Blakely acted with "deliberate cruelty"—a circumstance that Blakely had not admitted and that no jury had decided—increased his sentence to 90 months. In overturning this sentence (and thereby striking down dozens of state sentencing laws and affecting thousands of cases), the Court said the imposition of additional time violated Mr. Blakely's right to a jury trial.

In a handful of states, sentencing is determined by a jury. After the verdict is rendered, the jury is reconvened, and attorneys present evidence relevant to the sentencing decision. The jury then deliberates until it agrees on a recommended punishment. In cases involving the death penalty, jurors, rather than judges, decide the sentence (*Ring v. Arizona*, 2002).

The Appellate Process

Involvement of guilty defendants within the legal system does not end when they are sentenced to a prison term or to probation. To protect the rights of those who may have been convicted unjustly, society grants any defendant the opportunity to appeal a verdict to a higher level of court. Appeals are also possible in virtually every civil suit.

As in earlier steps in the legal process, a conflict of values occurs as appeals are pursued. One goal is equality before the law—that is, to administer justice consistently and fairly. But appellate courts also try to be sensitive to individual differences in what at first glance appear to be similar cases. Appellate courts recognize that judges and juries can make errors. The appellate process can correct mistakes that impair the fairness of trials; it also helps promote a level of consistency in trial procedures.

When a decision is appealed to a higher court, the appellate judges read the transcript of the trial proceedings, the motions and accompanying documents filed by the attorneys, and written arguments, called briefs, from both sides about the issues on appeal. They then decide whether to overturn the original trial decision or to let it stand. Appellate judges rarely reverse a verdict on the basis of the facts of the case or the apparent legitimacy of that verdict. When they do reverse a verdict, it is usually because they believe that the trial judge made a procedural error, such as allowing controversial evidence to be presented or failing to allow the jury to consider some evidence that should have been included.

If a verdict in a criminal trial is overturned or reversed, the appeals court will either order a retrial or order that the charges be thrown out. In reviewing the decision in a civil case, an appellate court can let the decision stand, reverse it (rule in favor of the side that lost rather than the side that won), or make some other changes in the decision and remand (return) the case to a lower court for reconsideration. One possible conclusion in either civil or criminal appeals is that certain evidence should not have been admitted or that certain instructions should not have been given; hence, a new trial may be ordered.

Psychologists have had relatively little to say about the appellate process. Recent exceptions include a book about psychological aspects of Supreme Court decision making (Wrightsman, 2006) and a study of how judges assess whether prior rulings allowing confessions to be included in trials constituted reversible error (Wallace & Kassin, 2012).

Courtroom of the Future

With only minor variations, courtroom trials and appeals have followed these procedures for much of our nation's history. The trials of John Scopes (tried in 1925 for teaching the theory of evolution in a Tennessee public school science class), Julius and Ethel Rosenberg (tried in 1951 on espionage charges), and defendants facing charges across the United States today all follow essentially the same format. But recently, the introduction of emerging technologies into the legal system has begun to change the look of trials. Today, juries and judges expect attorneys to use more than yellow legal pads and grainy videos. Many jurors, especially younger jurors and those who are more tech-savvy, now expect to see and hear multimedia approaches (Griffin, 2008), and some judges want all documents presented during a trial to be scanned and displayed electronically. The courtroom of the future will look very different from that of the past; some contend that it already does (Feigenson & Spiesel, 2009).

Technologies being used in courts these days extend far beyond surveillance videos, which would have been novel only a few years ago. Newer technologies include

- videoconferencing that permits live, two-way video and audio communication between hearings and trials in courtrooms and remote sites—useful when witnesses and defendants are medically incapacitated, incarcerated, or unavailable during the trial.

- electronic and digital evidence, such as digital recordings, documents, and photographs, that allows judges and jurors to easily observe the evidence themselves, rather than hear others' descriptions of it.

- computer animations and simulations that feature computer-generated depictions of complex physical events like accidents and crimes, often accompanied by voice-overs from participants in the event.

- virtual environment technologies that allow observers to experience a re-creation of an event as if they were actually present when it occurred. Using video game technology, so-called "virtual reality" allows judges and jurors to virtually "walk" through a crime scene or accident site to gauge for themselves what could be seen from different points of view and under relevant lighting conditions.

Each of these high-tech methods raises interesting and complex psychological questions. What effect does remote viewing have on a judge or juror's ability to determine whether a witness is credible and sincere? Are nuances of body language and verbal expression adequately captured in videoconferencing, or are they missing? Does the person testifying at a remote site—a setting that lacks the trappings and formality of a courtroom—feel less obligated to show respect and tell the truth? Would courtroom participants with high-tech experience put more emphasis than others on digital media presented during a trial? Would their opinions carry more weight in the deliberation room? Do computer animations, simulations, and virtual reality reenactments make difficult or technical concepts easier to visualize and, hence, to understand? Might they also serve to cement one version of a contested event in observers' minds, making it harder to construe alternative explanations? In other words, might observers assume that animations, simulations, and virtual realities represent true and uncontroversial facts, rather than just one party's theory of the case (Wiggins, 2006)?

Lawyers and judges should be especially interested in the answers to these questions because according to the Federal Rules of Evidence (2009), evidence may not be introduced into a trial if its **probative value** (relevance to legal proof) is outweighed by any prejudicial effects on the opposing party or if it misleads or confuses the jury (Feigenson, 2010). Thus, it is imperative that judges have good information about the effects of high-tech evidence presentations on legal judgments.

Psychologists have begun to address some of these questions. One study examined the effects of computer animations on jurors' verdicts (Dunn, Salovey, & Feigenson, 2006). In cases involving a plane crash and an automobile accident, mock jurors saw either a computer-animated display of the crash site or a diagram of the scene. Further, the use of animations and diagrams by the plaintiff and defendant was varied, resulting in four versions of the mock trial: (1) plaintiff animation/defendant animation, (2) plaintiff animation/defendant diagram, (3) plaintiff diagram/defendant animation, and (4) plaintiff diagram/defendant diagram.

The results of these variations on verdicts in the plane crash case were unambiguous: When the plaintiff presented an animation and the defendant had only a diagram, 68% of jurors voted in favor of the plaintiff, whereas when both plaintiff and defendant used diagrams, only 32% sided with the plaintiff.

At least in this case, the animation increased the ease by which participants could visualize the events leading up to the crash, allowing the plaintiff to persuade them about the merits of his case. Interestingly, in the car accident case, the animations had far less impact on jurors' verdicts, probably because few of us need help in visualizing automobile accidents. From this study we can conclude that animations have a stronger impact on judgments when the subject matter is relatively unfamiliar to viewers and when only one side uses that evidence (Feigenson, 2010).

Why do animations persuade people in ways that diagrams cannot? Basic psychological theorizing about the **vividness effect** suggests that information has a greater impact on judgments and decisions when it is vivid and attention grabbing than when it is pallid and bland. Information presented in a highly imaginable way is more persuasive than simple verbal descriptions of the same material.

Virtual environments have also piqued psychologists' interests in the notion of **presence**, or the degree to which a user or observer has the impression of actually "being in another world" and present in the virtual environment. For virtual environments to be effective, they should realistically create this alternate reality. But think for a moment about how to objectively measure whether someone is experiencing an alternative reality. It quickly becomes clear why, despite efforts to capture the subjective experience of being present in another world, objective measures are, at present, lacking (Bailenson, Blascovich, Beall, & Noveck, 2006).

A concern about the use of virtual environments in court is that people who witness them may be so swept up in the experience and persuaded by the lifelike nature of these scenes that they have difficulty imagining or visualizing a different point of view. This notion, termed **experiential inflammatory bias**, suggests that in the least, both sides in a trial should be able to manipulate and alter any virtual environment introduced into evidence (Bailenson et al., 2006).

Although virtual environment technology is not yet routinely used in actual trials, that day may arrive soon. (We describe one case that incorporated some of these new technologies in Box 8.4.) Indeed, proponents believe that the technology is already mature enough to warrant its use in court: "If a picture is worth a thousand words, then a … virtual reality simulation should be worth at least ten thousand" (Bailenson et al., 2006, p. 265). The day has already arrived for animations, simulations, remote

---

B o x   8.4   THE CASE OF U.S. ARMY STAFF SERGEANT TERRENCE DILLON IN VIRTUAL REALITY

To treat his high cholesterol levels, U.S. Army Staff Sergeant Terrence Dillon underwent a surgical procedure in February 2002, in which doctors implanted a "new life stent." The stent was designed to cleanse blood of cholesterol and to dissolve cholesterol-forming plaque blocking the arteries. But for Dillon, the stent worked too well, loosening large amounts of plaque that clogged his circulatory system and causing a stroke. Dillon died in March, 2002. Shortly thereafter, the stent's manufacturer, New-Life MedTech, was criminally indicted for manslaughter (Horrigan, 2002).

In truth, none of this actually happened. But these facts served as the basis for a simulated trial, one feature of a legal technology program dubbed "Courtroom 21 Project" by the National Center for State Courts. The project provides technology information to lawyers and judges.

During the "trial," the defense argued that NewLife MedTech was not at fault and that blame lay with the surgeon who allegedly placed the stent in the wrong part of the artery. To bolster that argument, the defense offered the testimony of a nurse who donned a virtual reality headset and specialized goggles, giving him a three-dimensional view of the operating room and allowing him to describe the stent's placement. The prosecution countered by arguing that because the nurse's view of the surgery was obstructed, he was unable to see where the stent had been implanted. Because virtual environment technology allowed jurors themselves to watch a reenactment of the surgery on laptops, they could decide for themselves what the nurse was able to observe. Images were also projected to wide-screen monitors in the courtroom, allowing the judge, lawyers, trial-watchers, and even observers outside the courtroom to view the virtual operation and reach their own conclusions. Whether NewLife MedTech was convicted is largely irrelevant; the noteworthy fact is that the "trial" introduced many people to the courtroom of the future.

Critical Thought Questions

Why might evidence presented via virtual environment technology be more persuasive to decision makers than evidence presented verbally or even visually?

videoconferencing and other forms of digitally presented evidence. To what extent they will alter the way that trials are conducted is a question that will concern psychologists for some time to come.

SUMMARY

1. ***What are the major legal proceedings between arrest and trial in the criminal justice system?*** (1) An initial appearance, at which defendants are informed of the charges, of their constitutional rights, and of future proceedings; (2) a preliminary hearing, in which the judge determines whether there is enough evidence to hold the defendant for processing by the grand jury; (3) action by the grand jury, which decides whether sufficient evidence exists for the defendant to be tried; (4) an arraignment, involving a formal statement of charges and an initial plea by the defendant to these charges; (5) a process of discovery, requiring that the prosecutor reveal to the defense certain evidence; and (6) pretrial motions, which are attempts by both sides to win favorable ground rules for the subsequent trial.

2. ***What is bail, and what factors influence the amount of bail set?*** Bail is the provision, by a defendant, of money or other assets that are forfeited if the defendant fails to appear at trial. In determining whether to release a defendant prior to trial, the judge should consider the risk that the defendant will not show up for his or her trial. Judges also consider the seriousness of the offense and the defendant's prior record as well as the defendant's race and gender.

3. ***Why do defendants and prosecutors agree to plea bargain?*** Plea bargaining is an excellent example of the dilemma between truth and conflict resolution as goals of our legal system. The vast majority of criminal cases end between arrest and trial with the defendant pleading guilty to some (often reduced) charges. Plea bargaining benefits both defendants and prosecutors. Defendants who plead guilty often receive reductions in the charges or in their sentences; prosecutors secure a "conviction" without expending their time at trial.

4. ***What are settlement negotiations, and why are most civil lawsuits resolved through settlement rather than trial?*** Settlement negotiations are private discussions held between the attorneys representing disputing parties in a civil lawsuit. The objective of the negotiations is to resolve the dispute in a manner agreeable to both sides. Settlement negotiations are often preferable to trials because (1) a negotiated compromise is more appealing to most litigants than the uncertainty of a jury trial, and (2) judges have large caseloads (or dockets) and therefore prefer that participants in civil disputes resolve their differences themselves without using the considerable resources necessary to a trial.

5. ***What is the purpose of a trial?*** Every trial presents two contrasting views of the truth. Although at first glance, the purpose of a trial seems to be to determine truth, conflict resolution may be an equally valid purpose. This debate is exemplified by three contrasting images of a trial: (1) as a search for the truth, (2) as a test of credibility, and (3) as a conflict-resolving ritual.

6. ***What are the steps involved in a trial?*** Pretrial procedures include discovery, or the process of obtaining information about the case held by the other side. Once the jury is selected (a process called *voir dire*), the following sequence of steps unfolds in the trial itself:

   a. Opening statements by attorneys for the two sides (prosecution or plaintiff goes first)

   b. Direct examination, cross-examination, and redirect and recross of witnesses, with prosecution witnesses first, then defense witnesses

   c. Presentation of rebuttal witnesses and evidence

   d. Closing statements, or summations, by the two sides, usually in the order of prosecution, then defense, then prosecution again

   e. Judge's instructions to the jury (in some jurisdictions, these come before the closing statements)

   f. Jury deliberations and announcement of a verdict

   g. If the verdict is guilty, determination of the punishment

7. ***How has the introduction of emerging technologies changed the way that trials are conducted?*** Over time, the emergence of more sophisticated technologies into the legal system has begun to change the look of courtroom trials and appeals. As judges, lawyers, and jurors have become more tech-savvy, documentation and presentation methods of the past are being replaced by newer technologies such as computer animations and simulations, videoconferencing, virtual reality, and electronic and digital presentations of evidence. These high-tech methods have raised a number of interesting and complex psychological questions regarding the influence and effectiveness of technology in the courtroom.

KEY TERMS

anchoring and
    adjustment bias

arraignment

change of venue

charge bargaining

closing argument

discovery

exculpatory

experiential
    inflammatory bias

extralegal factors

focal concerns
    perspective

framing effects

grand jury

heuristics

impeachment

indictments

initial appearance

legal factors

matching heuristic

motion *in limine*

opening statements

overconfidence bias

perjury

plea bargains

preliminary hearing

preponderance of
    evidence

presence

preventive detention

probative value

rebuttal evidence

recross

redirect questioning

reservation price

self-serving bias

sentence bargaining

settlement negotiation

vividness effect

Chapter
9

Alternatives to Traditional Prosecution

ORIENTING QUESTIONS

1. What is alternative dispute resolution (ADR)? What are some types of ADR?
2. What is the Sequential Intercept Model?
3. What are the major stages (or intercepts) for community-based alternatives to standard prosecution?
4. What are the similarities and differences between community court and other kinds of problem-solving courts?

The previous chapter described the components of our legal system that have been in place for centuries. Although, valuing precedent as it does, the law is slow to change, the last three decades have witnessed various innovations that are important and useful. These will be discussed in the present chapter. The first major area—alternative dispute resolution— has been applied in both criminal and civil contexts. The second major area of discussion is community alternatives to standard prosecution. Our discussion of this area is framed within the Sequential Intercept Model, which identifies different points at which certain groups of individuals can be diverted from standard prosecution into an approach that is more rehabilitation oriented. The discussion will include relevant research findings, which are very important in considering the effectiveness of interventions at these different stages.

ALTERNATIVE DISPUTE RESOLUTION

If you watch cable and online news and entertainment, you might get the impression that most lawsuits are resolved by a trial by jury. In fact, most cases are resolved through negotiation or by alternative dispute resolution (ADR), and relatively few cases are settled in trials. In a 2001 study of courts in 46 randomly selected counties in 22 states, the National Center for State Courts found that the number of cases tried had decreased by 50% in 10 years (Post, 2004c).

The drop-off of trials in the federal courts— particularly civil trials—is even more dramatic. In 1962, 11.5% of federal civil cases were decided in a trial, compared with 6.1% in 1982, 1.8% in 2002, and only 1.2% in 2009 (Qualters, 2010). On the criminal side, trials also decreased, though not as sharply. In 1962, 15.4% of criminal cases went to trial; in 2002 only 4.7% involved a trial (Galanter, 2004).

These declines are attributable to several factors, including the perceived cost of litigation—the "transaction costs," in economists' language. Lawyers' fees to prepare for and try a case, as well as the fees paid to expert witnesses, often make a trial economically unfeasible. In addition, federal courts pressure litigants to settle or to plead guilty. The federal sentencing guidelines give criminal defendants an incentive to plead guilty because judges can decrease the length of a sentence on the basis of "acceptance of responsibility" (which normally requires a guilty plea) (Galanter, 2004). Finally, federal trials have decreased because it has been some years since Congress has passed sweeping legislation that creates liability for certain actions—legislation such as the Americans with Disabilities Act of 1990 (Qualters, 2010).

In civil cases, federal judges are required to attempt to resolve disputes through ADR, and in both state and federal courts, judges can require litigants to try to settle their cases without going to trial. Increasingly, American courts assume that cases will be settled, not tried, to the point where a trial is viewed "as a failure of the system" (Sanborn, 2002, p. 25). Edmund Ludwig, a judge with over 30 years of experience, describes it this way:

> Litigation represents a breakdown in communication, which consists in the civil area of the inability of the parties to work out a problem for themselves and in the criminal area, of ineffectively inculcating society's rules and the consequences for violating them. Trials are the method we have ultimately used to deal with those breakdowns. However, the goal of our system is not to try cases. Rather, it is to achieve a fair, just, economical, and expeditious result by trial or otherwise (Ludwig, 2002, p. 217).

Many cases are settled by **negotiation**, without the assistance of a third party. Negotiation might be formal, as happens when management and union representatives negotiate a labor contract, or informal, as when attorneys go back and forth in a series of phone calls to settle a personal injury claim. Another informal mechanism involves collaborative divorce, in which lawyers and psychologists work with a divorcing couple to finalize all issues without going to court. Typically, there is a heightened sense of trust, openness, and disclosure in collaborative divorce (Degoldi, 2008). We describe one example in Box 9.1.

As in trials, procedural justice considerations are important in successful negotiations. People care about both the outcome of negotiations and the fairness of the process. In a study in which law students role-played attorneys in a simulated negotiation about a contract dispute, participants thought negotiations were fair when they believed that they had been listened to and treated with courtesy, and when they

---

Box 9.1 THE CASE OF SARAH SMITH, DAVID BOYLE, AND THEIR SWIFT COLLABORATIVE DIVORCE

Whereas a full-scale divorce litigated in a courtroom can cost more than $75,000 and a negotiated divorce involving adversarial lawyers can total more than $25,000, Sarah Smith and David Boyle spent roughly $5,000 for their collaborative divorce in 2005. Smith and Boyle, who live in neighboring suburbs of Boston, were mainly concerned about the welfare of their children, ages 5 and 9 at the time. Together with their lawyers, Smith and Boyle worked out an arrangement by which the children spend time with each of them.

Lawyers are increasingly likely to embrace collaborative divorce. As of 2007, more than 20,000 had received training in collaborative law, which requires them to pledge to work together with their clients and other professionals to devise outcomes that are beneficial to all parties.

Children of a divorcing couple reap a secondary benefit from collaborative divorce. Psychologists have shown that an important factor in emotional well-being in children is the nature of the parents' post-divorce relationship (Baxter, Weston, & Qu, 2011). The extent of court involvement during the divorce (little, moderate or high levels of litigation) is associated with children's coping ability: the higher the level of court involvement, the less successful the coping ability (Bing, Nelson, & Wesolowski, 2009).

Critical Thought Question
What factors explain the increasing popularity of collaborative divorce as compared to traditional, adversarial methods of divorcing?

---

perceived the other party as trustworthy (Hollander-Blumoff & Tyler, 2008).

Arbitration

One form of ADR, binding **arbitration**, bears the closest resemblance to a trial. When the parties agree to binding arbitration, they agree to accept the decision of an arbitrator. Salary arbitration in major league baseball is a good example of binding arbitration. The contract between the owners and the players' union provides that players' salary disputes are settled by binding arbitration, and it further provides that the arbitrator must accept either the owner's offer or the union's offer but cannot split the difference. The parties have an incentive to make an offer as close as possible to the player's "value" (their estimate of the arbitrator's valuation of the player's worth). Although many cases require binding arbitration, other cases are resolved by nonbinding arbitration. If one of the parties is dissatisfied with the arbitrator's decision, that person may ask that the case be tried before a judge or jury.

Arbitration, whether binding or nonbinding, uses trial-like procedures. The parties present evidence and argue the case, and the arbitrator makes a decision. Though initially promoted as a way to avoid the contentiousness and expense of a trial, in recent years arbitration has been criticized for being overly formal and time consuming (Stipanowich, 2010). Other methods for resolving disputes, such as mediation (which we discuss later), are more streamlined.

Summary Jury Trial

The **summary jury trial** is an interesting variation on arbitration. The concept was created by Federal District Court Judge Thomas Lambros in the early 1980s as a result of his difficulty resolving two personal injury cases using other forms of ADR. The parties in these cases refused to settle, each assuming that it would get a more favorable verdict from a jury. Judge Lambros reasoned that chances for settlement would increase if the parties had a sense of what a jury would do. He instituted an abbreviated and expedited form of a jury trial that he suspected would be especially helpful in resolving relatively simple, lower-value cases.

A summary jury trial is much like a conventional jury trial, though shorter. A jury is empanelled, and the lawyers tell the jurors what the witnesses would say if they were present. The lawyers argue the case and try to answer the jurors' questions about the facts. The judge tells the jury what the law is and tries to answer jurors' questions about the law. The jurors then deliberate and decide the case. In the original conception of a summary jury trial, the "verdict" did not bind the parties, it was merely advisory. In recent years, verdicts have become binding and enforceable. Regardless of these variations, the intent is the same: the process educates the lawyers and clients on how a conventional jury might view the facts and the law. Once educated, the lawyers and their clients are more amenable to settling the case (National Center for State Courts, 2012).

The *American Bar Journal* has reported favorable comments from lawyers and judges who had availed themselves of this form of ADR (McDonough, 2004). Commenting on the summary jury trial, federal judge William Bertelsman said,

> I believe that substantial amounts of time can be saved by using summary jury trial in a few select cases. Also … the summary jury trial gives the parties a taste of the courtroom and satisfies their psychological need for a confrontation with each other. Any judge or attorney can tell you that emotional issues play a large part in some cases. When emotions are high, whether between attorneys or parties, cases may not settle even when a cost-benefit analysis says they should. A summary jury trial can provide a therapeutic release of this emotion at the expenditure of three days of the court's time instead of three weeks (*McKay v. Ashland Oil Inc.*, 1988, p. 49).

Mediation

Another form of ADR, **mediation** involves a neutral person (the mediator) who works with the litigants and their lawyers to achieve a settlement of the controversy. The mediator does not have authority, as an arbitrator does, to decide the controversy. Rather, the mediator acts as a facilitator. Mediation often involves *shuttle diplomacy*, a term associated with former Secretary of State Henry Kissinger. Much as Kissinger would "shuttle" between the two sides in international diplomacy, the mediator goes back and forth between the parties, meeting first with one side, then with the other, in an attempt to broker an agreement between the two (Hoffman, 2011).

One thinks of lawyers as eager to do battle—to slay their opponents with rhetorical swords. Increasingly though, disputants prefer procedures in which a neutral third party helps them to craft a resolution of their own; in short, people prefer mediation (Shestowsky, 2004). Why? People are **risk averse**; they work to avoid taking risks. They prefer that controversies be settled *by them* rather than decided *for them*. A mediator can assist in facilitating a resolution, and people prefer the certainty of a settlement over the uncertainty of arbitration or trial.

Mediation also has a role in divorce proceedings. An alternative to collaborative divorce (in which both parties employ their own lawyers, who agree to cooperate), a mediated divorce involves a third party who helps the couple to dissolve their marriage. Psychologists have assessed whether a mediated divorce leads to more desirable outcomes than litigation. One remarkable study assessed parent–child contact and co-parenting in families whose custody disputes had been resolved 12 years earlier by either mediation or litigation (Emery, Laumann-Billings, Waldron, Sbarra, & Dillon, 2001). Families who mediated custody showed more cooperation and flexibility than families who litigated. In particular, nonresidential parents who mediated had more contact with their

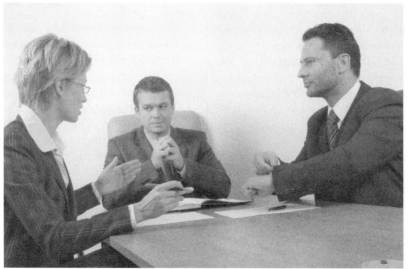

Mediator working with litigants to settle a case

children and were more intimately involved in parenting, and fathers who mediated were much more satisfied with their custody arrangements. Compared to litigated divorces, mediation apparently encourages parents to comply with divorce agreements, remained involved in their children's lives, and renegotiate relationships in a more adaptive way.

Beliefs about Alternative Dispute Resolution

What form of ADR do people tend to favor? The answer to this question is important because ADR procedures will be accepted and used only if they are respected and considered legitimate. A recent study investigated the preferences for different dispute resolution features among people involved in actual disputes. They indicated their preferences for a particular process and set of rules. The most consistent finding was that participants favored options that offered them control (e.g., a neutral third party helping disputants to arrive at *their own* resolutions, and processes that allow disputants to control *their own* presentation of evidence) (Shestowsky & Brett, 2008).

Should courts force litigants to try ADR before setting a case for trial? The reports from courts that mandate ADR are generally positive. Attorneys like the process, believing that it is fair and saves clients time and money (Boersema, Hanson, & Keilitz, 1991). The counterargument is that litigants have a constitutional right to trial by judge or jury. Judges are paid to enforce that right; mandating ADR undermines it. According to Federal Judge G. Thomas Eisele (1991), mandatory ADR can lead to an unintended effect: some lawyers (he calls them "piranhas") file meritless claims, knowing that their claims will have "settlement value" in mediation.

COMMUNITY ALTERNATIVES TO STANDARD PROSECUTION

We now move from ADR, which is practiced in both civil and criminal law, to community alternatives to standard prosecution (criminal law only). Have you ever wondered whether there was a more effective way than conviction and incarceration for our society to respond to certain kinds of offenders? Drug abuse was once considered an indication of poor motivation

and weak character; now it is treated as a disease. But what about the offender who continues to break the law by stealing, possessing substances that are illegal, and behaving in a way that reflects being high? If such an individual were successfully treated for drug abuse and monitored to ensure that she did not continue to behave in illegal ways, that would be a far better approach than incarceration. This is a description of the kind of offender who is well-suited for a drug court—a specialized kind of **problem-solving court**, developed to rehabilitate and monitor individuals in the community rather than incarcerate. Such problem-solving courts are discussed in this section.

There has been increasing attention over the last decade to community-based alternatives to conviction and imprisonment for certain individuals. As we will discuss, such community-based alternatives have developed because they are more humane, less expensive, and make our society safer (or at least do not increase the risk of crime). Typically these individuals are members of a certain subgroup whose experience or mental health disorder might account for a number of minor offenses committed by members of this group. For example, individuals with severe mental illness—schizophrenia, bipolar disorder, major depressive disorder, and other psychotic disorders—might have a greater likelihood of being arrested for domestic disturbances, encounters with police, and interactions with other citizens when the symptoms of such disorders are active. Individuals with serious drug problems may become involved in offenses such as theft, prostitution, and public intoxication for reasons related directly to the need to buy drugs and the consequences of taking them. Military veterans may become involved in offenses such as traffic violations, drug or weapon possession, or problematic interactions with police, fueled in part by posttraumatic stress disorder or traumatic brain injury. Each of these examples recognizes that some criminal offending involves acting upon symptoms that could be contained with targeted treatment and rehabilitation.

This is the basic philosophy underlying the development of community alternatives to standard criminal arrest, prosecution, and incarceration. Three major justifications have been offered for the development and expansion of such community alternatives. The first is humanitarian. In the words of the U.S. Supreme Court, the Eighth Amendment (one part of which states that "cruel and unusual punishments" may not be inflicted) must draw its meaning from the "evolving standards of decency" that characterize a "maturing society" (*Trop v. Dulles*, 1958). But *Trop v. Dulles* was a death penalty case. What about criminal offenses that are much less serious? For such less serious crimes, our society has identified behavioral health disorders that could be handled through standard criminal justice processing—but might also be addressed in a more humane and rehabilitative fashion through alternative approaches. Some offenders with severe mental illness are similar to general offenders in most of their rehabilitation needs (Skeem & Eno Louden, 2006). But those whose crimes involve influences that are specific to their disorders may be very good candidates for lower-intensity, briefer, and community-based interventions—particularly when they present a low risk for criminal offending, and this risk is reduced even further by treating the disorder.

The second justification for community-based alternatives to standard prosecution is cost. Put simply, it is much less expensive to monitor and treat an offender in the community than it is to incarcerate that individual. California, for example, currently spends about $2 billion annually on health care for offenders who are incarcerated in prison. This is more than $11,000 for each inmate (Kiai & Stobo, 2010), and does not include the non-health-care costs of operating prisons. Individuals who are provided with treatment and monitoring services in the community but do not need housing or board—and may be able to continue working—cost much less to rehabilitate.

The third justification involves the kind of specialized treatment services that can be provided in the community, as contrasted with those that can be delivered in a prison or jail. Correctional facilities house inmates who, as a group, have wide-ranging rehabilitation needs. More inmates need job training, housing assistance, or substance abuse rehabilitation, for example, than require the specific combination of medication, psychosocial skills intervention, co-occurring disorder treatment, and recovery that is optimal in working with inmates with severe mental illness. In addition, correctional facilities must prioritize security and rule compliance highly, which reduces the resources available for treatment and rehabilitation. When populations are more homogeneous (e.g., as in mental health or drug treatment settings), and security concerns are fewer, then specialized and intensive treatment is more feasible.

Community-Based Alternatives and the Sequential Intercept Model

One of the useful models describing community-based alternatives is the **Sequential Intercept Model** (Munetz & Griffin, 2006). It identifies five stages of the overall criminal justice process at which standard steps could be interrupted and a community treatment alternative substituted. These steps are: (1) law enforcement and emergency services; (2) post-arrest: initial detention/initial hearing and pre-trial services; (3) post-initial hearings: jail/prison, courts, forensic evaluations, and commitments; (4) re-entry from jails, prisons, and forensic hospitalization; and (5) community corrections and community support. This model is relatively new, so its impact has grown very recently. A review of the evidence for intervention effectiveness at each of these intercepts has been published (Heilbrun et al., 2012), and a book describing its applications has been completed (Griffin, Heilbrun, Mulvey, DeMatteo, & Schubert, in press). However, since this section focuses on community-based alternatives prior to incarceration, we will consider only the first three intercepts in this discussion.

Law Enforcement and Emergency Services (Intercept 1). When individuals with behavioral health disorders encounter police or other "first responders," it is the first step in the process that can result in arrest, criminal charges, conviction, and incarceration. Annual police encounters with citizens with mental health problems have been estimated at more than 300 encounters per 100,000 population across jurisdictions, with this rate increasing annually (Durbin, Lin, & Zaslavska, 2010). In some such encounters, arrest is unnecessary. What if police officers received specialized training in recognizing behavioral health symptoms—and interacting with such individuals in a way that did not result in the escalation of conflict, but instead perhaps yielded the opportunity for needed treatment? This is the goal of **specialized police responding**. In particular, the approach known as **Crisis Intervention Team (CIT)** (Compton, Bahora, Watson, & Oliva, 2008) provides police and other front-line responders with enhanced knowledge and behavioral skills for use when they encounter individuals who may be experiencing a behavioral health crisis. CIT is intended to increase the number of treatment-oriented dispositions and decrease the number of minor arrests in such cases,

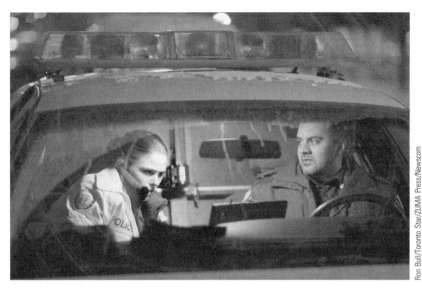

Police CIT (Crisis Intervention Team)

as well as decreasing the number of incidents in which the individuals or the police officers are harmed. For instance, an individual with bipolar disorder, off medication and in the midst of a manic episode, might be taken to the local psychiatric emergency room rather than arrested for disturbing the peace and battery on an officer if encountered by CIT-trained police. We share a representative story in Box 9.2, provided by a CIT-trained officer in Florida, describing the difference that such CIT training can make in correctional facilities as well as in the community.

What is the evidence that CIT is effective in diverting such individuals, resulting in more treatment dispositions and fewer arrests? Research on this topic has been summarized recently (Heilbrun et al., 2012) on several points related to CIT: characteristics and knowledge of CIT-trained officers; characteristics of diverted individuals; and outcomes such as the number of diverted individuals, services delivered to them, and number of arrests following police encounters. CIT-trained police officers reported better preparation for handling interactions with those experiencing a behavioral health crisis (Borum, Williams, Deans, Steadman & Morrissey, 1998), were more likely to help individuals obtain mental health services (Compton, Bahora, Watson, & Oliva, 2008), and were less likely to use physical force (Compton et al., 2008; Skeem & Bibeau, 2008). Jail days were fewer for such individuals, and costs were shifted from criminal justice to treatment sources; diverted

participants were also more likely to utilize mental health treatment (comply with medication, use hospital stay and emergency room visits, participate in counseling) and less likely to be treated for substance abuse on a residential basis (Steadman & Naples, 2005). Following such diversions, those who were diverted did not differ from others in their number of arrests over the next year (Teller, Munetz, Gil, & Ritter, 2006; Watson et al., 2010).

Post-Arrest: Initial Detention/Initial Hearing and Pre-trial Services (Intercept 2).   If an individual is arrested upon first encounter with police or another first responder, the second intercept identifies the point at which that person is brought to "first appearance" before a judge. This occurs before the individual enters a plea or proceeds to trial. In some jurisdictions, there is a specialized team that functions as part of the court system, identifying defendants who would be appropriate for diversion for behavioral health reasons. While some specialized problem-solving courts (e.g., drug court, mental health court, veterans' court, community court) function at this stage, it is more typical to have them take referrals at intercept 3. Accordingly, the second intercept is more likely to result in a diversion directly to treatment, or the assignment of specialized probation.

Intercept 2 has a number of studies using effectiveness criteria like those employed in studies on Intercept 1. Addressing outcomes for individuals who

---

Box 9.2 CIT FOR POLICE, FIRST RESPONDERS ... AND CORRECTIONAL OFFICERS

Please allow me to share this story with you. It is a little long, so be patient. The other day a 65-year-old transient female was arrested on two out-of-county misdemeanor warrants. It seems the woman was involved in a fight earlier in the day, which resulted in numerous cuts, bruises, and abrasions. Upon her arrest, she was initially transported to (a local medical facility) for medical clearance prior to being transported to the county jail. Unable to accurately detail the events leading to her arrest, she was subsequently treated and cleared from the hospital, then sent to directly to the county jail.

Upon arrival, the woman, who is elderly and petite in stature, now bruised and battered and obviously in some form of physical distress, is placed in a female dorm along with other offenders of various classifications. It always amazes me ... that most female offenders will come to the aid of the elderly and help them along with their personal needs. They help them shower, tend to personal needs, and even assist in changing their sheets and clothing. There seems to be an inmate code with the elderly and disabled. Well, as fate would have it, the woman begins to require additional needs which cannot be met in a county jail and this concern is finally brought to the attention of the supervisor by an attentive block officer.

Now here is where it starts to come together. The supervisor in this matter is CIT-trained and just knows in the pit of his stomach that something is wrong and just doesn't make sense. He immediately realizes that the woman needs supplementary care, medical attention, and proactive intervention. He instructs the officers to bring the female to booking, where she can be isolated from the general population. He then notifies the on-duty medic and initiates a 15-minute watch on her so she can be observed on a more regular basis. He instructs the female officers, with the assistance of some female inmates, to change her linen and clothing, which is soiled—and make her comfortable until the medic arrives. The woman appears to be resting comfortably on her bunk, but shortly after the supervisor notices she is extending her arm above her body as if to motion for assistance. The supervisor approaches the cell and realizes something is not right; he gets that gut feeling again. Her breath appears labored and she just had a look on her face that she was in need of some assistance, but was unable to ask. He summoned a female officer for additional aid and again notified the on-duty medic. Weak, frail, and pathetic, she is unable to properly communicate her concerns.

While ... the medical responders (are treating her, they learn) that the woman is asthmatic, suffers from emphysema, requires immediate oxygen, and was in pulmonary distress. The woman was immediately sent to the hospital. After returning, one of the female deputies assigned to the woman ... noticed that when she was assisting the woman with her change of clothing... (there) appeared to be some bruising on and about the woman's groin area. The Deputy then stated that "I think this woman was a victim of a sexual assault" and went on to say, "I wonder if they (hospital) did a rape kit on her?" After piecing various facts together, the supervisor, a trained CIT member, knew something was wrong. Shortly after, while officers were discussing what had happened, the classification officer mentioned that he had received a phone call from a victim in another matter, who stated something to the effect that the guy that assaulted her also tried to rape an elderly female the same night.

Now here is where it all finally comes together. The supervisor, aware of what might have happened to this woman, immediately contacted the Victim Services Advocate and the CID Detectives Bureau. After explaining the circumstances surrounding this matter, the detectives interviewed the woman in the safety of her hospital room. The victim's advocate immediately (pointed out that the perpetrator in this case) might very well be incarcerated in the very same jail on unrelated charges. Subsequently, the county which issued the charges against the woman rescinded the warrants and she was released and transferred to another hospital for treatment. The woman ultimately suffered a stroke while in the hospital and is currently being treated for her injuries and current medical condition. Without the intervention of a trained Crisis Intervention Team member, perhaps this end result would have been much different. Doctors stated that the woman was operating with only 1% lung capacity, and if (she had) gone untreated would not have made it through the night. The woman is alive today ... due to the actions of a CIT-trained individual.

Critical Thought Question
How might CIT training, which is increasingly provided to correctional officers as well as police and first responders, have made a difference in this case?

Source: www.floridacit.org (2008, January). Crisis intervention—affects everyone. Retrieved 5-22-12 from http://www.floridacit.org/Testimonials/Article%20FCSO%20.%20Crisis%20Intervention.pdf

---

receive diversion following arrest, investigators have examined services use, mental health, substance use, offending, and quality of life (Broner, Lattimore, Cowell, & Schlenger, 2004, Broner, Mayrl, & Landsberg, 2005); they have also employed criteria such as whether the individual had housing (National GAINS Center, 2002).

Almost all the existing research identifies differences between diverted and non-diverted individuals at this stage. It is not necessarily accurate to conclude that such differences are *attributable* to the diversion; that would require the use of experimental designs (using random assignment to condition) that are virtually impossible to implement in a criminal justice context. (Judges and clinical administrators are understandably reluctant to allow random assignment of defendants to condition, because an unfortunate outcome such as a serious offense committed by an individual in a no-treatment control group is hard to justify after the tragic event.) However, correlational designs, particularly when accompanied by a comparison group, can provide useful information on the strength (although not the causal direction) of the relationship between the diversion variable and the different outcomes. For example, the studies described later in this paragraph using a comparison group typically derive their groups from two sources—individuals who have been diverted, and those in a standard condition such as probation—and consider how these two groups fare on certain relevant outcomes. This is sometimes called a quasi-experimental design, but it does not have the genuine experimental attribute (random assignment to group) that allows the researcher to control all variables except the one of interest—diversion status—and hence draw conclusions about whether diversion causes differences in outcomes. For this intercept, several investigators noted that diverted individuals had more time in the community (Broner et al., 2005; Hoff, Baranosky, Buchanan, Zonana, & Rosenheck, 1999; Lamberti et al., 2001; Steadman & Naples, 2005), fewer hospital days in the community (Lamberti et al., 2001), fewer arrests (National GAINS Center, 2002; Shafer, Arthur, & Franczak, 2004), and less homelessness (National GAINS Center, 2002).

Post-Initial Hearings: Jail/Prison, Courts, Forensic Evaluations and Commitments (Intercept 3).   The third intercept in the Sequential Intercept Model is the most recognized of the five. This is the stage at which problem-solving courts (also called specialty courts) such as drug courts, mental health courts, homeless courts, domestic violence courts, and community courts have been developed. There have also been courts developed for other groups, such as veterans and prostitutes, but these problem-solving courts are sufficiently new that there has not been research investigating how well they work. Specialized problem-solving courts are also discussed later in this book in Chapter 15.

Problem-Solving Courts.   Certain offenders are summoned back to court and sent to prison again and again.

For them, the criminal justice system has become a dumping ground (Wiener, Winick, Georges, & Castro, 2010). Fed up with this model of "revolving-door" justice, states and communities increasingly are creating problem-solving courts (also called specialty courts) that combine the traditional criminal justice system with specialized treatment-oriented principles to address underlying causes of antisocial behavior (Casey & Rottman, 2005).

The premise of specialty courts is that the legal system should help troubled individuals cope with the chronic problems that brought them into contact with the criminal justice system in the first place. This collaborative, nonadversarial nature of specialty courts, in which judges work side by side with mental health professionals, community agencies, and offenders themselves, focuses more on meeting the ongoing needs of participants than on punishing them.

This approach, in which the law is used as a vehicle to improve people's lives, is called **therapeutic jurisprudence**. Examples include courts specialized to deal with issues of drugs, mental health, homelessness, and domestic violence, as well as veterans' issues, and courts that integrate these problems, for example, by applying mental health court techniques in domestic violence cases (Winick, Wiener, Castro, Emmert, & Georges, 2010). Regardless of the issue, all specialty courts involve a few common elements, including immediate interventions such as drug or alcohol counseling, frequent court appearances in a nonadversarial context, an interdisciplinary team approach, and a set of clearly defined objectives (Watson, Hanrahan, Luchins, & Lurigio, 2001).

Working together with mental health providers, attorneys, and probation officers, judges in these courts become social workers and cheerleaders as much as jurists. Rather than impose punishment, they offer opportunities for people to deal with their addictions, violent tendencies, and squabbles with their landlords (Hartley, 2008). Those who comply with the judges' orders may have their sentences reduced or dismissed.

Although some aspects of these courts are traditional—for instance, judges wear robes—many characteristics of specialty courts are unconventional. For example, the people who appear in court are often called clients rather than defendants. These "clients" are able to speak directly to the judge, rather than communicating through their attorneys. Judges often have a great deal of information about the clients and may

---

B o x 9.3 THE CASE OF A "CLIENT" OF JUSTICE MATTHEW D'EMIC

An immigrant from Barbados in his early 20s arrived in the New York courtroom of Justice Matthew D'Emic in 2003, facing a serious charge of arson after starting a fire that damaged a small public housing complex (Eaton & Kaufman, 2005). The man was delusional, believing that he was the son of God; he had been hospitalized nine times in five years. In a traditional courtroom, the case would have been disposed of by a guilty plea or verdict, and the defendant would have been sent to prison. But in the mental health court over which Justice D'Emic presided, something very different happened. The judge decided that the young man could safely return to live with his mother, provided that he continued to take his medications. Later, when the man complained of stomach cramps and began to miss appointments, the judge suggested that he change his medicine. The judge insisted that the man sign up for job training, allowing him to "graduate" from court with only a misdemeanor on his record. Most remarkably, Justice D'Emic gave the client his cell phone number and urged him to call if he got into a jam. The man said he used it just once, to ask the judge for advice about a woman he was considering marrying.

Critical Thought Question
What are the pros and cons of resolving this dispute in a mental health court, rather than through the workings of the traditional criminal justice system?

---

interact with them over a number of years. On occasion, a friendly relationship develops, as described in Box 9.3.

Drug Courts. The most common form of specialty court is drug court, created to deal with offenders whose crimes are related to addiction. Drug courts developed in response to an increase in antidrug law enforcement efforts and stiffer sanctions for drug offenders during the 1980s and 1990s. By 2011 there were more than 2,000 adult drug courts and 500 juvenile drug courts in the 50 states and many more in the planning phase (Shaffer, 2011).

Drug courts were developed to address the abuse of alcohol and other drugs and criminal activity related to addictions. Drug courts divert cases from the traditional criminal justice system and link drug-addicted offenders with treatment programs and extensive supervision. In exchange for successful completion of the program, the court may dismiss the original charge, reduce or set aside a sentence, assign some lesser penalty, or make a combination of these adjustments. The ultimate goal, in addition to improving the lives of drug-addicted individuals, is to reduce the number of drug offenders in prisons.

How successful are drug courts in reducing drug-related criminal activity? The findings are encouraging, though some drug courts work better than others. A **meta-analysis**—a statistical technique that combines the results of individual studies with similar research hypotheses—of 60 studies that compared a treatment

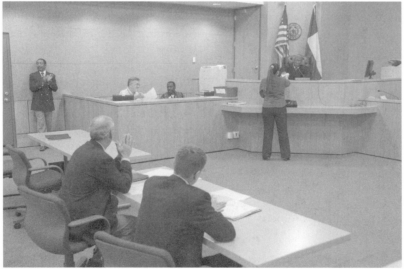

Drug court

Bob Daemmrich/PhotoEdit

condition to a control condition, and that included at least one measure of criminal behavior as an outcome measure, concluded that drug courts have a significant, though modest, effect on recidivism. Offenders assigned to drug court had a 45.5% recidivism rate, while the comparison group had a 54.5% recidivism rate (Shaffer, 2011). The most successful programs were those that excluded violent offenders, worked with and treated offenders who had not yet entered a plea, and employed well-qualified and competent staff who ensured that the program was delivered as designed and who interacted positively with participants.

According to Seattle Judge J. Wesley Saint Clair, "Drug courts work, and not because they're fuzzy—let me tell you, I can be a hard man to deal with." One offender to appear in Judge Saint Clair's courtroom was 36-year-old Jenifer Paris, who, after 22 years of heroin and cocaine use and stretches of prostitution and homelessness, was now clean. "You guys are the first people to believe in me … I'm full of gratitude for the opportunity and for you not kicking me out," she said, tearfully. Replied Judge Saint Clair with a hint of a smile, "We're not done yet" (Eckholm, 2008).

Problem-solving courts have particular appeal within communities, as judges often interact with treatment providers and advocacy groups in a way that is not usually seen in traditional courts. Judges like Judge Saint Clair often play a much more active role, setting aside judicial restraint and impartiality in favor of more direct involvement in the interventions and responses of problem-solving court participants.

Mental Health Courts. The number of individuals hospitalized long term for mental illness has dropped significantly in the past several decades. But **deinstitutionalization**, the long-term trend of closing mental hospitals and transferring care to community-based mental health treatment facilities, has left many mentally ill individuals without services or medication. As a result, the mentally ill have experienced higher rates of homelessness, unemployment, alcohol and drug use, and physical and sexual abuse. They also experience high rates of incarceration: 17% of men and 34% of women in jails suffer from a serious mental illness or post-traumatic stress disorder (Steadman, Osher, Clark Robbins, Case, & Samuels, 2009). Unfortunately, most local jails lack treatment resources and are highly stressful environments, especially for people suffering severe psychiatric illnesses.

According to the **criminalization hypothesis**, a subset of mentally ill offenders committed and were arrested for offenses *caused* by their untreated symptoms of mental illness. Mental health courts were developed for offenders dealing with serious mental illness and operate to "decriminalize" this population. By 2011, there were approximately 250 mental health courts in the United States, with more in the planning stage (Sarteschi, Vaughn, & Kim, 2011).

Following the drug court model, the first decision is whether to divert the offender from the regular criminal courts to mental health court–mandated treatment programs. This decision, which usually requires the consent of both the offender and the victim, is made after an evaluation of the offender and by considering the nature of the offense. If the offender is diverted, the mental health team prepares a treatment plan to lead to long-term psychiatric care and reintegration into society. Close monitoring is essential. Defendants are often assigned to a probation officer who is trained in mental health and who carries a greatly reduced caseload in order to provide a more intensive level of supervision and expertise. The charges are dismissed if the offender follows the treatment plan (Lurigio, Watson, Luchins, & Hanrahan, 2001).

Evaluations of mental health courts suggest that they have been moderately effective in linking individuals to treatment services and in reducing recidivism (Sarteschi et al., 2011), as long as the "full dose" of treatment is provided. People who completed a treatment program associated with a rural North Carolina mental health court were 88% less likely to recidivate than people who did not complete treatment (Hiday & Ray, 2010). Although findings are limited, it appears that mental health courts are also cost effective, reducing the need for services such as psychiatric emergency room visits and other crisis interventions.

There are two broad concerns associated with mental health courts, however. First, participants may feel coerced into participating. Redlich, Hoover, Summers, and Steadman (2010) interviewed 200 participants and found that although most said they agreed to participate, the majority were unaware that the program was voluntary and did not understand many of the nuances of the program, leading researchers to question whether diversion to mental health courts is truly voluntary.

The second concern involves the selection of participants. Specialty courts, including mental health courts, admit only a fraction of the people who are eligible, and admission decisions typically involve multiple perspectives and parties (e.g., clients, treatment providers, judges, prosecutors, defense attorneys, and victims) (Wolff, Fabrikant, & Belenko,

2011). Recent studies suggest that gender and racial bias may influence the way that potential clients are identified, recruited, and eventually selected to participate. Specifically, Caucasian males are overrepresented in mental health courts. According to a meta-analysis of 18 studies (Sarteschi et al., 2011), the majority of participants in mental health courts are Caucasian males in their mid-30s, whereas African-American males constituted the largest demographic group in prisons and jails in 2007 (Sabol & Couture, 2008) and psychiatric diagnoses are more prevalent among disadvantaged minority groups (Minsky, Vega, Miskimen, Gara & Escobar, 2003).

A related concern is the possibility that the selection processes, rather than the interventions provided, account for the modest positive outcomes associated with participating in mental health courts. This could happen if only those potential clients who accept their mental disorder and who are amenable to treatment are invited to participate. After evaluating the selection procedures in six demographically diverse mental health courts, Wolff et al. (2011) concluded that client selection might explain findings on the effectiveness of mental health courts.

Homeless Courts.   People living on the streets are frequently cited for public nuisance offenses such as drinking in public and loitering, and often fail to appear when summoned to court. As a result, they are unable to access vital services such as housing, employment opportunities, and public assistance.

Homeless courts were started in southern California in the late 1980s. They are designed to reach out to marginalized individuals, address the underlying problems that resulted in their homelessness, and reintegrate these people into society. Homeless "court" is typically held in shelters or agencies that serve this population. Rather than being fined or taken into custody, participants are given alternative sentences including assignment to programs and activities such as employment training, counseling, Alcoholics Anonymous meetings, and volunteer work.

New York City has created a variant on this approach termed community courts (discussed in more detail later in this section) in Times Square and the Red Hook area of Brooklyn (Post, 2004a). Meeting in a refurbished Catholic school, the judges, prosecutors, and defenders in the Red Hook community court see their goal as bettering the quality of life for citizens. They know the people of the community and make it a point to know the offenders and to make sure the offenders know them. "The clerk of court has been known to stop her car at street corners and tell defendants the judge has issued a warrant for them and they'd best get over to court" (Carter, 2004, p. 39). The result is a reduction in low-level crime and decreased recidivism by offenders. Some courts aim to reduce homelessness by dealing with landlord and tenant issues and addressing the underlying causes of homelessness—mental illness, poor job skills, and language barriers.

Domestic Violence Courts.   Historically, legal responses to domestic violence cases were fragmented with different court divisions issuing restraining orders, prosecuting perpetrators, and protecting children. Victims have been considered merely "witnesses" and the needs of children have been largely ignored (Casey & Rottman, 2005). In recent years, though, domestic violence courts have coordinated efforts to hold perpetrators accountable, enhance victim and child safety, and promote informed judicial decision making. Domestic violence court personnel work with community-based agencies to strengthen the entire community's response to domestic violence (Sack, 2002). There are now more than 300 domestic violence courts in the United States (Casey & Rottman, 2005).

Like other specialty courts, domestic violence courts involve judges and staff specially trained in the relevant domain, coordination among community resources, and close monitoring of the perpetrator both before and after case disposition. But domestic violence courts differ from other specialty courts in important respects. They start from the premise that offenders' behavior is learned rather than rooted in a treatable addiction or illness. Therefore, court proceedings are primarily adversarial rather than therapeutic. They often involve both victim and offender attempting to reach agreement on protection orders. The needs of children are considered, and co-occurring child abuse and neglect are addressed.

Although few studies have evaluated the effectiveness of domestic violence courts, including their ability to reduce recidivism (Wiener et al. 2010), victims, perpetrators, advocates, and judges have generally reacted positively. Both victims and perpetrators express satisfaction with the court processes and outcomes. Compared with traditional courts, domestic violence courts process cases faster and have higher rates of guilty pleas. In addition, perpetrators are more likely to comply with judge-ordered conditions (Casey & Rottman, 2005).

Community Courts.   In contrast to drug courts and mental health courts, each of which is characterized by jurisdiction over a very specific group, a community court is neighborhood-focused and designed to address local problems such as vandalism, prostitution, shoplifting, vagrancy, and the like. Community courts use problem solving and strive to create relationships with outside stakeholders such as residents, merchants, churches, and schools (Center for Court Innovation, 2012).

Community court participants generally like how they are treated in this kind of court. Participants see them as fairer than traditional courts (Frazer, 2006), and give them high marks in achieving goals such as working productively, assigning useful community service, and treating participants equally

(Justice Education Center, 2002). Perhaps one reason for such favorable ratings has been the use of alternative sanctions by community courts; they are less likely to incarcerate individuals as part of disposition of charges (Hakuta et al., 2008). Although such courts are slightly more expensive when measured by cost per case, they are also associated with higher levels of compliance with sanctions and greater reduction of particular outcomes such as prostitution, illegal vending, and other problems particular to community courts (Kralstein, 2005). We provide one example of a community court in Box 9.4.

Box 9.4 SEATTLE COMMUNITY COURT: CREATIVE SOLUTIONS FOR HIGH-IMPACT, LOW-LEVEL CRIME

When a minor crime is committed over and over, is it still too small for concern? Judge Fred Bonner, who presides over the Seattle Community Court, says that people in survival mode commit acts of theft to survive, and these small crimes often indicate larger societal problems that are significant. Many of the low-level crimes, such as theft and prostitution, committed in Seattle were by individuals who were homeless or mentally ill. "Criminal trespass, theft, prostitution, alcohol and drug-related crime—those were the main kinds of crimes we were dealing with," said Assistant City Attorney Tuere Sala. "They are what we call quality-of-life crimes—and they are usually crimes that are committed more out of a need to survive than an intention to injure others."

Although the intention of such offenses may not be to injure any one individual, the cumulative effect of this kind of offending on a community can be very substantial. "Even if you think it's a faceless crime," said defense attorney Nancy Waldman, "somebody is violated. If a business feels that way, they're more inclined to move their business away from any given district. It has an effect on the whole city." Seattle City Attorney Peter S. Holmes said, "This is a non-partisan issue: Everyone wants to reduce crime and save money, and that's ultimately what community court is about."

In the search for an appropriate response to Seattle's low-level crime, the Seattle Community Court opened in 2005 to serve the downtown district. "We took those individuals who had no place to go, who had spent many days in jail over the years," said Judge Bonner, "and we designed our program to address those needs." Like most community courts across the United States, by combining punishment with help, the Seattle Court seeks to address the social needs associated with crime, repair the harm done, and help transform offenders into productive members of the community. The Seattle Community Court handles only defendants who have committed low-level misdemeanors and do not present a public safety risk. Rather than paying a fine or spending time in jail, all defendants who agree to

participate in community court are assessed for social service needs and then must contact each social service link, such as community service opportunities identified during assessment. It is common practice in community courts to use alternatives to detention, such as community service, as a sanction. Participants in the Seattle Court have completed over 50,000 hours of community service, but Judge Bonner stresses the importance of developing such programs to also educate people about the effects that quality-of-life crime has on the community.

Seattle continues to develop its programs and services to address the needs of offenders as those needs change. "We've just developed a theft awareness class and life-skills training, which would constitute community service," said Judge Bonner, who added that Seattle Community Court also recently launched three stand-alone sites that provide young prostitutes with housing and classes on avoiding sexually transmitted diseases. They can earn community service hours at these sites, as well as receive literacy training and counseling. Seattle Community Court also has new protocols that allow for community service alternatives for individuals with disabilities. The court already partners with 25 community service organizations, and coordinators from the Seattle Community Court have recently started to expand options for individuals not physically able to perform traditional community service. For example, individuals who are unable to pick up trash could be required to answer phones or do filing. "Offenders find that they feel proud of putting in a full day's work," said Karen Murray, of the Associated Counsel for the Accused. "Then we can link them to employment services. Landlords and employers can see people's capacity to change." Seattle Community Court is also evolving to address the different needs that veteran offenders have. "We have a marvelous caseworker from the veterans' hospital coming to our court, and we're trying to do a docket right now just for veterans," said Murray. "They never had criminal histories before and suddenly they're coming back and they're acting out. Do we actually expect people to get off the plane and come back into society as though nothing happened? That's another role for community court in our time."

Another defining element of our time is the strained economic climate experienced throughout the country, and community courts are not immune to this struggle. "We have been suffering some serious budget issues here," said Judge Bonner, "but one of the things that the city council has said is, 'We don't want to reduce or cut community court.' It has been recognized that not only does it save the city money, it also saves lives."

In 2009, the Justice Management Institute issued an independent evaluation of Seattle Community Court. The report stated that individuals involved in the community court committed 66% fewer offenses within 18 months of community court intervention, while those in the control group (undergoing traditional prosecution, and receiving probation if convicted) showed an increase of 50%, suggesting that the court is significantly more effective at reducing the frequency of recidivism than the traditional court process. "The study adds to the value of understanding these kinds of interventions; even though they seem at the surface to be cost-intensive, that may actually not be the case," said Elaine Nugent-Borakove, president of the Justice Management Institute and primary researcher on the evaluation. Furthermore, the Seattle Mayor's Office of Policy and Management estimates that through reduced recidivism and jail use the community court saved the city $1,513,209 during the court's first three years of operation. "We're still studying why crime is down nearly double digits percentage-wise in Seattle over the past 16 months," said City Attorney Holmes, "but I have to think that community court is a factor." Holmes also discussed how community court may have helped alleviate the strain on funds. "When I was on the campaign trail in 2009, it was seen as inevitable that Seattle was going to break ground on a new jail with a price tag of 400 million dollars within the next five years. We have to give some credit to the community court diverting people from incarceration for the fact that Seattle is no longer seriously on the track to build a new jail."

For some who work in the court, the problem-solving approach is new. Craig Sims, chief of the Criminal Division, said, "When I came here in January 2010, I didn't know much about community court. I've been a prosecutor since the late nineties, working in the traditional mode of prosecution: Someone does something wrong, they go to court, they get prosecuted, they go to jail, and we move on to the next one. It was quite refreshing for me to collaborate with the court and the defense to figure out a different way to resolve lower-level crimes." "We're all partners in this," added Holmes, and the Seattle community can see the tangible benefits of this partnership. "We've had some wonderful public events," said Holmes. "Rather than spending time in jail, low-level offenders were out beautifying the community and giving back. Community murals have had unveiling events, heavily attended by local community groups and local media, and the community is able to feel less cynical about the criminal justice system."

"I like the fact that it's an opportunity court," said Sala. "You have an opportunity to make a difference, to change something. As a prosecutor, I would rather see that than the same offenders constantly coming back."

Critical Thought Question
How is community court similar to other kinds of problem-solving courts, such as drug court, mental health court, and veterans' court? How is it different?

Source: Sarah Schweig, Center for Court Innovation, www.courtinnovation.org

Veterans' Courts.   The newest version of specialty court, veterans' courts, was launched in 2008 to address the complicated psychological and legal problems of members of the U.S. military who have returned from war. There are now dozens of such courts across the country.

More than 2 million Americans have served in the wars in Iraq and Afghanistan, making these the largest deployments since the Vietnam War. Approximately one-third of them suffer from posttraumatic stress disorder (PTSD), traumatic brain injury, depression, or other mental illness, and one-fifth are addicted to drugs or alcohol (Marvasti, 2010). Sadly, only about half of the veterans with PTSD or depression have sought help, and of those, only about half received satisfactory care (Tanielian & Jayco, 2008). Given their training in the military to react immediately to any perceived threat, it is not surprising that thousands of returning veterans have reacted impulsively and violently in heated situations. Sometimes, as a result, they have been arrested and charged with serious criminal offenses, including child abuse, sexual assault, and homicide.

In a typical veterans' court, a district attorney may opt to defer prosecution or offer a plea bargain to a reduced charge if it is clear that the offense was related to the veteran's disability and the veteran agrees to seek treatment. Veterans who plead guilty to a nonviolent felony or misdemeanor are teamed with volunteer veteran mentors who ensure that the offender adheres to a strict regimen of counseling, personalized rehabilitation programs, and court appearances. Judges may issue alternative sentences that require offenders to seek psychological treatment. By completing the required program, an offender may avoid going to prison. Whether these provisions should be made available to veterans charged with felonies is a matter of ongoing debate. Because these programs are so new, there are very

Veterans' court

few studies of their effectiveness, though the sparse data that exist suggest that offenders who are diverted to veterans' court are less likely to reoffend than those whose cases go through the traditional criminal justice system (Mador, 2010).

Criticisms of Problem-Solving Courts.   Despite the apparent successes of problem-solving courts, they have also been criticized. One concern is that regardless of the type of specialty court, they are presided over by middle-class judges who inevitably reflect their own middle-class values and who may become inappropriately paternalistic in what they require of people (Eaton & Kaufman, 2005). Some have argued that problem-solving courts lack legitimacy because threatening punishment to coerce rehabilitation is unfair and because guilt or innocence is not determined by a trial (Casey, 2004). Prosecutors and public defenders have expressed concern over the "social worker" roles inherent in drug court philosophy; prosecutors feel pressured to favor rehabilitation of the offender over protection of society, and defenders feel pressured to plead their clients guilty and to inform the court of clients' failure to comply with the terms of probation (Feinblatt & Berman, 2001). Finally, social scientists worry about the lack of rigorous, empirical studies that assess *how* specialty courts influence (or fail to influence) offenders' conduct and what impact they have on the underlying social and psychological problems of offenders (Wiener et al., 2010).

In spite of these criticisms, problem-solving courts have shown remarkable growth and the ability to address some of the contributors to criminal

offending that respond to interventions. As a result, they have the potential to reduce recidivism rates and to improve the lives of participants and their families. Problem-solving courts will very likely continue to develop and evolve, focusing on the reasons why people are in court in the first place.

Research on Intercept 3 of the Sequential Intercept Model is the most mature and consistent of the intercepts described thus far. Specialty courts of different kinds have been studied, with the general focus on the particular characteristics of participants, the perceptions of favorability on the part of such participants, and outcomes such as cost, the nature of appropriate services delivered, and change in justice-relevant outcomes such as rearrest and subsequent incarceration. The evidence on the delivery of appropriate services, the perception of favorability on the part of participants, and the reduction of the incidence of subsequent arrest and incarceration seems largely favorable for drug courts, community courts, and mental health courts.

The Sequential Intercept Model describes two other points at which specialized interventions can occur for offenders in the community: during the transition from incarceration back to the community (the reentry process) and while on parole following release from incarceration. These are both discussed later in this book, in Chapter 15.

The Future of Community-Based Alternatives to Prosecution

The alternatives to traditional prosecution described in this chapter have grown substantially during the last two decades. Part of their appeal is their bipartisan nature. For conservative legislators who focus on public safety and cost, there is growing evidence that alternative approaches such as specialized police responding and problem-solving courts reduce the risk of criminal offending and also cost the criminal justice system less (although they may shift costs to systems that deliver rehabilitation services). For liberal legislators who might be inclined to emphasize rehabilitation, there is more specific treatment and rehabilitation associated with such alternative approaches. But such approaches have grown partly because the original areas of rehabilitation need (e.g., substance abuse, mental health) have been expanded to include a number of areas as well.

Will this trend continue? Will we see the development of "trauma courts" or other similar problem-solving courts? If so, we hope that research is used both in the development and the maintenance of these new courts, so our society has evidence that they work as intended. But it seems unlikely that the community alternatives approach will ever replace our traditional system of prosecution and incarceration, particularly for serious crime. Our society also values the importance of punishing criminal offending through incarceration.

SUMMARY

1. ***What is alternative dispute resolution (ADR)? What are some types of ADR?*** Alternative dispute resolution (ADR) is an umbrella term for alternatives to the court and jury as a means of resolving legal disputes. The most common forms are arbitration, in which a third party decides the controversy after hearing from both sides, and mediation, in which a third party tries to facilitate agreement between the disputants. The summary jury trial is another ADR mechanism.

2. ***What is the Sequential Intercept Model?*** The Sequential Intercept Model is a theoretical identification of the most relevant points of interception from the standard process of arrest, prosecution, conviction, and incarceration of criminal offenders.

3. ***What are the major stages (or intercepts) for community-based alternatives to standard prosecution?*** The intercepts that are relevant to community-based alternatives, diverting offenders from jail or prison into a rehabilitative community disposition, are (1) specialized law enforcement and emergency services responding; (2) post-arrest initial detention/hearing; and (3) jail/prison, courts, forensic evaluations, and commitments.

4. ***What are the similarities and differences between community court and other kinds of problem-solving courts?*** The underlying philosophy of all problem-solving courts reflects the view that identifying and rehabilitating a subset of criminal offenders can be accomplished less expensively, less restrictively, and more safely in the more rehabilitation-oriented problem-solving court than with the traditional criminal process. But most problem-solving courts accept a specific subgroup of offenders, based on their symptoms (e.g., mental health court, drug court) or experience (e.g., veterans' court), with the assumption that those in such groups have a specific constellation of rehabilitation needs which, if addressed, would make them less likely to reoffend. By contrast, community court is more heterogeneous, and may include a variety of groups of offender in need of rehabilitation for particular reasons that relate strongly to their risk for future offending.

KEY TERMS

arbitration

criminalization hypothesis

Crisis Intervention Team

deinstitutionalization

mediation

meta-analysis

negotiation

problem-solving court

risk averse

specialized police responding

summary jury trial

therapeutic jurisprudence

Chapter
10

Forensic Assessment in Juvenile and Criminal Cases

ORIENTING QUESTIONS

1. What is the scope of forensic psychology?

2. What is meant by competence in the criminal justice process?

3. How do clinicians assess competence?

4. What are the consequences of being found incompetent to proceed in the criminal justice process?

5. What is the legal definition of insanity?

6. How frequently is the insanity defense used, and how successful is it?

7. What are the major criticisms of the insanity defense, and what attempts have been made to reform it?

8. What are the important criteria in deciding on juvenile transfer?

THE SCOPE OF FORENSIC PSYCHOLOGY

Forensic psychologists use knowledge and techniques from psychology, psychiatry, and other behavioral sciences to answer questions about individuals involved in legal proceedings. In most cases, forensic assessment activities are performed by clinical psychologists, and the field of forensic psychology has prospered and matured considerably in the last 30 years (Heilbrun & Brooks, 2010; Heilbrun, Grisso, & Goldstein, 2009). For example,

- Forensic psychology is officially recognized as a specialty by the American Board of Professional Psychology and by the American Psychological Association.

- A revised version of specialty guidelines for the practice of forensic psychology has been approved (American Psychological Association, in press), updating the original version (Committee on Ethical Guidelines for Forensic Psychologists, 1991).

- Forensic psychology predoctoral training concentrations and postdoctoral fellowships are available, providing formal training in the field.

- The research and clinical literature on forensic practice have increased dramatically.

It appears likely that growth in this field will continue. There are several reasons for this. First, mental health experts have expertise in a variety of areas relevant to litigation. As scientists learn more about human behavior, attorneys will find new ways to use this information in various legal proceedings. In this and the following chapters, we focus on several topics that mental health professionals are called on to assess for individuals involved in court proceedings.

Second, forensic psychology is flourishing because the law permits, and even encourages, the use of expert testimony in a host of areas, including psychology, anthropology, criminology, engineering, toxicology, genetics, and medicine (National Research Council, 2009). Expert testimony is used in all these areas, but psychological topics have enjoyed particular prominence.

Finally, expert testimony by forensic psychologists thrives because it can be very lucrative. With hourly rates between $200 and $800, forensic experts can earn thousands of dollars per case. If one party in a lawsuit or criminal trial hires an expert, the other side usually feels pressure to respond with their own expert. Consequently, the use of psychological experts promotes the further use of such experts, and it has become a significant source of income for many professionals.

In general, a qualified expert can testify about a topic if such testimony is relevant to an issue in dispute and if the usefulness of the testimony outweighs whatever prejudicial impact it might have. If these two conditions are satisfied—as they must be for any kind of testimony to be admitted—an expert will be permitted to give opinion testimony if the judge believes that "scientific, technical, or other specialized knowledge will assist the trier of fact to understand the evidence or to determine a fact in issue" (Federal Rule of Evidence 702). The U.S. Supreme Court ruled in the 1993 case of *Daubert v. Merrell Dow* that federal judges could decide whether expert testimony has a sufficiently relevant and reliable scientific foundation to be admitted into evidence. For opinions offered by behavioral scientists and mental health experts, the *Daubert* standard suggests that admissible expert testimony should be grounded in scientifically based methods and theory (Melton, Petrila, Poythress, & Slobogin, 2007). In addition, the U.S. Supreme Court has held (in *Kumho Tire Co., Ltd v. Carmichael*, 1999) that this requirement

Box 10.1 THE CASE OF ANDREA YATES: TRAGEDY AND INSANITY

Andrea Yates with her family

On the morning of June 20, 2001, Andrea Yates, a 37-year-old wife and mother of five, said goodbye to her husband as he left for work. Before her mother-in-law arrived to help care for the children, who ranged in age from six months to seven years old, Yates filled the bathtub of her Texas home with water. Beginning with her middle son, Paul, she drowned each of her children in turn. She laid the four youngest children on the bed, covering them with a sheet. Her oldest boy was left floating lifelessly in the bathtub. She then called the police and her husband to tell them what she had done.

Prior to the killing of her children, Yates had a long history of severe mental illness. She reportedly suffered numerous psychotic episodes and had been diagnosed with schizophrenia and postpartum depression. These episodes resulted in several hospitalizations, including one just a month prior to the killings, and required psychotropic medications to help stabilize her ("The Andrea Yates Case," 2005).

Yates pled not guilty by reason of insanity to drowning three of her children; she was not charged in the other two deaths. Her insanity plea was based on her claim that she had no choice but to kill them while they were still innocents, to prevent them from burning in hell (Wordsworth, 2005). No one disputed that Yates systematically killed each of her children, but the question remained: Was she so disturbed by the symptoms of her severe mental illness that she could not be held criminally responsible for the murders?

At the conclusion of her trial, Yates was found guilty and sentenced to life in prison. After she had served three years of her sentence, however, the court declared a mistrial and Yates's conviction was overturned. During the trial, one of the psychiatric experts testified that the television show "Law and Order" had aired an episode in which a defendant had been acquitted by reason of insanity after drowning her children in the bathtub. Although the expert himself did not link this observation to Ms. Yates's thinking or motivation, the prosecutor did so in closing arguments. In fact, there had never been an episode of "Law and Order" with this specific story line. Yates was subsequently found not guilty by reason of insanity in a retrial, and is now hospitalized in the Texas state forensic hospital system.

Critical Thought Question
Why would it make a difference in the jury's consideration of the insanity defense for Andrea Yates if "Law and Order" had shown an episode in which an individual had drowned her children in a bathtub—and Ms. Yates had viewed this episode?

also applies to expert opinions that are provided by those with technical or professional skills, such as clinicians.

Expert testimony plays a crucial role in the insanity defense, one of the most difficult and controversial issues faced by courts and forensic evaluators. Our discussion of the insanity defense begins in Box 10.1, describing the case of Andrea Yates.

The question of whether Andrea Yates—or any criminal defendant—was insane at the time of a criminal offense is one of the most controversial questions

that forensic psychologists and psychiatrists are asked to help courts decide. The question has generated extensive research by social scientists. In this chapter, we discuss the construct of insanity—how it is defined, how claims of insanity are assessed by mental health professionals, and some of the implications of the insanity defense. Prior to that, we describe competence to stand trial, which is sometimes confused with insanity. We cover trial competence and insanity together in this chapter because these issues both occur in the criminal context, are raised together in some cases, and occur fairly close to one another within the sequence of criminal adjudication. We also discuss two other important issues that involve assessment by forensic psychologists: capital sentencing evaluations, and the transfer of juveniles from juvenile to criminal (adult) court. In Chapter 11, we explore several other forensic questions that clinicians assess, including questions that arise in civil litigation, divorce and child custody disputes, commitment hearings, and other types of legal proceedings.

COMPETENCE

The Andrea Yates case highlights the importance of evaluating a defendant's competence to stand trial. Did Yates understand the nature of her charges and the possible consequences of those charges? This question is particularly salient in light of an interview with Yates's mother, who recalled that Andrea Yates (while in prison for the murders of her children) asked her mother who would be watching them (Gibson, 2005). Questions were also raised about whether Yates was taking her antipsychotic medication at the time of the murders as well as during her trial.

What do we mean by competence to stand trial? How do clinicians assess this kind of legal competence? What legal standards should be applied? The question of a defendant's **competence** is the clinical-legal issue most frequently assessed in the criminal justice system. **Competence to stand trial** refers to a defendant's capacity to function meaningfully and knowingly in a legal proceeding. Defendants may be adjudicated (i.e., determined by a judge) to be incompetent if they are seriously deficient in one or more abilities, such as understanding the legal proceedings, communicating with their attorneys, appreciating their role in the proceedings, or making legally relevant decisions. Concerns about a defendant's competence are tied to one fundamental principle: Criminal proceedings should not continue against someone who cannot understand their nature and purpose, and thus cannot assist in defending against prosecution on these charges.

Competence is an important doctrine in our legal system, and the law requires defendants to be competent for several reasons (Melton et al., 2007). First, defendants must be able to understand the charges against them so that they can participate in the criminal justice system in a meaningful way,

making it more likely that legal proceedings will arrive at accurate and just results. Second, punishment of convicted defendants is morally acceptable only if they understand the reasons why they are being punished. Finally, the perceived fairness and integrity of our adversary system of justice requires participation by defendants who have the capacity to defend themselves against the charges of the state.

The accepted national standard for competence to stand trial is a "sufficient present ability to consult with [one's] attorney with a reasonable degree of rational understanding, and...a rational, as well as factual, understanding of the proceedings against [one]" (*Dusky v. United States*, 1960). With minor differences across jurisdictions, this is the standard for competence to stand trial in all American courts. It establishes the basic criteria for competence as the capacities for factual and rational understanding of the court proceedings and for consulting with one's attorney in a rational way. These criteria refer to *present* abilities rather than to the mental state of the defendant at the time of the alleged offense, which, as we will discuss later, is the focus of evaluations of a defendant's sanity.

The *Dusky* standard does not specify how the evaluator assessing competence should judge the sufficiency of rational understanding, ability to consult, or factual understanding. That is ultimately the role of the judge. However, to allow evaluators to provide courts with more detailed information in these areas, a number of courts and mental health groups have expanded on *Dusky* by listing more specific criteria related to competence. For example, evaluators may consider a number of relevant psycholegal abilities (Zapf & Roesch, 2009):

- Understanding
  - The roles of key participants within the legal process
  - The current charges faced by the defendant
  - The elements of an offense
  - The consequences of conviction
  - The rights waived in making a guilty plea
- Appreciation
  - The likelihood that he or she will be found guilty
  - The consequences for the defendant of being convicted

- The defendant's appraisal of the available legal defenses and their likely outcomes
- The defendant's appraisal of whether or not to testify
- The defendant's ability to make rational decisions regarding the specific case

■ Reasoning

- Distinguishing more relevant from less relevant information
- Seeking relevant information
- Weighing and evaluate various legal options and their consequences
- Making comparisons
- Providing reality-based justification for making particular case-specific decisions or conclusions

■ Assisting in one's defense

- Consulting with his or her lawyer
- Relating to the lawyer
- Planning legal strategy
- Engaging in his or her defense
- Challenging witnesses
- Testifying relevantly
- Managing his or her courtroom behavior

■ Decision-making abilities relevant to decisions likely to arise during the proceedings.

The issue of competence also arises when defendants plead guilty. By pleading guilty, defendants waive several constitutional rights: the right to a jury trial, the right to confront their accusers, the right to call favorable witnesses, and the right to remain silent. The Supreme Court has held that waiving such important rights must be done knowingly, intelligently, and voluntarily (*Johnson v. Zerbst*, 1938), and trial judges are required to question defendants about their pleas in order to establish clearly that they understand that they are waiving their constitutional rights by pleading guilty. A knowing, intelligent, and voluntary guilty plea also includes understanding the charges and the possible penalties that can be imposed, and requires the judge to examine any plea bargain to ensure that it is "voluntary" (i.e., that it represents a considered choice between constitutionally

permissible alternatives). For example, prosecutors can offer lighter sentences to a defendant in exchange for a guilty plea, but they cannot offer the defendant money to encourage a guilty plea.

Logically, **competence to plead guilty** would require that defendants understand the alternatives they face and have the ability to make a reasoned choice among them. In some respects, this standard is more demanding than that for competence to stand trial. Defendants standing trial must be aware of the nature of the proceedings and be able to cooperate with counsel in presenting the defense, paying attention to the proceedings and controlling their behavior over the course of a trial. This creates a strong demand for *attention*, *concentration*, and *behavioral control*. Defendants pleading guilty, on the other hand, must understand the possible consequences of pleading guilty instead of going to trial and must be able to make a rational choice between the alternatives. This underscores the importance of the defendant's *cognitive awareness* and *reasoning*.

Adjudicative Competence

Despite this, the U.S. Supreme Court ruled that the standard for competence to stand trial would be applied in federal courts to other competence questions that arise in the criminal justice process (*Godinez v. Moran*, 1993). In so doing, it rejected the idea that competence to plead guilty involves a higher standard than competence to stand trial. As a result of this decision, the terms *competence to plead guilty* and *competence to stand trial* have become somewhat confusing. Some scholars have suggested that **adjudicative competence** is a clearer description of the various capacities that criminal defendants need in different legal contexts (Bonnie, 1993; Hoge et al., 1997). The term competence to stand trial is still used frequently, although it acquired a broader meaning after the *Godinez* decision. We discuss adjudicative competence with the understanding that it is synonymous with competence to stand trial, post-*Godinez*. We begin this discussion with the case of Jared Loughner, described in Box 10.2.

Raising the Issue of Competence

The question of a defendant's competence can be raised at any point in the criminal process, and it can be raised by the prosecutor, the defense attorney,

Box 10.2   THE CASE OF JARED LOUGHNER: ASSESSING COMPETENCE

Jared Loughner following
his arrest

Jared Loughner was arrested after being wrestled to the ground in a grocery store parking lot in Tucson, Arizona on January 8, 2011, after he walked up to United States Congresswoman Gabrielle Giffords, an Arizona Democrat, and shot her. Following that, Mr. Loughner turned his gun on others in the crowd. Those dying in the shooting included John Roll, a federal judge in Tucson; 9-year-old Christina-Taylor Green; and four other bystanders. Twelve other individuals in addition to the congresswoman were injured.

Mr. Loughner was a troubled young man with a history of classroom outbursts at Pima Community College, which had expelled him, and bizarre postings on the Internet. Before he could be tried for these offenses, however, the issue of Mr. Loughner's competence to stand trial was raised. Among the questions that the mental health experts were asked to address, and the court ultimately had to decide, were whether Mr. Loughner indeed had a mental illness—and, if so, how the symptoms of that illness affected his capacities to understand his legal circumstances, assist counsel in his own defense, and make rational decisions in the process.

Judge Larry A. Burns of the U.S. District Court considered the findings of two mental health experts in the case: Christina Pietz, Ph.D., a psychologist appointed at the request of the prosecution, and Matthew Carroll, M.D., a psychiatrist appointed by the judge. Dr. Pietz reported that Mr. Loughner's thoughts were random and disorganized, that he experienced delusions, and that he responded to questions in an irrelevant fashion. Dr. Carroll also described delusions as well as bizarre thoughts and hallucinations. Both experts concluded that Mr. Loughner suffered from schizophrenia, a form of severe mental illness. They described these symptoms as seriously impairing Mr. Loughner's ability to understand his legal circumstances and assist counsel in his own defense. The judge adjudicated him incompetent to stand trial and committed him to the Federal Medical Center in Springfield, Missouri for treatment to improve his symptoms and restore these capacities.

Because of the horrific and widely publicized nature of these alleged offenses, there was (and will continue to be) a great deal of scrutiny of Mr. Loughner's case. The prosecution in such cases experiences pressure to consider the death penalty, and to bring the defendant to trial and convict. The defense may struggle in working with a severely mentally ill defendant, even one whose symptoms are in remission, because the defendant may continue to show irrational thinking and behavior that is not consistent with defense attorneys' strategic recommendations. A judge must balance the arguments of both prosecution and defense in a highly charged, widely scrutinized atmosphere. Such cases test the limits of our legal system in the pursuit of justice under very trying circumstances.

Critical Thought Question
Why does the highly publicized nature of an alleged offense like Jared Loughner's affect the proceedings on a question like competence to stand trial?

or the presiding judge. Once the question of incompetence is raised, the judge will order an evaluation of the defendant if a "bona fide doubt" exists that the defendant is competent. Judges consider the circumstances of each case and the behavior of each defendant when making this determination. However, if the question of competence is raised, an examination will usually be conducted. Because it is relatively easy to obtain such evaluations, attorneys often seek them for reasons other than a determination of competence. Competence evaluations are used for several tactical reasons: to obtain information about a possible

insanity defense, to guarantee the temporary incarceration of a potentially dangerous person without going through the cumbersome procedures of involuntary civil commitment, to deny bail, and to delay the trial as one side tries to gain an advantage over the other (Winick, 1996). Defense attorneys have questions about their clients' competence in up to 15% of felony cases (approximately twice the rate for defendants charged with misdemeanors); in many of these cases, however, the attorney does not seek a formal evaluation (Hoge et al., 1997; Poythress, Bonnie, Hoge, Monahan, & Oberlander, 1994).

Evaluating Competence

After a judge orders a competence examination, arrangements are made for the defendant to be evaluated by one or more mental health professionals. Although these evaluations were historically conducted in a special hospital or inpatient forensic facility, most evaluations over the last two decades have been conducted in the community on an outpatient (nonhospitalized) basis (Grisso, Cocozza, Steadman, Fisher, & Greer, 1994; Nicholson & Norwood, 2000). The transition from inpatient to outpatient facilities occurred because inpatient exams are more costly and time-consuming, and local outpatient evaluations are usually sufficient for evaluative purposes (Winick, 1996).

Physicians, psychiatrists, psychologists, and social workers are authorized by most states to conduct competence examinations, but psychologists are the professional group responsible for the largest number of reports (Nicholson & Norwood, 2000). Some data suggest that nonmedical professionals with relevant forensic specialty knowledge prepare reports of trial competence evaluations that are comparable in quality to those prepared by forensic psychiatrists (Lander & Heilbrun, 2009; Petrella & Poythress, 1983; Sanschagrin, Stevens, Bove, & Heilbrun, 2006).

Under the *Dusky* standard, the presence of mental illness or mental retardation does not guarantee that a defendant will be found incompetent to stand trial. The crucial question is whether the disorder impairs a defendant's ability to participate knowingly and meaningfully in the proceedings and to work with the defense attorney. A psychotic defendant might be competent to stand trial in a relatively straightforward case but incompetent to participate in a complex trial that would demand more skill and understanding. Consider the case of John Salvi, who, despite having an apparent psychotic disorder, was found competent to stand trial and was convicted of murdering two people and wounding five others during a shooting spree at two Massachusetts medical clinics that performed abortions. Salvi later committed suicide in prison. Apparently his symptoms (unlike those of Jared Loughner) did not substantially compromise his ability to understand the charges against him and the basic nature of his trial. Thus, he was found competent to stand trial.

Current competence evaluations focus on the defendant's present ability to function adequately in the legal process. This focus has been sharpened by the development of several structured tests or instruments specifically aimed at assessing the capacities relevant to competence to stand trial. Psychological testing remains a common ingredient in competence evaluations, and although clinicians have begun to use one or more of these specially designed competence assessment instruments in their practice, their use is not as widespread as it should be (Lander & Heilbrun, 2009; Skeem, Golding, Cohn, & Berge, 1998). There have been a number of such instruments historically. The most recent and best supported empirically are described in the following paragraphs.

Interdisciplinary Fitness Interview (IFI). The IFI and its revision, the IFI-R (Golding, 1993), are versions of a semi-structured interview that evaluates a defendant's abilities in five specific legal areas. It also assesses 11 categories of psychopathological symptoms. Evaluators rate the weight they attached to each item in reaching their decision about competence. These weights vary depending on the nature of the defendant's case; for example, hallucinations might impair a defendant's ability to participate in some trials, but they would have minor effects in others and would therefore be given slight weight. Golding, Roesch, and Schreiber (1984) found that interviewers using the IFI agreed on final judgments of competence in 75 of 77 cases evaluated. These judgments agreed 76% of the time with independent decisions about competence made later at a state hospital.

Fitness Interview Test—Revised. The Fitness Interview Test—Revised (FIT-R) is a structured interview for assessing a person's competence to stand trial. Like the IFI-R, it uses a structured professional judgment approach to assessing competence capacities. Using this approach, various areas are considered but not "scored," and there is not a total score that is related to a category or level of impairment. It was originally designed for use in Canada, but has been updated for use in the United States and Great Britain as well. It includes 16 items in three broad domains (Factual Knowledge of Criminal Procedure, Appreciation of Personal Involvement In and Importance Of the Proceedings, and Ability to Participate in Defense). Research on the FIT-R (Roesch, Zapf, & Eaves, 2006; Zapf & Roesch, 1997) suggests that it is a promising screening tool.

The MacArthur Measures of Competence. Growing out of the concept of adjudicative competence, which describes several interrelated components that need to be considered in the evaluation of competence, the *MacArthur Structured Assessment of the Competence of Criminal Defendants* (MacSAC-CD; Hoge et al., 1997) is a highly regarded research instrument. Most of the 82 items in the MacSAC-CD rely on a hypothetical vignette about which the defendant is asked questions that tap foundational and decisional abilities. Defendants are asked the questions in a sequence. Open-ended questions come first. If there is a wrong answer, correct information is provided to the defendant. Defendants are then asked additional open-ended questions to determine whether they now have the necessary understanding based on this disclosure; a series of true–false questions concludes each area of assessment. This format has several advantages. It offers a more standardized evaluation across different defendants, and it makes it possible to assess separately defendants' preexisting abilities as well as their capacity to learn and apply new information.

One major disadvantage of the MacSAC-CD is that it was developed as a research instrument and takes about two hours to complete, far too long to be used in clinical practice. To overcome this limitation, a 22-item clinical version of this measure, called the *MacArthur Competence Assessment Tool—Criminal Adjudication* (MacCAT-CA) was developed (Poythress et al., 1999). This instrument begins with a hypothetical vignette about a crime, upon which the first 16 items are based. These items assess the defendant's general understanding of the legal system and adjudicative process and his or her reasoning abilities in legal situations. The remaining six items are specific to the defendant's own legal situation.

The Evaluation of Competence to Stand Trial–Revised. The *Evaluation of Competence to Stand Trial–Revised* (ECST-R) (Rogers, Tillbrook, & Sewell, 2004) is a semi-structured interview that was developed using the *Dusky* criteria. Its three factors (factual understanding of proceedings, rational understanding of proceedings, and consultation with counsel) have been empirically tested using a statistical technique known as confirmatory factor analysis. It focuses on information that is specific to the case of the individual being evaluated (unlike the MacCAT-CA, which uses a general vignette involving two individuals who fight

in a bar). It also addresses the question of whether the evaluee is trying to exaggerate or fake deficits that might make that person appear incompetent to stand trial. Both the case specificity and the built-in measure of possible exaggeration are useful features of the ECST-R, which appears well supported by the relevant research (Norton & Ryba, 2010; Rogers, Grandjean, Tillbrook, Vitacco, & Sewell, 2001).

Competence Assessment for Standing Trial for Defendants with Mental Retardation. One specialized measure, the *Competence Assessment for Standing Trial for Defendants with Mental Retardation* (CAST-MR; Everington & Luckasson, 1992), was developed specifically for assessing defendants with mild to moderate mental retardation. Two validation studies have been conducted; although the number of participants has been small, the results have been somewhat encouraging (Grisso, 2003). In addition, the CAST-MR is the only specialized tool developed specifically for assessing trial competence with individuals with developmental disabilities.

One important issue being studied by researchers is the extent to which defendants can successfully fake incompetence on these tests. Some research suggests that although offenders can simulate incompetence, they often take such simulations to extremes, scoring much more poorly on specialized measures of competence capacities than their truly incompetent counterparts (Gothard, Rogers, & Sewell, 1995; Gothard, Viglione, Meloy, & Sherman, 1995). Therefore, very poor performance should make evaluators suspicious that a defendant might be exaggerating his or her deficiencies. As noted earlier, one specialized tool (the ECST-R) has a built-in measure to help the evaluator determine whether the defendant is exaggerating deficits. Research indicates that the ECST-R is sensitive to the exaggeration of both symptoms of mental illness and intellectual deficits (Vitacco, Rogers, & Gabel, 2009).

This issue has gained a great deal of attention because estimates of malingering (faking or grossly exaggerating) mental illness in competence evaluations have been estimated as nearly one in five (18%; Rogers, Salekin, Sewell, Goldstein, & Leonard, 1998). Therefore, screening tools have been developed to offer a more scientific method of detecting malingering in patients who are being evaluated for their competence to stand trial. One of these instruments is the Miller Forensic Assessment of Symptoms

Test (M-FAST; Miller, 2001). The M-FAST is a brief, 25-item structured interview that can accurately identify individuals who are attempting to feign mental disorders (see Miller, 2004). Empirical evidence thus far supports the use of the M-FAST in detecting malingering (Jackson, Rogers, & Sewell, 2005), but it is a screening instrument and should be used in conjunction with a wider array of assessments to determine whether the defendant is actually malingering.

Following the collection of assessment data, evaluators communicate their findings to the judge. Often, they submit a written report that summarizes the evidence on competence to stand trial, as well as the likelihood that appropriate treatment will sufficiently improve competence-relevant deficits. In controversial or strongly contested cases, it is more likely that there will be a formal competence hearing where the evaluating experts testify and are questioned by attorneys from both sides.

In formal competence hearings, who bears the burden of proof? Must prosecutors prove that defendants are competent, or are defendants required to prove their incompetence? In the 1992 case of *Medina v. California*, the U.S. Supreme Court held that a state can require a criminal defendant to shoulder the burden of proving that he or she is incompetent. But how stringent should that burden be? Most states established the criterion to be a "preponderance of the evidence," meaning that the defendant had to show that it was more likely than not that he or she was incompetent. But four states—Oklahoma, Pennsylvania, Connecticut, and Rhode Island—required a higher standard of proof: evidence that was "clear and convincing." Yet in 1996, the Supreme Court held that this higher standard was too stringent (*Cooper v. Oklahoma*, 1996).

Results of Competence Evaluations

About 70% of the defendants referred for evaluation are ultimately found competent to stand trial (Nicholson & Kugler, 1991; Melton et al., 2007); when very rigorous examinations are conducted, the rate of defendants found competent approaches 90%. Judges seldom disagree with clinicians' decisions about competence, and opposing attorneys often will **stipulate** (agree without further examination) to clinicians' findings (Melton et al., 2007).

One study asked judges, prosecutors, and defense attorneys to rank in order of importance eight items typically offered by expert witnesses in competence evaluations (e.g., clinical diagnosis of the defendant, weighing different motives and explanations, providing an ultimate opinion on the legal issue) (Redding, Floyd, & Hawk, 2001). The results revealed that judges and prosecutors agreed that the expert's ultimate opinion on the legal issue was one of the top three most important pieces of information the expert could provide.

Another study asked juvenile and criminal court judges ($N = 166$) about information they considered valuable in competence evaluations. Results showed that judges (1) consider clinicians' ultimate opinion to be an essential component of reports, (2) regard forensic and psychological testing as valuable, (3) seek similar but not identical characteristics in juvenile and adult competence evaluations, and (4) consider opinions about maturity to be an important component of competence evaluations in juvenile court (Viljoen, Wingrove, & Ryba, 2008). Depending upon how such "ultimate opinions" are used, this may suggest that mental health professionals exert great—perhaps excessive—influence on this legal decision.

What sort of person is most often judged to be incompetent? In his study of more than 500 defendants found incompetent to stand trial, Steadman (1979) described them as often "marginal" men who were undereducated and deficient in job skills, with long histories of involvement in both the legal and the mental health systems (see also Williams & Miller, 1981). Problems of substance abuse were common. Minorities were overrepresented. Others report relatively high percentages of psychosis, lower intelligence, and more problems with certain aspects of memory among incompetent defendants (Cooper & Zapf, 2003; Nestor, Daggett, Haycock, & Price, 1999; Roesch & Golding, 1980; Zapf & Roesch, 1998). Another consistent finding is that defendants deemed incompetent to stand trial (IST) are charged with more serious crimes than defendants in general. After an extensive review of competence research, Nicholson and Kugler (1991) described the typical defendant found IST to (1) have a history of psychosis for which previous treatment had been received; (2) exhibit symptoms of current serious mental disorder; (3) be single, unemployed, and poorly educated; and (4) perform poorly on specific competence assessment instruments. Another study compared hospitalized incompetent defendants to those receiving psychiatric treatment in jail, and to jail inmates who had not been referred for treatment. Compared with these other two groups, hospitalized incompetent defendants were more likely to have been diagnosed with schizophrenia, and more likely to have a history of prior mental health treatment (Hoge et al., 1997).

If a defendant referred for a competence evaluation is adjudicated competent to stand trial, the legal process resumes, and the defendant again faces the possibility of trial or disposition of charges through plea bargaining. If the defendant is found IST, however, the picture becomes more complicated. For crimes that are not serious, the charges are occasionally dropped, sometimes in exchange for requiring the defendant to receive treatment. In other cases, however, the defendant is hospitalized to be treated for restoration of competence, which, if successful, will result in the defendant proceeding with disposition of charges. Outpatient treatment of incompetent defendants is used less often, even though it might sometimes be justified.

Prior to the 1970s, defendants found incompetent were often confined in mental hospitals for excessive periods of time. (Sometimes such confinements were even longer than their sentences would have been had they stood trial and been convicted.) But the practice of providing long periods of hospitalization for defendants incompetent for trial was limited in 1972 when the U.S. Supreme Court decided the case of *Jackson v. Indiana*. This decision held that defendants who had been committed because they were incompetent to stand trial could not be held "more than a reasonable period of time necessary to determine whether there is a substantial probability that [they] will attain that capacity in the foreseeable future." As a result of this decision, the length of time an incompetent defendant can be confined is now limited, and many states have passed statutes that "limit" such hospitalization to a period not to exceed the maximum sentence that could have been imposed if the defendant were convicted of charges. In cases involving serious felony charges, such a period might well be 10 years or longer.

How successful are efforts to restore defendants' competence? One study evaluated an experimental group treatment administered to a sample of incompetent defendants sent to one of three Philadelphia facilities (Siegel & Elwork, 1990). In addition to receiving psychiatric medication, defendants assigned to these special treatment groups watched videotapes and received special instructions on courtroom procedures. They also discussed different ways of resolving problems that a defendant might face during a trial. A matched control group received treatment for their general psychiatric needs, but no specific treatment relevant to incompetence. Following their treatment, defendants participating in the special competence restoration group showed significant increases in their assessment scores compared to the controls. In addition, hospital staff judged 43% of the experimental subjects competent to stand trial after treatment compared to 15% of the control subjects. Other research, however, indicates that providing general legal information is about as effective as highly specialized programs focusing on individual deficits (Bertman et al., 2003). In general, most defendants have their adjudicative competence restored, usually with about six months of treatment (Melton et al., 2007), and the most important intervention for most defendants is the administration of appropriate psychotropic medication (Zapf & Roesch, 2009).

The real dilemma for IST defendants occurs when treatment is not successful in restoring competence and holds little promise of success in the future. At this point, all options are problematic. Theoretically, the previously-described *Jackson* ruling bars the indefinite confinement of an individual adjudicated incompetent to stand trial. The law varies across states as to how long such involuntary hospitalization is allowed, but many states permit the defendant to be hospitalized for a period up to the maximum sentence that he or she could have received if convicted of the charges. Once such a defendant has been hospitalized for this period, however, he or she can be found "unrestorably incompetent."

Typically, unrestorably incompetent defendants are committed to a hospital through involuntary civil commitment proceedings. Standards for this type of commitment are narrower than for being found IST, however. The state must show that the person is mentally ill and either imminently dangerous to self or others or so gravely disabled as to be unable to care for himself or herself.

Should an incompetent defendant not meet the criteria for involuntary hospitalization, what happens? Despite the ruling in the *Jackson* case, some states simply continue to confine incompetent defendants for indefinite periods. Although this "solution" might appease the public, we believe it jeopardizes defendants' due process rights and results in lengthy periods of punishment (disguised as treatment) without a conviction.

Several alternative procedures have been proposed to resolve this catch-22, including proposals to abolish the IST concept altogether (Burt & Morris, 1972); to allow defendants to seek trial continuances without going through an elaborate evaluation; or, under certain circumstances, to waive their right to be competent (Fentiman, 1986; Winick, 1996). One additional proposal (American Bar Association, 1984) is that a provisional trial be held for a defendant who is likely to be found unrestorably incompetent. This hearing would decide the question of guilt. If the defendant is found not guilty, he or she would be formally acquitted and could be further confined only through civil commitment. If proven guilty, the defendant would be subject to a special form of commitment that would recognize society's needs for secure handling of these persons.

Competent with Medication, Incompetent Without

For most defendants found IST, psychoactive medication has been the treatment of choice, as it is considered the best intervention for restoring defendants to competence in a reasonable period of time. Can incompetent defendants refuse this treatment? If medicated, will defendants be found competent to stand trial even though the medication, through its temporarily tranquilizing effects, might undercut a defense such as insanity? The U.S. Supreme Court case *Sell v. U.S.* (2003) concerns questions of competence and forced medication (Box 10.3).

Other Competence Issues

Because questions about competence can be raised at any point in the criminal process, several other competences are at issue in deciding whether a defendant can participate knowingly in different functions.

B o x 10.3 THE CASE OF CHARLES SELL: INVOLUNTARY MEDICATION TO RESTORE COMPETENCE?

Charles Sell, once a practicing dentist, had an extensive history of severe mental illness and was hospitalized several times. He was accused of fraud after he allegedly submitted fictitious insurance claims for payment. His competence to stand trial was evaluated, and he was found competent and released on bail. Subsequently, a grand jury indicted Sell on 13 additional counts of fraud and, later, attempted murder. During his bail revocation hearing, Sell's mental illness was markedly worse, and his behavior was "totally out of control," including "spitting in the judge's face" (2003, p. 2). His competence was again evaluated, at which time he was adjudicated incompetent to stand trial. He was hospitalized for treatment to help restore his competence. Hospital staff recommended antipsychotic medication, which Sell declined to take. The hospital administered these medications to him involuntarily. Sell challenged this in court, arguing that involuntary medication violates the Fifth Amendment right to "liberty to reject medical treatment" (p. 10). The lower court found that Sell was a danger to himself and others, that medication was the only way to render him less dangerous, that the benefits to Sell outweighed the risks, and that the drugs were substantially likely to return Sell to competence. The court further held that medication was the only viable hope of rendering Sell competent to stand trial and was necessary to serve the Government's interest in obtaining an adjudication on the issue of his guilt. Sell appealed and

this case was granted *certiorari* by the United States Supreme Court.

At the heart of this case is the question of whether it is a violation of a defendant's rights to be forcibly medicated in order to make that defendant competent to proceed to trial, with the associated possibility of conviction and incarceration in prison. But if the defendant cannot be restored to competence without medication, he or she may remain hospitalized, and thus also deprived of his or her liberty, for a lengthy period of time. In this decision, the Court weighed these considerations and outlined the conditions under which the government may forcibly administer psychotropic medication to render a mentally ill defendant competent to stand trial. The treatment must be (1) medically appropriate, (2) substantially unlikely to have side effects that may undermine the trial's fairness, and (3) necessary to significantly further important government trial-related interests.

Critical Thought Question
Assume that a defendant is hospitalized as incompetent to stand trial with a severe mental illness, and assume further that he is actively psychotic and declines to take prescribed medication while in the hospital. Finally, assume that he does not present a threat of harm toward others or himself. Under those circumstances, what are the advantages and disadvantages of forcing him to take psychotropic medication?

Competence for any legal function involves (1) determining what functional abilities are necessary, (2) assessing the context where these abilities must be demonstrated, (3) evaluating the implication of any deficiencies in the required abilities, and (4) deciding whether the deficiencies warrant a conclusion that the defendant is incompetent (Grisso, 1986). Mental health professionals are sometimes asked to evaluate each of the following competences (see also Melton et al., 2007).

Competence to Waive *Miranda* Rights. The waiver of *Miranda* rights is required in order for defendants in police custody to make a confession—and the waiver of these *Miranda* rights (Fifth Amendment right to avoid self-incrimination and Sixth Amendment right to counsel and trial) must be done in a knowing, intelligent, and voluntary fashion. A clinician's assessment of these abilities is challenging because, in most cases, the waiver and confession have occurred months before the professional's evaluation, requiring a reconstruction of the defendant's psychological condition at the time.

An aspect of a defendant's rights guaranteed by *Miranda* involves the Sixth Amendment right to be represented by counsel when he or she is in police custody. The same standard to waive this right—knowing, intelligent, and voluntary—is applied to the question of whether an individual had the capacity to waive the right to counsel before providing police with a confession.

A slightly different twist on the right to be represented by counsel involves the question of whether defendants can decide that they do not want a lawyer to represent them at trial. The Supreme Court has held that defendants have a constitutional right to waive counsel and represent themselves at trial, providing that they make this decision competently (*Faretta v. California*, 1975). In addition, the presiding judge must be convinced that the waiver of counsel is both voluntary and intelligent. Defendants do not have to convince the court that they possess a high level of legal knowledge, although some legal knowledge is probably important.

Competence to waive the right to counsel was at issue in the trial of Colin Ferguson, who was charged with murdering six passengers and wounding 19 more when he went on a killing rampage aboard a Long Island Rail Road train in December 1993. Ferguson insisted on serving as his own attorney,

after rejecting the "black rage" defense suggested by his lawyers. At first, Ferguson proved effective enough to have several of his objections to the prosecutor's case sustained. But then, giving new meaning to the old saying that a defendant who argues his own case has a fool for a client, Ferguson opened his case by claiming that "There were 93 counts to that indictment, 93 counts only because it matches the year 1993. If it had been 1925, it would be a 25-count indictment." This was a prelude to Ferguson's attempt at cross-examining a series of eyewitnesses, who, in response to his preposterous suggestion that someone else had been the murderer, answered time after time, "No, I saw the murderer clearly. It was you."

Competence to Refuse the Insanity Defense. In cases in which it is likely that the defendant was insane at the time of the offense, can the defendant refuse to plead insanity? If there is evidence that a defendant was not mentally responsible for criminal acts, do courts have a duty to require that the defendant plead insanity when the defendant does not want to do so? Courts are divided on this question. In some cases, they have suggested that society's stake in punishing only mentally responsible persons requires the imposition of an insanity plea even on unwilling defendants (*Whalen v. United States*, 1965). Other decisions (*Frendak v. United States*, 1979) use the framework of competence to answer this question—if the defendant understands the alternative pleas available and the consequences of those pleas, the defendant should be permitted to reject an insanity plea. This latter approach is followed in most courts.

This question was at the heart of the prosecution of Theodore Kaczynski, a reclusive mathematician who was dubbed the "Unabomber" for sending a series of mail bombs to universities and airlines between 1978 and 1995. Although the consensus of several experts was that Kaczynski suffered from paranoid schizophrenia, he adamantly refused to let his attorneys use an insanity defense, arguing that he did not want to be stigmatized, in his words, as a "sickie." Was Kaczynski competent to make this decision, or was Judge Garland E. Burrell, Jr. correct in ruling that Kaczynski's lawyers could control his defense, even over the defendant's persistent objections? It is doubtful that an insanity defense would have been successful—Kaczynski's own diary showed that he understood and intended to commit his crimes—but we will never know. Ultimately, to avoid the possibility of the death penalty, Kaczynski pled guilty to murder and was sentenced to life in prison.

Competence to Be Sentenced. For legal and humanitarian reasons, convicted defendants are not to be sentenced to punishment unless they are competent. In general, the standard for this competence is that defendants can understand the punishment and the reasons why it is being imposed, and can meaningfully execute their right to address the court at sentencing. Competence to be sentenced is often a more straightforward question for the clinician to evaluate than adjudicative competence, which involves issues of whether the accused can interact effectively with counsel and appreciate alternative courses of action.

Competence to Be Executed. A particularly controversial aspect of this area is determining whether a defendant is competent to be executed. The U.S. Supreme Court decided, in the case of *Ford v. Wainwright* (1986), that the Eighth Amendment ban against cruel and unusual punishments prohibits the execution of defendants while they are incompetent. Therefore, mental health professionals are at times called on to evaluate inmates waiting to be executed to determine whether they are competent to be executed. The practical problems and ethical dilemmas involved in these evaluations are enormous (Heilbrun, 1987; Heilbrun & McClaren, 1988; Mossman, 1987; Susman, 1992) and have led some psychologists to recommend that clinicians refrain from performing such evaluations.

Juvenile Competence to Stand Trial

Are juveniles competent to stand trial? Does it make a difference whether they are being processed in juvenile court or tried as adults? Do adolescents differ from adults in their abilities to participate in trials, and if so, what are these differences? These are questions posed by researchers (Grisso et al., 2003) when they studied a group of 927 adolescents in juvenile detention facilities and community settings. Participants were administered a specialized measure of competence for adults (the MacCAT-CA) as well as the MacArthur Judgment Evaluation (MacJen), which was designed to examine immaturity of judgment. Their research goal was to provide data on *competence to proceed* (comprehension of the purpose and nature of the trial process, ability to provide relevant information to counsel and to process information, and ability

Adolescent in Juvenile Court

to apply information to oneself without distortion or irrationality) and *decisional competence* (ability to make important decisions about waiver of constitutional rights and maturity of judgment).

Results indicated that participants who were age 15 and younger were significantly impaired in ways that compromised their abilities to function as competent defendants in a criminal (adult) proceeding. More specifically, one-third of 11–13-year-olds and one-fifth of 14–15-year-olds were as impaired in their functional legal capacities as mentally ill adults who were incompetent to stand trial. Below-average intelligence was also associated with deficits in these functional legal capacities. Since a large proportion of adolescents in the juvenile justice system have below-average IQ, the risk for incompetence is further increased when adolescents in this system are transferred into criminal court (Grisso et al., 2003).

These findings have fewer implications for adolescents in juvenile court. Since the expectations for competence in juvenile court are different—adolescents are being tried in a setting that is designed for juveniles—it is more likely that an adolescent with limited functional legal capacities would be adjudicated competent in juvenile court than if he or she were tried in adult criminal court.

THE INSANITY DEFENSE

Any society that respects the rights of individuals recognizes the possibility that some of its citizens cannot comprehend the consequences or the wrongfulness of their actions. Our legal system allows defendants who claim that they lack these abilities to invoke the insanity defense. Yet the truth in cases involving the insanity defense is elusive. For example, it may be very difficult to accurately gauge a defendant's mental state at the time of the offense, as must be done when a defendant uses insanity as a defense. The jury or judge must answer the question "What was he experiencing when he fired the gun?" rather than "Did he fire the gun?" How can we determine whether a defendant is legally insane? Can we know what a person's state of mind was when he or she committed an antisocial act? This becomes even more difficult when the fact finders—juries and judges—must determine not whether the person is currently insane but rather whether he or she was insane at the time of the crime, possibly months or years earlier.

This problem is further complicated by the reality that there are far fewer specialized tools specifically designed to assess insanity than there are to assess competence. One brief screening instrument—the Mental Status Examination at the Time of the Offense (Slobogin, Melton, & Showalter, 1984)—has been developed, but research on its reliability and validity is limited to one study. More research has been conducted on the Rogers Criminal Responsibility Scales (RCRAS; Rogers, 1986), a set of 25 scales that organize the many factors and points of decision that clinicians need to consider when assessing criminal responsibility. Although the RCRAS has clear limitations, it is the only formal instrument with some proven reliability and validity for guiding clinicians' decision-making process in insanity evaluations (Nicholson, 1999).

Another reason why truth is so elusive in cases of alleged insanity stems from the conflict between law and behavioral sciences as alternative pathways to knowledge. Insanity is a legal concept, not a medical or psychological one. In many states, a defendant could be hallucinating, delusional, and diagnosed as schizophrenic, but if the individual knew the difference between right and wrong, he or she would be legally sane. Thus, psychiatrists and clinical psychologists are called upon as forensic experts to provide information regarding a decision that is ultimately outside their professional/scientific framework. The therapeutic goals of psychiatry and clinical psychology (diagnosis and assessment that are probabilistic and complex) do not fit well with the legal system's demand for a straightforward "yes-or-no" answer (Heilbrun, 2001). Furthermore, although psychiatrists

and other mental health experts can offer diagnoses, the particular diagnosis is less important than the specific symptoms and their impact on the functional legal demands associated with the insanity standard (whether the defendant "knew" the behavior was wrong; in some states, additionally, whether the defendant could conform his or her conduct to the requirements of the law).

Rationale for the Insanity Defense

Insanity refers to the defendant's mental state at the time the offense was committed (as contrasted with *competence to stand trial*, which refers exclusively to the defendant's relevant legal capacities at the time of the trial or plea bargain). Why do we have laws about insanity at all? Wouldn't it be simpler to do away with insanity in the legal system? Allowing a criminal defendant to plead not guilty by reason of insanity reflects a fundamental belief that a civilized society should not punish people who do not know what they are doing or are incapable of controlling their conduct. Thus, the state must occasionally tell the victim's friends and family that even though it abhors the defendant's acts, some offenders do not deserve punishment. Before it can do that, however, a judgment about whether such persons were responsible for their actions must be made.

What is the legal standard for insanity? There is no single answer. The following sections describe several definitions currently in use. The legal standards that define criminal responsibility vary from state to state, but in all states, the defendant is initially presumed to be responsible for his or her alleged offense. Therefore, if pleading insanity, defendants have the duty to present evidence that would disprove the presumption of criminal responsibility in their case. A related legal issue is the assessment of **mens rea**, or the mental state of knowing the nature and quality of a forbidden act. To be a criminal offense, an act not only must be illegal but also must be accompanied by the necessary *mens rea*, or guilty mind.

Varying Insanity Defense Rules

The M'Naghten Rule: An Early Attempt to Define Insanity. In 1843, an Englishman named Daniel M'Naghten shot and killed the private secretary of the British prime minister. Plagued by paranoid delusions, M'Naghten believed that the Prime Minister,

Sir Robert Peel, was part of a conspiracy hatched by the Tory party against him. M'Naghten initially sought to escape his imagined tormentors by traveling through Europe. When that didn't work, he stalked the Prime Minister and, after waiting in front of his residence at No. 10 Downing Street, shot the man he thought was Peel.

M'Naghten was charged with murder, and his defense was to plead not guilty by reason of insanity. Nine medical experts, including the American psychiatrist Isaac Ray, testified for two days about his mental state, and all agreed that he was insane. On instructions from the lord chief justice, the jury rendered a verdict of not guilty by reason of insanity without even leaving the jury box to deliberate. M'Naghten was committed to the Broadmoor Asylum for the Insane, where he remained for the rest of his life.

The public was infuriated, as was Queen Victoria, who had been the target of several attempts on her life. She demanded a tougher test of insanity. Subsequent debate in the House of Lords led to what has come to be called the **M'Naghten rule**, which was announced in 1843, long before psychiatry became a household word. The M'Naghten rule, which became the standard for defining insanity in Great Britain and the United States, "excuses" criminal conduct if the defendant, as a result of a "disease of the mind," (1) did not know what he was doing (e.g., believed he was shooting an animal rather than a human), or (2) did not know that what he was doing was wrong (e.g., believed killing unarmed strangers was "right").

The M'Naghten rule (or a close variation) is used in 29 states and the federal jurisdiction (Packer, 2009), so it is by far the most frequently-employed legal standard for insanity in the United States. It has often been criticized on the basis that the cognitive focus ("knowing wrongfulness") is too limiting, and does not allow consideration of motivational and other influences affecting the control of behavior. There have been a number of alternative legal tests of insanity since the M'Naghten rule was first established, which are described in the sections that follow.

The Brawner Rule, Stemming from the Model Penal Code. A committee of legal scholars developed the Model Penal Code, which led to what is now called the **Brawner rule**. This rule states that a defendant is not responsible for criminal conduct if he, "at the time of such conduct as a result of mental disease or defect, [lacks] substantial capacity either

to appreciate the criminality [wrongfulness] of his conduct or to conform his conduct to the requirements of the law." This standard, or a variation, allows judges and juries to consider whether mentally ill defendants have the capacity to understand the nature of their acts or to behave in a lawful way. As of 2011, it was used in 18 states (FindLaw, 2012). Federal courts have also adopted the Brawner rule in a drastically altered form (which we describe later).

The Brawner test differs from the M'Naghten rule in three substantial respects. First, by using the term *appreciate*, it incorporates the emotional as well as the cognitive determinants of criminal actions. Second, it does not require that offenders exhibit a total lack of appreciation for the nature of their conduct, but only a lack of "substantial capacity." Finally, it includes both a cognitive element and a volitional element, making defendants' inability to control their actions a sufficient criterion by itself for insanity.

The Insanity Defense Reform Act. In the wake of the trial of John Hinckley, Jr., who attempted to assassinate President Ronald Reagan, the U.S. Congress enacted the Insanity Defense Reform Act (IDRA) in 1984. The law modified the existing insanity defense (eliminating the "volitional" prong and retaining the "cognitive" prong), with the expectation that fewer defendants would be able to use it successfully. The law did not abolish the insanity defense, but changed it substantially. In addition to eliminating the volitional prong, it also changed the insanity defense process as follows:

1. It prohibited experts from giving ultimate opinions about insanity (i.e., whether the defendant was insane at the time of the crime). Although this prohibition may have little effect on jurors, reformers believed it would prevent expert witnesses from having excessive influence over the jury's decision.
2. It placed on the defendant the burden to prove insanity, replacing the previous requirement that the prosecution must prove a defendant's sanity.

Empirical Research Relevant to Varying Insanity Defense Rules. What little research has been conducted on the Insanity Defense Reform Act suggests that it does not accomplish either what its proponents envisioned or what its critics feared. At least in mock jury studies, verdicts do not significantly differ regardless of whether the jurors have heard IDRA instructions, Brawner instructions, or no instructions (Finkel, 1989). In addition, states with the broadest test of insanity (Brawner) do not show higher rates of insanity acquittals than states with the narrowest test (M'Naghten) (Melton et al., 2007).

In theory, varying rules for insanity should influence jurors' understanding of the defense, but psychologists have questioned whether the typical juror can comprehend the legal language of these definitions and then apply them as intended by the courts. Elwork, Sales, and Suggs (1981) found jurors only 51% correct on a series of questions testing their comprehension of instructions regarding the M'Naghten rule. Ogloff (1991) obtained similar results: Regardless of what insanity rule was used, college students showed very low rates of recall and comprehension of crucial components in various insanity definitions. It may be that jurors (or mock jurors) do not understand the differences between these different tests very well, consistent with the broader conclusion that jurors do not understand the nuances of a variety of legal instructions that are provided to them (Lieberman, 2009).

The limited empirical evidence indicates that different standards of insanity also make little difference in verdicts. Although instructions have some effect on jury decision making in insanity cases, they tell only part of the story—and perhaps a minor part at that (Finkel & Slobogin, 1995; Ogloff, 1991; Roberts & Golding, 1991).

A much greater influence may be exerted by preexisting attitudes toward the insanity defense (Eno Louden & Skeem, 2007). This decision process is an example of how jurors are prone to interpret "facts" in the context of a personal story or narrative that "makes the most sense" to each of them subjectively. Differences among jurors in the individual narratives they weave about the same set of trial "facts" may be related, in turn, to the different attitudes they hold about the morality of the insanity defense and the punishment of mentally ill offenders (Roberts & Golding, 1991). For instance, one study found that jurors conceptualized the prototypical insanity defendant in one of three ways: (1) severely mentally disordered (SMD), characterized by extreme, chronic, uncontrollable mental illness and retardation that impair the defendant's ability to function in society; (2) morally insane (MI), typified by symptoms of psychosis and psychopathy, a categorization used to represent a malevolent, detached, and unpredictably violent offender; or (3) mental-state-centered (MSC), describing a defendant who suffered from varied, but clearly supported, impairments in his mental state at the time of his offense (Skeem & Golding, 2001). Jurors who held SMD- or MI-like prototypes made up the vast majority of the sample (79%), and they tended to believe that the insanity defense was frequently raised, was easily abused, and jeopardized public safety. By contrast, those jurors who held MSC-like prototypes (21%) were less likely to perceive the insanity defense as unjust and tended to believe that the constitutional rights ascribed to defendants were necessary components of the legal process.

Famous Trials and the Use of the Insanity Plea

Before reporting on the actual frequency and effectiveness of attempts to use the plea, we will review the results of several highly publicized trials that have molded public opinion about insanity pleas.

Trials in Which the Insanity Plea Failed. Among murder defendants who have pleaded insanity as a defense are Jack Ruby, whom millions of television viewers saw kill Lee Harvey Oswald, President John F. Kennedy's alleged assassin; Sirhan Sirhan, charged with the assassination of Robert F. Kennedy; John Wayne Gacy, who was convicted of killing 33 boys in Chicago; and Andrea Yates, charged with drowning her children in the bathtub. All these defendants were convicted of murder despite their pleas of insanity, although Ms. Yates was found not guilty by reason of insanity in a second trial granted after her appeal of her conviction in the first.

In the Jeffrey Dahmer case, jurors rejected a plea of insanity as a defense against murder charges. Dahmer admitted killing and dismembering 15 young men in Milwaukee over about a 10-year period, but his attorney, Gerald Boyle, argued that Dahmer was insane at the time—a sick man, not an evil one. Prosecutor Michael McCann disagreed, arguing that Dahmer knew that what he was doing was wrong. After listening to two weeks of evidence, including taped interviews in which Dahmer explained how he had dismembered his victims and expert testimony about Dahmer's mental condition, the jury ruled, by a 10–2 margin, that Jeffrey Dahmer was sane. He was subsequently sentenced to life in prison for his crimes, and was killed in prison by a fellow inmate.

Wisconsin defines insanity with the Brawner rule; consequently, to have found Dahmer insane, the jury would have had to conclude that he suffered a mental disorder or defect that made him unable either to appreciate the wrongfulness of his conduct or to control his conduct as required by the law. The jury rejected both conclusions, perhaps because of evidence that Dahmer was careful to kill his victims in a manner that minimized his chances of being caught. This cautiousness suggested that he appreciated the wrongfulness of his behavior *and* could control it when it was opportune to do so.

Several other famous defendants who might have attempted to escape conviction through use of the insanity plea did not do so. Among these are Son of Sam serial murderer David Berkowitz, cult leader Charles Manson, and Mark David Chapman, who killed John Lennon.

Trials in Which the Insanity Plea "Succeeded." Occasionally, when a judge or jury concludes that the defendant is not guilty by reason of insanity, the defendant spends only a short period of time in a treatment program. After being acquitted on charges of malicious wounding (for cutting off her husband's penis), Lorena Bobbitt was released from the mental hospital following only several weeks of evaluation to determine whether she met criteria for involuntary hospitalization (she did not).

But sometimes when the insanity plea "works," the defendant spends more time in an institution than he or she would have spent in prison if found guilty. In fact, this outcome has led defense attorneys to request that judges be required to instruct jurors that if the defendant is found not guilty by reason of insanity, he or she will probably be committed to a secure psychiatric hospital (Whittemore & Ogloff, 1995). The Supreme Court, however, has refused to require such an instruction (*Shannon v. United States*, 1994).

The case of John W. Hinckley, Jr. has had the greatest influence of any of those discussed in this chapter, triggering much of the court reform and legislative revision regarding the insanity plea since 1982. It is summarized in Box 10.4.

Even though the Hinckley case is one in which the insanity defense was successful in the narrow sense of the word, that outcome was largely a result of a decision by the presiding judge regarding the burden of proof. Judge Barrington Parker instructed the jury in accordance with then-existing federal law, which

required the prosecution to prove the defendant sane beyond a reasonable doubt. After listening to two months of testimony, the Hinckley jury deliberated for four days before finding the defendant not guilty by reason of insanity. Afterward, several jurors said that, given the instruction that it was up to the government prosecutors to prove Hinckley sane, the evidence was too conflicting for them to agree. They thought his meandering travels raised a question about his sanity, and both sides' expert psychiatric witnesses had testified that he suffered from some form of mental disorder.

Facts about the Insanity Defense

When the Insanity Defense Is Used. The insanity defense is most often used in cases in which the defendant is charged with a violent felony. In the largest study to date of insanity acquittees, data from NGRI acquittees from four states ($N = 1,099$) were obtained (Steadman et al., 1993). These investigators found that 22.5% of the insanity acquittees had been charged with murder and that a total of 64% had been charged with crimes against persons (murder, rape, robbery, or aggravated assault).

Available research consistently suggests that the majority of defendants found not guilty by reason of insanity (NGRI) have been diagnosed as psychotic, suggesting severe and probably chronic mental impairments (Melton et al., 2007). Steadman and colleagues (1993) reported that 67.4% of the insanity acquittees described in their study were diagnosed with a schizophrenic disorder and that another 14.9% were diagnosed with another major mental illness.

How often do criminal defendants being assessed for insanity try to fake a mental disorder? On the basis of his research, Rogers (1986, 1988) estimated that about one of four or five defendants being assessed for insanity engages in at least moderate malingering of mental disorders. This figure suggests that crafty conning is not rampant but is frequent enough to cause concern. As a result, psychologists have developed a number of assessment methods to detect persons who are trying to fake a mental disorder. These methods include special structured interviews, individual psychological tests, and specialized measures (Rogers, 2008). These techniques have shown promising results in distinguishing between subjects who were trying to simulate mental illness (to win

B o x   10.4   THE CASE OF JOHN W. HINCKLEY, JR. AND THE ATTEMPTED ASSASSINATION OF PRESIDENT REAGAN

Bob Daugherty/AP Photo

John W. Hinckley, Jr.

Television replays show John Hinckley's March 30, 1981, attempt to kill President Ronald Reagan. When Hinckley came to trial 15 months later, his lawyers didn't dispute the evidence that he had planned the attack, bought special bullets, tracked the president, and fired from a shooter's crouch. But he couldn't help it, they claimed; he was only responding to the driving forces of a diseased mind. Dr. William Carpenter, one of the defense psychiatrists, testified that Hinckley did not "appreciate" what he was doing; he had lost the ability to control himself.

The defense in John Hinckley's trial made several other claims:

1. Hinckley's actions reflected his pathological obsession with the movie *Taxi Driver*, in which Jodie Foster starred as a 12-year-old prostitute. The title character, Travis Bickle, is a loner who befriends Foster after he is rejected by the character played by Cybill Shepherd; he stalks a political candidate but eventually engages in a bloody shootout to rescue the Foster character. It was reported that Hinckley had seen the movie 15 times and that he so identified with the hero that he had been driven to reenact the fictional events in his own life (Winslade & Ross, 1983).

2. Although there appeared to be planning on Hinckley's part, it was really the movie script that provided the planning force. The defense argued, "A mind that is so influenced by the outside world is a mind out of control and beyond responsibility" (Winslade & Ross, 1983, p. 188).

3. The defense tried to introduce the results of a CAT scan—an image of Hinckley's brain using computerized axial tomography—to support its contention that he was schizophrenic. The admissibility of this evidence became a controversy at the trial. The prosecution objected, claiming that all the apparent scientific rigor of this procedure—the physical evidence, the numerical responses—would cause the jury to place undue importance on it. The prosecution also contended that there were no grounds for concluding that the presence of abnormal brain tissue necessarily denoted schizophrenia. Initially, the judge rejected the request to admit this testimony, but he later reversed the decision on the ground that it might be relevant.

Critical Thought Question

The Hinckley defense argued that he was so influenced by the movie "Taxi Driver" that he was not in control of his actions and therefore (under the prevailing insanity standard in federal court at that time) not guilty by reason of insanity. If you had been a member of the jury, how much weight would you have placed on evidence that he had seen the movie many times and seemed to be reenacting parts of it in his own life?

---

monetary incentives for being the "best" fakers) and those who were reporting symptoms truthfully.

In their large study, Steadman et al. (1993) observed that the decision to acquit by reason of insanity was most strongly influenced by clinical factors. They compared those who successfully employed the insanity defense with others who entered this plea but were nevertheless found guilty, and reported that 82% of the former group but only 38% of the latter group had been diagnosed with a major mental illness.

On the basis of research studies, we have learned more about defendants who are found not guilty by reason of insanity (NGRI). For instance,

1. Although most NGRI defendants have a record of prior arrests or convictions, this rate of previous criminality does not exceed that of other felons (Boehnert, 1989; Cohen, Spodak, Silver, & Williams, 1988).

2. Most NGRI defendants come from lower socioeconomic backgrounds (Nicholson, Norwood, & Enyart, 1991).

3. Most NGRI defendants have a prior history of psychiatric hospitalizations and have been diagnosed with serious forms of mental illness, usually psychoses (Nicholson et al., 1991; Steadman et al., 1993).

4. Most NGRI defendants have previously been found incompetent to stand trial (Boehnert, 1989).

5. Although most studies have concentrated on males, female defendants found NGRI have similar socioeconomic, psychiatric, and criminal backgrounds to their male NGRI counterparts (Heilbrun, Heilbrun, & Griffin, 1988).

Public Perceptions of the Insanity Defense

The American public has repeatedly expressed its dissatisfaction with the insanity defense. Several surveys have concluded that most U.S. citizens view the insanity defense as a legal loophole through which many guilty people escape conviction (Skeem & Golding, 2001; Bower, 1984; Hans & Slater, 1983). After John Hinckley was found not guilty by reason of insanity (NGRI), a public opinion poll conducted by ABC News showed that 67% of Americans believed that justice had not been done in the case; 90% thought Hinckley should be confined for life, but 78% believed he would eventually be released back into society.

The public's disapproval of the insanity defense appears to be stimulated by trials such as Hinckley's that receive massive publicity. Melton et al. (2007) reported the following three beliefs to be prevalent among the public: (1) A large number of criminal defendants use the insanity defense, (2) those defendants found NGRI are released back into society shortly after their NGRI acquittals, and (3) persons found insane are extremely dangerous.

How accurate are these views? Are they myths or realities? Given the interest and debate surrounding the insanity defense, it is surprising that so few empirical studies have been conducted to investigate its actual outcomes. But there are some data concerning each of these questions.

How Often Is the Plea Used, and How Often Is It Successful? The plea is used much less often than people assume. A survey of the use of the insanity defense in eight states between 1976 and 1985 found that although the public estimated that the insanity defense was used in 37% of the cases, the actual rate was only 0.9% (Silver, Cirincione, & Steadman, 1994). Consistent with these figures, the data reported from the states of California, Georgia, Montana,

and New York (Steadman et al., 1993) indicate that defendants in those states, over a 10-year period, entered an insanity plea in 0.9% of felony cases and were successfully acquitted as NGRI in 22.7% of the cases in which this plea was entered.

Studies such as these are particularly valuable because few individual states keep complete records on the use of the insanity plea and its relative success. The findings reported in these studies suggest that of the nine insanity pleas raised in every 1,000 criminal felony cases, about two will be successful.

To answer the question of how many people are acquitted by reason of insanity each year, Cirincione and Jacobs (1999) contacted officials in all 50 states and asked for the number of insanity acquittals statewide between the years 1970 and 1995. After persistent attempts to collect these data from a variety of sources, they received at least partial data from 36 states. Few states could provide information for the entire 25-year period, but the results shown in Table 10.1 were obtained.

What Happens to Defendants Who Are Found NGRI? Many mistakenly assume that defendants who are found NGRI go free. Steadman and Braff (1983) found that defendants acquitted on the basis of the insanity plea in New York had an average hospital stay of three years in a secure hospital. Researchers also found a clear trend for longer detentions of defendants who had committed more serious offenses: the average length of involuntary hospitalization was greater for those who had been charged with violent offenses (34.1 months) than for individuals with other categories of offenses (Steadman et al., 1993). The average length of confinement for all NGRI individuals was 28.7 months. But this figure undoubtedly underestimates the "true" average

T A B L E 10.1   Insanity Acquittals per 100,000 People
© Cengage Learning 2014

- The median number of insanity acquittals per state per year was 17.7.
- California and Florida had the highest annual averages (134 and 111, respectively).
- New Mexico (0.0) and South Dakota (0.1) had the lowest annual averages.
- Most of the acquittals were for felonies rather than misdemeanors.

period of confinement. Why? These data describe only individuals who were hospitalized and released—they cannot tell us about individuals who were hospitalized but not released. This points to one of the important differences between a criminal sentence, which often is determinate (of fixed length), and the hospital commitment following acquittal by reason of insanity, which is indeterminate (depending on the individual no longer meeting criteria for hospitalization).

Researchers have been particularly interested in learning whether defendants found not guilty by reason of insanity are confined for shorter periods than defendants who are found guilty of similar crimes. A survey of the use of the insanity defense across several states, covering nearly one million felony indictments between 1976 and 1985, sought answers to that question (Silver, 1995). On the basis of more than 8,000 defendants who pleaded insanity during this period, Silver (1995) found that compared to convicted defendants, insanity acquittees spent less time in confinement in four states and more time in confinement in three states.

Some states use a procedure known as *conditional release*, in which persons found NGRI are released to the community (following a period of hospital confinement) and are monitored and supervised by mental health personnel. Conditional release is the mental health system's counterpart to parole; it functions essentially like a form of outpatient commitment. According to one four-state follow-up of 529 persons found NGRI, about 60% of these individuals were conditionally released within five years of their confinement (Callahan & Silver, 1998). Of those released, the median period of hospital confinement was 3.6 years for violent offenders and 1.3 years for those charged with less serious offenses.

How Dangerous Are Defendants Found NGRI?

Because most defendants who are found NGRI are quickly committed to an institution following their acquittal, it is difficult to assess the risk they pose to public safety at that time. In addition, they are likely to receive treatment in the hospital to which they are committed, further complicating the question of their risk of reoffending without this treatment. The limited evidence available on this question suggests either no difference in recidivism rates between NGRI defendants and "regular" felons or slightly lower recidivism rates among the NGRI group (Cohen et al., 1988; Melton et al., 2007). For instance, in a year-long study examining rehospitalization and criminal recidivism in 43 NGRI acquittees, nearly half (47%) were rehospitalized, a minority of the patients (19%) were rearrested or had committed a new crime, and nearly a fourth of the patients (24%) were reintegrated into the community without difficulty (Kravitz & Kelly, 1999).

Thus, insanity acquittees continue to have legal and/or psychiatric problems, but their overall rate of criminal recidivism falls in the range found for criminals in general.

Current Criticisms of the Insanity Defense

Even if the insanity defense is not successful as often as presumed, legitimate concerns remain about its continued use. We will now evaluate several of these.

It Sends Criminals and Troublemakers to Hospitals and Then Frees Them.   Psychopathic killers can try to capitalize on the insanity plea to escape prison and eventually get released from the hospital. How often this happens is unknown. Some data indicate that persons found NGRI are confined more frequently and for longer periods than defendants convicted of similar crimes (Perlin, 1996). After confinement, acquittees also may undergo an additional period of conditional release.

The biggest problem with such insanity acquittals is that they are sometimes highly publicized, contributing to the public's perception that they "happen all the time," and that the insanity defense is therefore a constant threat to justice. Such acquittals are relatively rare, in reality. Furthermore, if in the interest of protecting society all NGRI defendants were kept hospitalized until they no longer showed symptoms of mental illness, then society would have to be willing to violate the rights of many mentally ill persons to protect against the violence of a few.

It Is a Defense Only for the Rich.   The parents of John W. Hinckley, Jr. spent between $500,000 and $1,000,000 on psychiatric examinations and expert psychiatric testimony in their son's trial—an amount that contributes to the perception of the insanity defense as a jail dodge for the rich. Of all the criticisms leveled at the insanity defense, this one is perhaps the most clearly contradicted by the data. A long line of studies has failed to find socioeconomic or racial bias in the use or the success of the insanity defense (Boehnert, 1989; Howard & Clark, 1985; Nicholson et al., 1991; Pasewark & Pantle, 1981; Steadman et al., 1993). In addition, this criticism is further weakened by the Supreme Court's 1985 ruling, in the case of *Ake v. Oklahoma*, that poor defendants who plead insanity are entitled to psychiatric assistance at state expense in pursuing this defense.

Although defendants who can afford to hire their own experts might be more likely to benefit from raising the issue of insanity, this is not a problem unique to the insanity defense. Defendants who can afford ballistics experts, chemists, and their own private detectives also have an advantage over poor defendants, but no one suggests that a defense based on ballistics evidence, blood analyses, or mistaken identity should be prohibited because of the expense.

It Relies Too Much on Psychiatric Experts. Several issues are pertinent here. One criticism is that testifying about insanity forces psychiatrists and clinical psychologists to give opinions about things they are not competent or trained to do—for example, to express "reasonable certainty" rather than probability about a person's mental condition, and to claim greater knowledge about the relationship between psychological knowledge and legal questions than is justified.

Within the field of psychology, there is debate on these matters. The debate centers on two related questions: (1) Can clinicians reliably and validly assess mental illness, mental retardation, neuropsychological disorders, and disorders occurring in childhood and adolescence? (2) Will this assessment permit the formulation of accurate opinions about a defendant's criminal responsibility for acts committed in the past? Researchers have found some support for the reliability and validity of psychologists' evaluations of criminal responsibility. Results from several studies revealed strong agreement (88% to 93%) between evaluators' recommendations and courts' decisions about defendants' criminal responsibility (see Viljoen, Roesch, Ogloff, & Zapf, 2003), which is important because courts' decisions are one kind of "outcome validation measure" in this kind of research.

Additionally, critics are concerned over the intrusion of psychology and psychiatry into the decision-making process. They want to reserve the decision for the judge or jury, the fact finder in the trial. This criticism is an example of the general concern

over the use and willingness of experts to answer legal questions for which they possess limited scientific evidence. One remedy proposed to solve this problem is to prevent experts from giving what is often called **ultimate opinion testimony**; that is, they could describe a defendant's mental condition and the effects it could have had on his or her thinking and behavioral control, but they could not state conclusions about whether the defendant was sane or insane. The federal courts, as part of their reforms of the insanity defense, now prohibit mental health experts from offering ultimate opinion testimony about a defendant's insanity. But does this prohibition solve any problems, or is it merely a "cosmetic fix" (Rogers & Ewing, 1989) that has few effects?

In a study of whether prohibiting ultimate opinion testimony affects jury decisions (Fulero & Finkel, 1991), subjects were randomly assigned to read one of 10 different versions of a trial, all of which involved a defendant charged with murdering his boss and pleading insanity as a defense. For our purposes, the comparisons among three different versions of the trial are of greatest interest. Some subjects read transcripts in which the mental health experts for both sides gave only *diagnostic testimony* (that the defendant suffered a mental disorder at the time of the offense); a second group read a version in which the experts gave a diagnosis and then also offered differing *penultimate opinions* about the effects this disorder had on the defendant's understanding of the wrongfulness of his act; a final group read a transcript in which the experts offered differing diagnoses, penultimate opinions, and *ultimate opinion testimony* about whether the defendant was sane or insane at the time of the killing. Did ultimate opinion testimony affect the subjects' verdicts? Not in this study; subjects' verdicts were not significantly different regardless of the type of testimony they read. The lack of difference could be interpreted as evidence that the prohibition of ultimate opinion testimony is unnecessary, or it could indicate that the ban streamlines the trial process without sacrificing any essential information.

Finally, there is the feeling that the process of assessing sanity in criminal defendants holds mental health professionals up to ridicule. When the jury sees a parade of mental health experts representing one side and then the other, their confidence in the behavioral sciences is jeopardized; this is also true for the general public, when they read about this process involving a number of different experts (Slater & Hans,

1984). Further, some experts, in an effort to help the side that has retained them, offer explanations of such an untestable nature that their profession loses its credibility with jurors and the public. However, in many cases involving claims of insanity, the experts retained by each side basically agree on the question of insanity. These cases receive less publicity because they often end in a plea agreement.

Revisions and Reforms of the Insanity Defense

Several reforms in the rules and procedures for implementing the insanity defense have been introduced. Proposals have ranged from abolition of the insanity defense (as has already been done in five states), to provision of a "guilty but mentally ill" verdict, to reform of insanity statutes, to maintenance of the present procedures. We review three reforms in this section.

The Guilty but Mentally Ill (GBMI) Verdict. Since 1976, about a quarter of the states have passed laws allowing juries to reach a verdict of guilty but mentally ill (GBMI) in cases in which a defendant pleads insanity. These GBMI rules differ from state to state, but generally they give a jury the following verdict alternatives for a defendant who is pleading insanity: (1) guilty of the crime, (2) not guilty of the crime, (3) NGRI, or (4) GBMI. Typically, a judge will sentence a defendant found GBMI exactly as he or she would another defendant found guilty of the same offense. In some jurisdictions, the GBMI-convicted individual starts his or her term in a hospital and then is transferred to prison after treatment is completed. In others, the individual simply receives treatment (if needed) while serving a prison sentence.

Proponents of GBMI verdicts hoped that this compromise verdict would decrease the number of defendants found NGRI. However, actual GBMI statutes have not produced decreases in NGRI verdicts in South Carolina or Michigan. One possible explanation for the lack of change in NGRI verdicts in states with GBMI statutes is that jurors do not understand the differences between the verdicts. One study examined jurors' knowledge about the two verdicts and found that only 4% of potential jurors correctly identified meanings and outcomes of both NGRI and GBMI verdicts (Sloat & Frierson, 2005).

Other problems have provoked a "second look" at the GBMI reform, leading to skepticism about its value (Borum & Fulero, 1999). If regular insanity instructions are confusing to jurors, the GBMI verdict only adds to the confusion by introducing the very difficult distinction for juries to make between mental illness that results in insanity and mental illness that does not. One possible effect of the GBMI verdict is that it raises jurors' threshold for what constitutes insanity, leading to a more stringent standard for acquitting defendants who use this defense (Roberts, Sargent, & Chan, 1993).

Also, the claim that the GBMI option will make it more likely that mentally ill offenders will receive treatment is largely a false promise. Overcrowding at hospitals in most states has impeded implementation of this part of the GBMI option. In one Michigan study, 75% of GBMI offenders went straight to prison with no treatment (Sales & Hafemeister, 1984). In Kentucky, in spite of a statute that appears to promise treatment to those found GBMI, the chair of the parole board filed an affidavit in 1991 stating that "from psychological evaluations and treatment summaries, the Board can detect no difference in treatment or outcome for inmates who have been adjudicated as 'Guilty But Mentally Ill,' from those who have been adjudicated as simply 'guilty'" (Runda, 1991).

The Defense of Diminished Capacity. Several states allow a defense of **diminished capacity**, which is a legal doctrine that applies to defendants who lack the ability to commit a crime purposely and knowingly. Like the insanity defense, diminished capacity often involves evidence that the defendant suffers a mental disorder. It differs from insanity in that it focuses on whether defendants had the state of mind to act with the purpose and the intent to commit a crime—that is, to consider the consequences of their contemplated actions—not on whether they knew the crime was wrong or whether they could control their behavior. Suppose M'Naghten knew that murder was wrong but, because of his mental condition, wasn't thinking clearly enough to intend to kill Peel's secretary. Under these conditions, he would not be insane, but he would lack the *mens rea* (the necessary specific intent) for first-degree murder, so he probably would have been convicted of second-degree murder or manslaughter.

The rationale for this defense is straightforward: Offenders should be convicted of the crime that matches their mental state, and expert testimony should be offered on the issue of their mental state. The majority of states permit expert testimony about a defendant's *mens rea*, thereby allowing clinicians to present testimony that could be used in support of a diminished-capacity defense (Melton et al., 2007). As long as proof of a defendant's *mens rea* is required, defendants are likely to put forward expert evidence about it, especially in those states that have abolished the insanity defense. Even when the diminished capacity defense "works," it still usually leads to a prison sentence.

Elimination of the Insanity Plea. Winslade and Ross (1983) reviewed seven trials (mostly for murder) in which the insanity defense was used and psychiatric testimony was introduced to justify it. On the basis of their analysis of the outcomes of these trials, Winslade and Ross recommend that the insanity defense be eliminated. They conclude that the possibility of an insanity defense often leads to injustice, for the following reasons:

1. Juries are asked to decide questions that predispose them to make arbitrary and emotional judgments because of either over-identification with or alienation from the defendant;

2. Psychiatrists and other mental health professionals are encouraged to offer opinions, guesses, and speculations under the banner of scientific expertise; and

3. Society's views about criminality and craziness are so intertwined that an insanity defense to a crime does not make much sense (p. 198).

Arguments against Eliminating the Plea. James Kunen (1983), a former public defender, challenges the proposal to eliminate the insanity defense, noting that "Anglo-American legal tradition … has required that to convict someone of a crime, the prosecution must prove not only that he did a particular act—such as pulling a trigger—but that he did it with a particular state of mind" (p. 157). Kunen argues that we cannot talk about guilt without bringing in the person's state of mind. If a defendant slashes his victim's throat, thinking that he is slicing a cucumber, we say that he committed an act but not that he was guilty of the intent to commit a crime. This is why, even in those few states that have abolished the insanity defense, defendants may still introduce evidence that they lacked the mental state required for the crime.

Some offenders are truly "not guilty by reason of insanity"; they do not know the "nature and quality of their acts"—they literally do not know what they are doing. Harvard law professor Alan Dershowitz has said, "I almost would be in favor of abolishing the insanity defense, except there really are a few genuinely crazy people who believe they're squeezing lemons when they're actually squeezing throats" (quoted in Footlick, 1978, p. 108). Of course, the actual number of such people is much smaller than the number of defendants who raise the NGRI defense.

We believe that the NGRI plea should be maintained as an option, modifications of the system should be restricted to those that clarify the rule, and defendants for whom the defense was successful should be evaluated. For example, the Insanity Defense Reform Act changed the law that required the prosecution to prove that John Hinckley was not insane. If an act similar to Hinckley's were committed today in a federal jurisdiction or in the vast majority of states, the defendant, not the prosecution, would bear the responsibility of proving the plea; otherwise, the defendant would be found guilty. States should carefully monitor people committed after NGRI verdicts to ensure that they are not released while still mentally ill and dangerous. All indications are that this precaution is being taken.

Capital Sentencing Evaluations

Although mental health professionals are involved in many aspects of the legal process, none has more implication for a defendant's life than capital sentencing evaluations, which have been described as literally "a life or death matter" (*Satterwhite v. Texas*, 1988, p. 1802). The U.S. Supreme Court, in *Eddings v. Oklahoma* (1982), held that a trial court must consider any potentially mitigating information—evidence that argues *against* a death sentence. Mitigating factors are defined as "… any aspect of a defendant's character or record, or any of the circumstances of the offense that the defendant proffered as a basis for a sentence less than death" (*Lockett v. Ohio*, 1978, p. 604). This leaves the forensic clinician with a very broad focus for the evaluation. They must consider information about a defendant's physical, cognitive, social, and developmental history. Understanding, judgment, impulsivity, and values are influenced by developmental, cognitive, neuropsychological, cultural, community, situational, and other life influences, and it is important to consider these dimensions as part of a capital sentencing evaluation.

Some jurisdictions also consider the question of a defendant's future risk to society, and forensic clinicians often evaluate and testify about these risks. Texas requires that the jury consider future risk in weighing a sentence of death (Cunningham, 2010).

In addition to considering factors encompassing mitigation and future violence risk, clinical evaluations must also address the question of eligibility for capital sentencing if the defendant may be intellectually disabled, which would exempt the defendant from the death penalty, consistent with the Supreme Court decision in *Atkins v. Virginia* (2002). It is also useful to consider the quality of such evaluations, given the enormous importance of the sentencing decision (DeMatteo, Murrie, Anumba, & Keesler, 2011).

JUVENILE TRANSFER

During the 1980s and 1990s, there was substantial reform in the juvenile and criminal justice systems in the United States to allow more frequent prosecution of juveniles in criminal (adult) court. Such reform was motivated largely by the perception that juvenile crime had increased—and become more serious. A "get tough" approach was adopted in the attempt to decrease the rate of juvenile offending. One aspect of this "do the crime, do the time" philosophy involved expansion of ways in which adolescent (under 18 years old) offenders could be **transferred** (also called certified or waived) into criminal court.

A number of criteria are described in state laws on juvenile transfer. Two of the most important are public safety and **treatment needs and amenability**. Another criterion often cited is **sophistication-maturity**. Those evaluating a juvenile for a possible transfer must focus on the risk of future offending, the interventions needed to reduce this risk, and the likelihood that the youth will respond favorably to such interventions. The extent to which a juvenile is mature—cognitively and psychosocially—and the degree to which he/she is "adult-like" in their criminal thinking and behavior can both affect their response to interventions. The risk/need/responsivity (RNR) model (Andrews & Bonta, 1990) is useful in this respect, as it prompts the evaluator to consider risk of reoffending and risk-relevant deficits (e.g., substance abuse, family problems, education/employment problems) carefully. This consideration can be facilitated by using an empirically supported specialized tool, such as the Structured Assessment of Violence Risk in Youth (SAVRY; Borum, Bartels, & Forth, 2005), the Youth Level of Service/Case Management Inventory (YLS/CMI; Hoge & Andrews, 2002), or the Risk-Sophistication-Treatment Inventory (Salekin, 2004).

Evaluating a youth being considered for transfer is a forensic evaluation. It involves a legal question that will be answered by the judge, just as competence and insanity do. With juveniles, this means that evaluators must pay particular attention to school and family functioning, often by obtaining school records and conducting interviews of family members. They should also obtain information in other important areas. Peers, for example, can have an important influence on an adolescent's behavior. Was the offense committed alone, or was the youth with peers who may have encouraged one another to offend—or at least refused to back down? Substance abuse is another very important risk factor for offending; both using drugs and selling drugs are areas that should be targeted for intervention. Determining whether such intervention will be effective with a particular individual is difficult. Whether intervention will help a particular youth to desist from offending may be judged partly from the individual's expressed motivation, capacity to admire and respect authority figures, and responses to previous interventions (Grisso, 1998).

States vary in their specification of the age at which an adolescent is eligible for prosecution in the criminal system. Some states do not have any age limit; others have passed legislation decreasing the age of eligibility. Most still use the age of 14 or 15, however. There are several justifications for transferring an adolescent into the criminal system: (1) a charge of homicide; (2) a charge of other specific violent felonies (e.g., sexual assault, armed robbery, aggravated battery); or (3) a history of prior juvenile offending, suggesting a failure to respond to interventions provided by the juvenile system. In addition, some states have a policy involving "once an adult, always an adult," under which any adolescent convicted (or even tried) in criminal court will be charged in criminal court for future offenses, regardless of their nature or that individual's age.

Juveniles can be transferred to criminal (adult) court in several different ways. The state legislature in a given jurisdiction can determine that certain offenses allegedly committed by an adolescent must be filed directly in adult court (Griffin, 2003). For example, a state legislature may pass a law dictating that certain serious felony charges (e.g., armed robbery, sexual battery) be prosecuted in criminal court if the defendant is over a certain age. This approach to transfer has been called **statutory exclusion**. As of 2008, 29 states had statutory exclusion for certain offenses (National Center for Juvenile Justice, 2008).

A second approach to transferring juveniles to criminal court has been termed **judicial discretion**. When this procedure is used, the juvenile court judge decides whether the youth should be transferred to criminal court. Some 45 states provide for this type of transfer (National Center for Juvenile Justice, 2008). In making such a decision, the judge typically considers statutorily specified influences such as the youth's risk to public safety, amenability to treatment, and maturity (Brannen et. al., 2006). Such factors can be evaluated by mental health professionals, and the results described in the report and in expert testimony, to help inform the judge in making this decision. Generally, judicial discretion transfer laws authorize, but do not mandate, a move to adult court. However, as of 2004, 15 states had established circumstances that make such transfers mandatory (National Center for Juvenile Justice, 2008).

A third approach to juvenile transfer is called **prosecutorial discretion**. Prosecutorial discretion requires prosecutors to decide whether cases are filed initially in juvenile or adult court. As of 2008, 15 states had established the option of prosecutorial discretion for certain offenses (National Center for Juvenile Justice, 2008).

Is putting juveniles in the adult system effective in reducing reoffending? Common sense might suggest that adolescents would be less likely to offend if they knew that offending could result in more severe punishment. But research has not supported this. Research on general deterrent effects has reflected no decline in juvenile crime after these transfer laws came into effect. One study found no differences in the juvenile homicide/manslaughter rates in the states with prosecutorial discretion policies in the first five years after transfer laws were enacted (Steiner & Wright, 2006). Housing juveniles with adult criminals may also promote criminal attitudes and motivations (Forst, Fagan, & Vivona, 1989). Juveniles detained in New York's adult system were 89% more likely to be rearrested for a violent offense and 44% more likely to be rearrested for a property offense than juveniles in the New York metropolitan area who were detained within New Jersey's juvenile court system (Fagan, 1996). Higher rates of recidivism have also been observed in other studies with youth detained in the adult correctional system (Bishop, Frazier, Lanza-Kaduce, & Winner, 1996; Mason & Chang, 2001; Myers, 2001). Research also suggests that juveniles in adult facilities were more likely to be sexually assaulted and physically assaulted than were youth in the juvenile facilities (Beyer, 1997).

Juvenile transfer may also occur in the other direction (when juveniles placed in adult court are returned to juvenile court). This procedure has been called **reverse transfer**. Many states provide this option, allowing the criminal court judge to review the case and determine whether the youth should remain in adult court. Some 25 states currently have reverse transfer procedures that allow juveniles in adult court to petition for transfer back to juvenile court (National Center for Juvenile Justice, 2008). Finally, 14 states and the District of Columbia have no reverse transfer mechanism (Snyder & Sickmund, 2006).

SUMMARY

1. ***What is the scope of forensic psychology?*** Forensic psychology is a specialty that involves the application of knowledge and techniques from the behavioral sciences to answer questions about individuals involved in legal proceedings. The range of topics about which psychological and psychiatric experts are asked to testify continues to grow, facilitated by the development of scientific research and specialized forensic assessment measures.

2. ***What is meant by competence in the criminal justice process?*** Adjudicative competence entails having a sufficient present ability to consult with one's attorney with a reasonable degree of rational understanding and with a rational, as well as factual, understanding of the proceedings. This

same standard is applied to the questions of whether a defendant is competent to plead guilty and whether a defendant is competent to stand trial, so the phrase "competence to stand trial" is often used to refer to the entire process of disposition of charges, not merely the trial.

3. ***How do clinicians assess competence?*** When mental health professionals assess a defendant's competence, they should use one of several specialized instruments designed specifically for the purpose of evaluating how well a defendant understands the charges and potential proceedings. These specific tests and structured interviews have made competence assessments more reliable, valid, and useful. Competence evaluations are sometimes complicated by such factors as malingering, amnesia, and the problem of whether incompetent defendants can be treated against their will. Other competence issues (e.g., competence to refuse the insanity defense and competence to be sentenced) can arise at different points in the criminal process.

4. ***What are the consequences of being found incompetent to proceed in the criminal justice process?*** When defendants are found incompetent to stand trial, they can be committed for a period of treatment designed to restore their competence. If later found competent, they will stand trial or dispose of their charges through the plea-bargaining process. If treatment is not successful in restoring competence, the state will usually attempt to commit the person to a mental hospital for a period of time. The alternatives that have been proposed for dealing with the unrestorably incompetent criminal defendant include waiving the right to be found incompetent to proceed to trial and using a special form of commitment for incompetent defendants who are judged at a provisional trial to be guilty of the crimes with which they are charged.

5. ***What is the legal definition of insanity?*** Two major definitions of insanity are used currently. The M'Naghten rule defines insanity as not knowing the difference between right and wrong: "To establish a defense on the grounds of insanity it must be clearly proved that, at the time of committing the act, the accused was laboring under such a defect of reason, from disease of the mind, as not to know the nature and quality of the

act he was doing, or, if he did know it, that he did not know what he was doing was wrong." A total of 29 states plus the federal jurisdiction use some version of the M'Naghten rule to define insanity. The Brawner rule states that a person is not responsible for a criminal act if, as a result of mental disease or defect, the person lacked "substantial capacity either to appreciate the criminality of his conduct or to conform his conduct to the requirements of the law." This rule or a variation of it is the standard in 18 states. Until 1984, it was also the federal standard, but the federal system now requires the defense to show that, as a result of a severe mental disease or defect, the defendant was unable to appreciate the nature and quality or the wrongfulness of his or her acts. Five states have outlawed insanity as a defense, although these states still allow the defendant to introduce evidence about his or her mental condition that is relevant to determining *mens rea*. Some highly publicized trials have led to "successful" use of the insanity defense. But many others who used this defense were found guilty.

6. ***How frequently is the insanity defense used, and how successful is it?*** The insanity plea is used much less frequently than people assume; it is attempted in fewer than 1% of cases, and it succeeds in only about 23% of these cases. When it does succeed, there is no guarantee that the defendant will be released from the hospital any sooner than he or she would have been paroled from prison.

7. ***What are the major criticisms of the insanity defense, and what attempts have been made to reform it?*** Some examples of early release of NGRI defendants have led to justified criticism of the procedure. Other criticisms are that insanity cannot be reliably and validly assessed and that the insanity defense relies too much on psychiatric testimony. Reforms include the Insanity Defense Reform Act and the adoption in several states of a "guilty but mentally ill" verdict, resulting (at least in theory) in the defendant's being treated in a state hospital until releasable and then serving the rest of the sentence in prison. A number of states also allow the diminished-capacity plea, a partial defense based on mental condition. But it also has been controversial.

8. ***What are the important criteria in deciding on juvenile transfer?*** One important consideration is

public safety—the risk that a youth would commit further offenses subsequent to rehabilitation in the juvenile system. A second related consideration is the youth's needs and likely response to interventions reducing the risk of future offending, often called "treatment needs and amenability." Many jurisdictions also cite a youth's "sophistication-maturity," involving the extent to which the developmental level and the approach to offending are similar to those of adults.

KEY TERMS

adjudicative competence

Brawner rule

competence

competence to plead guilty

competence to stand trial

diminished capacity

insanity

judicial discretion

M'Naghten rule

mens rea

prosecutorial discretion

reverse transfer

sophistication-maturity

statutory exclusion

stipulate

transferred

treatment needs and amenability

ultimate opinion testimony

Chapter
11

Forensic Assessment in
Civil Cases

ORIENTING QUESTIONS

1. What problems are associated with expert testimony, and what reforms have been proposed?
2. Under what conditions can a plaintiff be compensated for psychological damages?
3. What is workers' compensation, and how do mental health professionals participate in such cases?
4. What capacities are involved in civil competence?
5. What criteria are used for decisions about disputes involving child custody or parental fitness?
6. What steps are taken in civil commitment, and how well can clinicians assess the risk of dangerousness or violent behavior, a key criterion for civil commitment?

Whether a defendant is mentally competent to stand trial (often called *adjudicative competence*, because it refers to a defendant's capacities to dispose of charges either through a trial or via plea bargaining) and whether a defendant was insane at the time of an alleged criminal offense are perhaps the best-known legal questions that mental health professionals help courts decide. However, they are certainly not the only questions. Throughout earlier chapters, we examined other questions arising in the legal system that psychologists are often asked to consider. Is a given individual a good candidate to become a police officer? Will a person who is suffering from mental illness be violent in the future? How accurate is one's memory for, and testimony about, highly traumatic events likely to be? These questions—like those of competence and insanity—are often asked of forensic psychologists and psychiatrists, and they are usually answered through a combination of research knowledge and the results of individual assessments performed by forensic clinicians.

Different kinds of litigation are making use of scientific knowledge and expert opinion. Psychology and psychiatry are two fields in which the use of experts has proliferated. Melton, Petrila, Poythress, and Slobogin (2007) offer a comprehensive listing and description of the legal questions that are most often addressed in civil, juvenile/family, and criminal cases. In addition to the legal questions discussed in previous chapters, mental health experts are involved in hearings or trials in the areas of civil commitment; psychological damages in civil cases; psychological autopsies (i.e., determination of the extent to which psychological problems are attributable to a preexisting condition); negligence and product liability; trademark litigation; discrimination; guardianship and conservatorship (a guardianship-like arrangement for an individual's financial assets); child custody; adoption; termination of parental rights; professional malpractice; and other social issues such as sexual harassment in the workplace. Therefore, judges now often find themselves in the position of having to decide whether the expert testimony that an attorney seeks to introduce at trial meets the criteria that the U.S. Supreme Court has established as the modern standard for admitting scientific evidence and expert testimony.

In this chapter, we introduce some points about expert testimony in civil cases, and describe six areas of forensic assessment in which psychologists and psychiatrists are involved: (1) psychological damages to civil plaintiffs, (2) workers' compensation claims, (3) the assessment of civil competence, (4) psychological autopsy, (5) child custody and parental fitness, and (6) civil commitment and risk assessment. Although these areas do not receive the publicity commanded by adjudicative competence or insanity at the time of the offense, they illustrate several ways in which psychological expertise can be applied to important legal questions. For each of the six areas, we will

- Discuss the basic psycholegal questions that experts are expected to address.

- Describe the techniques typically used by forensic clinicians to evaluate these questions.

- Summarize the empirical evidence and legal status associated with the forensic activity.

EXPERTS IN THE ADVERSARIAL SYSTEM

In general, a qualified expert can testify about a topic if such testimony is relevant to an issue in dispute and if the usefulness of the testimony outweighs whatever prejudicial impact it might have. If these two conditions are met, an expert will be permitted to testify if the judge believes that the testimony is based on sufficiently relevant and reliable scientific evidence. In other words, under criteria established by the U.S. Supreme Court in *Daubert v. Merrell Dow Pharmaceuticals* (1993) and *Kumho Tire Co. v. Carmichael* (1999), the judge serves as a "gatekeeper" who must determine whether the theory, methodology, and analysis that are the basis of the expert's opinion measure up to scientific standards. If they meet this standard, the judge will probably admit relevant expert testimony; if they do not, the judge should not allow the testimony.

Judges generally do not perform this gatekeeper function well (Gatowski et al., 2001). Many judges lack the scientific training that *Daubert/Kumho* appears to require. Even with such training, the range of expert topics about which judges need information is staggering. As a result, many critics, including experts and judges themselves, believe that the difficulty of distinguishing valid from invalid scientific evidence will result in jurors too often being exposed to "expert" testimony that is based on little more than "junk science" (Grove & Barden, 1999; see Box 11.1).

There are clear advantages to having mental health professionals provide expert testimony. Mental health professionals have specialized knowledge and training that can provide the court with valuable information in a variety of cases. For example, some psychologists are trained to administer tests to determine malingering mental health or neuropsychological problems in workers' compensation cases or are experienced in conducting clinical interviews to assess parental fitness.

However, judges, lawyers, and mental health professionals themselves have expressed great concern about the reliability, validity, propriety, and usefulness of expert testimony and the forensic assessment on which it is based. Former federal appellate judge David T. Bazelon (1974) once complained that "psychiatry … is the ultimate wizardry … in no case is it more difficult to elicit productive and reliable testimony than in cases that call on the knowledge and practice of psychiatry." This view was echoed by Warren Burger (1975), a former chief justice of the United States Supreme Court, who chided experts for the "uncertainties of psychiatric diagnosis." Critiques of psychologists' expert testimony in this area can be found in several sources (Grisso, 2003; Tillbrook, Mumley, & Grisso, 2003).

What are the main problems with or objections to testimony by psychological or psychiatric experts? Smith (1989) cites the following potential problems:

1. The scientific foundation for much of the testimony offered in court is often less than adequate, leading to unreliable information and therefore potentially incorrect verdicts.

Expert Witness Testifies

B o x   11.1   THE CASE OF COLUMBINE SHOOTER ERIC HARRIS, ANTIDEPRESSANT MEDICATION, AND VIOLENCE: EXPERT OPINION OR JUNK SCIENCE?

In 2002, Mark Taylor, a survivor of the Columbine High School shooting, sued the pharmaceutical company that manufactures Luvox, the antidepressant drug that one of the shooters, Eric Harris, was taking at the time of the shooting. Is there scientific evidence that this drug caused Eric Harris to be violent? Peter Breggin, M.D., one of the experts involved in the litigation, thought so. Was his testimony impartial and based on good science? Or was it an example of expert bias, poor science, or both?

Breggin opined in a preliminary report filed with the U.S. District Court in Denver that Luvox triggered Harris's rampage. "Absent persistent exposure to Luvox, Eric Harris would probably not have committed violence and suicide," noted Breggin.

Breggin, a Washington, D.C.-area psychiatrist, described himself as a medical expert with 30 years of experience in product liability lawsuits involving psychiatric drugs. However, some of this history reflects the skepticism of legal fact finders about his impartiality. A Wisconsin judge in 1997 observed, "Dr. Breggin's observations are totally without credibility. I can almost declare him [to be a] fraud or at least approaching that. I cannot place any credence or credibility in what he has to recommend in this case." On the question of whether his opinion reflects good science, another court held in 1995 that "Dr. Breggin's opinions do not rise to the level of an opinion based on 'good science.' The motion to exclude his testimony as an expert witness should be granted." The question of Breggin's impartiality may be

Eric Harris and Dylan Klebold, Columbine High shooters

one reason that Taylor eventually dropped his lawsuit in exchange for a contribution from the pharmaceutical company to the American Cancer Society.

Critical Thought Questions
1. What are some of the characteristics you would expect from an expert whose testimony is grounded in science?
2. How might "litigation bias" influence an expert who was conducting the scientific research, as opposed to citing the research of others?
3. How might one court's critical language about an expert influence that expert's work on similar litigation matters in the future?

---

2. Much of the testimony is of limited relevance, therefore wasting court time and burdening an already crowded docket.

3. Experts are too often permitted to testify about "ultimate issues" (Is the defendant insane? Was the plaintiff emotionally damaged?), which should be left to juries to decide.

4. Expert testimony is frequently used to introduce information that would otherwise be prohibited because it is hearsay. (Experts are permitted to share this information with juries if it is the kind of information they routinely rely on in reaching expert opinions.)

5. The adversarial system compromises experts' objectivity. Experts readily testify to opinions that favor the side that retained them.

6. Expert testimony is very expensive, and relying on experts gives an advantage to the side with more money.

7. Testing the reliability and validity of expert opinions through cross-examination is inadequate because attorneys are usually not well equipped to conduct such cross-examination, and juries often fail to understand the significance of the information that is uncovered during the cross-examination.

8. The spectacle of experts disagreeing with one another in trial after trial ultimately reduces the public's esteem for mental health professionals.

Grisso (2003) has updated the discussion of criticisms that have been applied to forensic mental health assessment. Such criticisms have been called "the five I's": ignorance, irrelevance, intrusion, insufficiency, and incredibility. They refer to not knowing (or not using) the proper legal standard; providing evidence that goes beyond what is relevant to the proceeding; offering conclusions that impinge upon the court's domain; providing limited supporting evidence for one's conclusions; and offering conclusions that are not justified by the evidence one does provide. These criticisms are similar in many respects to those described by Smith (1989) over 20 years ago. Although Smith was talking about expert testimony and Grisso was referring to forensic assessment more broadly, their overlap underscores an important point: good expert testimony is based on a good evaluation.

In response to these concerns, some of which are also supported by empirical research discussed later in this chapter, several reforms of expert testimony have been proposed. Most of these suggestions are aimed at reducing the undue influence or excessive partisanship that can adversely affect expert testimony. As a result, the federal courts do not permit testimony on the "ultimate issue" of insanity in forensic cases. This change was part of the overall reform of federal law concerning insanity that occurred in 1984. Still, there

is little evidence that such limitation of expert testimony has much impact on the use or success of the insanity defense (Borum & Fulero, 1999) and it is even less likely to affect the kinds of cases we discuss in this chapter.

Most authors and sources of authority suggest that partisanship in expert witnesses should be reduced or eliminated entirely. But there are a few who do not. For instance, in his book subtitled *Behind the Scenes with an Expert Witness,* Tanay (2010) describes his own experience as a psychiatric expert—particularly on the legal question of insanity—and argues that the expert should be a strong advocate so that unjust jury verdicts are less likely. Reviewing this book, prominent psychologist Stan Brodsky (who has done a great deal of work on the topic of expert testimony) discusses the personal and idiosyncratic approach taken by Dr. Tanay to expert testimony. Such an approach, says Brodsky, makes for interesting reading—but it also involves more advocacy (and less impartiality) than is appropriate for the forensic expert.

Other suggestions have involved reducing the overly adversarial nature of expert testimony by limiting the number of experts on a given topic, requiring that the experts be chosen from an approved panel of individuals reputed to be objective and highly competent, and allowing testimony only from experts who have been appointed by a judge rather than hired by one of the opposing attorneys. Although these changes would appear to reduce the "hired gun" problem, it is not clear which experts would belong on an approved list, or whether being appointed by a judge ensures an expert's impartiality. Furthermore, some research suggests that jurors might already be inclined to discount the testimony of experts whom they perceive to be "hired guns" because of the high fees such experts are paid and their history of testifying frequently (Cooper & Neuhaus, 2000).

Several scholars have suggested that courts not permit clinical opinion testimony unless it can be shown that it satisfies standards of scientific reliability. The standard required by the *Daubert/Kumho* decisions has made this recommendation more feasible (Imwinkelried, 1994). Such a requirement might reduce the frequency of testimony by forensic psychologists and psychiatrists, but unless lawyers and judges are educated more thoroughly about scientific methodology, it is unlikely that many of them will be able to correctly apply the concepts described in *Daubert* (e.g., falsifiability, error rate) toward making informed distinctions between "good" and "bad" science (Gatowski, Dobbin, Richardson, Ginsburg, Merlino, & Dahir, 2001).

A more modest reform would involve simply banning any reference to witnesses as providing *expert* testimony, a term that suggests that jurors should give it extra credence. Instead, judges would always refer—in the presence of juries—to *opinion* testimony or witnesses.

In addition to deleting any mention of expert testimony, federal judge Charles Richey (1994) recommended that juries be read a special instruction before hearing any opinion testimony in order to reduce its possible prejudicial impact. Here is an example of his recommended instruction:

> Ladies and Gentlemen, please note that the Rules of Evidence ordinarily do not permit witnesses to testify as to their opinions or conclusions. Two exceptions to this rule exist. The first exception allows an ordinary citizen to give his or her opinion as to matters that he or she observed or of which he or she has firsthand knowledge. The second exception allows witnesses who, by education, training and experience, have acquired a certain specialized knowledge in some art, science, profession or calling to state an opinion as to relevant and material matters. The purpose of opinion witness testimony is to assist you in understanding the evidence and deciding the facts in this case. You are not bound by this testimony and, in weighing it, you may consider his or her qualifications, opinions and reasons for testifying, as well as all other considerations that apply when you evaluate the credibility of any witness. In other words, you should give it such weight as you think it fairly deserves and consider it in light of all the evidence in this case.

PSYCHOLOGICAL DAMAGES TO CIVIL PLAINTIFFS

When one party is injured by the actions of a second party, the injured individual can sue the second party to recover monetary damages as compensation for the injury. This action is covered by an area of civil law known as torts. A **tort** is a wrongful act that causes harm to an individual. The criminal law also exacts compensation for wrongful acts, but on behalf of society as a whole; by punishing an offender, the criminal law attempts to maintain society's overall sense of justice. Tort law, on the other hand, provides a mechanism to remedy the harms that individuals have suffered from wrongful acts by another party.

As illustrated by the O. J. Simpson case, both criminal punishment and civil remedies can be sought for the same act. Simpson was prosecuted by the state, under the criminal law, for murder; he was also sued for monetary damages by the surviving relatives of the victims, who alleged that he caused the wrongful deaths of Nicole Brown Simpson and Ronald Goldman.

Many kinds of behavior can constitute a tort. Slander and libel are torts, as are cases of professional malpractice, invasion of privacy, the manufacture of defective products that result in a personal injury, and intentional or negligent behavior producing harm to another person.

Four elements are involved in proving a tort in a court of law and all involve behavioral issues. First, torts occur in situations in which one individual owes a **duty**, or has an obligation, to another. For instance, a physician has a duty to treat patients in accordance with accepted professional standards, and individuals have a duty not to harm others physically or psychologically. Second, a tort typically requires proving that one party breached or violated a duty that was owed to other parties. The **breached duty** can be due to negligence or intentional wrongdoing. **Negligence** is behavior that falls below a standard for protecting others from unreasonable risks; it is often measured by asking whether a "reasonable person" would have acted as the civil defendant acted in similar circumstances. **Intentional behavior** is conduct in which a person meant the outcome of a given act to occur.) Third, the violation of the duty must have been the proximate cause of the harm suffered by a plaintiff. A **proximate cause** is one that constitutes an obvious or substantial reason why a given harm occurred. It is sometimes equated with producing an outcome that is "foreseeable." So if a given event would be expected to cause a given outcome, it is a proximate cause. Fourth, a **harm**, or loss, must occur, and the harm has to involve a legally protected right or interest for which the person can seek to recover damages that have been suffered. If it can be established that (1) there was a duty (2) that was breached, (3) which proximately caused the (4) resulting harm, then a tort can be proven in a civil lawsuit.

The damages a person suffers from a tort can involve destruction of personal property, physical injuries, and/or emotional distress (sometimes called "pain and suffering"). Historically, the law has always sought to compensate victims who are physically hurt or sustain property losses, but it was reluctant to allow compensation for emotional distress, largely out of concern that such damages are too easy to fake and too difficult to measure. In cases in which recovery for emotional damages has been allowed, the courts have historically required that a physical injury have accompanied the psychological harm or that a plaintiff who was not physically injured was at least in a "zone of danger." (For example, even if the plaintiff was not injured by the attack of an escaped wild animal, plaintiff was standing next to his or her children when the

animal attacked them.) More recently, however, a growing number of states are abandoning the "zone of danger" restriction and allowing recovery for psychological harm suffered when the individual was not within this zone of danger (Buckley & Okrent, 2004).

One case that received extensive international coverage illustrates this historical approach to emotional damages. On the afternoon of March 22, 1990, the *Aleutian Enterprise*, a large fishing boat, capsized in the Bering Sea. Within 10 minutes, the boat sank, killing nine crew members. Twenty-two sailors survived the disaster; of these men, two returned to work in a short time, but the other twenty filed a lawsuit against the company that owned the ship. Of the 20 plaintiffs, 19 consulted a psychologist or psychiatrist, and every one of these 19 individuals was subsequently diagnosed with posttraumatic stress disorder (PTSD) by his mental health professional (Rosen, 1995). (The defendant company hired its own psychologist, who evaluated the plaintiffs and diagnosed PTSD in only five of them and some other postincident disorder in three others.) The surviving sailors were entitled to recover for their psychological injuries because they had been in the "zone of danger."

In recent years, the courts have progressed to a view in which psychological symptoms and mental distress are more likely to be compensated regardless of whether the plaintiff suffered physical injuries. Two types of "purely" psychological injuries are now claimed in civil lawsuits: those arising from "negligent" behavior and those arising from "extreme and outrageous" conduct that is intended to cause distress. In the former type of case, plaintiffs are often allowed to sue for psychological damages if they are bystanders to an incident in which a loved one is injured (e.g., a parent sees her child crushed to death when a defective roller coaster—on which the child was riding—derails).

In the case of intentional torts causing psychological distress, a plaintiff must prove that a defendant intentionally or recklessly acted in an extreme and outrageous fashion (sometimes defined as "beyond all bounds of decency") to cause emotional distress. In addition, the plaintiff must prove that the distress is severe. In other words, the effects must be something more than merely annoying or temporarily upsetting (Merrick, 1985). What kinds of behavior might qualify? Courts have found that a debt collector who was trying to locate a debtor acted outrageously when he

---

B o x 11.2 THE CASE OF ANTITERRORISM OFFICER "JOHN DOE": RACIAL/ETHNIC AND RELIGIOUS DISCRIMINATION IN THE WORKPLACE

Discrimination in the workplace can occur for different reasons. Consider the case of "John Doe," an undercover police officer in the New York City Police Department (NYPD). Egyptian-born and Muslim, he was subjected to treatment that may have been discriminatory for ethnic and religious reasons. The NPYD has contained an undercover unit of investigators, most of whom are of Middle Eastern or Asian backgrounds, who use their language and cultural skills to investigate potential terrorist threats against New York City. But one Egyptian-born analyst in the unit filed a suit charging that he was subjected to hundreds of anti-Muslim and anti-Arab e-mail messages sent out by a city contractor over the course of three years. In an interview, "Mr. Doe" (who was not named because he is still in the unit) said he complained repeatedly to supervisors but that no one took action.

The lawsuit cites e-mail briefing messages sent out several times a day to members of the unit by Bruce Tefft, a former Central Intelligence Agency (CIA) official who has identified himself in the past as the Police Department's counterterrorism adviser. (The suit was filed against both the NYPD and Tefft.) The e-mail messages were sent to everyone in the division, according to the suit, which also alleges that the briefing messages were preceded by anti-Muslim and anti-Arab statements like, "Burning the hate-filled Koran should be viewed as a public service at the least" and "This is not a war against terrorism … it is against Islam and we are not winning." In one, he asked, "Has the U.S. threatened to vaporize Mecca?" and responded, "Excellent idea, if true." The lawsuit alleged that e-mails "ridiculed and disparaged the Muslim religion and Arab people, and stated that Muslim- and Arab-Americans were untrustworthy and could not reliably serve in law enforcement positions or handle sensitive data."

According to a NYPD spokesman, the police commissioner was not aware of the "offensive commentary" until the complaint was made. "As soon as the Police Department became aware of a complaint about the content of e-mail sent by an individual not employed by the Police Department, we took immediate action to block his e-mails, followed by a cease and desist letter to the individual and his employer, a consulting firm," he wrote.

Reportedly the department's contract with this advisor ended in 2003, but Tefft continued to send the e-mail messages on his own, circumventing attempts by the department to block them. Mr. Doe's lawyer commented, "It's incredible in this day and age that hundreds of racist e-mails could be sent to hundreds of NYPD officials over three years, and not one person did a thing to stop it."

This unit was profiled on "60 Minutes" and in the *Wall Street Journal* and the New York *Daily News*. Mr. Doe said, "The NYPD was happy to introduce us to the press—'Here these guys are, the best of the best, they are doing a great job.' But then they failed to protect us under this smear, this constantly daily attack against my religion and against good Muslim Arab-Americans, and I will say good because the majority are good."

Critical Thought Question

Can you apply a tort law framework in analyzing this lawsuit? What are the questions that a court will need to answer in deciding whether the lawsuit should be decided in favor of the plaintiff (the officer who filed the suit)?

---

posed as a hospital employee and told the debtor's mother that her grandchildren had been seriously injured in a wreck and that he needed to find the debtor to inform him of this fact (*Ford Motor Credit Co. v. Sheehan*, 1979).

In recent years, an increasing number of cases have dealt with psychological injuries resulting from the tort of sexual harassment, usually in the work-place. A plaintiff who claims to have been sexually harassed at work can sue the workers responsible for the harassment and can also sue the company itself, if the plaintiff can show that the company knew (or should have known) about the harassment and failed to stop it. These cases can be filed either in state courts or in federal courts, where Title VII of the federal Civil Rights Act of 1991 applies to companies with at least 15 employees. Plaintiffs can seek both **compensatory damages** (payment for injuries suffered) and **punitive damages** (punishment of the company for its failure to respond properly to the misconduct).

Of course, the tort of harassment is not always based on gender. It may incorporate other characteristics—including racial/ethnic group or religious beliefs, as we see in the case of antiterrorism officer "John Doe," described in Box 11.2.

Assessment of Psychological Damages

When a mental health professional assesses a plaintiff, the clinician will typically conduct an evaluation that, like most evaluations, includes a social history, a clinical interview, and a number of psychological tests and specialized forensic measures (Boccaccini & Brodsky, 1999; Melton et al., 2007). One major difference, however, between standard clinical evaluations and forensic assessments is the much greater use of third-party interviews and review of available records in forensic examinations. This practice is based on two basic considerations (Heilbrun, 2001; Melton et al., 2007). First, forensic experts must be sure that their opinions are based on accurate information, and self-reported information in the context of litigation is not necessarily accurate. Second, forensic experts are often asked to evaluate an individual's psychological condition at some specific time or in some particular situation in the past. Therefore, clinicians must use independent sources of information, when possible, to verify their descriptions and judgments about such matters.

Using data from these sources, the clinician arrives at an opinion about the psychological condition of the person in question. With the exception of greater reliance on third-party interviews and records, this part of the evaluation resembles a standard clinical evaluation of individuals assessed for diagnostic and treatment purposes. The more difficult question the clinician must answer in litigation, however, is whether the psychological problems were caused by the tort, aggravated by the tort, or existed before the tort. In fact, given that some research suggests that psychological problems make people more prone to accidents, the clinician needs to consider whether certain psychological conditions might have contributed to the plaintiff being injured in the first place.

There is no established procedure for answering these questions, although most clinicians try to locate records and other sources of information that help them describe the development of any disorder that is diagnosed. In some situations, a plaintiff might allege that he or she was targeted for harassment precisely because the defendants knew of some prior difficulty that made the plaintiff vulnerable to a particular kind of harassment. In such cases, the clinician must consider this additional information before reaching a conclusion about the significance of the prior psychological problem.

Another complication may affect the evaluations of individuals who claim to have suffered psychological harm: Plaintiffs may be motivated to exaggerate their symptoms in order to improve their chances of winning large awards. Sometimes such symptom

exaggeration or fabrication (called **malingering**) involves outright lying. In other cases, a genuine psychological disturbance is present, but the plaintiff exaggerates its seriousness. Occasionally no deception is intended at all; the plaintiff has simply become convinced that he or she is suffering from a disorder and responds to the evaluation in a way that is meant to convince the examiner to reach the same conclusion.

A meta-analysis found that the possibility of receiving compensation for an injury was associated with more frequent reports of pain (Rohling, Binder, & Langhinrichsen-Rohling, 1995). Similar findings were observed in a second meta-analysis, focusing in particular on mild traumatic brain injury (Belanger, Curtiss, Demery, Lebowitz, & Vanderploeg, 2005). Of course, such findings do not necessarily show that litigation involvement causes exaggeration. It might work in the other direction as well—individuals with more intransigent pain might be more likely to litigate their claims. Or a third influence might affect both; for instance, lifestyle might influence both recovery from injury and propensity toward litigation. But it is certainly possible that litigation involvement increases both the experience of pain and the report of such pain resulting from injury (Greene, 2008).

In a review of the ethics of attorneys "coaching" their clients on how to "beat" psychological tests in civil litigation cases, Victor and Abeles (2004) argued that these techniques are well within the ethical boundaries of legal practice and that attorneys often view such coaching as an important part of advocating for their clients. Another study found that some attorneys believe it to be malpractice *not* to coach their clients on the malingering scales of psychological assessments (e.g., the Minnesota Multiphasic Personality Inventory-2 [MMPI-2], often used in civil litigation) (Youngjohn, 1995). These coaching strategies may be effective. One study revealed that the F scale on the MMPI-2 (one of the instrument's validity scales designed to detect possible malingering) was not as effective at identifying coached malingerers as at identifying noncoached malingerers (Storm & Graham, 2000). Of course, forensic evaluators who suspect that coaching has occurred are likely to compensate by gathering additional information from sources other than self-report.

Spurred by results like these and by estimates from experienced clinicians that malingering and self-serving presentations are not at all uncommon in forensic evaluations (Rogers, 2008), some have recommended that clinicians be attentive in forensic contexts to the particular motivation of litigants and take extra steps to scrutinize their claims (Heilbrun, 2001; Williams, Lees-Haley, & Djanogly, 1999).

WORKERS' COMPENSATION

When a worker is injured in the course of his or her job, the law provides for the worker to be compensated through a streamlined system that avoids the necessity of proving a tort. This system is known as *workers' compensation law*. All 50 states and the federal government have some type of workers' compensation system in place. Prior to workers' compensation, a person who was injured at work had to prove that the employer was responsible for a tort in order to receive compensation. This was difficult because employers had several possible defenses to the worker's claim. They often blamed the employee's negligence or the negligence of another worker for the injury. In other cases, employers said that a worker's injuries were simply the unavoidable risks of particular jobs and that the worker was well aware of these risks at the time of employment. As a result, until early in the 20th century, many seriously injured workers and their families were denied any compensation for their work-related injuries.

Workers' compensation systems were developed around the beginning of the 20th century to provide an alternative to the tort system. In workers' compensation systems, employers contribute to a large fund that insures workers who are injured at work, and employers also waive their right to blame the worker or some other individual for the injury. For their part, workers give up their right to pursue a tort case against their employers, and if they are compensated, the size of the award they receive is determined by (1) the type and duration of the injury and (2) their salary at the time of the injury. Workers can seek compensation for

- physical and psychological injuries suffered at work
- the cost of whatever treatment is given
- lost wages
- the loss of future earning capacity

Injured on the job

Determining how much impairment in future earning capacity a given mental disorder or psychological condition might produce is very difficult. Physicians can assess the degree of impairment from a ruptured disc or a paralyzed arm, but how can we measure the degree or permanence of a mental disability? To bring some uniformity to these assessments, many states require evaluators to use the American Medical Association's *Guides to the Evaluation of Permanent Impairment* (AMA, 2007). The *Guide* provides five categories of impairment, ranging from "no impairment" to "extreme impairment," that clinicians can use to organize their descriptions of a claimant. In general, however, ratings of psychological impairments are hard to quantify reliably.

Both employers and employees should benefit from a process in which workers' claims can be resolved fairly quickly, which is a major goal of the workers' compensation system. Formal trials are not held, and juries do not resolve these cases; they are heard and decided by a hearing officer or commissioner. (These decisions can be appealed.) In theory, workers' compensation cases should be handled expeditiously, but they often drag on for years as both sides go through a process of hiring one or more experts to examine the worker and give opinions about the injuries and any disability suffered.

How do mental health professionals become involved in workers' compensation claims? Due to the fact that psychological injuries or mental disorders arising from employment can be compensated, clinicians are often asked to evaluate workers and render an opinion about the existence, cause, and implications of any mental disorders (Piechowski, 2011).

Claims for mental disability usually arise in one of two ways, though there is a third (less likely) basis for a claim as well. First, a physical injury can lead to a mental disorder and psychological disability. A common pattern in these *physical–mental* cases is for a worker to sustain a serious physical injury (e.g., a broken back or severe burns) that leaves the worker suffering chronic pain. As the pain and the disability associated with it continue, the worker also experiences associated psychological problems, usually depression and anxiety. These problems can worsen until they become full-fledged mental disorders, resulting in further impairments of the worker's overall functioning.

The second work-related pathway to mental disability is for an individual either to suffer a traumatic incident at work or to undergo a long period of continuing stress that leads to substantial psychological difficulties. A night clerk at a convenience store who is the victim of an armed robbery and subsequently develops posttraumatic stress disorder is an example of such *mental–mental* cases. Another example is the clerical worker who, following years of overwork and pressure from a boss, experiences an anxiety disorder.

In a third kind of case, known as *mental–physical*, work-related stress leads to the onset of a physical condition such as high blood pressure. Many states have placed restrictions on these types of claims, and psychologists are seldom asked to evaluate them.

The number of psychological claims in workers' compensation litigation has increased dramatically in the last two decades, and much of the increase can be attributed to a surge in mental–mental cases (Bonnie & Monahan, 1996, Melton et al., 2007). At least three explanations have been proposed to account for this increase in psychological claims. First, because more women have entered the workforce, and because women are more often diagnosed with anxiety and

depressive disorders than men, the rise in psychological claims might be due to the increased percentage of female workers. A second possibility is that a shift in the job market from manufacturing and industrial jobs to service-oriented jobs has produced corresponding increases in job-related interpersonal stressors and decreases in physical injuries. A third possibility is that claims of psychological impairments are motivated primarily by financial incentives, generating a range of cases in which genuine impairments are mixed in with exaggerated or false claims of disability.

Assessment in Workers' Compensation Claims

Some empirical studies have been conducted on the assessment of psychological damages in workers' compensation cases. They usually focus on one of the following questions:

- How do workers' compensation claimants score on standard psychological tests such as the MMPI-2 and the MMPI-2-RF?

- Are certain injuries or stressors associated with a particular pattern of psychological test scores?

- Can psychological tests distinguish claimants who are suffering from a bona fide disorder from those who are faking or exaggerating their problems?

- What factors threaten the impartiality of forensic evaluations in workers' compensation cases?

In a study relevant to the first bullet point, investigators analyzed archival MMPI-2s produced by 192 women and 14 men involved in litigation related to alleged workplace sexual harassment and discrimination. Among the women, 28% produced a "normal limits" profile. The remaining profiles produced four distinctive clusters of profiles representing different approaches to the test items (Long, Rouse, Nelsen, & Butcher, 2004). For example, the first cluster combined a defensive unwillingness to acknowledge problems with evidence of depression and physical complaints. The second cluster involved responding that was neither exaggerated nor defensive, and also featured evidence of depression and physical problems. Both the third and fourth clusters were marked by exaggeration of problems and reports of generalized psychopathology, although the fourth cluster featured very extreme exaggeration.

Regarding the association between injuries and test scores, the research does not suggest that particular injuries or claims are reliably linked with different patterns of test scores (Melton et al., 2007). One reason for the lack of distinguishing patterns might be that regardless of the injury or the stressor, most people manifest psychological distress through a mixture of physical complaints and negative emotions such as anxiety, depression, and feelings of isolation.

We now turn to the question of whether psychological tests can distinguish between claimants with bona fide disorders and those who are exaggerating. The MMPI-2 and MMPI-2-RF contain sets of items that are sometimes used to assess the test-taking attitudes of a respondent. These validity scales can be examined to determine whether respondents might have tried to fool the examiner by exaggerating or denying psychological problems. In workers' compensation cases, a main concern is that some plaintiffs might "fake bad" by exaggerating or inventing symptoms to improve their chances for an award.

Some research focuses on whether existing or new validity scales on the MMPI-2 can distinguish respondents who have genuine symptoms from those who are malingering. Tests such as the Validity Indicator Profile (Frederick, 1997, 2000; Frederick & Crosby, 2000) and the Test of Memory Malingering (Tombaugh, 1997) have been developed to detect malingering on cognitive and neuropsychological measures.

The typical case of a person trying to exaggerate or fake mental disorder involves the individual answering many items in the "bad" direction, thereby attempting to look as disturbed as possible. However, the strategy might be more complicated in the case of a person who is faking or exaggerating a disorder in a workers' compensation case. These individuals usually want to appear honest, virtuous, and free of any psychological problems that might have existed prior to the injury, while at the same time endorsing many symptoms and complaints that would establish that they had been harmed by a work-related incident. In other words, their motivation involves a combination of faking good and faking bad. A special validity scale composed of MMPI-2 items that tap this simultaneous fake-good/fake-bad strategy has been developed and has had some success in distinguishing between genuine and faked psychological injury claims (Lees-Haley, 1991; 1992; Nelson, Sweet, & Demakis, 2006), although others (Butcher, Arbisi,

Atlis, & McNulty, 2008) have argued that the scale is more likely to represent general maladjustment than malingering.

One study included a sample of MMPI-2s of worker's compensation and personal injury cases (N = 289) to consider the relationship of various indicators of exaggeration. The investigators concluded that malingering may take the form of inconsistent responding as well as symptom exaggeration, with patients evaluated at the request of plaintiff attorneys showing a seemingly greater degree of symptom exaggeration and inconsistent responding than did those referred by defense counsel (Fox, Gerson, & Lees-Haley, 1995).

The impartiality of psychological evaluations performed in workers' compensation cases can be threatened by several factors (Tsushima, Foote, Merrill, & Lehrke, 1996). Chief among these problems is that attorneys often retain the same expert to conduct evaluations of different cases. An expert who is repeatedly hired by the same attorney, whether a plaintiff's or defense attorney, may risk opining what the attorney wants rather than rendering impartial opinions about each case.

One study investigated this issue by examining whether psychological assessments of workers' compensation claimants were related to the side that had retained the expert. Hasemann (1997) collected and compared 385 reports that had been prepared by various mental health professionals. Of these reports, 194 had been conducted by defense-hired experts, 182 were completed by plaintiff-hired experts, and 9 evaluations could not be classified. Did plaintiff and defense experts differ in their opinions in these cases? Several results indicate that they did and that they might have been unduly influenced by the adversarial system.

Consider these three results:

- Plaintiff experts gave impairment ratings to claimants that were nearly four times larger than the impairment ratings assigned by defense experts.

- Defense experts concluded that MMPIs completed by claimants were invalid or malingered in 72% of their evaluations, whereas plaintiff experts reached this conclusion in 31% of their evaluations.

- Of the 19 experts who had conducted three or more evaluations, 17 tended to do so almost exclusively for one side. Ten showed partiality toward plaintiffs, conducting a total of 107 plaintiff evaluations and only 8 defense evaluations. Seven experts completed 147 assessments for the defense and only 36 for the plaintiffs.

Comparing the numbers of evaluations conducted for plaintiffs with the number conducted for defendants can be misleading however, because these numbers depend on the number of referrals from each side. A better measure of evaluator impartiality involves the proportion of "useful" opinions (i.e., opinions helpful to the referring attorney) relative to the overall number of referrals. For example, an evaluator who has conducted 90 evaluations for the defense and 10 for plaintiffs might appear less impartial than the evaluator who has done 50 for the defense and another 50 for plaintiffs. However, looking more closely at the "usefulness" proportion might reveal that the first evaluator has reached a conclusion favorable to the referring attorney in 50% of the defense cases and 45% of the plaintiff cases, whereas the second evaluator has favored the referring attorney in 98% and 100% of defense and plaintiff cases, respectively. Which evaluator appears less impartial?

Other influences can affect the apparent impartiality of forensic evaluations. Even if experts are reasonably impartial, attorneys may selectively introduce expert opinions depending on whether those opinions support their side. In order to consider this possibility, investigators would need to acquire the results of evaluations requested by attorneys but not subsequently presented as evidence. This is comparable to the "file drawer problem" encountered by investigators performing meta-analysis: Because research reporting nonsignificant differences is often not accepted for publication, such results tend to languish, unpublished, in a file drawer, which limits the accuracy of the investigator's ability to determine an overall "effect" of a research phenomenon based on all the evidence. Even if forensic evaluators can be reasonably impartial, they still conduct such evaluations in the context of an adversarial system, and decisions about whether to introduce such reports as evidence are often made by attorneys who are advocates for their clients.

It is these kinds of concerns that prompted the writing of a series of "best practice" books in forensic mental health assessment, published by Oxford University Press. These books describe several different kinds of civil questions relevant to this chapter. One

(Piechowski, 2011) focuses on evaluation for workplace disability. The second such book (Goodman-Delahunty & Foote, 2011) addresses the topic of workplace discrimination and harassment. A third (Kane & Dvoskin, 2011) describes the process of conducting evaluations for personal injury claims more broadly. These books discuss the steps that potential evaluators can take to promote thorough, accurate, and balanced evaluations on this topic. They do not, of course, ensure that future evaluations will be conducted as recommended. But they do identify best practices, as well as steps to avoid, so evaluators who wish to do this work in a way that is consistent with the strongest approaches developed in the field have a set of clear guides in this effort.

CIVIL COMPETENCIES

The concept of legal competence extends to many kinds of decisions that individuals are called on to make throughout their lives. When we discussed competence to stand trial, we focused on the knowledge that criminal defendants must have and the decisions they are required to make. However, the question of mental competence is raised in several noncriminal contexts as well; we refer to these other situations with the general term **civil competencies**.

The question of civil competence focuses on whether an individual has the capacity to understand information that is relevant to decision making in a given situation and then make an informed choice about what to do in that situation. Here are some questions that address issues of civil competence:

- Is a person competent to manage his or her financial affairs?
- Can an individual make competent decisions about his or her medical or psychiatric treatment?
- Is a person competent to execute a will and decide how to distribute property to heirs or other beneficiaries?
- Can a person make advance decisions about the kind of medical treatment he or she wants or does not want to receive if terminally ill or seriously injured?

Scholars who have studied this issue usually point to four abilities that contribute to competent decision making (Appelbaum & Grisso, 1995, Grisso, 2003). A competent individual is expected to be able to (1) understand basic information that is relevant to making a decision; (2) apply that information to a specific situation in order to anticipate the consequences of various choices; (3) use logical—or rational—thinking to evaluate the pros and cons of various strategies and decisions; and (4) communicate a personal decision or choice about the matter under consideration.

The specific abilities associated with each of these general criteria depend on the decision that a person must make. Deciding whether to have risky surgery demands different information and thinking processes than deciding whether to leave property to children or to a charitable organization.

Decisions about medical treatment that one might receive in the future, including the desire to have life-sustaining medical treatments discontinued, involve a special level of planning that has been encouraged by a 1990 federal statute known as the Patient Self-Determination Act. Planning about future medical treatments is formalized through what are known as **advance medical directives**, in which patients indicate what kinds of treatment they want should they later become incapacitated and incompetent to make treatment decisions.

The most controversial of these advance directives is the "living will," in which a patient essentially asserts that he or she prefers to die rather than to be kept alive on a ventilator or feeding tubes. The ethical and practical issues involved in determining patients' competence to issue advance medical directives are enormous, but the trend, revealed in Supreme Court decisions such as *Cruzan v. Director, Missouri Department of Health* (1990), is to recognize that patients have great autonomy in accepting or rejecting a variety of treatments and health care provisions (Hanson & Doukas, 2009).

Advance medical directives seem like a simple and direct way to communicate end-of-life decisions. But for living wills to be effective, individuals must be able to generate preferences that are stable over time and across changes in health. Unfortunately, individuals' predictions about what kind of care they might want in the future vary from one occasion to the next and are affected by the status of their present health.

In studies that examined the stability of advance directives, participants were asked to record their preferences for various life-sustaining treatments (e.g., cardiopulmonary resuscitation [CPR]) in different medical scenarios, such as coma). After an interval ranging from one month to two years, these individuals recorded their preferences again. The average stability of preferences across all judgments was 71%, suggesting that over time periods as short as two years, there were substantial changes in stated treatment preferences (Ditto et al., 2003). Of course, a person could change his or her preferences for good reason—perhaps as a result of some relevant intervening life experience such as a health crisis or a relative's need for life-sustaining treatment. However most people are unaware that their preferences change; they mistakenly believe that the preferences they express at the second interview are identical to those they provided at the first interview (Gready et al., 2000).

Preferences are also dependent on the context in which they are made. For example, when patients recently discharged from hospitals are asked about their desire for life-sustaining treatment, they show a characteristic "hospital dip;" they report less desire for interventions than they did prior to hospitalization—and less than they do several months after their discharge (Ditto, Jacobson, Smucker, Danks, & Fagerlin, 2006). Apparently people do not have stable preferences for future medical care.

Assessing Competence to Make Treatment Decisions

The question of competence to consent to treatment usually arises when a patient refuses treatment that seems to be medically and psychologically justified. Under these circumstances, the first step might be to break down the explanation of the treatment decisions facing the patient into smaller bits of information. (Research results have shown that patients can better understand treatment information when it is presented to them one element at a time.) Using this kind of presentation might facilitate a patient's appreciation of whether a recommended treatment would be in his or her best interest. Should an impasse between the patient and treating professionals still exist after such a presentation, it would be important to administer a clinical assessment instrument to determine whether a given patient lacks the necessary ability to reach a competent decision. Such an instrument—the MacArthur Competence Assessment Tool for Treatment Decisions (MacCAT-T)—is now commercially available (Grisso & Appelbaum, 1998a; 1998b).

The research for the MacCAT-T, conducted as part of a larger MacArthur Research Network on Mental Health and Law study on competencies, coercion, and risk assessment, focused on the capacities of individuals with severe mental disorders to make decisions and give informed consent about their own psychiatric treatment. Can persons with serious mental disorders make competent treatment decisions for themselves? Do their decision-making abilities differ from those of persons who do not suffer mental disorders?

Researchers in the MacArthur Treatment Competence Study developed a series of structured interview measures to assess the four basic abilities—understanding information, applying information, thinking rationally, and expressing a choice—involved in legal competence (Grisso, Appelbaum, Mulvey, & Fletcher, 1995). For example, here is an item that taps a person's ability to apply information to the question of whether he or she has a condition that could be effectively treated:

> "Most people who have symptoms of a mental or emotional disorder like your doctor believes you have can be helped by treatment. The most common treatment is medication. Other treatments sometimes used for such disorders are having someone to talk to about problems, and participating in group therapy with other people with similar symptoms." "… [D]o you believe that you have the kind of condition for which some types of treatment might be helpful?" "All right, you believe that … (paraphrase of the patient's expressed opinion). Can you explain that to me? What makes you believe that … (again paraphrase as above)?" For a patient who believes that treatment will not work because he or she is "just too sick," the interviewer would ask: "Imagine that a doctor tells you that there is a treatment that has been shown in research to help 90% of people with problems just as serious as yours. Do you think this treatment might be of more benefit to you than getting no treatment at all?" (Grisso et al., 1995, p. 133)

Standardized interviews, using items of this type, were conducted with three groups of patients—those with schizophrenia, those with major depression, and those with heart disease—and with groups of people from the community who were *not* ill but were demographically matched to the patient groups (Grisso & Appelbaum, 1995). Only a minority of the persons in all the groups showed significant impairments in competent decision making about various treatment options. However, the patients with schizophrenia and major depression tended to have a poorer understanding of treatment information and used less adequate reasoning in thinking about the consequences of treatment than did the heart patients or the members of the community sample. These impairments were more pronounced and consistent across different competence abilities for patients with schizophrenia than for patients with depression, and the more serious the symptoms of mental disorder (especially those involving disturbed thinking), the poorer the understanding.

These results obviously have implications for social policies involving persons with mental disorders. First, contrary to popular impressions, the majority of patients suffering from severe disorders such as schizophrenia and major depression appear to be capable of competent decision making about their treatment. On the other hand, a significant number of patients—particularly those with schizophrenia—show impairments in their decision-making abilities.

Assessing Competence to Execute a Will

Clinicians may also be asked to evaluate whether a person (called a "testator") was competent to execute a will; such competence is a requirement for the provisions of the will to be valid. Typically, challenges to this capacity are raised when there is suspicion that the testator lacked the necessary mental capacity to execute a valid will (Frolik, 1999; Melton et al., 2007).

In one example, Ronald Eisaman challenged his aunt's will in a Pennsylvania probate court, arguing that his aunt, Harriet Schott, lacked **testamentary capacity**. Schott executed a will in 1993, leaving the bulk of her estate to Eisaman. But she executed a second will in 1997, reducing his share to 50% and passing the remaining 50% to the corporation that owned the assisted-living facility where she resided prior to her death. The expert witnesses who testified about Schott's mental capacity were equivocal. Thus, the judge determined that Eisaman had not established that his aunt lacked testamentary capacity to change her will. The 1997 version was admitted to probate.

According to one study, situations that may raise concern about capacity to execute a will include the following: There is a radical change from a previous will (seen in 72% of cases); undue influence is alleged (56% of cases); the testator has no biological children (52% of cases); the testator executed the will less than a year prior to death (48% of cases); and the testator suffered from comorbid conditions such as dementia (40% of cases), alcohol abuse (28% of cases), or other neurological/psychiatric conditions (28% of cases) (Shulman, Cohen, & Hull, 2004).

The legal standard for testators' competence to execute a will is derived from *Banks v. Goodfellow* (1870), in which the court held as follows:

1. Testators must know at the time of making their wills that they are making their wills.
2. They must know the nature and extent of their property.
3. They must know the "natural objects of [their] bounty."
4. They must know the manner in which the wills they are making distribute their property.

This type of competence has a lower threshold than other competencies because it requires only that persons making a will have a general understanding of the nature and extent of their property and of the effect of their will on members of their family or others who may naturally claim to benefit from the property cited in the will (Melton et al., 2007). A person cannot be deemed incompetent to execute a will simply on the basis of the presence of a mental illness, unless there is clear evidence that the mental illness specifically interfered with the individual's ability to meet the standard set at the time the will was written.

Assessment of this competence focuses on the individual's functional abilities at the time his or her will was written. Melton and colleagues (2007) outline some strategies used by mental health professionals in assessing competence to execute a will. First, they recommend structuring the evaluation to conform to the associated legal elements. They suggest using the sources available (e.g., the testator, family, friends, records) to, first, determine the purpose of the will and why it was written at that time. Second, they recommend gathering information about the testator's property holdings, which may include asking questions about occupation and salary, tangible property, and intangibles (e.g., bank accounts, invest-

ments). Third, the clinician should determine the testator's "values and preferences" (p. 361) to better understand the family dynamics (e.g., with whom does the testator have a good relationship, with whom does he or she does not get along). This information can shed light on the testator's rationale for bequeathing his or her belongings to specific individuals. Finally, Melton and colleagues recommend that clinicians assess the general consequences of the dispositions outlined in the will.

One of the obvious difficulties in these types of evaluations is that the testator, the subject of the evaluation, is often deceased at the time the question of competence to execute the will arises. Thus, the sources of information will be different. If the testator is alive, he or she will be a primary informational source—but if he or she is deceased, the evaluator must gather information from family, friends, acquaintances, medical records, and other available sources without the testator's specific input.

PSYCHOLOGICAL AUTOPSIES

Like most clinical assessments, the typical forensic assessment involves a clinician interviewing, observing, and testing a client to arrive at an understanding of the case. However, in a few unusual circumstances, clinicians may be called on to give an opinion about a deceased person's state of mind as it existed at a specific time before death. Obviously, in these cases, the clinician must conduct an evaluation without any participation by the individual whose prior condition is in question. These evaluations are termed **psychological autopsies** (Ogloff & Otto, 1993).

Psychological autopsies originated in the 1950s when a group of social scientists in the Los Angeles area began assisting the coroner's office in determining whether suicide, murder, or accident was the most likely mode of death in some equivocal cases. Their use has spread over the years, and now they are encountered most often in cases such as determining the cause of death in situations where an insurance company could deny death benefits if the policy holder committed suicide; assessing claims in workers' compensation cases that stressful working conditions or work trauma contributed to a worker's death or suicide; evaluating a deceased individual's mental capacity to execute or modify a will; and assessing the validity of an argument occasionally made by criminal defendants that a victim's mode of death was suicide rather than homicide.

Although there is no standard format for psychological autopsies, most of them rely on information from two sources: interviews with third parties who knew the decedent, and prior records. General guidelines for what should be included in psychological autopsies have been published (La Fon, 2008). Some investigators concentrate on more recent data, generated close in time to the person's death. What was the person's mood? How was the person doing at work? Were there any pronounced changes in the person's behavior? Others—especially those who take a developmental perspective on behavior—look for clues early in the person's life. As a child, how did the person interact with his or her parents and siblings? What was the individual's approach to school? Peers? Hobbies and other activities?

As with any assessment technique, the first question to be considered is the reliability of the psychological autopsy. There are several reasons to suspect that the reliability of psychological autopsies is low.

For starters, the person in question is not available to be interviewed or tested. Obviously, the decedent's "true" state of mind is unknown; in fact, if it *were* known, the autopsy would be unnecessary. Also, the persons who are interviewed might not remember the past accurately, or they might have reasons to distort their answers.

A review of research on psychological autopsy studies (Foster, 2011) revealed specific life events (particularly interpersonal conflict) as risk factors for suicide, with some evidence that the greater the conflict, the higher the risk. However, limitations of psychological autopsy studies suggest the need for complementary research into life events prior to serious suicide attempts. One study addressed the question of reliability of psychological autopsy indirectly, using information from the investigation of the U.S.S. *Iowa* explosion (see Box 11.3).

How has testimony about psychological autopsies fared in court? In cases involving workers' compensation claims and questions of whether insurance benefits should be paid, the courts have usually admitted psychological autopsy testimony; in criminal cases or

---

B o x 11.3 THE CASE OF THE U.S.S. *IOWA*: GAUGING RELIABILITY OF THE PSYCHOLOGICAL AUTOPSY

On April 19, 1989, 47 U.S. Navy sailors were killed when an explosion ripped through turret 2 of the U.S.S. *Iowa*. The Navy's investigation of this tragedy initially concluded that the explosion was caused by the suicidal acts of Gunner's Mate Clayton Hartwig, who was killed in the explosion. The major foundation for this conclusion was a psychological autopsy conducted by FBI agents working at the National Center for the Analysis of Violent Crime. The Navy's conclusions were later evaluated by a congressional committee, which commissioned its own panel of 14 psychological and psychiatric experts to review the FBI's analysis. Partly on the basis of this panel's input, the congressional committee rejected the FBI analysis as invalid. Ultimately, the U.S. Navy also concluded that the cause of the explosion could not be determined.

Forensic psychologist Randy Otto and his colleagues asked 24 psychologists and psychiatrists to rate the reports of the 14 experts who reviewed the FBI analysis of the U.S.S. *Iowa* explosion (Otto, Poythress, Starr, & Darkes, 1993). Three raters judged each of the 14 reports, and although they failed to show precise agreement in how they thought the reports should be interpreted, they did achieve a moderate amount of broad agreement in their ratings. Note, however, that this agreement

The U.S.S. *Iowa*, damaged in an explosion

Thomas Jarrell/US Navy/DOD/Time Life Pictures/Getty Images

pertains only to how the raters interpreted the 14 panelists' reports, not to the contents or opinions in the reports themselves.

Critical Thought Question
What are the major challenges in conducting a psychological autopsy—and what kind of forensic mental health assessments in particular include such challenges?

in cases involving the question of whether a person had the mental capacity to execute a will, the courts have been more reluctant to permit the testimony (Ogloff & Otto, 1993). Judges are more hesitant to allow expert testimony in criminal cases than in civil ones, perhaps because the risks of prejudicial testimony are greater when one's liberties can be taken away. One reason for the courts' hesitancy in permitting psychological autopsy testimony in cases involving the validity of wills might be that, in such cases, the state of mind of the deceased is the critical question for the jury. Allowing expert testimony on this matter might therefore be viewed as invading the province of the jury, a perception that judges usually want to avoid.

CHILD CUSTODY AND PARENTAL FITNESS

The "Best Interests of the Child" in Custody Disputes

One of the growing areas of forensic psychology is the evaluation of families for the purpose of recommending the particular custodial arrangement that is in the best interests of a child whose parents are divorcing or separating. The increase in these cases is attributable to two facts. First, about 50% of marriages in the United States end in divorce. As of 2010, 34% of households with children in the United States were single-parent families and more than 60% of children born since 1986 will spend some time in a single-parent household (Annie E. Casey Foundation, 2010). Therefore, the issue of custody is a practical concern for millions of families. Second, from the end of the 19th century to about the middle of the 20th century, the prevailing assumption was that awarding custody of young children (sometimes called children of "tender years") to their mothers was usually in their best interests. This preference for maternal custody has diminished at the beginning of the 21st century; now many courts want to know about the parenting abilities of each parent before making a decision about custody (Furhman & Zibbell, in press).

Currently, the prevailing standard for custody decisions is the **future best interests of the child**. Although the child's "best interests" must be assessed

on a case-by-case basis, the Uniform Marriage and Divorce Act indicates that courts should consider the following criteria: (1) the wishes of the child; (2) the wishes of the child's parents; (3) the relationships between the child and the parents, siblings, and significant others who interact with the child; (4) the child's adjustment at home and school and in the community; and (5) the physical and mental health of the parties involved.

Child custody evaluations usually arise in situations in which divorcing parents disagree about which of them can better meet the needs of their children and should therefore have custody. Most states permit two kinds of custodial arrangements—sole and joint custody, each with two aspects (physical and legal). *Physical custody* refers to the living arrangement, whereas *legal custody* concerns the responsibility for decision making. In **sole custody**, the child will live only with one parent (although the other parent may be granted visitation rights), and/or all legal decision-making authority for that child will rest with one parent. In **joint custody**, both parents can retain parental rights concerning decisions about the child's general welfare, education, health care, and other matters (this is called joint legal custody), and the child can alternate living in the home of the mother and in the home of the father according to the schedule provided in the custody decision (this is called joint physical custody). Joint custody does not necessarily mean that the child spends equal time with each parent, however. Usually, one parent is designated the residential parent, and the child spends more time living at the home of that parent. In general, families that are functioning better at the time that custody is awarded are more likely to ask for joint custody than families that are experiencing ongoing difficulties (Gunnoe & Braver, 2001).

The three main differences between sole custody and joint custody are as follows:

1. Joint custody distributes the frequency of interaction more evenly between the children and each parent.

2. Joint custody requires more interactions between the divorced parents and generates more demands for cooperation concerning the children.

3. Joint custody results in more alterations in caregiving arrangements, along with more separations and reunions between children and parents (Clingempeel & Reppucci, 1982).

Psychologists have examined the effects of sole custody and joint custody on children and parents. Although the findings are not clear-cut, there appear to be several advantages to joint custody arrangements. In a meta-analysis of 21 studies, Bauserman (1997) concluded that children in joint custody fared better than children in sole custody on a number of measures related to adjustment and interpersonal relations. Fathers benefited from joint custody because they had more frequent contact with their children. Joint custody was advantageous for mothers because it afforded them greater opportunity for courtship; as a result, these mothers re-partnered more rapidly than mothers with sole responsibility for their children, a situation that may be economically beneficial for the children (Gunnoe & Braver, 2001).

Evidence on the effects of divorce on children comes from different kinds of research, including long-term longitudinal studies (Hetherington & Kelly, 2002; Wallerstein & Kelly, 1980), large-sample repeated surveys (Furstenberg, Peterson, & Nord, 1983; Zill, Morrison, & Coiro, 1993), smaller studies, retrospective perceptions of parents' separation or divorce (Braver, Ellman, & Fabricius, 2003; Marquardt, 2006), and meta-analyses (Amato, 2001; Amato & Keith, 1991; Bauserman, 2002). Researchers have also looked at the children of never-married parents (Insabella, Williams, & Pruett, 2003). Based on this evidence, it appears that the most significant effects of divorce on children occur in the first year or two. Temporary behavioral changes are frequent (Hetherington, Cox, & Cox, 1982; Wallerstein & Blakeslee, 2003), including problems in emotional regulation, disturbed sleep patterns, behavioral or academic problems, grief reactions, and loyalty conflicts (Wallerstein, Corbin, & Lewis, 1988). Most parents and children return to behavior that is more typical for them after this 1–2 year period (Laumann-Billings & Emery, 2000; Marquardt, 2006).

Both the well-being of the primary parent and the level of parental conflict are major factors influencing outcomes (Hetherington & Kelly, 2002). Children from families in which the parents had a great deal of conflict seem to do better following divorce than do children from low-conflict families (Amato, 2001; Amato, Loomis, & Booth, 1995). Importantly, around 75% of children whose parents divorce will not experience significant developmental challenges or long-term negative effects of the divorce (Kelly & Emery, 2003).

What makes it more or less likely that divorce will adversely affect the children involved? Risk and protective influences have been summarized (Furhman & Zibbell, in press) as follows:

Risk Factors:

- stress of the initial separation (Kelly & Emery, 2003)
- diminished parenting (Hetherington et al., 1982)
- loss of significant relationships (including extended family, e.g., grandparents), and friends (Amato & Booth, 2001)
- multiple moves (including change of schools and loss of friends) (Braver, Ellman, & Fabricius, 2003; Hetherington & Kelly, 2002)
- financial problems (the stress of which can affect parenting style or quality) (Duncan & Hoffman, 1985)
- either parent becoming involved with a new partner (Hetherington & Kelly, 2002; Kelly & Emery, 2003)
- parents with a low-conflict marriage (Amato et al., 1995)

Protective Factors:

- The custodial parent is competent and well adjusted (Hetherington & Kelly, 2002; Wallerstein & Kelly, 1980).
- The noncustodial parent has regular and consistent contact and (particularly important) takes an active interest in the activities and school performance of the child (Amato & Gilbreth, 1999; Nord, Brimhall, & West, 1997).
- The parents are cooperative, or at least keep the child from exposure to inter-parental conflicts (also particularly important) (Hetherington & Kelly, 2002).
- The custodial parent has extended family support (Hetherington & Kelly, 2002).

Assessment in Custody Disputes

Many mental health professionals regard child custody cases to be the most ethically and clinically difficult forensic evaluations they perform. First, the emotional stakes are extremely high, and both parents are often willing to spare no expense or tactic in the battle over which of them will win custody. The children involved are usually forced to live—for months, if not years—in an emotional limbo in which they do not know in whose home they will be residing, where they will be going to school, or how often they will see each parent.

Second, a thorough custody evaluation requires that the clinician evaluate the children, both parents, and others who have interacted with the child, such as relatives, teachers, and family health care providers. Often, not all the parties agree to be evaluated or do so only under coercion, resulting in a lengthy and sometimes tense process. Such tension can be worsened if the evaluation is requested by the attorney for one of the two divorcing spouses, which may lead the other spouse to perceive the evaluator as unfairly biased in favor of the spouse who retained this evaluator. An alternative arrangement—having the court order the evaluation and designate a neutral expert, with both parties agreeing to this appointment—can help to reduce this perception of bias.

Third, to render a valuable expert opinion, a clinician must be quite knowledgeable—about the children and parents under evaluation, but also about child development, bonding and attachment, family systems, the effects of divorce on children, adult and childhood mental disorders, and several different kinds of testing. Added to these factors are variations in what we have traditionally defined as a family. With increasing acceptance of different lifestyles and family structures, clinicians must often confront questions about whether parents' sexual orientation or ethnicity should have any bearing on custody decisions.

Finally, child custody evaluations are often highly adversarial, with each parent trying to expose all the faults of the other and each side vigorously challenging any procedures or opinion by an expert with which it disagrees. Clinicians who conduct custody evaluations must be prepared for challenges to their clinical methods, scholarly competence, and professional ethics. Even evaluators who operate under court appointment may have their findings challenged in some cases.

There are three major approaches to appointing evaluators: (1) A judge can appoint one clinician to conduct a custody evaluation that is available to all the parties, (2) each side can retain its own expert to conduct independent evaluations, or (3) the litigants can agree to share the expenses of hiring an expert to conduct one evaluation (Fuhrmann & Zibbell, in press). Historically, most clinicians have preferred either the first or the third option because they do not want to be subjected to the pressures that are brought to bear when separate experts are hired by each side (Keilin & Bloom, 1986). Attorneys tend to agree with this preference, believing that the second option leads to greater bias (LaFortune & Carpenter, 1998).

Specific guidelines for conducting custody evaluations have been developed by the American Psychological Association (2009), the Association of Family and Conciliation Courts (AFCC, 2007), and the American Academy of Child and Adolescent Psychiatry (AACAP, 1997). Although the methods used in custody evaluations vary depending on the specific issues in each case, most evaluations include the following components: (1) clinical, social history, and mental status interviews of the parents and the children; (2) standardized testing of the parents and the children; (3) observation of interactions between each parent and the children, especially when the children are minors; (4) assessments or interviews with other people who have had opportunities to observe the family (adult children of the parents, grandparents, neighbors, the family physician, schoolteachers, and other observers); and (5) documents or records that might be relevant to the case (medical records of children and parents, report cards, and arrest records).

In any forensic psychological evaluation, it is useful to include a specialized tool that has been developed to measure capacities associated with the legal decision. In child custody evaluations, these include parenting skills and capacities (for the parents) and needs (for the children). Although specialized approaches are available for child custody evaluations, these tests are of questionable validity (see Melton et al., 2007; Otto & Edens, 2003), so it remains for the field to develop a specialized measure that is consistent with the principles of scientific test development.

Custody evaluations are time-consuming. In a national survey of mental health professionals who conducted child custody evaluations, Ackerman and Ackerman (1997) found that experts spent an average of about 30 hours on each evaluation, which, another study found, may even have increased (Brey, 2009). Much of this time was devoted to interviewing and observing the parties in various combinations. In fact, more than two-thirds of the respondents indicated that they conducted individual interviews with each parent and each child, observed each parent interacting (separately) with each child, and conducted formal psychological testing of the parents and the children.

Experts also reported how often they recommended different kinds of custodial arrangements (Keilin & Bloom, 1986). Joint legal custody (parents share the decision making, but one parent maintains primary physical custody) was the most common recommendation (42.8%), and sole custody without visitation was the least often recommended alternative (4.6%). Sole custody with visitation (30.4%) and joint physical custody (21.7%) were among the other preferred recommendations. These findings were replicated and expanded in a subsequent study (Ackerman & Ackerman, 1997).

In recent years, divorced couples have sometimes returned to court to ask judges to resolve both ongoing and novel disputes. For example, Pamela Peck, a divorced mother, went to family court in Dallas to seek an injunction that would ban her ex-husband's girlfriend from spending the night at his house when his son was there. A Texas judge ruled in her favor, enjoining both parties from having overnight guests of the opposite sex when "in possession of" their 9-year-old son. One of the thorniest custody issues is whether a custodial parent can relocate. An example of a "move-away case" is described in Box 11.4.

Because divorce is a potent stressor for children and because protracted custody battles tend to leave a trail of emotionally battered family members in their wake, increasing attention is being given to helping parents and children cope with these transitions or to finding alternatives to custody fights (Grych & Fincham, 1992; Kelly, 1996; Silver & Silver, 2009). Many judges require divorcing couples to attempt to settle issues of custody, visitation, and support through mediation, a form of alternative dispute resolution that minimizes the adversarial quality of the typical custody dispute. If mediation fails, the couple can return to court and have the judge decide the issues. The benefits of custody mediation are that resolutions are reached more quickly, and with better compliance among the participants, than with adversarial procedures.

The Association of Family and Conciliation Courts (2007) has developed model standards for the practice of family and divorce mediation, indicating that a mediator shall (among other things)

- Recognize that mediation is based on the principle of self-determination by the participants.
- Conduct the mediation process in an impartial manner … disclose all actual and potential grounds of bias and conflicts of interest reasonably known to the mediator … structure the mediation process so that participants make decisions based on sufficient information and knowledge.
- Assist participants in determining how to promote the best interests of children.
- Recognize a family situation involving child abuse or neglect or domestic violence and take appropriate steps to shape the mediation process accordingly.
- Suspend or terminate the mediation process when the mediator reasonably believes that a participant is unable to effectively participate or for other compelling reasons.

Box 11.4 THE CASE OF *CIESLUK v. CIESLUK*: CAN A CUSTODIAL PARENT MOVE AWAY?

When Michelle and Christopher Ciesluk were divorced in 2002, they arranged to share joint legal custody of their son, Connor, who lived primarily with his mother. But when Michelle Ciesluk lost her job with Sprint in early 2003 and the company offered to rehire her, provided that she was willing to move from Colorado to Arizona, Christopher Ciesluk objected. He opposed the move, fearing he would lose any relationship with his son and would miss his son's school and athletic activities. Unfortunately for Ms. Ciesluk, neither the Colorado legislature nor the courts made it easy for her. In 2001, the legislature abolished a legal presumption that a custodial parent has the right to move away, and an appellate court ruled that a parent who wishes to move must demonstrate a *direct* beneficial effect on the child. (The more commonly used test requires the parent to show that the move would have an *indirect* effect on the child, typically by enhancing the custodial parent's job opportunities.) Michelle Ciesluk was not able to meet that test, so she remained in Colorado with her son, working for $10 an hour as an administrative assistant and feeling that her "whole life is on hold" (Eaton, 2004). In 2005, the Colorado Supreme Court reversed the decision by the appellate court and sent the case back to the trial court (*Ciesluk v. Ciesluk*, 2005).

Critical Thought Question
In the Ciesluk case, which of the risk factors for adverse childhood adjustment are increased by each of the alternatives (mother moving versus mother staying)? Which of the protective factors are increased by each alternative?

Research generally supports the favorable adjustment of those who go through mediation. Two reviews of a decade of research (Hahn & Kleist, 2000; Kelly, 1996) indicate that families that go through mediation to determine custody have better adjustment than those going through the more traditional child custody litigation process. A recent meta-analysis (Shaw, 2010) showed that mediation is a beneficial alternative to litigation for couples who are divorcing. Outcomes considered in this meta-analysis include satisfaction with process and outcome, emotional satisfaction, spousal relationship, and understanding children's needs.

Assessing Fitness to Be a Parent

Evaluations of parental fitness involve different questions than those involved in the typical custody dispute (Condie, 2003). In every state, the agency responsible for the protection of children will intervene if it receives a credible report that a child is being abused or neglected. After an investigation, the agency might file a petition asking a court to remove the child from the home and arrange placement with a relative or in foster care. In such cases, the issue before the court is whether the child should be left with the parents or removed from the home because of parental unfitness.

The issue for the evaluator is what arrangement protects the child's well-being, while properly respecting the rights of the parents. Although parental rights are important, the state must protect children from parents who cannot or will not provide adequate food, shelter, and supervision. The state must also protect children from parents who abuse them, physically or psychologically. A clinician might recommend that the child be placed temporarily in foster care and that the parents receive training in parenting skills as a condition of having the child returned to them. In extreme cases—those in which parents abandon a child or are clearly incapable of caring for a child—the state might seek to terminate parental rights. This is done most often when relatives or others wish to adopt the child (Heilbrun, Marczyk, & DeMatteo, 2002).

In an interesting twist on the usual circumstances of termination cases, 12-year-old Gregory Kingsley asked a Florida judge in 1992 to terminate his parents' right to function as parents on his behalf. Gregory had been removed from his home and placed in foster care, but when the state attempted to return him to his birth parents, Gregory objected and tried to sever his parents' ties to him. Courts had never before confronted the question of whether a 12-year-old can bring a termination petition, but both the trial judge and an appellate court ruled in Gregory's favor (Haugaard & Avery, 2002).

CIVIL COMMITMENT AND RISK ASSESSMENT

All 50 states and the District of Columbia have **civil commitment** laws that authorize the custody and restraint of persons who, as a result of mental illness, are a danger to themselves or others or who are so gravely disabled that they cannot care for themselves. This restraint is usually accomplished by compulsory commitment to a mental hospital. The courts also provide safeguards and rules for how these involuntary commitments are to be accomplished.

Many of these procedures were instituted in the 1970s in response to a concern that in the 1950s and 1960s, it was too easy to commit people to state psychiatric facilities. At that time, people who were mentally ill could be involuntarily committed whenever the state believed they needed treatment. Beginning around 1970, commitment proceedings began to be reformed, resulting in more legal rights for the mentally ill to resist compulsory commitment. A key case in this reform movement was *O'Connor v. Donaldson* (1975), in which the Supreme Court held that mental illness and a need for treatment were insufficient justifications for involuntarily committing mentally ill persons who were not dangerous.

Similar limits on involuntary hospitalizations were upheld by the Supreme Court in the 1990s (e.g., *Foucha v. Louisiana*, 1992). The standard for commitment changed from mental illness combined with a need for treatment, to mental illness that is associated with dangerousness or a grave lack of ability to care for oneself. This narrowing of the commitment standard, along with other societal influences during the last 40 years (e.g., the community mental health movement, deinstitutionalization), have resulted in fewer public hospital beds for mental health treatment, and shorter hospital stays.

Although the legislative changes of the 1970s were intended to protect the rights of the mentally ill, an exclusive concern with rights can sometimes leave patients without adequate care, housing, or the effective psychiatric treatment that can be provided in some hospitals (Turkheimer & Parry, 1992; Wexler, 1992). Resources in the community devoted to treatment and recovery for individuals with mental illness—focusing on such necessities as housing and employment as well as mental health care and case management—could have replaced the need for extended hospital care in most cases. Unfortunately, however, community-based resources for individuals with mental illness have not been increased substantially following the downsizing of public psychiatric hospitals, starting in the 1970s and continuing into the 2000s. As a consequence, some individuals have not had access to adequate treatment in either hospitals or in the community during these decades.

Four Types of Commitment Procedures

The law permits four types of civil commitment: (1) emergency detention, (2) voluntary inpatient commitment, (3) involuntary inpatient commitment, and (4) outpatient commitment. Emergency detention is the means by which most individuals are initially admitted to hospitals. A police officer, a mental health professional, or sometimes a private citizen can initiate involuntary detention of another person. Usually, the cause is actual or anticipated harmful behavior by the patient either against self (e.g., attempted suicide) or against others. An examination is performed by a physician or a qualified mental health professional. Patients committed on an emergency basis can be detained for only a specified length of time—usually two or three days—before a review takes place. At that time a preliminary hearing must be held before the patient can be confined any longer.

A person may volunteer to enter a psychiatric hospital, although he or she still must meet the criteria for hospitalization (typically some version of "mentally ill and in need of treatment"), but even those who are being hospitalized "voluntarily" may feel pressure from family, mental health personnel, or the legal system to enter the hospital. Individuals who have been provided with more information and given the chance to express their views report feeling less coercion, regardless of whether they are voluntarily or involuntarily hospitalized (Dennis & Monahan, 1996). While voluntarily hospitalized, the patient may find that the hospital has instigated commitment proceedings to challenge or delay release.

The third type of commitment—involuntary inpatient commitment—requires a court order. The criteria for obtaining an involuntary civil commitment vary from state to state; in general, however, the person must be mentally ill and must also be dangerous to self and others, or so gravely disabled as to be unable to provide for his or her own basic needs. Although the criterion of "dangerousness" is the most often discussed standard and therefore is deemed the most important for involuntary hospitalization, grave disability is the standard that determines most commitments (Turkheimer & Parry, 1992).

To obtain an involuntary commitment, the concerned persons must petition the court for a professional examination of the individual in question. A formal court hearing usually follows the examination. In most states, the hearing is mandatory, and persons whose commitment is sought can call witnesses and have their lawyer cross-examine witnesses who testify against them.

A fourth type of commitment procedure, known as outpatient commitment, is available in nearly all states and allows a patient to be mandated to receive treatment in an outpatient setting, such as a community mental health center, rather than in a hospital (Hiday & Goodman, 1982). Outpatient commitment often involves conditional release from a hospital. That is, formerly hospitalized patients are ordered to continue treatment in the community. It may also be used prior to hospitalization, as an alternative to inpatient commitment. This approach appears to have some promise. One study (Pollack, McFarland, Mahler, & Kovas, 2005) found that those released from involuntary hospitalization on outpatient commitment were more likely (relative to a group released without any kind of commitment) to use outpatient and residential mental health services and psychotropic medication. However, outpatient commitment should not simply be used as a mechanism for ensuring compliance with treatment if the individual does not meet the criteria (which typically have a public safety component).

Dangerousness and Risk Assessment

Dangerousness is one of the central constructs of mental health law. Whether a person is now or could in the future be dangerous is an issue that underlies many decisions in our system of justice, including questions of civil commitment. Although the law often uses the terms *dangerous* and *dangerousness*, these terms are difficult to define. They actually merge three distinct constructs: (1) risk factors (variables associated with the probability that violence or aggression will occur), (2) harm (the nature and severity of predicted and actual aggression), and (3) risk level (the probability that harm will occur) (National Research Council, 1989). In some combination, these factors provide a major justification for involuntarily committing the mentally ill to hospitals.

The construct of dangerousness to others recurs throughout the law. Dangerousness is the basis for requiring therapists to protect third parties from possible acts of violence against them by the patients of these therapists. It is also a reason for denying bail to certain defendants and the justification for hospitalizing defendants after they have been found not guilty by reason of insanity. Some states also use future dangerousness as one factor a jury can consider when deciding whether to sentence a convicted murderer to life in prison or death by execution.

Difficulties in Assessing Dangerousness

Because dangerousness is hard to define, we prefer to use the term *violence risk* and will do so throughout the remainder of this chapter. Can mental health experts accurately assess a person's present violence risk and then predict whether that person will be violent in the future? Is mental illness a sign that a person is likely to be violent? Do certain types of mental illness make a person more prone to violent behavior? These questions have been examined extensively by researchers for more than three decades, and they are at the heart of many real-life cases. For example, should the mental health professionals who treated John Hinckley have predicted that he posed a danger to President Reagan? What about Jeffrey Dahmer, who killed a number of young men and had sex with the bodies? Was his brutal behavior predictable, given his early psychological problems?

Clinicians who attempt to answer these questions perform **risk assessments**; using the best available data and research, they try to predict which persons are and which are not likely to behave violently in certain circumstances, give some estimate of the risk for violence, and offer suggestions on how to reduce the risk (Heilbrun, 2009; Monahan & Steadman, 1994).

Many factors make such predictions difficult. For example, the base rate of violence in some groups is

low, so clinicians are being asked to predict a phenomenon that rarely occurs. The clinical assessments of persons assessed for violence risk are often conducted in hospitals or prisons, whereas the environment where violence is relevant for those being considered for release is the community. The predictions have often been for long-term risk, which is harder to predict than violence risk over a shorter time frame.

The original consensus of researchers was that clinicians could not predict with accuracy the risk of violence. Leading scholars such as John Monahan (1984) of the University of Virginia summarized the research this way: "In one study after another, the same conclusion emerges: For every correct prediction of violence, there are numerous incorrect predictions" (Pfohl, 1984). Another early summary of the research on clinicians' ability to predict violence was that their predictions were wrong in two of every three cases in which a "yes" prediction of future violence was made.

Subsequent research changed the early pessimism about clinicians' ability to predict violence, however. Researchers have learned that these predictions can sometimes reach moderate to good levels of accuracy when certain conditions are present (Borum, 1996; Otto & Douglas, 2009). Specifically, clinicians who consider a set of factors that research has shown to be related to future violence can predict the risk for violence considerably better than was the case 30 years ago (Heilbrun, 2009). Specifically, when clinicians have information about a range of historical, personal, and environmental variables related to violence, when they limit their predictions to specific kinds of violent behavior, and when they concentrate on appraising risks in certain settings rather than in all situations, they can do so with a fair degree of accuracy. Although they still make a large number of errors, they do significantly better than chance.

One of the most important advances in the area of risk assessment has involved the development and use of such specialized risk assessment tools (Heilbrun, 2009). A number of specialized tools are now available (Otto & Douglas, 2009), some of which are actuarial. An actuarial tool (such as the Violence Risk Appraisal Guide; Harris, Rice, & Quinsey, 1993) uses specified risk factors that are rated and scored, with scores being combined into a final score that is then applied to the prediction in a way that is specified by a formula (which in turn has been developed through empirical research). Other tools (such as the HCR-20, which measures historical, clinical, and risk management variables [Webster, Douglas, Eaves, & Hart, 1997]) employ a "structured professional judgment." They do not combine scores on included variables to yield a total score. Rather, the evaluator is asked to make a judgment about risk in light of the status of these risk factors. Evidence indicates that good actuarial and structured professional judgment approaches to risk assessment are comparably accurate in predictions of violence (Heilbrun, Douglas, & Yasuhara, 2009).

SUMMARY

1. ***What problems are associated with expert testimony, and what reforms have been proposed?*** The main objections to expert testimony are that it invades the province of the jury, is too adversarial and thus not impartial, takes too much court time, introduces irrelevant information, and is often founded on an insufficient scientific base. Proposed reforms have focused on limiting the scope of expert testimony, reducing the partisanship involved in adversaries retaining their own experts, requiring judges to examine more strictly the scientific foundation of expert testimony, and referring to it as *opinion testimony* rather than as expert testimony. Limiting such testimony's scope and having judges consider the scientific foundation more carefully are proposals that have been implemented.

2. ***Under what conditions can a plaintiff be compensated for psychological damages?*** Plaintiffs can seek damages in civil trials if they allege that they have been victimized by a tort, which is a wrongful act that must be proved to have caused them harm. Although the law has historically been skeptical of claims for psychological harm and emotional distress unless they are accompanied by physical injuries, the more recent trend has been to allow plaintiffs to be compensated for emotional damages (without any physical injuries) resulting from intentionally outrageous or negligent conduct.

3. ***What is workers' compensation, and how do mental health professionals participate in such cases?*** Workers' compensation is a no-fault system now used by all states and in the federal system to provide a streamlined alternative for determining the compensation of workers who are injured in the course of their jobs. Formal trials are not held nor juries used in workers' compensation cases. Psychologists may testify in workers' compensation hearings about the extent, cause, and likely prognosis for psychological problems that have developed following a physical injury and/or work-related stress.

4. ***What capacities are involved in civil competence?*** Questions of civil competence focus on whether an individual has the mental capacity to understand information that is relevant to decision making in a given situation and then make an informed choice about what to do. The issue of civil competence is raised when it is not clear that an individual is capable of meeting the demands of a given task specified under civil law. Examples of such tasks include giving informed consent to current or future medical treatments, and executing a will.

5. ***What criteria are used for decisions about disputes involving child custody or parental fitness?*** The best interest of the child is the main criterion applied to disputes about which parent should have custody of a child following divorce. Evaluations of parental fitness address a different question: Should a parent's custody of a child be limited or terminated because of indications of parental unfitness? Many mental health professionals regard custody and parental fitness assessments as the most difficult evaluations they perform. For this reason, and in an attempt to reduce the stress of custody battles, custody mediation has been developed as a less adversarial means of resolving these disputes.

6. ***What steps are taken in civil commitment, and how well can clinicians assess the risk of dangerousness or violent behavior, a key criterion for civil commitment?*** Persons who are considered gravely disabled or dangerous to themselves or others may be committed to a state psychiatric hospital against their will, but

they have the right to a hearing shortly thereafter to determine whether they should be retained. After (or instead of) being hospitalized, some patients may be placed on outpatient commitment. Long-term predictions of violence risk are more difficult to make with accuracy, but there is a reliable association among historical, personal, and environmental factors and

dangerous behavior that provides a basis for reasonably accurate short-term assessments of risk. The use of structured risk assessment, whether through the use of a specialized actuarial risk assessment measure or a tool using structured professional judgment, can increase predictive accuracy beyond what is possible with unstructured judgment.

KEY TERMS

advance medical directives

breached duty

civil commitment

civil competencies

compensatory damages

dangerousness

duty

future best interests of the child

harm

intentional behavior

joint custody

malingering

negligence

proximate cause

psychological autopsies

punitive damages

risk assessments

sole custody

testamentary capacity

tort

Chapter
12

Preparing for Trials

ORIENTING QUESTIONS

1. How do juries' verdicts differ from those of judges?
2. What does the legal system seek in trial juries?
3. What stands in the way of jury representativeness?
4. What procedures are used in *voir dire*?

5. What personality and attitudinal characteristics of jurors, if any, are related to their verdicts?
6. What role do trial consultants play in a trial?
7. In what ways does pretrial publicity pose a danger to fair trials? How can these dangers be reduced?

Most disputes are resolved before they reach a courthouse because they are either diverted from the criminal justice system, plea bargained, or settled through alternative dispute resolution mechanisms such as mediation and negotiation. But some civil and criminal cases are resolved through a trial; moreover, the trial is a foundational aspect of our legal system and Constitution. Before a trial commences, various issues must be dealt with. We address three of these issues in this chapter: (1) whether the case should be decided by a jury or a judge; (2) if the choice is a jury, how a representative group of fair-minded citizens can be chosen to serve as jurors; and (3) what happens when those citizens are exposed to information about the case prior to setting foot in a courtroom. Each of these topics has been examined by psychological scientists.

WHO SHOULD DECIDE:
JURY OR JUDGE?

Before a trial begins, one choice looms large for all criminal defendants and most civil plaintiffs: should the case be heard by a judge or a jury? If the opposing party consents, defendants and plaintiffs can opt to have the verdict decided by a judge, in a proceeding called a **bench trial**. Three New York City police officers charged with the shooting death of Sean Bell in November 2006 chose the bench trial option. Bell and two friends died in a barrage of police bullets while standing outside a Queens strip club just hours before Bell's wedding. Learning of the officers' request, Reverend Al Sharpton remarked, "I think that it is stunning that these officers … do not want to face a jury of their peers whom they serve and by whom they are paid." The New York judge who presided over their trial acquitted all three, so

it is tempting to say that they gambled correctly. But did they? Might they have been equally (or even more) likely to have been acquitted by a jury? Later in this section we present data on the rates of conviction by juries versus judges that will help answer this question.

The preference for a bench trial over a jury trial may be influenced by race and ethnicity. When researchers asked approximately 1,500 Texas residents whether they would favor a bench trial or a jury trial, African Americans and Hispanics showed less support for a jury trial than Whites, perhaps reflecting the belief that the majority group's views, including any prejudices and biases, might predominate during deliberations. Minority group members may doubt that a jury is composed of a cross-section of the community and would be able to grasp their situations and understand their perspectives. Thus, judges appear to be the less risky choice (Rose, Ellison, & Diamond, 2008).

How Judges and Juries Compare

In general, does it matter who decides? Do juries and judges generally agree with each other? When they disagree, can we say who made the better decision?

In bench trials, a judge determines the verdict

Of course, jury verdicts are not systematically compared against some "correct," back-of-the-book answer—even if there were such a thing (which there is not!). Fortunately, we have some data that illustrate how frequently judges and jurors agree and why they might disagree.

The data were collected by Harry Kalven and Hans Zeisel (1966), professors at the University of Chicago, who carried out an extensive survey of the outcomes of jury trials. In a classic application of the methods of social science to understand legal decisions, Kalven and Zeisel asked each district court judge in the United States to provide information about recent jury trials over which he or she had presided. Of approximately 3,500 judges, only about 500 responded to a detailed questionnaire. But some judges provided information about a large number of trials, so the database consisted of approximately 3,500 trials.

Two questions are relevant to our discussion: (1) What was the jury's verdict? (2) Did the judge agree? In criminal trials, the judges reported that their verdict would have been the same as the jury's actual verdict in 75% of the cases (see Table 12.1 for detailed results). Thus, in three-fourths of the trials,

two independent fact-finding agents would have brought forth the same result. Similar consistency was found for civil trials, as illustrated in Table 12.2. This level of agreement suggests that jurors are not deviating to a great extent from their mandate to follow the law and use only the judge's instructions plus the actual evidence to reach their verdict.

One might speculate on an optimal level of agreement between judge and jury. What if they agreed 100% of the time? That undesirable outcome would reflect no difference whatsoever between judges' and juries' verdicts. But if judge and jury agreed only 50% of the time, given only two possible outcomes of guilty and not guilty (putting aside "hung" juries momentarily), it would reflect a level of agreement no better than that which would occur by chance. (Two independent agents, choosing yes or no at random, would agree 50% of the time by chance alone.) Appropriately enough, the 75% level of agreement is halfway between chance and perfect agreement.

Among the 25% of the criminal cases in which there was disagreement, 5.5% resulted in hung juries; that is, the jury members could not agree on a verdict. Thus, it is more appropriate to say that in

TABLE 12.1 Agreement of judges' and juries' verdicts based on 3576 criminal trials (in percentage of all trials). Jury verdicts shown in columns, judge verdicts shown in rows

Judge Verdict	Jury Verdict		
	Acquit	Convict	Hung
Acquit	**13.4**	2.2	1.1
Convict	16.9	**62.0**	4.4

SOURCE: Adapted from Kalven and Zeisel (1966, p. 56). Figures in bold show cases in which judge and jury agreed on the verdict.

TABLE 12.2 Agreement of judges' and juries' decisions in civil trials (as percentage of all trials). Jury verdicts shown in columns, judge verdicts shown in rows

Judge Verdict	Jury Verdict	
	Plaintiff	Defendant
Plaintiff	**47**	10
Defendant	12	**31**

SOURCE: Adapted from Kalven and Zeisel (1966, p. 63). Figures in bold show cases in which judge and jury agreed on the verdict.

only 19.5% of the criminal cases did the jury return a guilty verdict where the judge would have ruled not guilty, or vice versa.

In most of these discrepant decisions, the jury was more lenient than the judge. The judge would have convicted the defendant in 83.3% of these cases, whereas the jury convicted in only 64.2% of them. For every trial in which the jury convicted and the judge would have acquitted, there were almost eight trials in which the reverse was true.

The level of agreement between the jury and the judge was also high in civil trials, as we show in Table 12.2. Judges reported that their verdict would have favored the side favored by the jury in 78% of the civil suits analyzed by Kalven and Zeisel. Also important is the nearly equal likelihood of finding for the plaintiff; the jury ruled for the plaintiff in 59% of the cases, whereas the judge did so in 57%.

These figures are a healthy data-based response to the critics (Huber, 1990; Olson, 1991) who conclude that in civil suits, especially those involving personal injury claims, juries are overly sympathetic to plaintiffs. In fact, in certain kinds of cases, plaintiffs who go to trial before juries win infrequently.

Juries do occasionally make high awards to injured plaintiffs, sometimes higher than what judges would award (Hersch & Viscusi, 2004). These awards are sometimes publicized in print and discussed in blogs and on talk shows (Bailis & MacCoun, 1996). But in controlled studies, most juries make decisions—verdicts and awards—quite like those made by judges and experienced lawyers. There is little evidence that juries are especially pro-plaintiff, as several critics have claimed. In fact, some would argue that because the jury can apply its sense of community standards to a case, their award of damages in a civil case might actually be more fitting than a judge's award: "The appreciation of pain and suffering, and the likely impact on an individual's life and his or her ability to earn a living, are not matters which judges are any more qualified to assess than is a member of the public applying his or her life experience" (Watson, 1996, p. 457).

Determinants of Discrepancies

What accounts for the discrepancies between judge and jury? Are jurors less competent than judges and less able to apply the law in predictable ways? Or are there other, subtler factors at work? Kalven and Zeisel

attempted to answer these questions by delving more deeply into the judges' reactions to the cases and comparing them to the juries' verdicts.

A few of the jury–judge discrepancies resulted from facts that one party knew but the other did not. For example, in several cases, the judge was aware of the defendant's prior arrest record (a matter not introduced into evidence) and would have found him guilty, but the jury acquitted him. The reverse situation can also occur. Especially in a small community, a member of the jury might share with fellow jurors some information about a witness or a defendant that was not part of evidence and was not known to the judge at the time.

A second, smaller source of judge/jury discrepancies was the relative effectiveness of the two attorneys. In some trials, the jury was apparently swayed by the superiority of one lawyer over the other and produced a verdict that was, at least in the judge's opinion, contrary to the weight of the evidence. But it is not surprising that some number of jury verdicts would be determined by this extralegal factor, because jurors spend considerable time attending to the preparedness and demeanor of the attorneys.

Perhaps the most important explanation of judge–jury differences, accounting for roughly half of the disagreements, involves what Kalven and Zeisel called **jury sentiments**. They used this term to cover situations in which, *in the judge's view*, the jury's verdict was detrimentally affected by factors beyond the evidence and the law. (There is an implicit assumption here that the judge's decision was free of sentiments—a dubious claim, given that judges are all too human and subject to the same predispositions as most jurors.)

Jurors' sentiments play a role in decision making when jurors believe that the "crime" is just too trivial for any punishment or at least for the expected punishment, and find the defendant not guilty to ensure that he or she will not be punished. In one case included in the Kalven and Zeisel study, a man was brought to trial for stealing two frankfurters. Because this was his second crime, he would have been sentenced to prison. Whereas the judge would have found him guilty, the jury voted 10–2 for acquittal.

In other instances, jurors believe that the defendant has already been sufficiently sanctioned, and therefore punishment by the legal system is unnecessary. In a case of income tax evasion, the following series of misfortunes plagued the defendant between the crime and the trial: "His home burned, he was seriously injured, and his son was killed. Later he lost his leg, his wife became seriously ill, and several major operations were necessary … his wife gave birth to a child who was both blind and spastic" (Kalven & Zeisel, 1966, p. 305). The jury found the defendant not guilty of income tax evasion, apparently concluding that he had already suffered divine retribution. The judge would have found him guilty.

Jurors sometime acquit (when judges would have convicted) because they believe that a law is unfair. In trials for the sale of beer and liquor to minors who were in the military, juries concluded that there was minimal social harm. Apparently they felt that if a young man can be forced to die for his country, "he can buy and consume a bottle of beer" (Kalven & Zeisel, 1966, p. 273). Jury sentiments have surfaced in many cases involving "unpopular" crimes—for example, small misdemeanors such as gambling, and so-called victimless crimes such as prostitution. "Why waste our time over such minor affairs?" they might have been thinking.

So jury–judge discrepancies should probably not be attributed to a lack of competence on the part of juries. Such disagreements might more appropriately be attributed to the jury's interest in fairness, or its consideration of a range of factors that are broader than those considered by an individual judge (Shuman & Champagne, 1997).

The study by Kalven and Zeisel was a massive undertaking. But the actual data were collected between 1954 and 1961, and in the intervening decades, the methodological limitations of the study have become increasingly apparent:

1. Judges were permitted to choose which trial or trials they reported. Did they tend to pick those cases in which they disagreed with the jury, thus causing the sample's result to misrepresent the true extent of judge/jury disagreement?

2. Only approximately 500 judges out of 3,500 provided responses to the survey—an unrepresentative sampling of possible responses, leading us to question how well these results can be generalized to the entire population of judges and juries.

3. The membership of juries has changed; they are more heterogeneous today than in the past. This increased diversity might increase their rate *of disagreement* with the judge's position because

their broader experiences and cultural differences might give them insights or perspectives on the trial evidence to which judges do not have access (Hans & Vidmar, 1986). For example, a jury of African Americans may be less likely than a White judge to believe a White police officer's testimony that a drug dealer "dropped" a bag of cocaine.

4. As for *causes* of discrepancies between verdicts by the judge and jury, we have only the judge's beliefs about the jurors' feelings and sentiments (Hans & Vidmar, 1991).

Some New Data on Judge/Jury Differences

Updating Criminal Case Comparisons. A replication of this study was long overdue when researchers at the National Center for State Courts collected data from jurors, judges, and attorneys in more than 350 trials in four jurisdictions: Los Angeles, Phoenix, the Bronx (in New York City), and the District of Columbia (Eisenberg et al., 2005). They examined some of the same issues that Kalven and Zeisel had explored, including how often judges and juries agreed on verdicts in criminal trials.

Participants in felony trials completed questionnaires that asked about preferred verdicts and their evaluation of the evidence. There was a very high response rate (questionnaires were returned in 89% of cases), so we can be fairly certain that the data are representative of most trials. As before, judges stated, prior to hearing the juries' verdicts, whether they would opt to acquit or convict and what they thought about the evidence. One obvious advantage of this study over its predecessor is that all groups (judges, attorneys, and jurors alike) gave their views of the evidence, thus reducing an important concern about Kalven and Zeisel's work—that all the information about a trial came from the judge.

The most striking finding was how closely the new results mirrored those of the earlier study. The rate of jury/judge agreement was 70% (compared to Kalven and Zeisel's 75%). When there was disagreement, it also mirrored the earlier asymmetry: Juries were more lenient. They were more likely to acquit when judges opted to convict than they were to convict when judges would have acquitted (see Table 12.3).

TABLE 12.3 **Agreement of judges' and juries' verdicts based on 350 trials (National Center for State Court data, in percentage of all trials). Jury verdicts shown in columns, judge verdicts shown in rows**

Judge Verdict	Jury Verdict		
	Acquit	Convict	Hung
Acquit	**11.6**	5.0	1.9
Convict	16.0	**58.5**	6.9

SOURCE: Adapted from Eisenberg et al. (2005). Figures in bold show cases in which judge and jury agreed on the verdict.

Further scrutiny of the data collected by the National Center for State Courts revealed the circumstances in which jurors were more likely than judges to return "not guilty" verdicts (Givelber & Farrell, 2008). Jurors were more impressed than judges by the presence of a third-party defense witness (someone other than the defendant). Thus, when the defendant *and* another defense witness testified, jurors were 50% more likely than judges to acquit. Jurors were also impressed by the absence of a prior criminal record: when the defendant and another defense witness both testified *and* when the defendant had no prior record, jurors were 90% more likely to acquit!

A reasonable explanation for these differences is that jurors and judges assume their roles differently. While jury duty is a unique experience for a juror, judges have probably heard it all (or most of it) before. So jurors may take more seriously their instruction to acquit unless the prosecution can prove the case beyond a reasonable doubt, may feel sympathy for someone in the defendant's situation, and may possess a commonsense understanding of what motivates people to act impulsively.

Updating Civil Case Comparisons. There are also updated findings on how judges compare to juries in civil cases. One large-scale study examined plaintiff win rates (the proportion of cases in which the verdict favored the plaintiff) in federal cases tried before either juries or judges from 1979 to 1989 (Clermont & Eisenberg, 1992). For many types of cases, including contracts, property damage, civil rights, and labor disputes, plaintiffs' win rates were equivalent regardless of who decided.

But differences emerged in two types of cases—products liability and medical malpractice—where plaintiffs had more success with judges (48% win rate) than with juries (28% win rate). Researchers attributed these differences to **selection effects** by which the selection of cases tried by juries differed in important ways from those tried by judges. Because defense lawyers expected juries to be biased in favor of plaintiffs, they tended to settle cases in which the plaintiff had a strong case. That meant that on average, juries were left to decide relatively weaker cases for the plaintiff and appeared to make different decisions than judges. But taking selection effects into account, judges and juries may not actually be so different.

A related question is whether jury awards for punitive damages are different from awards assessed by judges, and whether the two groups differ on the reasons for those awards. Punitive damage awards are used to punish and deter corporations that have engaged in serious wrongdoing. Some punitive damage awards have been very high, and the Supreme Court has ruled on five occasions about whether they were excessively high.

The most comprehensive study of jury/judge agreement on punitive damages, conducted by Theodore Eisenberg and his colleagues (Eisenberg, LaFountain, Ostrom, Rottman, & Wells, 2002), analyzed data from nearly 9,000 trials that ended in 1996 in 45 of the nation's largest trial courts. The primary finding was that judges and juries did not differ substantially in these cases. They awarded punitive damages of about the same amount, although the range of the jury awards was somewhat greater than that of the judicial awards. These results call into question the notion that juries are unable to set reasonable limits on punitive damages.

Jurors also do about as well as judges in attending to the relevant evidence in these cases, setting aside any sympathy for the plaintiff, and focusing on the factors that *should* matter to the determination of punitive damages (i.e., the actions of the defendant).

Professor Jennifer Robbennolt (2002) asked judges and jury-eligible citizens to read a vignette about a patient who experienced harmful side effects of a medication prescribed for depression. The trial evidence included a memo demonstrating that employees of the defendant, an HMO (health maintenance organization), knew about the potential side effects of the drug but did not communicate them to the plaintiff. Research participants were told that the defendant's liability had already been determined and, if appropriate, they were to make awards of punitive damages.

The decision making of judges and of laypeople with regard to punitive damages was quite similar: their awards were of roughly the same magnitude and variability. Just as important, both groups used the evidence in appropriate ways. They based punitive damages on the nature of the defendant's conduct, rather than the extent of harm to the plaintiff.

Returning to the question we posed earlier—whether jurors perform as well as judges when deciding damage awards—we find little evidence that jurors' reasoning is much different from that of judges. Some studies suggest that jurors render erratic and unpredictable awards, in part because their decision-making processes are influenced by various cognitive biases (see, e.g., Sunstein, Hastie, Payne, Schkade, & Viscusi, 2002). But judges are also human, and apparently are affected by the same cognitive illusions as juries (Rachlinski, Johnson, Wistrich, & Guthrie, 2009). More generally, it is satisfying to know that Kalven and Zeisel's landmark study has withstood the test of time, even as the makeup of juries has changed in the intervening years.

When a lawsuit reaches the trial stage and the parties opt to have a jury, rather than judge, be the arbiter, specific procedures for selecting that jury come into play. We describe those procedures next, focusing on the psychological considerations and consequences of jury selection that begin not in the courtroom, but in the community.

JURY SELECTION BEGINS IN THE COMMUNITY: FORMING A PANEL, OR *VENIRE*

Jury selection begins before potential jurors arrive at the courthouse, as officials assemble a panel, or *venire*, of prospective jurors. Although each state, as well as the federal government, has its own procedures for determining how the panel of prospective jurors will be chosen, the general rule is the same: jury selection must neither systematically eliminate nor underrepresent any subgroups of the population.

To encourage representativeness, U.S. Supreme Court cases going back to 1880 (*Strauder v. West Virginia*) have forbidden systematic or intentional exclusion of religious, racial, and other **cognizable groups** (members of which, because of certain shared characteristics, might also hold unique perspectives on selected issues) from jury panels. But as recently as 50 years ago, the composition of most *venires* was homogeneous, with middle-aged, well-educated White men generally overrepresented (Beiser, 1973; Kairys, 1972).

Judicial and Legislative Reforms

In a series of decisions and lawmaking, the U.S. Supreme Court and the Congress established the requirement that the pool from which a jury is selected must be a representative cross-section of the community. These decisions were driven by two policy concerns, each of which includes psychological assumptions (Vidmar & Hans, 2007).

First, the government believed that if the pools from which juries were drawn represented a broad cross-section of the community, the resulting juries would be more heterogeneous. That is, they would be composed of people who were more diverse with respect to age, gender, ethnic background, occupation, and education. The courts assumed that this diversity would produce various benefits—for example, that minority group members might discourage majority group members from expressing prejudice. This assumption seems logical; casting a wider net will yield members of smaller religious and ethnic groups whose presence might reduce outright prejudicial remarks.

Another assumed benefit was that heterogeneous juries would be better fact finders and problem solvers. Extensive research on the dynamics of groups shows that, other things being equal, groups composed of people with differing abilities, personalities, and experiences are better problem solvers than groups made up of people who share the same background and perspectives (Antonio et al., 2004). Heterogeneous groups are more likely than homogeneous groups to evaluate facts from different points of view and to have richer discussions.

Does this also happen in juries? Apparently so. Samuel Sommers (2006) used actual jury pool members to examine the effects of racial heterogeneity on jury deliberations in a rape trial. He asked the jurors to take part in simulated (mock) trials in which he varied the racial mix of jurors and recorded their deliberations. Sommers found that mixed-race groups had several advantages over juries composed of only White jurors. First, the mixed-race groups had longer, more thorough deliberations and were more likely to discuss racially charged topics such as racial profiling. Second, White jurors on racially mixed juries mentioned more factual information and were more aware of racial concerns than were their counterparts on all-White juries. A follow-up study suggested that White jurors in diverse groups may actually process information differently than those in all-White groups (Sommers, Warp, & Mahoney, 2008). White jurors who expected to discuss a race-relevant topic in diverse groups showed better comprehension of relevant background information than did White jurors in all-White juries. On the basis of these studies, we can conclude that representative and diverse *venires* do, indeed, result in juries who undertake better, more thorough and accurate fact-finding and discussion (Sommers, 2008).

The second policy reason for the Court and Congress's decisions on representativeness is related to the *appearance* of legitimacy, rather than to the jury's actual fact-finding and problem-solving skills (Vidmar & Hans, 2007). Juries should reflect the standards of the community. When certain components of the community are systematically excluded from jury service, the community is likely to reject both the legal process and its outcomes as invalid.

We now know that the racial composition of a jury *can* affect public perceptions of the fairness and legitimacy of a trial and of the resulting verdict. To examine this issue, Leslie Ellis and Shari Diamond (2003) approached 320 adults in airports, bus and train stations, and parks, and asked them to take a short survey. Participants read a description of a shoplifting trial in which the racial makeup of the jury and the verdict were varied. Half of the respondents read that there were 12 Whites on the jury (racially homogeneous), and half read that there were 8 Whites and 4 African Americans (racially heterogeneous). In half of the descriptions, the jury's verdict was guilty and in the other half, not guilty. The researchers measured observers' perceptions of the fairness and legitimacy of the trial procedures. As shown in

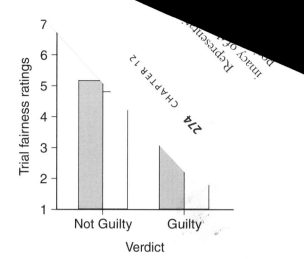

FIGURE 12.1 Effect of verdict and racial composition of jury on fairness ratings

Figure 12.1, when the verdict was not guilty, racial composition of the jury had no effect on fairness ratings. But when the verdict was guilty, the racial composition of the jury *was* important. Observers considered a trial with a homogeneous jury less fair than a trial with a heterogeneous jury (Ellis & Diamond, 2003). Different elements of the community must see that they are well represented among those entrusted with doing justice—that they have a voice in the process of resolving disputes (Hans, 1992).

The 1992 riots in Los Angeles that erupted after four White police officers were acquitted of assault in the beating of Black motorist Rodney King illustrate this problem dramatically. The jury eventually selected for the trial contained no Black jurors. After the jury found the police officers not guilty, the Black community rejected the verdict as invalid and angrily challenged the legitimacy of the entire criminal justice system. Shaken by the surprising verdicts and shocked by the ensuing riots, many Americans, regardless of their race, questioned the fairness of the jury's decision, in part because of the absence of Black citizens from its membership.

Defendants also reject the fairness of decisions made by juries whose members share few social or cultural experiences with them. Consider, for example, the probable reaction of a college sophomore, on trial for possession of marijuana, who is found guilty by a jury composed entirely of people in their fifties and sixties.

...tive juries not only preserve the legit-[...] the legal process but also solidify participants' positive feelings toward the process. If members of underrepresented groups—the poor, the elderly, racial minorities, youth—do not serve on juries, they are more likely to become angry and impatient with the legal process. For some participants, at least, the net result of serving on a jury is an increased appreciation for the jury as a worthwhile institution (Rose, 2005).

Representativeness of jury pools is a worthwhile goal. But how should courts go about forming the *venire* in order to reach this goal? For many years, voter registration lists were used as the primary source for jury pool selection. However, such lists underrepresent certain segments of the community because smaller percentages of young people, the poor, Latinos, and other minorities register to vote. Recently, other sources such as lists of licensed drivers, persons receiving public assistance, and unemployed people have supplemented voter lists as a source of prospective jurors (Mize, Hannaford-Agor, & Waters, 2007).

From those persons who are eligible for jury service, members of the *venire* are randomly selected and summoned to appear at the courthouse for jury service. But as many as half of qualified jurors ignore the jury summons, even though doing so constitutes a violation of law (Ellis & Diamond, 2003). Without doubt, people have concocted creative ways to escape jury service. Hemorrhoids are a frequently used excuse. Vincent Homenick, the chief jury clerk of the courthouse in Manhattan, once received a summons that someone had returned with the word "deceased" written on it, along with a plastic bag supposedly containing the ashes of the prospective juror (Green, 2004)! As Phoenix lawyer Patricia Lee Refo, chairwoman of the American Jury Project, put it aptly: "Everyone likes jury duty—just not this week."

Prospective jurors sometimes avoid jury service by claiming personal hardship. Some judges are sympathetic to claims of ill health, business necessity, vacation plans, and the like. But many other judges are unwilling to dismiss individual jurors because of perceived "hardships." During the jury selection for the O. J. Simpson civil trial, Judge Hiroshi Fujisaki responded to one prospective juror who had requested dismissal because she suffered from claustrophobia, "How big is your living room? Is it as big as this courtroom?" She remained in the pool. Another prospective juror complained of the likelihood of getting stiff from sitting too long. "That's why we take breaks," replied the unsympathetic judge.

When some prospective jurors are excused for reasons of hardship, the result is a winnowing down of the pool. Thus, even before the formal jury selection begins in a courtroom—that is, before jurors are questioned by attorneys and the judge—some people have been removed from the panel of prospective jurors. These removals can distort the representativeness of juries.

JURY SELECTION CONTINUES IN THE COURTROOM: THE *VOIR DIRE* PROCESS

Once the panel of prospective jurors has been assembled and summoned to the courthouse, selection issues change. The focus shifts from concerns about the representativeness of prospective jurors to questions about a given juror's ability and willingness to be fair and impartial (Diamond & Rose, 2005).

As part of the constitutional right to be tried by an "impartial" jury, a defendant is afforded the opportunity to screen prospective jurors to determine whether any of them are prejudiced. The forum in which the judge and/or the attorneys question prospective jurors is called **voir dire**, a French term that literally means "to see, to say" (i.e., to see what is said). *Voir dire* is conducted in a variety of ways, depending on a jurisdiction's rules and a judge's preferences. Who asks the questions, what questions are asked and how they are phrased, how long the questioning goes on, and whether the questions are posed to individual jurors or to a group are all matters left to judges' discretion.

The most limited form of *voir dire* involves a small number of questions asked in yes-or-no format only by the judge and features group rather than individual questioning of prospective jurors. An example: "Do any of you have an opinion at this time as to the defendant's guilt or innocence?" Yes-or-no questions are effective in controlling the answers of witnesses and reducing the time spent in *voir dire*, but they offer little insight into jurors' beliefs and attitudes. Also note that this form of questioning requires jurors to self-identify any biases and report them to the

A juror being questioned during jury selection

judge. Many jurors may be unaware of their predispositions and/or hesitant to state them in public; thus, both of these obligations may be difficult for jurors to fulfill.

Several studies show that limited *voir dire* has drawbacks as a means of identifying biased jurors (Johnson & Haney, 1994). One of the most compelling demonstrations came from a project initiated by District of Columbia Superior Court Judge Gregory Mize (1999). Prior to this study, Judge Mize, like many judges, conducted limited *voir dire* during which he asked questions in open court to a group of prospective jurors. He and the attorneys would then pose follow-up questions to those who responded affirmatively to the initial question. Judge Mize revised his procedures for the study by interviewing all prospective jurors, regardless of whether they had responded affirmatively to the first question. In doing so, he determined that a number of jurors who were silent in response to a preliminary question actually had a great deal to say when prompted individually. Among the responses:

- "I was frightened to raise my hand. I have taken high blood pressure medications for twenty years. I am afraid I'll do what others tell me to do in the jury room."

- "My grandson was killed with a gun so the topic of guns makes my blood pressure go up."

- And remarkably, this one: "I'm the defendant's fiancée."

Why is limited *voir dire* so ineffective at uncovering juror bias? Obviously, some jurors will fail to disclose important information because of privacy concerns, embarrassment, or a failure to recognize their own biases. But an important psychological dynamic, termed the **social desirability effect**, is also a factor at this stage. Most people want to present themselves in a positive, socially desirable way. This desire to appear favorably, especially in the presence of a high-status person such as a judge, shapes how people answer questions and influences what they disclose about themselves.

At the other extreme is extended *voir dire*, in which both the judge and attorneys ask open-ended questions that require elaboration, cover a wide range of topics, and question jurors individually. Extended *voir dire* has several advantages in uncovering biases. Open-ended questions (e.g., "What experiences have you had in your life that caused you to believe that a person was being discriminated against because of the color of his skin?") encourage jurors to talk more about their feelings and experiences. Individual questioning can result in disclosures that jurors might not otherwise offer. But extended *voir dire* can take a long time, so most courts tend not to favor it. Typical *voir dire* procedures involve a compromise between the limited and extended versions; both the attorneys and the judge pose questions to a group of prospective jurors, and then they ask brief follow-up questions of selected individuals.

Challenges for Cause and Peremptory Challenges. Technically, opposing attorneys do not select a jury; rather, the judge gives them the opportunity to exclude a number of potential jurors from the eventual jury. There are two mechanisms—challenges for cause and peremptory challenges—by which panelists are excluded from serving on a jury. We explain both in detail below. Here, we simply point out that after all the challenges have been made and ruled on, and some prospective jurors have been dismissed, the people who remain are sworn into service as the jury. Because attorneys strive to exclude those jurors who seem unfavorable to their client, the respective challenges tend to balance out and both extremes are eliminated, leaving a jury composed of people who are less biased and more open minded.

In any trial, each side can claim that particular jurors should be excluded because they are inflexibly biased or prejudiced or because they have a relationship to the parties or the issues that creates an appearance of bias. These exclusions are known as **challenges for cause**. For example, a relative or business associate of a defendant would be challenged, or excused, for cause. Additionally, the judge may excuse a panelist for cause without either attorney requesting it if the prospective juror is unfit to serve. In criminal cases, judges often inquire about whether prospective jurors have been crime victims and may excuse those who say that their own victimization experiences would affect their ability to be fair jurors. There is good reason to ask, because mock jurors who had been victims of the crime for which the defendant was being tried were more likely than nonvictims to convict (Culhane, Hosch, & Weaver, 2004).

One juror was deemed unfit to serve for a different reason: body odor. A Massachusetts judge dismissed the unsworn juror, saying "Given the strength of the body odor, I'm satisfied that the other jurors would be put at a distinct disadvantage in their efforts to concentrate." As one blogger put it, "Justice may be blind, but it retains a healthy sense of smell."

In most cases, judges are not quite so willing to dismiss jurors for cause. In fact, after a prospective juror has raised a concern about the ability to be fair and impartial (or after one of the attorneys has done so), the judge will typically ask the juror whether he or she can be impartial. Then, using the juror's assessment of those abilities and observing the juror's demeanor, the judge decides whether to dismiss that person for cause. But judges may have difficulty determining which jurors are truly impartial (Crocker & Kovera, 2010). In making that decision, judges may be overly reliant on the juror's expression of confidence. Small changes in the confidence that jurors express about their ability to be fair (e.g., "I would try" versus "Yes") can determine whether they will be excused for cause or remain on the jury. Unfortunately, jurors are not particularly insightful about their ability to be fair, and their confidence is not a reliable gauge of their bias (Rose & Diamond, 2008). So jurors who can be fair are sometimes dismissed, and those who cannot are sometimes retained—simply because of subtle variations in their responses to questions about impartiality.

In theory, each side has an unlimited number of challenges for cause. In reality, few prospective jurors are excused for reasons of bias. In a survey of New Mexico courts over a three-year period, only about 1 of every 20 jurors was dismissed for cause (Hans & Vidmar, 1986).

Each side may also exclude a designated number of prospective jurors "without a reason stated, without inquiry, and without being subject to the court's control" (*Swain v. Alabama*, 1965). This procedure is known as a **peremptory challenge**. The number of peremptory challenges allocated to each side varies from one jurisdiction to another and also by the type of case (civil or criminal) and seriousness of the charge.

Peremptory challenges have multiple purposes. First, they allow attorneys to challenge potential jurors whom they believe will be unsympathetic to their client, for whatever reason. The peremptory challenge has a second, largely symbolic function: When the parties in a lawsuit play a role in selecting the people who decide the outcome, they may be more satisfied with that outcome (Saks, 1997). The third function of peremptory challenges is to allow the attorney to begin to indoctrinate prospective jurors and influence those who ultimately will make up the jury. For example, Holdaway (cited in Blunk &

Sales, 1977, p. 44) explains how an attorney can ask a question that will acquaint the juror with relevant law but also phrase it to make a point consistent with the attorney's position. The question is "Do you agree with the rule of law that requires acquittal in the event there is reasonable doubt?" The real purpose of this question is to alert prospective jurors that reasonable doubt could exist in the case, and to make jurors aware of the rule so that they will look for reasonable doubt and then vote to acquit.

The Supreme Court has imposed more and more limits on the exercise of peremptory challenges. As a result, the overall status of this jury selection tool is in flux. Although opinions about the importance of the peremptory challenge remain divided—some experts favor its elimination altogether and others argue that it is crucial for fair trials—only a few researchers have examined the use of peremptory challenges in real trials. Among the questions asked: Are peremptory challenges used to remove minority jurors or other specific groups? Do the prosecution and defense repeatedly dismiss different types of jurors?

Answers come from a study that tracked the fate of 764 prospective jurors questioned during jury selection in 28 cases (Clark, Boccaccini, Caillouet, & Chaplin, 2007). Of this number, 234 were dismissed by the prosecution and 202 by the defense. More importantly, jurors' race seemed to factor into the exercise of peremptory challenges: only 10% of jurors excused by the defense were African American, compared to 48% of those excused by the prosecution.

Peremptory Challenges: No Exclusion on Account of Race or Gender. In a series of decisions, the Supreme Court has ruled that peremptory challenges may not be based *solely* on a juror's race or gender. Consequently, these challenges are "less peremptory" than they used to be. The decision regarding race was triggered by the case of James Batson, a Black man convicted of second-degree burglary by an all-White jury. During the *voir dire*, the prosecuting attorney used four of six peremptory challenges to dismiss all the Black persons from the *venire*. In *Batson v. Kentucky*, decided in 1986, the Court held that Batson was denied his Fourteenth Amendment right to equal protection by the prosecution's dismissal of Black members of the panel (Pizzi, 1987). In *Holland v. Illinois* (1990), the Court held that a White defendant could also complain about the exclusion of Blacks because the principle of representativeness was violated

by the arbitrary exclusion of *any* racial group. These decisions also reflect the Court's stance that systematic efforts by attorneys to exclude members of cognizable groups violate the constitutional rights of members of those groups. Simply stated, all citizens—regardless of race, religion, or creed—have the right to serve on juries.

In the *Batson* case, the Supreme Court developed a procedure for determining whether a peremptory challenge was racially based. When a defense attorney believes that the prosecution's peremptory challenge was motivated by racial factors, he or she initiates a so-called "*Batson* challenge," and the judge then asks the prosecutor for an explanation. The prosecutor typically advances a race-neutral explanation for the challenge—for example, that the prospective juror has a brother in prison or has filed a lawsuit against the police. The judge then determines whether the explanation is genuine, taking into account the other jurors who were not challenged by the attorney. For example, if a prosecutor stated that she dismissed a Black juror because he had been robbed, the judge would want to know why she had not dismissed a White juror who also had been robbed.

It might appear that creative prosecutors can always find "race-neutral" reasons for excluding minorities from the jury. Indeed, attorneys are unlikely to cite a prospective juror's race as the reason for exclusion. In an exhaustive analysis of every published decision of federal and state courts in the seven years after the *Batson* decision, Melilli (1996) found 2,994 *Batson* challenges but in only 1.8% of the sample had the attorney cited race as a factor.

Does a prospective juror's race really not matter to prosecutors, or are they simply unwilling to admit that it does? That question led to an experimental study in which college students, law students, and practicing attorneys assumed the role of a prosecutor trying a Black defendant (Sommers & Norton, 2007). They were given profiles of two prospective jurors, one Black and the other White, and had to use one remaining peremptory challenge. Although participants were more likely to challenge a Black juror than a White juror, they rarely cited race as a factor in their decision. Moreover, it was relatively easy for them to generate an ostensibly neutral explanation to justify their choice.

Psychological research on **social judgments** can help us understand why. People infrequently admit (even to themselves) that social category information

---

B o x 12.1   THE CASE OF THOMAS MILLER-EL AND THE DIFFICULTY OF PROVING RACIAL BIAS IN JURY SELECTION

Texas death row inmate Thomas Miller-El must have felt like a yo-yo, given the number of times his case bounced back and forth between the Fifth Circuit Court of Appeals and the Supreme Court. The issue was whether prosecutors engaged in purposeful discrimination during Miller-El's 1986 trial on charges that he robbed and murdered a hotel clerk in Irving, Texas. Probably no *voir dire* has been scrutinized as thoroughly as the one that occurred in this case.

Prosecutors in that trial used peremptory strikes to exclude 10 of the 11 Blacks who were eligible to serve on the jury, and Miller-El was convicted and sentenced to death. For years he contended that prosecutors used peremptory challenges in a biased way to keep African-American jurors off his jury panel, but courts rejected this claim four times. He eventually appealed to the Supreme Court.

This time, with the support of some unusual allies (including numerous federal prosecutors, judges, and the former director of the FBI), he found a receptive audience. In an 8–1 ruling and a rare victory for Miller-El, the Supreme Court found that the lower courts had failed to fully consider the evidence he offered to show racial bias, and it ordered the Fifth Circuit to reconsider Miller-El's claim (*Miller-El v. Cockrell*, 2003). (That evidence included a history of discrimination by Dallas prosecutors and a training manual from the Dallas District Attorney's Office that instructed prosecutors to exercise their peremptory strikes against minorities.) But when the Fifth Circuit judges undertook such reconsideration and examined all the reasons prosecutors gave for striking *venire* members, they concluded that Black and White jurors had been treated the same by prosecutors (*Miller-El v. Dretke*, 2004).

Miller-El again appealed to the Supreme Court, and again the high court ruled in his favor, overturning his conviction because of racial bias in jury selection. According to Justice David Souter, Miller-El's evidence of bias "is

Texas death row inmate Thomas Miller-El being told that he was granted a stay of execution in 2002.

too powerful to conclude anything but discrimination" (*Miller-El v. Dretke*, 2005). The case ended quietly in 2008 when Miller-El pled guilty to murder and aggravated robbery in exchange for a life sentence.

Critical Thought Question

In examining attorneys' peremptory challenges during the *voir dire* in Miller-El's trial, appellate justices read the trial transcript that provided a verbatim account of everything that was said in the courtroom. Why would it have been difficult for them to find evidence of racial bias in attorneys' choices about which jurors to excuse? In particular, would prospective jurors tend to answer *voir dire* questions in a manner that gives hints about their racially motivated beliefs? Why or why not? What other information could appellate justices use to assess whether peremptory challenges were exercised in a discriminatory way?

---

such as race influences their decisions (Norton, Vandello, & Darley, 2004), often because they want to appear to be unprejudiced and to avoid the social consequences of showing racial bias (Norton, Sommers, Apfelbaum, Pura, & Ariely, 2006). These findings suggest that in their self-reports, attorneys are unlikely to acknowledge considering the race of prospective jurors, even when race has been a factor in jury selection.

Recall that the judge, after hearing the prosecutor's explanation, must ultimately decide whether the attorney dismissed a prospective juror because of race.

Easily concocted, plausible, and (above all) race-neutral justifications leave judges with little reason to reject them, and archival analyses of actual *voir dire* proceedings show that judges are unlikely to find that peremptory challenges violate the *Batson* rule (Melilli, 1996). The case of Thomas Miller-El, detailed in Box 12.1, exemplifies the difficulty of proving racial bias in jury selection.

In 1994, the Supreme Court extended the logic of *Batson* to peremptory challenges based on another cognizable characteristic—gender. No longer could attorneys base their peremptory challenges solely on

The facts of this case are relatively simple: Teresia Bible gave birth to a child in May 1989; she named the child Phillip Rhett Bowman Bible, claimed that James E. Bowman, Sr. was the father, and filed a paternity suit against him to obtain child support. Even though a blood test showed that there was a 99.92% probability that he was the father, Mr. Bowman refused to acknowledge paternity, so a trial was held.

The jury pool was composed of 24 women and 12 men. After three jurors were dismissed for cause, the plaintiff used 9 of her 10 peremptory challenges to remove males, the defendant used 10 of his 11 challenges to remove women, and the resulting jury was composed of 12 women. (Note that in this case, it was men who were systematically excluded from the jury.) The jury

concluded that Mr. Bowman was the child's father and ordered him to pay child support of $415.71 per month.

Bowman appealed and the U.S. Supreme Court eventually ruled that peremptory challenges that were used to eliminate one gender were, like those used to exclude a race, unacceptable. The Court's decision acknowledged that peremptory strikes against women harken back to stereotypes about their competence and predispositions, traced from a long history of sex discrimination in the United States (Babcock, 1993).

Critical Thought Question
Given what you know about how attorneys support their exclusions in "Batson challenges," how might creative attorneys justify excluding jurors of a particular gender?

a jurors' gender. The leading case of *J. E. B. v. Alabama ex rel. T. B.* (1994) is described in Box 12.2.

How many different cognizable groups are there, and could limitations on peremptory challenges eventually be extended to cover all of them? In Houston, Texas, the attorney for accused murderer Jeffrey Leibengood asked to include only people less than five feet tall in the jury pool because his client's height was four feet six inches. The attorney told the judge, "We say a short person is subject to discrimination, and we hope to have two or three short people end up on the jury. *Batson* should be extended to include the little people" (quoted by Taylor, 1992, p. 43). The judge disagreed.

But a New York judge decided that Italian Americans were entitled to *Batson*-type protection (Alden, 1996), and a California law bans attorneys from removing jurors simply because they are homosexual. Still, attempts to apply the rule to obese jurors (*United States v. Santiago-Martinez*, 1995) and bilingual jurors (*Hernandez v. New York*, 1991; Restrepo, 1995) were denied.

Some courts have held that peremptory challenges based on religious affiliation violate state constitutions (e.g., *State v. Fuller*, 2004), but the Supreme Court has yet to rule that it is unconstitutional to base peremptory challenges on religious persuasion (or on any other classification, for that matter). Attorneys' discretion in jury selection remains relatively unfettered, except that jurors cannot be challenged because of their race or their gender.

Lawyers' Theories: Stereotypes in Search of Success. Do the jury selection strategies of attorneys conflict with the goal of having unbiased fact finders? Before we answer this question, we need to answer a more basic one: How do lawyers go about selecting or excluding jurors, and do their strategies work?

In everyday life, our impressions about others are governed largely by what psychologists have termed implicit personality theories. An **implicit personality theory** is a person's organized network of preconceptions about how certain attributes are related to one another and to behavior. Trial lawyers often apply their implicit personality theories to jury selection. For example, William J. Bryan (1971) advised prosecutors to "never accept a juror whose occupation begins with a P. This includes pimps, prostitutes, preachers, plumbers, procurers, psychologists, physicians, psychiatrists, printers, painters, philosophers, professors, phonies, parachutists, pipe-smokers, or part-time anythings" (p. 28). Another attorney vowed always to use a peremptory strike against any prospect who wore a hat indoors.

Implicit personality theories lead to stereotypes, when a person believes that all members of a distinguishable group (e.g., a religious, racial, sexual, age, or occupational group) have the same attributes. They also produce assumptions that two qualities are associated—for example, that slow-talking jurors are also unintelligent—when they actually may not be.

We tend to link qualities together and form our own implicit personality theories. Sometimes these judgments are rationally based; we may have had sufficient experience to draw a valid conclusion about the relationship. Other theories, however, such as the examples just presented, are only intuitive or are based on limited experiences and purely coincidental relationships and ignore within-group variability. But the emergence of implicit personality theories is almost inevitable when people form impressions of others and make interpersonal decisions. After all, human behavior is very complex and one must simplify it in some way.

The jury selection decisions in the trial of *J. E. B. v. T. B.* reflect the use of implicit personality theories and stereotypes. Ms. Bible's attorney dismissed male jurors, assuming they would be sympathetic to the man alleged to be the baby's father, whereas the defense dismissed female jurors because of similar beliefs that women would be biased in favor of another woman. But the courts prohibit the use of such stereotypes. In his majority opinion in the *J. E. B.* case, Justice Harry Blackmun wrote, "Virtually no support [exists] for the conclusion that gender alone is an accurate predictor of [jurors'] attitudes," and if gender does not predict a juror's predisposition, then there is no legitimacy to dismissing jurors on this basis only (quoted by Greenhouse, 1994, p. A10).

Lawyers must choose which prospective jurors to challenge with their quota of peremptory challenges. Hence, their own implicit personality theories come into play. Richard "Racehorse" Haynes, a highly successful lawyer, once defended two White Houston police officers charged with beating a Black prisoner to death. Like all lawyers, Haynes had his ideas about the kind of juror who would be sympathetic to his police officer clients, but his candor was a surprise. After the trial was over, Haynes was quoted as saying, "I knew we had the case won when we seated the last bigot on the jury" (Phillips, 1979, p. 77).

Even if they are allowed to question jurors individually, lawyers cannot know for certain whether they are being told the truth. By necessity, they fall back on their own impressions. What attributes do lawyers find important? Textbooks and journal articles on trial advocacy provide a wealth of folklore about jurors' characteristics and their relation to beliefs. Not surprisingly, characteristics that are visible or easily determined—age, gender, race, religion, occupation, country of origin—receive special attention, and attorneys are naively "advised" about how jurors with certain attributes tend to think.

In addition to applying their own theories of personality to juror selection, some attorneys use their understanding of group structure. For example, they play hunches about which jurors will be the most dominant during the deliberations. Who will be selected as foreperson if, as in most jurisdictions, that choice is left up to the jury? Understanding group dynamics is more complicated than relying on simple stereotypes of individual jurors, so lawyers who try to forecast group behavior also make assumptions. Some lawyers maintain a simple "one-juror verdict" theory—that is, they believe that the final group decision is usually determined by the opinions of one strong-willed, verbal, and influential juror. Lawyers who adhere to this maxim look for one juror who is likely to be both sympathetic and influential and then, during the trial, concentrate their influence attempts on that individual. In pursuing this search for a "key juror," the typical attorney follows one basic rule of thumb: "In general, an individual's status and power within the jury group will mirror his status and power in the external world" (Christie, 1976, p. 270).

If jurors themselves are asked who among them was most influential during their deliberations, three characteristics tend to emerge: male gender, an extroverted personality style, and height greater than that of their fellow jurors (Marcus, Lyons, & Guyton, 2000). It should come as no surprise then that Massachusetts senator and former presidential candidate John Kerry was elected to serve as foreperson in a 2005 trial in Suffolk County Superior Court. Fellow jurors described him as a "natural leader."

Another common attorney strategy is based on the assumption that jurors who are demographically or socially similar to a litigant will be predisposed to favor that litigant, a belief known as the **similarity–leniency hypothesis**. Does this rule of thumb hold true? Are jurors more likely to favor litigants with whom they share certain characteristics? One could make the opposite prediction in some cases—that sharing similar qualities with another might make a juror more skeptical of that person's excuses or justifications for behavior that the juror dislikes. Here, the so-called **black sheep effect** may apply: Although people generally favor individuals who are part of their in-group, they may sometimes strongly sanction those fellow members who reflect negatively on and embarrass the in-group.

Although the strength of evidence against a defendant is the most powerful predictor of jurors' sentiments

(Devine, Buddenbaum, Houp, Studebaker, & Stolle, 2009), similarity between jurors and defendants may also have an influence. The strength of that influence may depend on offenders' prior records. When the offender has committed previous wrongdoings, jurors render harsher judgments against members of their in-group than members of an out-group. This supports the black sheep effect: people distance themselves from others like them who are deviant in some way. But for offenders without prior wrongdoings, the similarity–leniency hypothesis seems more apt: jurors tend to view law-abiding members of their in-group more positively than members of an out-group (Gollwitzer & Keller, 2010).

Do Jurors' Demographic Characteristics Predict the Verdicts? Trial attorneys must make informed guesses about which prospective jurors will be more favorable to their side. To do so, they often rely on demographic features of jurors because many of these characteristics (e.g., age, race, gender, socioeconomic status [SES]) are easily observable (Kovera, Dickinson, & Cutler, 2002). Indeed, many attorneys actively select (or, rather, deselect) jurors on the basis of demographic information. When researchers (Olczak, Kaplan, & Penrod, 1991) gave attorneys mock juror profiles that varied along demographic lines (jurors' gender, age, marital status, and nationality) and asked them to rate the extent to which each profiled juror would be biased toward the defense or prosecution, they found that attorneys could do this task easily, focusing on one or two characteristics to the exclusion of others.

But though demographic characteristics of jurors and juries are *sometimes* related to their verdicts, the correlations are weak and inconsistent from one type of trial to another (Baldus, Woodworth, Zuckerman, Weiner, & Broffit, 2001; Devine, Clayton, Dunford, Seying, & Pryce, 2001). The relationships that emerge are usually small and offer no guarantee of success to the attorney who deals with only a few individuals and one trial at a time.

The relationship between demographic characteristics and verdicts also depends on the type of case. For example, in trials that involve issues such as child sexual assault, domestic violence, and sexual harassment, women are more likely than men to convict the perpetrators (Golding, Bradshaw, Dunlap, & Hodell, 2007), and in civil trials, women are more inclined than men to perceive that sexual harassment has occurred in the workplace (Wiener, Hurt,

Russell, Mannen, & Gasper, 1997). But gender is not a reliable predictor of verdicts or punitive damages in high-stakes civil litigation (Vinson, Costanzo, & Berger, 2008). The most consistent gender difference involves social influence rather than content; men are generally perceived by other jurors as more influential than women (Marcus et al., 2000).

Although few studies have examined the relationship between jurors' SES and their verdicts, the general consensus is that wealthy jurors are somewhat more likely than poorer jurors to assume that criminal defendants are guilty, particularly in trials involving theft, burglary, and fraud. Well-to-do jurors may have a desire to protect the social order and become wary of those who take what is not rightfully theirs (Devine, 2012). Laboratory research has shown that high-SES mock jurors are less harsh than low-SES jurors on civil defendants (Bornstein & Rajki, 1994). Perhaps the most powerful effect of SES occurs at the deliberation table, where jurors of higher status are regarded as more influential because of what others believe about their competence (York & Cornwell, 2006).

Using jurors' race to predict their verdicts is complicated because few studies have examined the decision making of non-White jurors (Sommers, 2007) and, as we described, the racial mix of the jury influences an individual juror's decision. Based on the existing data, we can tentatively conclude that Black jurors may be more lenient than Whites in the typical criminal case (Bothwell, 1999), but only if the defendant is also Black (Sommers & Ellsworth, 2000). In general, with regard to jurors' race as well as other demographic features, there is little evidence that these characteristics can consistently predict verdicts in criminal cases or damage awards in civil cases (Vinson et al., 2008).

Jurors' Personality and Attitudinal Characteristics as Predictors of Verdicts. Given that demographic variables have only a weak relationship to verdicts, one might wonder whether jurors' personality and attitudinal characteristics are better predictors. Personality characteristics are relatively stable patterns of behavior that describe "how people act in general" (Funder, 2004, p. 109). Attitudinal characteristics are evaluative reactions toward someone or something that are exhibited in feelings, beliefs, and intended actions (Olson & Zanna, 1993).

A number of studies concluded that enduring aspects of one's personality and attitudes may influence courtroom decisions, though usually only to a modest degree. Using simulated and real juries, this research has indicated that certain personality attributes of mock jurors such as Authoritarianism, the Need for Cognition, and Extraversion may be related to jurors' verdicts. Personality and attitudinal variables are somewhat better predictors of verdict decisions than are demographic factors (Lieberman & Olson, 2009), though the relationships between personality and attitudinal factors on the one hand, and verdicts on the other hand, are, at best, only modest.

Authoritarianism is one personality characteristic of jurors that is modestly correlated with their verdicts in criminal cases (Devine, 2012). People with an authoritarian personality adhere rigidly to traditional values, identify with and submit to powerful figures, and are punitive toward those who violate established norms. In terms of the legal system, authoritarian jurors are more likely to vote for conviction in mock jury experiments (Narby, Cutler, & Moran, 1993).

Authoritarian beliefs may be more powerful determinants of decisions in death penalty trials than in noncapital trials. In one study, prospective jurors reporting for jury duty in Florida read a condensed version of a capital case and recommended an appropriate sentence (life without parole or death). They also rated the extent to which various aggravating factors (those aspects of a crime that support a death sentence) and mitigating factors (aspects that support a life sentence) were present in the evidence (Butler & Moran, 2007). Jurors who scored high on a measure of Authoritarianism endorsed more aggravating factors and fewer mitigating factors, and were more likely to select a death sentence than their counterparts lower in Authoritarianism.

Interestingly, when highly authoritarian jurors encounter a defendant who symbolizes authority, their usual tendency to punish the defendant is reversed (Nietzel & Dillehay, 1986). In fact, about the only time that authoritarian mock jurors are not more conviction-prone than nonauthoritarians is in trials in which the defendant is a police officer. In such cases, the more authoritarian jurors tend to identify with the powerful and punitive image of the officer.

Another personality variable—the **Need for Cognition**—may influence how jurors evaluate evidence in a trial. The Need for Cognition refers to a person's inclination to engage in and enjoy effortful cognitive work (Cacioppo, Petty, Feinstein, & Jarvis, 1996). The Need for Cognition explains why some

people are motivated to think hard and analyze arguments thoroughly, and others are disinclined to do so. This concept is assessed by whether people agree with statements such as "I only think as hard as I have to" and "The notion of thinking abstractly is appealing to me." In a courtroom, the Need for Cognition can distinguish those jurors who scrutinize the evidence carefully and examine its weaknesses from jurors who accept trial testimony at face value and have little desire to pore over the evidence (DeWitt, Richardson, & Warner, 1997). Jurors with low Need for Cognition may pay more attention to witnesses' credentials than to the essence of their testimony.

The Need for Cognition influences how jurors process evidence presented by an expert witness. This evidence is often complicated, technical, or scientific, and may require effortful thinking on the part of jurors. When mock jurors read a summary of a sexual harassment trial in which an expert witness presented research that varied in terms of scientific rigor and quality, jurors high in Need for Cognition were attentive to the validity of the research. They evaluated the expert evidence more favorably when the research was valid, and tended to support the side that presented that evidence. On the other hand, jurors low in Need for Cognition were not attentive to flaws in the expert evidence and were less likely to support the side that presented the valid study (McAuliff & Kovera, 2008). One study showed that jurors who are low in Need for Cognition can be helped by a detailed cross-examination of an expert who presented flawed research during direct examination. These jurors are unlikely to process the expert testimony thoroughly themselves (Salerno & McCauley, 2009).

Psychologists have also examined the relationship between jurors' verdicts and other personality traits. For example, to test the impact of jurors' personality traits on verdicts in real cases and on attorneys' jury selection preferences, John Clark and his colleagues (2007) relied on the **Five-Factor Model of personality**, a generally accepted framework for describing personality characteristics (Costa & Widiger, 2002). The traits that form the model are (1) Openness to Experience, (2) Neuroticism, (3) Extraversion, (4) Conscientiousness, and (5) Agreeableness. According to this model, one's personality can be described by some combination of these traits.

Prior to *voir dire* in 28 real cases (11 criminal cases and 17 civil cases), the researchers asked prospective jurors to complete a questionnaire that measured these five traits. Court clerks provided information about which jurors were dismissed by the attorneys, which jurors remained to decide the case, and what the juries' verdicts were. Analyses revealed no differences in personality traits among those who were excused by the defense, those excused by the prosecution, and those who ultimately ended up on the jury. In real life, attorneys may pay little heed to prospective jurors' personality attributes, probably because these traits are largely hidden from view.

The second question addressed by this study was whether jurors' verdicts were related to their personality traits as measured by the Five-Factor Model. The answer: slightly. Whereas four of the five personality traits were inconsequential, Extraversion emerged as a moderately important factor in understanding juror influence and jury decisions. Jurors who opted for acquittals in criminal cases scored higher on measures of Extraversion than jurors who voted to convict, though none of the other personality traits were related to verdicts. Not surprisingly, jurors who scored high in Extraversion were also more likely to be selected as jury foreperson, and juries led by people high on this trait tended to deliberate longer.

In general then, laboratory studies suggest that some personality and attitudinal variables may be modestly related to individual jurors' verdicts, at least in criminal cases. The relationships are less strong in civil cases and, in both contexts, probably depend upon the type of case (Vinson et al., 2008). But the trials used in these studies were "close calls." That is, the evidence for each side was manipulated to be about equally persuasive—in such cases, individual juror characteristics may have their greatest influence (Penrod, 1990). In the real world, trial evidence is often so conclusive for one side that the jurors' personality dispositions may have less impact.

Attorney Effectiveness in _Voir Dire_. Attorneys take pride in their skill in selecting a proper jury. For example, a president of the Association of Trial Lawyers in America wrote, "Trial attorneys are acutely attuned to the nuances of human behavior, which enables them to detect the minutest traces of bias or inability to reach an appropriate decision" (Begam, 1977, p. 3). But findings from the study by Clark et al. (2007) are less encouraging on this point. Attorneys may overvalue the importance of demographic variables and undervalue the importance of

personality variables when making peremptory challenges.

As a result of research findings, social scientists are appropriately skeptical of how much lawyers can accomplish in _voir dire_. In a study of attorney effectiveness, experienced trial attorneys were observed to use juror selection strategies that were not different from or better than those used by inexperienced college and law students who were asked to evaluate mock jurors (Olczak et al., 1991). Trial attorneys did not appear to think any more accurately when making personality judgments than did nonprofessionals. Even when asked to perform a more realistic task—rating jurors from the videotapes of a previous _voir dire_—attorneys did no better than chance in detecting jurors who were biased against them (Kerr, Kramer, Carroll, & Alfini, 1991). In short, "attorneys cannot read jurors like open books" (Devine, 2012).

In another study evaluating the effectiveness of _voir dire_, Cathy Johnson and Craig Haney (1994) observed the full _voir dires_ in four felony trials in Santa Cruz, California. They also collected information on the criminal justice attitudes of jurors by administering Boehm's (1968) Legal Attitudes Questionnaire. By comparing the attitudes of persons who were retained as jurors with those of persons who were challenged by the prosecutor or defense attorney, they were able to gauge the effectiveness of each side's peremptory challenge strategy. Jurors who were peremptorily excused by prosecutors held stronger pro-defense attitudes than jurors excused by the defense. Jurors excused by the defense were more pro-prosecution than jurors excused by the prosecution. This would imply that attorneys had some success in determining which jurors were more favorable to their side. However, the overall score of the retained jurors was not significantly different from the average score of the first 12 jurors questioned or of a group of prospective jurors sampled at random. So although each side succeeded in getting rid of jurors most biased against it, the final result was a jury that would not have differed appreciably from a jury obtained by just accepting the first 12 people called or empanelling 12 jurors at random. (One wonders, then, whether _voir dire_ should be eliminated altogether! Undoubtedly, trial attorneys would object.)

Scientific Jury Selection: Does It Work Any Better? For years, trial lawyers have been "picking"

B o x 12.3 THE CASE OF CASEY ANTHONY, HER "TWO TRIALS," AND HER TRIAL CONSULTANT

On July 15, 2008, 2-year-old Caylee Anthony's maternal grandmother called 911 to report her missing. Her body was discovered several months later in a wooded area near her Orlando, Florida home. By that time, Caylee's mother, Casey, had been arrested and charged with her disappearance and death. Casey offered multiple explanations of her whereabouts, Caylee's disappearance, and her attempts to find her daughter.

In the period between Caylee's disappearance and Casey's trial on charges of murder and aggravated child abuse (among other charges) in 2011, the media had a heyday with this case. Because Florida has very liberal media access laws, all of the evidence in the case, including documents, photographs, and witness lists, was accessible online. Even before the judge had ruled on the relevance of the evidence and the potential for prejudice, commentators and bloggers were feasting on the details. They hid little of their disdain for Casey Anthony or their certainty of her guilt. Cable television executives made conscious decisions to feature the case prominently, banking on the old news adage, "If it bleeds, it leads" (Gabriel, 2011). *Time* magazine dubbed it the "social media trial of the century." Therefore, well before she was tried in a court of law, Anthony was tried in the court of public opinion.

Working as a *pro bono* (without charge) trial consultant on behalf of Anthony's defense team, Richard Gabriel had his hands full. He conducted a community attitude survey to assess public beliefs about the case and to determine what type of juror might be open-minded enough to consider a different perspective on Anthony's guilt. He also conducted pretrial focus groups to assess the effects of such extensive media penetration on prospective jurors' opinions. His work revealed that the more the prospective jurors were exposed to media hype about the case, the more they became suspicious of the *actual* evidence.

Casey Anthony's defense team eventually assembled a team of trial consultants, some of whom monitored the

Casey Anthony

televised *voir dire* and suggested follow-up questions and suggestions to aid the attorneys in exercising challenges for cause and peremptory challenges. Based on their pretrial research, consultants had determined that demographic factors of prospective jurors, such as gender, age, and race, would be largely irrelevant, and that ideal jurors for their side would be intelligent, skeptical, self-aware, and independent minded. They sought jurors who could set aside emotions and reason rationally, and who would conscientiously attend to the judge's instructions about the relevant rules and laws. One can never be certain what impact these choices had on the jury's composition, decision making, and eventual verdict, but they may have been critical: Casey Anthony was acquitted of the most serious charges (murder, aggravated child abuse) and convicted only on misdemeanor charges of lying to authorities.

Critical Thought Question

Based on what you have learned about effective jury selection strategies, how might the choices made by Casey Anthony's attorneys have led to her acquittal?

---

jurors on the basis of their own theories about how people behave. But recently, some attorneys (convinced of the importance of jury selection yet skeptical of their ability to do it well, or limited in the time they can devote to it) have hired social scientists as jury selection consultants. These consultants use empirically based procedures, such as small-group discussions called focus groups, shadow juries, systematic ratings of prospective jurors, and surveys of the community, to identify desirable and undesirable jurors (Lieberman, 2011). This collection of techniques is known as **scientific jury selection**. Although these

techniques were first used to aid defendants in several highly publicized "political" trials of the Vietnam War era (McConahay, Mullin, & Frederick, 1977), they are now frequently practiced in the full range of criminal and civil trials. They have been used in high profile cases including those involving Martha Stewart, hedge fund manager Raj Rajaratnam, and Casey Anthony (described in Box 12.3). They have also been employed in lower-profile cases.

Scientific jury selection raises a number of complex issues and generates significant controversy. Some critics claim that it subverts the criminal justice system because it favors the wealthy and well-heeled over individuals of modest means (Strier, 1999) and creates a perception among the public that the system is rigged (Brown, 2003). Others claim that it is ineffective (Kressel & Kressel, 2002; Saks, 1997). Not surprisingly, consultants (and some attorneys) dispute these claims, pointing out that public defenders have benefitted from their services and touting the value of professional training and experience: "We've collected a lot of research and we can spot things a lawyer wouldn't normally be paying attention to.... Most attorneys do just one or two trials a year, if they're lucky. But a good consultant has studied hundreds of juries and knows which behaviors and characteristics to look out for" (quote by consultant Dan Wolfe, cited by McCann, 2004). Moreover, because the American system of justice remains fundamentally adversarial, litigants are expected to present their version of the case as zealously as possible. So they should be able to use any legal means available to convince the jury to reach a favorable decision.

How effective *are* trial consultants at selecting juries? When attorneys in criminal trials first began to rely on empirically grounded scientific jury selection, they were often successful. Although the procedure seemed to work, the success rate may have been inflated by the following factors: (1) Many of the more widely discussed cases involved weak or controversial evidence against defendants. (2) Attorneys who made the extra effort to enlist jury consultation resources may also have been more diligent and thorough in other areas of their case preparation.

To assess the impact of trial consultants, ideally one would conduct an experiment in which two, identically composed juries would decide two identically tried cases, one that involved the services of a consultant and another that did not. By holding constant all aspects of the trial, including the nature of the evidence and the identities of the participants, and by varying only the involvement of a trial consultant, one might be able to reach some conclusion about that person's impact. Unfortunately, it is impossible to conduct such an experiment, so we may really never know with any precision or certainty whether and to what extent trial consultants are changing the outcomes of trials.

A few empirical studies have investigated the effectiveness of scientific jury selection, but their procedures were somewhat artificial. For example, Horowitz (1980) trained law students in either scientific

jury selection or traditional selection methods and investigated their performance in four criminal cases. Traditional selection methods included relying on past experiences, interactions with similar jurors in prior trials, and conventional wisdom. Those trained in scientific jury selection received pretrial survey responses and profiles showing the desirability of prospective jurors. Horowitz determined that neither approach was superior for all four trials: traditional methods were superior in cases in which there were weak links between demographic, personality, and attitudinal factors (e.g., in a murder case), whereas scientific methods were superior when those associations were strong (e.g., in a drug sale case).

A study of scientific jury selection used in a series of actual capital murder trials provides somewhat more data on the effectiveness of trial consultants. Nietzel and Dillehay (1986) examined the outcomes of 31 capital trials, some of which used a trial consultant and others did not. Juries recommended the death sentence in 61% of the trials in which consultants were not employed by the defense but in only 33% of the trials in which they were used. Of course, these cases differed on many variables besides the use of consultants, so it is not possible to conclude that different outcomes were due to their presence alone. But the results are consistent with claims that trial consultants might be effective in cases in which jurors' attitudes are particularly important, as they are when a jury is asked to choose between life and death. Clearly though, there is limited evidence of the effectiveness of scientific jury selection, and higher-quality, more contemporary studies are sorely needed.

In addition, the effectiveness of scientific jury selection depends on a number of variables over which the consultant has no control. These include how many peremptory challenges are allowed; the extent to which questions delve into matters beyond superficial demographic details of prospective panel members; whether attorneys act on the guidance of the consultant; and, perhaps most importantly, the extent to which jurors' attitudes and beliefs will determine the outcome of the case (Greene, 2002). The more freedom and flexibility inherent in the jury selection procedures and the more the case hinges on jurors' belief systems, the more room for consultants to ply their trade and the greater the chances they can succeed.

Still, trial-watchers and social scientists of the jury agree that in most cases the evidence is more important than jurors' attitudes or demographic characteristics (Jonakait, 2003; Kressel & Kressel, 2002) and that scientific jury selection may be of limited value in cases where the evidence is unambiguous. Richard Seltzer, a political scientist and trial consultant himself, acknowledged this indirectly: "Jurors cannot be predicted with the type of accuracy associated with experiments in physics" (2006).

Recognizing that jurors' demographic and personality characteristics do not correlate strongly with verdicts in general, many trial consultants have shifted their focus from advising lawyers about jury selection to providing services in realms other than jury selection (Lieberman, 2011). These include developing case themes and testing those themes and the demonstrative evidence in pretrial focus groups, preparing witnesses to testify in court, monitoring the effectiveness of evidence presentation during the trial, and interviewing jurors after the trial has ended. Consultants also assist attorneys during mediations.

PRETRIAL PUBLICITY

Legal cases have always attracted media attention, and the judicial system has struggled for centuries with the fallout of publicity that occurs prior to a trial. With the development of 24-hour news networks, thousands of cable and satellite channels, online news sources, social media, and blogs, trial-related information is more accessible to the public than ever before. As a result, the judicial system is experiencing new and growing concerns about the impact of this information on prospective jurors. A group of researchers estimates that the number of defendants who claim their case has been jeopardized by pretrial publicity has more than doubled in the past 20 years (Daftary-Kapur, Dumas, & Penrod, 2010).

One recent example involved the case of Michael Jackson's personal physician, Conrad Murray, who was charged with manslaughter in Jackson's death. Because Jackson's status as pop superstar seems to loom even larger in death than in life, the public was riveted by this case and by the question of whether Murray violated medical "standards of care" when he gave Jackson a lethal dose of the anesthetic propofol shortly before the singer's death.

Due to extensive publicity, it took two tries to select a jury for Murray's trial. In early 2011, after

three days of juror screening, the trial was aborted when only one prospective juror professed to lack knowledge of the case, and that person did not speak English. Jury selection resumed a few months later with similar results: when the judge asked 370 prospective jurors whether any was unaware of the case against the doctor, no one raised a hand. At this point, the focus shifted from finding "unaware" jurors to finding jurors who could put aside any knowledge of Jackson's life, fame, and death, and base their decision on evidence presented in the courtroom. But law professor Stan Goldman was skeptical. He said, "If you've got a jury of 12 people who have never heard of Michael Jackson, I'm not sure they qualify for jury duty." Yet a jury of 12 people *was* eventually selected, and after a six-week trial, Murray was convicted and sentenced to four years in prison. This trial highlights some of the challenges to the legal system's goal of forming fair and impartial juries when the case has attracted a great deal of pretrial publicity.

Conflicting Rights

Pretrial publicity highlights tensions between two cherished rights protected by the U.S. Constitution: freedom of the press as guaranteed by the First Amendment, and the right to a speedy and public trial before an impartial jury, as guaranteed by the Sixth Amendment. In the majority of cases, the liberties ensured by the First and Sixth Amendments are compatible and even complementary. The press informs the public about criminal investigations and trials, and the public learns the outcomes of these proceedings and gains increased appreciation for both the justness and the foibles of our system of justice.

On occasion, however, the First and Sixth Amendments clash. The press publishes information that, when disseminated among the public, threatens a defendant's right to a trial by impartial jurors. This can occur in cases in which defendants and/or victims, because of their fame or infamous acts (like Conrad Murray), have gained national reputations. More commonly, it happens when local media, online postings, blogs, and press releases disseminate information about a crime or the parties involved that is inflammatory, biased, emotion-laden, or factually erroneous. Examples of this information include details about a person's prior criminal record, a confession made by the accused, unfavorable statements regarding the defendant's character, and criticisms of the merits of pending cases.

The Supreme Court has considered several cases in which defendants claimed that their right to an impartial jury was impaired by inflammatory pretrial publicity. In one case, Jon Yount's confession that he had killed a high school student was published in two local papers in 1966. Prior to trial, Yount cited continuing publicity about the case and requested that the trial be moved to a different jurisdiction. The judge denied the motion despite the fact that 77% of prospective jurors admitted they had an opinion about Yount's guilt. Yount appealed his conviction, claiming that the publicity had made a fair trial impossible. The Supreme Court ruled against him, reasoning that a "presumption of correctness" should be given to the trial judge's opinion because, being present at the trial, the judge was in a better position to evaluate the demeanor, credibility, and, ultimately, the competence of prospective jurors (*Patton v. Yount*, 1984).

But in *Rideau v. Louisiana* (1963), the Court decided that dissemination of news that included information strongly pointing to the defendant's guilt violated his rights. On three occasions, a local TV station broadcast a 20-minute clip of Rideau, surrounded by law enforcement officials, confessing in detail to charges of robbery, kidnapping, and murder. Rideau's request for a change of venue was also denied, and Rideau was convicted and sentenced to death by a jury, of which at least three members had seen the televised confession. The Supreme Court reversed this decision, Rideau was granted a new trial, and he was eventually convicted of manslaughter, rather than murder. (In the 43 years he spent in prison prior to his 2005 release, Rideau transformed himself from an illiterate eighth-grade dropout to a national advocate for prison reform, a filmmaker, and an award-winning editor of Angola State Prison's renowned *Angolite* magazine. Perhaps most important, he acknowledged responsibility for his crime and apologized for the harm he caused [Green, 2005].)

Finally, in its most recent look at the potentially prejudicial effects of pretrial publicity (*Mu'Min v. Virginia*, 1991), the Supreme Court held that if prospective jurors claim they can be impartial, defendants do not have a constitutional right to ask them about the specifics of their exposure to pretrial publicity. According to the Court, such assurances are all that the Constitution requires.

Yet it is difficult to know how much trust to place in jurors' claims of impartiality. The problem is not that jurors lie about their beliefs, although some probably do. The issue is that people might not be aware of or admit the full measure of their prejudices in public. Prospective jurors would have to acknowledge that they received biasing information, know that they integrated those details with other pieces of information, and be able to reverse or control the biasing effects of this information—a very difficult cognitive task (Studebaker & Penrod, 2005).

Even if completely aware of their biases, prospective jurors might not be willing to disclose them in an open courtroom before a judge who encourages them to be fair and open-minded. They might experience **evaluation apprehension**, whereby they provide the answers that they perceive the judge wants to hear, regardless of whether their responses are truthful (Vidmar, 2002).

Effects of Pretrial Publicity

A large number of studies have measured the effects on jurors of various kinds of pretrial publicity presented in different media. Both experimental and field studies have been conducted. In experimental studies, participants are first exposed (or not exposed, in the control group) to some form of publicity and then are asked to assume the role of jurors in a simulated trial. In field studies, community-respondents are surveyed to assess the effects of naturally occurring publicity about an actual case. Taken together, these studies fairly convincingly point to the conclusion that jurors exposed to pretrial publicity are more likely than those not so exposed to favor the prosecution and prejudge the defendant as guilty.

Experimental Studies of the Effects of Pretrial Publicity. Using experimental procedures, researchers manipulate the presence and type of pretrial publicity and measure its impact on perceptions of witnesses and the defendant, evaluations of evidence, and the final verdict. Because all aspects of the trial except the publicity are held constant, scientists can assess whether variations in publicity cause differences in responses.

Many experimental studies have examined the effects of negative or antidefendant information in pretrial publicity on perceptions of the defendant. These studies generally show that pretrial publicity affects jurors' evaluations of the defendant's character and criminality, the extent to which they like or sympathize with him, their pretrial sentiments about his guilt, and their final verdicts (Steblay, Besirevic, Fulero, & Jiminez-Lorente, 1999). A few studies have explored the effects of positive or pro-defendant pretrial publicity. In one (Ruva & McEvoy, 2008), mock jurors who were exposed to positive publicity were less likely to convict the defendant than were jurors exposed to negative or no publicity.

Still other studies have attempted to explain why these effects occur. Three explanations seem reasonable. First, pretrial publicity may bias jurors' interpretations of the evidence to which they are exposed at trial. If pretrial publicity about the defendant is negative, jurors evaluate trial testimony in a manner adverse to the defendant yet consistent with the publicity (Hope, Memon, & McGeorge, 2004). In short, the publicity affects jurors' ability to determine the true probative value of the evidence. Second, jurors exposed to publicity come to believe, wrongly, that the pretrial information was actually presented as part of the evidence at trial. This is a **source monitoring** error: jurors are mistaken about the source of their information (Ruva, McEvoy, & Bryant, 2007). Finally, pretrial publicity often elicits emotional responses that are associated with jurors' verdicts. In one study, jurors who were exposed to anti-defendant information pretrial were angrier after the trial than jurors not exposed to this information, and as anger increased, so did guilt ratings (Ruva, Guenther, & Yarbrough, 2011).

An interesting question, given the pervasiveness of digital news sources and the declining readership of newspapers, is whether pretrial information conveyed on a screen has a different impact than information conveyed in print. In an experiment designed to test this question, participants were randomly assigned to one of three conditions that varied the format by which pretrial media information was presented about the Mount Cashel orphanage case, a highly publicized case in Canada concerning alleged sexual abuse by a group of Roman Catholic men who ran an orphanage in Newfoundland (Ogloff & Vidmar, 1994). The damaging pretrial material was presented to participants through (1) television, (2) newspaper articles, or (3) both TV and newspapers. Presentation of publicity via television had a greater biasing impact than the same information presented in print, but the

combined effects of TV and newspaper publicity had the greatest impact of all. Of additional interest was the finding that participants were generally unaware that their opinions had been biased by this material; those who had formed opinions about the trial were just as likely to say that they could be fair as were those who had not formed opinions.

To this point, we have considered the effects of **specific pretrial publicity**, showing that case-specific information made available prior to trial can affect the sentiments of jurors in that trial. But jurors can also be influenced by **generic prejudice**—that is, prejudice arising from media coverage of issues not specifically related to a particular case but thematically relevant to the issues at hand. Highly stigmatized conduct such as deviant sexual behavior or drug use in conservative communities can engender strong feelings among jurors that are unrelated to the facts of any particular case (Wiener, Arnot, Winter, & Redmond, 2006). In fact, Judge Abner Mikva of the Court of Appeals for the District of Columbia suggested that generic prejudice may be more problematic than specific pretrial publicity:

> Pretrial publicity is not the big difficulty. It is generic prejudice. I do not think you can get a fair child abuse trial before a jury anywhere in the country… I do not care how sophisticated or how smart jurors are, when they hear that a child has been abused, a piece of their mind closes up, and this goes for the judge, the juror, and all of us (cited by Doppelt, 1991, p. 821).

Psychological research seems to support Judge Mikva's assertion. For example, Wiener et al. (2006) found evidence of generic prejudice among mock jurors, and the effects of prejudice were greater in cases of sexual assault than homicide. Kovera (2002) showed that media exposure and preexisting attitudes interact: exposure to a story about a rape case influenced participants' appraisals of the witnesses and verdicts in a different rape case, but preexisting attitudes also affected the impact of the media on mock jurors' judgments.

Generic prejudice probably works by transferring preexisting beliefs and stereotypes about categories of people to a particular defendant in a trial setting (Vidmar, 2002). As a result, the facts of the case and the personal characteristics of the defendant go relatively unheeded. Racial and ethnic stereotypes are the most common forms of generic prejudice; for example, some people believe that an African-American defendant is more likely to be guilty of a crime than a White defendant, all other things being equal. Arab Americans on trial in the United States in the aftermath of 9/11 were also likely to have experienced some form of generic prejudice.

Field Studies of the Effects of Naturally Occurring Publicity. Serious crimes attract extensive news coverage, typically from the prosecutor's view of the case. Field studies, a research technique favored by trial consultants, can assess the saturation of a news story in a community by polling people about their knowledge of an actual crime. In some instances, polling occurs in the community where publicity is assumed to be widespread, as well as in jurisdictions farther from the crime, allowing for comparisons between respondents in two or more locales.

Whether surveying opinions about notorious crimes (Studebaker et al., 2002) or cases of only local interest (Vidmar, 2002), these studies consistently find that persons exposed to pretrial publicity possess more knowledge about the events in question, are more likely to have prejudged the case, and are more knowledgeable of incriminating facts that would be inadmissible at the trial. On rare occasions, when a field study demonstrates that the volume of publicity has been overwhelming and when a crime has touched the lives of large numbers of local residents, a judge will have no option but to move the trial. The Oklahoma City bombing case described in Box 12.4 is a good example.

In field studies, participants are typically asked about their knowledge of the crime in question, their perceptions of the defendant's culpability, and their ability to be impartial in light of their knowledge. (Responses may be of questionable validity, as we mentioned previously.) Surveys have revealed both specific prejudice, which stems from media coverage of a particular case (as in the Oklahoma City bombing), and more generic prejudice, which derives from mass media reports of social and cultural issues. Moran and Cutler (1991) showed that media descriptions of drug crimes influenced attitudes toward particular defendants who were charged with drug distribution. Cases involving sexual abuse also engender strong sentiments, fed in part by media coverage. Furthermore, generic prejudices can be engendered by publicity about jury damage awards and the controversy over tort reform in civil

cases. Nearly half of prospective jurors awaiting jury selection in Seattle said that their attitudes about tort reform were informed by the media; the more these individuals supported tort reform, the more negatively disposed they were to civil plaintiffs (Greene, Goodman, & Loftus, 1991).

Field studies have several strengths. For example, they use large and representative samples of prospective jurors, and they rely on naturally occurring publicity about actual cases. They also have a weakness: the data are correlational in nature and cannot indicate the direction of any relationship between exposure to publicity and prejudice. For example, does exposure to publicity lead to prejudicial sentiments about the defendant, or, alternatively, do people with an antidefendant bias voluntarily expose themselves to such publicity? Reasoning from Kovera's (2002) study on the interactive effects of the media and preexisting attitudes in a rape case, we suspect that both alternatives are possible.

Some scholars (e.g., Carroll et al., 1986) have suggested another weakness in field surveys. They argue that courts should not conclude that pretrial publicity biases jurors just because it affects their attitudes; to be truly prejudicial, it must also affect their verdicts. According to this logic, we need to know whether pretrial publicity effects persist through the presentation of trial evidence. Some evidence suggests that antidefendant biases held at the beginning of the trial persist through the presentation of evidence and may even influence the way the evidence is interpreted (Hope et al., 2004).

Using Multiple Methods to Assess Effects of Pretrial Publicity. Given the limitations of both experimental and field studies, a few researchers have opted to use multiple methods to understand effects of pretrial publicity in an actual trial as it occurred. One study focused on the case we described at the beginning of the chapter, involving three New York City police officers charged in the shooting death of Sean Bell on the morning of his wedding. The incident generated a great deal of controversy about the actions of the officers and, more broadly, about the treatment of African Americans by the New York City police. The three-stage study involved analyzing news articles, experimentally exposing residents of Boston (where case familiarity was almost nonexistent) to pretrial publicity, and measuring the impact of varying levels of naturally

Box 12.4   THE CASE OF TIMOTHY McVEIGH: DATA ON THE PREJUDICIAL EFFECTS OF MASSIVE PRETRIAL PUBLICITY

At 9:02 A.M. on April 19, 1995, a massive explosion destroyed the Murrah Federal Building in Oklahoma City. The bombing killed 163 people in the building (including 15 children in the building's day care center, which was visible from the street) as well as 5 people outside. The explosion trapped hundreds of people in the rubble and spewed glass, chunks of concrete, and debris over several blocks of downtown Oklahoma City. It was the country's most deadly act of domestic terrorism.

Approximately 75 minutes after the blast, Timothy McVeigh was pulled over while driving north from Oklahoma City because his car lacked license tags. Two days later, the federal government filed a complaint against McVeigh on federal bombing charges. By August 1995, McVeigh and codefendant Terry Nichols had been charged with conspiracy, use of a weapon of mass destruction, destruction by explosives, and eight counts of first-degree murder in connection with the deaths of eight federal law enforcement officials who had been killed in the blast.

The bombing, the heroic actions of rescue workers, and the arrest of McVeigh all generated a tremendous amount of publicity. Millions of Americans saw images of McVeigh, wearing orange jail garb and a bulletproof vest, being led through an angry crowd outside the Noble County Jail in Perry, Oklahoma. Predictably, McVeigh's defense team requested that the trial be moved from Oklahoma City to a more neutral (or at least a less emotionally charged) locale.

As part of their motion to move the trial, McVeigh's attorneys enlisted the help of a group of psychologists to provide information to the court about the extent and type of publicity in the Oklahoma City newspaper and in the papers from three other communities (Lawton, Oklahoma, a small town 90 miles from Oklahoma City; Tulsa; and Denver) (Studebaker & Penrod, 1997). Their media content analysis identified all articles pertaining to the bombing in these four papers between April 20, 1995, and January 8, 1996, and coded the content of the text, including positive characterizations of victims, negative characterizations of the defendant, reports of a confession, and emotionally laden publicity. They also measured the number of articles printed in each paper and the amount of space allotted to text and pictures (*United States v. McVeigh*, 1996).

The data were compelling: During the collection period, 939 articles about the bombing had appeared in

Timothy McVeigh

the Oklahoma City newspaper and 174 in the *Denver Post*. By a whopping 6,312–558 margin, the *Daily Oklahoman* had printed more statements of an emotional nature (e.g., emotional suffering, goriness of the scene) than the *Denver Post* (Studebaker & Penrod, 1997). On the basis of this analysis and other evidence presented at the hearing, Judge Richard Matsch moved the trial to Denver. In June 1997, McVeigh was convicted on all 11 counts and sentenced to death. He was executed in June 2001.

Critics have long suggested that studies of pretrial publicity lack usefulness because they do not measure the public's reactions to naturally occurring publicity. (As we pointed out, researchers often "expose" participants to news reports in the context of an experiment.) To address these concerns, Christina Studebaker and her colleagues conducted an online study to examine how differences in naturally occurring exposure to pretrial publicity affected public attitudes, evidence evaluation, and verdict and sentencing preferences in the *McVeigh* case (Studebaker et al., 2002). They found, among other things, that the closer people were to the bombing site, the more they knew about it and the more they believed that McVeigh was guilty. This study employs a novel methodology to explore important real-world effects of pretrial information.

Critical Thought Question
Why would prospective jurors with more knowledge about the case also be more likely to convict Timothy McVeigh?

occurring exposure in New York City residents (Daftary-Kapur, 2009).

Results showed that regardless of whether exposure was experimentally manipulated or naturally occurring, those who had read pro-prosecution

articles were more familiar with the case and more likely than those who read pro-defense articles to judge the defendants guilty prior to trial. Importantly, exposure occurred eight weeks before participants rendered verdicts, suggesting that the effects of pretrial publicity may be long lived. The study also lends external validity to laboratory studies in which exposure to media accounts is manipulated by researchers.

Remedies for the Effects of Pretrial Publicity

Given that pretrial publicity adversely affects juror impartiality, what procedures should be used to restore the likelihood of a fair trial for the defendant? Four alternatives are available.

1. *Continuance.* The trial can be postponed until a later date, with the expectation that the passage of time will lessen the effects of the prejudicial material. This view remains in vogue with some judges. But research indicates that although continuances may decrease jurors' reliance on factual pretrial publicity, they do not dampen jurors' recall or use of emotionally biasing information (Kramer, Kerr, & Carroll, 1990); furthermore, Daftary-Kapur (2009) showed that prejudicial effects of pretrial publicity can linger for at least eight weeks post-exposure.

2. *Expanded voir dire.* The most popular method for handling pretrial prejudice involves conducting a thorough *voir dire* of potential jurors in order to identify and dismiss those with particularly strong biases. But expanded *voir dire* may be of limited usefulness. Jurors may not recognize their own biases, and can hide their true feelings from an examiner if they so choose. They may also be hesitant to self-disclose in a public courtroom. Finally, Freedman, Martin, and Mota (1998) found that the impact of pretrial publicity actually increased, rather than decreased, when jurors were questioned about their exposure prior to trial.

3. *Judicial instructions.* A fairly simple remedy for the biasing effects of pretrial publicity is an instruction from the judge telling jurors to ignore what they learned about the case prior to trial and admonishing them to base their decision on the evidence. But cautionary instructions may also be insufficient to reduce the biasing effects of exposure to pretrial publicity. In one mock jury study, participants learned that a defendant was charged with killing his estranged wife and a neighbor (Fein, McCloskey, & Tomlinson, 1997). Before trial, half of the jurors read articles about the

murders and some also read an article in which the defense attorney complained about the negative publicity: "The coverage of this case serves as another fine example of how the media manipulates information to sell papers, and knowingly ignores acts which would point toward a defendant's innocence" (p. 1219). Despite judicial instructions to ignore pretrial information, jurors' verdicts were significantly influenced by it, unless the defense attorney had made them suspicious of the media's motives. In other words, mock jurors could follow the instruction only when they were given some reason to suspect that the pretrial information was biased.

On the basis of existing research, these three remedies appear to be largely ineffective. These methods probably fail as safeguards because of the way that people remember and use information to form impressions and make judgments (Studebaker & Penrod, 2005). Unless they have some reason to discount or ignore pretrial publicity when it is first encountered, most people will use it to help them interpret subsequent information and to make various pieces of information "fit" together in a coherent theme. Therefore, once the idea of a guilty perpetrator is established, it may become an organizing principle for the processing of additional information about the person. For these reasons, safeguards that attempt to remove an existing bias may never work as well as trying to find jurors who never had a bias to start with. The value of achieving this goal is why most social scientists prefer changes of venue.

4. *Change of venue.* A **change of venue**, the most extreme remedy for pretrial prejudice, is typically requested by defense attorneys in cases that have generated a great deal of biased publicity. Changing venue means that the trial is conducted in a different geographic jurisdiction and that jurors for the trial may be drawn from this new jurisdiction. But venue changes are expensive, inconvenient, and time-consuming, so judges are reluctant to grant them, though some evidence suggests that they are more easily persuaded when defense attorneys provide media analyses documenting the extent of news coverage (Spano, Daftary-Kapur, & Penrod, 2011).

Venue changes can result in significant variations in characteristics of the communities involved, as illustrated by the case of William Lozano, a Hispanic police officer who was convicted of killing an African American motorist in Miami. After his conviction was reversed because of pretrial publicity and he was granted a retrial, the case was first moved to Tallahassee (which has a much smaller Hispanic population than Miami) and eventually tried in Orlando (where the Hispanic population is more sizeable). The Florida appellate court reasoned that in cases in which race may be a factor and changes of venue are appropriate, trials should be moved to locations where the demographic characteristics are similar to those of the original location (*State v. Lozano*, 1993).

Psychologists can be enlisted to support a lawyer's motion for one or more of these protections against pretrial prejudices. When publicity is pervasive, a professionally conducted public opinion

survey is the technique of choice for evaluating the degree of prejudice in a community. Public opinion surveys gauge how many people have read or heard about a case, what they have read or heard, whether they have formed opinions, what these opinions are, and how their opinions influence perceptions of the case.

Public opinion surveys are also time consuming, and often require more resources than the typical client can afford. However, they usually yield valuable information. Obtaining a change of venue for a highly publicized case is probably the most effective procedure available for improving the chances for a fair trial. Moreover, even if the venue is not changed, the results of the survey can often be used in jury selection. Because of the multiple purposes for which they can be used, public opinion surveys are a popular tool among trial consultants.

SUMMARY

1. ***How do juries' verdicts differ from those of judges?*** The question of whether juries' and judges' verdicts differ significantly was answered in a massive empirical study by Harry Kalven and Hans Zeisel. In actual trials, 75% of the time the jury came to the same verdict that the judge would have reached. In 19.5% of trials, the judge and jury disagreed. In the vast majority of these disagreements, the jury was more lenient than the judge. The major source of discrepancies was what Kalven and Zeisel called "jury sentiments," or factors beyond the evidence and the law. Recent replications of this classic study showed remarkably similar results: In criminal cases, the judge and jury agreed on a verdict in 70% of trials, and when there was disagreement, jurors were more likely than judges to acquit.

2. ***What does the legal system seek in trial juries?*** The legal system seeks representative and unbiased juries. Both are hard to achieve. The jury selection process can, in some instances, create an unrepresentative jury.

3. ***What stands in the way of jury representativeness?*** The lists from which jurors' names were selected—originally only voter registration lists—underrepresent certain segments of society such as youth, older

adults, and minorities. Many people fail to respond to their jury summons. Others seek dismissal by claiming personal hardship. To make jury pools more representative, jurisdictions have broadened the sources of names of prospective jurors.

4. ***What procedures are used in voir dire?*** The goal of *voir dire* is an unbiased jury. Prospective jurors who have biases or conflicts of interest can be challenged for cause and discharged. Using peremptory challenges, each side may also dismiss a certain number of prospective jurors without giving any reason. Questioning of the prospective jurors is done at the discretion of the judge. In most trials, there is some combination of questions from the judge and the attorneys. When questioning jurors, most attorneys also try to sway them to their viewpoint through various ingratiation and indoctrination techniques.

5. ***What personality and attitudinal characteristics of jurors, if any, are related to their verdicts?*** In choosing jurors, lawyers base decisions on their implicit personality theories and stereotypes. According to laboratory studies, a few personality and attitude-related characteristics of jurors—Authoritarianism, Need for Cognition, and Extraversion—are related to their verdicts.

Attorneys tend not to focus on jurors' personality characteristics during jury selection, probably because they are difficult to identify.

6. ***What role do trial consultants play in a trial?***
Initially, practitioners of scientific jury selection tried to determine which demographic characteristics of jurors were related to sympathy for one side or the other in trials. More recently, consultants have broadened their work to include (1) pretrial assessments of reactions to the evidence and (2) the development of themes that organize the evidence for specific jurors likely to be swayed by this approach. There is some evidence that science-oriented consultation may be useful in cases in which jurors' attitudes about the evidence are especially important.

7. ***In what ways does pretrial publicity pose a danger to fair trials? How can these dangers be reduced?***
Freedom of the press and the right to a fair trial are usually complementary, but some trials generate so much publicity that the parties' right to an impartial jury is jeopardized. In addition, publicity about other cases or about social or cultural issues can create generic prejudice that can influence jurors' reasoning in a particular case. Psychologists have studied the effects of pretrial publicity on potential fact-finders and have also evaluated various mechanisms for reducing the negative effects of pretrial publicity. Change of venue, though the most costly remedy, may also be the most effective because it does not require jurors to disregard information to which they have been exposed.

KEY TERMS

Authoritarianism

bench trial

black sheep effect

challenges for cause

change of venue

cognizable groups

evaluation apprehension

Five-Factor Model of personality

generic prejudice

implicit personality theory

jury sentiments

Need for Cognition

peremptory challenges

pro bono

scientific jury selection

selection effects

similarity–leniency hypothesis

social desirability effect

social judgments

source monitoring

specific pretrial publicity

venire

voir dire

Chapter 13

Jurors and Juries

ORIENTING QUESTIONS

1. Describe the issue of jury competence.
2. What is the impact of extralegal information on jurors?
3. Can jurors disregard inadmissible evidence?

4. How can jurors be helped to understand their instructions?
5. What is meant by the statement "Bias is inevitable in jurors"?
6. What reforms of the jury system do psychologists suggest?

A trial by jury is the only right to appear in both the main body of the U.S. Constitution (Article 3) and the Bill of Rights (Sixth Amendment for criminal cases and Seventh Amendment for civil cases). The U.S. Supreme Court underscored the importance of the jury by stating that "[t]he guarantees of jury trial in the state and federal constitutions reflect a profound judgment about the way in which the law should be enforced and justice administered" (*Duncan v. Louisiana*, 1968, p. 149). More recently, the Supreme Court acknowledged the preeminent role of juries in our legal system when it announced that nearly any contested fact that increases the penalty for a crime must be determined by a jury (*Blakely v. Washington*, 2004).

Trial by jury is an institution that routinely draws ordinary citizens into the apparatus of the justice system. Although the number of U.S. cases decided by juries has dropped recently as a result of rising litigation costs and alternative dispute resolution, many countries around the world are changing their legal systems to include laypeople as jurors (Hans, 2008). In fact, jury trials have been reintroduced in Russia and Spain; are being instituted in Japan, South Korea, Venezuela, and Argentina; and form an integral part of the legal system in countries in Africa (e.g., Ghana, Malawi), Asia (e.g., Sri Lanka, Hong Kong), South America (e.g., Brazil), and Europe (e.g., England, Scotland, Ireland, Denmark). Jurors also decide many criminal cases in Canada.

Approximately two-thirds of Americans have been called to jury duty and approximately one-quarter have actually served as jurors (Harris Poll, 2008). For many jurors, their participation demands major sacrifices of income, time, and energy. In a massive class action lawsuit against the Ford Motor Corporation, one juror continued to attend the trial even after suffering injuries in a hit-and-run accident and in spite of requiring constant pain medication; another juror whose family moved out of the county opted to live in a hotel near the courthouse in order to continue hearing the case. On occasion, jury service can be extremely unpleasant: in 2009 a San Diego judge declared a mistrial in a kidnapping case after the defendant flung feces at the jury. Fortunately, he missed. Yet serving on a jury can also be educational and inspiring. Many jurors have a positive view of the court system after serving (Rose, Ellison, & Diamond, 2008). Occasionally, jury service even brings great personal satisfaction, as it did for Erika Ozer and Jeremy Sperling, who met in a New York City jury box in 2001 and were married in 2005.

The jury system casts its shadow well beyond the steps of the courthouse, because predictions about jury verdicts influence decisions to settle civil lawsuits and to accept plea bargains in criminal cases. Thus, the jury trial is an important and influential tradition; no other institution of government places power so directly in the hands of the people and allows average citizens the opportunity to judge the actions of their peers (Abramson, 1994).

Antecedents of the contemporary jury system may be seen in citizen juries used by the ancient Greeks and Romans, and formalized in English laws of 800 years ago. Despite this long history, the jury system has often been criticized. One commentator described the jury as, at best, 12 people of average ignorance. Another critic, Judge Jerome Frank, who served on the federal appeals court, complained that juries apply law they don't understand to facts they can't get straight. Even Mark Twain took a swing at the jury system. In *Roughing It*, he called the jury "the most ingenious and infallible agency for defeating justice that wisdom could contrive." One anonymous commentator asked rhetorically, "How would you like to have your fate decided by twelve people who weren't smart enough to get out of jury duty?" (cited by Shuman & Champagne, 1997).

The civil jury, in particular, has been vilified. In fact, one prominent scholar of the civil jury points out that "so many writings, both scholarly and journalistic, have been devoted to criticizing the institution of the civil jury that it becomes boring to recite the claims" (Vidmar, 1998, p. 849). According to Vidmar, civil juries have been criticized as incompetent, capricious, unreliable, biased, sympathy prone, confused, gullible,

Lucinda Naugle started smoking Benson and Hedges cigarettes in 1968 when she was 20 years old, believing that it made her look older and more sophisticated. She quit at age 45, but by then it was too late; she had contracted severe emphysema. She sued the manufacturer of Benson and Hedges, Philip Morris USA, claiming that it had committed fraud by hiding knowledge that smoking was addictive and harmful to smokers' health. Remember that the public knew little about the health hazards of cigarette smoking in 1968, so the critical issues in these cases are what tobacco industry insiders knew, when they knew it, and what they shared with the public.

When her case was tried before a jury in 2009, Ms. Naugle's condition was serious: she testified that she could not walk without struggling for breath and that she had to carry a walkie-talkie to the bathroom in case she needed help. She required a lung transplant that she was unable to afford—until the jury determined that Philip Morris was 90% responsible for Naugle's condition and awarded her $56 million in compensatory damages and $244 million in punitive damages.

As the largest single damage award in an individual lawsuit against a tobacco company, the verdict generated significant publicity and controversy. Its size stunned even the judge, who said, "From the moment I read the verdict and took a deep breath, I have considered that verdict and what I should do." Judges can reduce jury awards they deem excessive, and Judge Jeffrey Streitfeld, who presided over the trial in Broward County, Florida, vowed to do so. He called the jury award "excessive and shocking" and suspected that jurors were upset and inflamed by Philip Morris' "blame the smoker" defense. He may also have considered that more than 9,000 former smokers have filed similar lawsuits against the tobacco industry in courts across Florida.

Critical Thought Question
Why would the jury verdict in this case have generated significant controversy?

hostile to corporate defendants, and excessively generous to plaintiffs. We examine some of these claims later in this chapter.

Much of the public outcry focuses on the seemingly excessive nature of jury damage awards. For example, Marc Bluestone of Sherman Oaks, California, received a jury award of $39,000 after his mixed-breed dog, valued at $10, died a few days after returning home from a two-month stay at a pet clinic. Explains Steven Wise, a lawyer and animal rights activist: "The courts are beginning to realize that the bond between humans and animals is very powerful" (Hamilton, 2004). Other large damage awards have come in cases against the tobacco industry for its role in smokers' illnesses and deaths (Box 13.1).

To be sure, the jury system also has its defenders. Many authors (e.g., Bornstein & Robicheaux, 2008) point out that claims about juries are often based on anecdotes that are unrepresentative or fabricated and on studies that lack scientific validity. Most of us never hear about the hundreds of thousands of juries each year that toil out of the spotlight and, after careful deliberation, reach reasonable verdicts. In fact, as we point out in this chapter, the bulk of scientific evidence shows that juries generally do a commendable job (Bornstein & Greene, 2011).

Proponents further argue that trial by jury epitomizes what is special about the justice system in that it ensures public participation in the process. Verdicts reached by representative juries can and often do increase the legitimacy of the process in the eyes of the public, particularly in controversial trials. Juries can serve as a check on the arbitrary or idiosyncratic nature of a judge. Because juries do not give a reason for their verdicts (as judges are required to do), they retain a flexibility that is denied to judges. Finally, participating on a jury can both educate jurors and enhance their regard for the justice system. Alexis de Tocqueville (1900), a 19th-century French statesman, wrote, "I do not know whether the jury is useful to those who are in litigation, but I am certain it is highly beneficial to those who decide the litigation; and I look upon it as one of the most efficacious means for the education of the people which society can employ" (p. 290). Tocqueville was right: engaging in meaningful deliberations reinforces jurors' confidence in fellow citizens and public institutions (Gastil, Black, Deess, & Leighter, 2008).

Are juries capable of making fair and intelligent decisions, or are the criticisms justified? If they are, can the legal system do anything to improve the functioning of juries? Psychologists are in a good position to answer these questions because their studies of juror and jury decision making have become so plentiful that they occupy a central place in psychology and law research. From their findings, psychologists have been able to obtain a better picture of how the jury system works.

Over the past several decades, researchers have subjected the jury to careful scientific scrutiny by applying theories and principles of social psychology (e.g., stereotyping, attribution, social influence, conformity, and small-group behavior) and cognitive psychology (e.g., memory, reasoning, judgment, and decision making). In the cognitive realm, **dual–process models** of information processing capture individual jurors' thought processes as they attend to and evaluate evidence presented during a trial. A number of dual-process models exist (including one espoused by Nobel-Prize winning psychologist Daniel Kahneman in his 2011 book, *Thinking, Fast and Slow*), but they all propose two ways in which people process information—either by rationally and deliberately evaluating the content of the information, or by reacting to it quickly and intuitively, without careful analysis. The former requires motivation, effort, and ability; the latter does not.

One dual-process model, termed cognitive–experiential self theory, is especially relevant to decisions that jurors make (Groscup & Tallon, 2009). This theory suggests that when people rely on analysis and logical arguments, they are using a rationally based cognitive system that is active, deliberate, and effortful. On the other hand, when people rely on emotion, intuition, or stereotypical thinking from past events, they are using an experientially based system that is unconscious and effortless. The experiential mode is the default mode of processing, and jurors will shift to cognitive processing only if the importance of careful analysis is stressed to them. But they will revert to experiential processing when they are emotionally aroused (Epstein, 2003).

In this chapter, we elaborate on how jurors process information, make individual decisions, and then work with other jurors to reach verdicts. In particular, we focus on two broad questions: first, whether jurors and juries are competent to execute their duties properly, and, second, whether they are biased and prejudiced. Within each of these broad categories we examine several related issues and rely on research studies to answer the questions. Finally, we consider various proposals to reform the institution of the jury.

ARE JURIES COMPETENT?

Some commentators have suggested that juries in criminal cases make more mistakes than the public should tolerate, in part because they are faced with tough cases—cases in which the evidence is neither flimsy enough to warrant dismissal nor compelling enough to induce a guilty plea (Arkes & Mellers, 2002). Reexamining the data on jury–judge comparisons first presented by Harry Kalven and Hans Zeisel (1966; described in Chapter 12), Professor Bruce Spencer estimates that jury verdicts are incorrect in at least one out of every eight cases (Spencer, 2007). He asks, "Can we be satisfied knowing that innocent people go to jail for many years for wrongful convictions?" (Science Daily, 2007).

Psychologists have examined factors that affect the accuracy of jury verdicts. They have assessed the assumption that in reaching their verdicts, jurors rely only on the evidence and disregard information that is not evidence (e.g., preexisting beliefs; irrelevant facts about the defendant, victim, plaintiff, or witnesses; and any information that the judge asks them to disregard). They have determined whether jurors can listen attentively to expert testimony but not give it undue weight. They have asked whether, as the legal system assumes, jurors understand and correctly apply the judge's instructions on the law and have the necessary reasoning skills to understand protracted and complex cases.

To address these issues, psychologists have used a variety of methodologies, including questioning jurors after trials, analyzing archival records of past verdicts, and conducting field studies and jury simulation studies. In simulation studies, the researcher introduces and experimentally manipulates some piece of information (e.g., the defendant's race or gender, the presence of an alibi witness) and measures the extent to which that information, as well as the actual evidence, influences jurors' reasoning and verdicts. Although simulation studies sometimes cast this information in a more prominent light than would be likely in real trials (e.g., a defendant's physical appearance might seem salient in an abbreviated and simulated trial but would lose its impact in a lengthy proceeding), they are nonetheless useful techniques for exploring how jurors reason and make decisions. They involve random assignment of research participants to conditions (the "gold standard" in experimental methodology) and allow researchers to control what the participants experience. As a result, researchers learn precisely what effects their manipulations have on resulting jury performance.

On the basis of these studies, psychologists have learned something very important: jurors in both criminal and civil cases pay considerable attention to the strength of the evidence. In fact, **evidentiary strength** is probably the most important determinant of jurors' verdicts (Devine, 2012). Differences in strength of the evidence can have profound effects on jury verdicts: Some studies have shown a 70% increase in conviction rates as the evidence against the accused increases (Devine, Clayton, Dunford, Seying, & Pryce, 2001).

Professor Stephen Garvey and his colleagues (2004) analyzed the verdicts of 3,000 jurors in felony trials in four metropolitan areas to find out what explained jurors' first votes. They measured the strength of the evidence by asking the judge who presided in the case to estimate it. They then determined that the judge's assessment of the strength of the evidence was powerfully associated with the jurors' first votes: The stronger the evidence against the defendant, the more likely the juror was to convict. In the realm of civil litigation, jurors also place considerable weight on the evidence and, in particular, on the severity of the plaintiff's injury. More seriously injured plaintiffs engender more sympathy and receive greater compensation than less seriously injured plaintiffs (Bright & Goodman-Delahunty, 2011; Greene & Bornstein, 2003).

These findings are important because they speak to the question of whether jurors are competent to execute their duties as the law intends. One would hope that jurors would convict when the strength of the evidence against a defendant was strong, and that they would acquit when it was weak. Apparently they do just that.

Effects of Extralegal Information

But studies also document that jury decisions can also be influenced by irrelevant information about the defendant's background or appearance, by what jurors read in the newspaper, or by other sources of irrelevant information, all of which constitute **extralegal information**. For example, unattractive defendants may be more likely than attractive defendants to be convicted (Gunnell & Ceci, 2010).

Juror and jury decisions may also be influenced by a defendant's race. In one study, Black jurors rated White defendants as more aggressive, violent, and guilty than Black defendants, and White jurors were harsher on Black defendants than on White defendants, but only when the crime was *not* racially charged (Sommers & Ellsworth, 2000). When the

crime *was* racially charged, the defendant's race did not influence White jurors' verdicts. Professor Samuel Sommers (2007) interpreted the race-based results in the context of **aversive racism**, a social-psychological concept that proposes that most White jurors are motivated to avoid showing racial bias and, when cued about racial considerations (e.g., when the crime was racially charged or when jurors were instructed to avoid prejudice), they tend to render color-blind decisions. But without those explicit reminders to be objective, subtle racial biases influence their decisions.

What accounts for the fact that although evidence strength is, in many cases, the primary influence on jurors' decisions, extralegal evidence exerts its impact in other cases? According to the **liberation hypothesis** (Kalven & Zeisel, 1966), when the evidence in a case clearly favors one side or the other, juries will decide the case in favor of the side with the stronger evidence. But when the evidence is ambiguous (i.e., the prosecution and defense cases are evenly balanced), jurors are "liberated" and allowed to rely on their assumptions, sentiments, and biases. This is the circumstance in which extralegal evidence affects verdicts.

One can understand jurors' attention to extralegal information by applying the cognitive–experiential self theory we introduced earlier. When jurors deliberately focus on the arguments or evidence provided during a trial, they are relying on a rationally based system of information processing. That is likely to occur when the evidence is unambiguous and comprehensible. But when the evidence is contradictory or confusing, jurors may be more likely to rely on an experientially based system. In these circumstances, extralegal information can assert its influence.

Support for these ideas comes from posttrial questionnaire data collected from jurors, judges, and attorneys in 179 criminal cases. Professor Dennis Devine and his colleagues determined that extralegal factors such as demographics of the foreperson and exposure to pretrial publicity were related to jury verdicts only when the prosecution's evidence was not strong (Devine, Buddenbaum, Houp, Studebaker, & Stolle, 2009). In the face of ambiguity, jurors were more likely to use experiential processing, and extralegal information had an impact. But when the evidence was unambiguous—clearly favoring one side—they were likely to rely on the logic of the arguments and think rationally. As a result, extralegal evidence had less effect. Consistent with these findings, people who tend to process information experientially are more likely than rational processors to acknowledge that extralegal factors would affect their verdicts (Gunnell & Ceci, 2010). Psychologists have now examined the impact of various kinds of extralegal information in both criminal and civil cases.

Impact of Extralegal Information in Criminal Cases

The Influence of Prior-Record Evidence. In 2009, church custodian José Feliciano was a fugitive on charges related to assault on a 7-year-old girl in 1999. When the parish priest, Edward Hinds, learned of these charges, he threatened to fire Feliciano. This fact led Feliciano to stab Hinds multiple times, according to Chatham, New Jersey prosecutors. Feliciano was charged with murder, and prosecutors moved to introduce the 1999 charges to show that he was motivated to kill Hinds.

Once jurors have heard evidence about a defendant's prior criminal record or prior criminal charges, they may no longer be able to suspend judgment about that defendant and decide his or her fate solely on the basis of the evidence introduced at trial. Therefore, the prosecution is often not permitted to introduce evidence of a defendant's criminal record, for fear that jurors will be prejudiced by it and judge the current offense in light of those past misdeeds. However, if defendants opt to testify, then prosecutors may be able to question them about certain types of prior criminal involvement in order to impeach their credibility as witnesses. In that circumstance, the judge may issue a **limiting instruction** to the effect that evidence of a defendant's prior record can be used for limited purposes only: to gauge the defendant's credibility but not to prove the defendant's propensity to commit the charged offense. Defense attorneys and even some judges are decidedly suspicious of jurors' ability to follow this rule, as well they should be; limiting instructions are rarely effective. Thus, defendants with prior criminal records have three bad choices: take a plea bargain regardless of actual guilt, go to trial but do not testify, or testify and risk the possibility that jurors will learn about a prior record and be more likely to convict (Rickert, 2010).

Some of these possibilities have been assessed empirically by researchers who studied more than 300 criminal trials in four jurisdictions across the country: Los Angeles, Phoenix, the Bronx (New York City), and the District of Columbia (Eisenberg & Hans, 2009). They determined that the existence of a prior record affected a defendant's decision to testify, as 60% of those without criminal records testified on their own behalf, compared to only 45% with criminal records. They also determined that in about half of the cases in which defendants with prior records opted to testify, the jury learned about that prior record. This rarely occurred when defendants did not testify. Finally and most importantly, juries apparently relied on their knowledge of the prior record to convict defendants when other evidence in the case against them was weak. This suggests that a prior record can lead to a conviction even when the evidence in a case normally would not support this verdict.

Why does evidence of a prior record increase the likelihood of conviction on a subsequent charge? For some jurors, the prior record, in combination with allegations related to the subsequent charge, may show a pattern of criminality; together they point to an individual who is prone to act in an illegal or felonious manner. Other jurors, upon hearing evidence of a prior conviction, may need less evidence to be convinced of the defendant's guilt beyond a reasonable doubt on the subsequent charge. Prior-record evidence may lead a juror to think that because the defendant already has a criminal record, an erroneous conviction would not be serious. This juror might therefore be satisfied with a slightly less compelling demonstration of guilt.

The Impact of Character and Propensity Evidence. Evidence about a defendant's character—for example, that he is a kind and gentle person—is generally not admissible on the issue of whether the defendant committed a crime. There are exceptions, however. Character evidence can be used to provide evidence on guilt when it is relevant to the defendant, the alleged victim, or a witness. Of course, character evidence can be either glowing or damning. When admitted in trials, these types of character evidence affect jurors differently. Professor Jennifer Hunt and colleagues have shown that although positive character evidence has little impact on jurors' judgments, evidence about negative character traits increases the likelihood of conviction (Hunt & Budensheim, 2004; Maeder & Hunt, 2011). This is consistent with social-psychological findings that judgments are more

B o x **13.2** THE CASE OF CHARLES FALSETTA AND HIS PROPENSITY TO COMMIT SEX CRIMES

When Charles Falsetta was tried for rape and kidnapping in Alameda County Court, the prosecutor introduced evidence of two prior uncharged sexual assaults allegedly committed by Falsetta. In the first, the defendant was alleged to have begun jogging beside a woman, asked her where she was going, and then tackled and raped her. In the second incident, the defendant allegedly blocked the path of a woman as she walked to work and later jumped out from behind some bushes, grabbed her, threw her into the bushes, and sexually assaulted her. These incidents bore a striking resemblance to the Alameda County case in which the defendant was alleged to have stopped a 16-year-old girl as she was walking to her house from a convenience store. After initially refusing a ride, the girl eventually accepted and was driven to a darkened parking lot and raped. The defendant was convicted and appealed his conviction, contending that

the admission of evidence of other uncharged rapes violated his rights.

In an appeal to the California Supreme Court, Richard Rochman, the deputy attorney general who argued the case on behalf of the State of California, stated that because victims of sex offenses often hesitate to speak out and because the alleged crimes occur in private, prosecutors are often faced with a "he said, she said" credibility problem. Allowing prosecutors to present propensity evidence in these cases would give jurors the full picture of the defendant's past sexual misconduct, reasoned Rochman. The California Supreme Court agreed (*People v. Falsetta*, 1999).

Critical Thought Question
Why is propensity evidence *not* admissible in most cases, and why is it *admissible* in cases that involve sexual behavior?

influenced by negative information than by positive information.

Evidence of other crimes or wrongdoing (so-called **propensity evidence**) is also typically inadmissible because of its potential for prejudice. Thus, prosecutors may not suggest that because a defendant had the propensity to act in a criminal manner, he or she is guilty of the crime charged. However, sex crimes are treated differently. In 1994, Congress passed a law making evidence of other sex offenses admissible to show a defendant's propensity to commit the charged sex offense. (The promulgation of this law reflects a belief that some people have a propensity toward aggressive and sexual impulses.) The California legislature enacted a similar law, and the California Supreme Court upheld the law in the case described in Box 13.2.

What effect might propensity evidence have on jurors? In arguing in support of allowing propensity evidence in the *Falsetta* case, the California Attorney General assumed that jurors could properly use propensity evidence to gauge the defendant's disposition to commit sex crimes. Yet psychologists can point to a fundamental error in this assumption—the belief that this characteristic or trait is stable over time and that situational factors are irrelevant (Eads, Shuman, & DeLipsey, 2000). In short, making this assumption constitutes the fundamental attribution error.

Impact of Extralegal Information in Civil Cases

When individuals have a dispute with their landlord, their insurance company, or the manufacturer of a product that they allege to have caused them harm, they can attempt to resolve that dispute through the workings of the civil justice system. Although the vast majority of civil cases are resolved outside the courtroom, often in settlement discussions between the opposing lawyers, thousands of civil cases are tried before juries each year. Juries in these cases typically make two fundamental decisions: first, whether the defendant (or, in some instances, the plaintiff) is **liable**, meaning responsible for the alleged harm, and second, whether the injured party (typically the plaintiff) should receive any money to compensate his or her losses, and if so, in what amount. These monies are called **damages**.

In recent years psychologists have devoted considerable attention to the workings of civil juries. As a result, they are increasingly able to address the question of whether jurors are competent to decide civil cases fairly and rationally. Do jurors determine liability and assess damages in a rational way, or are they swayed by emotion and prejudice?

Determining Liability. An important decision that jurors must make in civil cases concerns the parties' respective responsibility for the harm that was suffered. When psychologists study juries' liability judgments, they are really asking how people assign responsibility for an injury. When a baby is stillborn, do jurors perceive the doctor to be at fault for not performing a caesarean section? Would the child have died anyway? When a smoker contracts lung cancer, do jurors blame the cigarette manufacturer for elevating the nicotine level in its product, or the smoker who knowingly exposed himself or herself to a dangerous product over the course of many years? Or do they blame both, as did the jurors described in Box 13.1?

Jurors should decide liability on the basis of the defendant's conduct. Were his or her actions reckless? Were they negligent? Were they malicious and evil? The severity of an injury or accident, sometimes referred to as **outcome severity**, though legally relevant to decisions about the damage award, should be irrelevant to a judgment concerning liability or legal responsibility. The defendant should not be saddled with a liability judgment against him or her simply because the plaintiff was seriously injured. But jurors tend to factor it into their decision about responsibility as well. In their simulation of an automobile negligence case, Greene and her colleagues found that the defendant was perceived to be more negligent when the plaintiff suffered more serious injuries (Greene, Johns, & Smith, 2001). These results are consistent with a meta-analysis (Robbennolt, 2000) showing that people attribute greater responsibility to a wrongdoer when the outcome of an incident is severe than when it is minor.

Why would people assign more responsibility to an individual as the consequences of his or her conduct become more serious? One explanation is **defensive attribution** (Fiske & Taylor, 1991), an explanation of behavior that defends us from feelings of vulnerability. As the consequences of one's actions become more severe and more unpleasant, we are likely to blame a person for their occurrence, because doing so makes the incident somehow more controllable and avoidable.

Although the legal system expects jurors to evaluate liability objectively, jurors' emotional reactions also influence their assessment of the facts and evidence. For example, jurors who are angered by evidence of wrongdoing and harm to others feel more sympathy for a plaintiff (Feigenson, Park, & Salovey, 2001) and less sympathy for a defendant (Bornstein, 1994). These experienced emotions are likely to interact with jurors' preexisting emotional states,

implying that the legal assumption of strict objectivity in how jurors evaluate evidence is probably inaccurate (Wiener, Bornstein, & Voss, 2006).

Assessing Damages. Pity the poor man. Michael Brennan, a St. Paul, Minnesota, bank president, was simply responding to nature's call when he was sprayed with more than 200 gallons of raw sewage as he sat on the toilet in the bank's executive washroom. The geyser of water came "blasting up out of the toilet with such force that it stood him right up," leaving Brennan "immersed in human excrement." He sued a construction company working in the bank at the time, but the jury awarded Brennan nothing. Why, then, did a jury award $300,000 to a workman who slipped from a ladder and fell into a pile of manure (a story aired on CBS's "60 Minutes")?

One of the most perplexing issues related to juries is how they assess damages (Greene & Bornstein, 2003; Vidmar & Wolfe, 2009). This complex decision seems especially subjective and unpredictable because people value money and injuries differently and because jurors are given scant guidance on how to award damages (Greene & Bornstein, 2000). The awards for punitive damages—intended to punish the defendant and deter future malicious conduct—are of special concern because the jury receives little instruction about how those awards should be determined. Consider the staggering $145 billion punitive damage award against the tobacco industry in a case brought by many state attorney generals in 2000. Even the judge in the case was amazed. "A lot of zeros," he observed dryly, after reading the verdict.

Psychologists have conducted research on this issue and have learned that few people get rich by suing for damages. In state court civil trials in 2005, the median damage award was $28,000 and only 4% of winning plaintiffs received more than $1 million (Langton & Cohen, 2008). Although the media are eager to tell us about multimillion-dollar damage awards, these colossal awards are very unusual. Also, the monies requested by the plaintiff—when grounded in quantitative evidence presented during the trial—serve as "anchor points" for jurors' damage awards. But when the requests are unsupported by the evidence, they are viewed as outrageous and are disregarded (Diamond, Rose, Murphy, & Meixner, 2011).

What factors do jurors consider in their decisions about damages? Data from interviews with actual jurors, simulation studies, and videotapes of actual jury deliberations show that, as in criminal cases, jurors put most weight on the evidence they hear in court. But in addition, they sometimes consider attorneys' fees and whether any loss is covered by insurance—issues that are theoretically irrelevant to decisions about the amount of damages to award. According to Professors Shari Diamond and Neil Vidmar (2001), discussions about insurance coverage are quite common in jury rooms. They examined the deliberations of 50 juries in Tucson as part of the landmark Arizona Jury Project (the research project evaluated reforms in jury trials that we describe later in this chapter). They determined that conversations about insurance occurred in 85% of these cases; often, jurors expressed concern about overcompensating plaintiffs whose medical bills had already been covered by their own insurance.

Another common (but theoretically forbidden) topic of discussion is attorneys' fees. Attorneys who represent plaintiffs in personal injury cases typically work on a contingent fee basis, meaning that they are paid only if they are successful in securing a settlement or damage award for their clients. In their analysis of the Arizona jury deliberations, Diamond and Vidmar (2001) found that the topic of attorneys' fees came up in 83% of jury discussions. Other research has shown, though, that although jurors discuss these issues, the resulting awards are not directly influenced (Greene, Hayman, & Motyl, 2008).

Can Jurors Disregard Inadmissible Evidence?

Anyone who has ever watched television shows depicting courtroom drama is familiar with the attorney's statement, "I object!" If the judge sustains an objection, the opposing attorney's objectionable question or the witness's objectionable response will not be recorded, and the judge will instruct, or admonish, the jury to disregard the material. But are jurors able to do so?

Inadmissible evidence is evidence that is presented in court but is unrelated to the substance of the case. Most of the empirical evidence indicates that a judge's admonition to disregard inadmissible evidence is relatively ineffective (Steblay, Hosch, Culhane, & McWerthy, 2006). On occasion, instructions to ignore inadmissible evidence actually backfire and result in jurors being *more* likely to use the inadmissible evidence than if they had not been told to ignore it (Lieberman & Arndt, 2000). For example, Broeder

(1959) presented a civil case in which mock jurors learned either that the defendant had insurance or that he did not. Half the subjects who were told that he had insurance were admonished by the judge to disregard that information. Juries who believed that the defendant lacked insurance awarded an average of $33,000 in damages. Juries who believed that he did have insurance awarded an average of $37,000. But those juries that were aware of the insurance but had been admonished to disregard it gave the highest average award, $46,000.

These findings imply that instructions to disregard certain testimony may heighten jurors' reliance on the inadmissible evidence. Psychologists have explained this phenomenon using **reactance theory** (Brehm & Brehm, 1981) which suggests that instructions to disregard evidence may threaten jurors' freedom to consider all available evidence. When this happens, jurors may respond by acting in ways that restore their sense of decision-making freedom. Interestingly, simply providing jurors with a reason for the inadmissibility ruling makes them more likely to comply with it.

Jurors' overreliance on evidence they are admonished not to use may also reflect a cognitive process described in **thought suppression** studies. Professor Daniel Wegner found that asking people "not to think of a white bear" increased the tendency to do just that. In fact, the harder people try to suppress a thought, the less likely they are to succeed (Wegner, 1994). Jurors may think more about inadmissible evidence as a direct consequence of their attempts to follow the judge's request to suppress thoughts of it (Clavet, 1996). An appellate court was aware of that possibility: "(the judge) could reasonably have believed that an instruction to the jurors to disregard what they had just heard … would have been just about as effective as a directive not to think about a pink elephant" (*Sowell v. Walker*, 2000, p. 448).

But what happens when individual jurors come together to deliberate? Will the process of discussing the case with others motivate jurors to follow the judge's instructions, or will the thoughts of white bears and pink elephants still prevail? As we describe later in this chapter, jury deliberations can indeed lessen the impact of inadmissible evidence (London & Nunez, 2000).

The jury's decision could also be influenced by many other irrelevant factors in the trial presentation, including pretrial publicity, the personal style and credibility of attorneys, the order of presentation of evidence, and the gender, race, age, physical appearance, and attractiveness of the litigants and other witnesses (Devine et al., 2009). In a sensational case stemming from the murder of wealthy fashion journalist Christa Worthington on Cape Cod in 2002 and the subsequent conviction of her African-American garbage collector, Christopher McCowen, jurors were summoned back to court a year after the trial to describe racially based remarks made during deliberations. Two White female jurors apparently referred to the defendant's race and size in justifying their verdict preferences. One juror, in the midst of a discussion about the physical evidence, allegedly pointed to a photograph of the bruising on the victim and "exclaimed that this is what happens 'when a 200-pound Black guy beats on a small woman'" (Sommers, 2009).

Judges implicitly assume that jurors are able to eliminate such irrelevant considerations from their decisions. But psychologists emphasize that, as active information processors, jurors desire to make a decision based on what they believe is just, not necessarily one that reflects only the legally relevant information. So, for example, when mock jurors were told to disregard certain evidence because of a legal technicality, they still allowed that evidence to influence their verdicts when they thought that it enhanced the accuracy of their decisions (Sommers & Kassin, 2001). Because jurors want to deliver fair and accurate verdicts, they may rely on information that *they* perceive to be relevant, regardless of whether that information meets the law's technical standards of admissibility. Although psychologists understand that jurors have difficulty performing the mental gymnastics required to use evidence for a limited purpose or ignore it altogether, they have not yet developed effective strategies to combat those problems (Daftary-Kapur, Dumas, & Penrod, 2010).

Effects of Expert Testimony

As society has become increasingly specialized and technical knowledge has accumulated rapidly, the judicial system has come to rely on expert witnesses to inform jurors about these advances. Experts typically testify about scientific, technical, or other specialized knowledge with which most jurors are not familiar. In accident cases, they may describe the nature and causes of various claimed injuries. In commercial cases, they may detail complex financial transactions and contractual arrangements. In criminal cases, they may describe procedures used to gather and test evidence such as blood, fingerprints, DNA, and ballistics, or scientific findings relevant to victims' or perpetrators' conduct.

A concern that arises when experts testify about highly specialized or technical matters is that because many jurors lack rigorous analytical skills, they may resort to unsystematic or effortless (i.e., experiential) processing, leading them to attend to peripheral or superficial aspects of experts' testimony including their credentials, appearance, personality, or presentation style, rather than the content of the testimony. But posttrial interviews, analysis of the questions asked by jurors, and observations of deliberations by the Arizona Jury Project showed that jurors spend considerable time focusing on the content of the expert's testimony rather than peripheral details (Vidmar & Diamond, 2001).

Another concern is that expert testimony will mesmerize jurors, causing them to discount their own common sense and rely too heavily on the opinions of the experts. Do jurors place undue weight on testimony from experts? A number of studies show that jurors do not defer to experts, but expert testimony does exert a small, reliable effect on their decisions (Vidmar, 2005). When prosecutors introduce expert testimony, convictions are more likely; when experts testify on behalf of the defense, the likelihood of conviction decreases. If jurors do not understand an expert's testimony, they simply tend to ignore it or to rely on more capable members of the jury whose experience or knowledge of scientific or technical information may improve the jury's functioning (Greene, 2009). So there is little reason to believe that it mesmerizes jurors.

When questioned about their reliance on expert testimony, jurors have stated that they evaluated the testimony on the basis of the experts' qualifications, the quality of the experts' reasoning, and the experts' impartiality (Shuman & Champagne, 1997). So it is fair to say that they do not routinely defer to the experts' assessments. A meta-analysis (Nietzel, McCarthy, & Kern, et al., 1999) supports this notion: Examining the effects of psychological expert testimony in 22 studies, Nietzel and his colleagues found little support for the concern that expert testimony will dominate jurors' decision making. Nor is it an expensive waste of time. Jurors appear to give reasoned and balanced consideration to experts whom they perceive as fair and professional. In Box 13.3, we describe

---

Box 13.3 **THE CASE OF DHARUN RAVI: EXPERT TESTIMONY FROM AN I.T. SPECIALIST**

In a case that galvanized concerns about suicide by gay teens, Rutgers University student Dharun Ravi used a webcam to remotely spy on his roommate kissing another man, and sent Twitter and text messages to other dormitory residents, encouraging them to watch when the roommate, Tyler Clementi, invited the man back two nights later. After discovering Ravi's actions, Clementi committed suicide by jumping off the George Washington Bridge, a mere three weeks into his freshman year. Ravi then deleted his text messages.

The controversy that swirled around this case for more than a year focused on whether this was a hate crime or simple boorish and childish behavior on Ravi's part. Eventually he was charged with 15 crimes.

One of the witnesses who testified for the prosecution at Ravi's 2012 trial was Douglas Rager, a former Rutgers University police detective and information technology expert. He established the trail of electronic evidence, including Twitter feeds, cell phone records, dining card swipes, and dormitory surveillance cameras, and provided a "net flow" analysis that described how the computers in the dormitory were connected. His testimony must have been useful to jurors, as they convicted Ravi on all 15 counts, including invasion of privacy, bias intimidation, lying to investigators, and tampering with evidence. Adding further controversy to an already contentious case, the judge sentenced Ravi to a mere 30 days

AP Photo/Mel Evans

Former Rutgers University study Dharun Ravi, convicted of using a webcam to spy on his roommate

in jail. Said Judge Glenn Berman, "I do not believe he hated Tyler Clementi. I do believe he acted out of colossal insensitivity."

Critical Thought Question
Given what you've learned about the ways that jurors use expert testimony, what do you suspect they focused on when discussing Detective Rager's testimony during deliberations?

---

a case in which expert testimony appeared to exert appropriate influence.

To this point, we have assumed that expert testimony is based on valid scientific methodologies. But judges, who ultimately decide what expert evidence is admitted into court (*Daubert v. Merrell Dow Pharmaceuticals, Inc.*, 1993), may not be accurate in assessing the quality of the science on which the expert relies and may allow unreliable expert testimony to be admitted into evidence. Are jurors able to distinguish between reliable scientific evidence and "junk science?"

This question was addressed in the context of a hostile work environment trial (McAuliff, Kovera, & Nunez, 2009). Mock jurors read a trial summary that included variations in the validity of the expert testimony: The expert's research was either valid, contained a confounding variable, lacked a control group, or involved experimenter bias. Jurors were sensitive to the missing control group but were

otherwise unable to distinguish the valid research from the flawed research. Even the introduction of opposing expert testimony fails to sensitize jurors to flaws in scientific methodology (Levett & Kovera, 2008). This suggests that jurors could benefit from clear and thorough explanations to assist them in understanding scientific expert testimony.

Jurors' Abilities to Understand Their Instructions

Jury instructions, provided by the judge to the jury near the end of a trial, play a crucial role in every case. They explain the laws that are applicable to the case and direct jurors to reach a verdict in accordance with those laws. Ironically, jurors are often treated like children during the evidence phase of the trial—expected to sit still and pay attention, and infrequently allowed to ask questions—but are treated like accomplished law students during the reading of the judge's instructions, when they are expected to understand the complicated legal terminology of the instructions. An appellate court acknowledged as much in granting a plaintiff a new trial in 2012. One judge called the jury instructions "a dreadful muddle" (Qualters, 2012).

Psychologists assess comprehension by providing instructions to jurors, typically in the context of a mock trial, and then testing them using true-false, multiple-choice, or open-ended questions (Devine, 2012). Results typically show that a serious weakness for many jurors is their inability to understand their instructions (Lieberman, 2009).

One source of confusion is the legal language itself. Often, the instructions simply repeat statutory language and therefore are full of legal terms that are unfamiliar to laypeople. (For example, in most civil cases, jurors are informed that the burden of proof is on the plaintiff to establish his or her case by a *preponderance* of the evidence; the word *preponderance* appears 0.26 times per million words in the English language!) In addition, consider this example of how jurors are instructed about the meaning of *proximate cause*, an important concept in civil trials: "a cause which, in a natural and continuous sequence, produced damage, and without which the damage would not have occurred." Do you think the average layperson would understand the meaning of that term? Despite the fact that juries work hard to understand their instructions, spending 20% or more of their deliberation time trying to decipher the meaning of the judge's instructions (Ellsworth, 1989), they sometimes get it wrong simply because they do not understand the legal jargon.

Another source of confusion lies in the way the instructions are conveyed to jurors. Typically, the jury listens passively as the judge reads the instructions aloud. They are almost never given the opportunity to ask questions in the courtroom to clarify misunderstandings they may have about the law. When jurors ask for assistance with the instructions in the course of deliberating, the judge is often unwilling to help, reasoning that rewording or clarifying the instructions could be grounds for appeal.

Judges generally assume that the instructions will have the intended effects of guiding jurors through the thicket of unfamiliar legal concepts. That was the sentiment of the U.S. Supreme Court in *Weeks v. Angelone* (2000). Lonnie Weeks confessed to killing a Virginia state trooper and was tried for capital murder. During the deliberations, jurors sent the judge a note asking for clarification of their instructions. The judge simply repeated the instruction. Two hours later, the jurors, some in tears, sentenced Weeks to death. Weeks appealed, citing the jury's apparent confusion about the instructions. But the appeal fell on deaf ears. Chief Justice William Rehnquist, author of the opinion, wrote that there was only a "slight possibility" that jurors had been confused by the trial judge's instructions. Ironically, a study conducted by Professor Stephen Garvey and his colleagues challenges that assumption. Simulating the Weeks case, Garvey and his colleagues concluded that the jury might not have sentenced Weeks to death had they received clarification of their instructions (Garvey, Johnson, & Marcus, 2000).

Can this situation be rectified? Could the instructions be rewritten, or could their presentation be revised so that jurors have a better chance of understanding and implementing them properly? Yes. A large number of research studies have focused on improving comprehension by modifying the language of the instructions. These studies borrow principles from the field of **psycholinguistics** (the study of how people understand and use language), including minimizing or eliminating the use of abstract terms, negatively modified sentences, and passive voice, and reorganizing the instructions in a more logical manner. These simplified instructions are easier for jurors to understand and use (Lieberman, 2009).

States have now begun to adopt reforms that focus on how judges communicate the law to jurors, and several states have revised portions of their jury instructions. California was the first state to finalize "plain-English" instructions for both civil and criminal trials (Post, 2004b). Consider these changes to the California civil jury instruction on "burden of proof":

> Old: "Preponderance of the evidence means evidence that has more convincing force than that opposed to it. If the evidence is so evenly balanced that you are unable to say that the evidence on either side of an issue preponderates, your finding on that issue must be against the party who had the burden of proving it."

> New: "When I tell you that a party must prove something, I mean that the party must persuade you, by the evidence presented in court, that what he or she is trying to prove is more likely to

be true than not true. This is sometimes referred to as 'the burden of proof.'"

Not surprisingly, simplified instructions enhance jurors' comprehension of the law and result in far fewer questions to the judge about what the jury instructions mean (Post, 2004b).

Another method for improving jurors' understanding of the instructions is to restructure how they are presented. Although instructions are typically read at the close of the trial, after the evidence has been presented and just before the jury retires to deliberate, some states now require judges to provide preliminary instructions before any of the evidence is presented, and many individual judges do so of their own accord (Dann & Hans, 2004).

Instructing the jury at the conclusion of the trial reflects a belief in the **recency effect**: that the judge's instructions will have a more powerful impact on a jury's decision when they are given late in the trial, after the presentation of evidence. The recency effect suggests that recent events are generally remembered better than more remote ones. Having just heard the judge's instructions, deliberating jurors would have them fresh in their minds and be more likely to make references to them.

Logical as it might seem, this idea has been questioned by a number of authorities. Roscoe Pound, former dean of the Harvard Law School, and others have proposed what is essentially a **schema** theory— that jurors should be instructed *before* the presentation of testimony, because this gives them a mental framework to appreciate the relevance or irrelevance of testimony as it unfolds. This line of reasoning gains support from research in cognitive psychology showing (1) that people learn more effectively when they know in advance what the specific task is, and (2) that schematic frameworks facilitate comprehension and recall (Bartlett, 1932; Neisser, 1976). Also, a number of judges (e.g., Frank, 1949) have objected to the customary sequence on the ground that instructions at the end of the trial are given after the jurors have already made up their minds. Judge E. Barrett Prettyman's (1960) position reflects this concern:

It makes no sense to have a juror listen to days of testimony only then to be told that he and his conferees are the sole judges of the facts, that the accused is presumed to be innocent, that the government must prove guilt beyond a reasonable doubt, etc. What manner of mind can go

back over a stream of conflicting statements of alleged facts, recall the intonations, the demeanor, or even the existence of the witnesses, and retrospectively fit all these recollections into a pattern of evaluations and judgments given him for the first time after the events; the human mind cannot do so (p. 1066).

The delivery of jury instructions at the beginning of the trial rests on the notion of a **primacy effect**— that instructions will have their most beneficial effect if they are presented first, because jurors can then compare the evidence they hear to the requirements of the law and apply the instructions to the evidence in order to reach a verdict. In this way, jurors know the rules of the trial and the requirements of the law before the trial commences.

At what point in the trial proceedings, then, *should* the judge instruct the jury? ForsterLee and Horowitz (2003) reported that mock jurors who received instructions at the beginning of the trial recalled and used more of the evidence than did jurors who were instructed after the evidence.

Preliminary instructions have other beneficial effects. In a study conducted in Los Angeles Superior Court, jurors who received pretrial instructions said that they were able to focus better during the trial (Judicial Council of California, 2004). Judges also believe that substantive preliminary instructions help jurors to follow the evidence (Dann & Hans, 2004).

We would argue that judicial preinstructions are vastly underutilized. There is no reason why general instructions about the law (e.g., burden of proof, assessment of the credibility of witnesses) should not be given at both the beginning and the end of trials. Interim instructions can be given as needed to explain issues that come up during the trial, and instructions that depend on the specific evidence in a trial can be given at the end (Ellsworth & Reifman, 2000).

Jurors' Willingness to Apply Their Instructions

Two questions arise pertaining to jurors' willingness to apply their instructions. First, must they follow the letter of the law if doing so violates their sense of justice and results in an unfair verdict? Second, how can judges insist, in the digital era, that jurors avoid online media during the trial, and once instructed, are jurors willing to obey those orders?

Jury Nullification.   The first question concerns **jury nullification**, the implicit power to acquit defendants despite evidence and judicial instructions to the contrary. Throughout history juries have occasionally ignored the law rather than enforced it, particularly when they believed the law was unjust. In the mid-1800s, juries acquitted abolitionists of helping slaves escape from the South even though the abolitionists' actions violated the fugitive slave law. The controversy resurfaced in the turbulent Vietnam War period when the government began to prosecute antiwar activists, usually on charges of conspiracy, and juries often acquitted. Jury nullification reflects acknowledgment that while the public trusts jurors to resolve the facts and apply the law in a given case, they also expect them to represent the conscience of the community (Abramson, 1994).

How would juries behave if they were informed that they have the option to disregard the law? Would there be "chaos in the courtroom," as opponents of nullification suggest, with jurors swayed by emotions and personal biases? A good way to assess the effects of nullification instructions is to consider the empirical evidence. What effect does explicit instruction about the jury's right to nullify have on verdicts in criminal cases? Does it unleash "chaos in the courtroom"?

These questions were addressed by Horowitz, Kerr, Park, and Gockel (2006) in a mock jury study of the impact of judicial instructions concerning jury nullification. Evidence in the case concerned the death of a terminally ill hospital patient who died as a result of a drug overdose. Jurors learned that the defendant, the patient's doctor, had acted either out of greed (killing the patient in order to gain access to his finances) or compassion (administering an overdose to relieve the patient's suffering). Jurors were then given either standard jury instructions with a reminder to focus on the evidence, or the standard instructions with a nullification addendum that told jurors they were free to use their conscience to reach a verdict. The nullification instructions unleashed jurors' emotional biases only in the euthanasia (i.e., mercy killing) case. In other words, when the prosecution seemed fair (i.e., when the doctor killed for greed), jurors tended to follow the law and convicted the defendant even when told they could disregard the law. These findings suggest that any "chaos" resulting from nullification instructions is limited: Jurors tend to rely on their feelings and sentiments and to nullify the law only when that law seems unjust.

The issue of race is a subtext to the nullification debate. There are notorious cases of nullification where White southern juries refused to convict members of the Ku Klux Klan and others who terrorized Blacks during the early years of the civil rights movement. One case concerns Byron de la Beckwith and the murder of civil rights leader Medgar Evers (see Box 13.4).

Jurors' Online Activities.   Do you know what this means?

> imho def glty
> jury dty cwot

You would be correct if you guessed, "In my humble opinion, the defendant is guilty. Jury duty is a complete waste of time." If you suspected that this message was texted from a courtroom during a trial, you would probably be correct. Jurors' use of smartphones, iPads™, and other devices to access blogs, Twitter, Facebook, MySpace, and other websites—whether to tweet minute-to-minute coverage of a trial, conduct Google searches on defendants, victims, attorneys, and excluded evidence, or simply pass the time—has increased exponentially in the past few years. During the 2009 trial of former Baltimore Mayor Sheila Dixon on corruption charges, five jurors "friended" one another on Facebook and posted comments even after being admonished by the judge. Nine of the twelve jurors in a high-profile federal drug trial in Florida admitted to doing online research in direct violation of the judge's orders. A prospective juror in West Virginia contacted a defendant via MySpace even *before* jury selection, telling him that "God has a plan for you and your life" (MacLean, 2011). At a minimum, these actions by jurors constitute willful disobedience of court rules. In some instances, they involve outright misconduct.

Web browsing and postings prior to, during, and after a trial raise concerns about whether a criminal defendant's Sixth Amendment right to a fair trial can be protected. When jurors rely on information that comes from unknown and unreliable sources—information that has not met formal rules for evidence admissibility and is not subjected to the adversarial context of a trial—has the integrity of the proceedings been threatened?

B o x 13.4 THE CASE OF BYRON DE LA BECKWITH: JURY NULLIFICATION AND RACE

Eager to see his children after a long day at work, civil rights leader Medgar Evers stepped out of his car in Jackson, Mississippi, on a hot June night in 1963 and was gunned down from behind by an assassin. The shooting ignited a firestorm of protest that ended in several more deaths and galvanized the civil rights movement.

The case against Byron de la Beckwith was strong but circumstantial. His rifle with his fingerprint was found at the scene, and a car similar to his was seen in the vicinity of Evers's home. But no one saw Beckwith pull the trigger, and his claim that he was 90 miles away at the time of the shooting was substantiated by two former police officers.

Beckwith was tried twice in 1964; both times the all-White, all-male jury deadlocked and failed to reach a verdict. This was an era of volatile race relations in which African Americans were excluded from jury service and in which attorneys for Ku Klux Klan members charged with killing civil rights leaders openly appealed to White jurors for racial solidarity. Beckwith's segregationist views were a common bond between himself and the juries that failed to convict him.

But things were different when Beckwith was retried in 1994. Despite the obstacles presented by stale evidence, dead witnesses, and constitutional questions, prosecutors put Beckwith on trial for the third time. This time, Beckwith's racist ideology was a liability. Despite pleas from defense attorneys that jurors not focus on Beckwith's sensational beliefs, a jury of eight Blacks and four Whites convicted him of murder in 1994. He was immediately sentenced to life in prison. Darrell Evers, the slain civil rights leader's son, who was nine years old at the time of the shooting, said he attended the trial to confront Beckwith: "He never saw my father's face. All he

Byron De La Beckwith, convicted in the slaying of civil rights leader Medgar Evers

saw was his back. I wanted him to see the face, to see the ghost of my father come back to haunt him."

Critical Thought Question
Contrast jury nullification in trials that occurred in the mid-1800s, in the early years of the civil rights movement, and in Beckwith's retrial in 1994. What do these examples have in common? How are they different?

Judges are concerned. Some courts now prohibit jurors' use of electronic devices during trials and others monitor jurors' online activities. Many judges have replaced their benign warnings to avoid newspapers and TV news programming during the course of the trial with something much more direct and sweeping. Jurors in California, for example, are told that they are prohibited from using "*any* electronic device or medium, *any* Internet service, *any* text or instant-messaging service, and *any* Internet chat room, blog, or website to exchange *any* information about the case until the panel is discharged" (California Civil Jury Instructions 100, 2011). For most jurors, such strongly worded instructions are sufficient; they abstain. But many jurors have deliberately disregarded the directive, and more than a few defendants have

argued, in appealing their convictions, that jurors' access to the Internet prejudiced their verdicts.

Though this issue has attracted scant scholarly attention, we can extrapolate from previous research to understand why it occurs and, perhaps, how to remedy it. Just as jurors chafe under instructions to disregard inadmissible evidence they deem pertinent, they are also annoyed by restrictions on accessing information online. Reactance theory suggests that such prohibitions may seem, especially for tech-savvy and "wired" jurors, to impair their ability to glean information needed to deliver a just verdict. Being restricted from accessing information online may actually impel some jurors to do just that. In fact, acknowledging that jurors are active information processors who want to make the right decisions helps to explain why they may quest for extralegal online information. It can provide clarity about a legal term, background and context information that jurors lack, and insights about the parties and their situations. Jurors perceive that it will help them render more just decisions (Morrison, 2011). So when the judge says, "Don't use the Internet," jurors have difficulty believing that the judge *really* means, "No Internet use" (MacPherson & Bonora, 2010).

Previous research also suggests some remedies. Psychologists know that pretrial instructions are effective in giving jurors a roadmap for the evidence they will hear. It follows that judges should instruct jurors about restrictions on Internet access—including reasons for those restrictions and consequences for ignoring them—when jurors first enter the courtroom for jury selection and at designated times throughout the trial. We suggest that judges should acknowledge jurors' desire to conduct online research and to share their experiences with their virtual communities. They should explain clearly that doing so introduces inconsistencies and inaccuracies into the proceedings, and they should remind jurors that defendants have a constitutional right to a trial by an impartial jury. Discussing these issues with jurors during *voir dire* and seeking a commitment to abide by the rules is important. We suspect that treating jurors in this way will effectively remedy many of the problems associated with this phenomenon, and quell the sense of "jurors gone wild" (MacLean, 2011).

Jurors' Abilities to Decide Complex Cases

Judge John V. Singleton looked up as his law clerk leaned against his office door as though to brace it closed. "You won't believe this," she said breathlessly, "but there are 225 lawyers out there in the courtroom!" (Singleton & Kass, 1986, p. 11). Judge Singleton believed it. He was about to preside over the first pretrial conference in *In re Corrugated Container Antitrust Litigation* (1980), at that time one of the largest and most complicated class action cases ever tried by a jury. A **class action case** involves many plaintiffs who collectively form a "class" and claim that they suffered similar injuries as a result of the defendants' actions. (A pending class action lawsuit involves more than 2,000 former NFL players and their families who allege that the National Football League knew about,

denied, and failed to warn them of the consequences of head injuries during their playing years.)

The case in Judge Singleton's court actually entailed three trials: a 15-week criminal trial that involved four major paper companies, 27 corporate officers, scores of witnesses, and hundreds of documents; a four-month-long class action trial with 113 witnesses and 5,000 exhibits; and a second class action trial involving plaintiffs who had opted out of the original class action lawsuit. Discovery and trials took five years. In the midst of this organizational nightmare, Judge Singleton worried about the "unsuspecting souls out there in the Southern District of Texas whose destiny was to weigh the facts under the complex antitrust law" (Singleton & Kass, 1986, p. 11).

Some of the loudest and most vehement criticisms of the jury center on its role in complex cases. In product liability and medical malpractice cases, for example, there are difficult questions related to causation (i.e., who or what actually caused the claimed injuries), and in business cases there are intricate financial transactions that must be dissected and evaluated. These cases often require the jury to render decisions on causation, liability, and damages for multiple plaintiffs, multiple defendants, or both (Vidmar, 1998). In criminal cases, the use of forensic evidence contributes to case complexity (Heise, 2004).

Many arguments have been made against the use of juries in complex cases. Some prominent examples include (1) the evidence is too difficult for a layperson to understand; (2) the general information load on juries is excessive because of the large number of witnesses, particularly expert witnesses, who testify in these cases; and (3) because of *voir dire* procedures that result in the exclusion of jurors with some understanding of or interest in the case, less-capable jurors are left to decide.

Data on juries in complex cases support some, but not all, of these concerns. Interview studies (e.g., Sanders, 1993) consistently point to a substantial range in the abilities of jurors to understand and summarize the evidence. Some jurors are willing and able to attend to the complicated nature of the testimony and the sometimes-arcane questions of law that they raise; others are overwhelmed from the beginning. Lempert (1993) systematically examined the reports of 12 complex trials. He concluded that in 2 of the 12 cases, the expert testimony was so complicated and esoteric that only professionals in the field could have understood it. On the other hand, Lempert found little evidence of jury befuddlement—and concluded that the juries' verdicts were largely defensible.

But jurors *are* confounded by the presence of multiple parties and claims. When Reiber and Weinberg (2010) presented hypothetical cases of varying complexity to individuals summoned for jury duty, they found that comprehension worsened as the number of parties and claims increased. Mock jurors had difficulty deciding a breach of contract case that involved a claim, an affirmative defense, a permissive counterclaim, and a third-party claim (no surprises there!). They managed capably to decide an automobile negligence case that involved a single plaintiff and single defendant.

These findings point to the need for attention to how a complex case is presented to the jury. A judge has wide discretion to set the tone and pacing of the trial, to implement procedures to assist the jury, and, ultimately, to ensure equal justice under law. Jury aids such as written summary statements of expert testimony and the opportunity to take notes can enhance the quality of jurors' decision making (ForsterLee, Kent, & Horowitz, 2005), as can other reforms discussed later in the chapter.

One would not expect a college student to pass a course without taking notes, asking questions to seek clarification, or discussing an interesting concept with a professor or fellow student. Yet all too often, jurors are handicapped by trial procedures that discourage or even forbid these simple steps toward better understanding. We suspect that jurors would have an easier time—and their verdicts would be more reasoned—if judges structured jurors' tasks to be more conducive to their learning (e.g., giving preinstruction and simplifying the language of the instructions). Fortunately, as we point out later in the chapter, some judges now do so.

ARE JURIES BIASED?

The Assumption of a Blank Slate

Courts assume that jurors can put aside any preconceptions about the guilt of a criminal defendant or the merits of civil defendants and plaintiffs when forming their judgments. In other words, jurors are assumed to enter a trial as "blank slates," free of overwhelming biases. (In criminal cases, the "blank slates" should be tinted at the outset by a presumption that the defendant is innocent of the charges.) If jurors cannot set aside their biases, they should be excused for cause.

The judge and the attorneys inquire about a prospective juror's biases during the jury selection process. A frequent question during *voir dire* takes the following form: "Do you believe that you, as a juror, can set aside any negative feelings you might have toward the defendant because he is (from the Middle East or a police officer or a used-car salesman—whatever the group membership is that possibly elicits prejudice) and make a judgment based on the law and the facts of this case?" If prospective jurors say yes, the judge usually believes them, and they are allowed to serve as jurors.

On occasion, prospective jurors have ties to the defendant that could influence their ability to be impartial. Consider the case against former Penn State assistant football coach Jerry Sandusky (see Box 13.5).

The courts assume that individual jurors can divest themselves of any improper "leaning" toward one side or the other, and that through jury selection procedures the ideal of open-minded jurors can be achieved. Courts also assume that attorneys can identify and dismiss prospective jurors whose preconceptions would affect their verdicts, so the trial can begin with a fair and unbiased jury. For various reasons, this optimism may be misguided. First, attorneys are motivated to select jurors who are favorable to their own side, rather than those who are neutral and thus unpredictable. Second, it is impossible for anyone to be entirely free of influence by past experiences and resulting prejudices.

Inevitability of Juror Bias

In a society that respects all persons, some biases (e.g., age, race, or gender bias) are clearly prejudicial and should be shunned. But many biases—including those based on expectations and experiences—may actually be inevitable. As we use the term here, **juror bias** is a juror's predisposition to interpret and understand information based on past experience. When people are exposed to new events, they respond by relying on past experiences. When they view a traffic accident, for instance, they may make judgments that one car ran a red light or that another car was in the wrong lane. They may assume that an accident involving teenaged drivers was caused by excessive speed or texting while driving.

Bias in responses to the actions of others is inevitable because people must make assumptions about the causes of behavior. Why was Emily so abrupt

Box 13.5 THE CASE OF JERRY SANDUSKY: THE SEARCH FOR UNBIASED JURORS

In one of the most anticipated criminal trials in recent years, Jerry Sandusky faced accusations of sexually molesting boys and young men over several years on the Penn State campus and at other locations. The trial was held in Bellefonte, Pennsylvania, approximately 12 miles from Penn State, where football is high profile and enormously profitable. Perhaps it was no surprise, then, that many prospective jurors had affiliations with and allegiances to Penn State. It was somewhat more surprising that so many were selected to serve on the jury. The group of 12 jurors and 4 alternates included a woman whose family has had Penn State football season tickets since the 1970s, a Penn State junior who was working in the athletic office and whose cousin played on the football team, two professors—one on the faculty for 24 years and another who retired, two women employed by the university, and three graduates of Penn State, including one who heard Jerry Sandusky speak at her graduation ceremony. Of course, having personal ties with the university does not necessarily render these jurors incapable of delivering fair verdicts. One wonders whether it was easy for them to do so—but they did convict Mr. Sandusky on 45 felony charges.

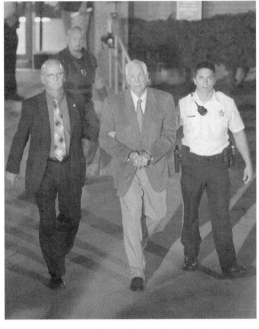

PAT LITTLE/Reuters/Landov

Former Penn State assistant football coach Jerry Sandusky being led out of courthouse after conviction on charges of child sexual abuse

Critical Thought Question
Why might court observers be concerned about the ability of these jurors to be objective?

---

when she spoke to me this morning? Why did Juan decide to buy a new car? Why did the defendant refuse to take a lie detector test? Every day, individuals make decisions on the basis of their assumptions about other people. College admission officers decide who will be admitted on the basis of applicants' credentials and academic promise. Criminal defense lawyers make recommendations to their clients on how to plead on the basis of their expectations about the reactions of prosecuting attorneys, judges, and jurors. Expectations about the outcomes of one's choices rest partly on one's biases.

People make assumptions about others to enable them to predict what others will do. These assumptions often provide explanations for other's behavior. Such processes also apply to the thoughts of jurors. When former Dallas Cowboys wide receiver Michael Irvin appeared before a grand jury wearing a mink coat, a lavender suit, and a bowler hat, jurors undoubtedly formed impressions of him on the basis

of his attire and judged his behavior in light of those impressions.

Virtually all descriptions of how a juror makes decisions in a criminal case propose that verdicts reflect two judgments on the part of jurors. One judgment is an estimate of the probability of commission—that is, how likely it is that the defendant actually committed the crime. Most jurors base their estimates of this probability on the strength of the evidence, but as we have noted, extralegal information and jurors' previous beliefs and experiences also have an impact on how they interpret the evidence (Finkel, 1995).

A second judgment by the criminal juror concerns reasonable doubt. Judges instruct jurors in criminal cases that they should deliver a not-guilty verdict if they have any reasonable doubt of the defendant's guilt. Because the legal system has difficulty defining reasonable doubt (a common, but not very informative, definition is that it is a doubt for which a person

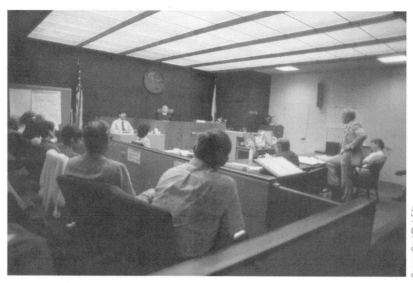

Spencer Grant/PhotoEdit

A jury listening to a witness testify during a trial

can give a reason), jurors apply their own standards for the threshold of certainty deemed necessary for conviction.

Because bias is inevitable, most jurors come to this task with either a pro-prosecution bias or a pro-defense bias. Jurors with a pro-prosecution bias view conflicting evidence in the case through the filter of their past experiences and beliefs, which make them more likely to think that the defendant committed the crime. Persons with pro-defense biases filter the same evidence in light of *their* past experiences and reactions, which make them more sympathetic to the defense.

To determine how bias affects verdicts, Lecci and Myers (2009) asked jury-eligible adults to complete the 29-item Pretrial Juror Attitudes Questionnaire (PJAQ), which includes statements such as "Criminals should be caught and convicted by any means necessary" and "Defense lawyers are too willing to defend individuals they know are guilty." Later, mock jurors watched a videotaped armed robbery trial, gave individual verdicts, deliberated as a jury, and gave postdeliberation individual verdicts. Jurors who voted guilty prior to deliberating were compared with those voting not guilty to see whether their personal biases differed. Indeed they did: jurors who convicted were more likely to endorse pro-prosecution sentiments on the PJAQ than jurors who acquitted. Biases revealed by the PJAQ predicted postdeliberation verdicts as well, suggesting that the deliberation process does little to

correct for individuals' bias. It appears that even when jurors all hear the same evidence during the trial, their personal beliefs and values affect their verdicts.

Personal predispositions may also affect the way evidence is evaluated. Professor Jane Goodman-Delahunty and colleagues found that mock jurors' beliefs about the death penalty influenced their perceptions of evidence (Goodman-Delahunty, Greene, & Hsiao, 1998). Participants watched the videotaped murder of a convenience store clerk that was captured on film. When asked about the defendant's motive and intentions, jurors who favored the death penalty were more likely than those who opposed it to "read" criminal intent into the actions of the defendant. For example, they were more likely to infer that the defendant intended to murder the victim and that his specific actions indicated premeditation. These findings remind us of the common situation in which two people experience the same event—a movie or a play, for example—and interpret the actions in very different ways, partly because of the "mindset" with which they watched or experienced that event. These beliefs, or schemas, can apparently influence the way jurors make sense of the evidence in a trial.

Psychologists have learned something interesting about how those schemas affect jurors' verdicts. When jurors are exposed to a new piece of evidence, they evaluate the evidence in a way that is consistent with their current verdict preferences rather than in an objective fashion. Assume that two jurors hear the same evidence that favors the prosecution's case. Also assume that Juror A favors the prosecution and Juror B favors the defense at that point in the trial. According to the notion of **predecisional distortion** (Carlson & Russo, 2001), these jurors will distort their evaluation of the evidence in a direction that supports their verdict choice. Thus, Juror A would evaluate this evidence as favoring the prosecution, whereas Juror B might evaluate it as favoring neither party, distorting his or her interpretation of the evidence away from its objective value (i.e., in favor of the prosecution) and in the direction of the side favored.

A powerful source of information which leads to premature beliefs and judgments about a defendant is prejudicial pretrial publicity (PTP). Ruva and LaVasseur (2012) exposed some mock jurors to anti-defendant PTP and subsequently analyzed what jurors said during deliberations. Those exposed to anti-defendant PTP were more likely than those not exposed to discuss ambiguous trial evidence in a manner that supported the prosecution.

Do jurors' biases predispose them to favor one side over another in a civil case? It seems natural for people to have feelings of compassion for injured persons and for these feelings to translate into favorable verdicts and lavish damage awards for plaintiffs. When jurors awarded $181 million in damages in 2012 to three workers injured in the explosion of a grain elevator in southern Illinois, did sympathy influence their thinking?

Surprisingly, perhaps, a variety of studies using different methodologies suggest that sympathy plays only a minor role in deliberations. In her study of claims by individuals against corporate defendants, Professor Valerie Hans (1996) interviewed jurors and ran experimental studies that manipulated variables related to this **sympathy hypothesis**. All the data pointed to the same conclusion: that the general public is "quite suspicious of, and sometimes downright hostile to, civil plaintiffs" (p. 244). A survey conducted by the consulting firm DecisionQuest yielded similar results: 84% of the 1012 people polled agreed with the statement "When people are injured, they often try to blame others for their carelessness." According to the same survey, potential jurors do not think highly of civil defendants, either. For example, more than 75% of respondents believe that corporate executives often try to cover up evidence of wrongdoing by their companies, and more respondents say that product warnings are intended to

protect manufacturers than say they are intended to keep consumers safe.

These findings raise another question: Do juries give larger awards when a defendant is wealthy? Some data would seem to support this so-called deep-pockets effect. Jury damage awards *are* consistently higher in products liability and medical malpractice cases than in automobile negligence cases. (The former group typically involves wealthy defendants, whereas the latter does not.) But a number of studies (e.g., Hans & Ermann, 1989; MacCoun, 1996) suggest that the wealth of the defendant alone is not the important variable. Rather, the public believes that businesses and corporations should be held to a higher standard of responsibility than individual defendants. Any inflation of awards against corporate defendants is apparently related to their status as a corporation and not to their wealth.

Can Deliberations Serve to De-bias Jurors?

We have shown that bias—including bias of any individual juror—is inevitable. Now we ask whether the process of deliberating with others can effectively reduce juror bias. There is reason to suspect that it can: when jurors must share their interpretations of the evidence publicly, they may become aware of their personal biases and work to set them aside. Deliberations may cause them to evaluate the evidence more carefully, correct misinterpretations, and challenge the biases and prejudices of others (Bornstein & Greene, 2011).

Psychologists have assessed the effects of deliberation by comparing the decisions of jurors who deliberate with the decisions of those who do not, and by comparing a single group of mock jurors prior to and after deliberating (Devine, 2012). The conclusion they draw from these studies is that deliberation can serve to correct individual biases. For example, London and Nunez (2000) assessed the impact of inadmissible evidence on jurors before and after deliberation. The defendant in their mock trial was charged with taking nude photographs of a child. This evidence was deemed admissible in one condition and inadmissible in another, and was not presented in a control condition. Prior to deliberations, jurors who were told that the photos were inadmissible were as likely to convict as jurors who were told the photos could be considered, demonstrating the powerful biasing effect of inadmissible evidence. But after deliberating, the conviction rate in the inadmissible evidence condition dropped significantly and was comparable to the control condition. Group discussion reduced the influence of inadmissible evidence, probably because jurors reminded each other of the mandate not to consider that evidence. Other studies have shown that biasing effects of pretrial publicity are also reduced by deliberations (e.g., Ruva, McEvoy, & Bryant, 2007).

Deliberating juries do not *always* make better decisions than individual jurors. Whether group deliberation reduces or amplifies bias may depend on the strength of the evidence (Kerr, Niedermeier, & Kaplan, 1999). When the evidence for either side in a trial is strong, deliberation seems to decrease bias that might exist in jurors' predeliberation sentiments. But when the evidence is ambiguous, deliberation seems to increase biases, probably because without hearing compelling evidence during the trial, jurors stick to their beliefs, values, and assumptions during the deliberations.

THE STORY MODEL

Although trial evidence is the primary determinant of verdicts, jurors' pretrial beliefs also affect their decisions. Now we describe how jurors make sense of the evidence that they hear *during* the trial. In many ways, the juror's task is like that of a mystery reader. The joy of reading a mystery comes from savoring each clue, combining it with prior clues, and evaluating its significance in the overall puzzle of who committed the crime. That is how most jurors operate. As they listen to the evidence, they form a schema, or mental structure that aids in the processing and interpretation of information. Just like mystery readers who remember clues that fit their hypothesis and forget clues that do not, jurors construct their own private stories about the evidence so that it makes sense to them; in the process, they pay inordinate attention to certain pieces of evidence while ignoring others.

Good lawyers know this. In fact, really great lawyers know that an important task is to convince the jury that their story, and not their opponent's story, is the right one. Famed criminal defense attorney "Racehorse" Haynes once said, "The lawyer with the best story wins."

Psychologists Reid Hastie and Nancy Pennington developed the **story model** to describe how individual jurors make a decision in a case (see, generally, Pennington & Hastie, 1993). It is the most widely endorsed model of juror decision making. Hastie and Pennington dubbed their model the story model because they suspected that the core cognitive process involved in juror decision making was construction of a story or narrative summary of the events in dispute. According to the model, jurors actively construct stories by considering three sources of information: the evidence presented during the trial, their personal experience in similar situations, and their broad knowledge of the elements of a story. After jurors learn about the verdict options in the case, they map their story onto the verdict options and determine which verdict fits best with their constructed story.

To illustrate the role of story construction in juror decision making, Hastie and Pennington interpreted the dramatic differences between White Americans' and African Americans' reactions to the verdict in the 1995 murder trial of O. J. Simpson. They suspected that because of their life experiences and beliefs, African Americans could more easily construct a story about police misconduct and police brutality than could White Americans. Thus, African Americans were more likely than Whites to accept the "defense story" that a racist police detective planted incriminating evidence on Simpson's property (Hastie & Pennington, 1996).

In one of their early empirical studies, Pennington and Hastie (1986) interviewed mock jurors who had seen a filmed reenactment of a murder trial and who were asked to talk out loud while making a verdict decision. The evidence summaries constructed by jurors had a definite narrative story structure, and, importantly, jurors who reached different verdicts had constructed different stories.

In a later study, Pennington and Hastie (1988) assessed whether the order in which evidence is presented influences jurors' judgments. Apparently so. They found that stories were easy to construct when the evidence was presented in a temporal order that matched the occurrence of the original events ("story order") but harder to construct when the evidence was presented in an order that did not match the sequence of the original events ("witness order").

Prosecutors and defense attorneys would be wise to familiarize themselves with these findings, because the study has significant implications for the practice of actual trials. When Pennington and Hastie manipulated the order of evidence, they affected the likelihood of a guilty verdict. For example, mock jurors were *most* likely to convict a criminal defendant when the prosecution evidence was presented in story order and the defense evidence in witness order. They were *least* likely to convict when the prosecution evidence was presented in witness order and the defense evidence in story order.

Is the story model a complete and accurate description of how jurors organize themselves to decide the verdict in a trial? No. For starters, it focuses only on *jurors* and does not address the complex nuances that come into focus when jurors deliberate as a jury. But as a framework for understanding the cognitive strategies employed by individuals to process trial information prior to deliberations, it is highly useful. Indeed, several other studies (e.g., Dunn, Salovey, & Feigenson, 2006; Huntley & Costanzo, 2003) have been inspired by its elegant theorizing.

JURY REFORM

Jury trials are conducted under strict rules developed over the years by statutes, case law, and tradition. These imperatives stem from the belief that justice is best served by an adversarial system in which the evidence presented to jurors is vetted through a neutral judge and limited by rules of the court. Under these rules, jurors were prohibited from investigating the facts themselves and asking questions during the trial, and they were warned not to discuss the evidence with anyone until they reach a verdict.

This model treats jurors as passive recipients of information who, like digital recorders, record a one-way stream of communication. Jurors were expected to process all incoming information impassively, without interpretation, until finally instructed by the judge to decide something. As we pointed out earlier, this conception of juror-as-blank-slate is largely wrong; jurors actively evaluate the evidence through the lens of their personal experiences and frames of reference, pose questions to themselves, and construct narratives or stories to help them understand the evidence and make a judgment about it.

Acknowledging that most jurors are active "thought processors," psychologists and other social scientists started suggesting reforms to the jury system in the 1970s. By the 1990s, judges were also beginning to question the traditional view of jurors as passive blank slates. Against this backdrop of increasing support for reform, creative court personnel and forward-thinking judges have implemented changes in trial procedures that take advantage of jurors' natural inclinations and provide tools to encourage jurors' active involvement in the process. Many of these reforms have now been implemented in courts across the country. Some are uncontroversial and benign: providing notebooks that list the witnesses and summarize their testimony in long or complex cases; giving pre-instructions or interim instructions during the course of a lengthy trial; allowing jurors to take notes; designating alternate jurors only after the presentation of evidence is completed; providing a written copy of the judge's instructions to each juror; and allowing jurors to examine the demonstrative evidence during their deliberations.

Two reforms have been more controversial: allowing jurors to pose questions to witnesses (questions are screened by the judge, who decides whether they are appropriate) and to discuss the evidence in the midst of trial. These reforms have also been implemented in many jurisdictions, and research studies have charted their effectiveness. Through such studies, psychologists have learned that these new practices contribute in beneficial ways to fair and accurate decisions.

Jurors questioned about the opportunity to submit written questions have been strongly supportive. Fully 83% of jurors surveyed by the Seventh Circuit American Jury Project between 2005 and 2008 reported that the opportunity to ask questions of witnesses enhanced their understanding of the facts (Seventh Circuit American Jury Project, 2008). Examining the questions jurors asked during 50 civil trials and how jurors discussed the answers during deliberations, Arizona Jury Project researchers found that questions helped to clarify conflicting evidence and produce a plausible description of the events in dispute. Discussion of these questions and answers did not dominate jurors' deliberations (Diamond, Rose, Murphy, & Smith, 2006). Allowing jurors to ask question may have the added benefit of reducing their inclination to seek answers online (MacPherson & Bonora, 2010). Finally, although some judges have worried that jurors will be offended by having a question disallowed or will speculate about why a submitted question could not be asked, jurors themselves tend to accept that decision and drop the issue (Diamond, Rose, & Murphy, 2004). Therefore, we see no serious drawbacks to allowing jurors to ask questions. Doing so can clarify their understanding of the evidence, enhance involvement in the trial process, and create an environment more conducive to learning.

The more radical reform permits jurors to discuss the evidence during the trial, rather than having to wait until formal deliberations begin. The rules are simple: All jurors must be present in the deliberation room during these discussions, and jurors must keep an open mind and avoid debating verdict options. Psychologists have described a number of potential advantages of such mid-trial discussions based on fundamental principles of cognitive and social psychology. In theory, juror discussions about the evidence can

- Improve comprehension by permitting jurors to sift through and organize the evidence into a coherent framework over the course of the trial.

- Improve recollection of the evidence and testimony by emphasizing and clarifying points made during trial.

- Promote greater cohesion among jurors, thereby reducing the time needed for deliberations (Bregant, 2009).

But there are also several potential drawbacks to jury discussions during trial, and these, too, are based on well-established psychological principles. They include the possibility that jury discussions may

- Facilitate the formation or expression of premature judgments about the evidence.

- Diminish the quality of the deliberations as jurors become more familiar with each other's views.

- Produce more interpersonal conflicts prior to formal deliberations (Bregant, 2009).

The first empirical test of this reform was a field experiment in which researchers randomly assigned approximately 100 civil jury trials to an experimental "trial discussion" condition and an equal number to a control "no discussion" condition (Hannaford, Hans, & Munsterman, 2000). Assessing jurors' impressions of this experience, researchers found that of those who were permitted to discuss the evidence, approximately 70% reported that their jury had at least one such discussion. So even when permitted to talk about the case, a sizeable minority of juries did not. Jurors who reported having discussions were quite positive about them. They said that trial evidence was remembered very accurately during these discussions, that discussions

helped them understand the evidence in the case, and that all jurors' points of view were considered during the course of the discussions. The perceived drawbacks were mostly logistical: Jurors said that there were difficulties in getting all members together at the same time. (After all, these short breaks represent the only time in the course of several hours that jurors may use the rest rooms or smoke a cigarette. Some people's desire for these comforts undoubtedly outweighed their interest in talking about the evidence!)

Useful data also come from the analysis of videotapes of 50 civil jury trials in Arizona (Diamond, Vidmar, Rose, Ellis, & Murphy, 2003). This study examined all mid-trial jury discussions, as well as the deliberations. These tapes make clear that during discussion jurors seek information from one another, raise questions they intend to ask, and talk about the not-yet-presented evidence they would like to hear. Such discussions led to modest enhancements in jurors' understanding of the evidence and did not result in premature judgments.

These findings provide a fascinating and previously unseen picture of the jury at work as it discusses the evidence in the midst of the trial and reaches a final verdict at the trial's conclusion. Predeliberation discussion may have the added benefit of reducing reliance on inadmissible evidence and other biases that interfere with jurors' ability to impartially consider subsequent evidence. In essence, they function *during* the trial in the same way that deliberations function *after* the trial—as a de-biasing mechanism (Bregant, 2009). We see few negative effects of mid-trial discussion, and believe that allowing jurors to talk about the case simply legitimizes what they are likely to do anyway.

THE JURY: SHOULD IT BE VENERATED OR VILIFIED? REVERED OR REVILED?

The jury system brings together multiple individuals with diverse backgrounds, experiences, and biases who pool their perceptions of the evidence to reach a verdict (Diamond, 2006). In this way, the trial jury is a remarkable institution and, in important respects, also a unique one. The use of average citizens to determine trial outcomes for rich and powerful figures such as corporate executive Rajat Gupta and hedge fund founder Raj Rajaratnam, convicted of insider trading and conspiracy, underscores our country's commitment to egalitarian values. It is no exaggeration to say that the trial jury is sanctified as one of our fundamental democratic institutions. Political scientist Jeffrey Abramson (1994), author of *We, the Jury*, put it eloquently:

> [T]here are all the jurors we never read about, who toil out of the limelight every day, crossing all kinds of racial and ethnic lines to defend a shared sense of justice. These examples convince me that the jury, far from being obsolete, is more crucial than ever in a multiethnic society struggling to articulate a justice common to [all] citizens. Though the jury system is a grand phenomenon—putting justice in the hands of

the people—we still have lessons to learn about how to design an institution that gathers persons from different walks of life to discuss and decide upon one justice for all (p. 5).

Although there remains much to learn, psychologists now know a good deal about how juries function. They know that juries don't always get it right; on occasion, jurors are overwhelmed by the sheer volume of evidence, misunderstand their instructions, and use evidence in inappropriate ways. They know that jurors' biases and prejudices can rise to the surface and color their judgments. But by and large, psychologists find little support for the extreme claims that charge juries with poor and irresponsible performance. On the contrary, it seems that the institution of the jury is worth defending and worth improving.

SUMMARY

1. *Describe the issue of jury competence.* Some commentators have wondered whether jurors and juries are overly attentive to extralegal information that, in theory, is irrelevant to the guilt decision in criminal cases and to the liability judgment in civil cases. Others have asked whether jurors will be mesmerized by the testimony of an expert or, conversely, that they will not understand such testimony and dismiss it outright. Whether jurors and juries are able to understand and apply their instructions is another question. Finally, some have asked whether jurors can decide the complicated issues that arise in so-called complex cases.

2. *What is the impact of extralegal information on jurors?* Research studies suggest that occasionally jurors are influenced by evidence of a defendant's prior record or character and propensity to commit crimes. In civil cases, evidence related to an accident victim's injury may influence the judgment of a defendant's liability.

3. *Can jurors disregard inadmissible evidence?* When a question posed or an answer offered during a trial is ruled inadmissible by the judge, jurors are instructed to disregard it. Psychological evidence indicates that it is difficult for jurors to disregard this testimony; in fact, the stronger the judge's admonition, the less effective it may be.

Deliberations tend to reduce reliance on inadmissible evidence.

4. *How can jurors be helped to understand their instructions?* Jurors can be instructed before the trial begins about the relevant elements of the law that they will apply to the facts they hear. Judges can provide written copies of the instructions for all jurors. Unfortunately, judges rarely answer jurors' questions about their instructions.

5. *What is meant by the statement "Bias is inevitable in jurors"?* Bias, as used here, refers to the human predisposition to make interpretations on the basis of beliefs and past experiences. Bias is inevitable because it is inescapable human nature to make assumptions about human behavior.

6. *What reforms of the jury system do psychologists suggest?* The information-processing demands placed on jurors should be simplified. More clearly worded instructions, in written as well as oral form, delivered at the beginning and at the conclusion of the trial would be helpful. Preinstructions and simplifying complex language may be especially helpful. During the trial, jurors should be able to pose questions that the judge would then ask of the witnesses. Finally, mid-trial discussion of the evidence helps jurors to organize the evidence in a thematic framework and thus improve their memory of the testimony.

KEY TERMS

aversive racism	extralegal information	limiting instruction	reactance theory
class action case	inadmissible evidence	outcome severity	recency effect
damages	juror bias	predecisional distortion	schema
defensive attribution	jury nullification	primacy effect	story model
dual-process models	liable	propensity evidence	sympathy hypothesis
evidentiary strength	liberation hypothesis	psycholinguistics	thought suppression

Chapter
14

Punishment and Sentencing

ORIENTING QUESTIONS

1. What are the purposes of punishment?
2. How are the values of discretion and fairness reflected in sentencing decisions?
3. What factors influence sentencing decisions?
4. What special factors are considered in the sentencing of juveniles? Of recidivist sex offenders?
5. How is the death penalty decided by juries?
6. In what ways has the Supreme Court recently limited the use of capital punishment, and what role have psychologists played in these decisions?

A sentencing decision comes near the end of a criminal prosecution and is typically made by a judge or magistrate. Options include probation, restitution, compensation, fines, community service, imprisonment, and others. The purpose of the sentence—punishment, deterrence, incapacitation, or rehabilitation, for example—depends on the nature of the crime, the characteristics and experiences of the offender, the temperament of the judge, and, in some cases, public sentiment. As you might suspect, judges have considerable latitude or discretion in the sentences they impose in this system, and disparities in sentence length can result. **Sentencing disparities** occur whenever similar offenders who committed similar crimes receive different sentences. Various efforts to reduce disparity, including maximum and minimum sentences, sentencing guidelines, and even revisions in sentencing guidelines have been instituted, with somewhat mixed success.

Great numbers of offenders in the United States are sentenced to prison. One of the most unusual is Sylvester Jiles, who, in 2010, was sentenced to 15 years for attempting to break into the Brevard County (FL) jail one week after he had been released from that very jail! Jiles begged jail officials to take him back into custody because he feared retaliation from his victim's family.

Oddities like Jiles aside, for most of the past 40 years no other industrialized country except Russia has imprisoned its citizens at the rate of the United States. This situation was a result of what Professor Craig Haney, a psychologist and a lawyer, called America's "rage to punish" (Haney, 2006, p. 4). According to Haney, "hundreds of thousands of people have been locked up in American jails and prisons who would not have been incarcerated (for the same misdeeds) in any other modern Western society" or "if they had committed their crimes at almost any other time in American history" (Haney, 2006, p. 11).

At the end of 2009, there were approximately 2.3 million people, including 200,000 women, in prisons and jails (compared with 1.5 million in 1995). About 3.2% of the population—1 in 32 adults—was under some form of correctional supervision (i.e., incarceration, probation, or parole). This is the highest documented incarceration rate in the world (Walmsley, 2009). Federal offenders are especially likely to be sentenced to prison (as opposed to probation or community confinement): 85% of federal offenders sentenced in 2007 went to prison; approximately one-third were illegal aliens awaiting deportation (Coyle, 2009). The crackdown on illegal immigration is partly responsible for the steep rise in the percentage of federal offenders who are Latinos, up from 24% in 1991 to 40% in 2007 (Lopez & Light, 2009).

Racial disparities continue to plague the criminal justice system. If past trends continue, it is predicted that 1 of every 3 African-American boys born today will spend some time in prison, as will 1 in 6 Latino males, and 1 in 17 White males. Although crime rates among females are much lower, racial disparities are still apparent: 1 of 18 African-American females, 1 in 45 Hispanic females, and 1 in 111 White females will spend time in prison (Bonczar, 2003). Some of the disproportion is related to greater involvement in criminal activities by people of color, but analysis of imprisonment data from 2004 suggests that nearly 40% of racial disparity in incarceration *cannot* be explained by that fact alone (Tonry & Melewski, 2008).

How should a society respond to individual criminals? With an inmate population over 2 million, does it make sense to continue locking up more offenders every year? Incarceration comes at a price; every dollar spent on corrections means one less dollar for public schools, health care, parks, and higher education.

Although philosophical questions about the costs and benefits of punishment and incarceration have been debated for many years, a convergence of social realities is now forcing criminal justice officials and legislators to seek new approaches to punishing criminals. One factor is the significant decline in crime rates since the early 1990s. With the decreasing salience of crime as an emotional and political issue, there has been a reduction in "tough on crime" rhetoric; there have also been modest developments in alternatives to harsh sentencing policies, particularly for drug offenses. A second factor driving reforms in sentencing is the worldwide recession. Fiscal constraints imposed on state budgets have forced policymakers to confront the high cost of imprisonment and examine the cost effectiveness of sentencing policies. For example, New Mexico lawmakers repealed the death penalty in 2009 in order to save money. In other states, legislators have voted to reduce the number of probationers sent to prison for violating conditions of their release, and to reduce the amount of time prisoners must serve before being considered for parole, particularly for nonviolent offenses (Mauer, 2011). As a result, over the past few years, state prison populations have begun to stabilize overall and actually to decline in a few states.

In this chapter and against this backdrop, we address the issues of punishment and sentencing by describing their multiple goals and purposes, some of which aim to exact retribution from an offender and others that favor practical ends such as deterrence, incapacitation, and rehabilitation. We describe the factors that judges consider in their sentencing decisions, and the specific issues that arise in sentencing of juvenile and sex offenders. Finally, we examine psychological aspects of the ultimate punishment, the death penalty.

THE PURPOSES OF PUNISHMENT

The crime control model of criminal justice has heavily influenced police, prosecutors, and many judges over the past 35 years. It interprets the primary aim of law enforcement as the apprehension and punishment of criminals so that they will not repeat their offenses and others will be deterred from similar acts. But as resources have dwindled, policymakers are increasingly interested in punishments that serve some beneficial function, particularly to the vast majority of offenders who reenter society after spending time behind bars.

These differing viewpoints illustrate the multiple purposes of punishment. Psychologists have identified at least seven different goals (see, for example, Greenberg & Ruback, 1984):

1. *General deterrence.* The punishment of an offender—and the subsequent publicity that comes with it—are assumed to discourage other potential lawbreakers. Some advocates of the death penalty, for example, believe that fear of death may be our strongest motivation; hence, they believe that the death penalty serves as a general deterrent to murder.

2. *Individual deterrence.* Punishment of the offender is presumed to keep that person from committing other crimes in the future. Some theories assume that many criminals lack adequate internal inhibitors; hence, punitive sanctions must be used to teach them that their behavior will be controlled—if not by them, then by society.

3. *Incapacitation.* If a convicted offender is sent to prison, society can feel safe from that felon while he or she is confined. One influential position (Wilson, 1975) sees a major function of incapacitation as simply to age the criminal—an understandable goal, given that the rate of offending declines with age.

4. *Retribution.* Society believes that offenders should not benefit from their crimes; rather, they should receive their "just deserts," or "that which is justly deserved." The moral cornerstone of punishment is that it should be administered to people who deserve it as a consequence of their misdeeds.

5. *Moral outrage.* Punishment can give society a means of catharsis and relief from the feelings of frustration, hurt, loss, and anger that result from being victims of crime; it promotes a sense of satisfaction that offenders have paid for what they have done to others.

6. *Rehabilitation.* One goal in sentencing has always been that offenders will recognize the error of

their ways and develop new skills, values, and lifestyles so that they can return to normal life and become law abiding. This has been a primary consideration in punishing juveniles.

7. *Restitution*. Wrongdoers should compensate victims for their damages and losses. Typical statutes require that defendants pay for victims' out-of-pocket expenses, property damage, and other monetary losses. Restitution is often a condition of probation.

Utilitarian Approaches

Most of these goals are **utilitarian**: They are intended to accomplish a useful outcome, such as compensating the victim, deterring crime, or incapacitating or rehabilitating the defendant. Utilitarian goals have a practical objective; they right the wrongs of past misconduct and reduce the likelihood of future criminal behavior.

Rehabilitation as a utilitarian goal has been in and out of favor throughout history. The basic notion is that offenders who receive treatment for the underlying causes of criminality will be less likely to reoffend. When it *was* the dominant goal, criminal sentences were expected to accomplish something other than incarceration and punishment.

Though the original purpose of prisons was to rehabilitate (many prisons are still called *correctional* institutions), high **recidivism** rates indicate that prisons have not been very effective at rehabilitating offenders. The extreme version of this view, dubbed the "nothing works" position, is attributed to Robert Martinson. He concluded, after reviewing a large number of outcome studies, that most attempts at offender rehabilitation fail (Martinson, 1974). Martinson's advocacy of another utilitarian approach—deterrence—led to a "get-tough" attitude toward offenders, and to increasingly punitive measures such as the three-strikes laws (laws stating that after a third criminal conviction, offenders go to prison for a very long time) and zero-tolerance policies enacted in the 1980s and 1990s. But after more than 30 years of this "get-tough" approach with no reduction in recidivism, the pendulum has begun to swing back slowly in the direction of rehabilitative policies. Psychologists now know that rehabilitation can be effective when it is tailored to an offender's age, race, criminal history, religion, and other personal attributes (Andrews &

Bonta, 2010). Unfortunately, many institutions continue to offer only one-size-fits-all interventions.

Retributive Approaches

Two of the punishment goals we described are **retributive**: they involve looking back at the offense and determining what the criminal "deserves" as a consequence of committing it. These goals are retribution (sometimes called "just deserts") and moral outrage, a close cousin of retribution (Kaplan, 1996). The notion of retribution implies that an offender deserves to be punished and that the punishment should be proportionate to the severity of the wrongdoing.

The stark contrast between utilitarian and retributive approaches raises the question of why we punish people. What are our motives for punishing others? Discovering how ordinary people think about this issue is important because those who draft sentencing laws should know what the public prefers (Carlsmith & Darley, 2008).

Psychologists have taken different approaches to answering this question. Some have simply asked people which philosophy they prefer and have assumed that respondents can report their true beliefs. But in studies that measured people's agreement with various sentencing policies, people tended to agree with all of them (Anderson & MacCoun, 1999)! Furthermore, people are sometimes unaware of the factors that influence their preferences (Wilson, 2002). An alternative research design involves considering the length of sentences that judges actually order and working backward from these sentences to identify the underlying motives (i.e., just deserts/retribution, deterrence, incapacitation). But this method can be fallible, too. Finally, other researchers have presented vignettes to respondents, varying the nature of the crime and details about the offender, and then measuring respondents' sentencing preferences.

Public Preferences for Deterrence and Retribution. Using a research technique called **policy capturing**, Carlsmith, Darley, and Robinson (2002) assessed the punishment motives of ordinary people. The specific motives for punishment that they contrasted were deterrence and retribution. Using vignettes that described a variety of harmful actions, the researchers attempted to understand (or "capture") the policies underlying the punishments that people assigned.

They varied different elements of the crimes described, elements that should or should not matter to respondents depending on which motive they preferred. For example, the magnitude of the harm should matter to people who are motivated by retribution, and the likelihood of reoffending should matter to those who are concerned with future deterrence. Carlsmith and his colleagues then measured the degree to which each respondent's sentence was influenced by these variables. The data showed a high sensitivity to factors associated with retribution and relative insensitivity to factors associated with deterrence. In fact, people actively seek information relevant to retribution (e.g., the magnitude of the harm and the perpetrator's intent) when they know that a crime has been committed and are asked to assign punishments (Carlsmith, 2006). People's preferences for punishment apparently focus on their sense of what an offender deserves.

Interestingly, that's not what people *say* about their punishment beliefs. Responding to opinion polls, people are more likely to indicate support for punishment that deters criminals than punishment that exacts retribution (Carlsmith, 2008). This suggests that people do not have a good sense of their own motivations for punishing others, and may explain why citizens enact legislation one year, then soon reject it as unjust and vote to repeal it shortly thereafter (Carlsmith & Darley, 2008).

Why do people say they support deterrence but act like they favor retribution? One possibility is that people have a limited awareness of their own reasons for their punishment preferences. As social psychologists have pointed out, when it comes to introspecting about why we behave in a particular way, "we are all strangers to ourselves" (Wilson, 2002). It may also be less socially acceptable to say that we favor a penalty based on reprisal and revenge than one based on notions of future good.

These findings appear to support the idea that many people actually favor punitive sanctions, and at least some politicians are happy to respond. Joe Arpaio, the controversial sheriff of Maricopa County, Arizona (Phoenix), is a "get-tough" icon. His philosophy, which has gained him national notoriety (as well as federal investigations into his management of funds), is to make jail so unpleasant that no one would want to come back—while simultaneously saving money. He sheltered prisoners in "leaky, dilapidated military-surplus tents set on gravel fields surrounded by barbed wire" and fed them "bologna

The only female chain gang in America

streaked with green and blue packaging dye" (Morrison, 1995). He established the first women's and juveniles' chain gangs. His "air posse" of 30 private planes tracks illegal immigrants and drug smugglers, leading Paul Gordon, the mayor of Phoenix, to accuse him of discriminatory harassment and improper searches and seizures.

Another retributive goal—moral outrage—allows society the satisfaction of knowing that offenders have been made to pay for the harms they caused. Professor Dan Kahan (1996) argued that for a sentence to be acceptable to the public, it must reflect society's outrage. He maintained that the expressive dimension of punishment is not satisfied by "straight" probation, "mere" fines, or direct community service. According to Kahan, probation appears to be no punishment, a fine appears to be a means to "buy one's way out," and community service is something everyone ought to do. Kahan argued that imposing a **shaming penalty** would allow society to express its moral denunciation of criminal wrongdoers.

Shaming is a traditional means by which communities punished offenders. In colonial days, those who committed minor offenses were put in stocks in a public place for several hours for all to see and ridicule. Serious offenders were branded or otherwise marked so they would be "shamed" for life. In Williamsburg, Virginia, thieves were nailed to the stocks by the ear; after a period of time the sheriff would rip the offender from the stocks, thus "ear-marking" the offender for life (Book, 1999).

The modern counterpart to shaming (without mutilation) is to allow offenders to avoid all or part of a jail sentence by publicly renouncing their crimes in a humiliating way. The impetus for these alternative sentences is twofold. First, judges have become frustrated with revolving-door justice: a large number of offenders who are released from prison eventually return, suggesting that their punishments had little long-term effectiveness. Second, judges are aware of the longstanding problem of prison overcrowding and the high costs of incarceration. The American Bar Association has urged judges to provide alternatives to incarceration for offenders who might benefit from them.

Some judges have been happy to oblige, and many of the sentences they have imposed are truly ingenious. Consider the following:

1. Men caught on surveillance cameras in the process of soliciting prostitutes in Oakland, California, have their faces plastered on bus stop signs and billboards (Stryker, 2005).

2. A Kentucky judge regularly gives "Deadbeat Dads"—fathers owing more than $10,000 in child support to more than three women—a choice: jail or a vasectomy (McAree, 2004).

Another innovative sentence is described in Box 14.1.

As you might expect, alternative sentences like these are highly controversial. Some lawyers—defense attorneys and prosecutors alike—applaud them, acknowledging that judges have discretion in sentencing and that incarceration is costly and does not always work. But others worry that the shaming

inherent in these sentences is sometimes extreme. Even Dan Kahan, the early proponent of shaming penalties, now shuns them (Kahan, 2006). He asserts that ordinary citizens prefer punishments that affirm, rather than denigrate, their core egalitarian values.

Still, shaming has intuitive appeal as a penal sanction because everyone has experienced shaming in childhood. Parents teach their children to "be good" by making them ashamed of their bad behavior. A child forced to confess to the store owner that he stole a piece of candy should associate theft with embarrassment from that time on (Book, 1999). However, the 21st century lacks the social cohesiveness of earlier societies in which shaming was effective in controlling behavior. For this reason, some perceive modern shaming as ineffective and unnecessarily cruel.

Some recent research suggests that it may also be counterproductive. When participants imagined or remembered themselves in situations where they were publicly reprimanded for wrongdoing, they expressed humiliation, even when the wrongful act was exposed to just one person. Importantly, that humiliation was associated not with feelings of shame or guilt, but rather with perceptions of unfair treatment, anger at others, and vengeful urges. Public condemnation shifts the focus from one's wrongdoing to perceived mistreatment by others (Combs, Campbell, Jackson, & Smith, 2010).

Apparently, the line between shaming and humiliation is rather blurred. An extreme example of counterproductive shaming: A 19-year-old was ordered to publish his name, photo, and offense in

---

B o x 14.1 THE CASE OF A CROOKED COUPLE AND THEIR SHAMING PENALTY

Over the course of her 16-year employment as an administrative assistant in the Harris County (Texas) District Attorney's Office, Eloise Mireles discovered a serious weakness in the office's accounting system. But rather than fix it, she and her husband Daniel opted to cheat the county out of more than $255,000. Eloise stole money orders and cashiers' checks intended to compensate crime victims, and Daniel deposited the checks in the couple's account. They spent the money on trips and tickets to concerts and sporting events. After pleading guilty to theft charges, they were ordered to spend six months in jail (one month per year for six years), stand at a busy Houston intersection for five hours at a time

(he on Saturdays and she on Sundays) wearing a sign that reads "I am a thief. I stole $255,000 from a crime victims' fund," and display a sign in front of their house that says "The occupants of this residence are convicted thieves." According to Daniel Mireles's attorney, this punishment suited his client just fine because Mireles would rather admit every day that he was wrong than go to prison (Rogers et al., 2010).

Critical Thought Question
Discuss the advantages and disadvantages of shaming as an approach to criminal sentencing in light of the goals of punishment discussed earlier in the chapter.

the local paper after his third DUI conviction. His mother saw the paper and left it on the breakfast table with a note saying she was ashamed of him. He wrote her a letter of apology and shot himself in the head (Braudway, 2004).

Restorative Approaches

Over the years, many people have become disenchanted with retributive justice. For one thing, punishing offenders in proportion to the severity of their offenses, although cathartic, has apparently done little to curb crime or reduce suffering. For another, inflicting punishment on offenders who "deserve" to be punished provides little opportunity for victims to be involved in the process or to have their own needs met. As a result, victims are often dissatisfied with their experiences in the criminal justice system (O'Hara, 2005).

In recent decades, a new approach has emerged that attempts to repair the damage caused by criminal offenses. This approach, called **restorative justice**, uses open dialogue to gain consensus about responsibility-taking and dispute resolution. The goals of restorative justice are to repair the harm and restore the losses caused by offensive activity, reintegrate offenders into society, and empower victims and the community to move from feelings of vulnerability and loss to a sense of understanding and closure (Umbreit, Vos, Coates, & Lightfoot, 2005).

Restorative justice is based on the premise that those who are most affected by crime—victims and offenders—should have a prominent role to play in resolving the conflict and that the community also has a stake in its outcome. Thus, it expands the circle of participants beyond the offender and the state, and encourages participants to use some combination of apology, remorse, and forgiveness to move beyond the harms caused by crime.

Restorative justice policies are used throughout the world (e.g., the Truth and Reconciliation Commissions in South Africa and Rwanda were based on these principles) and are now embedded in various components of many justice systems in the United States, including the criminal, civil, and juvenile justice systems (Sullivan & Tifft, 2006). We provide an example of a restorative procedure in Box 14.2.

How do people feel about achieving justice through a restorative process? Given the public's strong desire to punish offenders, is there support for procedures that focus on other justice goals? Although restorative justice has received much less empirical scrutiny than retributive justice (Roberts & Stalans, 2004), people apparently do value its role in repairing harm done to victims and communities. In fact, for less serious crimes, people prefer to respond with restorative measures, and even for more serious offenses, people prefer responses that combine restorative procedures and punitive sanctions (i.e., prison sentences), rather than either of these options alone

---

B o x 14.2 THE CASE FOR RESTORATIVE JUSTICE: HEALING A MOTHER WOUNDED BY TRAGEDY

On July 19, 2009, Sandy Eversole got the news that all parents fear and dread: her son David Mueller, a star athlete and college student, had been killed in an automobile accident. David was riding in a car driven by his friend Dylan Salazar, travelling nearly 100 mph on a Colorado Springs city street before running off the road. As expected, Sandy and her family were overwhelmed by grief in the first few months after the accident and then angered and frustrated by the claims settlement and criminal justice responses. She wanted to know what had happened that night and why, but after Salazar was sentenced to four years in a youth correctional facility, Sandy had no way to ask questions or seek solace. That changed when the District Attorney's office gave her an opportunity to meet with Salazar in a restorative justice session led by a trained mediator. Despite initial concerns about whether she

would be capable of controlling her rage, Sandy was able to tell Salazar what her family had endured. Also apprehensive, Salazar apologized and took responsibility for the accident. Reflecting on the experience, Sandy recalled, "Right away I could tell that he was full of remorse and sadness. It was hard to find out some of the details but I was glad I did. It was easy to forgive him after I saw his tears" (www.restorativemediationproject.org).

Critical Thought Question
Historically, victims have had little say in how criminal offenders are punished. Why? The restorative justice approach seeks to empower victims by giving them a voice in this matter. In your opinion, should victims' perspectives influence the punishment meted out to offenders?

(Gromet & Darley, 2006). The need to punish offenders does not preclude the desire to attend to the needs of others harmed by wrongdoing (Gromet & Darley, 2009).

Given the public's preference for both retribution and restoration, it is worthwhile examining how judges assign criminal punishments, to what extent their choices mirror public sentiment, and how psychological factors influence their decisions.

JUDICIAL DISCRETION IN SENTENCING

Criminal sentencing lies at the heart of society's efforts to ensure public order. Hoffman and Stone-Meierhoefer (1979) go so far as to state, "Next to the determination of guilt or innocence, a determination waived by a substantial proportion of defendants who plead guilty (around 90%), the sentencing decision is probably the most important decision made about the criminal defendant in the entire process" (p. 241).

Sentencing is a judicial function, but sentencing decisions are largely controlled by the legislative branch—Congress and state legislatures. The legislative branch dictates the extent of judges' discretion, and many legislators believe that judges should have little or no discretion. They emphasize retribution and argue that the punishment should fit the crime. Mandatory sentences, sentencing guidelines, and the abolition of parole have been the primary ingredients in these "get tough" schemes.

Other legislators maintain that the sentence should also fit the offender—in essence, that judges should have discretion to make the sentence fit both the crime and the criminal. Discretion allows judges to capitalize on their perceptions of an offender's personal and external circumstances so that sentencing decisions can "serve, within limits set by law, that elusive concept of justice which the law in its wisdom refuses to define" (Gaylin, 1974, p. 67). Those who advocate individually tailored sentences note that each offender is different and deserves to be treated as an individual: "Theories [that] place primary emphasis on linking deserved punishments to the severity of crimes, in the interest of treating cases alike ... lead to disregard of other ethically relevant differences between offenders—like their personal backgrounds and the effects of punishments on them and their families" (Tonry, 1996, p. 15).

Sentencing Policies

Some states have **indeterminate sentencing** schemes, in which judges exercise their discretion by imposing a variable period of incarceration for a given offense (e.g., 6–20 years), and a parole board determines the actual date of release. Such policies have been both hailed and criticized: hailed because they provide incentives for good behavior and encourage offenders to take advantage of available treatment programs to enhance the chances of earlier release, and criticized because they allow parole boards wide discretion in determining when the conditions of the sentence have been satisfied. When indeterminate sentencing works as it should, offenders are neither released early nor subjected to confinement beyond that necessary to ensure public protection.

In other states, the legislative branch has imposed a **determinate sentencing** system on the judiciary, effectively reducing judges' discretion. In these systems, offenders are sentenced for a fixed length of time determined by statutes and guidelines, and there is no parole. The primary goals of these sentences are retribution and moral outrage. There is little concern for the offender's personal characteristics, apart from his or her criminal record, and less potential for arbitrary or discriminatory decisions about when an offender should be released.

In a further attempt to reduce discretion, some states impose **mandatory minimum sentences** for certain offenses, including drug crimes. These policies require judges to sentence offenders to a minimum number of years in prison regardless of any extenuating circumstances. They, too, have been criticized as unjust. For example, a Utah judge was forced to sentence a first-time offender who had sold marijuana on three occasions to 61½ years in custody with no parole. The reason: He carried a gun during the marijuana sales. The statute imposed a 5-year minimum term for the first gun count and a minimum of 25 years for each subsequent count in addition to 6½ years for the sale of the marijuana. The judge noted that on the very day he sentenced the marijuana dealer to 61½ years, using the same guidelines he sentenced a murderer to a 21-year term (*United States v. Angelos*, 2004).

Review of more than 73,000 cases from 2010 revealed that 75% of offenders subjected to a mandatory minimum penalty were convicted of a drug trafficking offense (U.S. Sentencing Commission, 2011). The American Psychological Association (APA) has spoken out against mandatory minimum sentences: "[T]hey have done nothing to reduce crime or put big-time drug dealers out of business. What they have done … is to fill prisons with young, nonviolent, low-level drug offenders serving long sentences at enormous and growing cost to taxpayers" (Hansen, 1999, p. 14).

Current federal sentencing policy is based on the Sentencing Reform Act of 1984, which abolished parole and established a Sentencing Commission to develop mandatory sentencing guidelines. An overriding goal of the Sentencing Commission was to ensure uniformity of sentences. Federal judges were required to sentence offenders within a narrow range prescribed by a complicated analysis of the severity and circumstances of the crime, among other factors. But this scheme also proved to be controversial. In 2005, the U.S. Supreme Court decided that the mandatory nature of the guidelines was unconstitutional (*United States v. Booker*, 2005). Federal sentencing guidelines are now advisory rather than mandatory, meaning that they are among the factors that judges consider. In fact, judges still tend to follow the guidelines, although they are now able to consider more evidence than the guidelines would have permitted. When federal judges do diverge from the sentencing guidelines, though, their sentences are far more likely to be below the guidelines than above them. Meanwhile, the Sentencing Commission is considering alternatives to incarceration for offenders who are amenable to diversion and treatment.

Brian Gall benefited from judges' increased discretion in sentencing. In the late 1990s, while a student at the University of Iowa, Gall had been involved in a drug ring distributing Ecstasy. But he stopped using drugs, graduated from college, became a master carpenter, and started his own business in Arizona. After being tracked down by federal authorities, he turned himself in and pleaded guilty to conspiracy to distribute a controlled substance. The judge, taking Gall's circumstances into account, departed from the guidelines and imposed a sentence of 36 months of probation and no prison time. In 2007, the Supreme Court upheld the sentence, stating that federal judges have the authority to set any reasonable sentence as long as they explain their reasoning (*Gall v. United States*, 2007).

Sentencing Process

The procedure used in most courts for sentencing has several components. The judge receives a file on the offender that contains information about the offender's personal history and prior convictions (if any), and a number of documents describing various procedures (e.g., the date of the arraignment, the formal indictment). The judge reviews the file before the sentencing hearing.

At the hearing, recommendations for a sentence are presented, first by the prosecutor and then by the defense attorney. Statements are arranged in this order to give the defendant the final word before the judge makes a decision. But there may be an unexpected consequence of granting the prosecution the opportunity to make an initial recommendation. A large body of research has shown that initial numeric requests serve as powerful standards or "anchors" on subsequent judgments (Tversky & Kahneman, 1974). In fact, judges' sentencing decisions are highly influenced by the prosecutor's request for a lengthy sentence (Englich & Mussweiler, 2001), a finding that can be explained by a judgment process called **anchoring**.

Defense attorneys' sentencing recommendations are *also* influenced by the prosecutors' demands. When researchers asked lawyers to assume the role of defense attorneys in a simulated rape case, they found that though defense attorneys requested a lower punishment than prosecutors, they were still influenced by the level of the prosecutors' recommendation, and **assimilated** their own sentencing demands to those of the prosecutor (Englich, Mussweiler, & Strack, 2005). This behavior, in turn, will affect judges' decisions. So rather than being aided by going last, the defense may be hindered by having to follow, and counter, the prosecution's demand—its "anchor."

In addition to demands from the prosecutor and defense attorney, the sentencing judge has a probation officer's report and recommendation. The judge may ask the offender questions and will usually permit the offender to make a statement. In some cases, a forensic mental health professional may provide input on issues such as diminished capacity or coercion and duress (Krauss & Goldstein, 2007), particularly addressing questions such as whether the defendant was able to understand the wrongfulness of the crime, was able to conform his or her conduct to the requirements of the law, and has particular treatment or rehabilitation needs. On the basis of these sources of information and taking sentencing options into account, the judge then sentences the offender.

To this point, we have described a system of **front-end sentencing** by judges that mark the beginning of an offender's punishment. But another sanction, **back-end sentencing**, also merits attention. Back-end sentencing occurs when parolees are arrested for new crimes or violate the conditions of their parole and are returned to prison by state parole boards (Lin, Grattet, & Petersilia, 2010). Back-end sentencing is now responsible for approximately one-third of all prison admissions (Travis, 2007). Examination of these parole revocations shows that parole board officials, eager to protect themselves from public scorn, are especially harsh on sex offenders and serious and violent offenders, regardless of what these offenders did to violate their parole. Parole boards also consider offenders' gender and race when they ratchet penalties up and down (Lin et al., 2010). We discuss these sorts of implicit biases more thoroughly in the next section.

DETERMINANTS OF SENTENCING: RELEVANT AND IRRELEVANT

To what extent do judges, during sentencing, consider only factors relevant to the decision (e.g., seriousness of the crime committed) and to what extent do they also consider seemingly irrelevant factors like race, ethnicity, and gender? To answer this question, researchers have used a variety of procedures including observational studies, archival analyses of case records and sentencing statistics, interviews, and experiments in which they manipulate various facts in simulated cases or vignettes and ask sentencers to respond.

To be morally acceptable, punishment should be consistent with the seriousness of the crime. Sentences do correlate strongly with crime severity. Even in systems in which judges retain wide sentencing discretion, more serious crimes earn greater punishments, suggesting that judges focus on this important and relevant factor (Goodman-Delahunty & Sporer, 2010).

But factors other than the seriousness of the crime also influence sentencing. Should they? For example, should an offender's past be taken into account? Should it matter that a convicted offender was

deprived as a child, hungry, abused, and denied opportunities to go to school or look for work? An offender's criminal record is relevant in every jurisdiction, and most states require those with prior offenses to serve longer terms. California's famous "three strikes law" is an example. A third-time offender with two prior convictions for violent felonies can be sentenced to life imprisonment without parole, even if the third offense is minor (*Ewing v. California*, 2003), as the majority of them are.

Many people would agree that it shouldn't matter whether the defendant in any particular case is a man or woman; what should matter are the individual's criminal history and the seriousness of the offense. Indeed, determinate sentencing has evolved to ensure that extralegal factors such as the offender's race, social class, gender, or appearance do not result in variations in sentence length. But many of these factors, including the offender's gender and race, apparently influence sentencing decisions, often without conscious awareness of the judge. An archival analysis of cases involving 20,000 male and 3729 female offenders showed that females received less harsh sentences than males (Steffensmeier & Demuth, 2006). These gender effects vary according to the type of crime. Males are more likely than females to be sentenced to prison and serve longer sentences for property and drug offenses. But women are just as likely as men to be sentenced to prison for committing a violent offense (Rodriguez, Curry, & Lee, 2006).

What accounts for gender disparities? There is some evidence that they arise because judges' presentence reports contain a great deal of detail, which may be difficult to process. To manage the information overload, judges may rely on well-honed stereotypes and attributions about the case and the defendant's characteristics to aid their decisions (Steffensmeier & Demuth, 2006). According to the **focal concerns theory** of judicial decision making, judges focus on three main concerns in reaching sentencing decisions: (1) the defendant's culpability, (2) protection of the community (emphasizing incapacitation and general deterrence), and (3) practical constraints and consequences of the sentence, including concerns about disrupting ties to children and other family members.

Though it is not exactly clear how judges evaluate these focal concerns, evidence from field observations of sentencing hearings (Daly, 1994; Steffensmeier, Ulmer, & Kramer, 1998) suggests that judges may view most women as less likely to reoffend, understand women's crimes in the context of their own victimization (e.g., by coercive men, alcohol or drug problems), and perceive the social costs of detaining women as higher. In fact, judges now consider the social consequences of incarceration—particularly the effects on an offender's family—for both male and female offenders, and those who have familial caretaker roles are less likely to be incarcerated than those who are not caring for others (Freiburger, 2010).

Most of the research on the influence of gender on sentencing has focused on the gender of the *offender*, but crime victims' gender also has an impact on sentencing decisions. For example, among Texas offenders who were convicted of three violent crimes in 1991, offenders who victimized females received substantially longer sentences than those who victimized males (Curry, Lee, and Rodriguez, 2004). Because this analysis controlled for the type and severity of crime, the offenses perpetrated against women were not more serious or more deserving of a longer sentence. Rather, this difference may reflect some subtle form of sexism, paternalism, or an implicit belief that a female crime victim would suffer more than a male victim.

Another important demographic characteristic that influences sentencing decisions is the race of the offender. Determinate sentencing and sentencing guidelines have not been able to completely reduce racial disparity. A meta-analysis of the effects of race on sentencing decisions synthesized 71 separate studies and showed that African Americans were sentenced more harshly than Whites who committed comparable crimes (Mitchell, 2005). The disparity is larger for drug offenses (meaning that differences in sentence length for Blacks and Whites are larger for drug crimes than for other crimes). This situation may stem from media and political attention to the "crack epidemic" of the 1980s and 1990s, and public perception that the use and distribution of crack cocaine is associated with serious violent crime.

Psychologists have also wondered whether attribution theory and stereotypic beliefs of judges may explain the racial bias in sentencing decisions. According to attribution theory, people make assumptions about whether the cause of crime was a bad person or a bad environment and then convert their assumptions into sentencing decisions (Bridges & Steen, 1998). Judges may attribute the deviant behavior of minority offenders to negative attitudes and personality traits (rather than to environmental factors) and assume that these offenders are more likely

to repeat their crimes, thus believing that a longer sentence is more appropriate. Judges are not immune from stereotypical, superficial generalizations.

Another factor that influences judicial sentencing patterns is the way a conviction came about: whether by guilty plea or trial. Defendants who plead guilty are often given a reduced sentence, partly to encourage them to plead guilty and thereby reduce costs for court time and personnel. Using federal sentencing data for the years 2000–2002, Ulmer, Eisenstein, and Johnson (2010) determined that offenders who pled guilty received 15% shorter sentences than those convicted by trial. In addition to costing time and money, trials may also reveal more details pertaining to a defendant's blameworthiness and reduce his moral standing. One defense attorney explained that during trial, "you just sit here and think, 'You [the defendant] really should plead guilty because you're just such a jerk … and you're so arrogant and you're so unappreciative of the fact that you have nobody to blame but yourself, okay? Let's plead guilty, get up, cross your fingers behind your back, tell him [the judge] you're sorry, and cut your losses. Because the more he gets to see into your soul, the darker it's going to look for you" (Ulmer et al., p. 581).

Judges are human. When they have latitude in the punishments they can give, their backgrounds and personal characteristics may also influence their decisions (Tiede, Carp, & Manning, 2010). They may be prejudiced for or against certain groups—such as immigrants, antiwar protestors, or homosexuals. They may simply be uninformed. A Dallas judge told a reporter that he was giving a lighter sentence to a murderer because the victims were "queers." He was censured by the Texas State Commission on Judicial Conduct. A Maryland judge acquitted an alleged assailant on domestic violence charges after the victim failed to testify. He stated that one can't simply assume that a woman who is being hit didn't consent to the attack. "Sadomasochists sometimes like to get beat up," he said (Houppert, 2007).

SENTENCING JUVENILE OFFENDERS

The juvenile justice system differs from the adult system in some crucial ways. First, not all juveniles come into the system via arrests. Some are referred by school officials, social service agencies, or even by parents. Second, there is an emphasis on intervening with youthful offenders, rather than simply punishing them. Finally, early in a case, juvenile justice officials must decide whether to send it into the court system or divert the offender to alternative programs such as drug treatment, educational and recreational programs, or individual and group counseling.

If the choice is to involve the courts, then prosecutors recommend, or juvenile court judges decide, to transfer the case from juvenile court to criminal court. Sentencing procedures and options vary depending on whether the child is adjudicated in juvenile court or transferred to adult criminal court. Judges' beliefs about the deterrent effects of transfer—the possibility that juveniles will refrain from committing crimes because they fear being tried as adults—affect these decisions (Redding & Hensl, 2011). Surprisingly, more experienced judges see greater rehabilitative potential in juveniles and are less likely than inexperienced judges to transfer cases to criminal court.

Juvenile Court Dispositions

Nearly two-thirds of young people whose cases are adjudicated in juvenile court in 2007 were found to be delinquent (Puzzanchera, Adams, & Sickmund, 2010) and moved to the sentencing or **dispositional phase** of the case. Dispositional hearings typically combine adversarial procedures and attention to the particular needs—social, psychological, physical—of the child. They include "recommendations by probation and social workers; reports of social and academic histories; and interactions within the court among … the offender and his or her family, probation staff, and perhaps, psychologists and social workers" (Binder, Geis, & Bruce, 2001, p. 286). Issues of substance abuse, family dysfunction, mental health needs, peer relationships, and school problems may be addressed.

The goals of juvenile court dispositions—ensuring public safety and addressing children's needs—are reflected in the options available to juvenile court judges. These include (1) commitment to a secure facility; (2) probation, sometimes with intensive supervision; (3) referral to a group home or other lower security residential placement; (4) referral to day treatment or a mental health program; or (5) imposition of a fine, community service, or restitution.

When determining the appropriate disposition for a juvenile, judges may consider whether the parents are able to supervise the offender at home, assist in

rehabilitation efforts, and insist on school attendance. They may also consider the family's financial resources and the availability of community-based treatment programs and facilities (Campbell & Schmidt, 2000). In 2007, nearly 60% of juvenile offenders were sentenced to probation, and 25% were sentenced to some sort of out-of-home placement (Puzzanchera et al., 2010).

Juvenile court judges are also expected to assess offenders' rehabilitative needs and personal circumstances. Thus, one might expect that they would put considerable weight on offenders' psychosocial functioning, developmental maturity, responsibility taking, and gang involvement. But researchers who examined the effects of these factors on dispositional outcomes (i.e., probation and confinement) in a sample of 1,355 juvenile offenders found that legal factors (e.g., seriousness of the offense, whether the offender had prior court referrals) had the strongest influence on dispositions. Individual factors were not strongly linked to dispositional decisions (Cauffman et al., 2007). However, when judges adopt clinicians' recommendations for placement, they tend to put less weight on legal factors (O'Donnell & Lurigio, 2008).

Blended Sentencing

Juveniles who meet the criteria for transfer to adult criminal court are typically sentenced under **blended sentencing** statutes that combine the options available in juvenile court with those used in criminal court. These sentencing laws attempt to simultaneously address rehabilitation concerns and impose a "get tough" accountability (Redding & Mrozoski, 2005). In practice, this means that serious and violent young offenders can stay under juvenile court jurisdiction and receive more lenient sentences than if they were transferred to adult court. But they can also be subjected to harsh sentences if they commit new offenses, violate probation, or fail to respond to rehabilitation efforts (Trulson, Caudill, Belshaw, & DeLisi, 2011). Blended sentencing schemes provide incentives to offenders to avoid the more serious consequences of an adult sentence. Prosecutors often use the threat of transfer to adult criminal court to persuade juvenile offenders to plead guilty and accept a particular blended sentence (Podkopacz & Feld, 2001). Recent findings raise troubling questions about the effectiveness of blended sentencing, however, as roughly 50% of serious delinquents released early without continuing their sentence in adult prison were rearrested for a felony offense (Trulson, Haerle, DeLisi, & Marquart, 2011).

Life Sentences for Juvenile Offenders

Judges can also impose adult sanctions—sometimes very lengthy prison sentences—on offenders who were under 18 when they committed a serious crime. These sentences are a consequence of being tried as adults and convicted of murder or attempted murder. According to a report from the human rights organization Equal Justice Initiative, over 2,225 juveniles age 17 or younger have been sentenced to life imprisonment without parole in the United States; 73 of them were 13 or 14 when they committed their crimes (Equal Justice Initiative, 2007). But in 2012, the U.S. Supreme Court ruled that *mandatory* life sentences for juvenile offenders are unconstitutional (*Miller v. Alabama*, 2012).

These cases pit human rights and judicial reform advocates on the one hand against prosecutors and victims' rights groups on the other. Human rights groups argue that applying life-without-parole sentences to juveniles constitutes cruel and unusual punishment. Stephen Bright, director of the Southern Center for Human Rights, said, "It goes against human inclinations to give up completely on a young teenager.

It's impossible for a court to say that any 14-year-old never has the possibility to live in society." Prosecutors and victims groups say that such statutes are comforting to victims and make sense in their "adult-crime, adult-time" approach. But public sentiment is generally not supportive of life sentences for juveniles except in cases of murder (Greene & Evelo, 2011). We illustrate the complexity of these issues by describing the case of Jacob Ind, profiled on PBS's *Frontline* episode "When Kids Get Life," in Box 14.3.

SENTENCING SEX OFFENDERS

Many people believe that sex offenders are especially likely to reoffend, and therefore require different kinds of punishment than other offenders. But the truth is not so clear. A meta-analysis of 82 studies that traced the recidivism rates of 29,450 sex offenders up to six years postrelease (Hanson & Morton-Bourgon, 2005) showed that only 13.7% of sex offenders were arrested for another sexual offense in that period. Sexual deviancy and antisocial orientations (e.g., psychopathy, antisocial traits) were the

---

Box 14.3 THE CASE OF JACOB IND: WHEN A KID GETS LIFE

On the morning of December 17, 1992, 15-year-old Jacob Ind went to school in Woodland Park, Colorado, planning to tell a friend that he had just murdered his mother and stepfather and then to commit suicide. But the friend immediately went to the principal, who called the police, and 18 months later, Jacob was convicted of two counts of first-degree murder and sentenced to life without parole. According to Jacob's older brother, Charles, the murders ended years of physical and sexual abuse of both boys at the hands of their stepfather and of emotional betrayal by their mother. At Jacob's trial, Charles testified that their stepfather would wait for the boys to get home from school, then drag them into the bathroom, tie them with ropes to the toilet, and sexually molest them. Jacob claimed that his mother made it absolutely clear that she hated him and "[to] a child, that is more hurtful than getting hit across the face or getting beaten" (www.pbs.org).

Jacob Ind has now spent more than half his life in prison, including eight years in solitary confinement. (He was sent there shortly after arrival, when prison officials found a rope and a sharpened piece of rebar in his cell. The latter, he alleged, was for self-defense.) He has

earned a bachelor's degree in biblical studies and claims to be happier now than he ever imagined being. That's probably a good thing, considering the number of years he has left behind bars.

Critical Thought Question

Recent research on brain development shows that the adolescent brain is a work in progress, not fully mature with an intact frontal lobe—responsible for reasoning and judgment—until sometime between the ages of 25 and 30. Some psychologists (e.g., Scott & Steinberg, 2008) have argued that this means that adolescents are fundamentally different from adults and warrant differential treatment by the law. On the other hand, there is a great deal of variability in brain and behavioral development among same-aged teen-agers, and some older adolescents are comparable to young adults in psychological maturity. Should these factors be considered in determining the appropriate punishment for a juvenile offender? For Jacob Ind? Would your decision be affected by learning that psychologists are not particularly good at predicting adult functioning from snapshots of teenage behavior?

best predictors of sexual recidivism. The vast majority of convicted sex offenders were *not* rearrested for another sex crime within six years.

A 25-year follow-up study of sex offenders in Canada provides a more nuanced picture of sex offending patterns over many years. It found that the typical sex offender's criminal career spanned two decades, which suggests that recidivism can remain a problem over much of a sex offender's adult life (Langevin et al., 2004). Indeed, many sex offenders have committed more sex crimes than those for which they were arrested, so recidivism rates may underestimate actual rates of sexual offending.

There are several ways in which judges and corrections professionals treat sex offenders differently than other offenders, based on the belief that they are particularly likely to reoffend. Upon release from prison, sex offenders in many jurisdictions (1) are required to register with state officials, who then publicly notify the community about the location of the offender's residence; (2) are prohibited from living within certain distances of schools, day-care facilities, parks, and other locations frequented by children; and (3) can be involuntarily committed to a mental health facility following the completion of their sentence. In addition, sex offenders can be subjected to extraordinary sanctions, including enhanced sentences and mandatory treatments.

Registration and Notification

Convicted sex offenders are required to register with local law enforcement after they are released from prison and to notify authorities of subsequent changes of address. The period of required registration depends on the classification of the offender, which is a product of a formal risk assessment. In Kentucky, for example, high-risk offenders are required to register for life, whereas moderate- or low-risk offenders are required to register for 10 years after their formal sentence is completed. Unfortunately, many sex offenders do not register, and others fail to inform authorities when they move, and a lack of resources within jurisdictions hinders follow-up. One investigation revealed that California authorities have lost track of more than 33,000 sex offenders who were registered at one point (Curtis, 2003).

Notification is more controversial than registration. Community notification laws allow states to disseminate information about convicted sex offenders to the public. In some states (New Jersey, for example),

Steve Elwell, left, a registered sex offender in Cape May County, N.J., speaks out during a council meeting in opposition to a local ordinance that bans sex offenders from residing or loitering within 2,500 feet of schools and public areas.

police go door to door to notify neighbors that a high-risk sex offender has moved into the neighborhood (Witt & Barone, 2004). Most states and the federal government rely on the Internet as a means of notification. Typically, offenders' names are placed online for the period of their required registration, and law enforcement officials take no further steps to notify the community. But online notification appears to be plagued by the worst of two extremes. On the one hand, it is over-inclusive; the entire world can learn about the offender, even though only one or a few communities really need to know. On the other hand, online notification is under-inclusive; persons who cannot or do not regularly access the sex offender website will not be made aware of a sex offender living in the neighborhood.

Internet posting also raises serious concerns about invasion of privacy. No matter how minor the offense, states and the federal government post offenders' personal information (including their photos) online for all to see. A murderer could move to a new community, safe in the knowledge that his past, although a matter of public record, is not readily accessible to friends and neighbors. But a sex offender will know that his past is available to anyone in the world at the click of a mouse.

When someone learns that an offender is living nearby, the result may be public hysteria. After the community was notified about a released offender in Waterloo, Iowa, children started carrying bats and sticks as they walked to school; the recently released offender was threatened and was ultimately hounded out of the community (VanDuyn, 1999). Research shows that community notification has led to harassment and vigilantism directed at sex offenders, and has interfered with offenders' ability to find stable work and housing, important factors in reintegration into the community (Levenson & D'Amora, 2007). Furthermore, registration laws may also be ineffective. Enforcement of sex offender registration tends not to reduce the number of forcible rapes reported (Vasquez, Madden, & Walker, 2008), and as we describe in Box 14.4, does nothing to restrain some sex offenders from committing additional, horrific crimes.

Box 14.4 THE CASE OF JOHN ALBERT GARDNER III: REGISTERED SEX OFFENDER AND CONFESSED MURDERER

In 2000, 21-year-old John Albert Gardner III was convicted of luring a 13-year-old neighbor into his mother's home in an upscale community north of San Diego and punching and molesting the child. A psychiatrist who interviewed Gardner recommended a 30-year sentence, noting that Gardner lacked remorse and would continue to pose a danger to young women in the area. But prosecutors wanted to spare the victim from testifying and accepted a plea bargain that landed Gardner behind bars for five years. He was released in 2008 and registered as a sex offender.

Registration did little to quell Gardner's urges. Later that year he attempted to rape a jogger in a park near Escondido, California. Two months later, he killed 14-year-old Amber Dubois, who vanished while walking to school, and 17-year-old Chelsea King, whom Gardner admitted to raping and strangling in the same park. To avoid the death penalty, Gardner pleaded guilty to all of these crimes. King's parents championed legislation, fittingly named "Chelsea's Law," that allows life without parole sentences for offenders who kidnap, drug or use a weapon against a child and requires lifetime parole with GPS tracking for offenders who commit forcible sex crimes against children under age 14. Former Governor Arnold Schwarzenegger signed the law in 2010.

Convicted sex offender John Albert Gardner III

Critical Thought Question

Why, given that Gardner was registered as a sex offender and may have been listed on a sex offender registry website, would residents of surrounding communities have been unlikely to know that he was living nearby?

AP Photo/National Sex Offender Public web site

Residency Restrictions

In the best-selling novel *Lost Memory of Skin*, the main character is a young man, recently released from prison and on probation for soliciting an underage female, who is shackled to a GPS device and forbidden from living within 2,500 feet of places where children congregate. Though fictional, the story takes place in the all-too-real community of sex offenders that has sprung up under the Julia Tuttle Causeway in Miami.

One of the newest policy measures to manage the risk posed by sex offenders, residency restrictions have been enacted by most states and hundreds of communities. They establish a "buffer zone" in which sex offenders may not live around schools, parks, and even bus stops. Though the laws vary with regard to the size of the area, the group of offenders to whom they apply, and whether they also restrict places of employment, all such laws are premised on the idea that sex offenders are opportunistic and seek victims in public places. But an estimated 79–93% of sexual offenses are committed by a person known to the victim (Mercado, 2009), raising questions about the effectiveness of these laws. Residency restrictions result in other problems: they seriously reduce housing options in communities where nearly all residential properties are within the buffer zones (Chajewski & Mercado, 2009), and result in the clustering of sex offenders in more rural areas, making access to treatment more difficult and destabilizing offenders. Furthermore, they have not been shown to deter recidivism. Although residency restrictions may be a visible way for legislators to attempt to address sexual recidivism, empirical data suggest that they will have little impact.

Involuntary Commitment

Another form of sanction imposed on repeat sex offenders is involuntary commitment to a mental health facility after the prison term has been completed. Whereas prison sentences are intended to punish an offender for past bad acts, involuntary commitment is intended to protect the public from future harms.

The leading case on this topic is *Kansas v. Hendricks* (1997). Leroy Hendricks was "every parent's nightmare" (Kolebuck, 1998, p. 537). He was in his 60s when, in 1994, he was scheduled to be released from a Kansas prison where he had served 10 years for

child molestation, following a long history of sexually abusing children. In fact, he told a Kansas judge that only his death would guarantee that he would never commit another sexual offense on a child. Kansas had recently passed a Sexually Violent Predator (SVP) Act, allowing for the involuntary commitment of offenders suffering from a "mental abnormality" that would make them likely to commit predatory acts of sexual violence. A Kansas judge determined that Hendricks was a SVP and committed him to a mental hospital. (In *Kansas v. Hendricks*, the U.S. Supreme Court deemed the SVP Act to be constitutional.) After a decade-long stay in a sexual predator treatment program at a state hospital and in declining health, Hendricks was released to a supervised home setting in Lawrence, Kansas in 2005.

Professor Stephen Morse has raised concerns about the role of the *Hendricks* case in striking a balance between the due process and crime control models of criminal justice (Morse, 1998). He asserted that in its quest for public safety, society is now willing to punish people who are merely *at risk for* reoffending, in essence punishing them more severely than they deserve.

Yet, predictably, other states passed statutes similar to the Kansas statute. As of 2011, 20 states and the federal government had enacted some form of civil authorization for the involuntary commitment of sex offenders. Once such an individual is committed, release is rare. By 2007, almost 2,700 persons had been committed as SVPs, but only about 250 had been released, half on technical or legal grounds unrelated to treatment (Davey & Goodnough, 2007).

The Supreme Court's rulings on SVP laws make clear that selected individuals must have a "mental abnormality" or personality disorder that predisposes them to sexual violence and makes them oblivious to the prospect of further punishment (Slobogin, 2011). In making assessments of "mental abnormality," evaluators typically use the diagnostic criteria for pedophilia, paraphilia, or antisocial personality disorder set out in the *Diagnostic and Statistical Manual-IV* (Becker, Stinson, Tromp, & Messer, 2003).

The U.S. Supreme Court has also said that individuals subjected to SVP laws must be unable to control their behavior and thus, likely to commit future sexually violent crimes (*Kansas v. Crane*, 2002). How does one assess the likelihood of some possible event in the future? The risk of sexual reoffending is typically determined via formal risk assessment conducted around the time the offender is scheduled to be released from prison. They rely on measures of deviant sexual preferences and persistent antisocial behaviors. These tests compare a given individual to individuals who have similar characteristics and for whom the rates of recidivism are known. Several specialized actuarial measures or structured professional judgment measures have now been validated on sex offender populations (Otto & Douglas, 2010) and have been shown to be more accurate than clinical judgments (Hanson & Morton-Bourgon, 2009). Obviously, these instruments cannot predict with certainty that a given individual will behave in any particular way, but especially when combined with individualized clinical risk assessments, they can be quite useful in gauging the likelihood of future behavior (Slobogin, 2011).

Mandated Treatments for Sex Offenders

Unlike other offenders, sex offenders are often required to undergo treatment designed to "cure" them of their antisocial tendencies. Offenders sentenced to prison are required to participate in offender treatment programs or give up hope of parole. Offenders offered probation are required to participate in counseling sessions. These typically involve cognitive-behavioral interventions that require offenders to acknowledge wrongdoing and that challenge their rationalizations, minimizations (e.g., "no one was hurt"), and other erroneous beliefs that support the commission of the offense. Treatment may also include an assortment of behavior modification techniques, including aversive conditioning that pairs aversive stimuli such as mild electric shock with deviant sexual responses. Over time, the deviant behavior is expected to decrease. Treatment programs that focus on an offender's risk of reoffending and responsiveness to treatment have been successful in reducing recidivism (Hanson, Bourgon, Helmus, & Hodgson, 2009).

Some treatment programs have effectively reduced sexual offending by suppressing offenders' sex drive. This pharmacological approach, sometimes called **chemical castration**, involves administering hormones to reduce testosterone levels and thereby lower sex drive, sexual arousal, and sexual fantasizing. Therapists have also had some success using selective serotonin reuptake inhibitors (SSRIs) to reduce deviant sexual behavior. This class of drugs may reduce intrusive or obsessive thoughts associated with sexual offending (Marshall, Fernandez, Marshall, & Serran, 2006).

In the past, judges have sometimes given convicted sex offenders a choice: prison or hormone treatment. It is not surprising that some men have opted for the drugs, even though the possible side effects include lethargy, hot flashes, nightmares, hypertension, and shortness of breath (Keene, 1997).

California was the first state to pass a law requiring repeat child molesters (**pedophiles**) to be treated with hormones as a condition of parole. The California statute requires that clinicians assess offenders to determine whether they suffer from a condition (e.g., pedophilia) that creates a substantial risk of reoffending. If so, the California legislature reasoned, it makes sense to deny parole unless the offender agrees to the treatment. At the time the California Chemical Castration Bill was being considered, Assemblyman Bill Hoge, one of its sponsors, reasoned as follows:

> What we're up against is the kind of criminal who, just as soon as he gets out of jail, will immediately commit this crime again at least 90% of the time. So why not give these people a shot to calm them down and bring them under control? (Ayres, 1996, p. A1)

Although Assemblyman Hoge clearly overstated the probability of reoffending, there may be a certain logic in requiring sex offenders to take a drug that diminishes their sex drive.

THE DEATH PENALTY: THE ULTIMATE PUNISHMENT

The ultimate punishment, of course, is death. Citizens of the United States can be executed by the federal government and by the governments of 35 states. But capital punishment has had a controversial and volatile history in this country. Although a majority of Americans apparently favor capital punishment, and politicians and appellate judges have tended to make decisions that reflect that belief (Ogloff & Chopra, 2004), support for capital punishment may be waning. A 2010 Gallup Poll showed that when offered the choice between capital punishment and life imprisonment without the possibility of parole, only a slight majority of respondents favored the former (Gallup, 2011). The American Bar Association has called for a nationwide moratorium on capital punishment, citing concerns about the way the death penalty is administered. In 2011, Oregon Governor John Kitzhaber stated that he would not allow executions in his state during his term in office. A licensed physician, Kitzhaber noted that he had taken an oath to "do no harm" and deemed executions "morally wrong." In recent years, three states—New Jersey, New Mexico, and New York—have abolished the death penalty, and legislatures in several other states are considering that option. In late 2012, California voters will decide whether to replace capital punishment with life imprisonment.

The modern history of capital punishment in the United States began in 1972 when the U.S. Supreme Court effectively abolished the death penalty on the grounds that it constituted "cruel and unusual punishment" (*Furman v. Georgia*, 1972). After the *Furman* case, state legislatures revised their death penalty laws to address the Court's concern that capital punishment was being applied in an arbitrary and discriminatory fashion as a consequence of the "unbridled discretion" in sentencing given to juries.

To remedy this problem, states passed statutes that guided the sentencing discretion of juries in death penalty cases. (Whereas judges determine most criminal sentences, the choice between life and death in a capital case is made by a jury.) First, legislators made only certain crimes eligible for the death penalty. Second, they changed the structure of capital trials. Now, if a defendant is charged with one of these crimes, the trial is conducted in two phases. The jury decides the guilt or innocence of the defendant in the first phase (the "guilt phase"). If the defendant is found guilty, then the second phase, or "sentencing phase," of the trial is held. During this phase, the jury hears evidence of **aggravating factors** (elements of the crime, such as killing in an especially brutal or heinous manner, that make the defendant more likely to receive a death sentence) and **mitigating factors** (elements of the defendant's background or the crime, such as experiencing mental illness or acting under duress at the time of the offense, that make life imprisonment the more appropriate verdict). Specific aggravating and mitigating factors are listed in the statutes, but a jury is not required to consider only those factors in its deliberations. Before reaching a sentencing decision, jurors hear instructions from the judge on how to weigh the aggravating and mitigating factors. Generally, a jury cannot vote for a death sentence unless it determines that the prosecution has proven at least one aggravating factor. However, even if it decides that one or more aggravating factors were present, it may still, after considering the mitigating factors, return a sentence of life imprisonment.

Gurney on which the prisoner is executed by lethal injection

AP Photo/Wide World Photos

In 1976, in the case of *Gregg v. Georgia*, and in response to these newly enacted laws and procedures, the Supreme Court reinstituted the possibility of the death penalty. Since that time, the Court has issued many death penalty opinions, focusing often on the behavior of juries in death penalty cases (Haney & Wiener, 2004).

Following the *Gregg* decision, state after state began to execute those convicts who had been sentenced to die. The first to be executed, on January 17, 1977, was Gary Gilmore, in Utah, who gave up his right to challenge his conviction and resisted the efforts of his relatives to save him from the firing squad. (In 2010, Ronnie Lee Gardner was also executed by firing squad, telling a Utah judge "I lived by the gun, I murdered with a gun, so I will die by the gun.") Since the death penalty was reinstated in 1976, nearly 7,500 people have been sentenced to death and more than 1,225 people have been executed. The greatest number (98) were executed in 1999, and the rate of executions has declined since then. In 2010, 38 inmates were executed (Death Penalty Information Center, 2010). More than 80% of executions have occurred in southern states, and Texas alone accounts for more than one-third of them.

Concerns about Innocence

We do not know exactly how many innocent people have been sentenced to death. One estimate is that 2.3% of those sentenced to death may actually be innocent (Gross & O'Brien, 2008). Another estimate puts the figure at 5% (Risinger, 2007). We also do not know exactly how many innocent people have been executed, though some have. David Protess, a Northwestern University journalism professor, drew attention to the possibility of "executing the innocent" when students under his supervision tracked down and obtained confessions from true killers, thereby exonerating two men on death row. These investigations uncovered other instances of conviction of the innocent, and 13 inmates were ultimately exonerated from death row in Illinois, leading to Governor George Ryan's decision to commute the death sentences of all remaining Illinois death row inmates (Marshall, 2002). According to Ryan, "Our capital system is haunted by the demon of error: error in determining guilt and error in determining who among the guilty deserves to die."

The moratorium on executions gained momentum from a large-scale study, "A Broken System: Error Rates in Capital Cases" (Liebman, 2000). This study analyzed every capital conviction in the United States between 1973 and 1995 and revealed that serious mistakes had been made in two-thirds of the cases, a startling indictment of the criminal justice system. The most common problems included incompetent defense attorneys (37%), faulty jury instructions (20%), and misconduct on the part of prosecutors (19%). Of those defendants whose capital sentence was overturned because of an error, 82% received a sentence less than death at their retrials, including 7% who were found not guilty of the capital crime with which they had originally been charged.

Since executions resumed after the *Gregg* case, 138 people have been freed from death rows upon proof of their innocence (Death Penalty Information Center, 2010). Some of these condemned individuals were cleared when new evidence came to light or when witnesses changed their stories. DNA evidence is credited with proving the innocence of scores of death row inmates in the United States (Gross, Jacoby, Matheson, Montgomery, & Patil, 2005). Many of these cases involved defendants who had originally been convicted on the basis of faulty eyewitness identifications or false confessions.

As a result of these widely publicized errors, a number of states give death row inmates the right to postconviction DNA testing, though the Supreme Court has ruled that states are not required to do so (*District Attorney's Office for Third Judicial District v. Osborne*, 2009). In 2004, Congress established a grant program to help states defray the costs of such testing. The grant program bears the name of Kirk Bloodsworth, the first death row inmate exonerated by DNA testing. We tell his story in Box 14.5.

Not all cases end as satisfactorily as Bloodsworth's did. Consider the case of Todd Willingham, executed by the state of Texas in 2004 for allegedly setting a house fire that killed his three daughters. During Willingham's trial, forensic experts claimed that the fire had been intentionally set, yet well prior to Willingham's execution nationally recognized independent arson investigators questioned the validity of the scientific analysis used to convict him. They concluded that the fire was accidental (Grann, 2009).

Is the death penalty still justified if we know that innocent people have been executed? Some proponents

---

B o x 14.5 THE CASE OF KIRK BLOODSWORTH: THE WORTH OF HIS BLOOD AND HIS EXONERATION ON DEATH ROW

A Marine veteran, Kirk Bloodsworth had never been in trouble with the law when, in 1985, he was convicted of the rape and murder of a 9-year-old girl who had been strangled, raped, and beaten with a rock. Bloodsworth was sentenced to die in Maryland's gas chamber. Bloodsworth's arrest was based in part on an identification by an eyewitness from a police sketch that was compiled from the recollections of five other eyewitnesses. At trial, all five eyewitnesses testified that they had seen Bloodsworth with the victim. All were wrong.

In 1992, prosecutors in the case agreed to DNA testing in which blood found on the victim's clothing was compared to her own blood and to Bloodsworth's; testing excluded Bloodsworth as the perpetrator, and he was released from prison in 1993. DNA evidence ultimately led police to the true killer, Kimberly Ruffner, who was arrested in 2003. In an ironic twist to the story, Bloodsworth had known Ruffner in prison. When Ruffner was arrested, Bloodsworth was quoted as saying, "My God, I know him. He lifted weights for us. I spotted weights for him." (Levine, 2003, A01)

Kirk Bloodsworth (at left), the first death row inmate exonerated by DNA testing, being introduced at a rally

Critical Thought Question
Why do you suspect that Bloodsworth was wrongly convicted? Why do you suspect that he was sentenced to death?

---

insist that it is, invoking the analogy that administering a vaccine is justified even though a child might have an adverse—even lethal—reaction to it. Proponents of capital punishment suggest that even though innocent people are occasionally and mistakenly put to death, other compelling reasons justify maintaining this system of punishment.

Justifications for the Death Penalty

Many reasons have been advanced for endorsing the irrevocable penalty of death. While he was the mayor of New York City, Ed Koch contended that the death penalty "affirms life." By failing to execute murderers, he said, we "signal a lessened regard for the value of the victim's life" (quoted in Bruck, 1985, p. 20).

Most justifications for the death penalty reflect retributive beliefs (e.g., "an eye for an eye") and thus extend beyond the capacity of empirical research to prove or disprove. But a testable argument for capital punishment is the expectation that it will act as a deterrent to criminal activity. Proponents of this position suggest that (1) the death penalty accomplishes general, as well as specific, deterrence; (2) highly publicized executions have at least a short-term deterrent effect; and (3) murderers are such dangerous people that allowing them to live increases the risk of injury or death to other inmates and prison guards.

Using a variety of empirical approaches, social scientists have evaluated the deterrent effects of the death penalty, and their studies consistently lead to the conclusion that the death penalty does not affect the rate of crimes of violence (e.g., Zimring, Fagan, & Johnson, 2010). Evidence also contradicts the view that murderers are especially dangerous inmates. A good deal of data indicates that capital murderers tend to commit fewer violent offenses and prison infractions than parole-eligible inmates (Cunningham, 2010).

Not only is there little support for the deterrent effects of capital punishment, but some researchers contend that capital punishment actually *increases* crime, an effect known as **brutalization**. Brutalization theorists argue that executions increase violent crime by sending the message that it is acceptable to kill those who have wronged us. However, the evidence in support of brutalization effects is no stronger than the data in favor of deterrence (Radelet & Akers, 1996).

Equality versus Discretion in Application of the Death Penalty

Does the death penalty further the goal of equal treatment before the law? About a third of the states, plus the District of Columbia, do not permit it, and vastly different rates of executions occur in states that do. For example, even though the state of New Hampshire has the death penalty, no one has been executed or even sent to death row in that state since the penalty was reestablished. As we have noted, more than a third of all executions in the United States since 1977 have taken place in one state—Texas. So if equal treatment is the goal, it is safe to say that capital punishment has not furthered that goal. The death penalty is administered in only a minority of states and within those states, only in a subset of eligible cases. Furthermore, its determinants often seem inconsistent and unpredictable.

One concern is the issue of race. The victims of intentional homicide are equally divided between Blacks and Whites, yet the chance of a death sentence is much greater for criminals who kill Whites than those who kill Blacks. In fact, data from governmental and capital defense organizations show that between the late 1970s and the early 2000s, there was tremendous racial disparity in death sentences. So, for example, between 1990 and 1999, California offenders who killed Whites were more than three times more likely to receive the death penalty than offenders who killed Blacks, and more than four times more likely than offenders who killed Latinos (Pierce & Radelet, 2005).

The leading Supreme Court case on the issue of race and application of the death penalty, *McCleskey v. Kemp* (1987), considered this issue. The question was whether the death penalty discriminated against persons who murdered Whites. We describe McCleskey's case in Box 14.6.

Psychologists have determined that not all Black offenders are equally likely to be sentenced to death for killing a White person. Professor Jennifer Eberhardt and her colleagues showed to Stanford undergraduates the photographs of 44 Black offenders whose trials advanced to the penalty phase in Philadelphia between 1979 and 1999, and asked them to rate the stereotypicality of each offender's appearance. Controlling for other factors that influence sentencing, such as the severity of the murder and the defendant's and victim's socioeconomic status, researchers found that offenders whose appearance was rated as

---

Box 14.6 THE CASE OF WARREN McCLESKEY: DOES RACE MATTER?

Warren McCleskey, a Black man, was convicted in 1978 of armed robbery and the murder of a White police officer who had responded to an alarm while the robbery was in progress. McCleskey was sentenced to die in Georgia's electric chair. He challenged the constitutionality of the death penalty on the ground that it was administered in a racially discriminatory manner in Georgia. In the words of one of his attorneys, "When you kill the organist at the Methodist Church, who is White, you're going to get the death penalty, but if you kill the Black Baptist organist, the likelihood is that it will be plea bargained down to a life sentence" (quoted in Noble, 1987, p. 7).

The foundation for McCleskey's appeal was a comprehensive study of race and capital sentencing in the state of Georgia conducted by David Baldus, a law professor at the University of Iowa, and his colleagues. They analyzed the race of the offender and the race of the victim for about 2,000 murder and manslaughter convictions from 1973 to 1979 and concluded that those who killed Whites were 11 times more likely to receive the death penalty than those who killed Blacks (Baldus, Pulaski, & Woodworth, 1983). Anticipating the argument that the heinousness of the murders may explain this finding, Baldus and colleagues eliminated cases in which extreme violence or other aggravating circumstances virtually ensured the death penalty and cases in which overwhelming mitigating circumstances almost guaranteed a life sentence. For the remaining cases—which permitted the greatest jury discretion—they found that defendants were about four times more likely to be sentenced to death if their victims were White. Similar patterns have been reported for capital sentencing in several other states (Nietzel, Hasemann, & McCarthy, 1998).

Despite the mass of statistical evidence, the Supreme Court upheld McCleskey's death sentence. Because there was no evidence that individual jurors in his trial were biased, the Court was unwilling to assume that McCleskey's jury valued a White life more than a Black life.

Critical Thought Question

What legally irrelevant factors in McCleskey's case—in addition to the race of the victim—may have increased the likelihood that he would be sentenced to die for his crime?

more stereotypically Black were more likely to have received the death penalty than offenders whose appearance was less stereotypical (Eberhardt, Davies, Purdie-Vaughns, & Johnson, 2006). Apparently offenders' appearance can also lead to unequal treatment in the administration of capital punishment.

Capital Jury Decision Making

The *Furman* and *Gregg* cases, pivotal challenges to the constitutionality of the death penalty, focused attention on the role of the jury in capital cases. For this reason, it is not surprising that there has been intense public and scientific scrutiny of three important aspects of capital jury decision making: the racial composition of capital juries, the process of selecting jurors in capital cases, and the ability of those jurors to understand and apply the sentencing instructions they receive from the judge.

Racial Composition of Capital Juries. Psychologists have recently determined that not all jurors are equally likely to sentence a Black defendant to death. In simulated penalty-phase trials in which participants heard and saw trial evidence and jury instructions and then deliberated in small-group "juries," White male jurors were more likely than non-White and female jurors to vote to execute a Black defendant. This difference stems from the fact that White men are less able or inclined to empathize with a Black defendant. So during deliberations, these jurors tend to undermine a jury's willingness to consider mitigating factors (Lynch & Haney, 2011).

How Jurors are Selected in Capital Cases: "Death Qualification". During jury selection in cases in which the prosecutor seeks a death penalty, prospective jurors are required to answer questions about their attitudes toward capital punishment. This procedure is called **death qualification**. If jurors indicate extreme beliefs about the death penalty, they may be excused "for cause"—that is, dismissed from that case. More precisely, prospective jurors are excluded if their opposition to capital punishment would "prevent or substantially impair the performance of [their] duties as juror[s] in accordance with [their] instructions and [their] oath" (*Wainwright v. Witt*, 1985, p. 424). Prospective jurors dismissed for this reason are termed *excludables*, and those who remain are termed *death qualified*. (Another group of prospective jurors—those who would automatically impose

the death penalty at every opportunity—so-called "automatic death penalty" jurors—are also dismissed for cause, although they are fewer in number than "excludables.") Death-qualified jurors are qualified to impose the death penalty because they do not hold strong scruples or reservations about its use.

Death qualification raises some important questions. Recall that capital cases involve two phases but only one jury to decide both guilt and punishment. Although excludable jurors might be unwilling to impose the death penalty, many could fairly determine the guilt or innocence of the defendant. Yet death qualification procedures deny them the opportunity to make a decision. These procedures also raise concerns about the leanings of jurors who *do* assess guilt.

Intuitively, one might expect that death-qualified juries (those made up of people who are not opposed to the death penalty) would be somewhat more conviction prone than the general population. Indeed, research studies have demonstrated the conviction-proneness of death-qualified juries. Cowan, Thompson, and Ellsworth (1984) showed a filmed trial to mock jurors who were either death qualified or excludable, and who were then divided into juries. About half of the juries were composed entirely of death-qualified jurors; the others contained a few excludables. Three-fourths of the death-qualified juries found the defendant guilty, as did only 53% of the juries with excludable jurors. The "mixed" juries took a more serious approach to their deliberations, and were more critical of witnesses and better able to remember the evidence.

Death-qualified jurors differ from the general population in other important ways. They tend "to interpret evidence in a way more favorable to the prosecution and less favorable to the defense" (Thompson, Cowan, Ellsworth, & Harrington, p. 104), and are more upset about acquitting a guilty defendant than excludable jurors. Finally, as one's support for the death penalty increases, so do one's negative attitudes toward women, homophobic sentiments, and racist beliefs (Butler, 2007). Although these attitudes may not *overtly* affect jurors' judgments in capital cases, they could exert subtle and less conscious influences on the way that jurors process evidence and assess witness credibility.

Death qualification studies have consistently indicated that death-qualified juries are more disposed toward conviction than juries that include jurors with scruples against the death penalty. Lawyers for

Ardia McCree made that point before the U.S. Supreme Court (*Lockhart v. McCree*, 1986). At McCree's trial in Arkansas, the judge excluded eight prospective jurors who said that they could not, under any circumstances, impose a death sentence. McCree was convicted and sentenced to death. He appealed his conviction by arguing that the process of death qualification produced juries that were likely to be conviction prone and unrepresentative of the larger community (Bersoff, 1987).

In spite of the substantial body of empirical support for McCree's position, the Supreme Court held that the jury in McCree's trial was not an improper one. On the issue of representativeness, they noted that the only requirement was to have representative *venires*, not necessarily to have representative juries. Exclusion of groups who were "defined solely in terms of shared attitudes" was not improper.

The majority also rejected the claim that death-qualified juries were less than neutral in determining guilt and innocence. An impartial jury, Chief Justice William Rehnquist wrote, "consists of nothing more than jurors who will conscientiously apply the law and find the facts." He noted that McCree conceded that each of the jurors who convicted him met that test. Accordingly, the Supreme Court upheld the state's use of a death-qualified jury for the decision at the guilt phase.

How Capital Jurors Use Instructions. Jurors in capital cases receive a set of complex instructions that outline their duties and explain how to evaluate and weigh aggravating and mitigating circumstances to reach a sentencing decision. Several studies indicate that jurors do not adequately comprehend the instructions they receive about mitigating factors because, like other types of judicial instructions, mitigation instructions are couched in legal jargon and are unusually lengthy and grammatically complex (Lynch & Haney, 2009; Smith & Haney, 2011).

If jurors do not understand a judge's instructions about mitigation, they are more likely to rely on other, more familiar factors to guide their verdicts, such as the heinousness of the crime or extralegal considerations such as racial stereotypes, sympathy for victims, or the expertise of the lawyers. The race of the defendant and victim also appear to affect sentences to a significantly greater extent when comprehension of instructions is low. In a study by Lynch and Haney (2000), jury-eligible participants with poor comprehension of

instructions recommended death 68% of the time for Black-defendant/White-victim cases versus 36% of the time for White-defendant/Black-victim cases. Among participants who comprehended the sentencing instructions well, neither the race of the defendant nor that of the victim affected the sentences.

Jurors have particular difficulty understanding how to evaluate mitigating evidence presented during the sentencing phase of a capital case. Margaret Stevenson and colleagues analyzed the content of jury deliberations in a mock capital trial in which there was mitigating evidence that the defendant had been abused as a child. Approximately 40% of jurors relied on evidence of childhood maltreatment to argue for a life sentence, and approximately 60% either ignored it as a mitigating factor or used it as an aggravating factor to argue for a death sentence. They reasoned that being abused as a child increases the likelihood of violent behavior as an adult (Stevenson, Bottoms, Diamond, Stec, & Pimentel, 2008).

Would jurors fare better if these all-important instructions were presented in a different format? Richard Wiener and his colleagues posed this question. They tested various methods of improving jurors' **declarative knowledge** (their understanding of legal concepts) and **procedural knowledge** (their ability to know what to do in order to reach a sentencing decision) in a highly realistic trial simulation (Wiener et al., 2004). Their study involved both the guilt and sentencing phases of a capital murder trial based on an actual case, used death-qualified community members as jurors, and included jury deliberations. The modifications to the instructions involved (1) simplifying the language of the instructions, (2) presenting the instructions in a flowchart format so that jurors could understand the progression of decisions they were expected to make, (3) giving jurors the chance to review and practice using the instructions in a mock case so that they would gain some experience prior to the real trial, and (4) offering corrections to common misconceptions that jurors have about aggravating and mitigating circumstances. For example:

> [Some] people believe that an aggravating circumstance is a factor that aggravated or provoked the defendant to kill the victim. This definition is based on the common use of the word aggravation. However, this in an incorrect definition of aggravating circumstance and should not be used in imposing a sentence upon the defendant.

Each of these modifications was helpful in enhancing some aspect of jurors' declarative and procedural knowledge in capital cases.

Limiting Use of the Death Penalty

Another highly controversial aspect of the death penalty is its use in cases where the defendant, for reasons of mental illness, youth, or limited mental abilities, may not be fully culpable. In recent years, the Supreme Court has deemed the death penalty unconstitutional in cases involving defendants who are mentally retarded or mentally ill, or were under 18 years of age at the time of the murder. Psychologists often play a significant role in cases involving these defendants, evaluating and rendering expert opinions on questions concerning defendants' cognitive abilities and whether they meet diagnostic criteria for various psychiatric disorders.

Mental Retardation. In 1996, Daryl Atkins abducted and killed an airman from the Langley Air Force Base in Virginia. He was convicted and sentenced to death. His appeal to the U.S. Supreme Court focused on his limited mental abilities. In its opinion in the *Atkins* case (*Atkins v. Virginia*, 2002), the Supreme Court referred to definitions of *mental retardation* of the American Association of Mental Retardation and the American Psychiatric Association (*DSM-IV*). These definitions are based on three criteria: (1) manifestation prior to age 18; (2) below-average functioning in at least two adaptive skill areas such as communication, use of community resources, or work; and (3) an IQ level below 70–75. (Atkins's IQ was measured at different times as 59, 67, 74, and 76.)

Noting that many states prohibit the execution of the mentally retarded, the Supreme Court acknowledged that applying the death penalty to people with mental retardation does not further the legitimate goals of deterrence and retribution. The Court therefore declared that it was cruel and unusual punishment, in violation of the Eighth Amendment, to execute mentally retarded individuals (*Atkins v. Virginia*, 2002). This landmark ruling reflects awareness that those with mental retardation often cannot understand the consequences of their actions, the complex and abstract concepts involved in criminal law, or the finality of a death sentence.

Although the Court deemed such executions unconstitutional, it deferred judgment about whether

Daryl Atkins, defendant in Supreme Court case on execution of the mentally retarded

Atkins fit Virginia's definition of mental retardation. Thus, Atkins became one of the first death row inmates to have a jury trial on the question of whether he had mental retardation. If a jury were to deem him retarded, he would be spared the death penalty and sentenced to life imprisonment. Some of the evidence at Atkins's trial focused on his IQ.

One problem associated with reliance on IQ scores to assess mental retardation is that they are known to fluctuate over time (Ceci, Scullin, & Kanaya, 2003), just as Atkins's scores did. In fact, Evan Nelson, a clinical psychologist who tested Atkins in 1998 and 2004, surmised that his scores rose "as the result of a forced march towards increased mental stimulation provided by the case itself" (Liptak, 2005a). According to Dr. Nelson, "Oddly enough, because of his constant contact with the many lawyers that worked on his case, Mr. Atkins received more intellectual stimulation in prison than he did during his late adolescence and early adulthood." (Indeed, Atkins had dropped out of school after failing in his third attempt to pass 10th grade.)

In a 2005 trial in which the defense portrayed Atkins's capabilities as so limited that he was cut from the football team because he could not understand the plays, and the prosecution blamed his poor performance on alcohol and drugs, the jury decided that Atkins was *not* mentally retarded. But in the end, despite years of litigation, Atkins's sentence was commuted to life imprisonment because of prosecutorial misconduct.

Youthful Offenders. In the 18th and 19th centuries, death sentences were rarely carried out on children who were under 14 years of age at the time of the crime, but there was little reluctance to execute those who were 16 or 17 when the crime was committed. Of 287 juveniles executed in the United States prior to 1982, 248 were either 16 or 17 when they committed the offense for which they were executed (Streib, 1983).

In 1988, the Supreme Court drew the line at age 16, reasoning that contemporary standards of decency bar the execution of a child who was under age 16 at the time of the offense (*Thompson v. Oklahoma*, 1988). This ruling effectively allowed executions of those who were 16 or 17 when they committed their crimes. But even this standard was relatively short-lived, because the Court determined, in 2005, that it was cruel and unusual to execute any person who was younger than 18 at the time of the crime (*Roper v. Simmons*, 2005).

In his majority opinion in the *Roper* case, Justice Anthony Kennedy looked to the "evolving standards of decency that mark the progress of a maturing society." By that measure, the practice of executing juveniles had become outdated and even rare. In 2005, only 19 states allowed executions of convicted murderers who were under 18 at the time of the crime, and the United States was one of only a handful of countries in the world that condoned this practice.

Justice Kennedy also referred to psychological research findings concerning differences between juveniles and adults (e.g., Steinberg & Scott, 2003). He noted that "as any parent knows and as the scientific … studies … tend to confirm," young people lack maturity and the sense of responsibility of most adults, act in impetuous ways, and make ill-considered decisions. He commented on juveniles' vulnerability or susceptibility to negative influences and outside pressures, including peer pressure, and the fact that their characters are less well formed than those of adults. He concluded that "from a moral standpoint, it would be misguided to equate the failings of a minor with those of an adult, for a greater possibility exists that a minor's character deficiencies will be reformed" (*Roper v. Simmons*, 2005). The practical effect of sparing a youthful offender from execution is a life sentence without parole—potentially a very lengthy period of incarceration with little chance for redemption or release.

Mental Illness and Execution. Is it cruel and unusual punishment to execute an inmate who, due to mental illness, lacks a rational understanding of why he is being put to death? That was the question posed to the U.S. Supreme Court in the case of *Panetti v. Quarterman* (2007). (Earlier, in *Ford v. Wainwright* [1986], the Supreme Court held that it was unconstitutional to execute those who are incompetent for execution, but did not define the test for competence for execution.) In 1992, Scott Panetti killed his estranged wife's parents, with whom his wife had been living in Fredericksburg, Texas, and held his wife and 3-year-old daughter hostage in a lengthy police standoff. Panetti had a history of psychiatric problems prior to his conviction, including 14 hospital stays over 11 years. During earlier stages of the case, four mental health professionals agreed that Panetti suffered from impaired cognitive processes and delusions consistent with schizoaffective disorder. Scott Panetti believed that the government was executing him to prevent him from preaching the Gospel, not because he murdered his in-laws. Thus, the question for the Supreme Court was whether a person with serious mental illness, who may not understand the reason for his execution, can still be put to death.

The American Psychological Association (APA) teamed with the National Alliance on Mental Illness to assist the Court in developing standards for determining what level of mental illness should exempt an offender from execution. In its *amicus curiae* brief to the Supreme Court, the APA distinguished factual understanding from rational understanding. According to one of the authors of this book who consulted on the APA brief (Heilbrun), "factual understanding is about information. Rational understanding allows us to place that information in a meaningful context, without gross interference caused by certain symptoms of severe mental illness, or very serious impairment of intellectual functioning" (Medical News Today, 2007). The APA brief explained that some individuals who suffer from psychotic disorders have bizarre delusions that disrupt their understanding of reality and make it difficult or impossible for them to connect their criminal acts to punishment. The Supreme Court ruled that Panetti's delusions may have prevented him from understanding the reason for his punishment. That decision effectively means that defendants may not be executed if they do not understand *why* they are being put to death.

SUMMARY

1. ***What are the purposes of punishment?*** Punishment is associated with seven purposes: general deterrence, individual deterrence, incapacitation, retribution, expression of moral outrage, rehabilitation, and restitution. Although many citizens favor the punitive approaches of retribution and incapacitation, recidivism data suggest that they may not be effective. A new perspective on punishment, restorative justice, brings people together to repair the damage caused by wrongdoing.

2. ***How are the values of discretion and fairness reflected in sentencing decisions?*** The allocation of punishments is second only to the determination of guilt or innocence in importance to the criminal defendant. The sentencing process reflects many of the conflicts that permeate a psychological approach to the legal system. Historically, judges were given broad discretion in sentencing. Some judges were much more severe than the norm; others were more lenient. In recent years, concern over sentencing disparity led to greater use of determinate sentencing and tighter controls over judicial discretion in sentencing. Now, sentencing guidelines are merely advisory, however.

3. ***What factors influence sentencing decisions?*** Determinants of sentencing can be divided into relevant and irrelevant factors. For example, seriousness of the crime is a relevant factor, and there is a general relationship between it and the severity of the punishment. An offender's criminal history is another relevant determinant of the sentence. But a number of other, less relevant factors also are related to severity of sentence, such as race and gender of the offender and race and gender of the victim.

4. ***What special factors are considered in the sentencing of juveniles? Of recidivist sex offenders?*** Sentences for juvenile offenders are influenced by the jurisdiction in which the minor is sentenced (juvenile court, criminal court), the seriousness of the offense, the offender's rehabilitative needs, and professionals' recommendations. Because they are believed to be at high risk for reoffending, sex offenders have been singled out for special punishment including mandatory registration and community notification, residency restrictions, involuntary commitment, and enhanced sentences and treatments such as chemical castration.

5. ***How is the death penalty decided by juries?*** Jurors who oppose the death penalty regardless of the nature of the crime or the circumstances of the case are excluded from both the guilt phase and the sentencing phase of capital trials. Social science research has shown that the remaining so-called death-qualified jurors are conviction prone. But the Supreme Court has not been responsive to these findings. Capital juries tend to misunderstand their instructions, particularly regarding mitigating evidence. Finally, White male jurors are especially unsympathetic toward Black defendants in capital cases.

6. ***How has the Supreme Court limited the use of capital punishment, and what role have psychologists played in these decisions?*** The Supreme Court has deemed the death penalty unconstitutional in cases in which the defendant is mentally retarded or younger than 18 at the time of the crime. The Supreme Court has also indicated that executing those with mental illness may violate the Eighth Amendment if such defendants do not understand the reasons for their execution. Psychologists have been involved in these cases to assess offenders' cognitive abilities, diagnose mental illness, and provide data to the court about juveniles' decision making and judgment.

KEY TERMS

aggravating factors

anchoring

assimilated

back-end sentencing

blended sentencing

brutalization

chemical castration

death qualification

declarative knowledge

determinate sentencing

dispositional phase

focal concerns theory

front-end sentencing

indeterminate sentencing

mandatory minimum sentences

mitigating factors

pedophiles

policy capturing

procedural knowledge

recidivism

restorative justice

retributive

sentencing disparities

shaming penalty

utilitarian

Chapter
15

Juvenile and Adult Corrections

ORIENTING QUESTIONS

1. What are the important considerations in assessing juveniles prior to placement decisions?

2. What is the evidence for the effectiveness of interventions with juveniles in the community?

3. What are some characteristics of an effective treatment program?

4. How can risk/need/responsivity help to provide effective rehabilitative services for adults?

5. How do specialized problem-solving courts compare to other correctional interventions?

6. What are the differences between jails and prisons and what roles do psychologists play in these settings?

7. What kinds of interventions are delivered in jails and prisons?

8. What are some of the psychological consequences of imprisonment?

9. What are the priorities in preparing individuals for the transition from incarceration to community living (the reentry process)?

At the end of 2009, 1 in 32 Americans was in prison, on probation, or on parole, the highest per capita correctional rate in the world (Walmsley, 2009). Correctional systems disproportionately target young African-American males, with more Black men imprisoned or on parole or probation today than were enslaved in 1850, prior to the Civil War (Alexander et al., 2010). According to commentator Adam Gopnick, the "city of the confined and controlled, Lockuptown, is now the second largest in the United States" (Gopnick, 2012, p. 73).

In this final chapter, we discuss the process following a defendant's conviction for a criminal offense. This discussion will include both **adjudication of delinquency** (for juveniles) and **criminal conviction** (for adults). It will address the traditional aspects of corrections—**probation**, commitment to juvenile programs, incarceration in jail and prison for adults, and **parole** following release. But there have been some important innovations in correctional practice during the last decade—primarily in response to ballooning rates of incarceration—which we will also discuss. In particular, there is now more emphasis on **diversion** and **reentry** (returning from incarceration to the community) as well as increased specialization in the nature of parole and probation and the rehabilitative services delivered. These efforts have resulted from lawmakers' receptiveness to new models of correctional interventions and from increasingly rigorous analyses by psychologists and others of the effectiveness of these programs.

Four major justifications for correctional intervention have been traditionally cited: incapacitation, deterrence (both general, as it applies to others, and specific to the individual convicted); retribution; and rehabilitation. The role of psychology in addressing these goals is focused largely on deterrence and rehabilitation. The question of whether individuals undergoing juvenile or correctional intervention are deterred from committing further offenses is an important topic that psychological research can help address. It is related to the goal of rehabilitation. However, the rehabilitative question is broader: Has the individual gained skills, changed patterns of thinking, and decreased deficits? Such changes facilitate a more responsible lifestyle. Much of the discussion in this chapter, as it relates to both juveniles and adults, will address how psychology contributes to the broad goals of deterring future crime, enhancing public safety, and rehabilitation.

JUVENILE CORRECTIONS

Interventions for adjudicated delinquents involve delivering services designed to reduce the risk of future offending, and improve or eliminate deficits that are relevant to such risk. The goal of these interventions is to short-circuit the criminal trajectories of young offenders before they become career criminals. This can be done in different settings, ranging from the community to secure residential programs. (In some states, these programs are simply called juvenile prisons.)

It is useful to consider what such interventions might have in common. In 2004, the National Institutes of Health assembled a "state of the science" conference entitled *Preventing Violence and Related Health-Risking Social Behaviors in Adolescents*. Summarizing the evidence presented at this conference, the organizers concluded that there are certain characteristics shared by programs that are successful in reducing the rates of violence, antisocial behavior, and risky health behavior in adolescents:

- They are derived from sound theoretical rationales.

- They address strong risk factors (such as substance abuse, family problems, and educational problems).

- They involve long-term treatments, often lasting a year and sometimes much longer.

- They work intensively with those targeted for treatment and often use a clinical approach.

- They follow a cognitive behavioral strategy.

- They are multimodal and multicontextual (they use different kinds of interventions and deliver them in different contexts, such as home and school),

- They focus on improving social competency and other skill development strategies for targeted youth and/or their families.

- They are developmentally appropriate.

- They are not delivered in coercive institutional settings.

- They have the capacity for delivery with fidelity (meaning that services are delivered as intended).

Likewise, there are common elements of programs that appear to be ineffective:

- They fail to address strong risk factors.

- They are of limited duration.

- They aggregate high-risk youth in ways that facilitate contagion (i.e., the incarcerated youth are influenced by the antisocial behavior modeled by their peers).

- Their implementation protocols are not clearly articulated.

- Their staff are not well supervised or held accountable for outcomes.

- They are limited to scare tactics (e.g., Scared Straight) or toughness strategies (e.g., classic boot camps).

- They consist largely of adults lecturing at youth (e.g., the classic drug abuse resistance education program D.A.R.E.).

These are elements of interventions, both pro and con, that have a good deal of applicability to juvenile corrections. Consider them as we discuss strategies, procedures, and outcomes, and try to distinguish between what will be effective and what will not.

Assessing Risk and Needs in Juveniles

There are two important considerations that recur in juvenile forensic assessment: public safety and treatment needs/amenability. The former means that

courts, the juvenile system, and the larger society are rightly concerned with the question of whether the juvenile will reoffend following completion of the intervention. The second refers to the youth's deficits, problems, and symptoms, particularly those related to reoffense risk—and whether they can be improved or eliminated through intervention and within the time that is available until the youth "ages out" of eligibility for treatment as a juvenile (Grisso, 1998).

Social scientists have recognized that a number of influences are related to the risk of juvenile offending. For example, the Office of Juvenile Justice and Delinquency Prevention (OJJDP), in their 1995 *Guide for Implementing the Comprehensive Strategy for Serious, Violent, and Chronic Juvenile Offenders*, compared the factors used in eight different states to classify the risk for future offending in arrested juveniles. At least four of the states used factors that included age at first referral, number of prior referrals, and current offense (taken together, these provide an estimate of how long, how much, and how seriously the juvenile has offended). Other commonly used factors were drug/alcohol problems, school difficulties, negative peers, and family problems. These factors can be either static (with no potential to change through intervention) or dynamic (with the potential to change through intervention).

Focusing on both risk and risk-relevant needs is an approach that was formally conceptualized in the late 1980s. Andrews, Bonta, and Hoge (1990) described three separate considerations, which they termed **risk, need, and responsivity** (RNR). Risk means that the likelihood of committing future offenses should be evaluated, and those at highest risk should receive the most intensive interventions. Needs are the deficits (such as substance abuse, family problems, educational problems, and procriminal attitudes) that increase the risk of reoffending. These are sometimes called **criminogenic needs**. Responsivity involves the likelihood of a favorable response to the interventions, and the influences that may affect such responding. It is easy to see the conceptual relationship between the juvenile priorities of public safety, treatment needs, and treatment amenability on one hand, and the Andrews, Bonta and Hoge concepts of risk, need, and responsivity on the other. Accordingly, the RNR model is a very useful foundation for the evaluation of juveniles (Andrews & Hoge, 2010).

There are two specialized tools in particular that focus on the measurement of juvenile risk and needs: the Structured Assessment of Violence Risk in Youth (SAVRY) (Borum, Bartels, & Forth, 2005) and the Youth Level of Service/Case Management Inventory (Hoge & Andrews, 2002). Both prompt the user to consider historical factors, such as the nature of current and previous offending, as well as contextual factors (e.g., family, school, peers) and personal factors (e.g., substance abuse, anger, impulsivity, callousness, attitudes toward intervention, offending, and authority). The SAVRY also considers protective influences such as social support, attachment, resilience, and commitment to positive activities. A similar tool, the Risk–Sophistication–Treatment Inventory (Salekin, 2004), also prompts the evaluator to focus on influences related to risk and risk-relevant treatment needs. It includes "sophistication" (referring to the youth's adeptness and adult-like attitudes regarding offending), another factor that often appears in the law for decisions on juveniles.

Evaluating youth on the dimensions of risk and needs provides valuable information for several reasons. First, it structures the evaluation to require the psychologist to consider the influences that theory and research indicate are most strongly related to risk and needs. Second, it provides useful information for intervention planning. A specialized risk–needs tool could be used to help the court make a decision about placement, but could also be used by a program once the youth is placed to help determine what interventions should be provided to that individual. Third, it offers one approach to measuring progress and current status. A youth with deficits in certain areas who begins a program should be reevaluated at different times throughout the program to gauge whether he or she is making progress in important areas. This affects the assessment of current risk, as well as the needs for additional interventions following completion of the program. A careful evaluation of youth risk and needs is important for planning and future interventions at various levels in the juvenile system (Borum & Verhaagen, 2006).

Community-Based Interventions

There are a number of approaches to the rehabilitation and management of adjudicated delinquent youth in the community. Youth may be placed on probation, involving a specified set of conditions for which compliance is monitored by the probation officer assigned to the case. A variation on the standard conditions of probation involves **school-based probation**, in which the youth's attendance, performance, and behavior in school are monitored through the probation officer's personal visits to the school. Probation conditions may also include drug use monitoring (through testing blood or urine); substance abuse treatment; mental health treatment; and skills-based training in particular areas (e.g., anger management, decision making). Probation may also vary in intensity, with **intensive probation** involving more frequent monitoring contact.

Youths who are placed on probation typically live at home. Alternatively, a youth in a community-based placement might participate in a specific program or alternative school during the day but return home at night. Oakland's Evening Reporting Center for juvenile offenders is one such program. In order to remain in the community, adjudicated juveniles must report straight to the Center after school and remain there until 8 P.M. The program provides opportunities to participate in art, music, and sports; a sit-down dinner with caring adults; and a ride home at the end of each evening. Together, these components have contributed to reduced rates of incarceration, particularly for Oakland's minority youths (Porter, 2012).

There is a wide range of specific interventions and broader programs available in the community to youth adjudicated as delinquent. Rather than attempting to describe them all, we focus on three particular community-based interventions for delinquent youth that have been heavily researched: Multisystemic Therapy, Oregon Treatment Foster Care, and Functional Family Therapy. On the basis of this research, these interventions can be described as empirically supported, cost-effective, risk-reducing, and amenable to quality assurance monitoring (Sheidow & Henggeler, 2005).

MULTISYSTEMIC THERAPY (MST)

As the name implies, **Multisystemic Therapy** (Henggeler, Schoenwald, Borduin, Rowland, & Cunningham, 1998) focuses on multiple "systems": the individual, family, peer, school, and social networks as they relate to identified problems and risk factors for offending. It delivers services based in the home, school, or elsewhere in the community, with three to four therapists working in a team. This increases the frequency of participation well beyond what would be expected from having juveniles and their families come to the program or individual therapist's office. The training of therapists and supervisors in MST is highly standardized (Henggeler & Schoenwald, 1999), and the MST procedures are very clearly specified (Henggeler et al., 1998), so those receiving MST services are likely to receive them as they were intended to be delivered. (Researchers call this "treatment integrity.") Therapists are available 24/7, working to prevent problems or crises in the youth's life from having a major impact. Consequently, the rate of engaging and retaining families in treatment is very high; over the three to six months of direct service usually needed for MST, the retention rates are as high as 98% (Henggeler, Pickrel, Brondino, & Crouch, 1996; Henggeler et al., 1999).

As MST has become more popular, the amount of research on it has increased. This focus on treatment integrity has been important—particularly since studies have supported the link between adherence to MST treatment principles and favorable outcomes (Schoenwald, Henggeler, Brondino, & Rowland, 2000; Schoenwald, Sheidow, & Letourneau, 2003). In other words, there is a substantial "quality assurance" component built into MST; this intervention was being provided in more than 30 states and 10 nations as of 2009 (Henggeler, Sheidow, & Lee, 2010).

MST is one of the best-validated interventions for juveniles. Henggeler et al. (1986) reported that MST was more effective than usual diversion services on two outcomes: (1) improving both self-reported and observed family relations, and (2) decreasing youth behavior problems and time spent with deviant peers. It has also been shown to reduce recidivism by 43% and decrease placements outside the home by 64% over a 59-week period among juveniles charged with serious offenses (Henggeler, Melton, & Smith, 1992). The percentage of this MST group arrested over a longer outcome period (2.4 years) was about half that of the comparison group (Henggeler, Melton, Smith, Schoenwald, & Hanley, 1993).

A study in which participants were randomly assigned to either MST or individual counseling (the strongest kind of research design, with the random assignment to treatment versus control groups allowing the researcher to draw conclusions about the causal relationship between treatment and outcome) involved 176 chronic juvenile offenders (Borduin et al., 1995). It showed that MST produced better family functioning, better symptom reduction, and a 69% reduction in recidivism over a period of four years. Another randomized assignment study (Henggeler, Melton, Brondino, Scherer, & Hanley, 1997) with juveniles who had chronic histories of offending and were charged with a violent offense ($N = 155$) yielded similarly favorable results, including a reduction in mental health symptoms, a 26% reduction in recidivism, and a 50% reduction in incarceration over 1.7 years.

A long-term (22-year) follow-up of the differences between those who received MST and those who received another intervention has recently been completed (Sawyer & Borduin, 2011). The investigators included criminal and civil court outcomes for 176 serious and violent juvenile offenders who participated on average 21.9 (range = 18.3–23.8) years earlier in a clinical trial of MST, or who, alternatively, received individual therapy. Results showed that felony recidivism rates were significantly lower for MST participants than for individual therapy participants (34.8% vs. 54.8%, respectively) and that the frequency of misdemeanor offending was five times lower for MST participants. Also, the odds of involvement in family-related civil suits during adulthood were twice as high for IT participants as for MST participants.

There is also evidence that MST is effective with juveniles with substance abuse or dependence. Another study using random assignment to MST versus "treatment as usual" for substance-abusing juveniles ($N = 118$) (Henggeler, Pickrel, & Brondino, 1999) showed a decrease in drug use, a 50% decrease in time in out-of-home placement, and a 26% decrease in recidivism over a one-year period, while a longer follow-up (four years) yielded significantly reduced violent offending and significantly increased drug use abstinence in the MST group (Henggeler, Clingempeel, Brondino, & Pickrel, 2002). Finally, a study conducted by the Washington State Institute for Public Policy (Aos, Phipps, Barnoski, & Lieb, 2001) concluded that the MST intervention costs an average of $4,743 per family. Considering that cost, the evidence of its effectiveness, and the savings from not placing the juvenile outside the home, the study estimated cost savings of nearly $32,000 per youth and about $132,000 in additional savings from decreased costs to victims. We provide a case example in Box 15.1.

B o x 15.1 THE CASE OF MARCUS: A YOUTH TREATED IN THE COMMUNITY WITH MULTISYSTEMIC THERAPY

Marcus was 15 years old when he was arrested for stealing a bicycle from a classmate. This was his second arrest. A year earlier he had been arrested for possession of marijuana and received a disposition of six months of school-based probation, which required him to attend school (his probation officer periodically came to his school and checked whether he was there) and undergo urine tests for drug use.

Marcus completed his six-month probation without violating any of his conditions. However, despite this, he continued to have a number of difficulties in his life that increased the risk that he would continue to offend. His father had been absent from the family since Marcus was very young. He and his four siblings lived with his mother and grandmother. Because his mother had serious substance abuse problems herself, she was often unemployed and sometimes absent. The burden for supervising the children and supporting the family financially fell mainly on Marcus's grandmother. As she became older, she began to develop significant medical problems, and could not be as attentive to all the children as she had been previously.

Marcus's grades and behavior in school improved during the first six months of the ninth grade, but after the probation was finished, he began missing a number of school days and falling behind in his work. Marcus was measured in the Average range on a standard IQ test (higher than most juveniles who are arrested), but he found it hard to pay attention to written materials and when his teacher was talking. He tended to avoid doing his homework as a result. He preferred playing basketball with his friends, talking with girls from his neighborhood, and hanging out with older boys who sold drugs.

After he was arrested for his present offense, Marcus was evaluated by a psychologist appointed by the juvenile court judge. The psychologist concluded that Marcus had potentially serious problems with family, school, substance abuse, and negative peers, and diagnosed him with attention deficit disorder (ADD). However, he also had some strengths, including a close relationship with his grandmother, who was a strong role model; average intelligence; and an interest in sports. He was recommended for a community disposition that involved treatment with MST.

The judge adjudicated Marcus delinquent on the charge of stealing the bicycle and sentenced him to one year of juvenile probation. One condition of probation involved treatment with MST. Marcus's MST team included a case manager, a family therapist, a substance abuse counselor, and two other staff members responsible for working with Marcus in school and in the neighborhood. The case manager immediately made an appointment with a child psychiatrist, who diagnosed Marcus with attention deficit disorder and prescribed medication for the symptoms. One of his MST team members helped Marcus to join a community basketball league; his team practiced every day after school, and the gym was open for casual play (with adult supervision) after the season ended. His family therapist met with Marcus twice a week in his home to address the issues facing his family, including helping his grandmother schedule her medical appointments more effectively, providing access to job training and substance abuse support for his mother, and arranging for a regular supervision schedule involving Marcus's grandmother, mother, and all the children. During the second week of scheduled appointments, the family therapist and case manager found nobody at home at the time of each appointment. Therefore, they came to the home at 6:00 A.M. on Sunday and held a make-up meeting at that time.

By the end of the six-month MST session, Marcus was doing much better. His school attendance and behavior were consistently improved, his after-school hours were almost always spent playing basketball, his mother and grandmother were much more attentive to him and the other children, and he was able to concentrate on his homework more easily. Much of this improvement resulted because MST was administered in the home, school, and gym rather than the office of a therapist or probation officer. In addition, those administering the MST were careful to do it precisely as intended, and were firm about making sure that appointments were kept.

Critical Thought Question

What are some of the features of MST that make it effective for Marcus?

OREGON TREATMENT FOSTER CARE (OTFC)

Oregon Treatment Foster Care is another treatment intervention based in the community, developed in the 1980s as an alternative to "treatment as usual" (typically out-of-home placement) for juveniles charged with serious offenses. The procedures for delivering this intervention are described in a treatment manual (Chamberlain & Mihalic, 1998), which increases OTFC's treatment integrity. It involves placing juveniles with specially trained foster parents rather than in residential placement. Like MST, this intervention uses a team approach. The OTFC team includes a case manager and therapists, as well as foster parents who are available 24/7 over the 6–12 months usually needed. OTFC is designed to provide close supervision (including supportive relationships with adult mentors and reduced exposure to negative peers) within consistent limits. A variety of treatment modalities (including individual and group counseling, family therapy, and interventions to improve specific skills such as anger control and decision making) may be used. These are often conducted with the family, using both the foster parents and the biological parent(s), and in the school.

OTFC has been identified as a model treatment program by the U.S. Surgeon General (U.S. Public Health Service, 1999) and the *Blueprints for Violence Prevention* initiative (Mihalic, Irwin, Elliott, Fagan, & Hansen, 2001). One study involving OTFC (Chamberlain, 1990) treated 13- to 18-year-olds ($N = 16$) matched with a comparison group of 16 other juveniles treated in community residential treatment. Those in the OTFC group were less likely to be incarcerated and more likely to complete treatment over a two-year follow-up period. A second OTFC study (Chamberlain & Reid, 1998) involved random placement of youth ($N = 79$) between the ages of 12 and 17 into OTFC or treatment as usual. Youth treated with OTFC were more likely to complete treatment, spent more time with biological relatives and less time in detention over the next year, and were arrested less often during this period. OTFC is also a relatively cost-effective intervention. An analysis conducted by the Washington State Institute for Public Policy (Aos et al., 2001) estimated the cost per youth of about $2,000 (plus foster placement costs), which represents a savings of about $22,000 per youth relative to placement in group homes, and further savings of more than $87,000 in victim costs for each individual in OTFC.

FUNCTIONAL FAMILY THERAPY (FFT)

Functional Family Therapy is a third community-based intervention for juvenile offenders. It is somewhat older than either MST or OTFC, having been used for almost 30 years. It is provided by a single therapist, who has a caseload of 12–15 cases, with

weekly sessions over an average period of three months. As the name implies, it is family focused, and is often delivered in the home (Alexander et al., 1998). Quality assurance/treatment integrity is addressed by careful training of therapists, yearly on-site consultation, ongoing telephone consultation, feedback from families, and weekly supervision. As we have seen, such quality assurance is a component that is common to FFT, MST, and OTFC—each ensures that services are delivered as intended.

The OJJDP identified FFT as a model treatment program (Mihalic et al., 2001). An early study of FFT (Alexander & Parsons, 1973) involved a randomized trial of FFT delivered to 13- to 16-year-old status offenders (those committing offenses such as truancy or running away from home that would not be illegal if committed by an adult), with 46 families receiving FFT and another 40 receiving family-centered "treatment as usual." The recidivism rate for those receiving FFT was 50% lower than it was in the comparison group. A second study (Gordon, Arbuthnot, Gustafson, & McGreen, 1988) involved 54 youths who had committed more serious offenses. The comparison group was composed of randomly selected youth who had not been referred for family therapy, (a *no treatment control group*). The recidivism rate for those receiving FFT (11%) was substantially lower than for those in the group that did not receive treatment (80%).

The effectiveness of FFT depends on adherence to the model, however (Sexton & Turner, 2010). In a recent study, researchers compared the effectiveness of FFT to that of probation services in a community juvenile justice setting 12 months after treatment. FFT was effective in reducing youth behavioral problems—but only when the therapists adhered to the treatment model. High-adherent therapists delivering FFT had a statistically significant reduction of felony reoffending (35%) and violent reoffending (30%) when compared to the control condition. The low-adherent therapists, however, had significantly higher recidivism rates than either the FFT high-adherent or the control groups.

These and other studies indicate that FFT is associated with a significant reduction in recidivism when compared with those receiving "treatment as usual" and others receiving no treatment (Alexander et al., 1998). The same Washington State Institute for Public Policy report (Aos et al., 2001) noted earlier, which described the cost and savings associated with

MST and OTFC, indicated that FFT had an average cost of $2,161 per participant, saved an average of $14,149 in costs for intervention compared with standard treatment in the juvenile justice system, and saved another $45,000 in victim costs per participant.

How would Marcus (Box 15.1) have done with OTFC or FFT? Consider the similarities between these two approaches and MST on the dimensions described earlier in this chapter. All three directly target important influences such as substance abuse, family problems, and educational deficits. All three involve intensive work, including clinical interventions, and protocols to ensure that the planned interventions are actually delivered. (Remember the unscheduled 6:00 A.M. Sunday meeting with Marcus's family after missed appointments? This kind of extreme but effective response is sometimes necessary.) All three approaches use different interventions delivered in more than one setting, such as at home and in the school. These interventions are delivered in the community rather than an institution, and include goals that are developmentally appropriate. Finally, the interventions are carefully planned and monitored for consistency with the plan. Marcus probably would have responded favorably to any of these three empirically supported interventions.

Secure Residential Interventions

The previous section described three interventions that appear effective, both in terms of reducing the risk of reoffending and in saving money. So why not deliver most or all of juvenile interventions in the community, using MST, OTFC, or FFT? There are two answers to this question. First, not all communities offer these interventions. We cannot assume that because an effective intervention *could* be delivered in the community, it *will* be. Second, many judges would be inclined to place a youth in a secure residential facility as a consequence of a delinquency adjudication for a serious offense, even if that youth could possibly be treated in the community. Why? Community values (which judges represent) may support such a placement. The publicly perceived risk to society is lower when a youth is placed in a secure residential program, even though the actual risk (gauged through outcome research) may not be. Unfortunately, the impact of different placements for juveniles who commit serious offenses is a very difficult issue to answer through research. The ideal

study to help understand the impact of a given program or placement involves random assignment to such a program, comparing the outcomes to those from the "treatment as usual" group. Very few judges, juvenile system leaders, or legislators would support research that randomly placed serious offenders in the community (versus in residential placement) to determine the impact of each on subsequent reoffense risk.

Accordingly, we must describe residential placements and their effectiveness without the best kind of evidence. While this is inconvenient for researchers, it is probably appropriate for those who represent our society and are responsible for promoting its safety. It would be very helpful to have good evidence about program effectiveness, but certainly a tragedy if citizens were victimized by offending as a result of such research. This is the main reason why research with random assignment is difficult to do in the juvenile and criminal justice systems—and why researchers must be satisfied with comparing a given intervention to "treatment as usual" rather than "no treatment." In a study like this, no citizen is put at additional risk, which could be the case when "no treatment" is provided to a group of serious offenders.

A meta-analysis of the predictors of general recidivism in juveniles (Cottle, Lee, & Heilbrun, 2001) suggested a number of "treatment targets" that may be addressed at any stage of the intervention process. However, since residential placement is typically longer and more intensive, these issues may be particularly relevant for residential placement. The predictors (and treatment targets) include, in order of their strength, nonsevere pathology (such as conduct disorder, for example); family problems; ineffective use of leisure time; delinquent peers; and substance abuse. A smaller meta-analysis, focusing on predictors of recidivism in violent juvenile offenders (Heilbrun, Lee, and Cottle, 2005), identified cognitive and family therapies as more effective in reducing recidivism rates than usual services (e.g., those with other orientations; standard case management). This underscores an important weakness in residential interventions: If the juvenile is isolated from his or her family because of the location of the program, it is much more difficult to involve the family in a meaningful way. Conversely, one of the common features of the effective community-based interventions discussed earlier in this chapter is the close involvement of families in the intervention.

One meta-analysis of 32 studies of juvenile and adult treatment programs, many of them residential, found a reduction in recidivism in 75% of the studies (Redondo, Sanchez-Meca & Garrido, 1999). Behavioral and cognitive-behavioral treatments appear to be most effective in reducing recidivism. Lipsey's (1992) meta-analysis of the impact of intervention on general recidivism risk in juveniles included a large number of studies (443) and estimated a 10% decrease in delinquency rates for juveniles receiving some kind of intervention. More frequent contact and longer periods of treatment were associated with more favorable outcomes—but only to a certain extent. This suggests that there is a "drop-off" in effectiveness of the intervention after a certain time.

More structured and multimodal treatments also had a stronger impact. Lipsey and Wilson's (1998) meta-analysis of 83 treatment programs for institutionalized juvenile offenders found that the most effective treatments reduced violent recidivism risk by 15–20%. The most effective of the residential treatments involved interpersonal skills training and family-centered interventions. As was true for MST, OTFC, and FFT, the most effective treatment programs were attentive to quality assurance, making them consistent with the treatment model. Individual characteristics of the juveniles being treated had little effect on these outcomes.

This research tells us that residential placements for juveniles can be effective, particularly when they focus on skills training (in areas like anger control and decision making), vocational training, and educational and mental health needs, and also employ a treatment model that is "checked" through quality assurance. They should also be safe. If residents do not feel safe, it is very unlikely that rehabilitation efforts will be effective.

No comprehensive programs in juvenile residential settings have been studied through empirical research regarding their effectiveness. However, there have been studies of specific kinds of facilities, where youth are placed for mental health or substance abuse treatment—sometimes through court order (OJJDP, 2008). The OJJDP identified three residential programs supported by research. Two of the programs focused on the treatment of substance abuse and targeted both juveniles and other youths who were not involved in the juvenile justice system. Participation in either program resulted in reduced levels of drug and alcohol abuse, although one program did

not show a reduced rate of offending after one year (Morral, McCaffrey, & Ridgeway, 2004), and the second did not even consider reoffending as an outcome in the study (Morehouse & Tobler, 2000). The third effective residential program combined security with mental health treatment for adolescents who had not responded well to "treatment as usual" in Wisconsin's juvenile justice system (Caldwell & Van Rybroek, 2005). The goal was to interrupt the escalation of defiance and legal consequences. Individualized therapy, behavioral control, and motivational interviewing were among the approaches used in this program. Those treated in this program were significantly less likely to recidivate within two years when compared with other juveniles with similar offenses who had been assessed (but not treated) in this program. This may be a particularly useful approach for serious offenders who also have substantial mental health problems.

A primary goal of residential treatment for juveniles is to reduce the deficits that are associated with reoffending risk. One approach to addressing anger problems (Anger Replacement Training; Goldstein, 2004) can be delivered either in a residential or community setting. It involves meeting with a therapist three times weekly for 10 weeks, and focuses on the development of specific skills such as impulse control, anger control, and thinking ahead, as well as reasoning. Research has demonstrated reductions in anger problems in secure residential settings (Goldstein, 2004), although the impact on recidivism risk has not yet been studied (Heilbrun et al., 2011).

Another anger management program has been developed for girls in residential juvenile facilities. The Juvenile Justice Anger Management (JJAM) Treatment for Girls is an 8-week, 16-session group intervention that is delivered with careful attention to treatment integrity (through manuals and careful training of therapists) and intended to teach self-control, problem solving, and anger management (Goldstein, Dovidio, Kalbeitzer, Weil, & Strachan, 2007). A randomized controlled trial demonstrated significant reductions in anger, general aggression, verbal aggression, and indirect (relational) aggression for girls who completed the JJAM treatment in addition to treatment as usual, when compared with other girls who received only treatment as usual.

When should juveniles be placed in the community, and when should they be assigned to secure residential placements? This decision depends on several considerations. Higher risk juveniles, often with a history of prior offenses, may require more secure placement. A judge may decide that a single offense, if it is very serious, merits a secure placement. Sometimes it can be important to remove a juvenile from extremely problematic circumstances (involving family, peers, gangs, and the like) that would continue with a community placement. However, there are substantial costs (both to the individual adolescent and to society) associated with secure placements. Juveniles very often respond better to correctional interventions when they are delivered in the community and can involve important influences such as family and school. The case described in Box 15.2 highlights some of the complexities of secure placement.

This story raises some important questions about where juvenile correctional interventions should be made. When there are not proper resources and procedures in the community, interventions can be ineffective and put the public at continued risk. When there are not proper resources and procedures in secure settings, interventions are also ineffective and conditions can be brutal and dangerous. How can the necessary resources be obtained? (Lawsuits are one approach, as this story demonstrates.) How can they be most efficiently invested, so that interventions are

as effective as possible? Much of the discussion in this chapter centers on the most efficient ways to use resources to provide effective interventions.

Reentry

Behavioral treatments for delinquent youth provided in residential facilities frequently do not generalize to the community after discharge (Quinsey, Harris, Rice, & Cormier, 2006). The process of reentry into the community should include planning for aftercare services (in some states, called juvenile parole) that are important to ensure ongoing treatment in the community and reduced recidivism risk. There are six areas in particular that are important in the reentry planning process: family functioning, housing (if not living with the family), school or job, mental health and/or substance abuse services, monitoring, and social support. Addressing each of these areas can help provide a smoother, safer transition from the youth's placement back to the community. Promising approaches to such relevant aftercare include the intensive aftercare program, wraparound services, and several of the community interventions already discussed (MST, FFT).

Intensive aftercare was developed to address the needs of chronic and serious juvenile offenders who

---

Box 15.2 THE CASE OF THOMAS HARRIS: IMPRISONED, VIOLENT, AND SKEPTICAL

In the spring of 2008, 18-year-old Thomas Harris sat in a locked cell in an Ohio juvenile prison, a place he'd been for 2½ years. (This is longer than most juveniles are incarcerated, even for serious offenses.) In that time, he'd had group therapy approximately twice a month, had been beaten up 12 times, and had sustained a fractured leg and cut lip.

So when the agency that runs Ohio's juvenile prison agreed to improve the conditions for juvenile offenders—including offering better mental health and medical treatment and reducing violence—Harris was understandably skeptical. He said in a telephone interview from prison, "They tell us, 'We're going to hire more staff to make you feel safer and hire more social workers so we can get you on the road to success.' It never happens" (DeMartini, 2008).

Violence in the Ohio juvenile prison system had been escalating around this time. At the Marion County juvenile prison, juveniles attacked one another or a guard 504 times in 2007, up one-third from 2006. Violence may result from incarcerated juveniles' perceptions that they

must fight to protect themselves. Violent acts may be used by juveniles to establish themselves in the hierarchy or get what they want. Violent behavior may also stem from a feeling of being disrespected. Whatever the reasons why Thomas Harris and others are involved in violence, such behavior must be controlled and minimized for rehabilitation to be effective.

The agreement settled a class-action lawsuit filed against the Ohio prison system by a group of child-advocacy lawyers who claimed that the system was violent and ineffective. The new plan restricted how often and when prison staff can put juvenile offenders in solitary confinement, provided more medical and mental health services, and addressed overcrowding issues by releasing inmates who served their minimum sentence and progressed in therapy.

Critical Thought Question
Why is it particularly important that juveniles be placed in a facility that is rehabilitatively oriented?

are returning from residential placement. It used a graduated sanctions approach involving three steps: (1) prerelease planning; (2) a structured transition involving institutional and aftercare staff prior to, and following, release; and (3) long-term reintegrative activities to facilitate service delivery and social control (Altschuler & Armstrong, 1997). Studies addressing the impact of intensive aftercare (Altschuler, 1998) have produced mixed results. However, it also appears that many of the intensive aftercare interventions have not been consistent in providing appropriate and adequate treatment services. Accordingly, intensive aftercare remains an approach that appears promising and is consistent with both the emphasis on reentry planning and the "risk" principle of the RNR model ("treat the highest-risk individuals most intensely"). But the empirical evidence about its effectiveness has been limited.

"Wraparound services" involve the delivery of individualized services in the context of collaboration between agencies such as those responsible for mental health care, educational services, and juvenile corrections. In this approach, funding follows the adolescent's treatment, rather than being allocated to particular programs (Brown, Borduin, & Henggeler, 2001). Such services are useful particularly for youths with serious mental or emotional problems.

One example of wraparound services designed to serve emotionally disturbed youths in the juvenile justice system is Wraparound Milwaukee. Families are involved in these services, which use "care coordinators" to assist in obtaining needed services from the available providers. Research on the functioning of Wraparound Milwaukee has indicated that it improves functioning, reduces recidivism, and improves the coordination of service delivery between the juvenile justice, mental health, and child welfare systems (Goldman & Faw, 1999; Kamradt, 2000). It is also less costly than residential treatment (by about $5,000 per month) or inpatient psychiatric care (by about $15,000 per month) (Goldman & Faw, 1999).

ADULT CORRECTIONS

The justifications for sentencing and intervening with adult offenders are somewhat different than for those with juveniles. Retribution, in particular, has been strongly emphasized during the last three decades—and particularly since 9/11, when concerns about terrorism were added to societal attention to criminal offending. One commentator has referred to this era of harsh punishment as an *imprisonment binge* (Ayre, 1995); another calls it *the mean season of corrections* (Haney, 2006). We describe some of the psychological consequences to offenders, their families, and their communities in this chapter.

In many respects though, the role of psychology in adult corrections incorporates the same correctional priorities that were seen with juveniles. Deterrence and rehabilitation as broad goals translate into the need to assess risks and structure interventions to reduce risk-relevant deficits.

Assessing and Diverting Offenders

The risk–need–responsivity (RNR) model, discussed earlier in this chapter, applies as well to adult corrections as it does to juveniles. Offenders who are convicted of criminal offenses (or charged with offenses but diverted from standard prosecution) will be assessed at some time, either as part of the legal proceeding or postsentencing, to gauge their risk and rehabilitation needs. In the prison system, this is called **classification**. Following the offender's commitment to the state department of corrections, he or she typically is evaluated at a classification center before being placed in a particular prison. The "risk" assessed at that stage is typically the risk of escape or misconduct within the prison, as these have direct implications for the security level of the prison to which this individual is assigned.

The risk of reoffending—and the needs related to such risk—are important for the vast majority of offenders who will be released from prison and return to the community following completion of their sentences, or upon the granting of parole. Risk–needs assessment can be facilitated by using a specialized measure. One example of such a measure is the Level of Service/Case Management Inventory (LS/CMI; Andrews, Bonta, & Wormith, 2004).

The LS/CMI is composed of 58 items in the following areas: Criminal History, Education/Employment, Family/Marital, Leisure/Recreation, Companions, Alcohol/Drug Problem, Procriminal Attitude/Orientation, and Antisocial Pattern (Andrews et al., 2004). It has been validated on both males and females. The males ($N = 956$), drawn from three Canadian correctional facilities, had a mean age of 26.9 years, mean sentence length of 325.6 days, and mean number of convictions of 3.7. The females ($N = 1,414$) were from the medium-security institution for adult women operated by Ontario Ministry of Correctional Services; they had a mean age of 30.2 years and a mean sentence length of 322 days. LS/CMI total scores have been associated with (1) propensity for rules violations and assigned levels of supervision; (2) outcomes such as program outcome status, recidivism, and self-reported criminal activity in probation settings; (3) parole outcome; (4) the success of halfway house placements; and (5) maladjustment (Andrews & Bonta, 1995). This tool is useful in appraising risk for a variety of outcomes, including prison, various community settings, and under parole supervision.

Community-Based Interventions

Probation for adult offenders remains a frequent form of disposition of criminal charges, with the court placing the convicted offender on community supervision in lieu of incarceration. At the end of 2009, over 7.2 million adult men and women were supervised in the community. Most of these (over 80%) were on probation. The total population of offenders under supervision in the community grew by 103,100 (about 2%) during 2007. Offenses for those on probation included misdemeanors (51%), felonies (47%), and "other" (3%). The most frequent offenses of those on probation were drug charges (27%); this was also the most frequent offense for those on parole (37%). A total of 23% of those on probation were women; 55% were White, 29% African American, and 19% Hispanic (Bureau of Justice Statistics, 2008b).

Correctional supervision in the community involves monitoring adherence to specified conditions. This is true for both probation and parole. The number of conditions and the nature of the monitoring can vary, depending on the individual's needs. Standard conditions involve specifying how often individuals must meet with a parole or probation officer; where they will live; whether they will work (or receive another kind of financial support, such as Social Security disability); and certain activities that must be avoided (e.g., drinking or drug use, weapon possession). Additional conditions can be added as needed. For example, if the individual had a serious drug abuse problem, he might be required to

undergo urine screens and attend substance abuse treatment and Narcotics Anonymous meetings. An individual with a severe mental illness might be required to attend mental health treatment, take prescribed medication, and meet with a case manager.

Requiring adherence to specified conditions, and monitoring whether the individual actually does comply with these conditions, means that some individuals will violate the requirements of their probation or parole. If they do, there may be serious consequences, including the possibility of returning to a correctional facility. These consequences were made clear to offenders who violated the terms of their probation in Hawaii in the mid-2000s, when Judge Steven Alm decided to act swiftly when dealing with transgressors. But rather than sending people to prison, he arranged for offenders who tested positive for drugs or who missed appointments to be arrested within hours, subjected to a hearing within 72 hours, and, if found in violation of the terms of probation, sentenced to a short jail term. Judge Alm called the program HOPE (Hawaii's Opportunity Probation with Enforcement) and planned for a torrent of violation hearings. Happily, they did not materialize, and the rate of positive drug tests dropped by 93% for HOPE probationers, compared with a 14% decline for a comparison group (Rosen, 2010).

Those who do comply with the conditions of their probation or parole are more likely to be successful in returning, crime-free, to society. We describe a typical defendant on probation in Box 15.3.

Some people are required to undergo mental health treatment as a condition of community supervision. To what extent are probation and parole effective interventions for these individuals? This question was considered in some detail by Skeem and Louden (2006), who reviewed articles published between 1975 and 2005 on adults with mental illness on probation or parole. They concluded that the link between mental illness and supervision failure is complex and indirect (Dauphinot, 1996; Solomon & Draine, 1995; Solomon, Draine, & Marcus, 2002). However, they also noted that specialty agencies, in which offenders are assigned to officers with smaller caseloads, are more effective than traditional agencies. They are also more effective in linking probationers with treatment services and reducing the risk of probation violation, and possibly in reducing the short-term risk of parole violation. The use of specialized probation and parole services for these purposes is

---

B o x   15.3   THE CASE OF LOUISE FRANKLIN: A DEFENDANT ON PROBATION

Louise Franklin was a 24-year-old mother of three who was arrested for assault following an argument with a neighbor whom she thought was stealing from her. Prior to the disposition of her case, Ms. Franklin was evaluated by a probation officer with respect to her criminal history (she had no prior arrests), vocational status and financial circumstances (she was the sole source of support for her children), home and family circumstances, drug and alcohol use here, and medical/mental health history. Based on this evaluation (called a "presentence investigation"), and also using the results of a short actuarial tool to inform the court about reoffense risk level, Ms. Franklin was recommended for probation as a low-risk offender. The judge considered this recommendation and assigned a one-year period of probation following a plea bargain in which Ms. Franklin pled guilty to assault.

There were several "standard" conditions of probation imposed: having monthly meetings with her probation officer, obtaining permission from her probation officer prior to leaving the city, paying $250 in restitution to cover her victim's medical costs, and maintaining continued employment and her current residence. There was one additional condition specific to her probation: completing anger management group therapy. This condition was imposed because the judge observed that Ms. Franklin had been in two arguments (although not physical altercations) with other neighbors during the past year that resulted in police being contacted.

Ms. Franklin was glad that she was not incarcerated. She was also diligent about keeping her scheduled appointments with her probation officer. However, she insisted for the first three months that she had been unfairly treated, that her neighbor had started their dispute, and that she responded by slapping her neighbor (resulting in a fall and a trip to the emergency room) only to protect herself. She also had not paid the $250 in restitution by the six-month mark in her probationary year, when she was required to have done so. Her probation officer indicated to her in their sixth monthly

meeting that she must do so, or he would inform the court that she was in violation of the conditions of her probation. (This would result in a violation hearing and possible incarceration.) After this meeting, Ms. Franklin made arrangements to make this restitution payment within one week.

She attended weekly meetings of her anger management group for a total of 20 sessions, the scheduled duration of the group. She did not miss a meeting, and actively participated in the group. Her contributions reflected her initial feeling that she did not have a temper problem—she felt that others often provoked her, and she was justified in her reactions to such provocations. As the group progressed, however, Ms. Franklin began to see that others with similar perspectives did appear harsh and impulsive in their responses during the group sessions. She learned and practiced alternatives to angry dispute resolution, including identifying her own feelings better, avoiding confrontation when she was already angry, and avoiding "high-risk" situations, but dealing more openly and assertively with conflict, and "pausing and counting" before responding in situations in which unexpected confrontation occurred. She reported a noticeable decrease in the number of times she lost her temper after four months of being involved in this group. She also described the additional benefit of feeling more patient with her children. Her therapist reported to her probation officer that Ms. Franklin had satisfactorily completed anger management group therapy after six months. Ms. Franklin had satisfied all conditions of her probation after one year, so she was discharged from the supervision of the Department of Parole and Probation at that time.

Critical Thought Question

Some research has characterized the approach of probation officers who are particularly effective with clients with mental health problems as "firm but fair." How might this apply to Ms. Franklin's probation officer?

---

consistent with a larger trend, discussed throughout this chapter, of providing specialized rehabilitation services for individuals in particular clinical categories (e.g., severe mental illness, substance abuse). On that note, we now turn to specialized interventions in the community—drug courts and mental health courts—that are also outside the standard stream of prosecution and incarceration of criminal offenders.

Drug Courts in Corrections.   Since 1980, in part because of the "War on Drugs" that began in the United States in the 1970s and expanded into the

1980s, the number of those charged with and convicted of drug offenses has expanded dramatically. Jail and prison admissions more than tripled during this period (Harrison & Karberg, 2003), with drug offenses involved in about 60% of the federal cases and 30% of the state-level cases that are part of this increase (Harrison & Beck, 2002). Neither punishing drug offenders by incarcerating them for long periods (the *public safety* approach) nor providing treatment while conceptualizing drug addiction as a disease (the *public health* approach) has been particularly effective in reducing the prevalence of drug abuse and drug-related crime. About 70% of drug offenders reoffend within three years of release from prison (Martin, Butzin, Saum, & Inciardi, 1999), while prison drug rehabilitation programs have shown little reoffense risk–reduction impact and even less impact on reducing the rate of drug use relapse (Marlowe, 2002).

A community-based intervention that is both more effective and less costly than incarceration and prison rehabilitation would be welcome. Drug courts appear to be such an alternative. They are one form of "problem-solving courts," which have been influenced both by public safety and public health considerations. Consistent with the legal philosophy of therapeutic jurisprudence (Wexler & Winick, 1996), such courts consider how laws and legal decision makers can improve lives and solve problems and are designed to promote rehabilitation. Like the effective juvenile interventions described earlier in this chapter, drug courts are intended to provide an intensive and specific intervention targeting a very strong risk factor (substance abuse) for reoffending. Theoretically, for offenders with a serious substance abuse problem and a history of offending related directly to this problem, treating this risk factor (and ensuring that the right kind of treatment is delivered) should substantially reduce the risk of criminal reoffending.

Drug courts provide judicially supervised drug abuse treatment and case management services to nonviolent drug-involved offenders, taking them out of the standard "prosecution/conviction/incarceration" process. Participation is voluntary, and whether a defendant is eligible may be at the discretion of the prosecutor. San Francisco's "Back on Track" program is one such service. First-time, nonviolent, non–gang-affiliated drug offenders undergo a mandatory "personal responsibility program" that may include GED classes, community-based job training, parenting workshops and close court supervision to break the revolving door cycle of drug offending. Recidivism rates are less than 10% in a population in which recidivism typically top 50% (Harris, 2009).

Diversion in drug courts comes in two forms. First, those charged with a crime may be diverted entirely from prosecution, with the stipulation that they successfully complete the requirements imposed in drug court or face reinstatement of prosecution. Second, those who are convicted of a crime may be diverted to drug court to avoid prison or modify their probation conditions.

How well do they work? The research conducted during the last 15 years gives reason for optimism about this particular intervention. In essence, drug courts are more effective than virtually any other approach with substance-abusing offenders (Marlowe, DeMatteo, & Festinger, 2003). They seem particularly good at reducing drug use and criminal recidivism (e.g., Belenko, 2001, 2002; Belenko, DeMatteo, & Patapis, 2007; Government Accountability Office, 2005). Belenko (1998, 1999, 2001) described nearly 100 drug courts, concluding that about 60% of drug court clients attended at least one year of treatment, and approximately 50% graduated from the drug court program. These figures compare favorably to probation, where very few individuals (less than 10%) attend one year of treatment (Goldkamp, 2000). Belenko (1999, 2001) also reported that the frequency of positive urine screens for drug court clients (less than 10%) is lower than for those on probation, and that criminal recidivism rates for drug court clients are also lower than for similar offenders under other kinds of supervision in the community.

Two randomized controlled trials (the strongest kind of research design) indicate that drug court effectiveness is greater than standard criminal justice approaches to offenders with substance abuse. Drug court clients in one study (Turner, Greenwood, Fain, & Deschenes, 1999) were rearrested within three years at a rate of 33%, compared with 47% of those with drug problems on other probation conditions. A second study using random assignment to drug court (Gottfredson & Exum, 2002) reported that 48% of drug court clients, as compared with 64% of "treatment as usual" adjudicated control clients, were rearrested within one year, although the percentages of those arrested from each group were about the same by the end of the second year (Gottfredson, Najaka, & Kearley, 2003). In addition, a meta-analysis (Wilson, Mitchell, & Mackenzie, 2006) of 50 studies representing 55 drug court program evaluations found that the majority of studies reported lower rates of reoffending among drug court participants, with the average difference being 26% across all studies. Taken together, this research provides strong evidence that drug courts are more effective at reducing the rates of both substance abuse and reoffending over outcome periods of one year and perhaps longer, compared with more traditional forms of community supervision such as parole and probation.

Mental Health Courts in Corrections. Mental health courts handle both felony and misdemeanor offenders (Redlich, Steadman, Monahan, Petrila, & Griffin, 2005), although some courts exclude those charged with felonies. Juvenile mental health courts have also been developed (Cocozza & Shufelt, 2006). Mental health services that include psychotropic medication, case management, and individual and group therapy are among those delivered through such specialized courts, with progress monitored by the court. Despite local differences, most mental health courts feature (1) a specialized docket for selected offenders, (2) judicial supervision of clients, (3) regularly scheduled hearings, and (4) specific criteria that must be met if an individual is to remain in, and complete, the program (Thompson, Osher, & Tomasini-Joshi, 2007).

Mental health courts provide adjudication and monitoring for a particular group of defendants. In the context of corrections, how well do they work? There is less empirical evidence for the effectiveness of mental health courts than for drug courts. There are also fewer well-designed studies (particularly randomized controlled trials), and the operation of mental health courts varies more widely across different courts. Consequently, it is more difficult to draw conclusions about the operation of mental health courts (Heilbrun et al., 2011).

But there is some relevant research. Boothroyd, Poythress, McGaha, and Petrila (2003) compared mental health court offenders ($N = 121$) and criminal court offenders ($N = 101$). They reported that the percentage of individuals under mental health court jurisdiction who received behavioral health services increased from 36% to 53% after coming under mental health court jurisdiction, while only 28% of criminal court offenders received behavioral treatment. Another study compared mental health court clients charged with misdemeanors ($N = 368$) before and after coming under mental health court jurisdiction. It reported an increase in the hours of case management and medication management, and the days of outpatient service, as well as fewer crisis intervention services and inpatient days (Herinckx, Swart, Ama, Dolezal, & King, 2005).

Several other studies have focused on whether greater access to clinical services actually results in improved clinical functioning. In one study using random assignment of offenders ($N = 235$) to mental health court versus "treatment as usual" (criminal court), investigators found that participants in both conditions improved in satisfaction and independent functioning, but mental health court individuals reduced their drug use more and developed more independent living skills (Cosden, Ellens, Schnell, Yamini-Diouf, & Wolfe, 2003).

By contrast, another study comparing mental health court offenders ($N = 97$) with criminal court offenders ($N = 77$) did not find differences between the mental health functioning of these two groups, or the nature of the mental health services available to both groups (Boothroyd, Mercado, Poythress, Christy, & Petrila, 2005). The investigators suggested that one explanation for these results might be the fact that the mental health court judges did not have much control over whether the mental health services were actually delivered. If their explanation is correct, it underscores the importance of control over service delivery. It would not be particularly useful to develop a specialized mental health court and divert those with particular mental health needs into this court, unless there was some assurance that additional specialized mental health services were available to those under the jurisdiction of this specialized court.

Other research has focused on criminal recidivism as an outcome variable in studying the impact of mental health courts. There is also mixed evidence on this question. One study (Trupin & Richards, 2003) reported that mental health court clients had fewer arrests postdischarge than did criminal court clients, while another study (Christy, Poythress, Boothroyd, Petrila, & Mehra, 2005) reported that the number of arrests decreased for mental health court clients—but not significantly more than it did for those in criminal court. A third study (Cosden et al., 2003) used random assignment of offenders ($N = 235$) to either assertive community treatment (a particular form of mental health case management involving additional services and small caseloads, sometimes used as part of mental health court) or the standard case management services associated with criminal court. After one year, mental health court clients had significantly fewer arrests and convictions. After two years, however, these differences were much smaller, and both groups showed an increased number of arrests when compared with the first year (Cosden, Ellens, Schnell, & Yamini-Diouf, 2005).

One of the most important considerations in whether mental health court participation reduces criminal recidivism is whether the client actually completes the treatment required by the court; participants completing mental health court in one study were nearly four times less likely to reoffend than were those who did not graduate (Herinckx et al., 2005). Indeed, participants in mental health court who do not complete the program may not differ from those who are processed through traditional criminal court. For instance, Moore and Hiday (2006) reported that those who completed mental health court were rearrested at a rate about one-fourth that of those in criminal court after one year—and those who did *not* complete mental health court were rearrested at about the same rate as the criminal court clients. Other investigators (McNiel & Binder, 2007) also noted both the risk reduction impact of mental health court and the importance of successfully completing mental health court.

A principle of effective intervention discussed earlier in this chapter is treatment integrity. In order to be effective, interventions need to be delivered the way they were intended, and need to be completed. The data from completers versus noncompleters in mental health courts are consistent with this principle. If a defendant is processed through a mental health court and does not participate in the services required by the court, then we should not expect his or her outcome to be better than it would have been through standard prosecution and disposition.

This research suggests that mental health courts, like drug courts, can have a favorable impact on both symptoms amelioration and reoffense risk reduction—provided that services are delivered and clients

participate. Mental health courts vary more than drug courts in how they are administered across sites, however, and the supporting research is not as strong methodologically. Several studies indicate that the value of participation in mental health court is greatly limited when participants do not complete the program required by the court.

Institutional Interventions

There are several important differences between jails and prisons, even though both are secure institutional facilities that incarcerate individuals who have been convicted of criminal offenses. A jail is a community-based facility that houses both individuals who are pretrial (those who have been charged with offenses, but not yet convicted) and others who have been convicted of relatively minor offenses, usually with sentences no longer than a year. By contrast, a prison is part of a correctional system that is either operated by the state (usually a state department of corrections will include a number of prisons) or the federal government (which operates the Federal Bureau of Prisons within the Department of Justice). Those who are incarcerated in prison have all been convicted of criminal offenses. They have also received sentences that are longer than the relatively short sentences associated with jail inmates. Prison sentences can range from slightly over one year to life, and prisons also house those who have received a death sentence.

The Federal Bureau of Prisons (2012) provides a range of programs for inmates. These include

The United States Medical Center for Federal Prisoners in Springfield, Missouri

- Substance abuse treatment
- Educational and vocational training
- Skills development
- Religious programs
- Work programs

The nature of this programming reflects the view that the important influences contributing to reoffending risk include deficits in skills, work training, and experience; they also include problems with drugs or alcohol. Religion may serve as a protective factor for some individuals, offering a structure and set of beliefs that are inconsistent with criminal offending. Psychologists may play a role in the delivery of some of these services, particularly substance abuse treatment and skills development. Of course, psychologists may also be involved in the delivery of mental health services to inmates with mental and emotional disorders.

Many of the same kinds of services are provided in prisons operated by the states. For example, the New York Department of Corrections and Community Supervision (2012) has programs and services for inmates that include educational and vocational training, substance abuse treatment, parenting skills, anger management, domestic violence counseling, health education, sex offender treatment, religious services, and others. The substantial overlap between the kinds of rehabilitative services provided by federal and state facilities reflects the common aspects of views about the needs of offenders that would reduce their reoffense risk and promote the possibility that they will live responsible lives without offending, following their return to their communities.

Jails are in a somewhat different position with respect to providing rehabilitative services. While those in prison have been convicted of criminal offenses and are serving sentences, this is true for only a subset of individuals in jails. Some have been convicted of offenses that are less serious than those of individuals in state or federal prisons, so they serve shorter sentences in jail rather than prison. Others, however, are awaiting disposition of charges, and will be held in the jail for periods ranging from days (for those who have charges dismissed, for example, or who are able to post bond and are released from incarceration pending disposition of charges) to years (for some with serious charges which, for different reasons, take a longer time to resolve). Since jails

cannot anticipate whether their pretrial inmates will remain in the jail, they provide services focusing on immediate needs (e.g., medical and mental health care) rather than longer-term rehabilitation. This may be seen on the website of the nation's largest jail, operated by the Los Angeles County Sheriff's Department (2012). Medical and mental health services are provided, in additional to educational services. Psychologists are involved in delivering such services, but also in assessing inmates' needs and short-term risk for self-harm or violence toward others.

The functions carried out by psychologists also differ between jails and prisons. There are four broad purposes served by mental health professionals, particularly psychologists, in both jails and prisons: classification, consultation/crisis intervention, rehabilitation, and reentry planning. Because the nature of each function varies according to the facility, each will be discussed in terms of whether it is carried out in a jail or a prison.

The Role of Psychologists In Jails. There has been some fluctuation in the number of jail beds in the United States between the years 2000 and 2010. According to the Bureau of Justice Statistics (2011b), the total number of jail beds in the United States as of midyear 2010 was 748,728, an increase from an estimated 677,787 beds as of the same time in 2000 but a 2.4% decrease from the number held in 2009. In 2010, nearly 30% of these beds were contained in the 50 largest jails in the country, and about half of all jail inmates were incarcerated in the 6% of jails with a daily census of 1,000 or more inmates.

There is a much higher rate of severe mental illness in jail than in the general population (Bureau of Justice Statistics, 2006). For example, using inmate self-report of experiencing symptoms of severe mental illness such as hallucinations or delusions during the last 12 months, 17.5% of jail inmates reported the former and 13.7% the latter. These percentages are substantially higher than the percentage of adults over the age of 18 who report having experienced either symptom (3.1%). Another recent study (Steadman, Osher, Robbins, Case, & Samuels, 2009) estimated prevalence rates of serious mental illness among adult male and female inmates in five jails during two time periods: 2002–2003 and 2005–2006. A total of 822 admitted inmates at two jails in Maryland and three jails in New York were selected to receive the

Structured Clinical Interview for DSM-IV. Serious mental illness (defined as major depressive disorder; depressive disorder not otherwise specified; bipolar disorder I, II, and not otherwise specified; schizophrenia spectrum disorder; schizoaffective disorder; schizophreniform disorder; brief psychotic disorder; delusional disorder; and psychotic disorder not otherwise specified) was observed in 14.5% of male inmates and 31% of female inmates.

Given these numbers, we might expect that many of the psychological services provided to jail inmates would focus on those with mental disorders. Such services, described in a national survey of U.S. jails (Steadman & Veysey, 1997), include

- Screening, evaluation, classification
- Diversion (helping to determine whether a pre-trial inmate might meet criteria for a community-based program such as drug court or mental health court)
- Suicide prevention
- Crisis intervention
- Case management services/reentry (liaison with community treatment providers, planning for release, assistance with housing and transportation)
- Coordinating volunteers (teaching, mentoring, tutoring, guiding release)

- Teaching life skills
- Group therapy for inmates and their families

Larger jails with more resources might be able to offer most or all of these services, so a psychologist's role in such jails would be more varied. Smaller jails, by contrast, might be limited to screening, suicide prevention, and crisis intervention.

The Role of Psychologists in Prisons. The contemporary prison can trace its roots to London in the 19th century, when Jeremy Bentham developed the notion that incarceration could be considered part of punishment rather than just a means of holding an individual until trial (as jails do) or execution. Facilities at that time were sometimes called "penitentiaries," reflecting the goal of invoking penance from those who were confined in them.

Imprisoning offenders is not necessarily the most effective approach to reducing the risk of future offending. This is perhaps not a surprise. Among the goals of criminal sentencing and incarceration are retribution, incapacitation, and general deterrence. Although lengthy sentences and punitive prison conditions may be consistent with these goals, such conditions are not necessarily consistent with the goal of rehabilitation. A meta-analysis of over 100 studies (Smith, Goggin, & Gendreau, 2002) indicated that the rate of reoffending following release from

Aerial view of Pelican Bay prison

prison was 7% higher than following the completion of nonresidential sanctions.

Some approaches to prison-based rehabilitation are more effective than others, however. Bonta (1997) classified rehabilitation programs as either "appropriate" or "inappropriate" by determining their consistency with risk/need/responsivity principles discussed earlier in the chapter. Appropriate (RNR-consistent) treatments reduced criminal reoffending by an average of 50% when compared with inappropriate approaches. Appropriate treatment approaches were those that systematically assessed offender risk and needs with specialized tools (e.g., the Level of Service/Case Management Inventory; Andrews et al., 2004), targeted the criminogenic needs of offenders in treatment, and used cognitive-behavioral approaches to change deficits and increase strengths. By contrast, programs classified as inappropriate provided intensive services for low-risk offenders or targeted noncriminogenic needs such as self-esteem. Such interventions were associated with slight *increases* in recidivism. Bonta (1997) concluded that RNR-consistent interventions, whether provided in prison or in the community, reduce recidivism risk and protect the public in the process. The exclusive application of punitive approaches, by contrast, does not reduce reoffending risk and is therefore less useful for public safety—at least via the rehabilitation of offenders.

One other approach that shows promise, particularly in treating drug offenders in prison, is the **therapeutic community** (TC). This is an approach in which the staff, other clients, and physical setting are all part of the therapeutic environment. Group therapy, individual counseling, "community meetings" involving all residents, and specialized interventions to build skills in areas such as anger control, decision making, and recognizing high-risk situations are all used in the TC. Staff functions are not divided into those responsible for "security" versus those responsible for "treatment" (as is often the case in a secure hospital or correctional setting). Instead, all staff members are considered to be part of the rehabilitation process. All residents are likewise involved in maintaining an environment in which therapeutic goals are clear and important.

In correctional settings, the TC has most often been used to treat those with substance abuse problems. One quasi-experimental study (Welsh, 2007) focused on prison TC drug treatment program

participants ($N = 217$) and comparison group participants ($N = 491$) for two-year outcomes following release. Prison TC was effective even without mandatory community aftercare, although effects varied somewhat across different outcome measures and sites. TC interventions significantly reduced rearrest and reincarceration rates, but not drug relapse rates. Postrelease employment predicted a reduction in drug relapse and reincarceration.

One of the questions concerning the impact of rehabilitation in prison concerns "how much is enough?" Criminal sentences are imposed for a specific amount of time, not necessarily with rehabilitation as a primary determinant. But one interesting study (Bourgon & Armstrong, 2005) asked precisely this question: How much treatment is needed to reduce criminal reoffending? Researchers considered the recidivism rates of offenders in a Canadian prison ($N = 620$) who were followed up for one year after their release. While incarcerated, they had received either (1) no treatment, (2) 100 hours of treatment over 5 weeks, (3) 200 hours of treatment over 10 weeks, or (4) 300 hours of treatment over 15 weeks. Treatment programs were cognitive-behavioral, and focused on substance abuse, criminal attitudes, aggression, and criminal peers. Offenders' risk and needs had also been assessed as part of their incarceration. A total of 31% of offenders who received treatment in any dosage recidivated, compared with 41% who received no treatment. Offenders with different risk–needs levels required different amounts of treatment for an effective "dosage." In high-risk offenders with many criminogenic needs, for example, 300 hours of treatment reduced the observed rate of recidivism from 59% to 38%. By contrast, for medium-risk offenders with few criminogenic needs, 100 hours of treatment was sufficient to reduce recidivism from 28% to 12%—but more treatment was not associated with a further reduction in recidivism. For high- and medium-risk offenders with a moderate number of criminogenic needs, 200 hours of treatment was associated with a recidivism rate of 30%, as compared to 44% for similar offenders who received no treatment.

These results have several implications for rehabilitation in prison. First, just as in correctional interventions with juveniles, it is useful to employ a formal, structured approach to assessing relevant needs and intervening according to those needs. Second, it is possible to identify a "dosage effect" for relevant treatment, and to administer such treatment according to who is likely to receive the most benefit. Third, it is feasible to have a favorable impact over a relatively short period of time. Long sentences are not necessary to rehabilitate many of those who

are sentenced to prison—so the justification for keeping inmates in prison for a lengthy period must come from other reasons, such as retribution and deterrence. Box 15.4 concerns the incarceration and possible rehabilitation of a professional athlete.

B o x 15.4 THE CASE OF MICHAEL VICK: WAS HE REHABILITATED IN PRISON?

Michael Vick was the star quarterback for the Atlanta Falcons until he and his codefendants were arrested and charged with running a dogfighting kennel in Virginia. In September, 2007, while he was awaiting trial, Vick tested positive for marijuana. He was convicted of these charges in federal court, and received a sentence of 23 months in the federal system. He left Virginia in January 2008 to serve his sentence at a U.S. Bureau of Prisons facility in Leavenworth, Kansas.

How would the Bureau of Prisons have attempted to rehabilitate Michael Vick? First, he would have gone through "classification" (a period of assessment and individualized information gathering) to decide where he would be assigned. If he had a long sentence for a very serious charge, presented a substantial risk to harm others, or appeared to be an escape risk, he would probably have been assigned to a high-security facility. Apparently he did not meet these criteria, however, as Leavenworth is a minimum-security prison. Then, prison staff would have needed to decide what particular deficits contributed to his involvement in the dogfighting charges of which he was convicted.

Another issue was drug use. Given that Vick tested positive for marijuana three months before he was sentenced, he might have been referred for substance abuse treatment by prison staff. Bureau of Prisons policy on treating drug abuse involves having those in treatment (lasting at least 500 hours over a period of 6–12 months) set apart from the general prison population.

Michael Vick was released from federal prison in May 2009. His story is familiar to those who follow professional football, and many who do not. Following his release from prison, he returned to his home in Hampton, Virginia, where he served the two remaining months of his sentence on home confinement. He was subsequently signed by the Philadelphia Eagles as a back-up quarterback. During the 2010–2011 season, he moved from third-string quarterback to starter after the Eagles traded Donovan McNabb and Kevin Kolb suffered a concussion in the season-opening game.

In the previous edition of this book, we asked some important questions about Mr. Vick's transition from prison back into the community—the reentry process. Where would he live? How would he be employed? Was he genuinely remorseful for his offending? Could

Michael Vick

he live his life without future offending? Could he avoid people and situations that elevate his risk for reoffending?

The answers to these questions are now in. For Michael Vick, his return to the community, his family, and his profession seems to have gone well. How much of this is attributable to his months in prison? That is a difficult question, and certainly not one that can be answered without knowing more about Mr. Vick than can be judged from publicly available information. But his successful return to society and professional football does highlight one important reality: some individuals coming out of prison can (and do) take advantage of the "second chance" they are given to function as law-abiding citizens in our society.

Critical Thought Question
What difference does prior successful functioning make in rehabilitation of an offender?

Psychological Consequences of Imprisonment

The psychological effects of institutional confinement are complex. Vast differences in prison conditions are undoubtedly important: Incarceration in a well-run minimum-security prison with adequate programming and treatment options will have different effects than imprisonment in an overcrowded, mismanaged facility where staff members use highly punitive practices such as excessive surveillance and isolation to control inmates. The psychological vulnerability and resilience of inmates and the length of their confinement matter as well.

For a number of reasons, high-quality empirical studies of the psychological consequences of imprisonment are limited. First, it has been difficult to develop a standard measure to quantify the effects of long-term incarceration because they are so variable and subjective. Second, most studies have assessed the effects of incarceration among inmates still imprisoned (e.g., Bonta & Gendreau, 1990), and because prisoners can adapt and attempt to achieve a tolerable existence *inside* the prison, the full psychological implications of long-term confinement may be apparent only after release (Haney, 2006). It is too simplistic to assert that violent offenders will be more likely to be violent toward others in prison. One study found that although inmates convicted of assault, robbery, and certain other violent offenses were more likely to commit serious rules infractions in prisons, inmates convicted of homicide were not—and those convicted of sexual offenses were even less likely to commit such infractions (Sorenson & Davis, 2011).

But social scientists have learned something about the consequences of long-term incarceration. Many inmates show a particular pattern of coping mechanisms in response to high levels of prison stress. They may become hypervigilant in order to deal with the significant risks to their personal safety, learn to project a "tough-guy veneer," socially isolate themselves and suppress any signs of emotion, and become generally distrustful of others (McCorkle, 1992). None of these characteristics will facilitate their reintegration into society. Indeed, some evidence suggests that assigning an individual to a higher-security prison actually increases that individual's risk for reoffending (Bench & Allen, 2003; Chen & Shapiro, 2007). One study (Gaes & Camp, 2009) even used random assignment to prison security level to show that inmates

with a randomly-assigned higher security classification had a rate of returning to prison that was 31% higher than that of their counterparts who were assigned to a prison with a lower security level. There were no differences in the rates of serious institutional misconduct of these participants. These results are consistent with the influence of deviant peers and environmental strain, and inconsistent with specific deterrence theory.

Inmates report that their initial period of confinement is the most difficult (Harding & Zimmerman, 1989). Over time, a gradual process takes place in which prisoners adjust to their environment. Sociologist Donald Clemmer called this process **prisonization** and defined it as "the taking on in greater or less degree of the folkways, mores, customs, and general culture of the penitentiary" (Clemmer, 1958). This tends to happen without conscious awareness in inmates as they gradually learn to give up control of choices and decisions, and to depend on institutional rulemakers to provide structure and routine to their lives. One commentator likened it to a kind of "behavioral deep freeze" (Zamble, 1992) from which it is difficult to emerge, especially into the unstructured and unpredictable world that awaits an inmate upon release.

Psychologists have identified a number of other consequences of imprisonment. Impoverished conditions and arbitrary and abusive treatment diminish inmates' sense of identity and self-worth, causing some to project a reputation for toughness and others to appear distant and aloof. Still others externalize their rage and adopt aggressive and violent survival strategies (Toch, 1985). Although estimates of the frequency of prison rapes vary, there is little doubt that their consequences can be severe (King, 1992). Obviously, inmates with both diagnosed and unidentified psychiatric disorders are at heightened risk, and some inmates experience prison-related maladies in response to their harsh conditions. The secondary effects of incarceration extend to blameless spouses and the children of inmates. Having a parent in prison is a strong predictor of behavioral problems, including future lawbreaking (Mumula, 2000).

One scholar of correctional systems raised the intriguing possibility that prisons themselves serve to further the maladaptive and dysfunctional behavioral patterns that resulted in confinement in the first place:

> [T]he long-term effects of exposure to powerful and destructive situations, contexts, and structures

mean that prisons themselves also can act as criminogenic agents—in both their primary effects on prisoners and secondary effects on the lives of the persons who are connected to them…. Programs of prisoner change cannot ignore the situations and social conditions that prisoners encounter after they are released if there is to be any real chance of sustaining whatever positive growth or personal gains were achieved during imprisonment. (Haney, 2006, p. 8)

We discuss the problems associated with reentry into society next.

Reentry

The process of reentry focuses on preparing inmates to move from incarceration back into the community and to face a world that is fundamentally different from the one to which they adapted while in prison. To be successful, they must adjust quickly. Fortunately, and appropriately, there has been more emphasis on this transition during recent years. In this chapter, we have seen the importance of services delivered in the community—and planning so that services are delivered as needed and intended. Partly because of the relatively recent nature of the emphasis on reentry in corrections, there is limited empirical research regarding the effectiveness of reentry programs. Existing research in this area has recently been summarized (Heilbrun et al., in press).

The priorities for reentry begin with the goal of reducing the risk of reoffending. There are a number of ways to pursue this goal. Just as drug courts and mental health courts target specific constellations of clinical symptoms with the expectation that providing relevant services in these areas will reduce the symptoms, promote better adjustment, *and* reduce recidivism risk, the reentry process aims to target risk-relevant needs as the individual returns to the community. Released inmates account for a large proportion of the population with communicable health problems, for instance, HIV/AIDS and hepatitis B and C (Mellow, Mukamal, LoBuglio, Solomon, Osborne, 2008). Reentry services can promote the provision of necessary health care services. Reentry services can also yield significant cost savings when provided effectively. This is always an important consideration for local and state governments dealing with crime, especially during a recession.

Reentry can actually be considered broadly as including services provided during custody, in preparation for release, and during the period of community supervision and eventual discharge. The custody phase involves measuring offenders' risks, needs, and strengths upon entry to the correctional facility and providing interventions designed to reduce risk, address needs, and build strengths. The release phase includes *inmate release preparation*, with a parole plan for supervision, housing, employment, drug testing, and other considerations, and *release decision making*, regarding the parole decision. The community supervision/discharge phase involves *supervision and services*, *revocation decision making* (including graduated sanctions in response to infractions), and *discharge and aftercare*, when community correctional supervision is terminated. This section of the chapter focuses on the community supervision/discharge phase of reentry.

There were over 840,000 individuals on parole in the United States during 2010 (105,552 in the federal system and 735,124 in the states) (Bureau of Justice Statistics, 2011a). The number of those on probation and community supervision during 2009 has been estimated at greater than 7.2 million, however, reflecting the substantially larger number of offenders on this status (Bureau of Justice Statistics, 2010). Up to 2/3 of those on parole are rearrested within three years (Petersilia, 2001), underscoring the importance of the reentry process and its potential to reduce new offending. An inmate in the California Institute for Men, Dagoberto Noyola, 45, exemplifies both the benefit of reentry programs and the ease with which some inmates slip back into old patterns of behavior upon release. Noyola says that a program that taught him to provide drug counseling to high school students and land a job laying tile for a construction company enabled him to reintegrate into society on his last parole. But the career criminal landed behind bars again after a burglary conviction. Still, he is hoping to return to tiling when released again. Looking over a sea of inmates in the prison's gym, Noyola said "A lot of guys want to go out there and do good. Nobody wants to be in here" (Gould, 2011).

The "community classification center" is part of the trend toward greater structure in reentry. Such facilities accept inmates who are released from prison and returning to the community. However, rather than either placing them directly in the community or sending them home, the community classification centers provide assessment for a limited period of time, and structure the reentry process so that individuals receive housing and services that are consistent with their needs. Some limited evidence suggests that such centers do a good job in both providing treatment services and managing the risk of reoffending during the first 6–12 months in the community following prison (Wilkinson, 2001). Programs that target specific offender needs have also been associated with lower recidivism rates (Seiter & Kadela, 2003).

There have been other changes in practice consistent with contemporary approaches to reentry (Lowenkamp & Latessa, 2005). The Second Chance Act of 2007: Community Safety through Recidivism Prevention, which was signed into law by President Bush in April 2008, provides funding for improving reentry using approaches consistent with evidence-based policy (Burke & Tonry, 2006; Center for Effective Public Policy, 2007). Guidelines to assist in the reentry process have been published (Aos, Miller, & Drake, 2006; International Association of Chiefs of Police, 2006). The interest in using empirical evidence to guide the practice of reentry is strong, as it is in contemporary medicine and mental health under the rubric "evidence-based practice."

There has been a limited amount of empirical research on parole services provided in the reentry process. In the early 1990s, California started a community-based program to facilitate parolee success for reintegration into society (Zhang, Roberts, & Callanan, 2006). The investigators reported that those not participating in this program were 1.4 times more likely to be rearrested within 12 months on parole, and that meeting goals in four specified domains (which this program facilitated) was associated with the lowest risk for reincarceration. A second study (Martin, Lurigio, & Olson, 2003) focused on a community-based supervision facility providing relevant services (e.g., life skills training, violence prevention, literacy classes, job skills training, job placement services, and GED preparation) during the day. The findings of this study reflect the importance of sufficient time in a program. More clients remained arrest-free after a longer period in the program (70+ days) than after a shorter period (less than 10 days). This difference in the recidivism reduction between the two groups (25% reduction for the first versus 10% for the second) provides an estimate of the potential "dosage" impact of this program. A third study (Bouffard & Bergeron, 2006) described a small program targeting serious and violent offenders during reentry; the program provided more referrals to community-based services and increased drug testing frequency during parole. Participants were less likely

to test positive for drug use while on parole, had similar parole revocation rates, and had a 60% lower likelihood of postparole rearrest.

Research in this area reflects several trends for individuals with severe mental illness returning from prison to the community (Heilbrun et al., in press). The available evidence does support better criminal justice outcomes (whether rearrest or reincarceration) for participants in programs based upon either the Assertive Community Treatment (see, e.g., Lamberti, Deem, Weisman, & LaDuke, 2011) or Intensive Case Management (see, e.g., Steadman & Naples, 2005) models. Evidence on mental health outcomes is also generally favorable, although more mixed; some studies show consistently favorable mental health and community adjustment outcomes, while others suggest that certain health outcomes (e.g., hospital days) may actually be greater for those in specialized programs. The evidence in this area is generally promising, however, subject to the caveat that we clearly need more studies that are well-designed (including comparison/control groups and large samples) to support these conclusions with more confidence.

Reentry as applied to parole is growing in popularity. In fiscal year 2004–2005, for example, nearly 44,000 paroled offenders were required to attend a reentry program (National Offender Management Service, 2005). As yet, however, there is very limited information on the effectiveness of such programs. One study suggested that offenders who "fit" well with the reentry program (in terms of their risk and needs) were more likely to be recommended for placement (McGuire et al., 2008). This is good as far as it goes, but it would be even better if we had more information on the impact of the program on the services delivered, and whether the delivery of such services was related to rearrest.

Somewhat more research has been done on specialized parole services to individuals with mental disorders. A "firm but fair" approach to working with clients seems to distinguish more effective parole officers with this population (Skeem, Encandela, & Eno Louden, 2003; Skeem & Eno Louden, 2006). Graduated sanctions are used by both traditional and specialty parole/probation officers, but traditional officers generally respond to noncompliance with more punitive approaches (Eno Louden, Skeem, Camp, & Christensen, 2008). This relates to the differences between specialty agencies and traditional parole services; the former are more likely to focus on monitoring medication and treatment attendance and to use problem-solving strategies, and less likely to use threats of incarceration (Skeem, Emke-Francis, & Eno Louden, 2006). This appears particularly valuable with probationers who have co-occurring mental illness and substance abuse, as these individuals generally have poor relationships with professionals, and are more likely to feel coerced into treatment (Skeem, Eno Louden, Manchak, Vidal, & Haddad, 2009).

Several studies have addressed the results of specific programs, although none has been designed with random assignment to the program versus "treatment as usual." Accordingly, we cannot be confident that these reentry programs actually work as intended. One study, focusing on those with a history of violent offending, indicated that participants were less likely to test positive for drugs, and also less likely to be arrested, than were those from a comparison group (Bouffard & Bergeron, 2006). Several other studies noted various problems with noncompliance, however, including difficulty contacting participants following release from prison (Schram & Morash, 2002); having only a small percentage of participants actually receive an aftercare plan, and even fewer actually seek postrelease services (Haas & Hamilton, 2007); and less participation in referred services compared with the comparison group (Bouffard & Bergeron, 2006).

If community reentry programs are to be effective, it is very important that they be committed to the "quality assurance" process described for effective juvenile programs—ensuring that intended services are actually delivered as planned. One consideration is whether such services are voluntary or required as part of parole. One would expect that required participation would increase the overall compliance rate. However, there is some evidence for a self-selection process in which reentry services are voluntary, with the more motivated individuals seeking out and receiving services—and benefiting more. In one California program, for example, services to parolees were provided on a voluntary basis and included employment, substance abuse recovery, math and literacy skills, and housing services. Participants in at least one of these areas had a recidivism rate of 33.6%, compared to a recidivism rate of 52.8% among those not participating in this program (Zhang et al., 2006). These findings raise some complicated questions about whether parolees should be required to avail themselves of reentry services.

SUMMARY

1. ***What are the important considerations in assessing juveniles prior to placement decisions?*** The considerations that are most often considered by courts with juvenile placements are public safety and offenders' treatment needs and amenability to treatment. These factors, often cited in the law, overlap considerably with components of risk/need/responsivity, a well-supported approach to assessing and treating both juveniles and adults who have committed criminal offenses.

2. ***What is the evidence for the effectiveness of interventions with juveniles in the community?*** There is strong evidence for the effectiveness of three particular approaches to the community-based treatment of juveniles: Multisystemic Therapy, Oregon Treatment Foster Care, and Functional Family Therapy. These approaches are successful in both providing needed services for offenders, and reducing the risk of reoffending in those who receive them.

3. ***What are some characteristics of an effective program?*** Research has identified a number of

common elements in programs that are effective. They tend to use different treatment modalities, carefully train those who deliver services, use a team approach, monitor service delivery to ensure that services are actually being provided as intended and individuals do not drop out or miss appointments, and deliver services in family and school settings.

4. ***How can risk/need/responsivity help to provide effective rehabilitative services for adults?*** Assessment of risk helps determine who should be treated at a particular intensity (frequency of service) and dosage (total amount of service received). Assessment of needs helps to target the particular interventions that may be provided to individuals. Assessing responsivity helps a program to decide on the most applicable kinds of interventions—those to which inmates are likely to respond best.

5. ***How do specialized problem-solving courts compare to other correctional interventions?*** These courts serve specific populations—individuals with particular problems (such as substance abuse or mental illness), for whom the provision of

treatment services would both rehabilitate the individual and reduce the risk of reoffending. Service delivery and treatment participation are monitored by the court, giving participants a strong incentive to complete the planned course of treatment. These courts can either divert defendants from standard prosecution (unlike more conventional correctional dispositions) or function as a specialized form of community corrections similar to probation. In some jurisdictions, if a defendant does not satisfy the required conditions of the specialized problem-solving court, he or she may be returned to the traditional prosecution process.

6. *What are the differences between jails and prisons and what role do psychologists play in these settings?* A jail is a community-based setting that houses both pretrial defendants and inmates who have been convicted of minor offenses and sentenced to terms of less than two years. A prison is part of a state- or federal-level correctional system, housing only inmates who have been convicted of more serious offenses. There are four particular functions served by psychologists who work in either a jail or a prison: classification, consultation/crisis intervention, rehabilitation, and reentry planning. The nature, scope, and distribution of these tasks vary according to whether the facility is a jail or a prison; they can also vary according to the size and resources of the facility.

7. *What kinds of interventions are delivered in jails and prisons?* Because of heterogeneity in jail populations, jails generally cannot provide rehabilitative services whose delivery requires individuals to remain in the facility for predictable periods of time. Accordingly, they focus on providing present-state services (e.g., medical, mental health, educational, substance abuse).

Prisons, by contrast, can offer additional rehabilitative services that include more extensive educational and vocational training, skill building, and specialized interventions (e.g., for sexual offenders). Both kinds of facilities also offer religious services, which may have a protective influence for some individuals at risk of future offending.

8. *What are some of the psychological consequences of imprisonment?* Responses to imprisonment vary significantly as a function of the conditions of incarceration and inmates' psychological resilience and mental health. Many inmates experience adjustment problems early in their imprisonment; they may become hypervigilant, socially isolated, and emotionally suppressed. Exposure to prison violence and sexual offending can have a serious impact on psychological well-being. Individuals who are incarcerated for offenses such as assault and robbery (but not homicide or sexual offenses) may be more likely to behave violently toward others in a jail or prison.

9. *What are the priorities in preparing individuals for the transition from incarceration to community living (the reentry process)?* There are six areas in particular that are important in the reentry planning process. How is the family functioning, and will the individual live within it; if not, where will he or she be housed? Will the individual return to school, have a job, or be actively receiving any kind of job training? What mental health and/or substance abuse services are needed, and how will they be delivered? How will the individual be monitored for adherence to conditions specified in the plan? Will there be particular intensity to this monitoring, or specialized aspects (e.g., case management)? Finally, what kind of social support is available, and what peers will the individual be around?

KEY TERMS

adjudication of delinquency

classification

criminal conviction

criminogenic needs

diversion

Functional Family Therapy

intensive probation

Multisystemic Therapy

Oregon Treatment Foster Care

parole

prisonization

probation

reentry

risk, needs, and responsivity

school-based probation

Sequential Intercept Model

therapeutic community

Glossary

absolute judgment An eyewitness's process of deciding, when looking at a sequential lineup, whether any of the people shown in the lineup match the description of the perpetrator.

abuse excuse A legal tactic by which a person charged with a crime claims that past victimization justifies his or her present alleged offense.

acute stress disorder The development of anxiety-related, dissociative, and other symptoms that occurs within 1 month after exposure to an extreme traumatic event and whose duration is between 2 days and 4 weeks.

adjudication of delinquency The legal determination that a juvenile is culpable of an offense. When responsible for offending, juveniles are adjudicated delinquent; adults are found guilty.

adjudicative competence The legal capacities necessary for a defendant to stand trial or otherwise resolve criminal charges (see "competence to stand trial" and "competence to plead guilty").

advance medical directives Legal documentation in which an individual indicates the kinds of future medical treatments she will accept should she be incapacitated (and therefore be unable to make treatment decisions) at the time the treatment is needed.

adversarial system A system of resolving disputes in which the parties, usually represented by counsel, argue and present evidence to a neutral fact finder, who makes a decision based on the evidence and arguments presented by the parties; as distinguished from an inquisitorial system, in which the fact finder takes an active part in determining what occurred.

aggravating factors Conditions or components that make a criminal act more serious.

***amicus curiae* brief** A "friend-of-the-court" brief filed by a person or organization not a party to the litigation, but with a strong view on the subject matter in the case.

anchoring A cognitive bias that describes the common human tendency of individuals to rely too heavily, or "anchor," on a suggested piece of information (e.g., a dollar value in the context of damage awards) when making decisions.

anchoring and adjustment bias This occurs when individuals are strongly influenced or "anchored" by an initial starting value and when, in subsequent decisions, they do not sufficiently adjust their judgments away from this starting point.

anomie A sense of alienation or meaninglessness.

antisocial personality disorder A pervasive pattern of disregard for, and violation of, the rights of others that begins in childhood or early adolescence and continues into adulthood.

applied scientist An individual whose research focuses on solving problems rather than acquiring knowledge for the sake of understanding (see basic scientist).

arbitration A form of dispute resolution in which a neutral third party makes a decision that is binding on the two disputants.

archival analysis In psychology and law, a method of data collection that involves examination of previously decided issues and cases.

arraignment A formal statement of charges and an initial plea by the defendant to these charges.

assimilation The mental process in which an individual internalizes a current perception or conception into their preexisting representation.

attribution theory A theory in social psychology focusing on people's explanations for the causes of their behavior and the behavior of others.

authoritarianism A set of beliefs and characteristics that includes submissiveness to authority, demands for obedience from subordinates, intolerance of minorities and other outgroups, and endorsement of the use of power and punishment to ensure conformity to conventional norms.

autobiographical memory Memory for one's own life experiences.

aversive racism A description of those who believe in racial equality and view themselves as nonprejudiced, but have unconscious, negative beliefs about people of other races. In situations that elicit these negative beliefs, such individuals try to avoid acting on them or express them in subtle ways.

back-end sentencing Sentencing that occurs when parolees are arrested for new crimes or violate the conditions of their parole and are returned to prison by state parole boards as a consequence (as contrasted with front-end sentencing).

basic scientist A scientist who pursues knowledge motivated by scientific curiosity or interest in a scientific question, studying a phenomenon to better understand it rather than to solve a problem.

battered woman syndrome A collection of symptoms described in women who have experienced prolonged and extensive abuse from their partners.

behavioral confirmation An influence in which people's expectations cause them to act in ways that confirm those expectations.

best interests of the child The legal standard by which child custody decisions are made in the United States.

biological theory of crime An explanation for the causes of criminal behavior that uses heredity and constitutional characteristics of the lawbreaker.

bioterrorism A form of terrorism that uses biological "weapons," such as viruses and bacteria, to harm or threaten others.

black-letter law Basic principles of law generally accepted by courts and embodied in statutes.

black-sheep effect The tendency to be more punitive toward those members of one's group who violate the norms of the group.

blended sentencing A sentencing mechanism that allows judges, in sentencing juveniles tried as adults, to combine sanctions available in juvenile court with those used in criminal court.

borderline personality disorder A personality disorder characterized by impulsivity and instability in moods, behavior, self-image, and interpersonal relationships.

brain fingerprinting A procedure that involves the measurement of brain waves in response to a stimulus to assess whether the brain recognizes that stimulus.

***Brawner* rule** This rule states that a defendant is not responsible for criminal conduct when, because of a mental disease or defect, he or she lacks substantial capacity either to appreciate the criminality (wrongfulness) of the conduct or to conform his or her conduct to the requirements of the law (also known as the American Law Institute, or ALI, rule).

breached duty The violation, through either negligence or intentional wrongdoing, of a duty that one party legally owes to another party.

brutalization The proposition that the use of capital punishment actually increases the crime rate by sending a message that it is acceptable to kill those who have committed wrongful acts.

burnout A process occurring in response to prolonged stress; manifestations may include detachment from work and personal relationships, exhaustion, cynicism, and reduced productivity.

case law The body of previous legal decisions and legal principles developed from these earlier decisions, as contrasted with statutory laws (passed by the legislative branch and approved by the executive branch). Case law develops through the courts over time, based upon precedent, and tends to change slowly because of the legal principle of *stare decisis*.

challenges for cause Occurring during jury selection, such challenges can be made by an attorney seeking to excuse a potential juror on grounds of bias. In addition, a judge may excuse a prospective juror for cause without a request to do so from either attorney. There is no limit on the number of challenges for cause that an attorney can make (by contrast, see "peremptory challenges").

change of venue Moving a trial to another locality, usually because extensive pretrial publicity has prevented the assembling of an unbiased jury.

charge bargaining A form of plea bargaining in which a prosecutor reduces the number or severity of charges against a criminal defendant in exchange for a guilty plea.

chemical castration The use of injections of a female hormone into male rapists as a method of reducing their sex drive.

civil commitment The legal process involving the involuntary hospitalization of persons who are mentally ill and dangerous to themselves or others.

civil competencies This term applies to civil (noncriminal) legal contexts in which the question of mental competence for a specific task (e.g., making a will) is raised.

class action case A case that involves many plaintiffs who collectively form a "class" and who claim that they suffered similar injuries because of a defendant's actions.

classical conditioning A procedure in which one learns to associate a new response with a stimulus.

classical school of criminology The point of view, which evolved in the 1700s and 1800s, emphasizing the role of free will and cost-benefit analysis in determining criminal behavior.

classification The evaluation of convicted offenders by a correctional facility or parole office to assess the level of risk of criminal recidivism, institutional misconduct, and escape or noncompliance.

closing argument A summation of evidence, made by an attorney at the end of a trial.

cognitive interview A procedure used to assist victims in recalling aspects of a crime or other traumatic event.

cognitive load interviews Interviews that are designed to mentally tax a person through high cognitive demand. In such interviews it becomes difficult to simultaneously answer a question and maintain a lie.

cognizable groups Specific groups of persons, usually defined by demographic characteristics such as race or gender.

commonsense justice Ordinary citizens' basic notions of what is just and fair in contrast to the dictates of formal, statutory law.

community-based policing A policy that increases direct police/citizen contacts within a neighborhood.

compensatory damages The payment or restitution owed to a plaintiff for the damages and harm that have been determined to be caused by a civil defendant.

competence to plead guilty The ability of a defendant to understand the possible consequences of pleading guilty to criminal charges instead of going to trial, and to make a rational choice between the alternatives.

competence to stand trial Sufficient present ability to understand the legal proceedings in which one is involved and to consult with one's attorney with a reasonable degree of rational understanding.

compliant false confessions Confessions elicited when the suspect is induced to comply with the interrogator's demands to make an incriminating statement.

Concealed Knowledge Test An approach to interrogating criminal suspects focusing on relevant concealed knowledge in the suspect's mind, not the truthfulness of his/her statements. Such information is particularly important when only a guilty individual would know it.

concordance rate The extent of similarity in a behavior or characteristic between twins.

confirmation bias A tendency to search for information that confirms one's preconceptions.

confrontation clause Language in the Sixth Amendment of the United States Constitution that guarantees defendants the right to confront their accusers.

containment theory The proposition that societal pressure controls the rate of crime.

Control Question Test A polygraph technique in which the subject is asked a question that elicits an emotional response.

control theory The proposition that people will act in an antisocial way unless they are prevented from doing so.

countermeasures Techniques employed by a deceptive subject to "beat" the polygraph test in order to avoid detection (e.g., breathing strategies, complex mental calculations, thinking about something exciting or dangerous, or self-inflicted pain).

crime control model The model that emphasizes the reduction of crime rates and vindicating victims' rights by the efficient detection of suspects and the effective prosecution of defendants, to help ensure that criminal activity is being contained or reduced.

criminal conviction The outcome of a criminal prosecution that concludes in a judgment that the adult defendant is guilty of the crime charged.

criminal profiling The use of psychological principles as a crime investigation technique to guide police toward suspects who possess certain personal characteristics as suggested by evidence from the crime scene.

criminalization hypothesis The idea that untreated symptoms of mental illness result in behavior that is criminal, or is treated as criminal.

criminogenic needs The deficits (such as substance abuse, family problems, educational problems, and pro-criminal attitudes) that increase the risk of reoffending.

criminology The study of crime and criminal behavior.

Crisis Intervention Team (CIT) This program was designed by the Memphis Police Department (also known as the Memphis Model) to increase officer and public safety while attempting to redirect those with behavioral health problems from the judicial system to treatment-oriented alternatives. It involves training in more effective interactions with those experiencing behavioral health problems.

cycle of violence Behavior involving a pattern of periodic domestic violence, often exhibited by batterers, making their victims fearful of the battering they believe is inevitable.

damages Money awarded to a person injured by the unlawful act or negligence of another.

dangerousness A propensity to behavior that involves acts of physical violence or threats by one person against another. In some contexts, it is considered more broadly to include antisocial behavior of other kinds, including property damage, theft, and other illegal acts.

death qualification Questioning of prospective jurors during jury selection in death penalty cases regarding their attitudes toward capital punishment. Jurors endorsing extreme beliefs about the death penalty (such as an unwillingness to impose it under any circumstances) may be dismissed from consideration, leaving the remaining "death-qualified" pool of prospective jurors.

declarative knowledge In the context of jury behavior, jurors' understanding of legal concepts (as contrasted with procedural knowledge).

defensive attribution An explanation for behavior that enables people to deal with perceived inequities in others' lives and to avoid feelings of vulnerability.

deinstitutionalization The long-term trend of closing mental hospitals and transferring care to community-based mental health treatment facilities.

deliberative processes Thought processes that involve mental effort, concentration, motivation, and the application of learned rules.

determinate sentencing A sentence of confinement or probation for a fixed period of time specified by statute, as contrasted with an indeterminate sentence whose duration is determined by the offender's behavior.

diagnostic cues Cues that enable professionals to diagnose or distinguish among available alternatives (e.g., between psychopaths and nonpsychopaths, or between truth-tellers and liars).

differential association approach Criminal behavior requires socialization into a system of values conducive to violating the law; thus, the potential criminal develops definitions of behavior that make deviant conduct seem acceptable.

differential association reinforcement theory A learning-theory approach that asserts that criminal behavior is the result of socialization into a system of values that is conducive to violations of the law.

diminished capacity A variation of the insanity defense that is applicable if the defendant (in the words of the law) lacks the ability to "meaningfully premeditate the crime."

discovery A procedure in which the attorney for one side seeks to become aware of the materials used by the other side to form its case.

discretion The ability to act according to one's own judgment and conscience. In judicial decisions, discretion refers to a judge's consideration of factors that may lead to appropriate *variations* in how the system responds to offenses, as opposed to a decision based on predefined legal guidelines or rules.

dispositional attributions Explanations for others' behavior that focus on ability, personality, or even temporary states (such as fatigue or luck) to help understand the behavior.

dispositional phase The sentencing phase of the case in which hearings typically combine adversarial procedures and attention to the particular needs of the defendant.

dissociation The act of "escaping" from a traumatic event by extreme detachment.

distributive justice Concerns about what is right or just with respect to the allocation of goods within a society.

diversion The practice of officially stopping or suspending a case prior to court adjudication (without a formal trial) and referring the defendant to a community education,

treatment, or work program in lieu of adjudication or incarceration.

dizygotic twins (DZ) Commonly called fraternal twins, occurring when two eggs are fertilized.

double-blind testing procedures Experimental procedures in which both the participant and experimenter are unaware of the particular conditions being tested.

dual-process models Descriptions of two approaches to human information processing. Typically they propose both a rational, deliberate approach, and a quick, intuitive approach. The former requires motivation, effort, and ability; the latter does not.

due process model A perspective that emphasizes due process or procedural justice (fairness) under the law. In contrast to the crime control model, this model places stronger emphasis on defendants' rights.

duty The obligation that one party legally owes to another party.

ecological validity The extent to which the methods, materials, and setting of a research study resemble the real-life phenomena being investigated.

encoding The process of entering a perception into memory.

equality The principle that all who commit the same crime should receive the same consequences.

estimator variable The factors that are beyond the control of the justice system and whose impact on the reliability of the eyewitness can only be estimated (e.g., the lighting conditions at the time of the crime; whether the perpetrator was wearing a disguise).

euthanasia The act of killing an individual for reasons that are considered merciful.

evaluation apprehension Concern about the ways that others evaluate us.

evidence ploys Used in criminal interrogation, these are ruses that involve providing false information about their guilt to suspects, which can apparently cause them to doubt their memories and rely instead on external sources to infer what happened.

evidentiary strength Refers to the nature of the evidence regarding guilt in a legal proceeding, and is probably the most important determinant of jurors' verdicts.

exculpatory Tending to clear a defendant of fault or guilt.

executive function The cognitive ability to plan and regulate behavior.

experiential inflammatory bias The notion that people who witness the use of virtual environments may be so swept up in the experience and persuaded by the lifelike nature of these scenes that they have difficulty imagining or visualizing a different point of view.

experimental methodology Experimental research studies involve the manipulation of one or more factors (termed "independent variables"), observation of the effects of these factors on some behavior (termed "dependent variables"), and control of other relevant factors.

experimenter bias An experimenter's influence on the results of a research study.

expert witness A witness who has special knowledge beyond that of the ordinary lay person (juror) about a subject enabling him or her to give testimony regarding an issue that requires expertise to understand. Experts are permitted to give opinion testimony, while a nonexpert witness is typically limited to testimony about which he or she has direct knowledge through first-hand observation.

external validity A measure of whether the results of scientific research, conducted with a sample of the population, can be generalized to a larger group or that population.

extralegal factors Influences that are legally irrelevant in that they cannot serve as evidence in a legal proceeding (e.g., age, race, gender, and socioeconomic status).

extrinsic motivation The desire to pursue goals that would please and impress others.

extroversion The personality cluster characterized by outgoing orientation, enthusiasm, and optimism.

fabricated evidence False evidence presented by interrogators in order to elicit information from suspects.

false confession An admission of guilt to a crime for which the confessor is not culpable. False confessions occur for different reasons and they can be explained by different situational and dispositional factors.

false denial A guilty suspect's proclamation of innocence and denial of involvement in crimes for which he or she is actually responsible.

field studies Scientific research done in real-world settings, as contrasted with a more artificial environment. Field studies have more ecological validity (a greater resemblance to actual practice) but are more difficult to carefully control.

fitness-for-duty evaluation The psychological assessment of an employee conducted to determine whether that individual is mentally, emotionally, or behaviorally impaired, which might prevent the return to workplace duties. It is often used with those in dangerous occupations, such as police work, firefighters, and the military.

Five Factor Model of personality This descriptive model includes five broad factors or dimensions of personality. The personality dimensions (OCEAN) include Openness (intellect), Conscientiousness, Extraversion, Agreeableness, and Neuroticism (or emotional stability).

focal concerns theory A theory that explains the criminal activities of lower-class adolescent gangs as an attempt to achieve the ends that are most valued in their culture through behaviors that appear best suited to obtain those ends.

forensic evaluator A professional role played by psychologists, psychiatrists, and social workers when providing forensic mental health assessments and expert testimony on a variety of topics related to legal questions involving mental and emotional disorder, intellectual functioning, substance abuse, and other clinical disorders, as well as capacities that are directly related to the legal question.

forensic mental health assessment Evaluations conducted by a variety of professionals including psychiatrists, psychologists, and social workers. The assessments address a wide range of questions in civil, criminal, and family law (e.g., competency to stand trial, child custody, civil commitment, capital sentencing).

forensic psychologists These psychologists apply scientific findings and knowledge to questions and issues related to the legal system. Their work may include conducting forensic mental health assessments for courts and attorneys, providing treatment to those under the supervision of the legal system, offering consultation to law enforcement agencies and personnel, and other related tasks.

framing effects The way decision alternatives are presented (or framed)—as either gains or losses—can have a significant impact on a person's choice. Individuals are more willing to take chances when the decision alternatives are presented in terms of gains than in terms of losses.

front-end sentencing Sentencing imposed following conviction for a crime committed when the offender was not under correctional jurisdiction (as contrasted with back-end sentencing).

Functional Family Therapy A community-based intervention for juvenile offenders. It is provided weekly by a single therapist, over an average period of three months. It is family-focused, and is often delivered in the home.

functional magnetic resonance imaging A type of specialized neuroimaging that registers blood flow related to neural activity in the brain or spinal cord.

fundamental attribution error The belief that behavior is caused by stable factors internal to a person rather than by situational factors external to a person.

generic prejudice Prejudice arising from media coverage of issues not specifically related to a particular case but thematically relevant to the issues at hand.

grand jury A group of citizens who hear evidence in closed proceedings and decide whether to issue an indictment.

ground truth A clear and accurate measure of the outcome of interest in a study.

harm The losses or adversities suffered by a person who is the victim of wrongdoing.

hate crimes Criminal acts intended to harm or intimidate people because of their race, ethnicity, sexual orientation, religion or other minority group status.

heuristics A mental shortcut, "rule of thumb," or educated guess used to help solve a problem. These methods typically utilize experimentation and trial-and-error techniques.

hostile workplace harassment A form of workplace harassment that does not involve a specific response (see "*quid pro quo* harassment"), but instead involves gender harassment and unwanted sexual attention, resulting in an intimidating, hostile, or offensive working environment.

illusion of control Attorneys' perceptions that the outcomes of their cases are largely within their control.

illusory causation The inaccurate perception that two variables are causally related.

impeach To cross-examine a witness for the purpose of calling into question his or her credibility or reliability.

implicit personality theory A person's preconceptions about how certain attributes are related to one another and to behavior.

inadmissible evidence Evidence in a legal proceeding that the court holds cannot be admitted, and therefore cannot be considered by the fact finder.

indeterminate sentencing Sentencing scheme in which the judge imposes an indefinite period of incarceration for a given offense (e.g., 6–20 years) and the actual length of stay depends on the individual's behavior while incarcerated. Such behavior affects whether the individual will be released on parole or will serve the maximum sentence.

indictment An accusation issued by a grand jury charging the defendant with criminal conduct.

in-group bias The tendency to favor one's own group.

in-group/out-group differences An in-group shares a common identity and sense of belonging, while an out-group lacks these things.

initial appearance The constitutional right to be brought before a judge within 48 hours of arrest. The primary purpose is for the judge to review the evidence summarized by the prosecutor and determine whether there is sufficient reason to believe that the suspect may have committed the alleged offenses.

inquisitorial approach The legal system in which the judge plays a very active role in determining the accuracy of evidence before the court (as contrasted with the adversarial approach, in which the judge is a more passive evaluator of evidence presented in a trial).

insanity The principal legal doctrine permitting consideration of mental abnormality in assessing criminal liability. Those acquitted of criminal charges because they are found not guilty by reason of insanity are typically required to spend an indeterminate period of treatment in a secure mental health facility until they are no longer dangerous to self or others.

intensive probation Probation involving frequent monitoring and contact.

intention The offender's frame of mind in committing a criminal act.

intentional behavior Purposeful conduct in which a person meant the outcome of a given act to occur.

internalized false confessions An inaccurate confession that is genuinely believed. Internalized false confessions can result when, after hours of being questioned, badgered, and told stories about what "must have happened," the suspect begins to develop a profound distrust of his or her own memory.

intrinsic motivation Involves pursuing goals that involve internal or personal desires rather than external incentives.

intuitive processes Incidents of spontaneous mental processing that are often acted on but not given careful thought or effort.

jail diversion programs Programs attempting to divert certain groups of criminal offenders from jail incarceration into a rehabilitative, community-based alternative.

joint custody A legal outcome in which divorcing parents share or divide various decision-making and control responsibilities for their children.

judicial discretion A judge's ability to make decisions guided by personal values and beliefs (e.g., juvenile court judges use discretion to decide whether a youth should be transferred to criminal court).

juror bias The tendency of any juror to use irrelevant, inadmissible, or extralegal evidence or considerations in the course of legal decision making.

jury nullification An option allowing the jury to disregard both the law and the evidence, and acquit the defendant, if the jury believes that an acquittal is justified.

learned helplessness A condition in which people come to believe that they have no personal influence over what happens to them; consequently, they passively endure aversive treatment rather than to try to control it.

learning theory A form of criminological theory that emphasizes how specific criminal behaviors are learned directly from reinforcement and modeling influences.

legal factors Variables related to the offense or the offender's legal history.

legal formalism The model holding (in contrast to legal realism) that legal decision makers dispassionately consider the relevant laws, precedents, and constitutional principles, and that personal bias has no part in decision making.

legal realism The model holding (in contrast to legal formalism) that judges view the facts of cases in light of their attitudes and values, and make decisions accordingly.

liable Responsible or answerable for some action.

liberation hypothesis This hypothesis implies that when the strength of the evidence against a defendant is weak, jurors are free to rely on nonlegal information to inform their decisions.

limiting instruction An instruction to the jury placing explicit limitations on how certain evidence can be considered. For example, a judge may limit the consideration of a defendant's prior record to gauging the defendant's credibility only.

M'Naghten rule One test for the insanity defense. Under this rule, defendants may be deemed insane by the court if, because of a "disease of the mind," they (1) did not know what they were doing, or (2) did not know that what they were doing was wrong.

malingering The deliberate fabrication or exaggeration of physical or psychological symptoms in order to gain an advantage.

mandatory minimum sentences Sentencing schemes in which judges sentence offenders to a minimum number of years in prison following conviction for a given offense regardless of any extenuating circumstances or mitigating behavior while in prison.

mass murderer A person who kills four or more victims in one location during a period of time that lasts anywhere from a few minutes to several hours.

matching heuristic A process in which decision makers search through a subset of available case information and then make a decision based on only a small number of factors (e.g., offense severity and prior record), often ignoring other seemingly relevant information.

mediation A form of alternative dispute resolution in which a neutral third party helps the disputing parties agree on a resolution to their conflict.

mens rea A guilty mind. One of two elements that must be proven by the prosecution (the other being "a guilty act") in order to obtain a criminal conviction.

meta-analysis A statistical technique that combines the results of individual studies using similar variables and addressing similar questions.

mitigating factors Factors such as age, mental capacity, motivation, or duress that lessen the degree of guilt in a criminal offense and thus the nature of the punishment.

monozygotic twins (MZ) Commonly called identical twins,; multiple births that occur when a single egg is fertilized to form one zygote, which then divides into two embryos.

motion *in limine* A legal request for a judge to make a pretrial ruling on some matter of law expected to arise at the trial.

Multisystemic Therapy An empirically supported intervention for juvenile offenders implemented in multiple domains (e.g., family, school, structured activity) to reduce serious antisocial behavior and strengthen dysfunctional families.

Need for Cognition The inclination to engage in and enjoy effortful cognitive work.

negative incentives In the context of interrogations, tactics (such as accusations, attacks on the suspect's denials, and evidence fabrications) that interrogators use to convey that the suspect has no choice but to confess.

negligence Behavior that falls below a legal standard for protecting others from unreasonable risks; it is often measured by asking whether a "reasonable person" would have acted as the civil defendant acted in similar circumstances.

negotiation The process of conferring with another to attempt to settle a legal matter.

neuroticism A major dimension of personality involving the tendency to experience negative emotions such as anxiety, anger, and depression, often accompanied by distressed thinking and behavior.

open-ended questions This type of question does not specify or restrict the answers to be given; rather, respondents are prompted to suggest their own ideas for answers.

opening statement Not part of the evidence, these comments made by the lawyers on each side give an overview of the evidence that will be presented.

operant learning A form of learning in which the consequences of a behavior influence the likelihood of its being performed in the future.

Oregon Treatment Foster Care An empirically supported juvenile intervention that involves placing juveniles with specially trained foster parents rather than in residential placement.

other-race effect The tendency for people to less accurately recognize faces of other races.

outcome severity The severity of an accident or injury.

overconfidence bias The tendency to hold an unrealistically optimistic view of the likelihood of a favorable outcome in litigation. It applies to defendants who believe (incorrectly) that they have a good chance to win at trial, sometimes leading to rejection of reasonable plea offers from prosecutors.

parole The conditional release from prison of a person convicted of a crime prior to the expiration of that person's term of imprisonment, subject to both the supervision of the correctional authorities during the remainder of the term and a resumption of the imprisonment upon violation of the conditions imposed.

pedophile A person who derives gratification from sexual contact with children.

peremptory challenges Opportunities available to each attorney during jury selection to exclude potential jurors without having to give any reason. Their number, determined by the judge, varies from one jurisdiction to another.

perjury Lying while under oath.

photographic lineup A display of photographs of potential suspects that police often ask an eyewitness to examine to identify a suspect (also called a photospread).

photospread A display of photographs of potential suspects that police often ask an eyewitness to examine to identify a suspect (also called a photographic lineup).

physiognomic variability Perceived differences based on physical features.

plea bargains In exchange for the defendant's promise to forgo a trial, the government may promise to charge the defendant with a lesser crime or ask the judge for a reduced sentence. When the "bargain" is reached, the defendant pleads guilty and no trial is held.

policy capturing Research to determine (capture) policy preferences and inclinations (e.g., the punishment motives of ordinary people).

policy evaluator A role in which psychologists who have methodological skills in assessing policy provide data regarding the impact of such policy (e.g., degree of change, degree of effectiveness, design recommendations, observed outcomes).

polygraph (sometimes called "lie detector") An instrument for recording variations in several physiological functions that may indicate whether a person is telling the truth.

positive inducements Tactics used by interrogators to motivate suspects to see that an admission of guilt is in their best interest. It involves conveying that the suspect will receive some benefit in exchange for his confession.

positivist school of criminology A point of view that emphasized that criminal behavior by a person was determined, rather than a product of free will.

postdiction variable In the context of eyewitness memory, a variable (such as the speed of an identification) that does not directly affect the reliability of identification, but instead is a measure of some process that correlates with reliability.

post-event information Details about an event to which an eyewitness is exposed after the event has occurred.

posttraumatic stress disorder (PTSD) An anxiety disorder in which the victim experiences a pattern of intense fear reactions after being exposed to a highly stressful event.

precedent A ruling (or opinion) announced in a previous case that provides a framework in which to decide a current case. The expectation that a court should abide by precedent is called *stare decisis*.

predecisional distortion A phenomenon by which jurors' initial inclinations influence the way they interpret evidence presented during a trial.

predictive validity One form of psychometric validity, involving the accuracy with which a measure can predict something it should theoretically be able to predict.

preliminary hearing The step between arrest and trial. At a preliminary hearing, the prosecution must offer some evidence on every element of the crime charged and the judge must decide whether the evidence is sufficient to pursue the case further.

preponderance of evidence The standard of proof required in civil litigation, in which the evidence for one side must outweigh that on the other side by even a slight margin.

presence When used in reference to virtual reality, the degree to which a user or observer has the impression of actually "being in another world" due to the presentation in the virtual environment.

preventive detention The detention of accused persons who pose a risk of flight or dangerousness.

primacy effect The influence of information that is presented first, or early in a series.

primary deviance Behavior that violates a law or norm for socially acceptable conduct.

principle of proportionality The principle that the punishment should be consistently related to the magnitude of the offense.

prisonization The gradual process in which prisoners adjust to their environment (i.e., assimilate to the customs and culture of the penitentiary).

pro bono Without charge. A shortened version of *pro bono publico*, meaning "for the public good."

probabilistic estimates Attorneys' predictions about cases' outcomes, made far in advance of the known outcome and used to decide whether to accept the case.

probation The conditional freedom from incarceration following criminal conviction. It involves a specified set of conditions for which compliance is monitored by the probation officer assigned to the case. Probation conditions may include drug use monitoring, substance abuse treatment, mental health treatment, and skills-based training in particular areas (e.g., anger management, decision making).

probative value Tending to prove or actually proving.

problem-solving court A specialized kind of court focusing on the underlying behaviors of criminal defendants and seeking to rehabilitate them, thereby addressing the particular problems causing the offending. Examples include drug courts, mental health courts, domestic violence courts, homeless courts, and veterans' courts.

procedural justice The consideration of the fairness of the methods for resolving a dispute and allocating resources.

procedural knowledge Jurors' awareness of the correct process for reaching a decision (as contrasted with declarative knowledge).

propensity evidence Evidence of a defendant's past wrongdoings that suggest the defendant had the propensity, or inclination, to commit a crime.

prosecutorial discretion The authority of prosecutors to make decisions about certain aspects of criminal proceedings. In the context of juvenile offenders, it involves deciding whether cases involving serious charges are filed initially in juvenile or adult court.

proximate cause An obvious or substantially supported link between behavior and subsequent harm; a necessary element to establish in personal injury litigation.

psycholinguistics The psychological study of how people use and understand language.

psychological autopsy An attempt to determine the mode of death (whether an accident, suicide, homicide, or natural causes) by an examination of what was known about the behavior of the deceased.

psychological theories (of crime) Scientific principles that are formulated and applied to the analysis and understanding of cognitive and behavioral phenomena. For example, psychological theories of crime emphasize individual differences in behavior and the approaches to thinking, feeling, and decision making that make some people predisposed to committing criminal acts.

psychopathy A personality disorder characterized by a long-term pattern of antisocial behavior and personal characteristics such as shallow emotion, limited capacities for guilt and empathy, and failure to learn from experience.

psychoticism A major element in Eysenck's theory of personality, characterized by insensitivity, troublemaking, and lack of empathy.

punitive damages Financial compensation awarded to a prevailing party in civil litigation as a form of punishment for a specific act or omission.

quid pro quo harassment An implicit or explicit bargain in which the harasser promises a reward or threatens punishment in exchange for a specific response (often sexual in nature) from a workplace supervisee.

racial bias When police officers, prosecutors, jurors, and judges use an individual's race as the primary determinant for discretionary decisions or judgments of his or her behavior.

racial profiling The police practice of using race as a factor in determining actions such as traffic stops, arrests, and questioning of suspects.

rape shield laws Laws that prevent or restrict the questioning of an alleged rape victim during that person's time on the witness stand; specifically, questioning about the alleged victim's past sexual activities is prohibited or limited.

rape trauma syndrome A collection of behaviors or symptoms that are frequent aftereffects of having been raped.

reactance theory A theory proposing that, if something is denied or withheld from a person, the person's desire for it will increase.

rebuttal evidence Evidence presented to counter or disprove facts previously introduced by the adverse party.

recency effect The influence on memory and decision making of information that is presented last or later in a series.

recidivism In the context of criminal behavior, the commission of a new crime resulting in rearrest, reconviction, or reincarceration.

recross To cross-examine a witness a second time, after redirect examination.

redirect questioning Questioning by the original attorney that follows the opposing counsel's cross-examination.

reentry The process of returning from incarceration to the community.

relative judgment An eyewitness's process of deciding, when looking at a simultaneous lineup, which of the people shown in the lineup most closely resembles the perpetrator.

reminiscence effect When recalling previous experience, people often report (reminisce) new information on each recall attempt, suggesting that recollection is often incomplete on the first telling and that it is normal to produce unrecalled information in later interviews.

repression The process by which unpleasant thoughts or memories are moved outside of conscious awareness.

reservation price In negotiations, a negotiator's bottom line. Defendants in settlement negotiations typically have maximum amounts they are willing to pay and plaintiffs have minimum amounts they are willing to accept.

restorative justice An approach seeking to restore what has been lost through criminal offending. It includes programs designed to reconcile offenders with their victims, helping the offender appreciate the victim's pain and the victim to understand why the offender committed the crime.

retention interval The period of time between viewing an event and being questioned about it.

retributive approach The notion that punishment should be exacted on a person who has taken something from another.

retrieval The process by which a memory is returned to consciousness.

reverse transfer When juveniles initially placed in adult court are returned ("transferred back") to juvenile court.

risk assessment The assessment of the probability that a person will behave violently, often accompanied by suggestions for how to reduce the likelihood of violent conduct.

risk averse Seeking to minimize risk.

risk, needs, and responsivity (RNR) A theory that describes three separate considerations (risk, need, and responsivity) involving interventions for criminal offenders. Risk means that the likelihood of committing future offenses should be evaluated; those at highest risk should receive the most intensive interventions. Needs are the deficits (such as substance abuse, family problems, educational problems, and procriminal attitudes) that increase the risk of reoffending. Responsivity involves the likelihood of a favorable response to the interventions, and the influences that may affect such responding.

schema An individual's cognitive framework or set of preconceptions that helps that person attend to, organize, and interpret relevant information.

school-based probation A variation on the standard conditions of probation in which the youth's attendance, performance, and behavior in school are monitored through the probation officer's personal visits to the school.

scientific jury selection A process used by social scientists when acting as jury selection consultants. These consultants use empirically based procedures such as focus groups, shadow juries, systematic ratings of prospective jurors, and surveys of the community.

secondary deviance Creating or increasing the deviant identity of a person using official labels or formal legal sanctions.

secondary victimization A process in which post-event negative experiences with legal and medical authorities increase a victim's symptoms.

selective attention People have limited attentional capacity and cannot process all of the stimuli available at a given time, so they unconsciously select the information to which they will attend. The threatening aspect of a weapon is one example of something that would draw attention (see weapon focus effect).

self-defense A legal defense relied upon by criminal defendants typically charged with homicide; it asserts that the defendant's actions were justified by a reasonable belief that he or she was in imminent danger of death or bodily harm from an attacker.

self-determination theory of optimal motivation Theory describing situational and personality factors that cause positive and negative motivation and, eventually, changes in subjective well-being.

self-serving bias The tendency to interpret information or make decisions in ways that are consistent with one's own interests, rather than in an objective fashion.

sentence bargaining A form of plea bargaining in which a prosecutor recommends a reduced sentence in exchange for a guilty plea.

sentencing disparity The differences in the decisions of different judges in sentencing for the same crime.

Sequential Intercept Model The model assesses diversion needs for individuals with serious mental illness. It describes a number of points at which an intervention can be made to prevent further progress along the conventional criminal track. These points are (a) law enforcement and emergency services; (b) initial detention and initial hearings; (c) jail, courts, forensic evaluations, and forensic commitments; (d) reentry from jails, state prisons, and forensic hospitalization; and (e) community corrections and community support.

sequential presentation A lineup presentation in which the choices are shown one at a time.

serial killer A person who kills four or more victims on separate occasions, usually in different locations.

settlement negotiation Process used to resolve (settle) civil disputes without a trial, typically in private negotiations between attorneys representing the disputing parties.

shaming penalty A criminal sanction designed to embarrass an offender by publicizing the offense; shaming penalties are thought to express the community's moral outrage and to deter others from committing this type of crime.

similarity–leniency hypothesis The idea that fact finders treat those similar to themselves more leniently than they treat those they perceive as different from themselves.

simultaneous presentation A lineup presentation in which all choices are shown at the same time.

social desirability effect People's wishes to present themselves in a socially appropriate and favorable way and the influence of such wishes on their behavior.

social judgments Judgments incorporating information about social categories, such as race and gender.

social labeling theory The theory that the stigma of being branded deviant by society can influence an individual's belief about himself or herself.

social-psychological theory (of crime) A group of theories that propose that crime is learned in a social context; they differ about what is learned and how it is learned.

sociological theories (of crime) This group of theories maintains that crime results from social or cultural contexts (e.g., family, school/workplace, peer groups, community, and society). The various theories emphasize different social features and differ on the social causes of crime.

sole custody Awarding custody of a child to one parent only (as contrasted with joint custody, in which both parents have custodial involvement).

source confusion Confusion about the origin of a memory.

source monitoring The ability to accurately identify the source of one's memory.

specialized police responding Police conduct after receiving specialized training in recognizing behavioral health symptoms and interacting with individuals who display such symptoms in a way that deescalates conflict, making treatment alternative more likely and standard criminal prosecution less likely.

specific pretrial publicity Media coverage concerning the details of one specific case prior to trial.

spousal rape Sexual assault (rape) against a spouse.

spree killer A person who kills victims at two or more different locations with almost no time between the murders.

stare decisis The legal principle emphasizing the importance of decision making that is consistent with precedent; literally, "let the decision stand."

statutory exclusion A statute stipulating that certain serious offenses allegedly committed by an adolescent must be filed directly in adult court.

stimulation–seeking theory Theory suggesting that the thrill-seeking and disruptive behaviors of a psychopath serve to increase sensory input and raise arousal to a more tolerable level. As a result, the psychopathic person seems "immune" to many social cues that govern behavior.

stipulate To agree about a fact in a legal proceeding without further argument or examination.

Stockholm syndrome Feelings of dependency and emotional closeness that hostages sometimes develop toward their kidnappers in prolonged hostage situations.

storage That phase of the memory process referring to the retention of information.

story model The notion that people construct a story or narrative summary of the events in a dispute.

structural explanations A key concept of structural approaches is that certain groups of people suffer fundamental inequalities in opportunities that impair their ability to achieve the goals valued by society.

structured interviews Interviews in which the wording, order, and content of the questions are standardized in order to improve the reliability of the information obtained by an interviewer.

subcultural explanations The subcultural version of sociological theory maintains that a conflict of norms held by different groups causes criminal behavior. This conflict arises when various groups endorse subcultural norms, pressuring their members to deviate from the norms underlying the criminal law.

suggestive questions Questions asked in a way that provides cues regarding possible answers.

suicide by cop A crisis situation in which a citizen precipitates his or her own death by behaving in such a fashion that a police officer is forced to use lethal force.

sympathy hypothesis The assumption that jurors' decisions will be influenced by feelings of sympathy.

system variable In eyewitness identifications, a variable whose impact on an identification can be controlled by criminal justice system officials. Examples include the way a lineup is presented and the way a witness is questioned.

team policing A policy of less centralized decision making within police organizations.

terrorism The use of threats of violence to achieve certain organizational goals.

testamentary capacity Having the mental capacity to execute a will when the will is signed and witnessed, including the capacity to resist the pressures or domination of any person who might use undue influence on the distribution of the estate of the person writing the will.

therapeutic community A community-based approach in which all staff and participants are considered to be part of the treatment process. It has generally been used for drug offenders and domestic violence offenders. This approach may include group therapy, individual counseling, and drug testing with the objective of building skills in controlling anger, improving decision making, and recognizing high-risk situations.

therapeutic jurisprudence An approach to the law emphasizing the favorable mental health impact or otherwise "therapeutic" impact of the legal system upon its participants.

thought suppression The attempt to avoid thinking about something specific.

threat assessment A process that involves carefully considering the nature of the threat, the risk posed by the individual making it, and the indicated response to reduce the risk of harmful action.

tort A private or civil wrong or injury other than breach of contract, subject to civil litigation.

transferred The status of a juvenile charged with committing a serious offense when moved from juvenile court to criminal court.

treatment needs and amenability Rehabilitative needs and the likelihood of favorable response to interventions designed to reduce the risk of future criminal offending. It is an important consideration in decisions involving the transfer of juveniles.

trial consultants Social scientists who work as jury selection consultants, conduct community attitude surveys, prepare witnesses to testify, advise lawyers on their presentation strategies, and conduct mock trials.

truth bias The assumption that most statements are honest and truthful. In the context of interrogations, people are better at detecting truthful denials than accurately judging deceptive elaborations.

ultimate opinion testimony Testimony that offers a conclusion about the specific defendant or a specific witness, in contrast to testimony about a general phenomenon.

unconscious transference Generation of a memory that is based on the recall of past interactions with a suspect, so that an innocent person may be confused with an offender.

utilitarian approach The notion that criminal sentences should be designed to accomplish a useful outcome, such as compensating the victim or rehabilitating the offender.

validity scales Measures of an individual's approach to a psychological test, typically including the underreporting or overreporting of symptoms, problems, and unusual experiences.

venire A panel of prospective jurors drawn from a large list.

vicarious learning Learning by observing the actions of another person and their outcomes.

victimology The study of the process and consequences of victim's experiences, including recovery.

vividness effect Information has a greater impact on judgments and decisions when it is vivid and attention-grabbing than when it is pallid and bland. Information presented in a highly imaginable way is more persuasive than simple verbal descriptions of the same material.

voir dire The process by which the judge and/or attorneys ask potential jurors questions and attempt to uncover any biases.

voluntary false confessions False confessions that arise because people seek notoriety, desire to cleanse themselves of guilt feelings from previous wrongdoings, want to protect the real criminal, or have difficulty distinguishing fact from fiction.

weapon focus effect When confronted by an armed attacker, the victim's tendency to focus attention on the weapon and fails to notice other stimuli.

zero tolerance An approach to law enforcement in which the police attempt to arrest all lawbreakers, even those who have committed petty or nuisance crimes.

References

Abram, K. M., & Teplin, L. A. (1991). Co-occurring disorders among mentally ill jail detainees: Implications for public policy. *American Psychologist, 46,* 1036–1045.

Abram, K. M., Teplin, L. A., Charles, D. R., Longworth, S. L., McClelland, G. M., & Dulcan, M. K. (2004). Posttraumatic stress disorder and trauma in youth in juvenile detention. *Archives of General Psychiatry, 61,* 403–410.

Abram, K. M., Washburn, J. J., Teplin, L. A., Emanuel, K. M., Romero, E. G., & McClelland, G. M. (2007). Posttraumatic stress disorder and psychiatric comorbidity among detained youths. *Psychiatric Services, 58,* 1311–1316.

Abramson, J. (1994). *We, the jury.* New York: Basic Books.

Ackerman, M. J., & Ackerman, M. C. (1997). Child custody evaluation practices: A survey of experienced professionals (revisited). *Professional Psychology: Research and Practice, 28,* 137–145.

Adams, R. E., Rohe, W. M., & Arcury, T. A. (2005). Awareness of community-oriented policing and neighborhood perceptions in five small to midsize cities. *Journal of Criminal Justice, 33,* 43–54.

Ainsworth, P. (2001). *Offender profiling and crime analysis.* Portland, OR: Willan.

Ake v. Oklahoma, 105 S.Ct. 977 (1985).

Akers, R. L., Krohn, M. D., Lanz-Kaduce, L., & Radosevich, M. (1996). Social learning and deviant behavior: A specific test of a general theory. In D. G. Rojek & G. F. Jensen (Eds.), *Exploring delinquency: Causes and control* (pp. 109–119). Los Angeles: Roxbury.

Alden, B. (1996, September 9). Italian-Americans win "Batson" shield. *National Law Journal,* p. A8.

Alexander, J., Barton, C., Gordon, D., Grotpeter, J., Hansson, K., Harrison, R., et al. (1998). *Blueprints for violence prevention: Book three. Functional family therapy.* Boulder, CO: Center for the Study and Prevention of Violence.

Alexander, J., & Parsons, B. (1973). Short-term behavioral intervention with delinquent families: Impact on family process and recidivism. *Journal of Abnormal Psychology, 81,* 219–225.

Alexander, K., Quas, J., Goodman, G., Ghetti, S., Edelstein, R., Redlich, A., et al. (2005). Traumatic impact predicts long-term memory for documented child sexual abuse. *Psychological Science, 16,* 33–40.

Alexander, M. (2010). *The new Jim Crow: Mass incarceration in the age of colorblindness.* New York, NY: New Press.

Alhabib, S., Nur, U., & Jones, R. (2010). Domestic violence against women: Systematic review of prevalence studies. *Journal of Family Violence, 25,* 369–382.

Allan, A., Allan, M., Giles, M., Drake, D., & Froyland, I. (2005). An observational study of bail decision-making. *Psychiatry, Psychology and Law, 12,* 319–333.

Alleyne, V. (2007). Locked up means locked out: Women, addiction, and incarceration. *Women and Therapy, 29,* 181–194.

Allison, J. A., & Wrightsman, L. S. (1993). *Rape: The misunderstood crime.* Thousand Oaks, CA: Sage.

Allred, K., Mallozzi, J., Matsui, F., & Raia, C. (1997). The influence of anger and compassion on negotiation performance. *Organizational Behavior and Human Decision Processes, 70,* 175–187.

Almerigogna, J., Ost, J., Bull, R., & Akehurst, L. (2007). A state of high anxiety: How non-supportive interviewers can increase the suggestibility of child witnesses. *Applied Cognitive Psychology, 21,* 963–974.

Alpert, J. L., Brown, L. S., & Courtois, C. A. (1998). Symptomatic clients and memories of childhood abuse: What the trauma and child sexual abuse literature tells us. *Psychology, Public Policy, and Law, 4,* 941–995.

Altschuler, D. (1998). Intermediate sanctions and community treatment for serious and violent juvenile offenders. In R. Loeber & D. Farrington (Eds.), *Serious and violent juvenile offenders: Risk factors and successful interventions* (pp. 367–388). Thousand Oaks, CA: Sage.

Altschuler, D., & Armstrong, T. (1997). Aftercare not afterthought: Testing the IAP model. *Juvenile Justice, 3,* 115–122.

Amato, P. (2001). Children of divorce in the 1990s: An update of the Amato and Keith (1991) meta-analysis. *Journal of Family Psychology, 15,* 335–370.

Amato, P., & Booth, A. (2001). The legacy of parents' marital discord: Consequences for children's marital quality. *Journal of Personality and Social Psychology, 81*(4), 627–638.

Amato, P., & Gilbreth, J. (1999). Nonresident fathers and children's well-being: A meta-analysis. *Journal of Marriage and the Family, 61,* 557–573.

Amato, P., & Keith, B. (1991). Parental divorce and the well-being of children: a meta-analysis. *Psychological Bulletin, 110,* 26–46.

Amato, P., Loomis, L., & Booth, A. (1995). Parental divorce, marital conflict, and offspring well-being during early adulthood. *Social Forces, 73,* 895–915.

American Academy of Child and Adolescent Psychiatry (AACAP) (1997). *Practice parameters for child custody evaluation.* Retrieved from http://www.aacap.org/galleries/PracticeParameters/Custody.pdf

American Academy of Pediatrics (2009). Council on Communications and Media Policy Statement—Media Violence. *Pediatrics, 124,* 1495–1498.

American Bar Association (1984). *ABA criminal justice mental health standards.* Washington, DC: Author.

American Bar Association (1993). *ABA formal opinion 93–379.* Chicago, IL: Author.

American Bar Association (2010). *Model rules of professional conduct.* Washington, DC: Author.

American Bar Association Commission on Racial and Ethnic Diversity in the Profession (2006). *Goal IX Report 2005–2006: The status of racial and ethnic diversity in the American Bar Association.* Retrieved December 8, 2009, from http://www.abanet.org/minorities/publications/g9/GoalIX_0506.pdf

American Medical Association (2007). *Guides to the evaluation of permanent impairment* (6th ed.). Chicago, IL: Author.

American Psychiatric Association (2000). Diagnostic and statistical manual (4th ed., Text Revision). Washington, DC: Author.

American Psychological Association (2008). *Amendment to the reaffirmation of the American Psychological Association position against torture and other cruel, inhuman, or degrading treatment or punishment and its application to individuals defined in the United States Code as "enemy combatants."* Retrieved April 15, 2009, from http://www.apa.org/governance/resolutions/amend022208.html

American Psychological Association (2009). *Guidelines for child custody evaluations in family law proceedings.* Washington, DC: Author. Retrieved February 15, 2010, from http://www.apa.org/practice/guidelines/child-custody.pdf

American Psychological Association (2010). Guidelines for child custody evaluations in family law proceedings. *American Psychologist, 65,* 863–867.

American Psychological Association (2011). *Brief for the American Psychological Association, American Psychiatric Association, and National Association of Social Works as amici curiae in support of petitioners, Miller v. Alabama and Jackson v. Hobbs.* Retrieved July 13, 2012, from http://www.apa.org/about/offices/ogc/amicus/miller-hobbs.pdf

American Psychological Association (2012a). *Ethical principles of psychologists and code of conduct.* Retrieved July 17, 2012, from http://www.apa.org/ethics/code/index.aspx

American Psychological Association (2012b). *Specialty guidelines for forensic psychologists.* Retrieved July 17, 2012, from http://www.apa.org/practice/guidelines/forensic-psychology.aspx

Anderson, K. B., Cooper, H., & Okamura, L. (1997). Individual differences and attitudes toward rape: A meta-analytic review. *Personality and Social Psychology Bulletin, 23,* 295–315.

Anderson, M., & MacCoun, R. (1999). Goal conflict in juror assessments of compensatory and punitive damages. *Law and Human Behavior, 23,* 313–330.

The Andrea Yates case: Chronology of the Yates case. (2005, January 7). *Houston Chronicle,* p. A10.

Andrews, D. A., & Bonta, J. (1995). *LSI-R: The Level of Service Inventory-Revised.* Toronto, ON, Canada: Multi-Health Systems

Andrews, D. A., & Bonta, J. (2006). *The psychology of criminal conduct* (4th ed.). Newark, NJ: Lexis Nexis/Mathew Bender.

Andrews, D. A., & Bonta, J. (2010). Rehabilitating criminal justice policy and practice. *Psychology, Public Policy, and Law, 16,* 39–55.

Andrews, D. A., Bonta, J., & Hoge, R. D. (1990). Classification for effective rehabilitation: Rediscovering psychology. *Criminal Justice and Behavior, 17,* 19–52.

Andrews, D. A., Bonta, J., & Wormith, J. (2004). *The Level of Service/Case Management Inventory user's manual.* North Tonawanda, NY: Multi-Health Systems.

Andrews, D. A., & Hoge, R. (2010). *Evaluation for risk of violence in juveniles.* New York: Oxford University Press.

Andrews, J. A., Foster, S. L., Capaldi, D., & Hops, H. (2000). Adolescent and family predictors of physical aggression, communication, and satisfaction among young adult couples. *Journal of Consulting and Clinical Psychology, 68,* 195–208.

Annie E. Casey Foundation (2010). *Kids count data center.* Retrieved March 20, 2011, from http://datacenter. kidscount.org/data/acrossstates/Rankings.aspx?ind=107

Anti-Defamation League (2012). *State hate crimes statutory provisions.* Retrieved April 7, 2012, from http://www. adl.org/learn/hate_crimes_laws/map_frameset.html

Antonio, A., Chang, M., Hakuta, K., Kenny, D., Levin, S., & Milem, J. (2004). Effects of racial diversity on complex thinking in college students. *Psychological Science, 15,* 507–510.

Aos, S., Miller, M., & Drake, E. (2006). *Evidence-based adult corrections programs: What works and what does not.* Olympia, WA: Washington State Institute for Public Policy.

Aos, S., Phipps, P., Barnoski, R., & Lieb, R. (2001). *The comparative costs and benefits of programs to reduce crime.* Olympia, WA: Washington State Institute for Public Policy. (Document No. 01-05-1201)

Appelbaum, P. (2005). Law & psychiatry: Behavioral genetics and the punishment of crime. *Psychiatric Services, 56,* 25–27.

Appelbaum, P. (2007). The new lie detectors: Neuroscience, deception, and the courts. *Psychiatric Services, 58,* 460–462.

Appelbaum, P. S., & Grisso, T. (1995). The MacArthur Treatment Competence Study. I: Mental illness and competence to consent to treatment. *Law and Human Behavior, 19,* 105–126.

Arkes, H., & Mellers, B. (2002). Do juries meet our expectations? *Law and Human Behavior, 26,* 625–639.

Arrigo, B. A., & Claussen, N. (2003). Police corruption and psychological testing: A strategy for preemployment screening. *International Journal of Offender Therapy & Comparative Criminology, 47,* 272–290.

Asendorpf, J. B., Denissen, J. J. A. & van Aken, M. A. G. (2008). Inhibited and aggressive preschool children at 23 years of age: Personality and social transitions into adulthood. *Developmental Psychology, 44,* 997–1011.

Aspin, L., & Hall, W. (1994). Retention elections and judicial behavior. *Judicature, 77,* 306–315.

Associated Press (1988, January 13). Former Kansas woman identifies man in attack. *Kansas City Times,* p. B5.

Associated Press (2000, July 14). *Analysis of Philadelphia arrest: 59 blows in 28 seconds.* Retrieved July 18, 2005, from http://archives.cnn.com/2000/US/07/ 14/police.beating.02/index.html

Associated Press (2007a, April 26). *Man could face 30 days in jail for skipping out on jury duty.* Retrieved June 25, 2009, from http://abclocal.go.com/ktrk/story? section=news/bizarre&id=5248553

Associated Press (2007b). *More couples seeking kinder, gentler divorces.* Retrieved August 2, 2011, from http://www.msnbc.msn.com/id/22315262/ns/ health-behavior/t/more-couples-seeking-kinder- gentler-divorces/#.T7QfqUVYu5I

Association of Family and Conciliation Courts (2000). *Model standards of practice for family and divorce mediation.* Retrieved January 25, 2009, from http://www. afccnet.org/resources/resources_model_mediation.asp

Association of Family and Conciliation Courts (2006). *Model standards of practice for child custody evaluation.* Retrieved January 25, 2009, from http://www. afccnet.org/pdfs/Model%20Stds%20Child%20Cus tody%20Eval%20Sept%202006.pdf

Association of Family and Conciliation Courts (2007). Model standards of practice for child custody evaluation. *Family Court Review, 45,* 70–91.

Atkins v. Virginia, 536 U.S. 304 (2002).

Austen, I. (2008, July 16). *Blurry peek at questioning of a Guantanamo inmate.* Retrieved July 18, 2008, from http://www.nytimes.com/2008/07/16/world/ 16khadr.html?scp=1&sq=khadr&st=cse

Ayre, R. (1995). The prison crisis: An essay on the social and political foundations of criminal justice police. *Public Administration Quarterly, 19,* 42.

Ayres, B. D. (1996, August 27). California child molesters face "chemical castration." *The New York Times,* p. A1.

Babb, S. (2003). Fear and loathing in America: Application of treason law in times of national crisis and the case of John Walker Lindh. *Hastings Law Journal, 54,* 1721–1744.

Babcock, B. (1993). A place in the palladium: Women's rights and jury service. *University of Cincinnati Law Review, 61,* 1139–1180.

Badge of Life (2010). *2010 police suicide statistics from Badge of Life.* Retrieved from http://www.police suicideprevention.com/id48.html

Baer, R., Wetter, M., Nichols, J., Greene, R., & Berry, D. (1995). Sensitivity of MMPI-2 validity scales to underreporting of symptoms. *Psychological Assessment, 7,* 419–423.

Bailenson, J., Blascovich, J., Beall, A., & Noveck, B. (2006). Courtroom applications of virtual environments, immersive virtual environments, and collaborative virtual environments. *Law & Policy, 28,* 249–270.

Bailis, D., & MacCoun, R. (1996). Estimating liability risks with the media as your guide: A content analysis of media coverage of tort litigation. *Law and Human Behavior, 20,* 419–429.

Baker, L. (1983). *Miranda: Crime, law, and politics.* New York: Atheneum.

Baldas, T. (2004, November 15). Considering the alternatives. *National Law Journal,* p. 18.

Baldus, D. C., Pulaski, C., & Woodworth, G. (1983). Comparative review of death sentences: An empirical study of the Georgia experience. *Journal of Criminal Law and Criminology, 74,* 661–753.

Baldus, D. C., Woodworth, G., Zuckerman, D., Weiner, N. A., & Broffit, B. (1998). Race discrimination and the death penalty in the post-Furman era: An empirical and legal overview with recent findings from Philadelphia. *Cornell Law Review, 83,* 1638–1770.

Baldus, D. C., Woodworth, G., Zuckerman, D., Weiner, N. A., & Broffit, B. (2001). The use of peremptory challenges in capital murder trials: A legal and empirical analysis. *University of Pennsylvania Journal of Constitutional Law, 3,* 3–10.

Bandura, A. (1973). *Aggression: A social learning analysis.* Englewood Cliffs, NJ: Prentice Hall.

Bandura, A. (1976). Social learning analysis of aggression. In E. Ribes-Inesta & A. Bandura (Eds.), *Analysis of delinquency and aggression* (pp. 203–232). Hillsdale, NJ: Erlbaum.

Bandura, A. (1986). *Social foundations of thought and action: A social cognitive theory.* Englewood Cliffs, NJ: Prentice Hall.

Banks v. Goodfellow, L. R. 5 Q. B. 549 (1870).

Barbaree, H. E., & Marshall, W. L. (1991). The role of male sexual arousal in rape: Six models. *Journal of Consulting and Clinical Psychology, 59,* 621–630.

Barber, L., Grawitch, M., & Trares, S. (2009). Service-oriented and force-oriented emotion regulation strategies in police officers. *Applied Psychology in Criminal Justice, 5,* 182–202.

Bard, M. (1969). Family intervention police teams as a community mental health resource. *Journal of Criminal Law, Criminology, and Police Science, 60,* 24.

Bard, M., & Berkowitz, B. (1967). Training police as specialists in family crisis intervention: A community psychology action program. *Community Mental Health Journal, 3,* 209–215.

Barnett, O., Miller-Perrin, C., & Perrin, R. (2005). *Family violence across the lifespan: An introduction* (2nd ed.). Thousand Oaks, CA: Sage.

Barnow, S., Lucht, M., & Freyberger, H. (2001). Influence of punishment, emotional rejection, child abuse, and broken home on aggression in adolescence: An examination of aggressive adolescents in Germany. *Psychopathology, 34,* 167–173.

Barovick, H. (1998, June). DWB: Driving while black. *Time,* p. 35.

Barr, W. (1992, March). *Comments by the attorney general of the United States.* Speech delivered at the University of Kansas, Lawrence.

Bartlett, F. C. (1932). *Remembering: A study of experimental and social psychology.* New York: Cambridge University Press.

Bartoi, M. G., & Kinder, B. N. (1998). Effects of child and adult sexual abuse on adult sexuality. *Journal of Sex & Marital Therapy, 24,* 75–90.

Bartol, C. R. (1983). *Psychology and American law.* Belmont, CA: Wadsworth.

Bartol, C. R. (1991). Predictive validation of the MMPI for small-town police officers who fail. *Professional Psychology: Research and Practice, 22,* 127–132.

Bartol, C. R. (1996). Police psychology: Then, now, and beyond. *Criminal Justice and Behavior, 23,* 70–89.

Bartol, C. R., & Bartol, A. (2006). *Current perspectives in forensic psychology and criminal justice.* Thousand Oaks, CA: Sage.

Batson v. Kentucky, 476 U.S. 79 (1986).

Bauserman, R. (1997, October). *Child adjustment in joint custody versus sole custody arrangements: A meta-analytic review.* Paper presented at the 11th Annual Conference of the Children's Rights Council, Arlington, VA.

Bauserman, R. (2002). Child adjustment in joint-custody versus sole-custody arrangements: A meta-analytic review. *Journal of Family Psychology, 16,* 91–102.

Baxter, J., Weston, R., & Qu, L. (2011). Family structure, co-parental relationship quality, post-separation parental involvement and children's emotional well-being. *Journal of Family Studies, 17,* 86–109.

Bazelon, D. (1974). Psychiatrists and the adversary process. *Scientific American, 230,* 18–23.

Bechara, A., Damasio, H., Tranel, D., & Damasio, A. R. (1997). Deciding advantageously before knowing the advantageous strategy. *Science, 275,* 1293–1294.

Becker, J. V., Stinson, J., Tromp, S., & Messer, G. (2003). Characteristics of individuals petitioned for civil commitment. *International Journal of Offender Therapy and Comparative Criminology, 47,* 185–195.

Beech, A. R., Fisher, D. D., & Thornton, D. (2003). Risk assessment of sex offenders. *Professional Psychology: Research and Practice, 34,* 339–352.

Begam, R. (1977). Voir dire: The attorney's job. *Trial, 13,* 3.

Begany, J. J., & Milburn, M. A. (2002). Psychological predictors of sexual harassment: Authoritarianism, hostile sexism, and rape myths. *Psychology of Men and Masculinity, 3,* 119–126.

Beggs, S., & Grace, R. (2011). Treatment gains for sexual offenders against children predicts reduced recidivism:

A comparative validity study. *Journal of Consulting and Clinical Psychology, 79*, 182–192.

Behn, N. (1995). *Lindbergh: The crime.* New York: Onyx.

Beiser, E. N. (1973). Are juries representative? *Judicature, 57*, 194–199.

Belanger, H., Curtiss, G., Demery, J., Lebowitz, B., & Vanderploeg, R. (2005). Factors moderating neuro-psychological outcomes following mild traumatic brain injury: A meta-analysis. *Journal of the International Neuropsychological Society, 11*, 215–227.

Belenko, S. (1998). Research on drug courts: A critical review. *National Drug Court Institute Review, 1*, 1–42.

Belenko, S. (1999). Research on drug courts: A critical review: 1999 update. *National Drug Court Institute Review, 2*, 1–58.

Belenko, S. (2001). *Research on drug courts: A critical review: 2001 update.* New York: National Center on Addiction and Substance Abuse at Columbia University.

Belenko, S. (2002). Drug courts. In C. Leukefeld, F. Tims, & D. Farabee (Eds.), *Treatment of drug offenders: Policies and issues* (pp. 301–318). New York: Springer.

Belenko, S., DeMatteo, D., & Patapis, N. (2007). Drug courts. In D. Springer & A. Roberts (Eds.), *Handbook of forensic mental health with victims and offenders: Assessment, treatment, and research* (pp. 385–423). New York: Springer.

Bench, L., & Allen, T. (2003). Investigating the stigma of prison classification: An experimental design. *The Prison Journal, 83*, 307–382.

Benner, A. W. (1986). Psychological screening of police applicants. In J. T. Reese & H. A. Goldstein (Eds.), *Psychological services for law enforcement* (pp. 11–20). Washington, DC: U.S. Government Printing Office.

Ben-Shakhar, G. (2002). A critical review of the Control Questions Test (CQT). In M. Kleiner (Ed.), *Handbook of polygraph testing* (pp. 103–126). London: Academic Press.

Berkemer v. McCarty, 468 U.S. 420 (1984).

Berman, M. E. (1997). Biopsychosocial approaches to understanding human aggression: The first 30 years. *Clinical Psychology Review, 15*, 585–588.

Berman, M. E., Tracy, J. I., & Coccaro, E. F. (1997). The serotonin hypothesis of aggression revisited. *Clinical Psychology Review, 17*, 651–665.

Bersoff, D. N. (1987). Social science data and the Supreme Court: *Lockhart* as a case in point. *American Psychologist, 42*, 52–58.

Bertman, L., Thompson, J., Waters, W., Estupinan-Kane, L., Martin, J., & Russell, L. (2003). Effect of an individualized treatment protocol on restoration of competency in pretrial forensic inpatients. *Journal of the American Academy of Psychiatry and Law, 31*, 37–35.

Betts v. Brady, 316 U.S. 455 (1942).

Beyer, M. (1997). Experts for juveniles at risk of adult sentences. In P. Puritz, A. Capozello, & W. Shang (Eds.), *More than meets the eye: Rethinking assessment, competency, and sentencing for a harsher era of juvenile justice* (pp. 1–22). Washington, DC: American Bar Association, Juvenile Justice Center.

Bibas, S. (2004). Plea bargaining outside the shadow of trial. *Harvard Law Review, 117*, 2463–2547.

Binder, A. (1988). Juvenile delinquency. In M. R. Rosenzweig & L. W. Porter (Eds.), *Annual review of psychology* (pp. 253–282). Palo Alto, CA: Annual Reviews.

Binder, A., Geis, G., & Bruce, D. D. (2001). *Juvenile delinquency: Historical, cultural & legal perspectives.* Cincinnati, OH: Anderson.

Binder, J. R., Desai, R. H., Graves, W. W., & Conant, L. L. (2009). Where is the semantic system? A critical review and meta-analysis of 120 functional neuroimaging studies. *Cerebral Cortex, 19*, 2767–2796.

Bing, N., Nelson, W., & Wesolowski, K. (2009). Comparing the effects of amount of conflict on children's adjustment following parental divorce. *Journal of Divorce and Remarriage, 50*, 159–171.

Bishop, D. M., Frazier, C. E., Lanza-Kaduce, L., & Winner, L. (1996). The transfer of juveniles to criminal court: Does it make a difference? *Crime and Delinquency, 42*, 171–191.

Blair, I., Judd, C., & Chapleau, K. (2004). The influence of Afrocentric facial features in criminal sentencing. *Psychological Science, 15*, 674–679.

Blakely v. Washington, 124 S. Ct. 2348 (2004).

Blau, T. H. (1986). Deadly force: Psychosocial factors and objective evaluation. A preliminary effort. In J. T. Reese & H. A. Goldstein (Eds.), *Psychological services for law enforcement* (pp. 315–334). Washington, DC: U.S. Government Printing Office.

Blumenthal, J. A. (1998). The reasonable woman standard: A meta-analytic review of gender differences in perceptions of sexual harassment. *Law and Human Behavior, 22*, 33–58.

Blunk, R., & Sales, B. (1977). Persuasion during the voir dire. In B. Sales (Ed.), *Psychology in the legal process* (pp. 39–58). New York: Spectrum.

Boccaccini, M. T., & Brodsky, S. L. (1999). Diagnostic test usage by forensic psychologists in emotional injury cases. *Professional Psychology: Research and Practice, 30*, 253–259.

Boccaccini, M. T., Murrie, D., Clark, J., & Cornell, D. (2008). Describing, diagnosing, and naming psychopathy: How do youth psychopathy labels influence jurors? *Behavioral Sciences & the Law, 26*, 487–510.

Boehm, V. (1968). Mr. Prejudice, Miss Sympathy, and the authoritarian personality: An application of psychological measuring techniques to the problem of jury bias. *Wisconsin Law Review, 1968*, 734–750.

Boehnert, C. (1989). Characteristics of successful and unsuccessful insanity pleas. *Law and Human Behavior, 13*, 31–40.

Boersema, C., Hanson, R., & Keilitz, S. (1991). State court-annexed arbitration: What do attorneys think? *Judicature, 75*, 28–33.

Boire, R. (2005). Searching the brain: The Fourth Amendment implications of brain-based deception detection devices. *American Journal of Bioethics, 5*, 62–63.

Bonczar, T. (2003, August). *Prevalence of imprisonment in the U.S. population, 1974–2001*. Washington DC: U.S. Department of Justice, Bureau of Justice Statistics.

Bond, C., & DePaulo, B. (2006). Accuracy of deception judgments. *Personality and Social Psychology Review, 10*, 214–234.

Bonnie, R. J. (1993). The competence of criminal defendants: Beyond *Dusky* and *Drope*. *University of Miami Law Review, 47*, 539–601.

Bonnie, R. J., & Monahan, J. (1996). *Mental disorder, work disability, and the law*. Chicago, IL: The University of Chicago Press.

Bonnie, R. J., & Slobogin, C. (1980). The role of mental health professionals in the criminal process: The case for informed speculation. *Virginia Law Review, 66*, 427–522.

Bonta, J. (1997). *Offender rehabilitation: From research to practice*. Ottawa, Canada: Department of the Solicitor General of Canada. (User Report No. 1997-01)

Bonta, J., & Gendreau, P. (1990). Reexamining the cruel and unusual punishment of prison life. *Law and Human Behavior, 14*, 347–372.

Booij, L., Tremblay, R. E., Leyton, M., Seguin, J. R., Vitaro, F., Gravel, P., et al. (2010). Brain serotonin synthesis in adult males characterized by physical aggression during childhood: A 21-year longitudinal study. *PLoS ONE, 5*, ArtID e11255.

Book, A. S. (1999). Shame on you: An analysis of modern shame punishment as an alternative to incarceration. *William and Mary Law Review, 40*, 653–686.

Boothroyd, R., Mercado, C., Poythress, N., Christy, A., & Petrila, J. (2005). Clinical outcomes of defendants in mental health court. *Psychiatric Services, 56*, 829–834.

Boothroyd, R., Poythress, N., McGaha, A., & Petrila, J. (2003). The Broward mental health court: Process, outcomes, and service utilization. *International Journal of Law & Psychiatry, 26*, 55–71.

Borduin, C., Mann, B., Cone, L., Henggeler, S., Fucci, B., & Blaske, D. (1995). Multisystemic treatment of serious juvenile offenders: Long-term prevention of criminality and violence. *Journal of Consulting and Clinical Psychology, 63*, 569–578.

Borgida, E., & Brekke, N. (1985). Psycholegal research on rape trials. In A. Burgess (Ed.), *Research handbook on rape and sexual assault* (pp. 313–342). New York: Garland.

Bornstein, B. (1994). David, Goliath, and Reverend Bayes: Prior beliefs about defendants' status in personal injury cases. *Applied Cognitive Psychology, 8*, 232–258.

Bornstein, B. H., & Greene, E. (2011a). Consulting on damage awards. In R. Wiener & B. Bornstein (Eds.), *Handbook of trial consulting* (pp. 281–296). New York: Springer.

Bornstein, B. H., & Greene, E. (2011b). Jury decision making: Implications for and from psychology. *Current Directions in Psychological Science, 20*, 63–67.

Bornstein, B. H., & Rajki, M. (1994). Extra-legal factors and product liability: The influence of mock jurors' demographic characteristics and intuitions about the cause of an injury. *Behavioral Sciences & the Law, 12*, 137–147.

Bornstein, B. H., & Robicheaux, T. (2008). Crisis, what crisis? Perception and reality in civil justice. In B. Bornstein, R. Wiener, R. Schopp, & S. Willborn (Eds.), *Civil juries and civil justice: Psychological and legal perspectives* (pp. 1–22). New York: Springer.

Borum, R. (1996). Improving the clinical practice of violence risk assessment: Technology, guidelines, and training. *American Psychologist, 51*, 945–956.

Borum, R., Bartels, P., & Forth, A. (2005). *Structured assessment of violence risk in youth*. Lutz, FL: PAR.

Borum, R., Deane, M. W., Steadman, H. J., & Morrissey, J. (1998). Police perspectives on responding to mentally ill people in crisis: Perceptions of program effectiveness. *Behavioral Sciences & the Law, 16*, 393–406.

Borum, R., & Fulero, S. M. (1999). Empirical research and the insanity defense and attempted reforms: Evidence toward informed policy. *Law and Human Behavior, 23*, 375–394.

Borum, R., & Verhaagen, D. (2006). *Assessing and managing violence risk in youth*. New York: Guilford.

Borum, R., Williams, M., Deans, M., Steadman, H., & Morrissey, J. (1998). Police perspectives on responding to mentally ill people in crisis: Perceptions of program effectiveness. *Behavioral Sciences & the Law, 16*, 393–405.

Bothwell, R. K. (1999). The ethnic factor in voir dire. In W. F. Abbott & J. Batt (Eds.), *A handbook of jury research* (pp. 10.1–10.11). Philadelphia, PA: ALI-ABA.

Bottoms, B. L., Golding, J. M., Stevenson, M. C., Wiley, T. R. A., & Yozwiak, J. A. (2007). A review of factors affecting jurors' decisions in child sexual abuse cases. In J. D. Read, D. Ross, M. Toglia, & R. Lindsay (Eds.), *The psychology of eyewitness memory*. Mahwah, NJ: Lawrence Erlbaum.

Bouffard, J., & Bergeron, L. (2006). Reentry works: The implementation and effectiveness of a serious and violent offender reentry initiative. *Journal of Offender Rehabilitation, 44*, 1–29.

Bourgon, G., & Armstrong, B. (2005). Transferring the principles of effective treatment into a "Real World" prison setting. *Criminal Justice and Behavior, 32*, 3–25.

Bower, B. (1984). Not popular by reason of insanity. *Science News, 126*, 218–219.

Boyer, P. J. (2000, January 17). DNA on trial. *The New Yorker*, pp. 42–53.

Brank, E., & Scott, L. (2012). Let's make a deal: The psychology of plea agreements. *APA Monitor, 43*(4), 31.

Brannen, D., Salekin, R., Zapf, P., Salekin, K., Kubak, F., & DeCoster, J. (2006). Transfer to adult court: A national study of how juvenile court judges weight pertinent *Kent* criteria. *Psychology, Public Policy, and Law, 12*, 332–355.

Braudway, B. (2004). Scarlet letter punishments. *Campbell Law Review, 27*, 63–90.

Braun, K., Ellis, R., & Loftus, E. (2002). Make my memory: How advertising can change our memories of the past. *Psychology and Marketing, 19*, 1–23.

Braver, S., Ellman, I., & Fabricius, W. (2003). Relocation of children after divorce and children's best interests: New evidence and legal considerations. *Journal of Family Psychology, 17*, 206–219.

Bregant, J. (2009). Let's give them something to talk about: An empirical evaluation of predeliberation discussions. *University of Illinois Law Review*, 1213–1241.

Brehm, S. S., & Brehm, J. (1981). *Psychological reactance*. New York: Academic Press.

Brennan, P. A., & Raine, A. (1997). Biosocial bases of antisocial behavior: Psychophysiological, neurological, and cognitive factors. *Clinical Psychology Review, 17*, 589–604.

Breslau, N., Chilcoat, H. D., Kessler, R. C., & Davis, G. C. (1999). Previous exposure to trauma and PTSD effects of subsequent trauma: Results from the Detroit Area Survey of Trauma. *American Journal of Psychiatry, 156*, 902–907.

Breslau, N., Kessler, R. C., Chilcoat, H. D., Schultz, L. R., Davis, G. C., & Andreski, P. (1998). Trauma and posttraumatic stress disorder in the community: The 1996 Detroit Area Survey of Trauma. *Archives of General Psychiatry, 55*, 626–632.

Breslau, N., Lucia, V., & Alvarado, G. (2006). Intelligence and other predisposing factors in exposure to trauma and posttraumatic stress disorder: A follow-up study to age 17 years. *Archives of General Psychiatry, 63*, 1238–1245.

Brewer, N., & Burke, A. (2002). Effects of testimonial inconsistencies and eyewitness confidence on mock-juror judgments. *Law and Human Behavior, 26*, 353–364.

Brewer, N., Keast, A., & Sauer, J. (2010). Children's eyewitness identification performance: Effects of a Not Sure response option and accuracy motivation. *Legal and Criminological Psychology, 15*, 261–277.

Brewster, J., & Stoloff, M. (2003). Relationship between IQ and first-year overall performance as a police officer. *Applied H. R. M. Research, 8*, 49–50.

Brey, T. (2009). Child custody evaluation practices: A survey of psychologists. *Dissertation Abstracts International: Section B: The Sciences and Engineering, 69*(7-B), 4410.

Bridges, G., & Steen, S. (1998). Racial disparities in official assessments of juvenile offenders: Attribution stereotypes as mediating mechanisms. *American Sociological Review, 63*, 554–570.

Brigham, J., & Wasserman, A. (1999). The impact of race, racial attitude, and gender on reactions to the criminal trial of O. J. Simpson. *Journal of Applied Social Psychology, 29*, 1333–1370.

Bright, D., & Goodman-Delahunty, J. (2011). Mock juror decision making in a civil negligence trial: The impact of gruesome evidence, injury severity, and information processing route. *Psychiatry, Psychology and Law, 18*, 439–459.

Broder, J. (2004, June 21). Starting over, 24 years after a wrongful conviction. *The New York Times*. Retrieved June 27, 2004, from http://www.nytimes.com/2004/06/ 21/national/

Brodsky, S. (2011). The feisty expert witness. *PsycCRITIQUES, 56*, 13.

Broeder, D. W. (1959). The University of Chicago jury project. *Nebraska Law Review, 38*, 744–760.

Broeder, D. W. (1965). Voir dire examinations: An empirical study. *Southern California Law Review, 38*, 503–528.

Broner, N., Lattimore, P., Cowell, A., & Schlenger, W. (2004). Effects of diversion on adults with co-occurring mental illness and substance use: outcomes from a national multi-site study. *Behavioral Sciences & the Law, 22*, 519–541.

Broner, N., Mayrl, D., & Landsberg, G. (2005). Outcomes of mandated and nonmandated New York City diversion for offenders with alcohol, drug, and mental disorders. *The Prison Journal, 85*, 18–49.

Bronner, G., Peretz, C., & Ehrenfeld, M. (2003). Sexual harassment of nurses and nursing students. *Journal of Advanced Nursing, 42*, 637–644.

Brown v. Board of Education, 347 U.S. 483 (1954).

Brown v. Entertainment Merchants Association, Case # 08-1448 U.S. Supreme Court (2011).

Brown, L. T. (2003). Racial discrimination in jury selection: Professional misconduct, not legitimate advocacy. *Review of Litigation, 22,* 209–317.

Brownmiller, S., & Alexander, D. (1992, January/February). *From Carmita Wood to Anita Hill.* Ms., pp. 70–71.

Brown, T., Borduin, C., & Henggeler, S. (2001). Treating juvenile offenders in community settings. In J. Ashford, B. Sales, & W. Reid (Eds.), *Treating adult and juvenile offenders with special needs* (pp. 445–464). Washington, DC: American Psychological Association.

Brubacher, M. R., Fondacaro, M. R., Brank, E. M., Brown, V. E., & Miller, Scott, A. M. (2009). Procedural justice in resolving family disputes: Implications for childhood bullying. *Psychology, Public Policy, and Law, 15,* 149–167.

Brubacher, S., Glisic, U., Roberts, K., & Powell, M. (2011). Children's ability to recall unique aspects of one occurrence of a repeated event. *Applied Cognitive Psychology, 25,* 351–358.

Bruck, D. (1985, May 20). The death penalty: An exchange. *New Republic,* pp. 20–21.

Bruck, M., Ceci, S., & Hembrooke, H. (1998). Reliability and credibility in young children's reports: From research to policy and practice. *American Psychologist, 53,* 136–151.

Bruck, M., Ceci, S., & Hembrooke, H. (2002). The nature of children's true and false narratives. *Developmental Review, 22,* 520–554.

Brunner, H., Nelen, M., Breakefield, X., Ropers, H., & van Oost, B. (1993). Abnormal behavior associated with a point mutation in the structural gene for monoamine oxidase A. *Science, 262,* 578–580.

Bryan, P. (2005). *Constructive divorce: procedural justice and sociolegal reform.* Washington, DC: American Psychological Association.

Bryan, W. J. (1971). *The chosen ones.* New York: Vantage Press.

Buckley, W., & Okrent, C. (2004). *Torts and personal injury law* (3rd ed.). Clifton Park, NY: Thomson Delmar Learning:.

Budd, K., Clark, J., & Connell, M. (2011). *Evaluation of parenting capacity in child protection.* New York: Oxford University Press.

Bureau of Justice Statistics (2002). *Rape and sexual assault: Reporting to police and medical attention, 1992–2000.* Washington, DC: U.S. Department of Justice.

Bureau of Justice Statistics (2003). *Community policing.* Retrieved from http://bjs.ojp.usdoj.gov/index .cfm?ty=tp&tid=81

Bureau of Justice Statistics (2005a). *National crime victimization survey.* Washington, DC: U.S. Department of Justice, Office of Justice Programs, Bureau of Justice.

Bureau of Justice Statistics (2005b). *State and local law enforcement statistics.* Retrieved July 18, 2005, from http://www.ojp.usdoj.gov/bjs/sandlle.htm#education

Bureau of Justice Statistics (2006). *Special report: Mental health problems of prison and jail inmates.* Retrieved January 26, 2009, from http://www.ojp.usdoj.gov/ bjs/pub/pdf/mhppji.pdf

Bureau of Justice Statistics (2008a). *Criminal victimization, 2007.* Retrieved January 26, 2009, from http://www. ojp.usdoj.gov/bjs/pub/pdf/cv07.pdf

Bureau of Justice Statistics (2008b). *Jail inmates at midyear 2007.* Retrieved February 9, 2009, from http:// www.ojp.usdoj.gov/bjs/abstract/jim07.htm

Bureau of Justice Statistics (2008c). *Probation and parole statistics.* Retrieved January 29, 2009, from http:// www.ojp.usdoj.gov/bjs/pandp.htm

Bureau of Justice Statistics (2010a). *Criminal victimization, 2010.* Retrieved from http://bjs.ojp.usdoj.gov/index .cfm?ty=tp&tid=31

Bureau of Justice Statistics (2010b). *Press release.* Retrieved July 14, 2011, from http://bjs.ojp.usdoj.gov/content/ pub/press/corrections09pr.cfm

Bureau of Justice Statistics (2011a). *Adults on parole, federal and state by state, 1975–2010.* Retrieved January 10, 2012, from http://bjs.ojp.usdoj.gov/index .cfm?ty=pbdetail&iid=1997

Bureau of Justice Statistics (2011b). *Criminal victimization in the United States, 2008.* Washington, DC: U.S. Department of Justice.

Bureau of Justice Statistics (2011c). *Jail inmates at midyear 2010—statistical tables.* Retrieved January 12, 2012, from http://bjs.ojp.usdoj.gov/content/pub/pdf/ jim10st.pdf

Burger, W. E. (1975). Dissenting opinion in *O'Connor v. Donaldson. U. S. Law Week, 42,* 4929–4936.

Burgess, A. W., & Holmstrom, L. L. (1974). *Rape: Victims of crisis.* Bowie, MA: Robert J. Brady.

Burke, P., & Tonry, M. (2006). *Successful transition and reentry for safer communities: A call to action for parole.* Silver Spring, MD: Center for Effective Public Policy.

Burnet v. Coronado Oil and Gas Co., 52 S.Ct. 443 (1932).

Burt, M. R. (1980). Cultural myths and supports for rape. *Journal of Personality and Social Psychology, 38,* 217–230.

Burt, R., & Morris, N. (1972). A proposal for the abolition of the incompetency plea. *University of Chicago Law Review, 40,* 66–95.

Bush v. Schiavo, 885 So. 2d 321 (Fla. 2004).

Buss, A. H. (1966). *Psychopathology.* New York: Wiley.

Buss, D. M., & Malamuth, N. M. (Eds.). (1996). *Sex, power, conflict: Evolutionary and feminist perspectives.* New York: Oxford University Press.

Butcher, J., Arbisi, P. A., Atlis, M. M., & McNulty, J. L. (2008). The construct validity of the Lees-Haley Fake Bad Scale: Does this scale measure somatic malingering and feigned emotional distress? *Archives of Clinical Neuropsychology, 23*, 855–864.

Butler, B. (2007). Death qualification and prejudice: The effect of implicit racism, sexism, and homophobia on capital defendants' right to due process. *Behavioral Sciences & the Law, 25*, 857–867.

Butler, B., & Moran, G. (2007). The impact of death qualification, belief in a just world, legal authoritarianism, and locus of control on venirepersons' evaluations of aggravating and mitigating circumstances in capital trials. *Behavioral Sciences and the Law, 25*, 57–68.

Butler, W. M., Leitenberg, H., & Fuselier, D. G. (1993). The use of mental health consultants to police hostage negotiation teams. *Behavioral Sciences & the Law, 11*, 213–221.

Byrne, C. A., Resnick, H. S., Kilpatrick, D. G., Best, C. L., & Saunders, B. E. (1999). The socioeconomic impact of interpersonal violence on women. *Journal of Consulting and Clinical Psychology, 67*, 362–366.

Cacioppo, J. T., Petty, R. E., Feinstein, J. A., & Jarvis, W. B. G. (1996). Dispositional differences in cognitive motivation: The life and times of individuals varying in Need for Cognition. *Psychological Bulletin, 119*, 197–253.

Caetano, R., McGrath, C., Ramisetty-Mikler, S., & Field, C. A. (2005). Drinking, alcohol problems and the five-year recurrence and incidence of male-to-female and female-to-male partner violence. *Alcoholism: Clinical & Experimental Research, 29*, 98–106.

Caldwell, M., & Van Rybroek, G. (2005). Reducing violence in serious juvenile offenders using intensive treatment. *International Journal of Psychiatry and Law, 28*, 622–636.

Calhoun, K., Atkeson, B., & Resick, P. (1982). A longitudinal examination of fear reactions in victims of rape. *Journal of Counseling Psychology, 29*, 656–661.

California Civil Jury Instructions (2011). Retrieved June 12, 2012 from http://www.courts.ca.gov/partners/documents/caci_2012_edition.pdf

California v. Cahill, 5 Cal. 4th 497 (1993).

Callahan, L. A., & Silver, E. (1998). Factors associated with the conditional release of persons acquitted by reason of insanity: A decision tree approach. *Law and Human Behavior, 22*(2), 147–163.

Campbell, M. A., & Schmidt, F. (2000). Comparison of mental health & legal factors in the disposition outcome of young offenders. *Criminal Justice & Behavior, 27*, 688–715.

Campbell, R., Sefl, T., Barnes, H. E., Ahrens, C. E., Wasco, S. M., & Zaragoza-Diesfeld, Y. (1999). Community services for rape survivors: Enhancing psychological well-being or increasing trauma? *Journal of Consulting and Clinical Psychology, 67*, 847–858.

Canter, D., Alison, L., Alison, E., & Wentink, N. (2004). The organized/disorganized typology of serial murder: Myth or model? *Psychology, Public Policy and Law, 10*, 293–320.

Caperton v. A. T. Massey Coal, 556 U.S. 868 (2009).

Carlsmith, K. (2006). The roles of retribution and utility in determining punishment. *Journal of Experimental Social Psychology, 42*, 437–451.

Carlsmith, K. (2008). On justifying punishment: The discrepancy between words and actions. *Social Justice Research, 21*, 119–137.

Carlsmith, K., & Darley, J. (2008). Psychological aspects of retributive justice. *Advances in Experimental Social Psychology, 40*, 193–236.

Carlsmith, K., Darley, J., & Robinson, P. (2002). Why do we punish: Deterrence and just deserts as motives for punishment. *Journal of Personality and Social Psychology, 83*, 284–299.

Carlson, C., Gronlund, S., & Clark, S. (2008). Lineup composition, suspect position, and the sequential lineup advantage. *Journal of Experimental Psychology: Applied, 14*, 118–128.

Carlson, K., & Russo, J. (2001). Biased interpretation of evidence by mock jurors. *Journal of Experimental Psychology: Applied, 7*, 91–103.

Carnevale, P. (2008). Positive affect and decision frame in negotiation. *Group Decision and Negotiation, 17*, 51–63.

Carr, P. L., Ash, A. S., Friedman, R. H., Szalacha, L., Barnett, R. C., Palepu, A., et al. (2000). Faculty perceptions of gender discrimination and sexual harassment in academic medicine. *Annals of Internal Medicine, 132*, 889–896.

Carroll, J. S., Kerr, N. L., Alfini, J. J., Weaver, F. M., MacCoun, R. J., & Feldman, V. (1986). Free press and fair trial: The role of behavioral research. *Law and Human Behavior, 10*, 187–201.

Carter, T. (2004, June). Red Hook experiment. *American Bar Association Journal, 90*, 37–42.

Carter, T. (2005, February). Mud and money. *American Bar Association Journal, 91*, 40–45.

Casey, P., & Rottman, D. (2005). Problem-solving courts: Models and trends. *The Justice System Journal, 26*, 35–56.

Casey, T. (2004). When good intentions are not enough: Problem-solving courts and the impending crisis of legitimacy. *Southern Methodist University Law Review, 57*, 1459–1519.

Caspi, A., McClay, J., Moffitt, T., Mill, J., Martin, J., Craig, I., et al. (2002). Role of genotype in the cycle of violence by maltreated children. *Science, 297*, 851–854.

Castelli, P., Goodman, G., & Ghetti, S. (2005). Effects of interview style and witness age on perceptions of children's credibility in sexual abuse cases. *Journal of Applied Social Psychology, 35*, 297–319.

Catton, B. (1965). *Foreword to Twenty Days by D. Kunhardt & P. Kunhardt.* New York: Harper & Row.

Cauffman, E., Piquero, A., Kimonis, E., Steinberg, L., Chassin, L., & Fagan, J. (2007). Legal, individual, and environmental predictors of court disposition in a sample of serious adolescent offenders. *Law and Human Behavior, 31*, 519–535.

Ceci, S. J., Huffman, M., Smith, E., & Loftus, E. (1994). Repeatedly thinking about a non-event: Source misattribution among preschoolers. *Consciousness and Cognition, 3*, 388–407.

Ceci, S. J., Kulkofsky, S., Klemfuss, J. Z., Sweeney, C. D., & Bruck, M. (2007). Unwarranted assumptions about children's testimonial accuracy. *Annual Review of Clinical Psychology, 3*, 307–324.

Ceci, S. J., Scullin, M., & Kanaya, T. (2003). The difficulty of basing death penalty eligibility on IQ cutoff scores for mental retardation. *Ethics & Behavior, 13*, 11–17.

Cecil, J. (2005). Ten years of judicial gatekeeping under *Daubert. American Journal of Public Health, 95*(S1), S74–S80.

Center for Court Innovation (2012). *Community court.* Retrieved from http://www.courtinnovation.org/topic/community-court

Center for Effective Public Policy (2007). *Increasing public safety through successful offender reentry: Evidence-based and emerging practices in corrections.* Washington, DC: Author.

Cernkovich, S. A., & Giordano, P. C. (1996). School bonding, race, and delinquency. In D. G. Rojek & G. F. Jensen (Eds.), *Exploring delinquency: Causes and control* (pp. 210–218). Los Angeles: Roxbury.

Chajewski, M., & Mercado, C. (2009). An evaluation of sex offender residency restriction functioning in town, county, and city-wide jurisdictions. *Criminal Justice Policy Review, 20*, 44–61.

Chamberlain, P. (1990). Comparative evaluation of specialized foster care for seriously delinquent youths: A first step. *Community Alternatives: International Journal of Family Care, 2*, 21–36.

Chamberlain, P., & Mihalic, S. (1998). *Blueprints for violence prevention: Book eight. Multidimensional treatment foster care.* Boulder, CO: Center for the Study and Prevention of Violence.

Chamberlain, P., & Reid, J. (1998). Comparison of two community alternatives to incarceration for chronic juvenile offenders. *Journal of Consulting and Clinical Psychology, 66*, 624–633.

Chan, J., & LaPaglia, J. (2011). The dark side of testing memory: Repeated retrieval can enhance eyewitness suggestibility. *Journal of Experimental Psychology: Applied, 17*, 418–432.

Charman, S., Carlucci, M., Vallano, J., & Gregory, A. (2010). The selective cue integration framework: A theory of postidentification witness confidence assessment. *Journal of Experimental Psychology: Applied, 16*, 204–218.

Chen, M. K., & Shapiro, J. (2007). Do harsher prison conditions reduce recidivism? A discontinuity-based approach. *American Law and Economics Review, 9*, 1–29.

Chicago Police Department (2004). *Traumatic incidents stress management program.* Retrieved January 11, 2006, from http://directives.chicagopolice.org/directives/data/a7a57be2-12abe584-90812-abe5-851cc873b7528b11.html

Choi, A., & Edleson, J. L. (1996). Social disapproval of wife assaults: A national survey of Singapore. *Journal of Comparative Family Studies, 27*(1), 73–88.

Christie, R. (1976). Probability v. precedence: The social psychology of jury selection. In G. Bermant, C. Nemeth, & N. Vidmar (Eds.), *Psychology and the law: Research frontiers* (pp. 265–281). Lexington, MA: Lexington Books.

Christy, A., Poythress, N., Boothroyd, R., Petrila, J., & Mehra, S. (2005). Evaluating the efficiency and community safety goals of the Broward County mental health court. *Behavioral Sciences & the Law, 23*, 1–17.

Ciesluk v. Ciesluk, 113 P. 3d 135 (2005).

Cirincione, C., & Jacobs, C. (1999). Identifying insanity acquittals: Is it any easier? *Law and Human Behavior, 23*, 487–497.

CIT National Advisory Board (2006). *Crisis intervention team core elements.* Memphis, TN: University of Memphis CIT Center.

Clark, J., Boccaccini, M. T., Caillouet, B., & Chaplin, W. F. (2007). Five-factor model personality traits, jury selection, and case outcomes in criminal and civil cases. *Criminal Justice and Behavior, 34*, 641–660.

Clark, S. (2005). A re-examination of the effects of biased lineup instructions in eyewitness identification. *Law and Human Behavior, 29*, 395–424.

Clark, S. (2012). Costs and benefits of eyewitness identification reform: Psychological science and public policy. *Perspectives on Psychological Science, 7*, 238–259.

Clark, S., & Davey, S. (2005). The target-to-fillers shift in simultaneous and sequential lineups. *Law and Human Behavior, 29*, 151–172.

Clayton, L., Dunford, B., Seying, R., & Pryce, 1). Jury decision making: 45 years of empirical h on deliberating groups. *Psychology, Public and Law, 7*, 622–727.

, Holland, R., Corneille, O., Rondeel, E., & man, C. (2012). Mood effects on dominated s: Positive mood induces departures from logical *Journal of Behavioral Decision Making, 25*, 74–81.

S., Richardson, J. T., & Warner, L. G. (1997). scientific evidence and controversial cases: al psychological examination. *Law & Psychology*, *21*, 1–28.

(2003). Psychological models of professional n making. *Psychological Science, 14*, 175–180.

(2005). From discretion to disagreement: ning disparities in judges' pretrial decisions. *oral Sciences & the Law, 23*, 367–386.

, & Ayton, P. (2001). Bailing and jailing the fast ugal way. *Journal of Behavioral Decision Making*, 1–168.

S. (2006). Beyond fantasy and nightmare: A t of the jury. *Buffalo Law Review, 54*, 717–763.

S., & Rose, M. (2005). Real juries. *Annual* / *of Law and Social Sciences, 1*, 255–284.

S., Rose, M., & Murphy, B. (2004). Jurors' wered questions. *Court Review, 41*, 20–29.

S., Rose, M., Murphy, B., & Meixner, J. (2011). ge anchors on real juries. *Journal of Empirical Legal* s, *8*, 148–178.

S., Rose, M., Murphy, B., & Smith, S. (2006). questions during trial: A window into juror ng. *Vanderbilt Law Review, 59*, 1925–1972.

S., & Vidmar, N. (2001). Jury room ruminations bidden topics. *Virginia Law Review, 87*, 1915.

S., Vidmar, N., Rose, M., Ellis, L., & Murphy, 03). *Civil juror discussions during trial: A study of* a's rule 39(f) from videotaped discussions and *tions.* Retrieved October 5, 2005, from http:// law.northwestern.edu/diamond/papers/ a_civil_discussions.pdf

v. United States, 530 U.S. 428 (2000).

J., Poole, D., & Laimon, R. (2005). Children's and testimony. In N. Brewer & K. Williams , *Psychology and Law: An empirical perspective* 51–175). New York: Guilford.

F., & Gottesman, I. (1991). Biological and c contributors to violence: Widom's untold tale. *logical Bulletin, 109*, 125–129.

torney's Office for the Third Judicial District v. ne, U.S. Supreme Court 08-6 (2009).

Ditto, P., Jacobson, J., Smucker, W., Danks, J., & Fagerlin, A. (2006). Context changes choices: A prospective study of the effects of hospitalization on life-sustaining treatment preferences. *Medical Decision Making, 26*, 313–322.

Ditto, P., Smucker, W., Danks, J., Jacobson, J., Houts, R., Fagerlin, A., et al. (2003). Stability of older adults' preferences for life-sustaining medical treatment. *Health Psychology, 22*, 605–615.

Donat, P. L. N., & D'Emilio, J. (1992). A feminist redefinition of rape and sexual assault: Historical foundations and change. *Journal of Social Issues, 48*, 9–22.

Doppelt, J. (1991). Generic prejudice: How drug war fervor threatens the right to a fair trial. *American University Law Review, 40*, 821–836.

Dougall, A. L., Hayward, M. C., & Baum, A. (2005). Media exposure to bioterrorism: Stress and the anthrax attacks. *Psychiatry, 68*, 28–43.

Douglas, J., Burgess, A. W., Burgess, A. G., & Ressler, R. (2006). *Crime classification manual: A standard system for investigating and classifying violent crimes* (2nd ed.). New York: Wiley.

Douglas, J. E., Ressler, R. K., Burgess, A. W., & Hartman, C. R. (1986). Criminal profiling from crime scene analysis. *Behavioral Sciences & the Law, 4*, 401–421.

Douglass, A., Brewer, N., & Semmler, C. (2009). Moderators of post-identification feedback effects on eyewitnesses' memory reports. *Legal and Criminological Psychology, 15*, 279–292.

Dragowski, E., Halkitis, P., Grossman, A., & D'Augelli, A. (2011). Sexual orientation victimization and posttraumatic stress symptoms among lesbian, gay, and bisexual youth. *Journal of Gay & Lesbian Social Services: The Quarterly Journal of Community & Clinical Practice, 23*, 226–249.

Driscoll, D. M., Kelly, J. R., & Henderson, W. L. (1998). Can perceivers identify likelihood to sexually harass? *Sex Roles, 38*, 557–588.

Drizin, S., & Colgan, B. (2004). Tales from the juvenile confession front: A guide to how standard police interrogation tactics can produce coerced and false confessions from juvenile suspects. In G. D. Lassiter (Ed.), *Interrogations, confessions, and entrapment* (pp. 127–162). New York: Kluwer Academic/Plenum.

Drizin, S., & Leo, R. (2004). The problem of false confessions in the post-DNA world. *North Carolina Law Review, 82*, 891–1007.

Duncan, G. J., & Hoffman, S. D. (1985). Economic consequences of marital instability. In M. David & T. Smeeding (Eds.), *Horizontal equity, uncertainty, and well-being* (pp. 427–469). Chicago, IL: University of Chicago Press.

Duncan v. Louisiana, 391 U.S. 145 (1968).

Clavet, G. J. (1996, August). *Ironic effects of juror attempts to suppress inadmissible evidence.* Paper presented at the meeting of the American Psychological Association, Toronto, ON, Canada.

Cleary, H., Woolard, J., Jarvis, J., & Vidal, S. (2011, March). *An observational study of interview characteristics and Miranda in juvenile interrogations.* Paper presented at American Psychology-Law Society, Miami, FL.

Clemmer, D. (1958). *The prison community.* New York: Rinehart.

Clermont, K., & Eisenberg, T. (1992). Trial by jury or judge: Transcending empiricism. *Cornell Law Review, 77*, 1124–1177.

Clingempeel, W. G., & Reppucci, N. D. (1982). Joint custody after divorce: Major issues and goals for research. *Psychological Bulletin, 92*, 102–127.

Cloninger, C., Dragan, M., & Przybeck, T. (1993). A psychobiological model of temperament and character. *Archives of General Psychiatry, 50*, 975–990.

Cloninger, C., Sigvardsson, S., Bohman, M., & vonKnorring, A. (1982). Predisposition to petty criminality in Swedish adoptees. II: Cross-fostering analysis of gene-environment interaction. *Archives of General Psychiatry, 39*, 1242–1249.

Cloud, J. (1998). Of arms and the boy. *Time*, p. 152.

Clow, K., Leach, A., & Ricciardelli, R. (2012). Life after wrongful conviction. In B. Cutler (Ed.), *Conviction of the innocent: Lessons from psychological research* (pp. 327–341). Washington, DC: American Psychological Association.

Cloward, R. A., & Ohlin, L. E. (1960). *Delinquency and opportunity: A theory of delinquent gangs.* New York: Free Press.

CNN (1998, April 23). Ray's death won't end assassination controversy. Retrieved June 10, 2009, from http:// www.cnn.com/US/9804/23/james.earl.ray.reax/

CNN (2004, June 25). No charges against man beaten during arrest. Retrieved June 20, 2005, from http://www. cnn.com/2004/US/West/06/25/lapd.video/ index.html

Cochrane, R., Tett, R., & Vandecreek, L. (2003). Psychological testing and the selection of police officers. *Criminal Justice and Behavior, 30*, 511–537.

Cocozza, J., & Shufelt, J. (2006, June). *Juvenile mental health courts: An emerging strategy.* Retrieved July 3, 2008, from http://www.ncmhjj.com/pdfs/publications/ JuvenileMentalHealthCourts.pdf

Cohen, M. I., Spodak, M. K., Silver, S. B., & Williams, K. (1988). Predicting outcome of insanity acquittees released to the community. *Behavioral Sciences & the Law, 6*, 515–530.

Cohen, T., & Reaves, B. (2006). *Felony defendants in large urban counties, 2002.* Washington, DC: U.S. Department of Justice, Bureau of Justice Statistics.

Colangelo, J. (2009). The recovered memory controversy: A representative case study. *Journal of Child Sexual Abuse, 18*, 103–121.

Colbach, E. (1981). Integrity checks on the witness stand. *Bulletin of the American Academy of Psychiatry and the Law, 9*, 285–288.

Colorado v. Connelly, 107 S.Ct. 515 (1986).

Combs, D., Campbell, G., Jackson, M., & Smith, R. (2010). Exploring the consequences of humiliating a moral transgressor. *Basic and Applied Social Psychology, 32*, 128–143.

Committee on Ethical Guidelines for Forensic Psychologists (1991). Specialty guidelines for forensic psychologists. *Law and Human Behavior, 15*, 655–665.

Compton, M., Bahara, M., Watson, A., & Oliva, J. (2008). A comprehensive review of extant research on Crisis Intervention Team (CIT) programs. *Journal of the American Academy of Psychiatry and Law, 36*, 47–55.

Compton, M., Demir Neubert, B., Broussard, B., McGriff, J., Morgan, R., & Oliva, J. (2011). Use of force preferences and perceived effectiveness of actions among crisis intervention team police officers and non-CIT officers in an escalating psychiatric crisis involving a subject with schizophrenia. *Schizophrenia Bulletin, 37*, 737–745.

Condie, L. O. (2003). *Parenting evaluations for the court: Care and protection matters.* New York: Springer.

Conger, R. (1980). Juvenile delinquency: Behavior restraint or behavior facilitation? In T. Hirschi & M. Gottfredson (Eds.), *Understanding crime: Current theory and research* (pp. 131–142). Newbury Park, CA: Sage.

Conover, T. (2003, June 29). In the land of Guantanamo. *The New York Times Sunday Magazine*, p. 40.

Cooper, J., & Neuhaus, I. M. (2000). The hired gun effect: Assessing the effect of pay, frequency of testifying, and credentials on the perception of expert testimony. *Law and Human Behavior, 24*, 149–172.

Cooper v. Oklahoma, 116 S.Ct. 1373 (1996).

Cooper, V., & Zapf, P. (2003). Predictor variables in competency to stand trial decisions. *Law and Human Behavior, 27*, 423–436.

Copson, G., Badcock, R., Boon, J., and Britton, P. (1997). Articulating a systematic approach to clinical crime profiling. *Criminal Behaviour and Mental Health, 7*, 13–17.

Cordon, I., Saetermoe, C., & Goodman, G. (2005). Facilitating children's accurate responses: Conversational rules and interview style. *Applied Cognitive Psychology, 19*, 249–266.

Cornell, D. (2003). Guidelines for responding to student threats of violence. *Journal of Educational Administration, 41*, 705–719.

Cornell, D. (2006). *School violence: Fears versus facts.* New York: Routledge.

Corrado, R. R., Vincent, G. M., Hart, S. D., & Cohen, I. M. (2004). Predictive validity of the Psychopathy Checklist: Youth version for general and violent recidivism. *Behavioral Sciences & the Law, 22*, 5–22.

Cosden, M., Ellens, J., Schnell, J., & Yamini-Diouf, Y. (2005). Efficacy of a mental health treatment court with assertive community treatment. *Behavioral Sciences & the Law, 23*, 199–214.

Cosden, M., Ellens, J., Schnell, J., Yamini-Diouf, Y., & Wolfe, M. (2003). Evaluation of a mental health court with assertive community treatment. *Behavioral Sciences & the Law, 21*, 415–427.

Costa, P. T., Jr., & Widiger, T. A. (2002). *Personality disorders and the five-factor model of personality* (2nd ed.). Washington, DC: American Psychological Association.

Costanzo, M., Shaked-Schroer, N., & Vinson, K. (2010). Juror beliefs about police interrogations, false confessions, and expert testimony. *Journal of Empirical Legal Studies, 7*, 231–247.

Cottle, C., Lee, R., & Heilbrun, K. (2001). The prediction of criminal recidivism in juveniles: A meta-analysis. *Criminal Justice and Behavior, 28*, 367–394.

Cougle, J., Resnick, H., & Kilpatrick, D. (2009). PTSD, depression, and other comorbidity in relation to suicidality: Cross-sectional and prospective analyses of a national probability sample of women. *Depression and Anxiety, 26*, 1151–1157.

Cowan, C. L., Thompson, W. C., & Ellsworth, P. C. (1984). The effects of death qualification on jurors' predispositions to convict and on the quality of deliberation. *Law and Human Behavior, 8*, 53–79.

Coy v. Iowa, 487 U.S. 1012 (1988).

Coyle, M. (2009). *New report shows sharp rise in prison time for federal offenders.* Retrieved February 13, 2009, from www.law.com

The Criminal Justice/Mental Health Consensus Project. (2005). *Mental health resources.* Retrieved November 20, 2008, from http://justicecenter.csg.org/resources/mental_health

Crocker, C., & Kovera, M. (2010). The effects of rehabilitative voir dire on juror bias and decision making. *Law and Human Behavior, 34*, 212–226.

Crosbie-Burnett, M. (1991). Impact of joint versus sole custody and quality of coparental relationship on adjustment of adolescents in remarried families. *Behavioral Sciences & the Law, 9*, 439–449.

Cruzan v. Director, Missouri Department of Health, 497 U.S. 261 (1990).

Cuffe, S. P., Addy, C. L., Garrison, C. Z., Waller, J. L., Jackson, K. L., McKeown, R. E., et al. (1998). Prevalence of PTSD in a community sample of older adolescents. *Journal of the American Academy of Child & Adolescent Psychiatry, 37*, 147–154.

Culhane, C. E., Hosch, H. M., & Weaver, W. G. (2004). Crime victims serving as jurors: Is there bias present? *Law and Human Behavior, 28*, 649–659.

Cunningham, M. (2010). *Evaluation for capital sentencing.* New York: Oxford University Press.

Curry, T., Lee, G., & Rodriguez, S. (2004). Does victim gender increase sentence severity? Further explorations of gender dynamics and sentencing outcomes. *Crime and Delinquency, 50*, 319–343.

Curtis, Kim. (2003, January 8). *California loses track of 33,000 sex offenders.* Retrieved from http://www.deseretnews.com/article/958174/California-loses-track-of-33000-sex-offenders.html

Cutler, B. (2011). *Conviction of the innocent: Lessons from psychological research.* Washington, DC: American Psychological Association.

Cutler, B., & Kovera, M. (2011). Expert psychological testimony. *Current Directions in Psychological Science, 20*, 53–57.

D'Agostino, C. (1986). Police psychological services: Ethical issues. In J. T. Reese & H. A. Goldstein (Eds.), *Psychological services for law enforcement* (pp. 241–248). Washington, DC: U.S. Government Printing Office.

Daftary-Kapur, T. (2009). *The influence of pre- and post-venire publicity on juror decision making* (Doctoral dissertation). Available from proquest dissertations and theses database. (UMI No. AAT3378557).

Daftary-Kapur, T., Dumas, R., & Penrod, S. (2010). Jury decision-making biases and methods to counter them. *Legal and Criminological Psychology, 15*, 133–154.

Daicoff, S. (1999). Making law therapeutic for lawyers: Therapeutic jurisprudence, preventive law, and the psychology of lawyers. *Psychology, Public Policy, and Law, 5*, 811–848.

Daly, K. (1994). *Gender, crime, and punishment.* New Haven, CT: Yale University Press.

Dann, B., & Hans, V. (2004). Recent evaluative research on jury trial innovations. *Court Review, 41*, 12–19.

Dantzker, M. (2010). Differences in pre-employment screening protocols used and reasons for their use between police and clinical psychologists. *Dissertation Abstracts International: Section B: The Sciences and Engineering, 71*(3-B), 2042.

Danziger, S., Levav, J., & Avnaim-Pesso, L. (2011). Extraneous factors in judicial decisions. *Proceedings of the National Academy of Sciences of the United States of America, 108*, 6889–6892.

Darley, J., Sanderson, C., & LaMantha, P. (1996). Community standards for defining attempt: Inconsistencies with the Model Penal Code. *American Behavioral Scientist, 39*, 405–420.

Daubert v. Merrell Dow Pharmaceuticals, Inc., 113 S.Ct. 2786 (1993).

Dauphinot, L. (1996). *The efficacy of community correctional supervision for offenders with severe mental illness.* Unpublished doctoral dissertation, University of Texas at Austin, Austin, TX.

Davey, M., & Goodnough, A. (2007). *Doubts rise as states hold sex offenders after prison.* Retrieved March 24, 2009, from http://www.nytimes.com/2007/03/04/us/04civil.html

Davis, S., & Bottoms, B. (2002). Effects of social support on children's eyewitness reports: A test of the underlying mechanism. *Law and Human Behavior, 26*, 185–215.

Day, M., & Ross, M. (2011). The value of remorse: How drivers' responses to police predict fines for speeding. *Law and Human Behavior, 35*, 221–234.

Death Penalty Information Center (2010). *Facts about the death penalty.* Retrieved March 26, 2010, from http://www.deathpenaltyinfo.org

Deci, E. L., & Ryan, R. M. (2000). The "what" and "why" of goal pursuits: Human needs and the self-determination of behavior. *Psychological Inquiry, 11*, 227–268.

Deffenbacher, K., Bornstein, B., McGorty, E., & Penrod, S. (2008). Forgetting the once-seen face: Estimating the strength of an eyewitness's memory representation. *Journal of Experimental Psychology: Applied, 14*, 139–150.

Deffenbacher, K., Bornstein, B. H., & Penrod, S. D. (2006). Mugshot exposure effects: Retroactive interference, mugshot commitment, source confusion, and unconscious transference. *Law and Human Behavior, 30*, 287–307.

Deffenbacher, K., Bornstein, B. H., Penrod, S. D., & McGorty, E. (2004). A meta-analytic review of the effects of high stress on eyewitness memory. *Law and Human Behavior, 28*, 687–706.

Degold, B. (2008). Lawyers' emerging experiences of interdisciplinary collaborative separation and divorce. *Psychiatry, Psychology and Law, 15*, 396–414.

Deitz, S. R., Russell, S. A., & Hammes, K. M. (1989, August). *Who's on trial? Information processing by jurors in rape cases.* Paper presented at the meeting of the American Psychological Association, New Orleans.

DeMatteo, D., Murrie, D., Anumba, N., & Keesler, M. (2011). *Forensic mental health assessments in death penalty cases.* New York: Oxford University Press.

Dunn, M., Salovey, P., & Feigenson, N. (2006). The jury persuaded (and not): Computer animation in the courtroom. *Law & Policy, 28*, 228–248.

Durbin, J., Lin, E., & Zaslavska, N. (2010). Police-citizen encounters that involve mental health concerns: Results of an Ontario police services survey. *Canadian Journal of Community Mental Health, 29*, 53–71.

Durkin, E. (2011). *Kiss our ashes: Many smokers plan to ignore sweeping ban in city parks.* Retrieved June 19, 2012, from http://www.nydailynews.com/new-york/kiss-ashes-smokers-plan-ignore-sweeping-ban-city-parks-article-1.146021

Dusky v. United States, 362 U.S. 402 (1960).

Dutton, D. G. (1995). Male abusiveness in intimate relationships. *Clinical Psychology Review, 15*, 567–582.

Dutton, D. G. (2000). *The domestic assault of women* (3rd ed.). Vancouver: University of British Columbia Press.

Dvoskin, J., Skeem, J., Novaco, R., & Douglas, K. (2011). *Using social science to reduce violent offending.* New York: Oxford University Press.

Eads, L., Shuman, D., & DeLipsey, J. (2000). Getting it right: The trial of sexual assault and child molestation cases under Federal Rules of Evidence 413–415. *Behavioral Sciences & the Law, 18*, 169–216.

Earnshaw, V. A., Pitpitan, E. V., & Chaudoir, S. R. (2011). Intended responses to rape as functions of attitudes, attributions of fault, and emotions. *Sex Roles, 64*, 382–393.

Eaton, L. (2004, August 8). Divorced parents move, and custody gets trickier. *The New York Times*, p. 1. Retrieved June 25, 2009, from http://www.nytimes.com/2004/08/08/nyregion/divorced-parents-move-and-custody-gets-trickier.html?pagewanted=all

Eaton, L., & Kaufman, L. (2005, April 26). In problem-solving courts, judges turn therapist. *The New York Times*, p. A1.

Eberhardt, J., Davies, P., Purdie-Vaughns, V., & Johnson, S. (2006). Looking deathworthy: Perceived stereotypicality of Black defendants predicts capital-sentencing outcomes. *Psychological Science, 17*, 383–386.

Ebreo, A., Linn, N., & Vining, J. (1996). The impact of procedural justice on opinions of public policy: Solid waste management as an example. *Journal of Applied Social Psychology, 26*, 1259–1285.

Eckhardt, C. L., Barbour, K. A., & Davison, G. C. (1998). Articulated thoughts of maritally violent and nonviolent men during anger arousal. *Journal of Consulting and Clinical Psychology, 66*, 259–269.

Eckholm, E. (1985, July 4). Stockholm syndrome: Hostages' reactions. *Lawrence Journal-World*, p. 6.

Eckholm, E. (2008, October 14). Courts give addicts a chance to straighten out. *The New York Times*. Retrieved October 15, 2008, from www.nytimes.com/2008/10/15/us/15drugs.html

Eddings v. Oklahoma, 436 U.S. 921 (1982).

Edkins, V. (2011). Defense attorney plea recommendations and client race: Does zealous representation apply equally to all? *Law and Human Behavior, 35*, 413–425.

Eisele, G. T. (1991). The case against mandatory court-annexed ADR programs. *Judicature, 75*, 34–40.

Eisenberg, T., Hannaford-Agor, P., Hans, V., Waters, N., Munsterman, T., Schwab, S., et al. (2005). Judge-jury agreement in criminal cases: A partial replication of Kalven and Zeisel's *The American Jury. Journal of Empirical Legal Studies, 2*, 171–207.

Eisenberg, T., & Hans, V. (2009). Taking a stand on taking the stand: The effect of prior criminal record on the decision to testify and on trial outcomes. *Cornell Law Review, 94*, 1353–1390.

Eisenberg, T., LaFountain, N., Ostrom, B., Rottman, D., & Wells, M. (2002). Juries, judges, and punitive damages: An empirical study. *Cornell Law Review, 87*, 743–782.

Ekman, P., & O'Sullivan, M. (1991). Who can catch a liar? *American Psychologist, 46*, 913–920.

Eley, T. C. (1997). General genes: A new theme in developmental psychopathology. *Current Directions in Psychological Science, 6*, 90–95.

Ellis, D., Choi, A., & Blaus, C. (1993). Injuries to police officers attending domestic disturbances: An empirical study. *Canadian Journal of Criminology, 35*, 149–168.

Ellis, L. (1989). *Theories of rape: Inquiries into the causes of sexual aggression.* New York: Hemisphere.

Ellis, L. (1991). A synthesized (biosocial) theory of rape. *Journal of Consulting and Clinical Psychology, 59*, 631–642. doi: 10.1037/0022-006K.59.5.631

Ellis, L., & Diamond, S. (2003). Race, diversity, and jury composition: Battering and bolstering legitimacy. *Chicago-Kent Law Review, 78*, 1033–1058.

Ellison, K., & Buckhout, R. (1981). *Psychology and criminal justice.* New York: Harper & Row.

Ellsworth, P. C. (1989). Are twelve heads better than one? *Law and Contemporary Problems, 52*, 205–224.

Ellsworth, P. C., & Mauro, R. (1998). Psychology and law. In D. Gilbert, S. Fiske, & G. Lindzey (Eds.), *The handbook of social psychology* (Vol. 2, pp. 684–732). Boston, MA: McGraw-Hill.

Ellsworth, P. C., & Reifman, A. (2000). Juror comprehension and public policy: Perceived problems and proposed solutions. *Psychology, Public Policy, and Law, 6*, 788–821.

Elwork, A., Sales, B. D., & Suggs, D. (1981). The trial: A research review. In B. D. Sales (Ed.), *The trial process* (pp. 1–68). New York: Plenum.

Emery, R. E. (1982). Interparental conflict and the children of discord and divorce. *Psychological Bulletin, 92,* 310–330.

Emery, R. E., Laumann-Billings, L., Waldron, M., Sbarra, D., & Dillon, P. (2001). Child custody mediation and litigation: Custody, contact, and coparenting 12 years after initial dispute resolution. *Journal of Consulting and Clinical Psychology, 69,* 323–332.

Englich, B., & Mussweiler, T. (2001). Sentencing under uncertainty: Anchoring effects in the courtroom. *Journal of Applied Social Psychology, 31,* 1535–1551.

Englich, B., Mussweiler, T., & Strack, F. (2005). The last word in court: A hidden disadvantage for the defense. *Law and Human Behavior, 29,* 705–722.

Ennis, B. J., & Litwack, T. R. (1974). Psychiatry and the presumption of expertise: Flipping coins in the courtroom. *California Law Review, 62,* 693–752.

Eno Louden, J., & Skeem, J. (2007). Constructing insanity: Jurors' prototypes, attitudes, and legal decision-making. *Behavioral Sciences & the Law, 25,* 449–470.

Eno Louden, J., Skeem, J., Camp, J., & Christensen, E. (2008). Supervising probationers with mental disorder: How do agencies respond to violations? *Criminal Justice and Behavior, 35,* 832–847.

Epstein, S. (2003). Cognitive-experiential self-theory of personality. In T. Milton & M. Lerner, (Eds.), *Comprehensive handbook of psychology,* Volume 5: Personality and Social Psychology (pp. 159–184). Hoboken, NJ: Wiley.

Equal Justice Initiative (2007). *Cruel and unusual: Sentencing 13- and 14-year-old children to die in prison.* Montgomery, AL: Author.

Eron, L. (1990). Understanding aggression. *Bulletin of the International Society for Research on Aggression, 12,* 59.

Evans, J. R., Meissner, C. A. Brandon, S. E., Russano, M. B., & Kleinman, S. M. (2010). Criminal versus HUMINT interrogations: The importance of psychological science to improving interrogative practice. *Journal of Psychiatry and Law, 38,* 215–249.

Everington, C. T., & Luckasson, R. (1992). *Competence assessment for standing trial for defendants with mental retardation (CAST-MR) test manual.* Columbus, OH: International Diagnostic Systems.

Ewing v. California, 538 U.S. 11 (2003).

Ewing, C. (1987). *Battered women who kill: Psychological self-defense as legal justification.* Lexington, MA: Lexington Books.

Eysenck, H. J. (1964). *Crime and personality.* Boston, MA: Houghton Mifflin.

Eysenck, H. J., & Gudjonsson, G. H. (1989). *The causes and cures of criminality.* New York: Plenum.

Fagan, J. (1996). The comparative advantage of juvenile versus criminal court sanctions on recidivism among adolescent felony offenders. *Law & Policy, 18,* 79–113.

Farah, M. (2005). Neuroethics: The practical and the philosophical. *Trends in Cognitive Science, 9,* 34–40.

Fare v. Michael C., 442 U.S. 707 (1979).

Faretta v. California, 422 U.S. 806 (1975).

Farrington, D. P. (1995). The development of offending and antisocial behavior from childhood: Key findings from the Cambridge Study in Delinquent Development. *Journal of Child Psychology and Psychiatry, 360,* 929–964.

Farwell, L. (2011). Brain fingerprinting: Corrections to *Rosenfeld. The Scientific Review of Mental Health Practice, 8,* 56–68.

Farwell, L. A., & Smith, S. S. (2001). Using brain MERMER testing to detect knowledge despite efforts to conceal. *Journal of Forensic Sciences, 46,* 135–143.

FBI Academy. (2002). *Countering terrorism: Integration of practice and theory.* Retrieved July 22, 2005, from http://www.apa.org/releases/countering_terrorism.pdf

Federal Bureau of Investigation (2010). *Crime in the United States.* Retrieved from http://www.fbi.gov/stats-services/publications

Federal Bureau of Investigation (2011a). *Crime in the United States 2010.* Retrieved from http://www.fbi.gov/about-us/cjis/ucr/crime-in-the-u.s/2010/crime-in-the-u.s.-2010/violent-crime/rapemain

Federal Bureau of Investigation (2011b). *FBI releases 2010 statistics on law enforcement officers killed and assaulted.* Retrieved from http://www.fbi.gov/about-us/cjis/ucr/leoka/2010/fbi-releases-2010-statistics-on-law-enforcement-officers-killed-and-assaulted

Federal Bureau of Prisons (2012). *Inmate matters.* Retrieved from http://www.bop.gov/inmate_programs/

Federal Rules of Evidence (2009). *Federal Rules of Evidence.* St. Paul: West.

Feeley, M. M. (1983). *Court reform on trial.* New York: Basic Books.

Feige, D. (2006, June 7). *Witnessing guilt, ignoring innocence?* Retrieved July 28, 2008, from http://www.nytimes.com/2006/06/06/opinion/06feige.html?_r=1&scp=11&sq=david%20feige&st=cse&oref=slogin

Feigenson, N. (2010). Visual evidence. *Psychonomic Bulletin & Review, 17,* 149–154.

Feigenson, N., Park, J., & Salovey, P. (2001). The role of emotions in comparative negligence judgments. *Journal of Applied Social Psychology, 31,* 576–603.

Feigenson, N., & Spiesel, C. (2009). *Law on display: The digital transformation of legal persuasion and judgment.* New York: New York University Press.

Fein, S., McCloskey, A. L., & Tomlinson, T. M. (1997). Can the jury disregard that information? The use of suspicion to reduce the prejudicial effects of pretrial publicity and inadmissible testimony. *Personality and Social Psychology Bulletin, 23,* 1215–1226.

Feinblatt, J., & Berman, G. (2001). *Responding to the community: Principles for planning and creating a community court.* Washington, DC: U.S. Department of Justice.

Feldman, M. P. (1977). *Criminal behavior: A psychological analysis.* New York: Wiley.

Feldmann, T. B. (2001). Characteristics of hostage and barricade incidents: Implications for negotiation strategies and training. *Journal of Police Crisis Negotiations, 1,* 3–33.

Feldman-Summers, S., & Ashworth, C. D. (1981). Factors related to intentions to report rape. *Journal of Social Issues, 37,* 71–92.

Felitti, V. J., Anda, R. F., Nordenberg, D., Williamson, D. F., Spitz, A. M., Edwards, V., et al. (1998). Relationship of childhood abuse and household dysfunction to many of the leading causes of death in adults: The adverse childhood experiences (ACE) study. *American Journal of Preventive Medicine, 14,* 245–258.

Felson, R., Ackerman, J., & Gallagher, C. (2005). Police intervention and the repeat of domestic assault. *Criminology: An Interdisciplinary Journal, 43,* 563–588.

Fentiman, L. (1986). Whose right is it anyway? Rethinking competency to stand trial in light of the synthetically sane insanity defendant. *University of Miami Law Review, 40,* 1109–1169.

Findlaw (2012). *The insanity defense among the states.* Retrieved May 30, 2012, from http://criminal.findlaw.com/crimes/more-criminal-topics/insanity-defense/the-insanity-defense-among-the-states.html

Finkel, N. (1989). The Insanity Defense Reform Act of 1984: Much ado about nothing. *Behavioral Sciences & the Law, 7,* 403–419.

Finkel, N. (1995). *Commonsense justice: Jurors' notions of the law.* Cambridge, MA: Harvard University Press.

Finkel, N., & Groscup, J. L. (1997). When mistakes happen: Commonsense rules of culpability. *Psychology, Public Policy, and Law, 3,* 65–125.

Finkel, N., & Slobogin, C. (1995). Insanity, justification, and culpability toward a unifying theme. *Law and Human Behavior, 19,* 447–464.

Finnila, K., Mahlberga, N., Santtilaa, P., Sandnabbaa, K., & Niemib, P. (2003). Validity of a test of children's suggestibility for predicting responses to two interview situations differing in their degree of suggestiveness. *Journal of Experimental Child Psychology, 85,* 32–49.

Finz, S., & Walsh, D. (2004, December 15). *The stuff of crime novels finally has an end.* Retrieved September 1, 2005, from www.sfgate.com

Fischer, K. (1989). Defining the boundaries of admissible expert psychological testimony on rape trauma syndrome. *University of Illinois Law Review, 3,* 691–734.

Fisher, R. P., & Geiselman, R. E. (1992). *Memory enhancing techniques for investigative interviewing: The cognitive interview.* Springfield, IL: Thomas.

Fiske, S., & Taylor, S. (1991). *Social cognition* (2nd ed.). New York: McGraw-Hill.

Fitzgerald, L. F., Buchanan, N. T., Collinsworth, L. L., Magley, V. J., & Romos, A. M. (1999). Junk logic: The abuse defense in sexual harassment litigation. *Psychology, Public Policy, and Law, 5,* 730–759.

Fitzgerald, L. F., Gelfand, M., & Dragow, F. (1995). Measuring sexual harassment: Theoretical and psychometric advances. *Basic and Applied Social Psychology, 17,* 425–445.

Florence v. Board of Chosen Freeholders, 132 S.Ct. 1510 (2012).

Flynn, C., & Heitzmann, D. (2008). Tragedy at Virginia Tech: Trauma and its aftermath. *The Counseling Psychologist, 36,* 479–489.

Foa, E. B., Hearst-Ikeda, D., & Perry, K. J. (1995). Evaluation of a brief cognitive behavioral program for the prevention of chronic PTSD in recent assault victims. *Journal of Consulting and Clinical Psychology, 63,* 948–955.

Foa, E. B., & Kozak, M. J. (1986). Emotional processing of fear: Exposure to corrective information. *Psychological Bulletin, 99,* 20–35.

Follingstad, D. R. (1994, March 10). *The use of battered woman syndrome in court.* Workshop for the American Academy of Forensic Psychology, Santa Fe, NM.

Footlick, J. (1978, May 8). Insanity on trial. *Newsweek,* pp. 108–112.

Ford v. Wainwright, 477 U.S. 399 (1986).

Ford Motor Credit Co. v. Sheehan, 373 So. 2d 956 (Fla. App. 1979).

Ford, W. (1998). *Managing police stress.* Walnut Creek, CA: The Management Advantage.

Forgas, J. (2011). Affective influences on self-disclosure: Mood effects on the intimacy and reciprocity of disclosing personal information. *Journal of Personality and Social Psychology, 100,* 449–461.

Forst, M., Fagan, J., & Vivona, T. S. (1989). Youth in prisons and training schools: Perceptions and consequences of the treatment-custody dichotomy. *Juvenile and Family Court Journal, 40,* 1–14.

ForsterLee, L., & Horowitz, I. (2003). The effects of jury-aid innovations on juror performance in complex civil trials. *Judicature, 86,* 184–190.

Forsterlee, L., Kent, L., & Horowitz, I. (2005). The cognitive effects of jury aids on decision-making in complex civil litigation. *Applied Cognitive Psychology*, *19*, 867–884.

Foster, T. (2011). Adverse life events proximal to adult suicide: A synthesis of findings from psychological autopsy studies. *Archives of Suicide Research*, 15, 1–15.

Foucha v. Louisiana, 112 S.Ct. 1780 (1992).

Fox, D., Gerson, A., & Lees-Haley, P. (1995). Interrelationship of MMPI-2 validity scales in personal injury claims. *Journal of Clinical Psychology*, *51*, 42–47.

Fox, J. A., & Levin, J. (1998). Multiple homicide: Patterns of serial and mass murder. *Crime and Justice*, *23*, 407–455.

Fox, J. A., & Levin, J. (2005). *Extreme killing: Understanding serial and mass murder*. Beverly Hills, CA: Sage.

Frank, J. (1949). *Courts on trial*. Princeton, NJ: Princeton University Press.

Frazer, M. (2006). *The impact of the community court model on defendant perceptions of fairness: A case study at the Red Hook Community Justice Center*. New York: Center for Court Innovation.

Frazier, P. A., & Borgida, E. (1985). Rape trauma syndrome evidence in court. *American Psychologist*, *40*, 984–993.

Frazier, P. A., & Borgida, E. (1988). Juror common understanding and the admissibility of rape trauma syndrome evidence in court. *Law and Human Behavior*, *12*, 101–122.

Frazier, P. A., Cochran, C. C., & Olson, A. M. (1995). Social science research on lay definitions of sexual harassment. *Journal of Social Issues*, *51*, 21–37.

Frazier, P. A., & Haney, B. (1996). Sexual assault cases in the legal system: Police, prosecutor, and victim perspectives. *Law and Human Behavior*, *20*, 607–628.

Frederick, R. (1997). *Validity Indicator Profile manual*. Minnetonka, MN: NSC Assessments.

Frederick, R. (2000). Mixed group validation: A method to address the limitations of criterion group validation in research on malingering detection. *Behavioral Sciences & the Law*, *18*, 693–718.

Frederick, R., & Crosby, R. (2000). Development and validation of the Validity Indicator Profile. *Law and Human Behavior*, *24*, 59–82.

Frederick, S. (2005). Cognitive reflection and decision making. *Journal of Economic Perspectives*, *19*, 25–42.

Freedman, J., Martin, C., & Mota, V. (1998). Pretrial publicity: Effects of admonition and expression pretrial opinions. *Legal and Criminological Psychology*, *3*, 255–270.

Freiburger, T. (2010). The effects of gender, family status, and race on sentencing decisions. *Behavioral Sciences and the Law*, *28*, 378–395.

Freiburger, T., Marcum, C., & Pierce, M. (2010). The impact of race on pretrial decision. *American Journal of Criminal Justice*, *35*, 76–86.

Frendak v. United States, 408 A. 2d 364 (D.C. 1979).

Freud, S. (1961). *The complete psychological works of Sigmund Freud* (Vol. 19). London: Hogarth.

Friedman, R., Anderson, C., Brett, J., Olekalns, M., Goates, N., & Lisco, C. (2004). The positive and negative effects of anger on dispute resolution: Evidence from electronically mediated disputes. *Journal of Applied Psychology*, *89*, 369–376.

Frolik, L. A. (1999). Science, common sense, and the determination of mental capacity. *Psychology, Public Policy, and Law*, *5*, 41–58.

Fulero, S. M., & Finkel, N. J. (1991). Barring ultimate issue testimony: An "insane" rule? *Law and Human Behavior*, *15*, 495–508.

Fuhrmann, G., & Zibbell, R. (2011). *Evaluation for child custody*. New York: Oxford University Press.

Funder, D. C. (2004). *The personality puzzle* (3rd ed.). New York: Norton.

Furman v. Georgia, 408 U.S. 238 (1972).

Furstenberg, F., Peterson, J., Nord, C., & Zill, N. (1983). The life course of children of divorce. *American Sociological Review*, *48*, 656–668.

Gabriel, R. (2011). American justice or American Idol? Two trials and two verdicts in the Casey Anthony case. *The Jury Expert*, *23*, 1–7.

Gaes, G., & Camp, S. (2009). Unintended consequences: Experimental evidence for the criminogenic effect of prison security level placement on post-release recidivism. *Journal of Experimental Criminology*, *5*(2), 139–162.

Gaines, L. K., & Falkenberg, S. (1998). An evaluation of the written selection test: Effectiveness and alternatives. *Journal of Criminal Justice*, *26*, 175–183.

Galanter, M. (2004). The vanishing trial: An examination of trials and related matters in state and federal courts. *Journal of Empirical Legal Studies*, *1*, 459–570.

Galberson, W. (2011, August 8). By helping a girl testify in a rape trial, a dog ignites a legal debate. *New York Times*. Retrieved June 5, 2012, from http://www.nytimes.com/2011/08/09/nyregion/dog-helps-rape-victim-15-testify.html?pagewanted=all

Galinsky, A., Maddux, W., Gilin, D., & White, J. (2008). Why it pays to get inside the head of your opponent. *Psychological Science*, *19*, 378–384.

Gall v. United States, 552 U.S. 38 (2007).

Gallagher, M. (2008). *Thousands of resentencings narrow gap between crack, powder cocaine penalties*. Retrieved December 23, 2008, from www.law.com

Gallagher, W. (1996). *I.D.: How heredity and experience make you who you are*. New York: Random House.

Gallup (2011). *Death penalty*. Retrieved December 28, 2011, from http://www.gallup.com/poll/1606/death-penalty.aspx

Gardner, J., Scogin, F., Vipperman, R., & Varela, J. G. (1998). The predictive validity of peer assessment in law enforcement: A 6-year follow-up. *Behavioral Sciences & the Law, 16*, 473–478.

Garofalo, R. (1914). *Criminology* (R. W. Millar, Trans.). Boston, MA: Little, Brown.

Garrett, B. (2008). Judging innocence. *Columbia Law Review, 108*, 55–142.

Garrett, B. (2010). The substance of false confessions. *Stanford Law Review, 62*, 1051–1119.

Garrett, B. (2011). *Convicting the innocent: Where criminal prosecutions go wrong*. Cambridge, MA: Harvard University Press.

Garvey, S., Hannaford-Agor, P., Hans, V., Mott, N., Munsterman, G. T., & Wells, M. (2004). Juror first votes in criminal trials. *Journal of Empirical Legal Studies, 1*, 371–399.

Garvey, S. P., Johnson, S. L., & Marcus, P. (2000). Correcting deadly confusion: Responding to jury inquiries in capital cases. *Cornell Law Review, 85*, 627–655.

Gastil, J., Black, L., Deess, E., & Leighter, J. (2008). From group member to democratic citizen: How deliberating with fellow jurors reshapes civic attitudes. *Human Communication Research, 34*, 137–169.

Gatowski, S. I., Dobbin, S. A., Richardson, J. T., Ginsburg, G. P., Merlino, M. L., & Dahir, V. (2001). Asking the gatekeepers: A national survey of judges of judging expert evidence in a post-*Daubert* world. *Law and Human Behavior, 25*, 433–458.

Gaylin, W. (1974). *Partial justice: A study of bias in sentencing*. New York: Vintage.

Gazal-Ayal, O., & Sulitzeanu-Kenan, R. (2010). Let my people go: Ethnic in-group bias in judicial decisions - Evidence from a randomized natural experiment. *Journal of Empirical Legal Studies, 7*, 403–428.

Geis, G., & Bienen, L. B. (1998). *Crimes of the century*. Boston: Northeastern University Press.

Gelles, R. J., & Cornell, C. P. (1985). *Intimate violence in families*. Newbury Park, CA: Sage.

George, J. A. (2008). Offender profiling and expert testimony: Scientifically valid or glorified results? *Vanderbilt Law Review, 61*, 221–260.

Georgia v. McCollum, 112 S.Ct. 2348 (1992).

Geraerts, E., Bernstein, D., Merckelbach, H., Linders, C., Raymaekers, L., & Loftus, E. (2008). Lasting false beliefs and their behavioral consequences. *Psychological Science, 19*, 749–753.

Geraerts, E., Schooler, J., Merckelbach, H., Jelicic, M., Hauer, B., & Ambadar, Z. (2007). The reality of recovered memories: Corroborating continuous and discontinuous memories of childhood sexual abuse. *Psychological Science, 18*, 564–568.

Gerber, M. R., Ganz, M. L., Lichter, E., Williams, C. M., & McCloskey, L. A. (2005). Adverse health behaviors and the detection of partner violence by clinicians. *Archives of Internal Medicine, 165*, 1016–1021.

Gergen, K. J. (1994). Exploring the postmodern: Perils or potentials? *American Psychologist, 49*, 412–416.

Gerry, M., Garry, M., & Loftus, E. (2005). False memories. In N. Brewer & K. Williams (Eds.), *Psychology and law: An empirical perspective* (pp. 222–252). New York: Guilford.

Giaconia, R. M., Reinherz, H. Z., Silverman, A. B., Pakiz, B., Frost, A. K., & Cohen, E. (1995). Traumas and posttraumatic stress disorder in a community population of older adolescents. *Journal of the American Academy of Child & Adolescent Psychiatry, 34*, 1369–1380.

Gibson, C. (2005, January 7). *Andrea Yates case interview with Andrea Yates's mother* [ABC News Transcript, Good Morning America]. Retrieved August 7, 2005, from http://www.lexisnexis.com/us/lnacademic/results/docview/docview.do?docLinkInd=true&risb=21_T8239962496&format=GNBFI&sort=RELEVANCE&startDocNo=1&resultsUrlKey=29_T8239962499&cisb=22_T8239962498&treeMax=true&treeWidth=0&csi=8277&docNo=7

Gideon v. Wainwright, 372 U.S. 335 (1963).

Gidycz, C., Rich, C., Orchowski, L., King, C., & Miller, A. (2006). The evaluation of a sexual assault self-defense and risk-reduction program for college women: a prospective study. *Psychology of Women Quarterly, 30*, 173–186.

Gilovich, T., Kerr, M., & Medvec, V. H. (1993). Effect of temporal perspective on subjective confidence. *Journal of Personality and Social Psychology, 64*, 552–560.

Gist, R. M., & Perry, J. D. (1985). Perspectives on negotiation in local jurisdictions. Part 1: A different typology of situations. *FBI Law Enforcement Bulletin, 54*, 21.

Givelber, D. (2001). The adversary system and historical accuracy: Can we do better? In S. Westervelt & J. Humphrey (Eds.), *Wrongly convicted: Perspectives on failed justice* (pp. 253–268). New Brunswick, NJ: Rutgers University Press.

Givelber, D., & Farrell, A. (2008). Judges and juries: The defense case and differences in acquittal rates. *Law and Social Inquiry, 33*, 31–52.

Glamser, D. (1997, January 27). Washington State testing therapy for sex felons. *USA Today*, p. 3A.

Gless, A. G. (1995). Some post-*Daubert* trial tribulations of a simple county judge: Behavioral science evidence in trial courts. *Behavioral Science & the Law*, 13, 261–291.

Glymour, B., Glymour, C., & Glymour, M. (2008). Watching social science: The debate about the effects of exposure to televised violence on aggressive behavior. *American Behavioral Scientist*, 51, 1231–1259.

Godinez v. Moran, 113 S.Ct. 2680 (1993).

Golding, J. M., Bradshaw, G. S., Dunlap, E. E., & Hodell, E. C. (2007). The impact of mock jury gender composition on deliberations and conviction rates in a child sexual assault trial. *Child Maltreatment*, 12, 182–190.

Golding, S. L. (1993). Interdisciplinary Fitness Interview-Revised: A training manual. State of Utah Division of Mental Health.

Golding, S. L., Roesch, R., & Schreiber, J. (1984). Assessment and conceptualization of competency to stand trial: Preliminary data on the Interdisciplinary Fitness Interview. *Law and Human Behavior*, 8, 321–334.

Goldinger, S., He, Y., & Papesh, M. (2009). Deficits in cross-race face learning: Insights from eye movements and pupillometry. *Journal of Experimental Psychology: Learning, Memory, and Cognition*, 35, 1105–1122.

Goldkamp, J. (2000). The drug court response: Issues and implications for justice change. *Albany Law Review*, 63, 923–961.

Goldman, S., & Faw, L. (1999). Three wraparound models as promising approaches. In B. Burns & S. Goldman (Eds.), *Promising practices in wraparound for children with serious emotional disturbance and their families. Systems of care: Promising practices in children's mental health, 1998 series* (Vol. 4, pp. 35–78). Washington, DC: American Institutes for Research Center for Effective Collaboration and Practice.

Goldstein, A. P. (2004). Evaluations of effectiveness. In A. P. Goldstein, R. Nensen, B. Daleflod, & M. Kalt (Eds.), *New perspectives on aggression replacement training* (pp. 230–244). Chichester, UK: Wiley.

Goldstein, N. E. S., Dovidio, A., Kalbeitzer, R., Weil, J., & Strachan, M. (2007). An anger management intervention for female juvenile offenders: Results of a pilot study. *Journal of Forensic Psychology Practice*, 7, 1–28.

Goldstein, R., Grant, B., Ruan, W., Smith, S., & Saha, T. (2006). Antisocial Personality Disorder with childhood- versus adolescence-onset conduct disorder: From the National Epidemiologic Survey on alcohol and related conditions. *Journal of Nervous and Mental Disease*, 194, 667–675.

Gollwitzer, M., & Keller, L. (2010). What you did only matters if you are one of us: Offenders' group membership moderates the effect of criminal history on punishment severity. *Social Psychology*, 41, 20–26.

Goodman, G. S., Pyle-Taub, E., Jones, D., England, P., Port, L., Rudy, L., et al. (1992). Testifying in criminal court: Emotional effects of criminal court testimony on child sexual assault victims. *Monographs of the Society for Research in Child Development*, 57(5, Serial No. 229), i, ii, v, 1–159.

Goodman, G. S., Quas, J., & Ogle, C. (2010). Child maltreatment and memory. *Annual Review of Psychology*, 61, 325–251.

Goodman, G. S., Tobey, A., Batterman-Faunce, J., Orcutt, H., Thomas, S., & Shapiro, C. (1998). Face-to-face confrontation: Effects of closed-circuit technology on children's eyewitness testimony and jurors' decisions. *Law and Human Behavior*, 22, 265–203.

Goodman-Delahunty, J. (1998). Approaches to gender and the law: Research and applications. *Law and Human Behavior*, 22, 129–143.

Goodman-Delahunty, J., & Foote, W. (2011). *Evaluation for workplace discrimination and harassment*. New York: Oxford University Press.

Goodman-Delahunty, J., Granhag, P. A., Hartwig, M., & Loftus, E. F. (2010). Insightful or wishful: Lawyers' ability to predict case outcomes. *Psychology, Public Policy, and Law*, 16, 133–157.

Goodman-Delahunty, J., Greene, E., & Hsiao, W. (1998). Construing motive in videotaped killings: The role of jurors' attitudes toward the death penalty. *Law and Human Behavior*, 22, 257–271.

Goodman-Delahunty, J., & Sporer, S. (2010). Unconscious influences in sentencing decisions: A research review of psychological sources of disparity. *Australian Journal of Forensic Sciences*, 42, 19–36.

Gopnick, A. (2012, January 30). The caging of American: Why do we lock up so many people? *The New Yorker*, pp. 72–77.

Gordon, D., Arbuthnot, J., Gustafson, K., & McGreen, P. (1988). Home-based behavioral-systems family therapy with disadvantaged juvenile delinquents. *American Journal of Family Therapy*, 16, 243–255.

Gordon, R. A. (1986, August). *IQ commensurability of black – white differences in crime and delinquency*. Paper presented at the meeting of the American Psychological Association, Washington, DC.

Gothard, S., Rogers, R., & Sewell, K. W. (1995). Feigning incompetency to stand trial: An investigation of the Georgia Court Competency Test. *Law and Human Behavior*, 19, 363–374.

Gothard, S., Viglione, D. J., Meloy, J. R., & Sherman, M. (1995). Detection of malingering in competency to stand trial evaluations. *Law and Human Behavior, 19,* 493–506.

Gottfredson, D., & Exum, M. (2002). The Baltimore city drug treatment court: One-year results from a randomized study. *Journal of Research in Crime and Delinquency, 39,* 337–356.

Gottfredson, D., Najaka, S., & Kearley, B. (2003). Effectiveness of drug courts: Evidence from a randomized trial. *Criminology & Public Policy, 2,* 171–196.

Gottfredson, L. (1986, August). *IQ versus training: Job performance and black – white occupational inequality.* Paper presented at the meeting of the American Psychological Association, Washington, DC.

Gould, J. (2011). *As California fights prison overcrowding, some see a golden opportunity.* Retrieved June 12, 2012, from http://www.time.com/time/nation/article/0,8599,2094840,00.html

Government Accountability Office (2005). *Adult drug courts: Evidence indicates recidivism reductions and mixed results for other outcomes.* Washington, DC: Author.

Grann, D. (2009, September 7). Trial by fire: Did Texas execute an innocent man? *The New Yorker,* pp. 42–63.

Gray, E. (1993). *Unequal justice: The prosecution of child sexual abuse.* New York: Macmillan.

Gready, R., Ditto, P., Danks, J., Coppola, K., Lockhart, L., & Smucker, W. (2000). Actual and perceived stability of preferences for life-sustaining treatment. *Journal of Clinical Ethics, 11,* 334–346.

Greathouse, S., & Kovera, M. (2009). Instruction bias and lineup presentation moderate the effects of administrator knowledge on eyewitness identification. *Law and Human Behavior, 33,* 70–82.

Greely, H. (2005). Premarket approval for lie detections: An idea whose time may be coming. *American Journal of Bioethics, 5,* 50–52.

Greely, H., & Illes, J. (2007). Neuroscience-based lie detection: The urgent need for regulation. *American Journal of Law and Medicine, 33,* 377–421.

Green, A. (2004, August 30). The waiting room: August. *The New Yorker,* pp. 37–38.

Green, B., Grace, M., Lindy, J., Gleser, G., & Leonard, A. C. (1990). Risk factors for PTSD and other diagnoses in a general sample of Vietnam veterans. *American Journal of Psychiatry, 147,* 729–733.

Green, S. (2005, January 31). When justice is delayed. *National Law Journal,* p. 22.

Greenberg, M. S., & Ruback, R. B. (1984). Criminal victimization: Introduction and overview. *Journal of Social Issues, 40,* 1–8.

Greene, E. (2002). How effective? Review of *Stack and sway: The new science of jury consulting. Judicature, 85,* 1–3.

Greene, E. (2008). "Can we talk?" Therapeutic jurisprudence, restorative justice, and tort litigation. In B. Bornstein & R. Wiener (Eds.), *Civil juries and civil justice: Empirical perspectives* (pp. 235–258). New York: Springer.

Greene, E. (2009). Psychological issues in the civil trial. In J. Lieberman & D. Krauss (Eds.), *Jury psychology: Social aspects of trial processes.* Vol.1: Psychology of the Courtroom (pp. 183–206). Burlington, VT: Ashgate.

Greene, E., & Bornstein, B. (2000). Precious little guidance: Jury instructions on damage awards. *Psychology, Public Policy, and Law, 6,* 743–768.

Greene, E., & Bornstein, B. (2003). *Determining damages: The psychology of jury awards.* Washington, DC: American Psychological Association.

Greene, E., & Bornstein, B. (2011, April). Cloudy forecasts: Predicting case outcomes. *Trial, 47,* 28–33.

Greene, E., Chopra, S., Kovera, M., Penrod, S., Rose, V., Schuller, R., et al. (2002). Jurors and juries: A review of the field. In J. Ogloff (Ed.), *Taking psychology and law into the twenty-first century* (pp. 225–285). New York: Kluwer Academic/Plenum.

Greene, E., & Ellis, L. (2007). Decision making in criminal justice. In D. Carson, B. Milne, F. Pakes, K. Shalev, & A. Shawyer (Eds.), *Applying psychology to criminal justice* (pp. 183–200). Chichester, UK: Wiley.

Greene, E., & Evelo, A. J. (2011, March). *Attitudes regarding the appropriateness of life sentences for juvenile offenders.* Paper presented at International Congress on Psychology and Law, Miami, FL.

Greene, E., Goodman, J., & Loftus, E. (1991). Jurors' attitudes about civil litigation and the size of damage awards. *American University Law Review, 40,* 805–820.

Greene, E., Hayman, K., & Motyl, M. (2008). "Shouldn't we consider …?" Jury discussions of forbidden topics and effects on damage awards. *Psychology, Public Policy, and Law, 14,* 194–222.

Greene, E., Johns, M., & Smith, A. (2001). The effects of defendant conduct on jury damage awards. *Journal of Applied Psychology, 86,* 228–237.

Greene, E., & Loftus, E. (1985). When crimes are joined at trial. *Law and Human Behavior, 9,* 193–207.

Greene, J. A. (1999). Zero tolerance: A case study of police policies and practices in New York City. *Crime and Delinquency, 45,* 171–187.

Greenhouse, L. (1994, April 20). High court bars sex as standard of picking jurors. *The New York Times,* pp. A1, A10.

Gregg v. Georgia, 428 U.S. 153 (1976).

Gregory, W. L., Mowen, J. C., & Linder, D. E. (1978). Social psychology and plea bargaining: Applications, methodology, and theory. *Journal of Personality and Social Psychology, 36*, 1521–1530.

Griffin, M. (2008, March). *Old dogs and new tricks: Demographic variables and interest in technology implementation in the courtroom.* Paper presented at the annual conference of American Psychology-Law Society, Jacksonville, FL.

Griffin, P. (2003). *Trying and sentencing juveniles as adults: An analysis of state transfer and blended sentencing laws.* Pittsburgh, PA: National Center for Juvenile Justice.

Griffin, P., Heilbrun, K., Mulvey, E., DeMatteo, D., & Schubert, C. (Eds.). (in press). *Criminal justice and the Sequential Intercept Model: Promoting community alternatives for people with severe mental illness.* New York: Oxford University Press.

Grills-Taquechel, A., Littleton, H., & Axsom, D. (2011). Social support, world assumptions, and exposure as predictors of anxiety and quality of life following a mass trauma. *Journal of Anxiety Disorders, 25*, 498–506.

Grisso, T. (1986). *Evaluating competencies: Forensic assessments and instruments.* New York: Plenum.

Grisso, T. (1998). *Forensic assessment of juveniles.* Sarasota, FL: Professional Resource Press.

Grisso, T. (2003). *Evaluating competencies: Forensic assessments and instruments* (2nd ed.). New York: Kluwer/Plenum.

Grisso, T., & Appelbaum, P. S. (1995). The MacArthur Treatment Competence Study. III: Abilities of patients to consent to psychiatric and medical treatments. *Law and Human Behavior, 19*, 149–174.

Grisso, T., & Appelbaum, P. (1998a). *Assessing competence to consent to treatment: A guide for physicians and other health professionals.* New York: Oxford University Press.

Grisso, T., & Appelbaum, P. (1998b). *MacArthur competence assessment tool for treatment (MacCAT-T).* Sarasota, FL: Professional Resource Press.

Grisso, T., Appelbaum, P. S., Mulvey, E. P., & Fletcher, K. (1995). The MacArthur Treatment Competence Study. II: Measures of abilities related to competence to consent to treatment. *Law and Human Behavior, 19*, 127–148.

Grisso, T., Cocozza, J. J., Steadman, H. J., Fisher, W. H., & Greer, A. (1994). The organization of pretrial forensic evaluation services: A national profile. *Law and Human Behavior, 18*, 377–394.

Grisso, T., & Saks, M. J. (1991). Psychology's influence on constitutional interpretation: A comment on how to succeed. *Law and Human Behavior, 15*, 205–211.

Grisso, T., Steinberg, L., Woolard, J., Cauffman, E., Scott, E., Graham, S., et al. (2003). Juveniles' competence to stand trial: A comparison of adolescents' and adults' capacities as trial defendants. *Law and Human Behavior, 27*, 333–363.

Gromet, D., & Darley, J., (2006). Restoration and retribution: How including retributive components affects the acceptability of restorative justice procedures. *Social Justice Research, 19*, 395–432.

Gromet, D., & Darley, J. (2009). Punishment and beyond: Achieving justice through the satisfaction of multiple goals. *Law and Society Review, 43*, 1–38.

Groscup, J., & Tallon, J. (2009). Theoretical models of jury decision-making. In J. Lieberman & D. Krauss (Eds.), *Jury psychology: Social aspects of trial processes.* Vol.1: Psychology of the Courtroom (pp. 41–66). Burlington, VT: Ashgate.

Gross, J., & Hayne, H. (1996). Eyewitness identification by 5- to 6-year-old children. *Law and Human Behavior, 20*, 359–373.

Gross, S., Jacoby, K., Matheson, D., Montgomery, N., & Patil, S. (2005). Exonerations in the United States 1989 through 2003. *Journal of Criminal Law and Criminology, 95*, 523–560.

Gross, S., & O'Brien, B. (2008). Frequency and predictors of false conviction: Why we know so little, and new data on capital cases. *Journal of Empirical Legal Studies, 5*, 927–962.

Groth, A. N. (with Birnbaum, H. J.). (1979). *Men who rape.* New York: Plenum.

Grove, W. M., & Barden, R. C. (1999). Protecting the integrity of the legal system: The admissibility of testimony from mental health experts under *Daubert/Kumho* analyses. *Psychology, Public Policy, and Law, 5*, 224–242.

Grych, J. H., & Fincham, F. D. (1992). Interventions for children of divorce: Toward greater integration of research and action. *Psychological Bulletin, 111*, 434–454.

Gudjonsson, G. H. (2010). The psychology of false confessions: A review of the current evidence. In G. D. Lassiter & C. Meissner (Eds.), *Police interrogations and false confessions* (pp.31–47). Washington, DC: American Psychological Association.

Gudjonsson, G. H., & Copson, G. (1997). The role of the expert in criminal investigation. In J. L. Jackson & D. A. Bekerian (Eds.), *Offender profiling: Theory, research, and practice* (pp. 61–76). Chichester, UK: Wiley.

Gudjonsson, G. H., & MacKeith, J. (1982). False confessions: Psychological effects of interrogation. In A. Trankell (Ed.), *Reconstructing the past: The role of psychologists in criminal trials* (pp. 253–269). Deventer, The Netherlands: Kluwer.

Gudjonsson, G., & Pearse, J. (2011). Suspect interviews and false confessions. *Current Directions in Psychological Science, 20*, 33–37.

Gunnell, J., & Ceci, S. (2010). When emotionality trumps reason: A study of individual processing style and juror bias. *Behavioral Sciences and the Law, 28,* 850–877.

Gunnoe, M. L., & Braver, S. L. (2001). The effects of joint legal custody on mothers, fathers, and children, controlling for factors that predispose a sole maternal vs. joint legal award. *Law and Human Behavior, 25,* 25–43.

Gunter, G. (1985, January 25). Voices across the USA. *USA Today,* p. 12A.

Gutek, B. A. (1995). How subjective is sexual harassment? An examination of rater effects. *Basic and Applied Social Psychology, 17,* 447–467.

Gutek, B. A., & O'Connor, M. (1995). The empirical basis for the reasonable woman standard. *Journal of Social Issues, 51,* 151–166.

Guthrie, C., Rachlinski, J., & Wistrich, A. (2001). Inside the judicial mind. *Cornell Law Review, 86,* 777–830.

Guthrie, C., Rachlinski, J., & Wistrich, A. (2007). Blinking on the bench: How judges decide cases. *Cornell Law Review, 93,* 1–43.

Guthrie, C., Rachlinski, J. J., & Wistrich, A. J. (2009). The "hidden judiciary": An empirical examination of the executive branch of justice. *Duke Law Journal, 58,* 1477–1530.

Haarr, R. N. (2005). Factors affecting the decision of police recruits to "drop out" of police work. *Police Quarterly, 8,* 431–453.

Haas, S., & Hamilton, C. (2007, May). *The use of core correctional practices in offender reentry: The delivery of service delivery and prisoner preparedness for release.* Charleston, WV: Mountain State Criminal Justice Research Services.

Hahn, R., & Kleist, D. (2000). Divorce mediation: Research and implications for family and couples counseling. *The Family Journal, 8,* 165–171.

Haj-Yahia, M. M. (2003). Beliefs about wife-beating among Arab men in Israel: The influence of their patriarchal ideology. *Journal of Family Violence, 18,* 193–206.

Hakuta, J., Soroushian, V., & Kralstein. (2008). *Do community courts transform the justice response to misdemeanor crime? Testing the impact of the Midtown Community Court.* New York: Center for Court Innovation.

Hall, G. C., & Hirschman, R. (1991). Toward a theory of sexual aggression: A quadripartite model. *Journal of Consulting and Clinical Psychology, 59,* 662–669.

Hall, S., & Sales, B. (2008). *Courtroom modifications for child witnesses: Law and science in forensic evaluations.* Washington, DC: American Psychological Association.

Halligan, S. L., Michael, T., Clark, D. M., & Ehlers, A. (2003). Posttraumatic stress disorder following assault: The role of cognitive processing, trauma memory, and appraisals. *Journal of Consulting and Clinical Psychology, 71,* 419–431.

Hamilton, A. (2004, December 13). Woof, woof, your honor. *Time,* p. 46.

Haney, C. (2006). *Reforming punishment: Psychological limits to the pains of imprisonment.* Washington, DC: American Psychological Association.

Haney, C., & Wiener, R. (2004). Death is different: An editorial introduction to the theme issue. *Psychology, Public Policy, and Law, 10,* 373–378.

Hannaford, P., Hans, V., & Munsterman, G. T. (2000). Permitting jury discussions during trial: Impact of the Arizona reform. *Law and Human Behavior, 24,* 359–382.

Hans, V. P. (1992). Judgments of justice. *Psychological Science, 3,* 218–220.

Hans, V. P. (1996). The contested role of the civil jury in business litigation. *Judicature, 79,* 242–248.

Hans, V. P. (2008). Jury systems around the world. *Annual Review of Law and Social Science, 4,* 275–297.

Hans, V. P., & Ermann, M. D. (1989). Responses to corporate versus individual wrongdoing. *Law and Human Behavior, 13,* 151–166.

Hans, V. P., Kaye, D., Dann, B., Farley, E., & Albertson, S. (2011). Science in the jury box: Jurors' comprehension of mitochondrial DNA evidence. *Law and Human Behavior, 35,* 60–71.

Hans, V. P., & Slater, D. (1983). John Hinckley, Jr., and the insanity defense: The public's verdict. *Public Opinion Quarterly, 47,* 202–212.

Hans, V. P., & Vidmar, N. (1986). *Judging the jury.* New York: Plenum.

Hans, V. P., & Vidmar, N. (1991). The American jury at twenty-five years. *Law and Social Inquiry, 16,* 323–351.

Hansen, M. (1999, April). Mandatories going, going … going. *American Bar Association Journal, 85,* 14.

Hanson, R., Bourgon, G., Helmus, L., & Hodgson, S. (2009). The principles of effective correctional treatment also apply to sexual offenders: A meta-analysis. *Criminal Justice and Behavior, 36,* 865–891.

Hanson, R. K., & Morton-Bourgnon, K. E. (2005). The characteristics of persistent sexual offenders: A meta-analysis of recidivism studies. *Journal of Consulting and Clinical Psychology, 73,* 1154–1163.

Hanson, R. K., & Morton- Bourgnon, K. E. (2009). The accuracy of recidivism risk assessment for sexual offenders: A meta-analysis of 188 prediction studies. *Psychological Assessment, 21,* 1–21.

Hanson, S. S. and Doukas, D. J. (2009). Advance directives. In V. Ravitsky, A. Fiester, & A. Caplan (Eds.), *The Penn Center Guide to Bioethics* (pp. 749–760). New York: Springer.

Harding, T., & Zimmerman, E. (1989). Psychiatric symptoms, cognitive stress and vulnerability factors: A study in a remand prison. *British Journal of Psychiatry, 155,* 36–43.

Hare, R. D. (2003). *The Hare Psychopathy Checklist—Revised (PCL-R)* (2nd ed.). Toronto, ON: Multi-Health Systems.

Hare, R. D., & McPherson, L. M. (1984). Violent and aggressive behavior by criminal psychopaths. *International Journal of Law and Psychiatry, 7,* 35–50.

Hare, R. D., & Neumann, C. (2008). Psychopathy as a clinical and empirical construct. *Annual Review of Clinical Psychology, 4,* 217–246.

Hare, T. A., O'Doherty, J., Camerer, C. F., Schultz, W., & Rangel, A. (2008). Dissociating the role of the orbitofrontal cortex and the striatum in the computation of goal values and prediction errors. *Journal of Neuroscience, 28,* 5623–5630.

Harpold, J. A., & Feemster, S. L. (2002). Negative influences of police stress. *FBI Law Enforcement Bulletin, 71* (9), 1–7. Retrieved July 18, 2005, from http://www.fbi.gov/publications/leb/2002/sept2002/sept02leb.htm#page_2

Harrington v. Iowa, 659 NW 2d 509 (Iowa, 2003).

Harris Interactive and GLSEN (2005). *From teasing to torment: School climate in America, a survey of students and teachers.* New York: GLSEN. Downloaded from http://www.des.emory.edu/mfp/302/302GLSEN2.pdf

Harris v. Forklift Systems, Inc., 510 U.S. 17 (1993).

Harris v. New York, 401 U.S. 222 (1971).

Harris, G. T., Rice, M. E., & Quinsey, V. L. (1993). Violent recidivism of mentally disordered offenders: The development of a statistical prediction instrument. *Criminal Justice and Behavior, 20,* 315–335.

Harris, K. (2009, June 26). *San Francisco DA: 'Back on Track' saves money and reduces crime.* Retrieved from http://www.latimes.com/news/opinion/opinionla/la-oew-harris26-2009jun26,0,73758.story

Harris Poll (2008, January 21). Just under three in five Americans believe juries can be fair and impartial all or most of the time. *Harris Poll #9.* Retrieved January 16, 2009, from http://www.harrisinteractive.com/harris_poll/index.asp?PID=861

Harrison, P., & Beck, A. J. (2002). *Prisoners in 2001. Bureau of Justice Statistics Bulletin.* Washington, DC: U.S. Department of Justice.

Harrison, P. M., & Karberg, J. C. (2003, April). *Prison and jail inmates at midyear 2002. Bureau of Justice Statistics Bulletin.* Washington, DC: U.S. Department of Justice.

Hart, S., Michie, C., & Cooke, D. (2007). The precision of actuarial risk assessment instruments: Evaluating the "margins of error" of group versus individual predictions of violence. *British Journal of Psychiatry, 190,* s60–s65.

Hartcollis, A. (2006, April 13). Excuses from jury pool? He's heard them all. *The New York Times.* Retrieved from http://www.nytimes.com/2006/04/13/nyregion/13clerk.html?pagewanted=print

Hartley, R. (2008). Dedication for the special issue on problem-solving courts. *Criminal Justice Review, 33,* 289–290.

Hartwig, M. (2011). Methods in deception detection research. In B. Rosenfeld & S. Penrod (Eds.), *Research methods in forensic psychology* (pp. 136–155). Hoboken, NJ: Wiley.

Hartwig, M., Granhag, P., Stromwall, L, & Kronkvist, O. (2006). Strategic use of evidence during police interrogations: When training to detect deception works. *Law and Human Behavior, 30,* 603–619.

Hasemann, D. (1997). *Practices and findings of mental health professionals conducting workers' compensation evaluations.* Unpublished doctoral dissertation, University of Kentucky, Lexington, KY.

Hastie, R., & Pennington, N. (1996). The O. J. Simpson stories: Behavioral scientists' reflections on *The People of the State of California v. Orenthal James Simpson. University of Colorado Law Review, 67,* 957–975.

Hatch, D. E. (2002). *Officer-involved shootings and use of force: Practical investigative techniques.* Boca Raton, FL: CRC.

Hatcher, C., Mohandie, K., Turner, J., & Gelles, M. G. (1998). The role of the psychologist in crisis/hostage negotiations. *Behavioral Sciences & the Law, 16,* 455–472.

Haugaard, J. J., & Avery, R. J. (2002). Termination of parental rights to free children for adoption: Conflicts between parents, children, and the state. In B. Bottoms, M. Kovera, & B. McAuliff (Eds.), *Children, social policy, and U.S. Law* (pp. 131–152). Boston: Cambridge University Press.

Haw, R., & Fisher, R. (2004). Effects of administrator—witness contact on eyewitness identification accuracy. *Journal of Applied Psychology, 89,* 1106–1112.

Hawkins, H. C. (2001). Police officer burnout: A partial replication of Maslach's burnout inventory. *Police Quarterly, 4,* 343–360.

Hazelwood, R. R., & Douglas, J. E. (1980). The lust murderer. *FBI Law Enforcement Bulletin, 49,* 18–22.

Hazelwood, R. R., & Michaud, S. (2001). *Dark dreams.* New York: Macmillan.

Hazelwood, R. R., Ressler, R. K., Depue, R. L., & Douglas, J. C. (1995). Criminal investigative analysis: An overview. In A. W. Burgess & R. R. Hazelwood (Eds.), *Practical aspects of rape investigation: A multidisciplinary approach* (2nd ed., pp. 115–126). Boca Raton, FL: CRC.

Heider, F. (1958). *The psychology of interpersonal relations.* New York: Wiley.

Heilbrun, K. (1987). The assessment of competency for execution: An overview. *Behavioral Sciences & the Law, 5,* 383–396.

Heilbrun, K. (2001). *Principles of forensic mental health assessment.* New York: Kluwer Academic/Plenum.

Heilbrun, K. (2009). *Evaluation for risk of violence in adults.* New York: Oxford University Press.

Heilbrun, K., & Brooks, S. (2010). Forensic psychology and forensic science: A proposed agenda for the next decade. *Psychology, Public Policy, and Law, 16,* 219–253.

Heilbrun, K., DeMatteo, D., Yasuhara, K., Brooks Holliday, S., Shah, S., King, C., et al. (2012). Community-based alternatives for justice-involved individuals with severe mental illness: Review of the relevant research. *Criminal Justice and Behavior, 39,* 351–419.

Heilbrun, K., Douglas, K., & Yasuhara, K. (2009). Violence risk assessment: Core controversies. In J. Skeem, K. Douglas, & S. Lilienfeld (Eds.), *Psychological science in the courtroom: Controversies and consensus* (pp. 333–357). New York: Guilford.

Heilbrun, K., Dvoskin, J., & Heilbrun, A. (2009). Mass killings on college campuses: Public health, threat/risk assessment, and preventing future tragedies. *Psychological Injury and Law, 2,* 93–99.

Heilbrun, K., Goldstein, N., DeMatteo, D., Hart, A., Riggs Romaine, C., & Shah, S. (2011). Interventions in forensic settings: Juveniles in residential placement, defendants in drug courts or mental health courts, and defendants in forensic hospitals as Incompetent to Stand Trial. In Barlow, D. (Ed.), *Oxford handbook of clinical psychology* (pp. 649–679). New York: Oxford University Press.

Heilbrun, K., Grisso, T., & Goldstein, A. (2009). *Foundations of forensic mental health assessment.* New York: Oxford University Press.

Heilbrun, K., Heilbrun, P., & Griffin, N. (1988). Comparing females acquitted by reason of insanity, convicted, and civilly committed in Florida: 1977–1984. *Law and Human Behavior, 12,* 295–312.

Heilbrun, K., Lee, R., & Cottle, C. (2005). Risk factors and intervention outcomes: Meta-analyses of juvenile offending. In K. Heilbrun, N. Sevin-Goldstein, & R. Redding (Eds.), *Juvenile delinquency: Prevention, assessment, and intervention* (pp. 111–133). New York: Oxford University Press.

Heilbrun, K., Marczyk, G., & DeMatteo, D. (2002). *Forensic mental health assessment: A casebook.* New York: Oxford University Press.

Heilbrun, K., & McClaren, H. (1988). Assessment of competency for execution? A guide for mental health professionals. *Bulletin of the American Academy of Psychiatry and the Law, 16,* 206–216.

Heise, M. (2004). Criminal case complexity: An empirical perspective. *Journal of Empirical Legal Studies, 1,* 331–369.

Henggeler, S., Clingempeel, W., Brondino, M., & Pickrel, S. (2002). Four-year follow-up of multi-systemic therapy with substance-abusing and substance-dependent juvenile offenders. *Journal of the American Academy of Child and Adolescent Psychiatry, 41,* 868–874.

Henggeler, S., Melton, G., Brondino, M., Scherer, D., & Hanley, J. (1997). Multisystemic therapy with violent and chronic juvenile offenders and their families: The role of treatment fidelity in successful dissemination. *Journal of Consulting and Clinical Psychology, 65,* 821–833.

Henggeler, S., Melton, G., & Smith, L. (1992). Family preservation using multisystemic therapy: An effective alternative to incarcerating serious juvenile offenders. *Journal of Consulting and Clinical Psychology, 60,* 953–961.

Henggeler, S., Melton, G., Smith, L., Schoenwald, S., & Hanley, J. (1993). Family preservation using multisystemic treatment: Long-term follow-up to a clinical trial with serious juvenile offenders. *Journal of Child and Family Studies, 2,* 283–293.

Henggeler, S., Pickrel, S. G., & Brondino, M. J. (1999). Multisystemic treatment of substance abusing and dependent delinquents: Outcomes, treatment fidelity, and transportability. *Mental Health Services Research, 1,* 171–184.

Henggeler, S., Pickrel, S. G., Brondino, M. J., & Crouch, J. (1996). Eliminating (almost) treatment dropout of substance abusing or dependent delinquents through home-based multisystemic therapy. *American Journal of Psychiatry, 153,* 427–428.

Henggeler, S., Rodick, J., Borduin, C., Hanson, C., Watson, S., & Urey, J. (1986). Multisystemic treatment of juvenile offenders: Effects on adolescent behavior and family interaction. *Developmental Psychology, 22,* 132–141.

Henggeler, S., Rowland, M., Randall, J., Ward, D., Pickrel, S., Cunningham, P., et al. (1999). Home-based multisystemic therapy as an alternative to the hospitalization of youths in psychiatric crisis: Clinical outcomes. *Journal of the American Academy of Child and Adolescent Psychiatry, 38,* 1331–1339.

Henggeler, S. , & Schoenwald, S. K. (1999). The role of quality assurance in achieving outcomes in MST programs. *Journal of Juvenile Justice and Detention Services, 14,* 1–17.

Henggeler, S., Schoenwald, S. K., Borduin, C. M., Rowland, M. D., & Cunningham, P. B. (1998). *Multisystemic treatment of antisocial behavior in children and adolescents.* New York: Guilford.

Henggeler, S., Sheidow, A., & Lee, T. (2010). Multisystem therapy. In J. Bray & M. Stanton (Eds.), *The Wiley-Blackwell handbook of family psychology*. Retrieved January 15. 2010, from http://onlinelibrary.wiley.com/book/10.1002/9781444310238.

Henry, M., & Rafilson, F. (1997). The temporal stability of the National Police Officer Selection Test. *Psychological Reports, 81*, 1259–1265.

Herbert, B. (2010, March 2). *Watching certain people*. Retrieved July 13, 2012, from http://www.nytimes.com/2010/03/02/opinion/02herbert.html

Herinckx, H., Swart, S., Ama, S., Dolezal, C., & King, S. (2005). Rearrest and linkage to mental health services among clients of the Clark County Mental Health Court Program. *Psychiatric Services, 56*, 853–857.

Hernandez v. New York, 111 S.Ct. 1859 (1991).

Hersch, J., & Viscusi, W. (2004). Punitive damages: How judges and juries perform. *Journal of Legal Studies, 33*, 1–36.

Hershkowitz, I., Lamb, M., Orbach, Y., Katz, C., & Horowitz, D. (2012). The development of communicative and narrative skills among preschoolers: Lessons from forensic interviews about child abuse. *Child Development, 83*, 611–622.

Hetherington, E. M., & Arasteh, J. D. (Eds.). (1988). *Impact of divorce, single parenting, and step-parenting on children*. Hillsdale, NJ: Erlbaum.

Hetherington, E. M., Cox, M., & Cox, R. (1982). Effects of divorce on parents and children. In M. Lamb (Ed.), *Non-traditional families* (pp. 223–288). Hillsdale, NJ: Erlbaum.

Hetherington, E., & Kelly, J. (2002). *For better or worse: Divorce reconsidered*. New York: Norton.

Hickey, E. (2009). *Serial murderers and their victims*. Belmont, CA: Wadsworth.

Hiday, V. A., & Goodman, R. R. (1982). The least restrictive alternative to involuntary hospitalization, outpatient commitment: Its use and effectiveness. *Journal of Psychiatry and Law, 10*, 81–96.

Hiday, V. A., & Ray, B. (2010). Arrests two years after a well-established mental health court. *Psychiatric Services, 61*, 463–468.

Higgins, M. (1999, March). Tough luck for the innocent man. *ABA Journal, 85*, 46–52.

Hill, C., Memon, A., & McGeorge, P. (2008). The role of confirmation bias in suspect interviews: A systematic evaluation. *Legal and Criminological Psychology, 13*, 357–371.

Hille, C. A. (2010). Law enforcement-related stress and relationship satisfaction. *Dissertation Abstracts International Section A: Humanities and Social Sciences, 71*(2–A), 729.

Ho, T. (2001). The interrelationships of psychological testing, psychologists' recommendations, and police departments' recruitment decisions. *Police Quarterly, 4*, 318–342.

Hoff, R., Baranosky, M., Buchanan, J., Zonana, H., & Rosenheck, R. (1999). The effects of a jail diversion program on incarceration: A retrospective cohort study. *Journal of the American Academy of Psychiatry and the Law, 27*, 377–386.

Hoffman, D. (2011). Mediation and the art of shuttle diplomacy. *Negotiation Journal, 27*, 263–309.

Hoffman, P. B., & Stone-Meierhoefer, B. (1979). Application of guidelines to sentencing. In L. E. Abt & I. R. Stuart (Eds.), *Social psychology and discretionary law* (pp. 241–258). New York: Van Nostrand Reinhold.

Hogarth, J. (1971). *Sentencing as a human process*. Toronto, ON: University of Toronto Press.

Hoge, R., & Andrews, D. (2002). *The Youth Level of Service/Case Management Inventory (YLS/CMI) user's manual*. North Tonawanda, NY: Multi-Health Systems.

Hoge, S. K., Bonnie, R. J., Poythress, N., Monahan, J., Eisenberg, M., & Feucht-Haviar, T. (1997). The MacArthur adjudicative competence study: Development and validation of a research instrument. *Law and Human Behavior, 21*, 141–179.

Hoge, S. K., Poythress, N., Bonnie, R., Monahan, J., Eisenberg, M., & Feucht-Haviar, T. (1997). The MacArthur adjudicative competence study: Diagnosis, psychopathology, and competence-related abilities. *Behavioral Sciences & the Law, 15*, 329–345.

Hogg, A., & Wilson, C. (1995). *Is the psychological screening of police applicants a realistic goal? The successes and failures of psychological screening*. Payneham, Australia: National Police Research Unit. (National Police Research Unit Report Series No. 124).

Holander-Blumoff, R., & Tyler, T. (2008). Procedural justice in negotiation: Procedural fairness, outcome acceptance, and integrative potential. *Law and Social Inquiry, 33*, 473–500.

Holland v. Illinois, 493 U.S. 474 (1990).

Holmes, M. D., & Smith, B. W. (2008). *Race and police brutality*. Albany, NY: SUNY Press.

Holmes, O. (1881). *The common law*. Boston, MA: Little, Brown.

Holmes, R. M., & DeBurger, J. (1988). *Serial murder*. Newbury Park, CA: Sage.

Homant, R. J., & Kennedy, D. B. (1998). Psychological aspects of crime scene profiling. *Criminal Justice and Behavior, 25*, 319–343.

Honts, C. (2004). The psychophysiological detection of deception. In P. Granhag & L. Stromwell (Eds.),

Detection of deception in forensic contexts (pp. 103–123). London: Cambridge University Press.

Honts, C. J., & Alloway, W. (2007). Information does not affect the validity of a comparison question test. *Legal and Criminological Psychology*, *12*, 311–320.

Honts, C. & Kircher, J. (2011). Research methods for psychophysiological deception detection. In B. Rosenfeld & S. Penrod (Eds.), *Research methods in forensic psychology* (pp. 105–121). Hoboken, NJ: Wiley.

Honts, C., Raskin, D., & Kircher, J. (1994). Mental and physical countermeasures reduce the accuracy of polygraph tests. *Journal of Applied Psychology*, 79, 252–259.

Hope, L., Memon, A., & McGeorge, P. (2004). Understanding pretrial publicity: Predecisional distortion of evidence by mock jurors. *Journal of Experimental Psychology: Applied*, *10*, 111–119.

Hope, L., & Wright, D. (2007). Beyond unusual? Examining the role of attention in the weapon focus effect. *Applied Cognitive Psychology*, *21*, 951–961.

Hopt v. Utah, 110 U.S. 574 (1884).

Horowitz, I. A. (1980). Juror selection: A comparison of two methods in several criminal cases. *Journal of Applied Social Psychology*, *10*, 86–99.

Horowitz, I. A., Kerr, N., Park, E., & Gockel, C. (2006). Chaos in the courtroom reconsidered: Emotional bias and juror nullification. *Law and Human Behavior*, *30*, 163–181.

Horrigan, D. (2002, May). Technology on trial: Operating in virtual reality. *Law Technology News*. Retrieved June 25, 2009, from http://ltn-archive.hotresponse. com/may02/technology_on_trial_p21.html

Horwitz, A., Widom, C., McLaughlin, J., & White, H. (2001). The impact of childhood abuse and neglect on adult mental health: A prospective study. *Journal of Health and Social Behavior*, *42*, 184–201.

Hotelling, K. (1991). Sexual harassment: A problem shielded by silence. *Journal of Counseling and Development*, *69*, 497–501.

Houppert, K. (2007). *Deluded judge suggests domestic violence victim wanted to be hit*. Retrieved February 21, 2009, from http://www.alternet.org/ blogs/peek/66153/

Houston, C. (1935). The need for Negro lawyers. *Journal of Negro Education*, *4*, 49–52.

Howard, R. C., & Clark, C. R. (1985). When courts and experts disagree: Discordance between insanity recommendations and adjudications. *Law and Human Behavior*, *9*, 385–395.

Huber, G., & Gordon, S. (2004). Accountability and coercion: Is justice blind when it runs for office? *American Journal of Political Science*, *48*, 247–263.

Huber, P. (1990). *Liability: The legal revolution and its consequences*. New York: Basic Books.

Huesmann, L. R., Eron, L. D., Lefkowitz, M. M., & Walder, L. O. (1984). Stability of aggression over time and generations. *Developmental Psychology*, *20*, 1120–1134.

Huesmann, L. R., Eron, L. D., & Yarmel, P. W. (1987). Intellectual functioning and aggression. *Journal of Personality and Social Psychology*, *52*, 232–240.

Huesmann, L. R., Moise-Titus, J., Podolski, C., & Eron, L. D. (2003). Longitudinal relations between children's exposure to TV violence and their aggressive and violent behavior in young adulthood: 1977–1992. *Developmental Psychology*, *39*, 201–221.

Hughes, T. A., Wilson, D. J., & Beck, A. J. (2001). *Trends in state parole, 1990— 2000*. Washington, DC: U.S. Department of Justice, Bureau of Justice Statistics.

Hunt, J. S., & Budesheim, T. L. (2004). How jurors use and misuse character evidence. *Journal of Applied Psychology*, *89*, 347–361.

Hunter, J., & Hunter, R. (1984). Validity and utility of alternative predictors of job performance. *Psychological Bulletin*, *96*, 72–98.

Huntley, J., & Costanzo, M. (2003). Sexual harassment stories: Testing a story-mediated model of juror decision-making in civil litigation. *Law and Human Behavior*, *27*, 29–51.

Ilies, R., Hauserman, N., Schwochau, S., & Stibal, J. (2003). Reported incidence rates of work-related sexual harassment in the United States: Using meta-analysis to explain reported rate disparities. *Personnel Psychology*, *56*, 607–631.

Imwinkelried, E. J. (1994). The next step after *Daubert*: Developing a similarly epistemological approach to ensuring the reliability of nonscientific expert testimony. *Cardozo Law Review*, *15*, 2271–2294.

In re Corrugated Container Antitrust Litigation, 614 F2d 958 (5th Circuit, 1980).

Inbau, F., Reid, J., Buckley, J., & Jayne, B. (2004). *Criminal interrogation and confessions* (4th ed.). Gaithersburg, MD: Aspen.

Innocence Project (2008). *Understand the causes: Eyewitness misidentification*. Retrieved July 23, 2008, from http:// www.innocenceproject.org/understand/ Eyewitness-Misidentification.php

Insabella, G., Williams, T., & Pruett, M. K. (2003). Individual and co-parenting differences between divorcing and unmarried fathers: Implications for court services. *Family Court Review*, *41*, 290–306.

International Association of Chiefs of Police (2006). *Building an offender reentry program: A guide for law enforcement*. Washington, DC: U.S. Bureau of Justice Assistance.

Inwald, R. (1992). *Inwald Personality Inventory technical manual* (Rev. ed.). Kew Gardens, NY: Hilson Research.

Inwald, R. (2008). The Inwald Personality Inventory (IPI) and Hilson Research Inventories: Development and rationale. *Aggression and Violent Behavior, 13*, 298–327.

Inwald, R., Knatz, H., & Shusman, E. (1983). *Inwald Personality Inventory manual.* New York: Hilson Research.

Irwin, J. (1970). *The felon.* Englewood Cliffs, NJ: Prentice Hall.

J.D.B. v. North Carolina, No. 09–1112 U.S. S. Ct (2011).

J.E.B. v. Alabama ex rel. T.B., 511 U.S. 127 (1994).

Jackson v. Denno, 378 U.S. 368 (1964).

Jackson v. Indiana, 406 U.S. 715 (1972).

Jackson, R. L., Rogers, R., & Sewell, K. W. (2005). Forensic applications of the Miller Forensic Assessment of Symptoms Test (MFAST): Screening for feigned disorders in competency to stand trial evaluations. *Law and Human Behavior, 29*, 199–210.

Jackson, S. E., & Maslach, C. (1982). After-effects of job-related stress: Families as victims. *Journal of Occupational Behavior, 3*, 63–77.

Jackson, S. E., & Schuler, R. S. (1983, March–April). Preventing employee burnout. *Personnel, 60*, 58–68.

Jacobson, J., Dobbs-Marsh, J., Liberman, V., & Minson, J. (2011). Predicting civil jury verdicts: How attorneys use (and misuse) a second opinion. *Journal of Empirical Legal Studies, 8*, 99–119.

James, D. J. (2004). *Bureau of Justice Statistics special report: Profile of jail inmates, 2002.* Washington, DC: U.S. Department of Justice.

Janus, E., & Prentky, R. (2003). Forensic use of actuarial risk assessment with sex offenders: Accuracy, admissibility and accountability. *American Criminal Law Review, 40*, 1443–1499.

Jeffers, H. P. (1991). *Who killed Precious?* New York: Pharos.

Jeffreys, B., & Rozen, M. (2006, January 30). The big show: Jury selection crucial element in imminent Lay-Skilling trial. *Texas Lawyer.*

Jenkins, P., & Davidson, B. (1990). Battered women in the criminal justice system: An analysis of gender stereotypes. *Behavioral Sciences & the Law, 8*, 161– 170.

Joe Arpaio 2004. (2004). Retrieved September 1, 2005, from http://www.reelectjoe.com

Johnson v. Zerbst, 304 U.S. 458 (1938).

Johnson, C., & Haney, C. (1994). Felony voir dire: An explanatory study of its content and effect. *Law and Human Behavior, 18*, 487–506.

Johnson, R. (2006). Confounding influences on police detection of suspiciousness. *Journal of Criminal Justice, 34*, 435–442.

Jonakait, R. N. (2003). *The American jury system.* New Haven, CT: Yale University Press.

Jones, E. E. (1990). *Interpersonal perception.* New York: Freeman.

Jones, E. E., Williams, K., & Brewer, N. (2008). "I had a confidence epiphany!" Obstacles to combating post-identification confidence inflation. *Law and Human Behavior, 32*, 164–176.

Jones, J. S., Wynn, B. N., Kroeze, B., Dunnuck, C., & Rossman, L. (2004). Comparison of sexual assaults by strangers versus known assailants in a community-based population. *American Journal of Emergency Medicine, 22*, 454–459.

Judicial Council of California (2004). *Final report: Task force on jury system improvements.* San Francisco, CA: Author.

Justice Education Center, Inc. (2002). *Evaluation of the Hartford Community Court.* Hartford, CT: Author.

Kadri, S. (2005). *The trial: A history, from Socrates to O. J. Simpson.* New York: Random House.

Kahan, D. (1996). What do alternative sanctions mean? *University of Chicago Law Review, 63*, 591–653.

Kahan, D. (2006). What's really wrong with shaming sanctions. *Texas Law Review, 84*, 2075–2095.

Kahneman, D. (2011). *Thinking, fast and slow.* New York: Farrar, Straus, & Giroux.

Kairys, D. (1972). Juror selection: The law, a mathematical method of analysis, and a case study. *American Criminal Law Review, 10*, 771–806.

Kalven, H., & Zeisel, H. (1966). *The American jury.* Boston, MA: Little, Brown.

Kamisar, Y., LaFave, W. R., & Israel, J. (1999). *Basic criminal procedure: Cases, comments and questions.* St. Paul, MN: West.

Kamradt, B. J. (2000). Wraparound Milwaukee: Aiding youth with mental health needs. *Juvenile Justice Journal, 7*, 14–23.

Kane, A., & Dvoskin, J. (2011). *Evaluation for personal injury claims.* New York: Oxford University Press.

Kang, H., Natelson, B., Mahan, C., Lee, K., & Murphy, F. (2003). Post–traumatic stress disorder and chronic fatigue syndrome-like illness among Gulf War veterans: A population-based survey of 30,000 veterans. *American Journal of Epidemiology, 157*, 141–148.

Kansas v. Crane, 534 U.S. 407 (2002).

Kansas v. Hendricks, 117 S. Ct. 2013 (1997).

Kaplan, J. (1996). *Criminal law.* Boston, MA: Little, Brown.

Kaplow, J., & Widom, C. (2007). Age of onset of child maltreatment predicts long-term mental health outcomes. *Journal of Abnormal Psychology, 116*, 176–187.

Karlsen, C. (1989). *The devil in the shape of a woman: Witchcraft in colonial New England.* New York: W.W. Norton & Co.

Kassin, S. (2005). On the psychology of confessions: Does innocence put innocents at risk? *American Psychologist, 60,* 215–228.

Kassin, S., Drizin, S., Grisso, T., Gudjonsson, G., Leo, R., & Redlich, A. (2010). Police-induced confessions: Risk factors and recommendations. *Law and Human Behavior, 34,* 3–38.

Kassin, S. M., & Gudjonsson, G. (2004). The psychology of confessions: A review of the literature and issues. *Psychological Science in the Public Interest, 5,* 33–67.

Kassin, S. M., & Kiechel, K. L. (1996). The social psychology of false confessions: Compliance, internalization, and confabulation. *Psychological Science, 7,* 125–128.

Kassin, S., Leo, R., Meissner, C., Richman, K., Colwell, L., Leach, A., et al. (2007). Police interviewing and interrogation: A self-report survey of police practices and beliefs. *Law and Human Behavior, 31,* 381–400.

Kassin, S., & Neumann, K. (1997). On the power of confession evidence: An experimental test of the "fundamental difference" hypothesis. *Law and Human Behavior, 21,* 469–484.

Kassin, S., & Norwick, R. (2004). Why suspects waive their *Miranda* rights: The power of innocence. *Law and Human Behavior, 28,* 211–221.

Kassin, S. M., & Wrightsman, L. S. (1985). Confession evidence. In S. M. Kassin & L. S. Wrightsman (Eds.), *The psychology of evidence and trial procedure* (pp. 67–94). Newbury Park, CA: Sage.

Katz, J. (1988). *Seductions of crime.* New York: Basic Books.

Keast, A., Brewer, N., & Wells, G. L. (2007). Children's metacognitive judgments in an eyewitness identification task. *Journal of Experimental Child Psychology, 97,* 286–314.

Kebbell, M., & Milne, R. (1998). Police officers' perception of eyewitness factors in forensic investigations. *Journal of Social Psychology, 138,* 323–330.

Kebbell, M., & Wagstaff, G. (1998). Hypnotic interviewing: The best way to interview eyewitnesses? *Behavioral Sciences & the Law, 16,* 115–129.

Keene, B. (1997). Chemical castration: An analysis of Florida's new "cutting-edge" policy towards sex criminals. *Florida Law Review, 49,* 803–820.

Keilin, W. G., & Bloom, L. J. (1986). Child custody evaluation practices: A survey of experienced professionals. *Professional Psychology, Research and Practice, 17,* 338–346.

Kellerman, A. L., & Mercy, J. M. (1992). Men, women, and murder: Gender-specific differences in rates of fatal violence and victimization. *Journal of Trauma, 33,* 1–5.

Kellough, G., & Wortley, S. (2002). Remand for plea: Bail decisions and plea bargaining as commensurate decisions. *British Journal of Criminology, 42,* 186–210.

Kelly, J. (1996). A decade of divorce mediation research. *Family Court Review, 34,* 373–385.

Kelly, J., & Emery, R. (2003). Children's adjustment following divorce: Risk and resilience perspectives. *Family Relations, 52,* 352–362.

Kennedy v. Louisiana, 554 U.S. 407 (2008).

Kennedy, L. (1985). *The airman and the carpenter: The Lindbergh kidnapping and the framing of Richard Hauptmann.* New York: Viking.

Kerr, N., Kramer, G. P., Carroll, J. S., & Alfini, J. J. (1991). On the effectiveness of voir dire in criminal cases with prejudicial pretrial publicity: An empirical study. *American Law Review, 40,* 665–701.

Kerr, N. L., Niedermeier, K. E., & Kaplan, M. F. (1999). Bias in jurors vs. bias in juries: New evidence from the SDS perspective. *Organizational Behavior and Human Decision Processes, 80,* 70–86.

Kessler, R., Berglund, P., Delmer, O., Jin, R., Merikangas, K., & Walters, E. (2005). Lifetime prevalence and age-of-onset distributions of DSM-IV disorders in the National Comorbidity Survey Replication. *Archives of General Psychiatry, 62,* 593–602.

Kessler, R., Sonnega, A., Bromet, E., Hughes, M., & Nelson, C. (1995). Posttraumatic stress disorder in the National Comorbidity Survey. *Archives of General Psychiatry, 52,* 1048–1060.

Kiai, J., & Stobo, J. (2010). Prison healthcare in California. *UC Health,* Retrieved January 22, 2010, from http://universityofcalifornia.edu/sites/uchealth/2010/01/22/prison-health-care-in-california/

Kilpatrick, D. G., Resick, P., & Veronen, L. (1981). Effects of a rape experience: A longitudinal study. *Journal of Social Issues, 37,* 105–112.

Kimonis, E., Frick, P., & Barry, C. (2004). Callous-unemotional traits and delinquent peer affiliation. *Journal of Consulting and Clinical Psychology, 72,* 956–966.

King, M. (1992). Male rape in institutional settings. In G. Mezey & M. King (Eds.), *Male victims of sexual assault* (pp. 67–74). Oxford: Oxford University Press.

Kiser, R. (2010). *Beyond right and wrong.* Berlin, Germany: Springer-Verlag.

Kleinberg, H. (1989, January 29). It's tough to have sympathy for Bundy. *Lawrence Journal-World,* p. 5A.

Kleiner, M. (2002). *Handbook of polygraph testing.* New York: Academic Press.

Kleinmuntz, B., & Szucko, J. J. (1984). Lie detection in ancient and modern times: A call for contemporary scientific study. *American Psychologist, 39,* 766–776.

Klockars, C. (1985). *The idea of police.* Thousand Oaks, CA: Sage.

Koch, K. (2000). Zero tolerance. *CQ Researcher, 10,* 185.

Kolebuck, M. D. (1998). *Kansas v. Henricks:* Is it time to lock the door and throw away the key for sexual predators? *Journal of Contemporary Health and Law Policy, 14,* 537–561.

Kopelman, S., Rosette A. S., & Thompson, L. (2006). The three faces of Eve: An examination of the strategic display of positive, negative, and neutral emotions in negotiations. *Organizational Behavior and Human Decision Processes, 99,* 81–101.

Kopfinger, S. (2007). *PTSD victim tells gripping story.* Retrieved May 15, 2009, from http://lancasteronline.com/article/local/208863_PTSD-victim-tells-gripping-story.html

Korobkin, R., & Doherty, J. (2009). Who wins in settlement negotiations? *American Law and Economics Review, 11,* 162–209.

Kovera, M. (2002). The effects of general pretrial publicity on juror decisions: An examination of moderators and mediating mechanisms. *Law and Human Behavior, 26,* 43–72.

Kovera, M., Dickinson, J., & Cutler, B. (2002). Voir dire and jury selection. In A. Goldstein (Ed.), *Comprehensive handbook of psychology: Forensic psychology* (Vol. 11, pp. 161–175). New York: Wiley.

Kovera, M., Russano, M., & McAuliff, B. (2002). Assessment of the commonsense psychology underlying *Daubert:* Legal decision makers' abilities to evaluate expert evidence in hostile work environment cases. *Psychology, Public Policy, and Law, 8,* 180–200.

Kraemer, G. W., Lord, W. D., & Heilbrun, K. (2004). Comparing single and serial homicide offenses. *Behavioral Sciences & the Law, 22,* 325–343.

Kramer, G. M., Wolbransky, M., & Heilbrun, K. (2007). Plea bargaining recommendations by criminal defense attorneys: Evidence strength, potential sentence, and defendant preference. *Behavioral Sciences & the Law, 25,* 573–585.

Kramer, G. P., Kerr, N. L., & Carroll, J. S. (1990). Pretrial publicity, judicial remedies, and jury bias. *Law and Human Behavior, 14,* 409–438.

Kralstein, D. (2005). *Community court research: A literature review.* New York: Center for Court Innovation.

Krauss, D., & Goldstein, A. (2007). The role of forensic mental health experts in federal sentencing proceedings. In A. Goldstein (Ed.), *Forensic psychology: Emerging topics and expanding roles* (pp. 359–384). Hoboken, NJ: Wiley.

Kravitz, H. M., & Kelly, J. (1999). An outpatient psychiatry program for offenders with mental disorders found Not Guilty by Reason of Insanity. *Psychiatric Services, 50,* 1597–1605.

Kressel, N., & Kressel, D. (2002). *Stack and sway: The new science of jury consulting.* Boulder, CO: Westview.

Krings, F., & Facchin, S. (2009). The moderating role of sexism and personality. *Journal of Applied Psychology, 94,* 501–510.

Kroner, D., Mills, J., & Reddon, J. (2005). A Coffee Can, factor analysis, and prediction of antisocial behavior: The structure of criminal risk. *International Journal of Law and Psychiatry, 28,* 360–374.

Kulik, C., Perry, E., & Pepper, M. (2003). Here comes the judge: The influence of judge personal characteristics on federal sexual harassment case outcomes. *Law and Human Behavior, 27,* 69–86.

Kulka, R., Schlenger, W., Fairbanks, J., Hough, R., Jordan, B., Marmar, C., et al. (1990). *Trauma and the Vietnam War generation: Report of findings from the National Vietnam Veterans Readjustment Study.* New York: Brunner/Mazel.

Kumho Tire Co. v. Carmichael, 526 U.S. 137 (1999).

Kunen, J. (1983). *"How can you defend those people?" The making of a criminal lawyer.* New York: Random House.

Kurtz, H. (2004, October 29). Bill O'Reilly, producer settle harassment suit: Fox host agrees to drop extortion claim. *The Washington Post.* Retrieved September 1, 2005, from http://www.washingtonpost.com/wp-dyn/articles/A7578–2004Oct28.html

Kushner, M., Riggs, D., Foa, E., & Miller, S. (1992). Perceived controllability and the development of posttraumatic stress disorder (PTSD) in crime victims. *Behavior Research & Therapy, 31,* 105–110.

La Fon, D. (2008). *Psychological autopsies: Science and practice.* Boca Raton, FL: CRC.

La Rooy, D., Katz, C., Malloy, L., & Lamb, M. (2010). Do we need to rethink guidance on repeated interviews? *Psychology, Public Policy, and Law, 16,* 373–392.

Lafler v. Cooper, U.S. Supreme Court No. 10–209 (2012).

Lafortune, K. A., & Carpenter, B. N. (1998). Custody evaluations: A survey of mental health professionals. *Behavioral Sciences & the Law, 16,* 207–224.

Lake, D. A. (2002, Spring). Rational extremism: Understanding terrorism in the twenty-first century. *Dialog-IQ, 15–29.*

Lamar, J. V. (1989, February 6). "I deserve punishment." *Time,* p. 34.

Lamb, H. R., Weinberger, L. E., & DeCuir, W. J. (2002). The police and mental health. *Psychiatric Services, 53,* 1266–1271.

Lamb, M., Hershkowitz, I., Orbach, Y., & Esplin, P. (2008). *Tell me what happened: Structured investigative interviews of child victims and witnesses.* Chichester, UK: Wiley.

Lamb, M., Sternberg, K., Orbach, Y., Esplin, P., Stewart, H., & Mitchell, S. (2003). Age differences in children's responses to open-ended invitations in the course of forensic interviews. *Journal of Consulting and Clinical Psychology, 71,* 926–934.

Lamb, S. (2003). The psychology of condemnation: Underlying emotions and their symbolic expression in condemning and shaming. *Brooklyn Law Review, 68,* 929–958.

Lamberti, J., Deem, A., Weisman, R., & LaDuke, C. (2011). The role of probation in forensic assertive community treatment. *Psychiatric Services, 62,* 418–421.

Lamberti, J., Weisman, R., Schwarzkopf, S., Price, N., Ashton, R., & Trompeter, J. (2001). The mentally ill in jails and prisons: Towards an integrated model of prevention. *Psychiatric Quarterly, 72,* 63–77.

Lambros, T. (1993). The summary jury trial: An effective aid to settlement. *Judicature, 77,* 6–8.

Lampinen, J., Judges, D., Odegard, T., & Hamilton, S. (2005). The reactions of mock jurors to the department of justice guidelines for the collection and preservation of eyewitness evidence. *Basic and Applied Social Psychology, 27,* 155–162.

Lampinen, J., Neuschatz, J., & Cling, A. (2012). *The psychology of eyewitness identification.* New York: Taylor and Francis.

Lander, T., & Heilbrun, K. (2009). The content and quality of forensic mental health assessment: Validation of a principles-based approach. *International Journal of Forensic Mental Health, 8,* 115–121.

Landstrom, S., & Granhag, P. (2010). In-court versus out-of-court testimonies: Children's experiences and adults' assessments. *Applied Cognitive Psychology, 24,* 941–955.

Lane, S. (2006). Dividing attention during a witnessed event increases eyewitness suggestibility. *Applied Cognitive Psychology, 20,* 199–212.

Langevin, R., Curnoe, S., Federoff, P., Bennett, R., Langevin, M., Peever, C., et al. (2004). Lifetime sex offender recidivism: A 25-year-follow-up study. *Canadian Journal of Criminology and Criminal Justice, 46,* 531–552.

Langton, L., & Cohen, T. (2008). *Civil bench and jury trials in state courts, 2005.* Washington, DC: U.S. Department of Justice. (Bureau of Justice Statistics Special Report No. NCJ 223851)

Larochelle, S., Diguer, L., Laverdiere, O., & Greenman, P. (2011). Predictors of psychological treatment non-completion among sexual offenders. *Clinical Psychology Review, 31,* 554–562.

Larson, J. (2004, April 10). Behind the death of Timothy Thomas: Shooting of 19-year-old brings to light pattern of ticketing that raises questions of racial profiling. *Dateline NBC.* Retrieved September 24, 2005, from http://www.msnbc.msn.com/id/ 4703574/

Larson, J. A. (1932). *Lying and its detection.* Chicago, IL: University of Chicago Press.

Lassiter, G. D. (2010). Psychological science and sound public policy: Video recording of custodial interrogations. *American Psychologist, 65,* 768–779.

Lassiter, G. D., Diamond, S., Schmidt, H., & Elek, J. (2007). Evaluating videotaped confessions: Expertise provides no defense against the camera-perspective effect. *Psychological Science, 18,* 224–226.

Lassiter, G. D., & Geers, A. (2004). Bias and accuracy in the evaluation of confession evidence. In G. D. Lassiter (Ed.), *Interrogations, confessions, and entrapment* (pp. 197–214). New York: Kluwer/Plenum.

Lassiter, G. D., Ware, L., Ratcliff, J., & Irvin, C. (2009). Evidence of the camera perspective bias in authentic videotaped interrogations: Implications for emerging reform in the criminal justice system. *Legal and Criminological Psychology, 14,* 157–170.

Laumann-Billings, L., & Emery, R. (2000). Distress among young adults from divorced families. *Journal of Family Psychology, 14,* 671–87.

Lecci, L., & Myers, B. (2009). Predicting guilt judgments and verdict change using a measure of pretrial bias in a videotaped mock trial with deliberating jurors. *Psychology, Crime and Law, 15,* 619–634.

Lees-Haley, P. (1991). A fake bad scale on the MMPI-2 for personal injury claimants. *Psychological Reports, 68,* 203–210.

Lees-Haley, P. (1992). Efficacy of MMPI-2 validity scales and MCMI-2 modifier scales for detecting spurious PTSD claims: F, F-K, Fake Bad Scale, Ego Strength, Subtle-Obvious subscales, DIS, and DEB. *Journal of Clinical Psychology, 48,* 681–689.

Leipold, A., & Abbasi, H. (2006). The impact of joinder and severance on federal criminal cases: An empirical study. *Vanderbilt Law Review, 59,* 347–404.

Leippe, M. R., Eisenstadt, D., Rauch, S. M., & Stambush, M. A. (2006). Effects of social-comparative memory feedback on eyewitnesses' identification confidence, suggestibility, and retrospective memory reports. *Basic and Applied Social Psychology, 28,* 201–220.

Leistico, A., Salekin, R., DeCoster, J., & Rogers, R. (2008). A large-scale meta-analysis relating the Hare measures of psychopathy to antisocial conduct. *Law and Human Behavior, 32,* 28–45.

Lemert, E. M. (1951). *Social pathology.* New York: McGraw-Hill.

Lemert, E. M. (1972). *Human deviance, social problems, and social control* (2nd ed.). Englewood Cliffs, NJ: Prentice Hall.

Lempert, R. (1993). Civil juries and complex cases: Taking stock after twelve years. In R. E. Litan (Ed.), *Verdict: Assessing the civil jury system* (pp. 181–247). Washington, DC: The Brookings Institution.

Leo, R. (2007). The problem of false confession in America. *The Champion, 31.* Retrieved July 22, 2008, from http://www.nacdl.org/Champion.aspx?id=1093

Leo, R. (2008). *Police interrogation and American justice.* Cambridge, MA: Harvard University Press.

Leo, R., & Ofshe, R. (1998). The consequences of false confessions: Deprivations of liberty and miscarriages of justice in the age of psychological interrogation. *Journal of Criminal Law and Criminology, 88,* 429–496.

Leonard, K. E., Quigley, B. M., & Collins, R. L. (2002). Physical aggression in the lives of young adults. *Journal of Interpersonal Violence, 17,* 533–550.

Lerner, M. J. (1970). The desire for justice and reactions to victims. In J. Macaulay & L. Berkowitz (Eds.), *Altruism and helping behavior* (pp. 205–229). Orlando, FL: Academic Press.

Lerner, M. J. (1980). *The belief in a just world.* New York: Plenum.

Levenson, J., & D'Amora, D. (2007). Social policies designed to prevent sexual violence: The emperor's new clothes? *Criminal Justice Policy Review, 18,* 168–199.

Levenson, R., & Dwyer, L. (2003). Peer support in law enforcement: Past, present, and future. *International Journal of Emergency Mental Health, 5,* 147–152.

Levett, L., & Kovera, M. (2008). The effectiveness of opposing expert witnesses for educating jurors about unreliable expert evidence. *Law and Human Behavior, 32,* 363–374.

Levine, S. (2003, September 26). Death-row inmate hears hoped-for-words: We found killer. *The Washington Post,* p. A01.

Lewin, C., & Herlitz, A. (2002). Sex differences in face recognition: Women's faces make the difference. *Brain & Cognition, 50,* 121–128.

Lewin, T. (1994, October 21). Outrage over 18 months for a killing. *The New York Times,* p. A18.

Lewis, A. (1964). *Gideon's trumpet.* New York: Knopf.

Lewis, A. (2005, June 21). Guantanamo's long shadow. *The New York Times,* p. A23.

Lieberman, J. (2009). The psychology of the jury instruction process. In J. Lieberman & D. Krauss (Eds.), *Jury psychology: Social aspects of trial processes* (pp. 129–156). Burlington, VT: Ashgate.

Lieberman, J. (2011). The utility of scientific jury selection: Still murky after 30 years. *Current Directions in Psychological Science, 20,* 48–52.

Lieberman, J., & Arndt, J. (2000). Understanding the limits of limiting instructions: Social psychological explanations for the failures of instructions to disregard pretrial publicity and other inadmissible evidence. *Psychology, Public Policy, and Law, 6,* 677–711.

Lieberman, J., & Olson, J. (2009). The psychology of jury selection. In J. Lieberman & D. Krauss (Eds.), *Jury psychology: Social aspects of trial processes* (pp. 97–128). Burlington, VT: Ashgate.

Liebman, J. S. (2000). *A broken system: Error rates in capital cases, 1973—1995.* Retrieved October 1, 2005, from http://ccjr.policy.net/cjedfund/jpreport/

Lilly, J. R., Cullen, F. T., & Ball, R. A. (1989). *Criminological theory: Context and consequences.* Newbury Park, CA: Sage.

Lin, J., Grattet, R., & Petersilia, J. (2010). "Back-end sentencing" and reimprisonment: Individual, organizational, and community predictors of parole sanction decisions. *Criminology, 48,* 759–795.

Lind, E. A. (1975). The exercise of information influence in legal advocacy. *Journal of Applied Social Psychology, 5,* 127–143.

Lind, E. A. (1982). The psychology of courtroom procedure. In N. L. Kerr & R. M. Bray (Eds.), *Psychology in the courtroom* (pp. 13–37). Orlando, FL: Academic Press.

Lind, E. A., Erickson, B. E., Friedland, N., & Dickenberger, M. (1978). Reactions to procedural models for adjudicative conflict resolution. *Journal of Conflict Resolution, 22,* 318–341.

Lind, E. A., Thibaut, J., & Walker, L. (1973). Discovery and presentation of evidence in adversary and non-adversary proceedings. *Michigan Law Review, 71,* 1129–1144.

Lind, E. A., & Tyler, T. R. (1988). *The social psychology of procedural justice.* New York: Plenum.

Lindsay, D., Hagen, L., Read, J., Wade, K., & Garry, M. (2004). True photographs and false memories. *Psychological Science, 15,* 149–154.

Lindsay, D. S., & Read, J. D. (1995). "Memory work" and recovered memories of childhood sexual abuse: Scientific evidence and public, professional, and personal issues. *Psychology, Public Policy, and Law, 1,* 846–908.

Lipsey, M. (1992). Juvenile delinquency treatment: A meta-analytic inquiry into the variability of effects. In T. Cook, H. Cooper, S. Cordray, H. Hartmann, L. Hedges, R. Light, et al. (Eds.), *Meta-analysis for explanation: A casebook* (pp. 83–128). New York: Russell Sage Foundation.

Lipsey, M., & Wilson, D. (1998). Effective intervention for serious juvenile offenders: A synthesis of research. In R. Loeber & D. Farrington (Eds.), *Serious and violent juvenile offenders: Risk factors and successful interventions* (pp. 313–345). Thousand Oaks, CA: Sage.

Liptak, A. (2005a). *Inmate's rising I.Q. score could mean his death.* Retrieved February 8, 2005, from http://www.nytimes.com/2005/02/06/national/06atkins.html/

Littleton, H., Axsom, D., & Grills-Taquechel, A. (2009). Sexual assault victims' acknowledgment status and revictimization risk. *Psychology of Women Quarterly, 33,* 34–42.

Lockett v. Ohio, 438 U.S. 604 (1978).

Lockhart v. McCree, 476 U.S. 162 (1986).

Loeber, R., & Stouthamer-Loeber, M. (1986). Family factors as correlates and predictors of juvenile conduct problems and delinquency. In M. Tonry & N. Morris (Eds.), *Crime and justice: An annual review of research* (Vol. 7, pp. 29–149). Chicago, IL: University of Chicago Press.

Loewenstein, G., Issacharoff, S., Camerer, C., & Babcock, L. (1993). Self-serving assessments of fairness and pre-trial bargaining. *Journal of Legal Studies, 22,* 135–159.

Loftus, E. F. (1974). Reconstructing memory: The incredible witness. *Psychology Today, 8,* 116–119.

Loftus, E. F. (1975). Leading questions and the eyewitness report. *Cognitive Psychology, 7,* 560–572.

Loftus, E. F. (1979). *Eyewitness testimony.* Cambridge, MA: Harvard University Press.

Loftus, E. F. (1984). Expert testimony on the eyewitness. In G. L. Wells & E. F. Loftus (Eds.), *Eyewitness testimony: Psychological perspectives* (pp. 273–282). New York: Cambridge University Press.

Loftus, E. F., & Pickrell, J. E. (1995). The formation of false memories. *Psychiatric Annals, 25,* 720–725.

Lombroso, C. (1876). *L' Uomo delinquente.* Milan: Hoepli.

London, K., Bruck, M., Ceci, S., & Shuman, D. (2005). Disclosure of child sexual abuse: What does the research tell us about the ways that children tell? *Psychology, Public Policy, and Law, 11,* 194–226.

London, K., & Nunez, N. (2000). The effect of jury deliberations on jurors' propensity to disregard inadmissible evidence. *Journal of Applied Psychology, 85,* 932–939.

Long, B., Rouse, S., Nelsen, R., & Butcher, J. (2004). The MMPI-2 in sexual harassment and discrimination litigants. *Journal of Clinical Psychology, 60,* 643–657.

Lopez, M., & Light, M. (2009). *A rising share: Hispanics and federal crime.* Washington, DC: Pew Research Center. Retrieved from http://pewhispanic.org/files/reports/104.pdf

Los Angeles County Sheriff's Department (2012). *Home page.* Retrieved June 3, 2012, from http://app4.lasd.org/iic/ajis_search.cfm

Lowenkamp, C., & Latessa, E. (2005, April). Developing successful reentry programs: Lessons learned from the "what works" research. *Corrections Today, 67,* 72–77.

Ludwig, E. (2002). The changing role of the trial judge. *Judicature, 85,* 216–217.

Luna, K., & Migueles, M. (2008). Typicality and misinformation: Two sources of distortion. *Psicologica, 29,* 171–187.

Lurigio, A. J., & Skogan, W. G. (1994). Winning the hearts and minds of police officers: An assessment of staff perceptions of community policing in Chicago. *Crime and Delinquency, 40,* 315–330.

Lurigio, A. A., Watson, A., Luchins, D., & Hanrahan, P. (2001). Therapeutic jurisprudence in action. *Judicature, 84,* 184–189.

Lynam, D., Moffitt, T., & Stouthamer-Loeber, M. (1993). Explaining the relation between IQ and delinquency: Class, race, test motivation, school failure, and self-control. *Journal of Abnormal Psychology, 102,* 187–196.

Lynch, M., & Haney, C. (2000). Discrimination and instructional comprehension: Guided discretion, racial bias, and the death penalty. *Law and Human Behavior, 24,* 337–358.

Lynch, M., & Haney, C. (2009). Capital jury deliberation: Effects on death sentencing, comprehension, and discrimination. *Law and Human Behavior, 33,* 481–496.

Lynch, M., & Haney, C. (2011). Mapping the racial bias of the White male capital juror: Jury composition and the "empathic divide." *Law and Society Review, 45,* 69–102.

Lynch, T. (2003, Fall). The case against plea bargaining. *Regulation, 26,* 24–27.

MacCoun, R. J. (1996). Differential treatment of corporate defendants by juries: An examination of the "deep pockets" hypothesis. *Law and Society Review, 30,* 121–161.

MacCoun, R. J. (1999). Epistemological dilemmas in the assessment of legal decision making. *Law and Human Behavior, 23,* 723–730.

MacLean, P. (2011). *Jurors gone wild: An epidemic of juror blogging, texting, and tweeting infuriates judges and defense counsel—and fuels motions for retrial.* Retrieved June 11, 2012, from http://www.callawyer.com/clstory.cfm?pubdt=NaN&eid=914907&evid=1

MacPherson, S., & Bonora, B. (2010, November). The wired juror, unplugged. *Trial,* 40–45.

Madden-Derdich, D. A., Leonard, S. A., & Gunnell, G. A. (2002). Parents' and children's perceptions of family processes in inner-city families with delinquent youths: A qualitative investigation. *Journal of Marital and Family Therapy, 28,* 355–370.

Madon, S., Guyll, M., Scherr, K., Greathouse, S., & Wells, G. (2011, March). *The differential impact of proximal and distal consequences on the elicitation of criminal confessions.* Paper presented at American Psychology-Law Society, Miami, FL.

Mador, J. (2010, March 22). *New veterans' court aims to help soldiers struggling at home.* Retrieved July 1, 2011, from www.minnesota.public.radio.org/display/web/2010/03/22/veterans-court/

Magdol, L., Moffitt, T. E., Caspi, A., Newman, D. L., Fagan, J., & Silva, P. A. (1997). Gender differences in rates of partner violence in a birth cohort of 21-year-olds: Bridging the gap between clinical and epidemiological approaches. *Journal of Consulting and Clinical Psychology, 65,* 68–78.

Maeder, E., & Hunt, J. (2011). Talking about a black man: The influence of defendant and character witness race on jurors' use of character evidence. *Behavioral Sciences and the Law, 29,* 608–620.

Magdol, L., Moffitt, T. E., Caspi, A., & Silva, P. A. (1998). Developmental antecedents of partner abuse: A prospective-longitudinal study. *Journal of Abnormal Psychology, 107,* 373–389.

Mailer, N. (1979). *The executioner's song.* Boston, MA: Little, Brown.

Malpass, R. S., & Devine, P. G. (1981). Eyewitness identification: Lineup instructions and the absence of the offender. *Journal of Applied Psychology, 66,* 482–489.

Mandracchia, J., & Morgan, R. (2011). Understanding criminals' thinking: Further examination of the Measure of Offender Thinking Styles-Revised. *Assessment, 18,* 442–452.

Marcus, D. R., Lyons, P. M., & Guyton, M. R. (2000). Studying perceptions of juror influence *in vivo*: A social relations analysis. *Law and Human Behavior, 24,* 173–186.

Maricopa County Sheriff's Office (2005). *Sheriff Joe Arpaio.* Retrieved October 5, 2009, from http://www.mcso.org/index.php?a=GetModule& mn=sheriff_bio

Marlowe, D. B. (2002). Effective strategies for intervening with drug abusing offenders. *Villanova Law Review, 47,* 989–1026.

Marlowe, D. B., DeMatteo, D., & Festinger, D. (2003). A sober assessment of drug courts. *Federal Sentencing Reporter, 16,* 113–128.

Marquardt, E. (2006). *Between two worlds: The inner lives of children of divorce.* New York: Three Rivers Press.

Marshall, L. (2002). Do exonerations prove that the system works? *Judicature, 86,* 83–89.

Marshall, W., Fernandez, Y., & Cortoni, F. (1999). Rape. In V. Van Hasselt & M. Hersen (Eds.), *Handbook of psychological approaches with violent offenders* (pp. 245–266). New York: Kluwer/Plenum.

Marshall, W. L., Fernandez, Y., Marshall, L., & Serran, G. (2006). *Sexual offender treatment: Controversial issues.* West Sussex, UK: Wiley.

Marshall, W. L., Jones, R., Ward, T., Johnston, P., & Barbaree, H. E. (1991). Treatment outcome with sex offenders. *Clinical Psychology Review, 11,* 465–485.

Martin, C., Lurigio, A., & Olson, D. (2003). An examination of rearrests and reincarcerations among discharged day reporting center clients. *Federal Probation, 67,* 24–30.

Martin, S. S., Butzin, C. A., Saum, C. A., & Inciardi, J. A. (1999). Three-year outcomes of therapeutic community treatment for offenders in Delaware. *The Prison Journal, 79,* 294–320.

Martinson, R. (1974). What works? Questions and answers about prison reform. *Public Interest, 35,* 22.

Martinson, R. (1979). New findings, new views: A note of caution regarding sentencing reform. *Hofstra Law Review, 7,* 243.

Marvasti, J. (2010). Combat trauma and PTSD in veterans: Forensic aspect and 12-step program. *American Journal of Forensic Psychiatry, 31,* 5–30.

Maryland v. Craig, 110 S.Ct. 3157 (1990).

Maslach, C., & Jackson, S. E. (1984). Burnout in organizational settings. In S. Oskamp (Ed.), *Applied social psychology annual* (pp. 133–154). Newbury Park, CA: Sage.

Mason, C., & Cheng, S. (2001). *Re-arrest rates among youth sentenced in adult court.* Miami, FL: Miami-Dade County Public Defender's Office.

Mauer, M. (2011). Sentencing reform: Amid mass incarcerations–guarded optimism. *Criminal Justice, 26,* 27–36.

Mauer, M., & King, R. S. (2007, July). *Uneven justice: State rates of incarceration by race and ethnicity.* Retrieved October 25, 2008, from http://www.sentencing project.org

Maxfield, M. G., & Widom, C. S. (1996). The cycle of violence: Revisited 6 years later. *Archives of Pediatrics & Adolescent Medicine, 150,* 390–395.

Maxwell, C. D., Garner, J. H., & Fagan, J. A. (2002). The preventive effects of arrest on intimate partner violence: Research, policy and theory. *Criminology and Public Policy, 2,* 51–80.

Mazzoni, G., & Memon, A. (2003). Imagination can create false autobiographical memories. *Psychological Science, 14,* 186–188.

McAllister, H. (2008). Plea bargaining. In B. Cutler (Ed.), *Encyclopedia of psychology and law* (pp. 559–561). Thousand Oaks, CA: Sage Publications.

McAree, D. (2004, May 31). Deadbeat dads face ban on procreation. *National Law Journal,* p. 4.

McAuliff, B. D., & Kovera, M. B. (2008). Juror need for cognition and sensitivity to methodological flaws in expert evidence. *Journal of Applied Social Psychology, 38,* 385–408.

McAuliff, B. D., Kovera, M. B., & Nunez, G. (2009). Can jurors recognize missing control groups, confounds, and experimenter bias in psychological science? *Law and Human Behavior, 33,* 247–257.

McAuliff, B. D., Nicholson, E., Amarilio, D., & Ravenshenas, D. (2012). Supporting children in U.S. legal proceedings: Descriptive and attitudinal data from a national survey of victim/witness assistants. *Psychology, Public Policy, and Law,* Advance online publication.

McCandless, S. R., & Sullivan, L. P. (1991, May 6). Two courts adopt new standard to determine sexual harassment. *National Law Journal*, pp. 18–20.

McCann, J. (1998). A conceptual framework for identifying various types of confessions. *Behavioral Sciences & the Law, 16*, 441–453.

McCann, T. (2004, August 21). *Jury consultants try to turn voir dire into a science.* Retrieved October 1, 2005, from http://www.zmf.com

McCleskey v. Kemp, 107 S. Ct. 1756 (1987).

McConahay, J. B., Mullin, C., & Frederick, J. (1977). The uses of social science in trials with political and racial overtones: The trial of Joan Little. *Law and Contemporary Problems, 41*, 205–229.

McCorkle, R. (1992). Personal precautions to violence in prison. *Criminal Justice and Behavior, 19*, 160–173.

McCoy, A. (2006). *A question of torture: CIA interrogation, from the cold war to the war on terror.* New York: Metropolitan Books/Henry Holt.

McCrae, R., & Costa, P. (1990). *Personality in adulthood.* New York: Guilford.

McDonough, M. (2004, October). Summary time blues. *American Bar Association Journal, 90*, 18.

McGuire, J., Bilby, C., Hatcher, R., Hollin, C., Hounsome, J., & Palmer, E. (2008). Evaluation of structured cognitive-behavioural treatment programmes in reducing criminal recidivism. *Journal of Experimental Criminology, 4*, 21–40.

McKay v. Ashland Oil Inc., 120 F.R.D. 43 (E.D. Ky. 1988).

McKinley, J. (2009). *Smoking ban hits home. Truly.* Retrieved April 22, 2009, from http://www.nytimes.com/2009/01/27/us/27belmont.html

McLachlan, K., Roesch, R., & Douglas, K. (2011). Examining the role of interrogative suggestibility in *Miranda* rights comprehension in adolescents. *Law and Human Behavior, 35*, 165–177.

McLaurin v. Oklahoma State Regents for Higher Education, 339 U.S. 637 (1950).

McLoughlin, N., Rucklidge, J. J., Grace, R. C., & McLean, A. P. (2010). Can callous unemotional traits and aggression identify children at high risk of antisocial behavior in a low socioeconomic group? *Journal of Family Violence, 25*, 701–712.

McNally, R., & Geraerts, E. (2009). A new solution to the recovered memory debate. *Perspectives on Psychological Science, 4*, 126–134.

McNatt, D. (2000). Ancient Pygmalion joins contemporary management: A meta-analysis of the result. *Journal of Applied Psychology, 85*, 314–322.

McNiel, D., & Binder, R. (2007). Effectiveness of a mental health court in reducing criminal recidivism and violence. *American Journal of Psychiatry, 164*, 1395–1403.

McQuiston-Surrett, D., Malpass, R., & Tredoux, C. (2006). Sequential vs. simultaneous lineups: A review of the methods, data, and theory. *Psychology, Public Policy, and Law, 12*, 137–169.

McQuiston-Surrett, D., & Saks, M. (2009). The testimony of forensic identification science: What expert witnesses say and what factfinders hear. *Law and Human Behavior, 33*, 436–453.

Meddis, S. S., & Kelley, J. (1985, April 8). Crime drops but fear on rise. *USA Today*, p. A1.

Medical News Today (2007). *What level of mental illness should preclude execution and how to determine it?* Retrieved April 1, 2009, from www.medicalnewstoday.com

Medina v. California, 112 S.Ct. 2572 (1992).

Mednick, S. A., & Christiansen, K. O. (Eds.). (1977). *Biosocial bases of criminal behavior.* New York: Gardner.

Meijer, E., & Verschuere, B. (2010). The polygraph and the detection of deception. *Journal of Forensic Psychology Practice, 10*, 325–338.

Meissner, C., & Brigham, J. (2001). Thirty years of investigating the own-race bias in memory for faces: A meta-analytic review. *Psychology, Public Policy, and Law, 7*, 3–35.

Meissner, C., & Kassin, S. (2004). "You're guilty, so just confess!" Cognitive and behavioral confirmation biases in the interrogation room. In G. D. Lassiter (Ed.), *Interrogations, confessions, and entrapment* (pp. 85–106). New York: Kluwer Academic/Plenum.

Meissner, C., & Redlich, A. (2011, March). *A meta-analytic review of the influence of accusatorial vs. information-gathering.* Paper presented at American Psychology-Law Society, Miami, FL.

Meissner, C., Russano, M., & Narchat, F. (2010). The importance of laboratory science for improving the diagnostic value of confession evidence. In G. D. Lassiter & C. Meissner (Eds.), *Police interrogations and false confessions* (pp. 111–126). Washington, DC: American Psychological Association.

Meissner, C., Sporer, S., & Susa, K. (2008). A theoretical review and meta-analysis of the description-identification relationship in memory for faces. *European Journal of Cognitive Psychology, 20*, 414–455.

Meissner, C., Tredoux, C., Parker, J., & MacLin, O. (2005). Eyewitness decisions in simultaneous and sequential lineups. *Memory and Cognition, 33*, 783–792.

Melilli, K. (1996). *Batson* in practice: What we have learned about *Batson* and peremptory challenges. *Notre Dame Law Review, 71*, 447–503.

Mellow, J., Mukamal, D. A., LoBuglio, S. F., Solomon, A. L., & Osborne, J. W. L. (2008, May). *The jail administrator's toolkit for reentry.* Washington, DC: Urban Institute.

Meloy, J. R., & Felthous, A. R. (2004). Introduction to this issue: Serial and mass homicide. *Behavioral Sciences & the Law, 22*(3), 289–290.

Meloy, J. R., Hempel, A. G., Gray, B. T., Mohandie, K., Shiva, A., & Richards, T. C. (2004). A comparative analysis of North American adolescent and adult mass murderers. *Behavioral Sciences & the Law, 22*(3), 291–309.

Melton, G., Petrila, J., Poythress, N., & Slobogin, C. (2007). *Psychological evaluations for the courts: A handbook for mental health professionals and lawyers* (3rd ed.). New York: Guilford.

Memon, A., Bartlett, J., Rose, R., & Gray, C. (2003). The aging eyewitness: Effects of age on face, delay, and source-memory ability. *The Journals of Gerontology Series B: Psychological Sciences and Social Sciences, 58B,* P338–P345.

Memon, A., Meissner, C., & Fraser, J. (2010). The cognitive interview: A meta-analytic review and study space analysis of the past 25 years. *Psychology, Public Policy, and Law, 16,* 340–372.

Mercado, C. (2009, Summer). Are residence restrictions an effective way to reduce the risk posed by sex offenders? *AP-LS News.* Retrieved from http://www.ap-ls.org/publications/newsletters/aplsnews.sum2009.pdf

Meritor Savings Bank v. Vinson, 106 S.Ct. 2399 (1986).

Merrick, R. A. (1985). The tort of outrage: Recovery for the intentional infliction of mental distress. *Behavioral Sciences & the Law, 3,* 165–175.

Mertens, R., & Allen, J. J. B. (2008). The role of psychophysiology in forensic assessments: Deception detection, ERPs, and virtual reality mock crime scenarios. *Psychophysiology, 45,* 286–298.

Merton, R. K. (1968). *Social theory and social structure.* New York: Free Press.

Meyer, P. (1982). *The Yale murder.* New York: Empire Books.

Michels, S. (2006, June 16). *Judicial elections turn expensive, polarized, nasty.* Retrieved July 1, 2011, from http://www.usnews.com/usnews/news/articles/060616/16judicial.htm

Mihalic, S., Irwin, K., Elliott, D., Fagan, A., & Hansen, D. (2001). *Blueprints for violence prevention.* Boulder, CO: Center for the Study and Prevention of Violence.

Milgram, S. (1963). Behavioral study of obedience. *Journal of Abnormal and Social Psychology, 67,* 371–378.

Miller v. Alabama, 132 S. Ct. 1733 (2012).

Miller, A. (1988, April 25). Stress on the job. *Newsweek,* pp. 40–45.

Miller, G. R., & Boster, F. J. (1977). Three images of a trial: Their implications for psychological research.

In B. D. Sales (Ed.), *Psychology in the legal process* (pp. 19–38). New York: Spectrum.

Miller, H. A. (2001). *M-FAST: Miller Forensic Assessment of Symptoms Test professional manual.* Odessa, FL: Psychological Assessment Resources.

Miller, H. A. (2004). Examining the use of the M-FAST with criminal defendants incompetent to stand trial. *International Journal of Offender Therapy and Comparative Criminology, 48,* 268–280.

Miller, J., & Lynam, D. (2001). Structural models of personality and their relation to antisocial behavior: A meta-analytic review. *Criminology, 39,* 765–798.

Miller, W. B. (1958). Lower-class culture as a generating milieu of gang delinquency. *Journal of Social Issues, 14,* 5–19.

Miller v. Alabama, 132 S.Ct. 2455 (2012).

Miller-El v. Cockrell, 537 U.S. 322 (2003).

Miller-El v. Dretke, 361 F. 3d 849 (5th Cir. 2004); 545 U.S. 231 (2005).

Mills, R. B., McDevitt, R. J., & Tonkin, S. (1966). Situational tests in metropolitan police recruit selection. *Journal of Criminal Law, Criminology, and Police Science, 57,* 99–104.

Milstein, V. (1988). EEG topography in patients with aggressive violent behavior. In T. E. Moffitt & S. A. Mednick (Eds.), *Biological contributions to crime causation.* Dordrecht, Netherlands: Martinus Nihjoff.

Minsky, S., Vega, W., Miskimen, T., Gara, M., & Escobar, J. (2003). Diagnostic patterns in Latino, African American, and European American psychiatric patients. *Archives of General Psychiatry, 60,* 637–644.

Miranda v. Arizona, 384 U.S. 486 (1966).

Mitchell, D., and Smith, L. (2007). *When mediation fails: The summary jury trial alternative.* Retrieved from http://www.nmbar.org/AboutSBNM/sections/Employment LaborLaw/Enewsletters/SJTARTICLENov07.pdf

Mitchell, O. (2005). A meta-analysis of race and sentencing research: Explaining the inconsistencies. *Journal of Quantitative Criminology, 21,* 439–466.

Mitchell, P. (1976). *Act of love: The killing of George Zygmanik.* New York: Knopf.

Mize, G. (1999, Spring). On better jury selection: Spotting UFO jurors before they enter the jury room. *Court Review, 36,* 10–15.

Mize, G. E., Hannaford-Agor, P., & Waters N. L. (2007). *The State-of-the-States Survey of Jury Improvement Efforts: A compendium report.* Williamsburg, VA: National Center for State Courts.

Moffitt, T., & Lynam, D. (1994). The neuropsychology of conduct disorder and delinquency: Implications for understanding antisocial behavior. In D. Fowles,

P. Sutker, & S. Goodman (Eds.), *Psychopathy and antisocial behavior: A developmental perspective* (pp. 233–262). New York: Springer-Verlag.

Mohamed, F., Faro, S., Gordon, N., Platek, S., Ahmad, H., & Williams, J. (2006). Brain mapping of deception and truth telling about an ecologically valid situation: Functional MR imaging and polygraph investigation-initial experience. *Radiology, 238*, 679–688.

Monahan, J. (1984). The prediction of violent behavior: Toward a second generation of theory and practice. *American Journal of Psychiatry, 141*, 10–15.

Monahan, J. (2012). The individual risk assessment of terrorism: Conceptual and methodological challenges. *Psychology, Public Policy, and Law, 18*, 167–205.

Monahan, J., & Steadman, H. (Eds.). (1994). *Violence and mental disorder: Developments in risk assessment*. Chicago, IL: University of Chicago Press.

Monahan, J., Steadman, H. J., Robbins, P. C., Appelbaum, P., Banks, S., Grisso, T., et al. (2005). An actuarial model of violence risk assessment for persons with mental disorders. *Psychiatric Services, 56*, 810–815.

Monahan, J., & Walker, L. (2005). *Social science in law: Cases and materials* (6th ed.). Westbury, NY: Foundation Press.

Monahan, K. C., Steinberg, L., & Cauffman, E. (2009). Affiliation with antisocial peers, susceptibility to peer influence, and antisocial behavior during the transition to adulthood. *Developmental Psychology, 45*, 1520–1530.

Moore, D., Kurtzberg, T., Thompson, L., & Morris, M. (1999). Long and short routes to success in electronically mediated negotiations: Group affiliations and good vibrations. *Organizational Behavior and Human Decision Processes, 77*, 22–43.

Moore, M., & Hiday, V. (2006). Mental health court outcomes: A comparison of re-arrest and re-arrest severity between mental health court and traditional court participants. *Law and Human Behavior, 30*, 659–674.

Moore, S. (2007, October 1). *DNA exoneration brings change in legal system*. Retrieved July 23, 2008, from http://www.nytimes.com/2007/10/01/us/01exonerate.html?scp=1&sq=%22dna%20exonera tion%20brings%20change%22&st=cse

Moran, G., & Cutler, B. L. (1991). The prejudicial impact of pretrial publicity. *Journal of Applied Social Psychology, 21*, 345–367.

Morehouse, E., & Tobler, N. (2000). Preventing and reducing substance use among institutionalized adolescents. *Adolescence, 35*, 1–28.

Morgan, A. B., & Lilienfeld, S. O. (2000). A meta-analytic review of the relation between antisocial behavior and neuropsychological measures of executive function. *Clinical Psychology Review, 20*, 113–136.

Morgan, C., Hazlett, G., Doran, A., Garrett, S., Hoty, G., Thomas, P., et al. (2004). Accuracy of eyewitness memory for persons encountered during exposure to highly intense stress. *International Journal of Law and Psychiatry, 27*, 265–279.

Morral, A., McCaffrey, D., & Ridgeway, G. (2004). Effectiveness of community-based treatment for substance abusing adolescents: 12-month outcomes from a case-control evaluation of a Phoenix academy. *Psychology of Addictive Behaviors, 18*, 257–268.

Morrison, C. (2011). Jury 2.0. *Hastings Law Journal, 62*, 1579–1632.

Morrison, P. (1995, August 21). The new chain gang. *National Law Journal*, pp. A1, A22.

Morse, S. J. (1978). Law and mental health professionals: The limits of expertise. *Professional Psychology, 9*, 389–399.

Morse, S. J. (1998). Fear of danger, flight from culpability. *Psychology, Public Policy, and Law, 4*, 250–267.

Morton, R., & Hilts, M. (Eds.) (2008). *Serial murder: Multidisciplinary perspectives for investigators*. Washington, DC: U.S. Department of Justice, Federal Bureau of Investigation.

Mossman, D. (1987). Assessing and restoring competency to be executed: Should psychiatrists participate? *Behavioral Sciences & the Law, 5*, 397–410.

Mulford, C. L., Lee, M. Y., & Sapp, S. C. (1996). Victim-blaming and society-blaming scales for social problems. *Journal of Applied Social Psychology, 26*, 1324–1336.

Mullen, P. (2004). The autogenic (self-generated) massacre. *Behavioral Sciences & the Law, 22*, 311–323.

Mulvey, E., & Cauffman, E. (2001). The inherent limits of predicting school violence. *American Psychologist, 56*, 797–802.

Mu'Min v. Virginia, 111 S.Ct 1899 (1991).

Mumula, C. (2000). *Incarcerated parents and their children*. Washington, DC: U.S. Department of Justice.

Munetz, M., & Griffin, P. (2006). Use of the sequential intercept model as an approach to decriminalization of people with serious mental illness. *Psychiatric Services, 57*, 544–549.

Murray, J. (2008). Media violence: The effects are both real and strong. *American Behavioral Scientist, 51*, 1212–1230.

Murray, J., & Farrington, D. (2010). Risk factors for conduct disorder and delinquency: Key findings from longitudinal studies. *The Canadian Journal of Psychiatry, 55*, 633–642.

Murrie, D., Boccaccini, M., Johnson, J., & Janke, C. (2008). Does interrater (dis)agreement on Psychopathy Checklist scores in sexual violent predator trials suggest partisan allegiance in forensic evaluations? *Law and Human Behavior, 32*, 352–362.

Murrie, D., Cornell, D., & McCoy, W. (2005). Psychopathy, conduct disorder, and stigma: Does diagnostic labeling influence juvenile probation officer recommendations? *Law and Human Behavior, 25*, 323–342.

Mustard, D. (2001). Racial, ethnic, and gender disparities in sentencing: Evidence from the U.S. federal courts. *Journal of Law and Economics, 44*, 285–314.

Myers, B., Latter, R., & Abdollahi-Arena, M. K. (2006). The court of public opinion: Lay perceptions of polygraph testing. *Law and Human Behavior, 30*, 509–523.

Myers, D. L. (2001). *Excluding violent youths from juvenile court: The effectiveness of legislative waiver.* New York: LFB Scholarly.

Myers, M., Stewart, D., & Brown, S. (1998). Progression from conduct disorder to antisocial personality disorder following treatment for adolescent substance abuse. *American Journal of Psychiatry, 155*, 479–486.

Nadler, J. (2005). Flouting the law. *Texas Law Review, 83*, 1399–1441.

Narby, D. J., Cutler, B. L., & Moran, G. (1993). A meta-analysis of the association between authoritarianism and jurors' perceptions of defendant culpability. *Journal of Applied Psychology, 78*, 34–42.

Nardulli, P., Eisenstein, J., & Fleming, R. (1988). *The tenor of justice: Criminal courts and the guilty plea process.* Champaign: University of Illinois Press.

Nash, A. R., & Wade, K. A. (2009). Innocent but proven guilty: Eliciting internalized false confessions using doctored-video evidence. *Applied Cognitive Psychology, 23*, 357–371.

National Advisory Commission on Criminal Justice Standards and Goals. (1973). *Corrections.* Washington, DC: U.S. Government Printing Office.

National Archive of Criminal Justice Data. (2010). *National criminal victimization survey, 2010.* Retrieved February 18, 2011, from http://www.icpsr.umich.edu/icpsrweb/NACJD/studies/31202/documentation

National Association of Drug Court Professionals. (2012). *Featured drug court graduate.* Retrieved March 20, 2012, from http://www.nadcp.org/act/share-your-drug-court-story-1

National Center for Education Statistics. (2003). *Indicators of school crime and safety: 2003.* Retrieved September 1, 2005, from http://nces.ed.gov/

National Center for Education Statistics. (2004). *Crime and safety in America's public schools: Selected findings from the School Survey on Crime and Safety.* Retrieved September 1, 2005, from http://nces.ed.gov/

National Center for Juvenile Justice (2008). *Different from adults: An updated analysis of juvenile transfer and blended sentencing laws, with recommendations for reform.* Retrieved December 13, 2009, from http://www.modelsforchange.net/publications/181

National Center for State Courts. (2012). *Short, summary & expedited: The evolution of civil jury trials.* Retrieved April 9, 2012, from http://www.ncsc.org/~/media/Files/PDF/Information%20and%20Resources/Civil%20cover%20sheets/Monograph%20FINAL%20Electronic%20Version.ashx

National GAINS Center. (2002). *The Nathaniel Project: An alternative to incarceration program for people with serious mental illness who have committed felony offenses.* Delmar, NY: Author.

National Institutes of Health. (2004). *Preventing violence and related health-risking social behaviors in adolescents: An NIH state-of-the-science conference.* Retrieved February 4, 2009, from http://consensus.nih.gov/2004/2004YouthViolencePreventionSOS023html.htm

National Offender Management Service. (2005). *Annual report for accredited programmes 2004–2005.* London: Author.

National Probation Directorate Interventions Unit, National Offender Management Service. National Research Council. (1989). *Improving risk communication.* Washington, DC: National Academy Press.

National Registry on Exonerations. (2012). Retrieved May 22, 2012, from http://www.law.umich.edu/special/exoneration/Pages/about.aspx

National Research Council. (2003). *The polygraph and lie detection.* Washington, DC: National Academy of Sciences.

National Research Council. (2009). *Strengthening forensic science in the United States: A path forward.* Washington, DC: Author.

National Science Board. (2008). *Research and development: National trends and international linkages. Science and Engineering Indicators 2008.* Arlington, VA: National Science Foundation.

National Women's Study. (2000). *National Institute on Drug Abuse.* Retrieved October 1, 2005, from http://data.library.ubc.ca/java/jsp/database/production/detail.jsp?id=528

Neisser, U. (1976). *Cognition and reality: Principles and implications of cognitive psychology.* San Francisco: Freeman.

Nelson, N. W., Sweet, J. J., & Demakis, G. J. (2006). Meta-analysis of the MMPI-2 Fake Bad Scale: Utility in forensic practice. *The Clinical Neuropsychologist, 20*, 39–58.

Nestor, P. G., Daggett, D., Haycock, J., & Price, M. (1999). Competence to stand trial: A neuropsychological inquiry. *Law and Human Behavior, 23*, 397–412.

Nettler, G. (1974). *Explaining crime.* New York: McGraw-Hill.

Neuschatz, J., Lawson, D., Fairless, A., Powers, R., Neuschatz, J., Goodsell, C., et al. (2007). The mitigating effects of suspicion on post-identification feedback and on retrospective eyewitness memory. *Law and Human Behavior, 31,* 231–247.

Neuschatz, J. S., Lawson, D. S., Swanner, J. K., Meissner, C. A., & Neuschatz, J. S. (2008). The effects of accomplice witnesses and jailhouse informants on jury decision making. *Law and Human Behavior, 32,* 137–149.

New York Department of Corrections and Community Supervision. (2012). *Home page.* Retrieved from http://www.doccs.ny.gov/

Newton, E. (2009). *Ban on drooping drawers faces legal challenge.* Retrieved April 20, 2009, from http://www.nytimes.com/2009/04/13/us/13pants.html

Nicholson, R. A. (1999). Forensic assessment. In R. Roesch, S. D. Hart, & J. R. Ogloff (Eds.), *Psychology and law: The state of the discipline* (pp. 122–173). New York: Kluwer/Plenum.

Nicholson, R. A., Briggs, S. R., & Robertson, H. C. (1988). Instruments for assessing competency to stand trial: How do they work? *Professional Psychology: Research and Practice, 19,* 383–394.

Nicholson, R. A., & Kugler, K. E. (1991). Competent and incompetent criminal defendants: A quantitative review of comparative research. *Psychological Bulletin, 109,* 355–370.

Nicholson, R. A., & Norwood, S. (2000). The quality of forensic psychological assessments, reports, and testimony: Acknowledging the gap between promise and practice. *Law and Human Behavior, 24,* 9–44.

Nicholson, R. A., Norwood, S., & Enyart, C. (1991). Characteristics and outcomes of insanity acquittees in Oklahoma. *Behavioral Sciences & the Law, 9,* 487–500.

Niedermeier, K. E., Horowitz, I. A., & Kerr, N. L. (1999). Informing jurors of their nullification power: A route to a just verdict or judicial chaos? *Law and Human Behavior, 23,* 331–352.

Nietzel, M. T. (1979). *Crime and its modification: A social learning perspective.* New York: Pergamon.

Nietzel, M. T., & Dillehay, R. C. (1982). The effects of variations in voir dire procedures in capital murder trials. *Law and Human Behavior, 6,* 1–13.

Nietzel, M. T., & Dillehay, R. C. (1986). *Psychological consultation in the courtroom.* New York: Pergamon.

Nietzel, M. T., Hasemann, D., & McCarthy, D. (1998). Psychology and capital litigation: Research contributions to courtroom consultation. *Applied and Preventive Psychology, 7,* 121–134.

Nietzel, M. T., McCarthy, D., & Kern, M. (1999). Juries: The current state of the empirical literature. In R. Roesch, S. D. Hart, & J. R. P. Ogloff (Eds.), *Psychology and law: The state of the discipline* (pp. 25–52). New York: Kluwer/Plenum.

Nishith, P., Mechanic, M. B., & Resick, P. A. (2000). Prior interpersonal trauma: The contribution to current PTSD symptoms in female rape victims. *Journal of Abnormal Psychology, 109,* 20–25.

Nix, C. (1987, July 9). 1000 new officers graduate to New York City streets. *New York Times,* p. 15.

Nobile, P. (1989, July). The making of a monster. *Playboy,* 41–45.

Noble, K. B. (1987, March 23). High court to decide whether death penalty discriminates against blacks. *New York Times,* p. 7.

Nord, C. W., Brimhall, D., & West, J. (1997). *Fathers' involvement in their children's schools.* Washington, DC: National Center for Education Statistics.

Nordheimer, J. (1989, January 25). Bundy is put to death in Florida, closing murder cases across U.S. *New York Times,* pp. A1, A11.

Norton, K., & Ryba, N. L. (2010). An investigation of the ECST-R as a measure of competence and feigning. *Journal of Forensic Psychology Practice, 10*(2), 91–106.

Norton, M., Sommers, S., Apfelbaum, E., Pura, N., & Ariely, D. (2006). Colorblindness and interracial interaction: Playing the "political correctness game." *Psychological Science, 17,* 949–953.

Norton, M., Vandello, J., & Darley, J. (2004). Casuistry and social category bias. *Journal of Personality and Social Psychology, 87,* 817–831.

Obiakor, F., Merhing, T., & Schwenn, J. (1997). *Disruption, disaster, and death: Helping students deal with crises.* Reston, VA: Council for Exceptional Children.

O'Connell, C. (2004). *Murder trial renews division between Ivy Leaguers, blue-collar locals.* Retrieved October 11, 2005, from http://www.courttv.com/trials/pringwilson/cambridge_091704_ctv.html

O'Connor v. Donaldson, 422 U.S. 563 (1975).

Odinot, G., Wolters, G., & Lavender, T. (2009). Repeated partial eyewitness questioning causes confidence inflation but not retrieval-induced forgetting. *Applied Cognitive Psychology, 23,* 90–97.

Odinot, G., & Wolters, G. (2006). Repeated recall, retention interval and the accuracy confidence relation in eyewitness memory. *Applied Cognitive Psychology, 20,* 973–985.

O'Donnell, P., & Lurigio, A. (2008). Psychosocial predictors of clinicians' recommendations and judges' placement orders in a juvenile court. *Criminal Justice and Behavior, 35,* 1429–1448.

Offe, H., & Offe, S. (2007). The comparison question test: Does it work and if so how? *Law and Human Behavior, 31,* 291–303.

Office of Juvenile Justice and Delinquency Prevention. (1995). *Guide for implementing the comprehensive strategy for serious, violent, and chronic juvenile offenders.* Washington, DC: Author.

Office of Juvenile Justice and Delinquency Prevention. (2008). *Model programs guide.* Retrieved June 11, 2008, from http://www.dsgonline.com/mpg2.5/mpg_index.htm

Ogloff, J. R. P. (1991). A comparison of insanity defense standards on juror decision making. *Law and Human Behavior, 15,* 509–532.

Ogloff, J. R. P., & Chopra, S. (2004). Stuck in the dark ages: Supreme Court decision making and legal developments. *Psychology, Public Policy, and Law, 10,* 379–416.

Ogloff, J. R. P., & Finkelman, D. (1999). Psychology and law: An overview. In R. Roesch, S. D. Hart, & J. R. Ogloff (Eds.), *Psychology and law: The state of the discipline* (pp. 1–20). New York: Kluwer.

Ogloff, J. R. P., & Otto, R. (1993). Psychological autopsy: Clinical and legal perspectives. *Saint Louis University Law Journal, 37,* 607–646.

Ogloff, J. R. P., & Vidmar, N. (1994). The impact of pretrial publicity on jurors: A study to compare the relative effects of television and print media in a child sex abuse case. *Law and Human Behavior, 18,* 507–525.

O'Hara, E. (2005). Victim participation in the criminal process. *Journal of Law and Policy, 13,* 229–247.

O'Keefe, M., Klebe, K., Stucker, A., Sturm, K., & Leggett, W. (2011). *One-year longitudinal study of the psychological effects of administrative segregation.* Washington, DC: Department of Justice. Retrieved July 17, 2012, from https://www.ncjrs.gov/pdffiles1/nij/grants/232973.pdf

Olczak, P. V., Kaplan, M. F., & Penrod, S. (1991). Attorneys' lay psychology and its effectiveness in selecting jurors: Three empirical studies. *Journal of Social Behavior and Personality, 6,* 431–452.

Olsen-Fulero, L., & Fulero, S. (1997). Commonsense rape judgments: An empathy-complexity theory of rape juror story making. *Psychology, Public Policy, and Law, 3,* 402–427.

Olson, J., & Zanna, M. (1993). Attitudes and attitude change. *Annual Review of Psychology, 44,* 117–154.

Olson, W. K. (1991). *The litigation explosion.* New York: Dutton.

Oppel, R. (2011, September 26). *Sentencing shift gives new leverage to prosecutors.* Retrieved March 22, 2012, from http://www.nytimes.com/2011/09/26/us/tough-sentences-help-prosecutors-push-for-plea-bargains.html?pagewanted=all

Orchowski, L. M., Gidycz, C. A., & Raffle, H. (2008). Evaluation of a sexual assault risk reduction and self-defense program: A prospective analysis of a revised protocol. *Psychology of Women Quarterly, 32,* 204–218.

Ornstein, P. A., Ceci, S. J., & Loftus, E. F. (1998). Adult recollections of childhood abuse: Cognitive and developmental perspectives. *Psychology, Public Policy, and Law, 4,* 1025–1051.

Osman, S. (2011). Predicting rape empathy based on victim, perpetrator, and participant gender, and history of sexual aggression. *Sex Roles, 64,* 506–515.

Ostrov, E. (1986). Police/law enforcement and psychology. *Behavioral Sciences & the Law, 4,* 353–370.

Otto, R., & Douglas, K. (Eds.). (2009). *Handbook of violence risk assessment tools.* New York: Routledge.

Otto, R., & Douglas, K. (2010). *Handbook of violence risk assessment.* New York: Routledge.

Otto, R., & Edens, J. (2003). Parentiwng capacity. In T. Grisso, *Evaluating competencies* (2nd ed., pp. 229–308). New York: Springer.

Otto, R., Poythress, N., Starr, K., & Darkes, J. (1993). An empirical study of the reports of APA's peer review panel in the congressional review of the *USS Iowa* incident. *Journal of Personality Assessment, 61,* 425–442.

Owen, D. (2004). *Criminal minds: The science and psychology of profiling.* New York: Barnes & Noble Books.

Packer, H. L. (1964). Two models of the criminal process. *University of Pennsylvania Law Review, 113,* 1–68.

Packer, I. (2009). *Evaluation of criminal responsibility.* New York: Oxford University Press.

Panetti v. Quarterman, 551 U.S. 930 (2007).

Parker, R. (2004). Alcohol and violence: Connections, evidence and possibilities for prevention. *Journal of Psychoactive Drugs* (Suppl. 2), 157–163.

Pasewark, R. A., & Pantle, M. L. (1981). Opinions about the insanity plea. *Journal of Forensic Psychology, 8,* 63.

Paterson, H. M., & Kemp, R. I. (2006). Comparing methods of encountering post-event information: The power of co-witness suggestion. *Applied Cognitive Psychology, 20,* 1083–1099.

Patton v. Yount, 467 U.S. 1025 (1984).

Peak, K., Bradshaw, R., & Glensor, R. (1992). Improving citizen perceptions of the police: "Back to the basics" with a community policing strategy. *Journal of Criminal Justice, 20,* 24–40.

Pennington, N., & Hastie, R. (1986). Evidence evaluation in complex decision making. *Journal of Personality and Social Psychology, 51,* 242–258.

Pennington, N., & Hastie, R. (1988). Explanation-based decision making: Effects of memory structure on judgment. *Journal of Experimental Psychology: Learning, Memory, and Cognition, 14,* 521–533.

Pennington, N., & Hastie, R. (1993). The story model for juror decision making. In R. Hastie (Ed.), *Inside the juror: The psychology of juror decision making* (pp. 192–221). New York: Cambridge University Press.

Penrod, S. D. (1990). Predictors of jury decision making in criminal and civil cases: A field experiment. *Forensic Reports, 3*, 261–278.

Penrod, S. D., Loftus, E. F., & Winkler, J. (1982). The reliability of eyewitness testimony: A psychological perspective. In N. L. Kerr & R. M. Bray (Eds.), *The psychology of the courtroom* (pp. 119–168). Orlando, FL: Academic Press.

People v. Falsetta, 986 P. 2d 182 (1999).

Perkonigg, A., Kessler, R. C., Storz, S., & Wittchen, H. U. (2000). Traumatic events and post-traumatic stress disorder in the community: Prevalence, risk factors and comorbidity. *Acta Psychiatrica Scandinavica, 101*, 46–59.

Perlin, M. (1996). The insanity defense: Deconstructing the myths and reconstructing the jurisprudence. In B. D. Sales & D. W. Shulman (Eds.), *Law, mental health, and mental disorder* (pp. 341–359). Pacific Grove, CA: Brooks/Cole.

Perry v. Schwarzenegger, Case # 09-02292 JW (N. D. CA, 2011).

Petersilia, J. (2001). When prisoners return to communities: Political, economic, and social consequences. *Federal Probation, 65*, 3–8.

Peterson, C., Parsons, T., & Dean, M. (2004). Providing misleading and reinstatement information a year after it happened: Effects on long-term memory. *Memory, 12*, 1–13.

Petherick, W. (2005). *The science of criminal profiling.* New York: Barnes & Noble.

Petrella, R. C., & Poythress, N. G. (1983). The quality of forensic evaluations: An interdisciplinary study. *Journal of Consulting and Clinical Psychology, 51*, 76–85.

Pezdek, K. (2012). Fallible eyewitness memory and identification. In Cutler, B. (Ed.), *Conviction of the innocent: Lessons from psychological research* (pp. 105–124). Washington, DC: American Psychological Association.

Pfohl, S. J. (1984). Predicting dangerousness: A social deconstruction of psychiatric reality. In L. A. Teplin (Ed.), *Mental health and criminal justice* (pp. 201–225). Newbury Park, CA: Sage.

Phillips, A. (2004, February 8). Training to be police officers: What does it take to join the force? These cadets are finding out. *The Austin American Statesman.* Retrieved July 15, 2005, from http://www.statesman.com/opinion/content/editorial/cadets/0208apdcadets.html

Phillips, C. (Producer). (2006, October 1). *Dexter* [Television Series]. Long Beach, CA: Showtime Network.

Phillips, D. A. (1979). *The great Texas murder trials: A compelling account of the sensational T. Cullen Davis case.* New York: Macmillan.

Phillips, M., McAuliff, B., Kovera, M., & Cutler, B. (1999). Double-blind photoarray administration as a safeguard against investigator bias. *Journal of Applied Psychology, 84*, 940–951.

Pickel, K., (2009). The weapon focus effect on memory for female versus male perpetrators. *Memory, 17*, 664–678.

Pickel, K., French, T., & Betts, J. (2003). A cross-modal weapon focus effect: The influence of a weapon's presence on memory for auditory information. *Memory, 11*, 277–292.

Piechowski, L. (2011). *Evaluation of workplace disability.* New York: Oxford University Press.

Pierce, G., & Radelet, M. (2005). The impact of legally inappropriate factors on death sentencing for California homicides, 1990–1999. *Santa Clara Law Review, 46*, 1–47.

Pinizzotto, A. J., & Finkel, N. J. (1990). Criminal personality profiling: An outcome and process study. *Law and Human Behavior, 14*, 215–234.

Pizzi, W. T. (1987). Batson v. Kentucky: Curing the disease but killing the patient. In P. K. Kurland, G. Casper, & D. Hutchinson (Eds.), *The Supreme Court review, 1987* (pp. 97–156). Chicago: University of Chicago Press.

Platt, J. J., & Prout, M. F. (1987). Cognitive-behavioral theory and interventions for crime and delinquency. In E. K. Morris & C. J. Braukmann (Eds.), *Behavioral approaches to crime and delinquency: A handbook of application, research, and concepts* (pp. 477–497). New York: Plenum.

Plessy v. Ferguson, 163 U.S. 537 (1896).

Plumm, K., & Terrance, C. (2009). Battered women who kill: The impact of expert testimony and empathy induction in the courtroom. *Violence Against Women, 15*, 186–205.

Podkopacz, M., & Feld, B. (2001). The back door to prison: Waiver reform, blended sentencing, and the law of unintended consequences. *Journal of Criminal Law & Criminology, 91*, 997–1071.

Police Psychological Services Section. (2004). *Psychological fitness-for-duty evaluation guidelines.* Retrieved July 1, 2005, from www.policepsych.com/fitforduty.pdf

Pollack, D., McFarland, B., Mahler, J., & Kovas, A. (2005). Outcomes of patients in low-intensity, short-duration involuntary outpatient commitment program. *Psychiatric Services, 26*, 863–866.

Porter, B. (1983). Mind hunters. *Psychology Today, 17*, 44–52.

Porter, R. (2012). *Giving juvenile offenders a second chance at Oakland's Youth UpRising.* Retrieved from http://oaklandlocal.com/posts/2012/03/giving-juvenile-offenders-second-chance-oaklands-youth-uprising-community-voices

Post, C. G. (1963). *An introduction to the law.* Englewood Cliffs, NJ: Prentice Hall.

Post, L. (2004a, June 7). Courts mix justice with social work. *National Law Journal,* p. 1.

Post, L. (2004b, November 8). *Spelling it out in plain English.* Retrieved November 11, 2004, from www.law.com/jsp/nlj

Post, L. (2004c, June 21). Report: Civil trials fall by half. *National Law Journal,* p. 6.

Poythress, N., Monahan, J., Bonnie, R., Otto, R. K., & Hoge, S. K. (2002). *Adjudicative competence: The MacArthur Studies.* New York: Kluwer/Plenum.

Poythress, N. G., Bonnie, R. J., Hoge, S. K., Monahan, J., & Oberlander, L. B. (1994). Client abilities to assist counsel and make decisions in criminal cases: Findings from three studies. *Law and Human Behavior, 18,* 437–452.

Poythress, N. G., Nicholson, R., Otto, R. K., Edens, J. F., Bonnie, R. J., Monahan, J., et al. (1999). *The MacArthur Competence Assessment Tool—Criminal Adjudication: Professional Manual.* Odessa, FL: Psychological Assessment Resources.

Pozzulo, J., & Dempsey, J. (2009). Witness factors and their influence on jurors' perceptions and verdicts. *Criminal Justice and Behavior, 36,* 923–934.

Prentky, R. A., & Knight, R. A. (1991). Identifying critical dimensions for discriminating among rapists. *Journal of Consulting and Clinical Psychology, 59,* 643–661.

President's Commission on Law Enforcement and Administration of Justice. (1967). *Toward a just America.* Washington, DC: U.S. Government Printing Office.

Prettyman, E. B. (1960). Jury instructions—First or last? *American Bar Association Journal, 46,* 10–66.

Pryor, J. B. (1987). Sexual harassment proclivities in men. *Sex Roles, 17,* 269–290.

Pryor, J. B., Giedd, J. L., & Williams, K. B. (1995). A social psychological model for predicting sexual harassment. *Journal of Social Issues, 51,* 69–84.

Puzzanchera, C., Adams, B., & Sickmund, M. (2010). *Juvenile Court Statistics, 2006–2007.* Pittsburgh, PA: National Center for Juvenile Justice.

Pynes, J., & Bernardin, H. (1992). Entry-level police selection: The assessment center is an alternative. *Journal of Criminal Justice, 20,* 41–52.

Qualters, S. (2010, September 22). Two federal judges offer differing takes on declining trial numbers. *New York Law Journal.* Retrieved from http://www.newyorklawjournal.com/PubArticleNY.jsp?id=1202472305785

Qualters, S. (2012, March 8). *Seventh Circuit gives plaintiff new trial in bias case.* Retrieved June 9, 2012, from http://www.law.com/jsp/law/LawArticleFriendly.jsp?id=1202545092993&slreturn=1

Quas, J., Goodman, G., Ghetti, S., Alexander, K., Edelstein, R., Redlich, A., et al. (2005). Childhood sexual assault victims: Long-term outcomes after testifying in criminal court. *Monographs of the Society for Research in Child Development, 70* (2, Serial No. 280), 1–145.

Quas, J., Malloy, L., Melinder, A., Goodman, G., D'Mello, M., & Schaaf, J. (2007). Developmental differences in the effects of repeated interviews and interviewer bias on young children's event memory and false reports. *Developmental Psychology, 43,* 823–837.

Quas, J., & Schaaf, J. (2002). Children's memories of experienced and nonexperienced events following repeated interviews. *Journal of Experimental Child Psychology, 83,* 304–338.

Quay, H. C. (1965). Personality and delinquency. In H. C. Quay (Ed.), *Juvenile delinquency* (pp. 139–169). Princeton, NJ: Van Nostrand.

Quinlivan, D., Neuschatz, J., Cutler, B., Wells, G., McClung, J., & Harker, D. (2012). Do pre-admonition suggestions moderate the effect of unbiased lineup instructions? *Legal and Criminological Psychology, 17,* 165–176.

Quinlivan, D., Neuschatz, J., Jimenez, A., Cling, A., Douglass, A., & Goodsell, C. (2009). Do prophylactics prevent inflation? Post-identification feedback and the effectiveness of procedures to protect against confidence-inflation in ear-witnesses. *Law and Human Behavior, 33,* 111–121.

Quinn, J. (1996). "Attitudinal" decision making in the federal courts: A study of constitutional self-representation claims. *San Diego Law Review, 33,* 701–754.

Quinsey, V., Harris, G., Rice, M., & Cormier, C. (2006). *Violent offenders: Appraising and managing risk* (2nd ed.). Washington, DC: American Psychological Association.

Rabe-Hemp, C., & Schuck, A. (2007). Violence against police officers: Are female officers at greater risk? *Police Quarterly, 10,* 411–428.

Rachlinski, J., Johnson, S., Wistrich, A., & Guthrie, C. (2009). Does unconscious racial bias affect trial judges? *Notre Dame Law Review, 84,* 1195–1231.

Radelet, M., & Akers, R. (1996). Deterrence and the death penalty: The views of the experts. *Journal of Criminal Law and Criminology, 87,* 1–16.

Radelet, M., Bedau, H., & Putnam, C. (1992). *In spite of innocence: Erroneous convictions in capital cases.* Boston, MA: Northeastern University Press.

Rafilson, F., & Sison, R. (1996). Seven criterion-related validity studies conducted with the National Police Officer Selection Test. *Psychological Reports, 78,* 163–176.

Raine, A. (2002). Annotation: The role of prefrontal deficits, low autonomic arousal, and early health factors in the development of antisocial and aggressive behavior in children. *Journal of Child Psychology & Psychiatry, 43,* 417–434.

Raine, A., Lencz, T., Bihrle, S., Lacasse, L., & Colletti, P. (2000). Reduced prefrontal gray matter volume and reduced autonomic activity in antisocial personality disorder. *Archives of General Psychiatry, 57,* 119–127.

Raine, A., Meloy, J., & Buchsbaum, M. (1998). Reduced prefrontal and increased subcortical brain functioning using positron emission tomography in predatory and affective murderers. *Behavioral Sciences & the Law, 16,* 319–332.

Raine, A., Venables, P., & Williams, M. (1989). Relationships between N1, P300, and contingent negative variation recorded at age 15 and criminal behavior at age 24. *Psychophysiology, 27,* 567–574.

Rainville, J., Sobel, J. B., Hartigan, C., & Wright, A. (1997). The effect of compensation involvement on the reporting of pain and disability by patients referred for rehabilitation of chronic low back pain. *Spine, 22,* 2016–2024.

Ramirez, G., Zemba, D., & Geiselman, R. E. (1996). Judge's cautionary instructions on eyewitness testimony. *American Journal of Forensic Psychology, 14,* 31–66.

Rasul v. Bush, 542 U.S. 466 (2004).

Reaves, B. (2006). *Violent felons in large urban counties.* Washington, DC: U.S. Department of Justice, Bureau of Justice Statistics.

Reckless, W. C. (1967). *The crime problem* (4th ed.). New York: Meredith.

Redding, R. E., Floyd, M. Y., & Hawk, G. L. (2001). What judges and lawyers think about the testimony of mental health experts: A survey of the courts and bar. *Behavioral Sciences & the Law, 19,* 583–594.

Redding, R. E., & Hensl, K. B. (2011). Knowledgeable judges make a difference: Judicial beliefs affect juvenile court transfer decisions. *Juvenile and Family Court Journal, 62,* 15–24.

Redding, R., & Mrozoski, B. (2005). Adjudicatory and dispositional decision making in juvenile justice. In K. Heilbrun, N., Goldstein, & R. Redding (Eds.), *Juvenile delinquency: Prevention, assessment, and intervention* (pp. 232–256). New York: Oxford University Press.

Reddy, M., Borum, R., Berglund, J., Vossekuil, B., Fein, R., & Modzeleski, W. (2001). Evaluating risk for targeted violence in schools: Comparing risk assessment, threat assessment, and other approaches. *Psychology in the Schools, 38,* 157–172.

Redlich, A. (2010). The susceptibility of juveniles to false confessions and false guilty pleas. *Rutgers Law Review, 62,* 943–957.

Redlich, A. D., Hoover, S., Summers, A., & Steadman, H. J. (2010). Enrollment in mental health courts: Voluntariness, knowingness, and adjudicative competence. *Law and Human Behavior, 34,* 91–104.

Redlich, A., Silverman, M., Chen, J., & Steiner, H. (2004). The police interrogation of children and adolescents. In G. D. Lassiter (Ed.), *Interrogations, confessions, and entrapment* (pp. 107–126). New York: Kluwer Academic/Plenum.

Redlich, A., Steadman, H., Monahan, J., Petrila, J., & Griffin, P. (2005). The second generation of mental health courts. *Psychology, Public Policy, & Law, 11,* 527–538.

Redlich, A., Steadman, A., Monahan, J., Robbins, P., & Petrila, J. (2006). Patterns of practice in mental health courts: A national survey. *Law and Human Behavior, 30,* 347–362.

Summers, A., & Hoover, S. (2010). Self-reported false confessions and false guilty pleas among offenders with mental illness. *Law and Human Behavior, 34,* 79–90.

Redondo, S., Sanchez-Meca, J., & Garrido, V. (1999). The influence of treatment programs on the recidivism of juvenile and adult offenders: A European meta-analytic review. *Psychology, Crime and Law, 5,* 251–278.

Reiber, M., & Weinberg, J. (2010). The complexity of complexity: An empirical study of juror competence in civil cases. *University of Cincinnati Law Review, 78,* 929–968.

Reibstein, L., & Foote, D. (1996, November 4). Playing the victim card. *Newsweek,* pp. 64, 66.

Reid, J. E., & Inbau, F. E. (1966). *Truth and deception: The polygraph ("lie-detector") technique.* Baltimore: Williams & Wilkins.

Reid, S. T. (1976). *Crime and criminology.* Hinsdale, IL: Dryden.

Reisberg, D., & Heuer, F. (2007). The influence of emotion on memory for forensic settings. In M. Toglia, J. Read, D. Ross, & R. Lindsay (Eds.), *The handbook of eyewitness psychology: Memory for events.* Mahwah, NJ: Erlbaum.

Reppucci, N.D., Meyer, J., & Kostelnik, J. (2010). Custodial interrogation of juveniles: Results of a national survey of police. In G. D. Lassiter & C. Meissner (Eds.), *Police interrogations and false confessions* (pp. 67–80). Washington, DC: American Psychological Association.

Resnick, H. S., Kilpatrick, D. G., Dansky, B. S., Saunders, B., & Best, C. L. (1993). Prevalence of civilian trauma and posttraumatic stress disorder in a representative national sample of women. *Journal of Consulting and Clinical Psychology, 61*, 984–991.

Ressler, R. K., Burgess, A. W., & Douglas, J. E. (1988). *Sexual homicide: Patterns and motives*. Lexington, MA: Lexington Books.

Restrepo, L. F. (1995, April 17). Excluding bilingual jurors may be racist. *National Law Journal*, pp. A21, A22.

Reuben, R. (1996, August). The lawyer turns peace-maker. *American Bar Association Journal, 82*, 54–55.

Rhode Island v. Innis, 446 U.S. 291 (1980).

Ribes-Inesta, E., & Bandura, A. (Eds.). (1976). *Analysis of delinquency and aggression*. Hillsdale, NJ: Erlbaum.

Rice, C. (2012). *Power concedes nothing: One woman's quest for social justice in America, from the kill zones to the courtroom*. New York: Scribner.

Richardson, A., & Budd, T. (2003). Young adults, alcohol, crime and disorder. *Criminal Behaviour & Mental Health, 13*, 5–16.

Richey, C. R. (1994). Proposals to eliminate the prejudicial effect of the use of the word "expert" under the federal rules of evidence in civil and criminal jury trials. *Federal Rules Decisions, 154*, 537–562.

Richter, E., & Humke, A. (2011). Demonstrative evidence: Evidence and technology in the courtroom. In R. Wiener & B. Bornstein (Eds.), *Handbook of trial consulting* (pp. 187–202). New York: Springer.

Rickert, J. (2010). Denying defendants the benefit of a reasonable doubt: Federal rule of evidence 609 and past sex crime convictions. *Journal of Criminal Law and Criminology, 100*, 213–242.

Rideau v. Louisiana, 373 U.S. 723 (1963).

Rider, A. O. (1980). The firesetter: A psychological profile. *FBI Law Enforcement Bulletin, 49*, 123.

Ring v. Arizona, 536 U.S. 584 (2002).

Risinger, D. M. (2007). Innocents convicted: An empiri-cally justified factual wrongful conviction rate. *Journal of Criminal Law and Criminology, 97*, 761–806.

Risinger, D., & Loop, J. (2002). Three card monte, Monty Hall, modus operandi, and "offender profiling": Some lessons of modern cognitive science for the law of evidence. *Cardozo Law Review, 24*, 193–253.

Risling, G. (2008). *Jury convicts mother of lesser charges in MySpace suicide case*. Retrieved February 15, 2009, from http://www.law.com

Robbennolt, J. (2000). Outcome severity and judgments of "responsibility": A meta-analytic review. *Journal of Applied Social Psychology, 30*, 2575–2609.

Robbennolt, J. (2002). Punitive damage decision making: The decisions of citizens and trial court judges. *Law and Human Behavior, 26*, 315–342.

Robbennolt, J. (2003). Apologies and legal settlement: An empirical examination. *Michigan Law Review, 102*, 460–516.

Robbennolt, J., & Davidson, S. (2011). Legal research techniques for social scientists. In B. Rosenfeld & S. Penrod (Eds.), *Research methods in forensic psychology* (pp. 3–25) . New York: Wiley.

Robbennolt, J., & Taksin, M. (2010). Can judges deter-mine their own impartiality? *Monitor on Psychology, 41*(2), 24.

Robertiello, G. & Terry, K. (2007). Can we profile sex offenders? A review of sex offender typologies. *Aggression and Violent Behavior, 12*, 508–518.

Roberts, A. L., Gillman, S. E., Breslau, J., Breslau, N., & Koenen, K. C. (2011). Race/ethnic differences in exposure to traumatic events, development of post-traumatic stress disorder, and treatment-seeking for post-traumatic stress disorder in the United States. *Psychological Medicine: A Journal of Research in Psychiatry and the Allied Sciences, 41*, 71–83.

Roberts, C. F., & Golding, S. L. (1991). The social construction of criminal responsibility and insanity. *Law and Human Behavior, 15*, 349–376.

Roberts, C. F., Sargent, E. L., & Chan, A. S. (1993). Verdict selection processes in insanity cases: Juror construals and the effects of guilty but mentally ill instructions. *Law and Human Behavior, 17*, 261–275.

Roberts, J., & Stalans, L. (2004). Restorative sentencing: Exploring the views of the public. *Social Justice Research, 17*, 315–334.

Robertson, C. T. (2010). Blind expertise. *New York University Law Review, 85*, 175–257.

Robertson, C., & Yokum, D. (2011). *Effect of blinded experts on mock jurors' assessments of credibility and verdicts in civil trials*. Arizona Legal Studies Discussion Paper No. 11-30. Retrieved July 17, 2012, from http://papers.ssrn.com/sol3/papers.cfm?abstract_id=1884765

Rodriguez, F., Curry, T., & Lee, G. (2006). Gender differences in criminal sentencing: Do effects vary across violent, property, and drug offenses? *Social Sciences Quarterly, 87*, 318–339.

Roesch, R., & Golding, S. L. (1980). *Competency to stand trial*. Urbana: University of Illinois Press.

Roesch, R., & Golding, S. L. (1987). Defining and asses-sing competence to stand trial. In I. Weiner & A. Hess (Eds.), *Handbook of forensic psychology* (pp. 378–394). New York: Wiley.

Roesch, R., Zapf, P., & Eaves, D. (2006). *Fitness Interview Test-Revised (FIT-R): A structured interview for assessing competency to stand trial*. Sarasota, FL: Professional Resource Press.

Rogers, R. (1986). *Conducting insanity evaluations.* New York: Van Nostrand.

Rogers, R. (1988). *Clinical assessment of malingering and deception.* New York: Guilford.

Rogers, R. (Ed.). (1997). *Clinical assessment of malingering and deception* (2nd ed.). New York: Guilford.

Rogers, R. (2001). *Handbook of diagnostic and structured interviewing* (2nd ed.). New York: Guilford.

Rogers, R. (Ed.). (2008). *Clinical assessment of malingering and deception* (3rd ed.). New York: Guilford.

Rogers, R., & Ewing, C. P. (1989). Ultimate opinion proscriptions: A cosmetic fix and a plea for empiricism. *Law and Human Behavior, 13,* 357–374.

Rogers, R., Grandjean, N., Tillbrook, C., Vitacco, M,. & Sewell, K. (2001). Recent interview-based measures of competency to stand trial: A critical review augmented with research data. *Behavioral Sciences & the Law, 19,* 503–518.

Rogers, R., Rogstad, J., Gillard, N., Drogin, E., Blackwood, H., & Shuman, D. (2010). "Everyone knows their *Miranda* rights": Implicit assumptions and countervailing evidence. *Psychology, Public Policy, and Law, 16,* 300–318.

Rogers, R., Rogstad, J., Steadham, J, & Drogin, E. (2011). In plain English: Avoiding recognized problems with *Miranda* comprehension. *Psychology, Public Policy, & Law, 17,* 264–285.

Rogers, R., Salekin, R. T., Sewell, K. W., Goldstein, A., & Leonard, K. (1998). A comparison of forensic and nonforensic malingerers: A prototypical analysis of exploratory models. *Law and Human Behavior, 22,* 253–267.

Rogers, R., Sewell, K., & Gillard, N. (2010). *Structured interview of reported symptoms: Professional manual* (2nd ed.). Lutz, FL: Psychological Assessment Resources.

Rogers, R., & Shuman, D. (2000). *Conducting insanity evaluations* (2nd ed.). New York: Guilford.

Rogers, R., Tillbrook, C., & Sewell, K. (2004). *Evaluation of Competence to Stand Trial—Revised: Professional manual.* Lutz, FL: Psychological Assessment Resources.

Rohling, M. L., Binder, L. M., & Langhrinrichsen-Rohling, J. (1995). Money matters: A meta-analytic review of the association between financial compensation and the experience and treatment of chronic pain. *Health Psychology, 14,* 537–547.

Roper v. Simmons, 543 U.S. 551 (2005).

Rose, M. (2005). A dutiful voice: Justice in the distribution of jury service. *Law and Society Review, 39,* 601–634.

Rose, M., & Diamond, S. (2008). Judging bias: Juror confidence and judicial rulings on challenges for cause. *Law and Society Review, 42,* 513–548.

Rose, M., Ellison, C., & Diamond, S. (2008). Preferences for juries over judges across racial and ethnic groups. *Social Science Quarterly, 89,* 372–391.

Rosen, G. M. (1995). The *Aleutian Enterprise* sinking and posttraumatic stress disorder: Misdiagnosis in clinical and forensic settings. *Professional Psychology: Research and Practice, 26,* 82–87.

Rosen, J. (2010, January 10). *Prisoners of parole.* Retrieved July 22, 2011, from http://www.nytimes.com/2010/01/10/magazine/10prisons-t.html?_r=1&pagewanted=all

Rosenbaum, A., & Gearan, P. J. (1999). Relationship aggression between partners. In V. B. Van Hasselt & M. Hersen (Eds.), *Handbook of psychological approaches with violent offenders: Contemporary strategies and issues* (pp. 357–372). New York: Kluver Academic/Plenum.

Rosenfeld, J. P. (2005). Brain fingerprinting: A critical analysis. *Scientific Review of Mental Health Practice, 4,* 20–37.

Rosenfeld, J., Soskins, M., Bosh, G., & Ryan, A. (2004). Simple effective countermeasures to P300-based tests of detection of concealed information. *Psychophysiology, 41,* 205–219.

Rosenmerkel, M., Durose, M., & Farole, D. (2009). *Felony sentences in state courts, 2006.* Bureau of Justice Statistics Report NCJ 226846. Washington, DC: Department of Justice.

Rosenthal, R., & Jacobson, L. (1968). *Pygmalion in the classroom: Teacher expectation and pupils' intellectual development.* New York: Holt.

Rotundo, M., Nguyen, D., & Sackett, P. (2001). A meta-analytic review of gender differences in perceptions of sexual harassment. *Journal of Applied Psychology, 86,* 914–922.

Rowland, J. (1985). *The ultimate violation.* New York: Doubleday.

Rubin, D., & Boals, A. (2010). People who expect to enter psychotherapy are prone to believing that they have forgotten memories of childhood trauma and abuse. *Memory, 18,* 556–562.

Runda, J. (1991). Personal affidavit filed with authors. Lexington: University of Kentucky Press.

Rushton, J. (1996). Self-report delinquency and violence in adult twins. *Psychiatric Genetics, 6,* 87–89.

Russell, B., & Melillo, L. (2006). Attitudes toward battered women who kill: Defendant typicality and judgments of culpability. *Criminal Justice and Behavior, 33,* 219–241.

Ruva, C., Guenther, C., & Yarbrough, A. (2011). Positive and negative pretrial publicity: The roles of impression formation, emotion, and predecisional distortion. *Criminal Justice and Behavior, 38,* 511–534.

Ruva, C., & LeVasseur, M. (2012). Behind closed doors: The effect of pretrial publicity on jury deliberations. *Psychology, Crime and Law 18,* 431–452.

Ruva, C., & McEvoy, C. (2008). Negative and positive pretrial publicity affect juror memory and decision making. *Journal of Experimental Psychology: Applied, 14,* 226–236.

Ruva, C., McEvoy, C., & Bryant, J. (2007). Effects of pretrial publicity and collaboration on juror bias and source monitoring errors. *Applied Cognitive Psychology, 21,* 45–67.

Ryan, W. (1970). *Blaming the victim.* New York: Vintage.

Sabol, W. J., & Couture, H. (2008). *Prison Inmates at Midyear 2007* (NCJ 221944). Retrieved November, 30, 2010, from U.S. Department of Justice, Office of Justice Programs: http://bjs.ojp.usdoj.gov/content/pub/pdf/pim07.pdf

Sack, E. (2002). *Creating a domestic violence court: Guidelines and best practices.* San Francisco, CA: Family Violence Prevention Fund.

Sacks, D., Bushman, B., & Anderson, C. (2011). Do violent video games harm children? Comparing the scientific amicus curiae "experts" in *Brown v. Entertainment Merchants Association. Northwestern University Law Review, 106,* 1–12.

Saks, M. (1997). What do jury experiments tell us about how juries (should) make decisions? *Southern California Interdisciplinary Law Journal, 6,* 1–53.

Salekin, R. (2004). *The Risk-Sophistication-Treatment Inventory.* Lutz, FL: Psychological Assessment Resources.

Salekin, R. T., Rogers, R., & Sewell, K. W. (1997). Construct validity of psychopathy in a female offender sample: A multitrait–multimethod evaluation. *Journal of Abnormal Psychology, 107,* 576–585.

Salekin, R., Trobst, K., & Krioukova, M. (2001). Construct validity of psychopathy in a community sample: A nomological net approach. *Journal of Personality Disorders, 15,* 425–441.

Salerno, J., & McCauley, M. (2009). Mock jurors' judgments about opposing scientific experts: Do cross-examination, deliberation, and need for cognition matter? *American Journal of Forensic Psychology, 27,* 37–60.

Sales, B. D., & Hafemeister, T. (1984). Empiricism and legal policy on the insanity defense. In L. A. Teplin (Ed.), *Mental health and criminal justice* (pp. 253–278). Newbury Park, CA: Sage.

Sales, B. D., & Shuman, D. W. (1993). Reclaiming the integrity of science in expert witnessing. *Ethics and Behavior, 3,* 223–229.

Salfati, C. G., & Canter, D. V. (1999). Differentiating stranger murders: Profiling offender characteristics from behavioral styles. *Behavioral Sciences & the Law, 17,* 391–406.

Samenow, S. E. (1984). *Inside the criminal mind.* New York: Times Books.

Sanborn, H. (2002, October). The vanishing trial. *American Bar Association Journal, 87,* 24–27.

Sanders, J. (1993). The jury decision in a complex case: *Havener v. Merrell Dow Pharmaceuticals. The Justice System Journal, 16,* 45.

Sanschagrin, K., Stevens, T., Bove, A., & Heilbrun, K. (2006, March). *Quality of forensic mental health assessment of juvenile offenders: An empirical investigation.* Paper presented at the annual conference of the American Psychology-Law Society, Tampa, Florida.

Santiago, J.M., McCall-Perez, F., Gorcey, M., & Beigel, A. (1985). Long-term psychological effects of rape in 35 rape victims. *American Journal of Psychiatry, 142,* 1338–1340.

Santobello v. New York, 404 U.S. 257 (1971).

Sarteschi, C. M., Vaughn, M. G., & Kim, K. (2011). Assessing the effectiveness of mental health courts: A quantitative review. *Journal of Criminal Justice, 39,* 12–20.

Satterwhite v. Texas, 108 S. Ct. 1792 (1988).

Sawyer, A., & Borduin, C. (2011). Effects of multisystemic therapy through midlife: A 21.9-year follow-up to a randomized clinical trial with serious and violent juvenile offenders. *Journal of Consulting and Clinical Psychology, 79,* 634–652.

Schiavo ex rel. Schindler v. Schiavo, No. 05-116282005 WL 713153 (11th Circuit 2005).

Schmidt, F., Hunter, J., McKenzie, R., & Muldrow, T. (1979). Impact of valid selection procedures on workforce productivity. *Journal of Applied Psychology, 64,* 609–626.

Schoenwald, S., Henggeler, S., Brondino, M., & Rowland, M. (2000). Multisystemic therapy: Monitoring treatment fidelity. *Family Process, 39,* 83–103.

Schoenwald, S., Sheidow, A., & Letourneau, E. (2003). Toward effective quality assurance in multisystemic therapy: Links between expert consultation, therapist fidelity, and child outcomes. *Journal of Clinical Child and Adolescent Psychology, 33,* 94–104.

Schram, P. J., & Morash, M. (2002). Evaluation of a life skills program for women inmates in Michigan. *Journal of Offender Rehabilitation, 34,* 47–70.

Schuller, R., McKimmie, B., & Janz, T. (2004). The impact of expert testimony in trials of battered women who kill. *Psychiatry, Psychology and Law, 11,* 1–12.

Schwartz, J. (2009, March 18). *As jurors turn to Web, mistrials are popping up.* Retrieved March 23, 2009, from http:// www.nytimes.com/2009/03/18/us/18juries.html

Schweitzer, N., & Saks, M. (2009). The gatekeeper effect: The impact of judges' admissibility decisions on the persuasiveness of expert testimony. *Psychology, Public Policy and Law, 15,* 1–18.

Science Daily. (2007, June 28). New study shows how often juries get it wrong. *Science Daily.* Retrieved June 5, 2012, from http://www.sciencedaily.com/releases/2007/06/070628161330.htm

Scott, C., & Holmberg, T. (2003). Castration of sex offenders: Prisoners' rights versus public safety. *Journal of the American Academy of Psychiatry and the Law, 31,* 502–509.

Scott, E., & Steinberg, L. (2008). *Rethinking juvenile justice.* Cambridge, MA: Harvard University Press.

Seamon, J., Philbin, M., & Harrison, L. (2006). Do you remember proposing marriage to the Pepsi machine? False recollections from a college walk. *Psychonomic Bulletin & Review, 13,* 752–756.

Seedman, A. A., & Hellman, P. (1974). *Chief!* New York: Arthur Fields Books.

Segal, J., & Spaeth, H. (1993). *The Supreme Court and the attitudinal model.* New York: Cambridge University Press.

Seiter, R. P., & Kadela, K. R. (2003). Prisoner reentry: What works, what does not, and what is promising. *Crime & Delinquency, 49,* 360–388.

Sell v. U.S., 539 U.S. 166 (2003).

Seltzer, R. (2006). Scientific jury selection: Does it work? *Journal of Applied Social Psychology, 36,* 2417–2435.

Semmler, C., Brewer, N., & Douglass, A. (2012). Jurors believe eyewitnesses. In Cutler, B. (Ed.), *Conviction of the innocent: Lessons from psychological research* (pp. 185–209). Washington, DC: American Psychological Association.

Seventh Circuit American Jury Project. (2008). Retrieved January 30, 2009, from www.7thcircuitbar.org/associations/1507/files/7th%20Circuit%20American%20Jury%20Project%20Final%20Report.pdf

Sexton, T. & Turner, C. (2010). The effectiveness of functional family therapy for youth with behavioral problems in a community practice setting. *Journal of Family Psychology, 24,* 339–348.

Shafer, M., Arthur, B., & Franczak, M. (2004). An analysis of post-booking jail diversion programming for persons with co-occurring disorders. *Behavioral Sciences and the Law, 22,* 771–785.

Shaffer, D. K. (2011). Looking inside the black box of drug courts: A meta-analytic review, *Justice Quarterly, 28,* 493–521.

Shannon v. United States, 114 S.Ct. 2419 (1994).

Shaw, J., Appio, L., Zerr, T., & Pontoski, K. (2007). Public eyewitness confidence can be influenced by the presence of other witnesses. *Law and Human Behavior, 31,* 629–652.

Shaw, L.A. (2010). Divorce mediation outcome research: A meta-analysis. *Conflict Resolution Quarterly, 27,* 447–467.

Sheidow, A., & Henggeler, S. (2005). Community-based treatments. In K. Heilbrun, N. Goldstein, & R. Redding (Eds.), *Juvenile delinquency: Prevention, assessment, and intervention* (pp. 257–281). New York: Oxford University Press.

Sheldon, K., & Krieger, L. (2004). Does legal education have undermining effects on law students? Evaluating changes in motivation, values, and well being. *Behavioral Sciences & the Law, 22,* 261–286.

Sheldon, K., & Krieger, L. (2007). Understanding the negative effects of legal education on law students: A longitudinal test of self-determination theory. *Personality and Social Psychology Bulletin, 33,* 883–897.

Sheley, J. F. (1985). *America's "crime problem": An introduction to criminology.* Belmont, CA: Wadsworth.

Sheppard, B. H., & Vidmar, N. (1980). Adversary pretrial procedures and testimonial evidence: Effects of lawyer's role and Machiavellianism. *Journal of Personality and Social Psychology, 39,* 320–332.

Sheppard, B. H., & Vidmar, N. (1983, June). *Is it fair to worry about fairness?* Paper presented at the meeting of the Law and Society Association, Denver, CO.

Sherman, L. W., & Berk, R. A. (1984). *The Minneapolis domestic violence experiment.* Washington, DC: Police Foundation.

Shestowsky, D. (2004). Procedural preferences in alternative dispute resolution: A closer, modern look at an old idea. *Psychology, Public Policy, and Law, 10,* 211–249.

Shestowsky, D., & Brett, J. (2008). Disputants' perceptions of dispute resolution procedures: An *ex ante* and *ex post* longitudinal empirical study. *Connecticut Law Review, 41,* 63–107.

Shulman, K. I., Cohen, C. A., & Hull, I. (2004). Psychiatric issues in retrospective challenges of testamentary capacity. *International Journal of Geriatric Psychiatry, 20,* 63–69.

Shuman, D. (2000). The role of apology in tort law. *Judicature, 83,* 180–189.

Shuman, D. W., & Champagne, A. (1997). Removing the people from the legal process: The rhetoric and research on judicial selection and juries. *Psychology, Public Policy, and Law, 3,* 242–258.

Shusman, E., Inwald, R., & Landa, B. (1984). Correction officer job performance as predicted by the IPI and MMPI. *Criminal Justice and Behavior, 11,* 309–329.

Siegel, A. M., & Elwork, A. (1990). Treating incompetence to stand trial. *Law and Human Behavior, 14,* 57–65.

Silver, E. (1995). Punishment or treatment? Comparing the lengths of confinement of successful and unsuccessful insanity defendants. *Law and Human Behavior, 19,* 375–388.

Silver, E., Cirincione, C., & Steadman, H. J. (1994). Demythologizing inaccurate perceptions of the insanity defense. *Law and Human Behavior, 18,* 63–70.

Silver, R. B. & Silver, D. B. (2009). The Sieve Model: An innovative process for identifying alternatives to custody evaluations. *Conflict Resolution Quarterly, 26,* 333–348.

Singleton, J. V., & Kass, M. (1986). Helping the jury understand complex cases. *Litigation, 12,* 11–13, 59.

Skagerberg, E., & Wright, D. (2008). Co-witness feedback in lineups. *Applied Cognitive Psychology, 21,* 489–497.

Skeem, J., & Bibeau, L. (2008). How does violence potential relate to Crisis Intervention Team responses to emergencies? *Psychiatric Services, 59,* 201–204.

Skeem, J., Emke-Francis, P., & Eno Louden, J. (2006). Probation, mental health, and mandated treatment: A national survey. *Criminal Justice and Behavior, 33,* 158–184.

Skeem, J., Encandela, J. & Eno Louden, J. (2003). Perspectives on probation and mandated mental health treatment in specialized and traditional probation departments. *Behavioral Sciences and the Law, 21,* 429–458.

Skeem, J., & Eno Louden, J. (2006). Toward evidence-based practice for probationers and parolees mandated to mental health treatment. *Psychiatric Services, 57,* 333–342.

Skeem, J., Eno Louden, J., Manchak, S., Vidal, S., & Haddad, E. (2009). Social networks and social control of probationers with co-occurring mental and substance abuse problems. *Law and Human Behavior, 33,* 122–135.

Skeem, J. L., & Golding, S. L. (2001). Describing jurors' personal conceptions of insanity and their relationship to case judgments. *Psychology, Public Policy, and Law, 7,* 561–621.

Skeem, J. L., Golding, S. L., Cohn, N. B., & Berge, G. (1998). Logic and reliability of evaluations of competence to stand trial. *Law and Human Behavior, 22,* 519–548.

Skeem, J., & Louden, J. (2006). Toward evidence-based practice for probationers and parolees mandated to mental health treatment. *Psychiatric Services, 57,* 1–10.

Skogan, W. G. (2006). *Police and community in Chicago: A tale of three cities.* New York: Oxford University Press.

Slater, D., & Hans, V. P. (1984). Public opinion of forensic psychiatry following the *Hinckley* verdict. *American [Journa]l of Psychiatry, 141,* 675–679.

Sloat, L. M., & Frierson, R. L. (2005). Juror knowledge and attitudes regarding mental illness verdicts. *Journal of the American Academy of Psychiatry and Law, 33,* 208–213.

Slobogin, C. (2011). Prevention of sexual violence by those who have been sexually violent. *International Journal of Law and Psychiatry, 34,* 210–216.

Slobogin, C., & Fondacaro, M. (2011). *Juveniles at risk: A plea for preventive justice.* New York: Oxford University Press.

Slobogin, C., Melton, G., & Showalter, S. R. (1984). The feasibility of a brief evaluation of mental state at the time of the offense. *Law and Human Behavior, 8,* 305–321.

Smith, A. (2008). *Case of a lifetime: A criminal defense lawyer's story.* New York: Palgrave Macmillan.

Smith, A., & Haney, C. (2011). Getting to the point: Attempting to improve juror comprehension of capital penalty phase instructions. *Law and Human Behavior, 35,* 339–350.

Smith, C. A., & Farrington, D. C. (2004). Continuities in antisocial behavior and parenting across three generations. *Journal of Child Psychology & Psychiatry, 45,* 230–247.

Smith, P., Goggin, C., & Gendreau, P. (2002). *The effects of prison sentences and intermediate sanctions on recidivism: General effects and individual differences.* Ottawa, ON: Public Safety Canada. (User Report 2002-01).

Smith, P. H., White, J. W., & Holland, L. J. (2003). A longitudinal perspective on dating violence among adolescent and college-age women. *American Journal of Public Health, 93,* 1104–1109.

Smith, S. (1989). Mental health expert witnesses: Of science and crystal balls. *Behavioral Sciences & the Law, 7,* 145–180.

Snyder v. Phelps, 131 S.Ct. 1207 (2011).

Snyder, H. N., & Sickmund, M. (1999). *Juvenile offenders and victims: 1999 national report.* Washington, DC: U.S. Department of Justice, Office of Juvenile Justice and Delinquency Prevention.

Snyder, H., & Sickmund, M. (2006). *Juvenile offenders and victims: 2006 national report.* Washington, DC: U.S. Department of Justice, Office of Justice Programs, Office of Juvenile Justice and Delinquency Prevention. (NCJ No. 212906).

Solomon, P., & Draine, J. (1995). Jail recidivism in a forensic case management program. *Health and Social Work, 20,* 167–173.

Solomon, P., Draine, J., & Marcus, S. (2002). Predicting incarceration of clients of a psychiatric probation and parole service. *Psychiatric Services, 53,* 50–56.

Solomon, R. C. (1990). *A passion for justice.* Reading, MA: Addison-Wesley.

Sommers, S. (2006). On racial diversity and group decision making: Identifying multiple effects of racial composition on jury deliberations. *Journal of Personality and Social Psychology, 90,* 597–612.

Sommers, S. (2007). Race and decision making of juries. *Legal and Criminological Psychology, 12,* 171–187.

Sommers, S. (2008). Determinants and consequences of jury racial diversity: Empirical findings, implications, and directions for future research. *Social Issues and Policy Review, 2,* 65–102.

Sommers, S. (2009). *Consequential conversations III.* Retrieved January 28, 2009, from http://blogs. psychologytoday.com/blog/science-of-small-talk/ 200901/consequential-conversations-part-iii

Sommers, S. R., & Ellsworth, P. C. (2000). Race in the courtroom: Perceptions of guilt and dispositional attributions. *Personality and Social Psychology Bulletin, 26,* 1367–1379.

Sommers, S., & Kassin, S. (2001). On the many impacts of inadmissible testimony: Selective compliance, need for cognition, and the overcorrection bias. *Personality and Social Psychology Bulletin, 27,* 1368–1377.

Sommers, S., & Norton, M. (2007). Race-based judgments, race-neutral justifications: Experimental examination of peremptory use and the *Batson* challenge procedure. *Law and Human Behavior, 31,* 261–273.

Sommers, S., Warp, L., & Mahoney, C. (2008). Cognitive effects of racial diversity: White individuals information processing in heterogeneous groups. *Journal of Experimental Social Psychology, 44,* 1129–1136.

Sorenson, J. & Davis, J. (2011). Violent criminals locked up: Examining the effect of incarceration on behavioral continuity. *Journal of Criminal Science, 39,* 151–158.

Sorenson, S. B., & White, J. W. (1992). Adult sexual assault: Overview of research. *Journal of Social Issues, 48,* 1–8.

Soskis, D. A., & Van Zandt, C. R. (1986). Hostage negotiation: Law enforcement's most effective nonlethal weapon. *Behavioral Sciences & the Law, 4,* 423–436.

Sowell v. Walker, 755 A. 2d 438 (2000).

Spano, L., Daftary-Kapur, T., & Penrod, S. (2011). Trial consulting in high-publicity cases. In B. Rosenfeld & S. Penrod (Eds.), *Research methods in forensic psychology* (pp. 215–236). New York: Wiley.

Spence, S. A., Kaylor-Hughes, C., Brook, M., Lankappa, S. T., & Wilkinson, I. D. (2008). "Munchausen's syndrome by proxy" or a "miscarriage of justice"? An initial application of functional neuroimaging to the question of guilt versus innocence. *European Psychiatry, 23,* 309–314.

Spencer, B. (2007). Estimating the accuracy of jury verdicts. *Journal of Empirical Legal Studies, 4,* 305–329.

Spilbor, J. M. (2004, October 28). *The sexual harassment case against Fox News's Bill O'Reilly: Why winning may be O'Reilly's costliest option.* Retrieved September 1, 2005, from http://writ.news.findlaw.com/commentary/ 20041028_spilbor.html

Spohn, C. (2000). Thirty years of sentencing reform: The quest for a racially neutral sentencing process. In J. Horney (Ed.), *Criminal justice 2000: Policies, processes, and decisions of the criminal justice system* (Vol. 3, pp. 427–501). Washington DC: U.S. Department of Justice, National Institute of Justice.

Sporer, S. (2001). Recognizing faces of other ethnic groups: An integration of theories. *Psychology, Public Policy, and Law, 7,* 170–200.

Sporer, S., & Schwandt, B. (2006). Paraverbal indicators of deception: A meta-analytic synthesis. *Applied Cognitive Psychology, 20,* 421–446.

Sporer, S., & Schwandt, B. (2007). Moderators of nonverbal indicators of deception: A meta-analytic synthesis. *Psychology, Public Policy, and Law, 13,* 1–34.

Sprague, J., & Walker H. (2000). Early identification and intervention for youth with antisocial and violent behavior. *Exceptional Children, 66,* 367–380.

Stamps, V., Abeling, N., van Gennip, A., van Cruchten, A., & Gurling, H. (2001). Mild learning difficulties and offending behavior—is there a link with monoamine oxidase A deficiency? *Psychiatric Genetics, 11,* 173–176.

State v. Damms, 100 N.W. 2d 592 (Wisc. 1960).

State v. Fuller, 862 A. 2d 1130 (N.J. 2004).

State v. Henderson (No. 062218), (N.J. Supreme Court 2011).

State v. Lozano, 616 So. 2d 73 (Fla. App. 1993).

State v. Michaels, 642 A. 2d 1372 (N.J., 1994).

Steadman, H. J. (1979). *Beating a rap? Defendants found incompetent to stand trial.* Chicago, IL: University of Chicago Press.

Steadman, H. J., & Braff, J. (1983). Defendants not guilty by reason of insanity. In J. Monahan & H. J. Steadman (Eds.), *Mentally disordered offenders: Perspectives from law and social science* (pp. 109–132). New York: Plenum.

Steadman, H. J., Deane, D. W., Borum, R., & Morrissey, J. P. (2000). Comparing outcomes of major models of police responses to mental health emergencies. *Psychiatric Services, 51,* 5, 645–649.

Steadman, H. J., Keitner, L., Braff, J., & Arvanites, T. M. (1983). Factors associated with a successful insanity plea. *American Journal of Psychiatry, 140,* 401–405

Steadman, H. J., McGreevy, M., Morrissey, J., Callahan, L., Robbin, P., & Cirincione, C. (1993). *Before and after Hinckley: Evaluating insanity defense reform.* New York: Guilford.

Steadman, H., & Naples, M. (2005). Assessing the effectiveness of jail diversion programs for persons with serious mental illness and co-occurring substance use disorders. *Behavioral Sciences & the Law, 23,* 163–170.

Steadman, H. J., Osher, F. C., Robbins, P. C., Case, B., Samuels, S. (2009). Prevalence of serious mental illness among jail inmates. *Psychiatric Services, 60,* 761–765.

Steadman, H. J., Rosenstein, M. J., MacAskill, R. L., & Manderscheid, R. W. (1988). A profile of mentally disordered offenders admitted to inpatient psychiatric services in the United States. *Law and Human Behavior, 12,* 91–99.

Steadman, H. J., & Veysey, B. (1997). *Providing services for jail inmates with mental disorders.* Retrieved February 8, 2009, from http://www.ncjrs.gov./txtfiles/162207.txt

Steblay, N. (1997). Social influence in eyewitness recall: A meta-analytic review of lineup instruction effects. *Law and Human Behavior, 21,* 283–298.

Steblay, N., Besirevic, J., Fulero, S., & Jiminez-Lorente, B. (1999). The effects of pretrial publicity on jury verdicts: A meta-analytic review. *Law and Human Behavior, 23,* 219–235.

Steblay, N., Dysart, J., & Wells, G. (2011). Seventy-two tests of the sequential lineup superiority effect: A meta-analysis and policy discussion. *Psychology, Public Policy, and Law, 17,* 99–139.

Steblay, N., Hosch, H., Culhane, S., & McWerthy, A. (2006). The impact on juror verdicts of judicial instruction to disregard inadmissible evidence: A meta-analysis. *Law and Human Behavior, 30,* 469–492.

Steffensmeier, D., & Demuth, S. (2006). Does gender modify the effects of race-ethnicity on criminal sanctioning? Sentences for male and female White, Black, and Hispanic defendants. *Journal of Quantitative Criminology, 22,* 241–261.

Steffensmeier, D., Ulmer, J., & Kramer, J. (1998). The interaction of race, gender, and age and criminal sentencing: The punishment cost of being young, black, and male. *Criminology, 36,* 763–797.

Steinberg, L., & Scott, E. (2003). Less guilty by reason of adolescence: Developmental immaturity, diminished responsibility, and the juvenile death penalty. *American Psychologist, 58,* 1009–1018.

Steiner, B., & Wright, E. (2006). Assessing the relative effects of state direct file waiver laws on violent juvenile crime: Deterrence or irrelevance? *The Journal of Criminal Law and Criminology, 96,* 1451–1477.

Stevens, R. (1983). *Law school: Legal education in America from the 1850s to the 1980s.* Chapel Hill, NC: University of North Carolina Press.

Stevenson, M., Bottoms, B., Diamond, S., Stec, I., & Pimentel, P. (2008, March). *How jurors discuss a defendant's childhood maltreatment when they are deliberating on death.* Paper presented at the annual conference of the American Psychology-Law Society, Jacksonville, FL.

Stinchcomb, J. (2004). Searching for stress in all the wrong places: Combating chronic organizational stressors in policing. *Police Practice and Research, 5,* 259–277.

Stinson, V., & Cutler, B. (2011). Training of trial consultants. In R. Wiener & B. Bornstein (Eds.), *Handbook of trial consulting* (pp. 331–350). New York: Springer.

Stipanowich, T. (2010). Arbitration: The "new litigation." *University of Illinois Law Review, 2010,* 1–58.

Stockdale, M. S., Visio, M., & Batra, L. (1999). The sexual harassment of men: Evidence for a broader theory of sexual harassment and sex discrimination. *Psychology, Public Policy, & Law, 5,* 630–664.

Stolle, D., & Studebaker, C. (2011). Trial consulting and conflicts of interest: An introduction. In R. Wiener & B. Bornstein (Eds.), *Handbook of trial consulting* (pp. 351–370). New York: Springer.

Storm, J., & Graham, J. (2000). Detection of coached general malingering on the MMPI-2. *Psychological Assessment, 12,* 158–165.

Stormo, K. J., Lang, A. R., & Stritzke, W. G. K. (1997). Attributions about acquaintance rape: The role of alcohol and individual differences. *Journal of Applied Social Psychology, 27,* 279–305.

Strauder v. West Virginia, 100 U.S. 303 (1880).

Straus, M. (2011). Gender symmetry and mutuality in perpetration of clinical-level partner violence: Empirical evidence and implications for prevention and treatment. *Aggression and Violent Behavior, 16,* 279–288.

Straus, M. A., & Gelles, R. J. (1988). How violent are American families? Estimates from the National Family Violence Resurvey and other studies. In G. T. Hotaling, D. Finkelhor, J. T. Kirkpatrick, & M. A. Straus (Eds.), *Family abuse and its consequences* (pp. 14–36). Thousand Oaks, CA: Sage.

Streib, V. (1983). Death penalty for children: The American experience with capital punishment for crimes committed while under age eighteen. *Oklahoma Law Review, 36,* 613–641.

Strier, F. (1996). *Reconstructing justice: An agenda for trial reform.* Westport, CN: Quorum.

Strier, F. (1999). Whither trial consulting? Issues and projections. *Law and Human Behavior, 23,* 93–115.

Strier, F. (2001). Why trial consultants should be licensed. *Journal of Forensic Psychology Practice, 1*, 69–76.

Strier, F. (2011). Reform proposals. In R. Wiener & B. Bornstein (Eds.), *Handbook of trial consulting* (pp. 371–392). New York: Springer.

Stromwall, L. & Willen, R. (2011). Inside criminal minds: Offenders' strategies when lying. *Journal of Investigative Psychology and Offender Profiling, 8*, 271–281.

Stryker, J. (2005). *Using shame as punishment. Have sex, get infamous.* Retrieved from http://articles.sfgate.com/2005-03-13/opinion/17365359_1_shame-prostitution-legal-system

Studebaker, C. A., & Penrod, S. D. (1997). Pretrial publicity: The media, the law and common sense. *Psychology, Public Policy, and Law, 3*, 428–460.

Studebaker, C., & Penrod, S. (2005). Pretrial publicity and its influence on juror decision making. In N. Brewer & K. Williams (Eds.), *Psychology and law: An empirical perspective* (pp. 254–275). New York: Guilford.

Studebaker, C., Robbennolt, J., Penrod, S., Pathak-Sharma, M., Groscup, J., & Devenport, J. (2002). Studying pretrial publicity effects: New methods for improving ecological validity and testing external validity. *Law and Human Behavior, 26*, 19–42.

Sullivan, C. M., & Bybee, D. I. (1999). Reducing violence using community-based advocacy for women with abusive partners. *Journal of Consulting and Clinical Psychology, 67*, 43–53.

Sullivan, D., & Tifft, L. (2006). Introduction: The healing dimension of restorative justice. A one-world body. In D. Sullivan & L. Tifft (Eds.), *Handbook of restorative justice: A global perspective* (pp. 1–16). London: Routledge.

Sunstein, C., Hastie, R., Payne, J., Schkade, D., & Viscusi, W. (2002). *Punitive damages: How juries decide.* Chicago, IL: University of Chicago Press.

Susman, D. (1992). *Effects of three different legal standards on psychologists' determinations of competency for execution.* Unpublished doctoral dissertation, University of Kentucky, Lexington.

Sutherland, E. H. (1947). *Principles of criminology* (4th ed.). Philadelphia, PA: Lippincott.

Sutherland, E. H., & Cressey, D. R. (1974). *Principles of criminology* (9th ed.). New York: Lippincott.

Swahn, M. H., Whitaker, D. J., Pippen, C. B., Leeb, R. T., Teplin, L. A., Abram, K. M., et al. (2006). Concordance between self-reported maltreatment and court records of abuse or neglect among high-risk youths. *American Journal of Public Health: Mental Health for Individuals and Communities, 96*, 1849–1853.

Swain v. Alabama, 380 U.S. 202 (1965).

Sydeman, S. J., Cascardi, M., Poythress, N. G., & Ritterband, L. M. (1997). Procedural justice in the context of civil commitment: A critique of Tyler's analysis. *Psychology, Public Policy, and Law, 3*, 207–221.

Tanay, E. (2010). *American legal injustice: Behind the scenes with an expert witness.* Lanham, MD: Jason Aronson.

Tanha, M., Beck, C., Figueredo, A., & Raghavan, C. (2010). Sex differences in intimate partner violence and the use of coercive control as a motivational factor for intimate partner violence. *Journal of Interpersonal Violence, 25*, 1836–1854.

Tanielian, T., & Jayco, L., (Eds.) (2008). *Invisible wounds of war: Psychological and cognitive injuries, their consequences, and services to assist recovery.* Santa Monica: RAND Corporation.

Tarasoff v. Regents of the University of California, 529 P. 2d 553 (1974), 551 P. 2d 334 (1976).

Taylor, G. (1992, March 2). Justice overlooked. *National Law Journal*, p. 43.

Taylor, S. E., Klein, L. C., Lewis, B. P., Gruenewald, T. L., Gurung, R. A. R., & Updegraff, J. A. (2000). Biobehavioral responses to stress in females: Tend-and-befriend, not fight-or-flight. *Psychological Review, 107*, 411–429.

Tehrani, J., & Mednick, S. (2000). Genetic factors and criminality. *Federal Probation, 64*, 24–28.

Tellegan, A., & Ben-Porath, Y. (2008). *MMPI-2-RF technical manual.* Minneapolis, MN: University of Minnesota Press.

Teller, J., Munetz, M., Gil, K., & Ritter, C. (2006). Crisis Intervention Team training for police officers responding to mental disturbance calls. *Psychiatric Services, 57*, 232–237.

Temcheff, C. E., Serbin, L. A., Martin-Storey, A. Stack, D. M., Hodgins, S., Ledingham, J., et al. (2008). Community and pathways from aggression in childhood to family violence in adulthood: A 30-year longitudinal study. *Journal of Family Violence, 23*(4), 231–242.

Tennessee v. Garner, 471 U.S. 1 (1985).

Teplin, L. A. (1984). The criminalization of the mentally ill: Speculation in search of data. In L. A. Teplin (Ed.), *Mental health and criminal justice* (pp. 63–85). Newbury Park, CA: Sage.

Teplin, L. (2000, July). Keeping the peace: Police discretion and mentally ill persons. *National Institute of Justice Journal*, 8–15.

Terman, L. M. (1917). A trial of mental and pedagogical tests in a civil service examination for policemen and firemen. *Journal of Applied Psychology, 1*, 17–29.

Terpstra, D. E., & Baker, D. D. (1987). A hierarchy of sexual harassment. *Journal of Psychology, 121*, 599–605.

Terpstra, D. E., & Baker, D. D. (1988). Outcomes of sexual harassment charges. *Academy of Management Journal, 31*, 185–194.

Terpstra, D. E., & Baker, D. D. (1992). Outcomes of federal court decisions on sexual harassment. *Academy of Management Journal, 35*, 181–190.

Terrell, J., & Weaver, C. (2008). Eyewitness testimony in civil litigation: Retention, suggestion, and misinformation in product identification. *North American Journal of Psychology, 10*, 323–346.

Thibaut, J., & Walker, L. (1975). *Procedural justice: A psychological analysis*. Hillsdale, NJ: Erlbaum.

Thomas, C. (1996, April 8). *Judging*. Invited address, School of Law, University of Kansas, Lawrence, KS.

Thompson, M., Osher, F., & Tomasini-Joshi, D. (2007). *Improving responses to people with mental illnesses: The essential elements of a mental health court*. New York: Council of State Governments Justice Center.

Thompson v. Oklahoma, 487 U.S. 815 (1988).

Thompson, W. C., Cowan, C. L., Ellsworth, P. C., & Harrington, J. C. (1984). Death penalty attitudes and conviction proneness: The translation of attitudes into verdicts. *Law and Human Behavior, 8*, 95–113.

Thornton, H. (1995). *Hung jury: The diary of a Menendez juror*. Philadelphia, PA: Temple University Press.

Tiede, L., Carp, R., & Manning, K. L (2010). Judicial attributes and sentencing-deviation cases: Do sex, race, and politics matter? *Justice System Journal, 31*, 249–272.

Tillbrook, C., Mumley, D., & Grisso, T. (2003). Avoiding expert opinions on the ultimate legal question: The case for integrity. *Journal of Forensic Psychology Practice, 3*, 77–87.

Tjaden, P., & Thoennes, N. (2000). *Full report of the prevalence, incidence, and consequences of violence against women*. Washington, DC: National Institute of Justice, Office of Justice Programs. (NCJ 13781).

Tjaden, P., & Thoennes, N. (2006). *Extent, nature, and consequences of rape victimization: Findings from the National Violence Against Women Survey*. Washington, DC: National Institute of Justice, Office of Justice Programs.

Toch, H. (1985). Warehouses for people? *The Annals of the American Academy of Political and Social Science, 478*, 58–72.

Tombaugh, T. (1997). *TOMM: Test of Memory Malingering manual*. Toronto, ON: Multi-Health Systems.

Tonry, M. (1996). *Sentencing matters*. New York: Oxford University Press.

Tonry, M. (2010). The social, psychological, and political causes of racial disparities in the American criminal justice system. *Crime and Justice, 39*, 273–312.

Tonry, M., & Melewski, M. (2008). The malign effects of drug and crime control policies on Black Americans. *Crime and Justice, 37*, 1–44.

Toobin, J. (1996, December 9). Asking for it. *New Yorker*, pp. 55–60.

Toot, J., Dunphy, G., Turner, M., & Ely, D. (2004). The SHR Y-chromosome increases testosterone and aggression, but decreases serotonin as compared to the WKY Y-chromosome in the rat model. *Behavioral Genetics, 34*, 515–524.

Torbet, P., Gable, R., Hurst, H., Montgomery, I., Szymanski, L., & Thomas, D. (1996). *State responses to serious and violent juvenile crime*. Washington, DC: U.S. Department of Justice, Office of Juvenile Justice and Delinquency Prevention.

Torres, A., Boccaccini, M., & Miller, H. (2006). Perceptions of the validity and utitility of criminal profiling among forensic psychologists and psychiatrists. *Professional Psychology: Research and Practice, 37*, 51–58.

Travis, J. (2007). Back-end sentencing: A practice in search of a rationale. *Social Research, 74*, 631–44.

Trivedi, S. B. (2011). Intellectual differences between violent and nonviolent juveniles: Utilizing the Wechsler Abbreviated Scale of Intelligence: A study of three ethnic groups. *Dissertation Abstracts International: Section B: The Sciences and Engineering, 71*(10-B), 6454.

Trop v. Dulles, 356 U.S. 86 (1958).

Trope, Y., & Liberman, N. (2003). Temporal construal. *Psychological Review, 110*, 403–421.

Trulson, C., Caudill, J., Belshaw, S., & DeLisi, M. (2011). A problem of fit: Extreme delinquents, blended sentencing, and the determinants of continued adult sanctions. *Criminal Justic Policy Review, 22*, 263–284.

Trulson, C., Haerle, D., DeLisi, M., & Marquart, J. (2011). Blended sentencing, early release, and recidivism of violent institutionalized delinquents. *Prison Journal, 92*, 255–278.

Trupin, E., & Richards, H. (2003). Seattle's mental health courts: Early indicators of effectiveness. *International Journal of Law & Psychiatry, 26*, 33–53.

Tsushima, W. T., Foote, R., Merrill, T. S., & Lehrke, S. A. (1996). How independent are independent psychological examinations? A workers' compensation dilemma. *Professional Psychology: Research and Practice, 27*, 626–628.

Tuohy, A. P., Wrennall, M. J., McQueen, R. A., & Stradling, S. G. (1993). Effect of socialization factors on decisions to prosecute: The organizational adaptation of Scottish police recruits. *Law and Human Behavior, 17*, 167–182.

Turkheimer, E., & Parry, C. D. H. (1992). Why the gap? Practice and policy in civil commitment hearings. *American Psychologist, 47*, 646–655.

Turner, S., Greenwood, P., Fain, T., & Deschenes, E. (1999). Perceptions of drug court: How offenders view ease of program completion, strengths and weaknesses, and the impact on their lives. *National Drug Court Institute Review, 2,* 61–85.

Tversky, A., & Kahneman, D. (1974). Judgment under uncertainty: Heuristics and biases. *Science, 185,* 1124–1131.

Tyler, T., & Huo, Y. (2002). *Trust in the law: Encouraging public cooperation with the police and court.* New York: Russell Sage Foundation.

Tyler, T., Sherman, L., Strang, H., Barnes, G., & Woods, D. (2007). Reintegrative shaming, procedural justice, and recidivism: The engagement of offenders' psychological mechanisms in the Canberra RISE drinking-and-driving experiment. *Law and Society Review, 41,* 553–586.

Uchida, C., & Brooks, L. (1988). *Violence against the police: Assaults on Baltimore County Police, 1984–86, final report.* Washington, DC: U.S. Department of Justice.

Ulmer, J., Eisenstein, J., & Johnson, B. (2010). Trial penalties in federal sentencing: Extra-guidelines factors and district variation. *Justice Quarterly, 27,* 560–592.

Umbreit, M., Vos, G., Coates, R., & Lightfoot, E. (2005). Restorative justice in the 21st century: A social movement full of opportunities and pitfalls. *Marquette Law Review, 89,* 251–304.

United States Sentencing Commission. (2011). *Report to Congress: Mandatory minimum penalties in the federal criminal justice system.* Retrieved January 8, 2012, from http://www.ussc.gov/Legislative_and_Public_ Affairs/Congressional_Testimony_and_Reports/ Mandatory_Minimum_Penalties/20111031_RtC_ Mandatory_Minimum.cfm

United States v. Angelos, 345 F. Supp. 2d 1227 (2004).

United States v. Booker, 125 S. Ct. 735 (2005).

United States v. Lea, 249 F. 3d 632 (2001).

United States v. McVeigh, 918 F. Supp. 1467 (1996).

United States v. Salerno, 481 U.S. 739 (1987).

United States v. Santiago-Martinez, 94–10350 (9th Cir. 1995).

United States v. Scheffer, 118 S. Ct. 1261 (1998).

United States v. Telfaire, 469 F. 2d 552 (1972).

U.S. Department of Justice. (1999). *Eyewitness evidence: A guide for law enforcement.* Washington, DC: Author.

U.S. Public Health Service. (1999). *Mental health: A report of the Surgeon General.* Rockville, MD: U.S. Department of Health and Human Services, National Institutes of Health, National Institute of Mental Health.

Valentine, T., Pickering, A., & Darling, S. (2003). Characteristics of eyewitness identification that predict the outcome of real lineups. *Applied Cognitive Psychology, 17,* 969–993.

VanDuyn, A. L. (1999). The scarlet letter branding: A constitutional analysis of community notification provisions in sex offender statues. *Drake Law Review, 47,* 635–659.

Varela, J. G., Scogin, F. R., & Vipperman, R. K. (1999). Development and preliminary validation of a semi-structured interview for the screening of law enforcement candidates. *Behavioral Sciences & the Law, 17,* 467–481.

Vecchi, G. (2009). Conflict and crisis communication: A methodology for influencing and persuading behavioral change. *Annals of the American Psychotherapy Association, 12,* 34–42.

Vecchi, G., Van Hasselt, V., & Romano, S. (2005). Crisis (hostage) negotiation: Current strategies and issues in high-risk conflict resolution. *Aggression and Violent Behavior, 10,* 533–551.

Verlinden, S., Hersen, M., & Thomas, J. (2000). Risk factors in school shootings. *Clinical Psychology Review, 20,* 3–56.

Victor, T. L., & Abeles, N. (2004). Coaching clients to take psychological and neuropsychological tests: A clash of ethical obligations. *Practice Issues in Forensic Psychology, 35,* 373–379.

Vidmar, N. (1998). The performance of the American civil jury: An empirical perspective. *Arizona Law Review, 40,* 849–899.

Vidmar, N. (2002). Case studies of pre- and midtrial prejudice in criminal and civil litigation. *Law and Human Behavior, 26,* 73–106.

Vidmar, N. (2005). Expert evidence, the adversary system, and the jury. *American Journal of Public Health, 95,* S137–S143.

Vidmar, N. (2011). The psychology of trial judging. *Current Directions in Psychological Science, 20,* 58–62.

Vidmar, N., & Diamond, S. (2001). Juries and expert evidence. *Brooklyn Law Review, 66,* 1121–1180.

Vidmar, N., & Hans, V. P. (2007). *American juries: The verdict.* Amherst, NY: Prometheus.

Vidmar, N., & Wolfe, M. (2009). Punitive damages. *Annual Review of Law and Social Sciences, 5,* 179–199.

Viljoen, J., Klaver, J., & Roesch, R. (2005). Legal decisions of preadolescent and adolescent defendants: Predictors of confessions, pleas, communication with attorneys, and appeals. *Law and Human Behavior, 29,* 253–277.

Viljoen, J. L., Roesch, R., Ogloff, J. R. P., & Zapf, P. A. (2003). The role of Canadian psychologists in conducting fitness and criminal responsibility evaluations. *Canadian Psychology, 44,* 369–381.

Viljoen, J., Wingrove, T., & Ryba, N. (2008). Adjudicative competence evaluations of juvenile and adult defendants: Judges' views regarding essential components of competence reports. *The International Journal of Forensic Mental Health, 7,* 107–119.

Vinson, K. V., Costanzo, M. A., & Berger, D. E. (2008). Predictors of verdict and punitive damages in high-stakes civil litigation. *Behavioral Sciences & the Law, 26,* 167–186.

Violanti, J. M., & Aron, F. (1994). Ranking police stressors. *Psychological Reports, 75,* 824–826.

Vitacco, M. J., Rogers, R. & Gabel, J. (2009). An investigation of the ECST-R in male pretrial patients: Evaluating the effects of feigning on competency evaluations. *Assessment, 16,* 249–257.

Vitale, J. E., & Newman, J. P. (2001). Using the Psychopathy Checklist—Revised with female samples: Reliability, validity, and implications for clinical utility. *Clinical Psychology: Science & Practice, 8,* 117–132.

Vrij, A., Granhag, P., & Porter, S. (2010). Pitfalls and opportunities in nonverbal and verbal lie detection. *Psychological Science in the Public Interest, 11,* 89–121.

Vrij, A., Leal, S., Granhag, P. A., Mann, S., Fisher, R. P., Hillman, J., & Spery, K. (2009). Outsmarting the liars: The benefit of asking unanticipated questions. *Law and Human Behavior, 33,* 159–166.

Vrij, A., Leal, S., Mann, S., & Granhag, P. (2011). A comparison between lying about intentions and past activities: Verbal cues and detection accuracy. *Applied Cognitive Psychology, 25,* 212–218.

Vrij, A., Mann, S., Fisher, R., Leal, S., Milne, B., & Bull, R. (2008). Increasing cognitive load to facilitate lie detection: The benefit of recalling an event in reverse order. *Law and Human Behavior, 32,* 253–265.

Vasquez, B., Maddan, S., & Walker, J. (2008). The influence of sex offender registration and notification laws in the United States: A time-series analysis. *Crime and Delinquency, 54,* 175–192.

Wade, K., Garry, M., Read, J., & Lindsay, D. (2002). A picture is worth a thousand lies: Using false photographs to create false childhood memories. *Psychonomic Bulletin & Review, 9,* 597–603.

Wainwright v. Witt, 469 U.S. 412 (1985).

Walker, L. E. (1979). *The battered woman.* New York: Harper & Row.

Walker, L. E. (2009). *The battered woman syndrome* (3rd ed.). New York: Springer.

Walker, L., La Tour, S., Lind, E. A., & Thibaut, J. (1974). Reactions of participants and observers to modes of adjudication. *Journal of Applied Social Psychology, 4,* 295–310.

Wallace, D., & Kassin, S. (2012). Harmless error analysis: How do judges respond to confession errors? *Law and Human Behavior, 36,* 151–157.

Wallerstein, J., & Blakeslee, S. (2003). *What about the kids? Raising your children before, during, and after divorce.* New York: Hyperion.

Wallerstein, J., Corbin, S., & Lewis, J. (1988). Children of divorce: A ten-year study. In Hetherington, M. & Arasteh, J. (Eds.), *Impact of divorce, single parenting, and stepparenting on children.* (pp. 197–214). Hillsdale, NJ: Erlbaum.

Wallerstein, J., & Kelly, J. (1980). *Surviving the breakup:* New York: Basic Books.

Walmsley, R. (2009). *World prison population list* (8th ed.). London: International Centre for Prison Studies.

Walsh, B. (2012). *Oil spill: Why the BP settlement is just the beginning of the end.* Retrieved April 3, 2012, from http://ecocentric.blogs.time.com/2012/03/03/oil-spill-why-the-bp-settlement-is-just-the-beginning-of-the-end/

Walster, E. (1966). Assignment of responsibility for an accident. *Journal of Personality and Social Psychology, 3,* 73–79.

Walters, G. (2002). The Psychological Inventory of Criminal Thinking Styles (PICTS): A review and meta-analysis. *Assessment, 9,* 278–291.

Waltz, J., Babcock, J. C., Jacobson, N. S., & Gottman, J. M. (2000). Testing a typology of batterers. *Journal of Consulting and Clinical Psychology, 68,* 658–669.

Wang, J., Iannotti, R., Luk, J., & Nansel, T. (2010). Co-occurrence of victimization from five subtypes of bullying: Physical, verbal, social exclusion, spreading rumors, and cyber. *Journal of Pediatric Psychology, 35,* 1103–1112.

Ward, S. (2007). Pulse of the legal profession. *American Bar Association Journal.* Retrieved October 11, 2008, from http://www.abajournal.com/magazine/article/pulse_of_the_legal_profession/

Warmelink, L., Vrij, A., Mann, S., Leal, S., Forrester, D., & Fisher, R. P. (2011). Thermal imaging as a lie detection tool at airports. *Law and Human Behavior, 35,* 40–48.

Warner, W. J. (2005, April). Polygraph testing: A utilitarian tool. *FBI Law Enforcement Bulletin, 74,* 4.

Warren, E. (1977). *The memoirs of Earl Warren.* Garden City, NY: Doubleday.

Warren, P., Tomaskovic-Devey, D., Smith, W., Zingraff, M., & Mason, M. (2006). Driving while Black: Bias processes and racial disparity in police stops. *Criminology: An Interdisciplinary Journal, 44,* 709–738.

Wasco, S. M. (2004). An ecological study of repeated sexual victimization among college women. *Dissertation Abstracts International: Section B: The Sciences and Engineering, 65*(3-B), 1565.

Waterman, A., Blades, M., & Spencer, C. (2001). Interviewing children and adults: The effect of question format on the tendency to speculate. *Applied Cognitive Psychology, 15,* 521–531.

Watson, A., Hanrahan, P., Luchins, D., & Lurigio, A. (2001). Mental health courts and the complex issues of mentally ill offenders. *Psychiatric Services*, *52*, 477–481.

Watson, A., Ottati, V., Morabito, M., Draine, J., Kerr, A., & Angell, B. (2010). Outcomes of police contacts with persons with mental illness: The impact of CIT. *Administration and Policy in Mental Health and Mental Health Services Research*, *37*, 302–317.

Watson, P. (1996). The search for justice—A case for reform in the civil justice system in Britain. *ILSA Journal of International and Comparative Law*, *2*, 453.

Webster, C. D., Douglas, K. S., Eaves, D., & Hart, S. D. (1997). *HCR-20: Assessing risk for violence* (Version 2). Vancouver: Mental Health, Law, and Policy Institute (Simon Fraser University).

Weeks v. Angelone, 120 S. Ct. 1290 (2000).

Wegner, D. M. (1994). Ironic processes of mental control. *Psychological Review*, *101*, 34–52.

Weinberger, L., Sreenivasan, S., Garrick, T., & Osran, H. (2005). The impact of surgical castration on sexual recidivism risk among sexually violent predatory offenders. *Journal of the American Academy of Psychiatry and the Law*, *33*, 16–36.

Weir, J. A., & Wrightsman, L. S. (1990). The determinants of mock jurors' verdicts in a rape case. *Journal of Applied Social Psychology*, *20*, 901–919.

Weiser, B. (2011, August 24). In New Jersey, rules are changed on witness IDs. *New York Times*. Retrieved May 22, 2012, from http://www.nytimes.com/2011/08/25/nyregion/in-new-jersey-rules-changed-on-witness-ids.html

Weiss, P., Hitchcock, J., Weiss, W., Rostow, C., & Davis, R. (2008). The Personality Assessment Inventory Borderline, Drug, and Alcohol Scales as predictors of overall performance in police officers: A series of exploratory analyses. *Policing & Society*, *18*, 301–310.

Weiss, W., Davis, R., Rostow, C., & Kinsman, S. (2003). The MMPI-2 L scale as a tool in police selection. *Journal of Police and Criminal Psychology*, *18*, 57–60.

Weissman, H. N. (1991). Child custody evaluations: Fair and unfair professional practices. *Behavioral Sciences & the Law*, *9*, 469–476.

Weitzer, R., & Tuch, S. A. (1999). Race, class, and perceptions of discrimination by the police. *Crime & Delinquency*, *45*, 494–507.

Wells, G. (1978). Applied eyewitness testimony research: System variables and estimator variables. *Journal of Personality and Social Psychology*, *36*, 1546–1557.

Wells, G. L. (1993). What do we know about eyewitness identification? *American Psychologist*, *48*, 553–571.

Wells, G., & Luus, C. (1990). Police lineups as experiments: Social methodology as a framework for properly conducted lineups. *Personality and Social Psychology Bulletin*, *16*, 106–117.

Wells, G., & Quinlivan, D. (2009). Suggestive eyewitness identification procedures and the Supreme Court's reliability test in light of eyewitness science: 30 years later. *Law and Human Behavior*, *33*, 1–24.

Wells, G. L., Small, M., Penrod, S., Malpass, R. S., Fulero, S. M., & Brimacombe, C. A. E. (1998). Eyewitness identification procedures: Recommendations for lineups and photospreads. *Law and Human Behavior*, *22*, 603–647.

Wells, G., Memon, A., & Penrod, S. (2006). Eyewitness evidence: Improving its probative value. *Psychological Science in the Public Interest*, *7*, 45–75.

Wells, G., Steblay, N., & Dysart, J. (2011). A test of the simultaneous vs. sequential lineup methods. *An Initial Report of the AJS National Eyewitness Identification Field Studies*. Des Moines, IA: American Judicature Society.

Wells, G., Wrightsman, L., & Miene, P. (1985). The timing of the defense opening statement: Don't wait until the evidence is in. *Journal of Applied Social Psychology*, *15*, 758–772.

Welsh, W. (2007). A multisite evaluation of prison-based therapeutic community drug treatment. *Criminal Justice and Behavior*, *34*, 1481–1498.

Wexler, D. B. (1992). Putting mental health into mental health law: Therapeutic jurisprudence. *Law and Human Behavior*, *16*, 27–38.

Wexler, D., & Winick, B. (Eds.). (1996). *Law in a therapeutic key: Developments in therapeutic jurisprudence*. Durham, NC: Carolina Academic Press.

Whalen v. United States, 346 F. 2d 812 (1965).

White, J. W., & Sorenson, S. B. (1992). A sociocultural view of sexual assault: From discrepancy to diversity. *Journal of Social Issues*, *48*, 187–195.

Whittemore, K. E., & Ogloff, J. R. P. (1995). Factors that influence jury decision making: Disposition instructions and mental state at the time of the trial. *Law and Human Behavior*, *19*, 283–303.

Whren et al. v. United States, 517 U.S. 806 (1996).

Widom, C. S. (1989). Child abuse, neglect, and adult behavior: Research design and findings on criminality, violence, and child abuse. *American Journal of Orthopsychiatry*, *59*, 355–367.

Widom, C. S. (1992). *The cycle of violence: National Institute of Justice Research in brief*. Washington, DC: U.S. Department of Justice.

Widom, C., Schuck, A., & White, H. (2006). An examination of pathways from childhood victimization to violence: The role of early aggression and problematic alcohol use. *Violence and Victims*, *21*, 675–690.

Wiener, R. (2011). Trial consulting and discrimination law: An untapped opportunity. In R. Wiener & B. Bornstein (Eds.), *Handbook of trial consulting* (pp. 245–280). New York: Springer.

Wiener, R., Arnot, L., Winter, R., & Redmond, B. (2006). Generic prejudice in the law: Sexual assault and homicide. *Basic and Applied Social Psychology, 28,* 145–155.

Wiener, R., & Bornstein, B. (2011). *Handbook of trial consulting.* New York: Springer.

Wiener, R., Bornstein, B., & Voss, A. (2006). Emotion and the law: A framework for inquiry. *Law and Human Behavior, 30,* 231–248.

Wiener, R., & Gutek, B. (1999). Advances in sexual harassment research, theory, and policy. *Psychology, Public Policy, and Law, 5,* 507–518.

Wiener, R., Hurt, L., Russell, B., Mannen, K., & Gasper, C. (1997). Perceptions of sexual harassment: The effects of gender, legal standard, and ambivalent sexism. *Law and Human Behavior, 21,* 71–94.

Wiener, R., Rogers, M., Winter, R., Hurt, L., Hackney, A., Kadela, K., et al. (2004). Guided jury discretion in capital murder cases: The role of declarative and procedural knowledge. *Psychology, Public Policy, and Law, 10,* 516–576.

Wiener, R., Winick, B., Georges, L., & Castro, A. (2010). A testable theory of problem-solving courts: Avoiding past empirical and legal failures. *International Journal of Law and Psychiatry, 33,* 417–427.

Wiggins, E. (2006). The courtroom of the future is here: Introduction of emerging technologies in the legal system. *Law & Policy, 28,* 182–191.

Wikstrom, P., Ceccato, V., Hardie, B., & Treiber, K. (2010). Activity fields and the dynamics of crime: Advancing knowledge about the role of the environment in crime causation. *Journal of Quantitative Criminology, 26,* 55–87.

Wilcock, R., Bull, R., & Vrij, A. (2007). Are old witnesses always poorer witnesses? Identification accuracy, context reinstatement, own-age bias. *Psychology, Crime, and Law, 13,* 305–316.

Wilkinson, R. (2001). Offender reentry: A storm overdue. *Corrections Management Quarterly, 5,* 46–51.

Will, G. (1984, January 22). Fitting laws to dynamic society likened to trousers on 10-year-old. *Lawrence Journal-World,* p. 6.

Williams, C. W., Lees-Haley, P. R., & Djanogly, S. E. (1999). Clinical scrutiny of litigants' self-reports. *Professional Psychology: Research and Practice, 30,* 361–367.

Williams, L. M. (1994). Recall of childhood trauma: A prospective study of women's memories of child sexual abuse. *Journal of Consulting and Clinical Psychology, 62,* 1167–1176.

Williams, W., & Miller, K. S. (1981). The processing and disposition of incompetent mentally ill offenders. *Law and Human Behavior, 5,* 245–261.

Wilson, J. Q. (1975). *Thinking about crime.* New York: Basic Books.

Wilson, J. Q., & Herrnstein, R. (1985). *Crime and human nature.* New York: Simon & Schuster.

Wilson, T. (2002). *Strangers to ourselves: Discovering the adaptive unconscious.* Cambridge, MA: Harvard University Press.

Wilson, A. E., Calhoun, K. S., & Bernat, J. A. (1999). Risk recognition and trauma-related symptoms among sexually revictimized women. *Journal of Consulting and Clinical Psychology, 67,* 705–710.

Wilson, D., Mitchell, O., & Mackenzie, D. (2006). A systematic review of drug court effects on recidivism. *Journal of Experimental Criminology, 2,* 459–487.

Wingrove, T., Korpas, A., & Belli, R. (2011). The use of survey research in trial consulting. In R. Wiener & B. Bornstein (Eds.), *Handbook of trial consulting* (pp. 93–120). New York: Springer.

Winick, B. (1996). Incompetency to proceed in the criminal process: Past, present, and future. In B. D. Sales & D. W. Shulman (Eds.), *Law, mental health, and mental disorder* (pp. 310–340). Pacific Grove, CA: Brooks/Cole.

Winick, B., Wiener, R., Castro, A., Emmert, A., & Georges, L. (2010). Dealing with mentally ill domestic violence perpetrators: A therapeutic jurisprudence judicial model. *International Journal of Law and Psychiatry 33,* 428–439.

Winslade, W. J., & Ross, J. W. (1983). *The insanity plea.* New York: Scribners.

Wistrich, A., Guthrie, C., & Rachlinski, J. (2005). Can judges ignore inadmissible information? The difficulty of deliberately disregarding. *University of Pennsylvania Law Review, 153,* 1251–1345.

Witherspoon v. Illinois, 391 U.S. 510 (1968).

Witt, P., & Barone, N. (2004). Assessing sex offender risk: New Jersey's methods. *Federal Sentencing Reporter, 16,* 170.

Wogalter, M., Malpass, R., & McQuiston, D. (2004). A national survey of U.S. police on preparation and conduction of identification lineups. *Psychology, Crime, and Law, 10,* 69–82.

Wolf, S. M. (2009). A study of the differences in trauma related symptoms in adult female rape victims across levels of support systems. *Dissertation Abstracts International: Section B: The Sciences and Engineering, 69*(12-B), 7828.

Wolff, N., Fabrikant, N., & Belenko, S. (2011). Mental health courts and their selection processes: Modeling variation for consistency. *Law and Human Behavior, 35,* 402–412.

Women in Prison Project. (2009). New York, NY: Correctional Association of New York. Retrieved March 20, 2010, from http://www.correctionalassociation. org/publications/download/wipp/factsheets/ Wome_in_Prison_Fact_Sheet_2009_FINAL.pdf

Wood, J., Schreiber, N., Martinez, Y., McLaurin, K., Strok, R., Velarde, L., et al. (1998, March). *Child interviewing techniques in the McMartin Preschool and Kelly Michaels cases: A quantitative comparison.* Paper presented at the conference of the American Psychology Law Society, Redondo Beach, CA.

Woodrell, D. (1996). *Give us a kiss.* New York: Henry Holt.

Woodworth, M., & Porter, S. (2000). Historical foundations and current applications of criminal profiling in violent crime investigations. *Expert Evidence, 7,* 241–264.

Worden, A., & Carlson, B. (2005). Attitudes and beliefs about domestic violence: Results of a public opinion survey. *Journal of Interpersonal Violence, 20,* 1219–1243.

Wordsworth, A. (2005, January 7). Child-killer unfairly convicted, court rules: Expert witness misled jury in Andrea Yates trial. *National Post, Toronto Edition,* p. A13.

Worsnop, R. L. (1993, February 5). Community policing. *CQ Researcher,* p. 97.

Wrightsman, L. (2006). *The psychology of the Supreme Court.* New York: Oxford University Press.

Wrightsman, L. (2010). The Supreme Court on Miranda rights and interrogations: The past, the present, and the future. In G. D. Lassiter & C. Meissner (Eds.), *Police interrogations and false confessions* (pp. 161–178). Washington, DC: American Psychological Association.

Wrightsman, L., & Kassin, S. (1993). *Confessions in the courtroom.* Thousand Oaks, CA: Sage.

Wyatt, G. E., Guthrie, D., & Notgrass, C. M. (1992). Differential effects of women's child sexual abuse and subsequent sexual revictimization. *Journal of Consulting and Clinical Psychology, 60,* 167–173.

www.abanet.org. (2005).

www.adversity.net. (2002).

www.floridacit.org. (2008, January). *Crisis intervention— affects everyone.* Retrieved http://www.floridacit.org/ Testimonials/Article%20FCSO%20.%20Crisis% 20Intervention.pdf

www.nalp.org. (2005).

www.pbs.org (2007). *Profiles five stories.* Retrieved from www. wgbh/pages/frontline/when kids get life/five/ind/

Yochelson, S., & Samenow, S. E. (1976). *The criminal personality: A profile for change* (Vol. 1). New York: Aronson.

York, E., & Cornwell, B. (2006). Status on trial: Social characteristics and influence in the jury room. *Social Forces, 85,* 455–477.

Youngjohn, J. (1995). Confirmed attorney coaching prior to neuropsychological evaluation. *Assessment, 2,* 279–283.

Zamble, E. (1992). Behavior and adaptation in long-term prison inmates. *Criminal Justice and Behavior, 19,* 409–425.

Zapf, P., & Roesch, R. (1997). Assessing fitness to stand trial: Institution-based evaluations and brief screening interview. *Canadian Journal of Community Mental Health, 16,* 53–66.

Zapf. P., & Roesch, R. (1998). Fitness to stand trial: Characteristics of remands since the 1992 Criminal Code amendments. *Canadian Journal of Psychiatry, 43,* 287–293.

Zapf, P., & Roesch, R. (2009). *Evaluation of competence to stand trial.* New York: Oxford University Press.

Zezima, K., & Carey, B. (2009, September 10). Ex-priest challenges abuse conviction on repressed memory. *New York Times.* Retrieved May 28, 2012, from http://www.nytimes.com/2009/09/11/us/11priest. html?ref=paulrshanley

Zhang, S., Roberts, R., & Callanan, V. (2006). Preventing parolees from returning to prison through community-based reintegration. *Crime & Delinquency, 52,* 551–571.

Zhao, J., Lovrich, N., & Thurman, Q. (1999). The status of community policing in American cities: Facilitators and impediments revisited. *Policing: An International Journal of Police Strategies and Management, 22,* 74–92.

Zill, N., Morrison, D., & Coiro, M. (1993). Long-term effects of parental divorce on parent-child relationship, adjustment, and achievement in young adulthood. *Journal of Family Psychology, 7,* 91–103.

Zimring, F., Fagan, J., & Johnson, D. (2010). Executions, deterrence, and homicide: A tale of two cities. *Journal of Empirical Legal Studies, 7,* 1–29.

Zinger, I., & Forth, A. E. (1998). Psychopathy and Canadian criminal proceedings: The potential for human rights abuses. *Canadian Journal of Criminology, 40,* 237–277.

Zukov, I., Ptacek, R., & Fischer, S. (2008). EEG abnormalities in different types of criminal behavior. *Activitas Nervosa Superior, 50,* 110–113.

Zulawski, D. E., & Wicklander, D. E. (2001). *Practical aspects of interview and interrogation.* Boca Raton, FL: CRC Press.

Name Index

C

Cacioppo, J. T., 282
Caetano, R., 80
Cahill, R. E., 8
Caillouet, B., 277
Caldwell, M., 354
Calhoun, K., 135
Calhoun, K. S., 136
California Civil Jury Instructions 100, 308
Callahan, L., 229, 230, 231
Callahan, L. A., 232
Callanan, V., 368, 369
Camerer, C., 187
Camerer, C. F., 160
Camp, J., 368
Camp, S., 366
Campbell, G., 324
Campbell, M. A., 330
Campbell, R., 136
Canter, D., 153
Canter, D. V., 153
Capaldi, D., 79
Caperton v. A. T. Massey Coal, 36
Carey, B., 116
Carlsmith, K., 30, 322, 323
Carlson, B., 128
Carlson, C., 104
Carlson, K., 313
Carlucci, M., 106
Carnevale, P., 188
Carp, R., 38, 329
Carpenter, B. N., 259
Carr, P. L., 139
Carroll, J. S., 283, 289
Carter, T., 36, 208, 211
Cascardi, M., 31
Case, B., 77, 78, 207, 362
Casey, P., 205, 208
Caspi, A., 54, 79, 80, 127, 128
Castelli, P., 112
Castro, A., 205, 208, 211
Caudill, J., 330
Cauffman, E., 48, 66, 225, 330
Ceccato, V., 64
Ceci, S., 110, 298, 299
Ceci, S. J., 114, 342
Cecil, J., 20
Center for Court Innovation, 209, 210
Center for Effective Public Policy, 368
Center on Juvenile and Criminal
    Justice, 8
Central Intelligence Agency (CIA), 155
Cernkovich, S. A., 66
Chajewski, M., 334
Chamberlain, P., 351, 352
Champagne, A., 270, 295, 303
Chan, A. S., 234
Chan, J., 99
Chang, M., 272
Chapleau, M., 12
Chaplin, W. F., 277
Charles, D. R., 127

Charman, S., 106
Chassin, L., 330
Chaudoir, S. R., 132
Chen, M. K., 366
Chibnall, J. T., 72, 74, 75
Chilcoat, H. D., 127
Choi, A., 79, 128
Chopra, S., 335
Christensen, E., 368
Christiansen, K. O., 55
Christie, R., 280
Christy, A., 360
Cirincione, C., 229, 230, 231
Clark, C. R., 233
Clark, D. M., 126
Clark, J., 58, 277
Clark, S., 102, 103, 104, 105
Claussen, N., 72
Clavet, G. J., 302
Clayton, L., 281, 298
Cleary, H., 163
Clemmer, D., 366
Clermont, K., 271
Cling, A., 105, 106
Clingempeel, W., 350
Clingempeel, W. G., 257
Cloninger, C., 53, 56
Cloud, J., 47
Clow, K., 96
Cloward, R. A., 52
CNN, 71
Coates, R., 325
Coccaro, E. F., 55
Cochran, C. C., 141
Cochrane, R., 73
Cocozza, J., 360
Cocozza, J. J., 219
Cohen, C. A., 255
Cohen, E., 127
Cohen, I. M., 59
Cohen, M. I., 230, 232
Cohen, T., 175, 301
Cohn, N. B., 219
Coiro, M., 258
Colangelo, J., 114
Colgan, B., 166, 171
Colletti, P., 54
Collins, R. L., 127
Collinsworth, L. L., 142
Colorado Department of Corrections, 20
Colwell, L., 169
Combs, S., 324
Committee on Ethical Guidelines for
    Forensic Psychologists, 214
Compton, M., 78, 202, 203
Conant, L. L., 160
Condie, L. O., 261
Cone, L., 350
Conger, R., 59
Conyers, J., 9
Cooke, D., 182
Cooper v. Oklahoma, 221
Cooper, H., 132

Cooper, J., 245
Cooper, V., 221
Coppola, K., 253
Copson, G., 148
Corbin, S., 258
Cormier, C., 355
Corneille, O., 188
Cornell, C. P., 80
Cornell, D., 47, 48, 58
Cornwell, B., 281
Corrado, R. R., 59
Cortoni, F., 131
Cosden, M., 360
Costa, P., 56
Costanzo, M., 171, 315
Costanzo, M. A., 281, 283
Cottle, C., 353
Cougle, J., 126
Courtois, C. A., 114
Couture, H., 207
Cowan, C. L., 340
Cowell, A., 204
Cox, M., 258
Cox, R., 258
Coy v. Iowa, 112
Craig, I., 54
Cressey, D. R., 60
Crocker, C., 276
Crosby, R., 251
Crouch, J., 350
*Cruzan v. Director, Missouri Department of
    Health*, 253
Cuffe, S. P., 127
Culhane, C. E., 276
Culhane, S., 302
Cullen, F. T., 52, 63
Cunningham, M., 236, 338
Cunningham, P. B., 349, 350
Curnoe, S., 332
Curry, T., 328, 329
Curtis, K., 332
Curtiss, G., 248
Cutler, B., 19, 103, 105, 107, 281
Cutler, B. L., 282

D

D'Agostino, C., 87
D'Amora, D., 333
D'Augelli, A., 121
D'Emilio, J., 133
D'Mello, M., 110
Daftary-Kapur, T., 286, 290, 291, 303
Daggett, D., 221
Dahir, V., 242, 245
Daicoff, S., 42
Daly, K., 328
Damasio, A. R., 54
Damasio, H., 54
Danks, J., 253
Dann, B., 306
Dansky, B. S., 126

Subject Index

Deinstitutionalization, 207, 261
Deliberation room, 191
Deliberations, 305, 313–314
Deliberative process decision-making, 38
Delinquency and Opportunity (Ohlin and Cloward), 52
Delinquents, 330
D'Emic, Matthew, 206
Demographic characteristics, 123
Denver Post, 290
Department of Homeland Security, 103
Department of Justice, 361
Department of Motor Vehicles, 178
Department of Parole and Probation, 358
Depo-Provera, 138
Dershowitz, Alan, 144
De Salvo, Albert, 148
Determinate sentencing, 326
Deterrence, 321, 322–323
  general, 321
  individual, 321
  public preferences for, 322–325
De Tocqueville, Alexis, 296
Devine, Dennis, 298
Dexter (television series), 50
Dexter in the Dark, 50
Diagnostic and Statistical Manual-IV, 334
Diagnostic cues, 155
Diagnostic testimony, 233
Diallo, Amadou, 89
Diamond, Shari, 273, 302
Dickerson v. United States, 163
Differential association approach, 60
Differential association reinforcement theory, 60
Differential opportunity, 52
Dillon, Terrence, 194
Diminished capacity, 234–235
Disclosure, 140
Discovery, 177, 190
Discretion
  defined, 9
  Parole board's, 11
  value of, 10–12
Discrimination
  gender, 141, 143
  peremptory challenges, 278–279
  racial, 121
  religious, 121, 247
"Disease of the mind," 227
Dispositional attributions, 120
Dispositional phase, 330
Dissociation, 113
Distributive justice, 31
District Attorney's Office for Third Judicial District v. Osborne, 94, 337
Diversion, 33, 347
Divorce
  children, effects on, 258–260
  mediation, 260
  protective factors, 258
  risk factors, 258

Dixon, Sheila, 307
Dizygotic twins, 53
DNA, 303
  exoneration, 166
  exoneration based on, 95, 100, 337–338
  post conviction testing, 337
Dobson, James, 57
Doe, John, 247
Dog the Bounty Hunter (TV program), 179
Domestic homicide, 130. *See also* Domestic violence
Domestic violence
  borderline personality disorder, 129
  causes of, 128–129
  cycle of violence, 129
  exaggerated beliefs, 128
  homicide, 130
  media, 60–61
  myths, 79–80, 128
  police intervention, 80–81
  police officers and, 79
  self-defense, 130–131, 138
  Spouse Assault Replication Program, 81
  statistics, 127–128
Domestic violence courts, 208
Double-blind testing procedures, 105
Drew, Lori, 122
Drug abuse. *See* Substance abuse
Drug abuse resistance education (D.A.R.E.) program, 348
Drug courts, 206–207, 358–359
  development, reasons for, 206, 359
  diversion in, 359
  effectiveness study, 359
  substance abuse treatment, 359
  success rate, 206–207
Drug Enforcement Agency (DEA), 155
Drug smugglers, 323
DSM-IV, 342
Dual-process theory of attitude change, 297
Due process
  incompetence, 223
  model, 8, 334
  officers, 87
Duncan v. Louisiana, 295
Dupree, Cornelius, 95, 96
Durkheim, Emile, 52
Dusky standard, 216, 219
Dusky v. United States, 216
Dutton, Donald, 129
Duty, 246. *See also* Tort law
Dysfunctional family, 58

E

"Ear-marking," 323
Ebbinghaus, Hermann, 98
Eberhardt, Jennifer, 339
Ecological validity, 100
Economic recession, 120
ECST-R. *See* Evaluation of Competence to Stand Trial–Revised

Eddings v. Oklahoma, 235
Education, lawyers, 39, 42
Edwards, John, 186
EEG. *See* Electroencephalogram
Eighth Amendment
  community alternatives to standard prosecution and, 201–202
  competence for death penalty, 235–236
  excessive bail, 179
  protection against "cruel and unusual punishment," 87
Eisaman, Ronald, 254
Eisele, Thomas G., 201
Eisenberg, Theodore, 271
Electroencephalogram (EEG), 54, 161
Ellis, Leslie, 273
Emergency detention, 262
Emergency services
  mental health disorders (individuals) and, 202–203
Encoding memory, 97–98
Equality *vs.* discretion, 8–12
Equal Justice Initiative, 331
Equal protection rights, 277
Estimator variable, 100
Ethical Principles of Psychologists and Code of Conduct (EPPCC), 17
Ethnic bias, 272
Ethnicity in child custody, 259
Euthanasia
  defined, 28
  jury emotional bias, 307
  mercy killing, 27–28
Evaluation apprehension, 287
Evaluation of Competence to Stand Trial–Revised (ECST-R), 220
Evening Reporting Center, 349
Evers, Darrell, 308
Evers, Medgar, 307–308
Eversole, Sandy, 325
Evidence
  assessing damage through, 301–302
  electronic and digital, 193
  exculpatory, 177
  eyewitness, 102
  full disclosure of, 178
  grand jury, 176
  nullification, 307
  preponderance of, 305
  prior record, 299
  propensity, 299–300
  sex offenders, 300
Evidence ploys, 170
Evidentiary strength, 298
Evolutionary theory, 133
Ewing v. California, 10, 328
Exaggerating deficits, 220
Excludables, 340
Exculpatory evidence, 177
Executive function, 58
Exoneration
  compensation, 95

Redirect questioning, 190
Reentry
 adult, 367–369
 community classification center, 367
 custody phase, 367
 defined, 347
 goal of, 367
 juvenile, 355–356
 release phase, 367
 risk-relevant needs, 367
Refo, Patricia Lee, 274
Regents of the University of California v. Tarasoff, 17, 18
Registration, 332–333
Rehabilitation, 321–322, 363–364
Rehnquist, William, 305, 341
Relative judgment, 104
Reminiscence effect, 110
"Removal without replacement," 104
Reporters, 33, 34
Repression, 113–115
Repression interpretation, 114
Resendiz, Angel Maturino, 150
Reservation price, 187
Residency restrictions, 334
Residential interventions, 353–355
 goal of, 354
 recidivism, reduction in, 354
 studies regarding, 354
 weakness of, 353
Resnick, Heidi, 126
Restitution, 322
Restorative justice, 325
Retention interval, 98
Retribution, 321, 322–323, 356
Retrieval of information, 99
Reverse transfer, 237
Rhode Island v. Innis, 165
Rice, Connie, 90
Richardson, Terri, 135
Richey, Charles R., 245
Rideau v. Louisiana, 287
Ridgway, Gary, 151
Rights
 to an attorney, 7
 discover truth or resolve conflicts, 12–14
 equality *vs.* discretion, 8–12
 individuals *vs.* common good, 6–8
 traffic violation, 7
Right to liberty, 7
Rihanna, 127
Ring v. Arizona, 192
Risk assessments, 262–264
Risk averse, 200
Risk/need/responsivity (RNR), 236, 348, 356
Risk-Sophistication-Treatment Inventory, 236, 349
RNR. *See* Risk/need/responsivity
Robbennolt, Jennifer, 272
Roberts, John, 7
Rochman, Richard, 300

Rogers Criminal Responsibility Assessment Scales (RCRAS), 226
Roll, John, 218
Roper v. Simmons, 10, 343
Rosenberg, Ethel, 193
Rosenberg, Julius, 193
Rosenheimer, Edward, 4
Roughing It, 295
Rowland, Judith, 135–136
Ruby, Jack, 228
Rudolph, Eric, 13
Ruffner, Kimberly, 338
Rutgers University, 304
Ryan, George, 337
Ryan, William, 120

S

Sala, Tuere, 209–210
Salvi, John, 219
Samenow, Stanton E., 55–56
Same-sex marriage, 6
Sandusky, Jerry, 176, 310, 311
Santobello v. New York, 184
Satterwhite v. Texas, 235
SAVRY. *See* Structured Assessment of Violence Risk in Youth
Schema, 306, 312, 314
Schiavo, Terri, 34, 35
Schizophrenia, 215, 218, 222, 224, 254
School-based probation, 349
Schools
 bullying, 121–122
 peer victimization, 141
 safety, 122
 shooting sprees, 46–47
 violence in, 46–48
Schott, Harriett, 254
Schwarz, Charles, 71
Schwarzenegger, Arnold, 333
Science Daily (American news website), 297
Scientific jury selection, 283–286
Scopes, John, 192
Seattle Community Court, 209
Secondary deviance, 63
Secondary victimization, 136
Second Chance Act of 2007: Community Safety through Recidivism Prevention, 368
Seedman, Al, 73
Selection effects, 271
Selective attention, 97
Selective serotonin reuptake inhibitors (SSRIs), 335
Self-defense, 130–131
Self-determination theory of optimal motivation, 42
Self-exoneration, 62
Self-serving bias, 187
Sell, Charles, 223
Sell v. U.S., 223
Seltzer, Richard, 286
Sentence bargaining, 182

Sentencing
 aggravating and mitigating factors, 336
 bargaining, 182
 blended, 330–331
 competence, 225
 death penalty, 335–338
 determinants of, 328–329
 determinate, 12
 disparities, 320
 disparity, 12
 indeterminate, 326
 judge's role, 12, 192
 judicial discretion in, 326–328
 phase, 336
 process
  forensic psychologists, 327
  lawyer presentations, 327
  offender file, 327
  probation officer's report, 327
 racial bias, 12
 restorative justice, 325
 retribution, 321, 322–323
 severity of crime, 329
 sex offenders, 331–335
 shaming, 323–324
Sentencing demands assimilation, 327
Sentencing disparities, 320
Sentencing Reform Act of 1984, 327
Sequential Intercept Model
 community alternatives to standard prosecution and, 202–211
 law enforcement and emergency services, 202–203
 post-arrest, 203–205
 post-initial Hearings, 205–206
Sequential presentation, 103
Serial killers, 150–151
SES. *See* Socioeconomic status
Settlement negotiations, 175, 185–186
Seven-factor temperament and character model, 56
Seventh Circuit American Jury Project, 315
Seven-year syndrome, 86
Severely mentally disordered (SMD), 228
Sex education, 139
Sex offenders
 assessments, 334–335
 involuntary commitment, 334–335
 recidivism, 331–332, 334
 registration, 332–333
 treatments, 138, 335
Sexting, 3
Sexual aggression, 132, 133, 135
Sexual assaults. *See also* Rape
 as children, 128–129, 136
 defined, 140–141
 DNA, 94–95
 generic prejudice, 288–289
 prior record, 300
 treatment for rapist, 138–139
 U.S. Equal Employment Opportunity Commission, 139
Sexual conservatism, 132